«« GAME FREAK »»

CONCEPT ART

Welcome to a behind-the-scenes look from the creators of *Pokémon Sun* and *Pokémon Moon*

The creators at GAME FREAK inc. in Japan put countless hours into developing the characters for each new generation of Pokémon games. Once they have an idea for a character, an artist needs to bring that character to life by planning out all the details of his or her outfit and expressions to be reflected in the games. In the following pages, you can take an exclusive peek at these concept artwork pieces to see where the characters from *Pokémon Sun* and *Pokémon Moon* were first given their unique looks.

! The following section contains concept artwork for *Pokémon Sun* and *Pokémon Moon*. This artwork may include characters and information that could spoil some of the secrets you'll uncover during your grand adventure in the Alola region. You may wish to hold off on viewing this art until you've completed your island challenge!

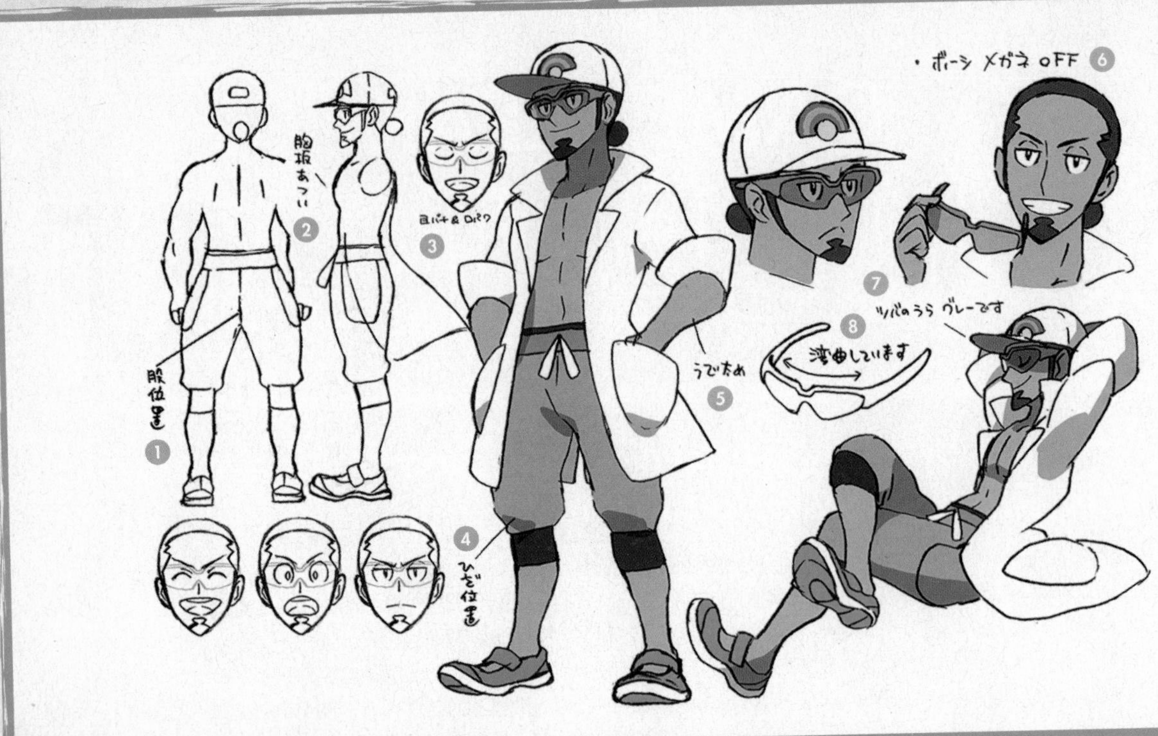

PROFESSOR KUKUI

1. Pants loose from here **2.** Thick chested **3.** Eyes closed, mouth open **4.** Knees **5.** Thick arms **6.** Without the glasses and hat **7.** Underside of cap is gr
8. Curved

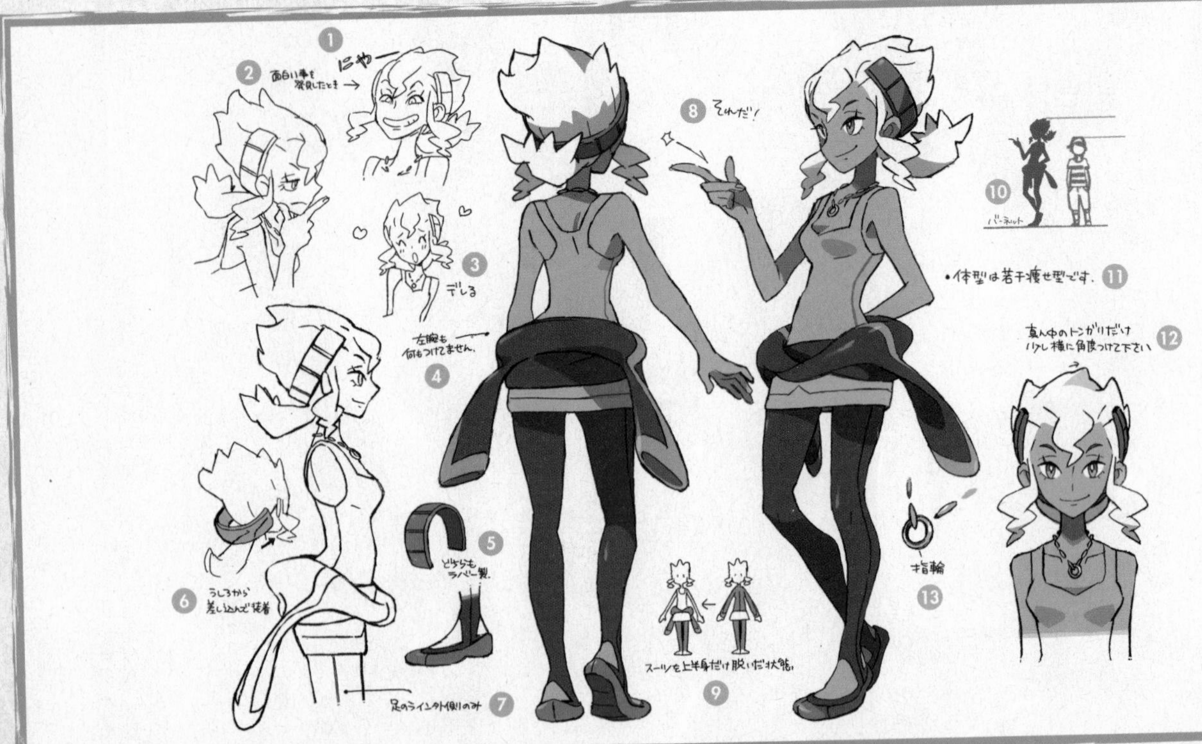

PROFESSOR BURNET

1. *Grin* **2.** When she's discovered something that amuses her **3.** *Flush* **4.** Nothing on her left arm either **5.** Both are made of rubber **6.** Worn by bei
on from behind **7.** Seams on the outside of the leg only **8.** That's it! **9.** Has just the top part of her suit off **10.** Burnet **11.** Body shape a bit on the skinny
12. The middle spike alone should be angled slightly to the side, please! **13.** Ring

HAU

1. Dahaha! **2.** Snap clips **3.** Henley neckline **4.** Serious **5.** Warm **6.** Angry **7.** Shocked **8.** Snickering **9.** Normal **10.** Eyes closed, mouth open **11.** Pattern

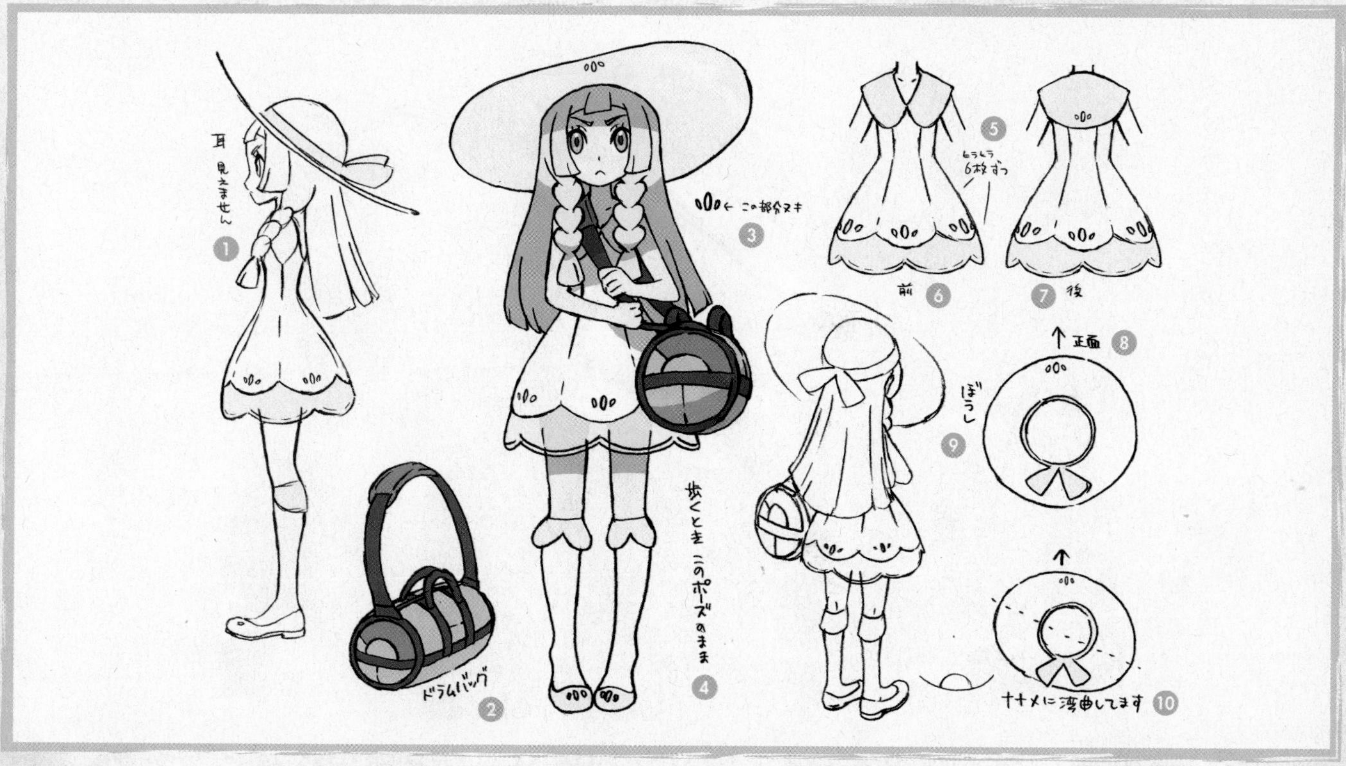

LILLIE

1. Ears not visible **2.** Duffel bag **3.** This part is cut out **4.** Keeps this pose while walking **5.** Six panels on each layer **6.** Front **7.** Back **8.** Front **9.** Hat **10.** Hat curves up at an angle

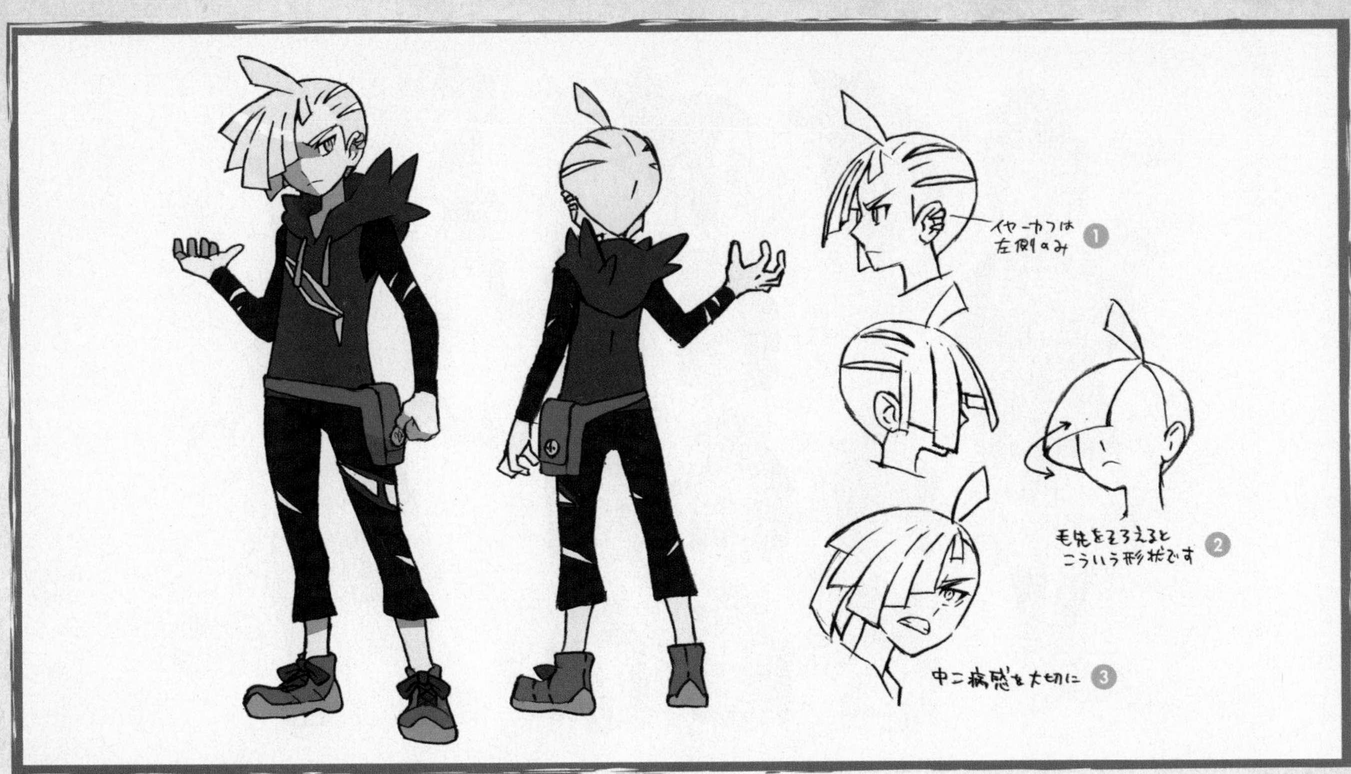

GLADION

1. Ear cuffs on the left ear only **2.** If trimmed to the same length, the bangs would be like this **3.** Gotta express that middle-school arrogance and being emo

MOM

1. Laughing face **2.** You forgot this! **3.** Normal face **4.** Acts like she's dancing the hula while she does laundry **5.** Happy **6.** Eyes closed **7.** Welcome home **8.** Mouth open

ILIMA

1. Ilima **2.** Incredible! **3.** *Sparkle* **4.** *Sparkle* **5.** Ends of hair are rounded **6.** Left handed **7.** From behind left ear **8.** Captain symbol **9.** Hair passes through the hole in top and bottom **10.** Finger gloves **11.** Leather **12.** Both reach to about the second knuckle **13.** Palm **14.** Bag **15.** Hangs from belt loop **16.** Leather projects out a little here

LANA

1. Lana **2.** No whites in her eyes **3.** Freckles **4.** Um... **5.** *Flush* **6.** Likes her alone time, too **7.** Sisters! **8.** Rubber sandals worn by Fishermen (too big for her) **9.** String hairband **10.** Where it ties together is hidden in her hair **11.** Wearing a sailor shirt over the top **12.** Captain symbol **13.** Like a key ring (hanging from string on her pants) **14.** She might look small, but she's surprisingly strong! **15.** Her good friend Mallow **16.** Pattern on the pants from Hawaiian waves

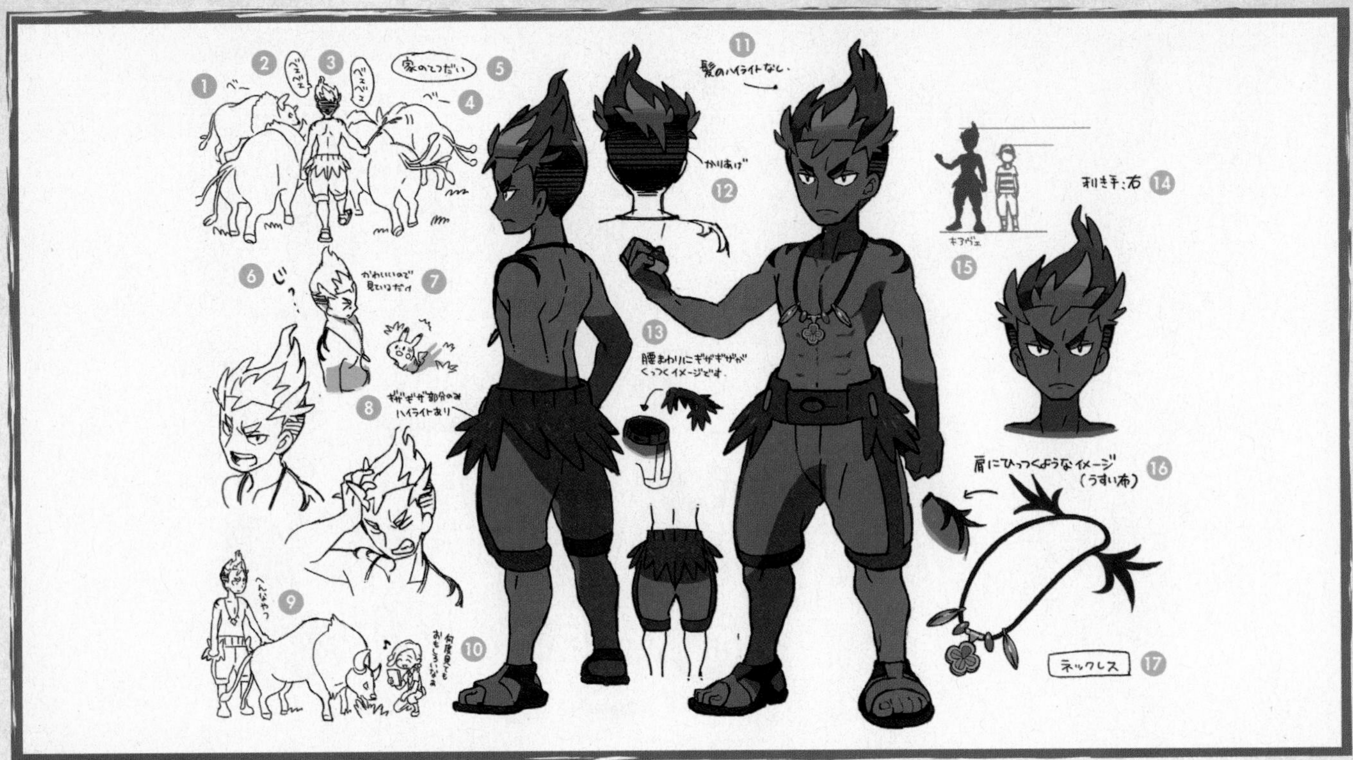

KIAWE

1. Moooo **2.** Yeah, yeah **3.** Moo-moo **4.** Moooo **5.** Helping out at home **6.** *Stare* **7.** So cute that all he can do is stare **8.** Highlights on this ragged part only **9.** What a weirdo **10.** I never get tired of watching this fellow! **11.** No highlights in hair **12.** Close cropped here **13.** This ragged bit attaches around the waist **14.** Right-handed **15.** Kiawe **16.** They cling to his shoulders (thin cloth) **17.** Necklace

MALLOW

1. Hairband looks like a flower decoration (Note: It's not a real flower) **2.** One piece **3.** Elastic string passes through the hole and is tied off **4.** Middle part is a bit thicker **5.** Middle ⟷ Outside **6.** Show damage in the same way **7.** Back **8.** She wears it like a badge, hooked onto her clothes **9.** Mallow **10.** Pocket can't hold much more than small Berries **11.** Whaaat?! **12.** Boooo!

SOPHOCLES

1. Captain's symbol is just stuck on, so it projects outward **2.** Sophocles **3.** Gyargh! I don't know! **4.** Has a habit of mussing up his hair when he's upset **5.** Eyebrows when he is feeling troubled **6.** Pull out the metal fitting **7.** Projection keyboard and screen **8.** Can be used anywhere that you have a flat surface

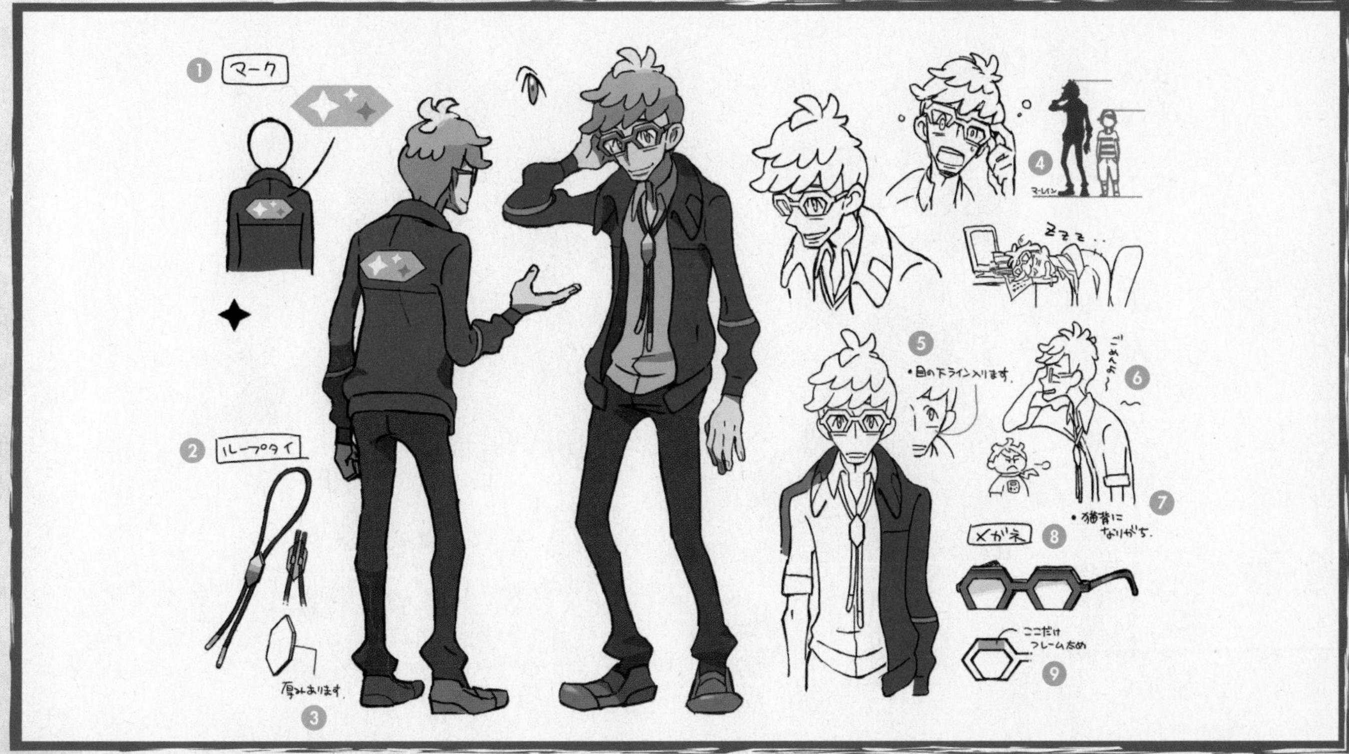

MOLAYNE

1. Design **2.** Bolo tie **3.** Has some thickness **4.** Molayne **5.** There's a line below the eye **6.** So-o-orry... **7.** Tends to slouch **8.** Glasses **9.** Frame is thicker just here

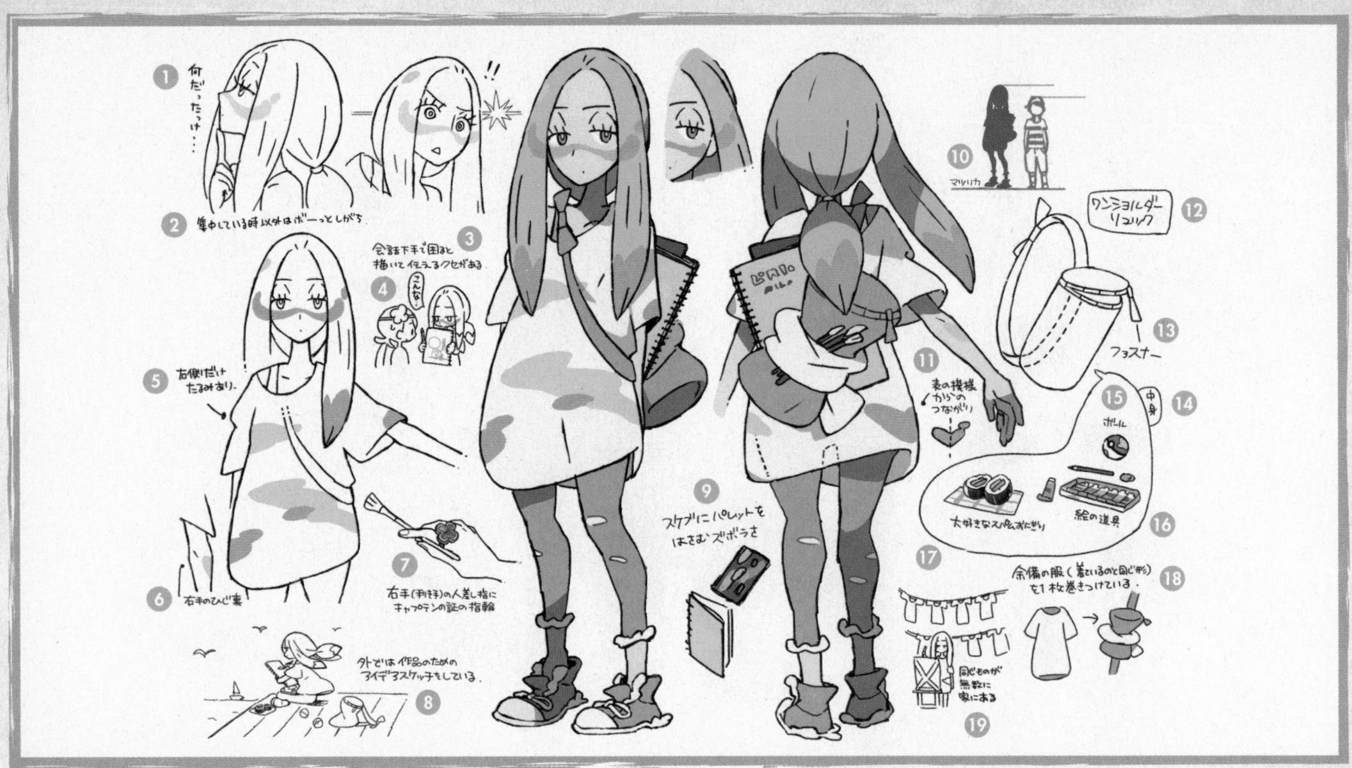

MINA

1. What was I gonna do next...? **2.** When not focused, she tends to space out **3.** Uses pictures to express herself when words fail her in conversation **4.** I-is that...? **5.** Droops off her right shoulder only **6.** Back of her right elbow **7.** Wears her captain symbol as a ring on the pointer finger of her dominant right hand **8.** Doing a rough sketch for a painting outside **9.** Sloppiness shown in how she keeps her palette wedged in her sketchbook **10.** Mina **11.** Connects to the pattern in the front **12.** One-strap backpack **13.** Zipper **14.** Contents **15.** Balls **16.** Art supplies **17.** Her favorite spam musubi **18.** Has an extra shirt (same design as the one she's wearing) wrapped around it **19.** Has countless of the same shirt at home

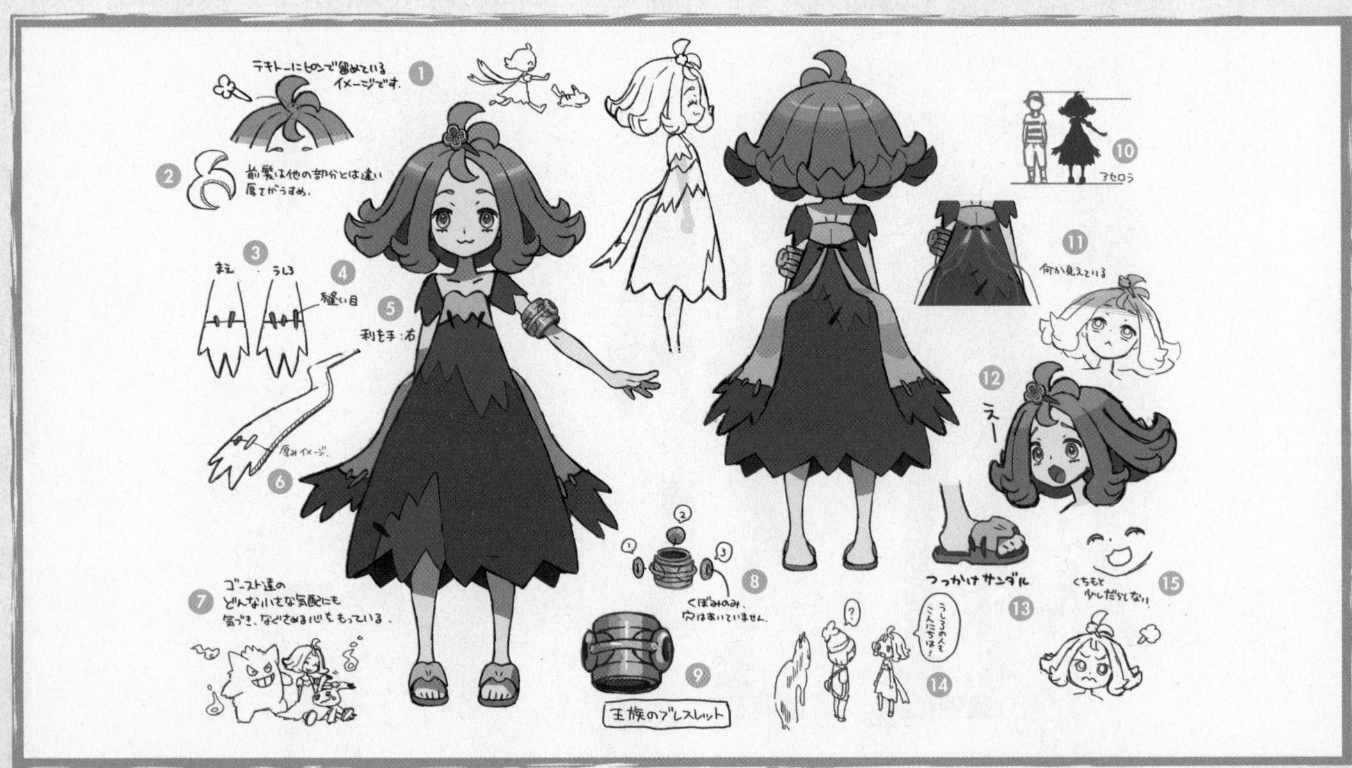

ACEROLA

1. She's just pinned it up wherever **2.** Bangs are a bit different than the other parts of her hair (thinner) **3.** Front Back **4.** Stitched together **5.** Right-handed **6.** Illustration of thickness **7.** Notices even the slightest presence of a ghost and comforts them **8.** Just indents, not holes **9.** Royal bracelet **10.** Acerola **11.** She can see something there... **12.** What?! **13.** Slip-on sandals **14.** And hello to the person behind you, too! **15.** The look around her mouth is a bit careless

GUZMA

1. Pants loose from here **2.** Knees around here

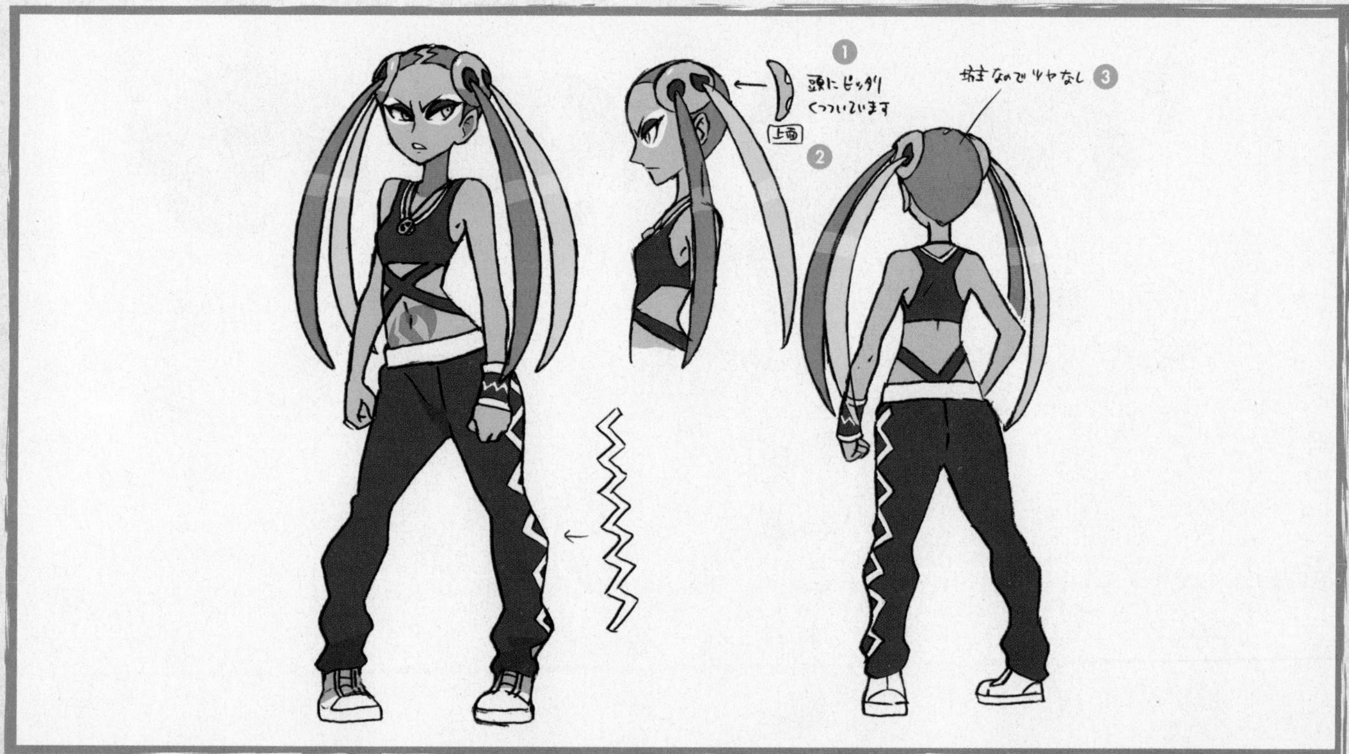

PLUMERIA

1. Fits tight against the head **2.** From above **3.** Crop-cut hair, so no shine here

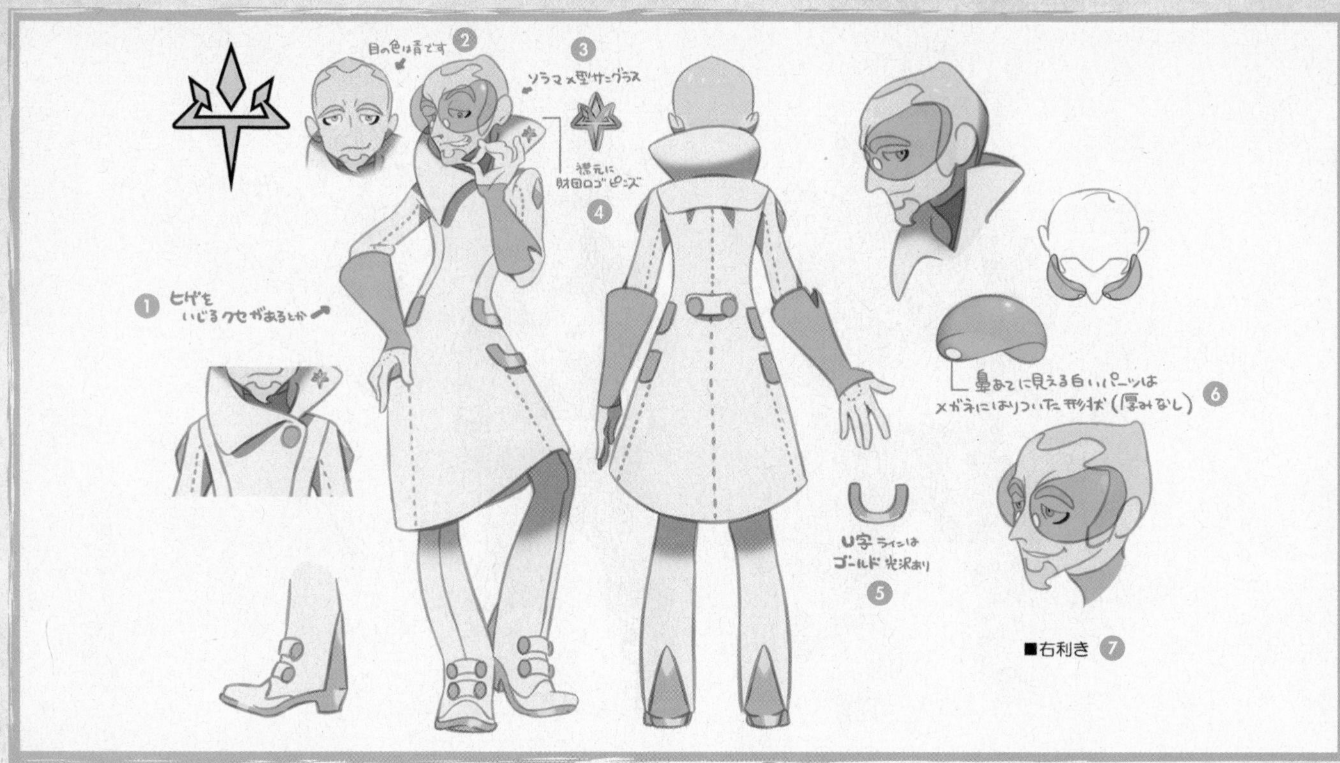

FABA

1. Has a habit of tweaking his beard **2.** Eye color is blue **3.** Fava bean-shaped sunglasses **4.** Foundation logo pin on his collar **5.** U-shaped line is gold and shiny **6.** White parts you can see against his nose are stuck on the glasses (no thickness) **7.** Right-handed

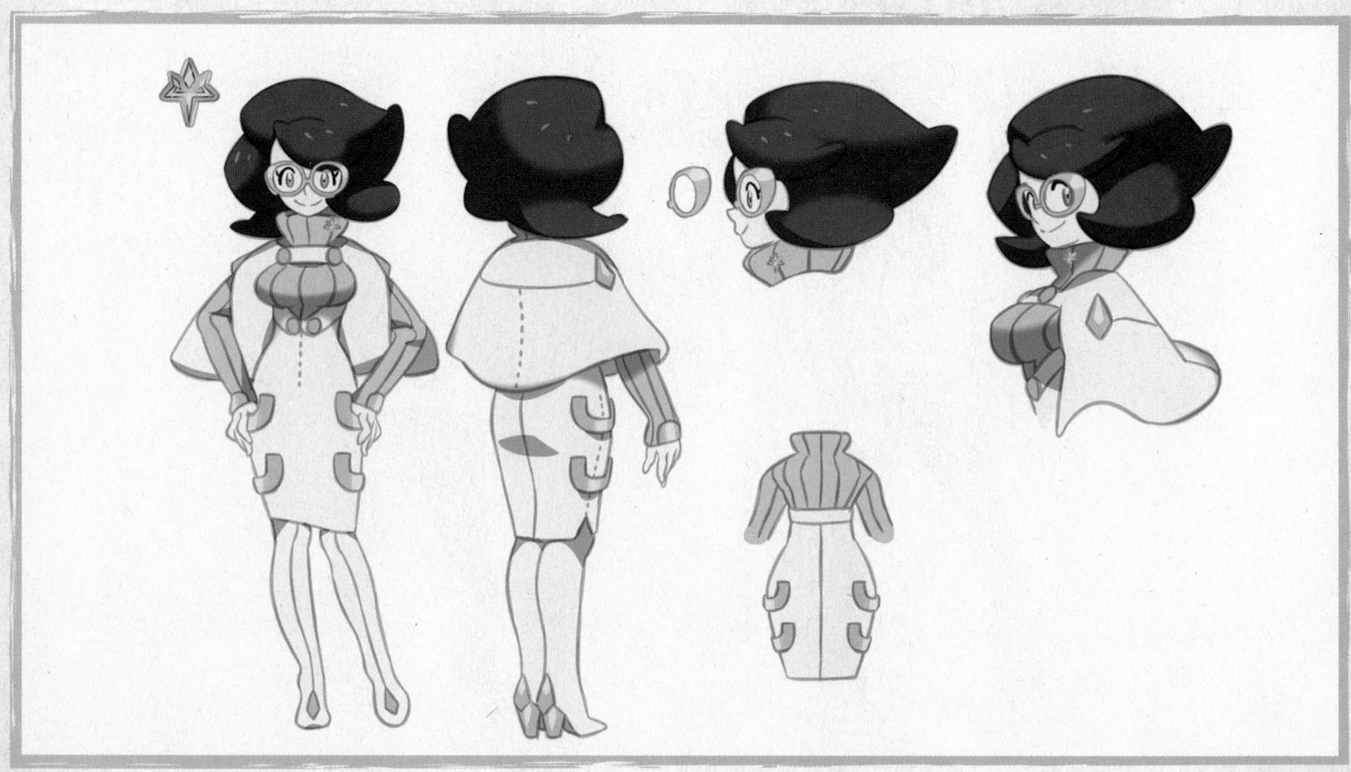

WICKE

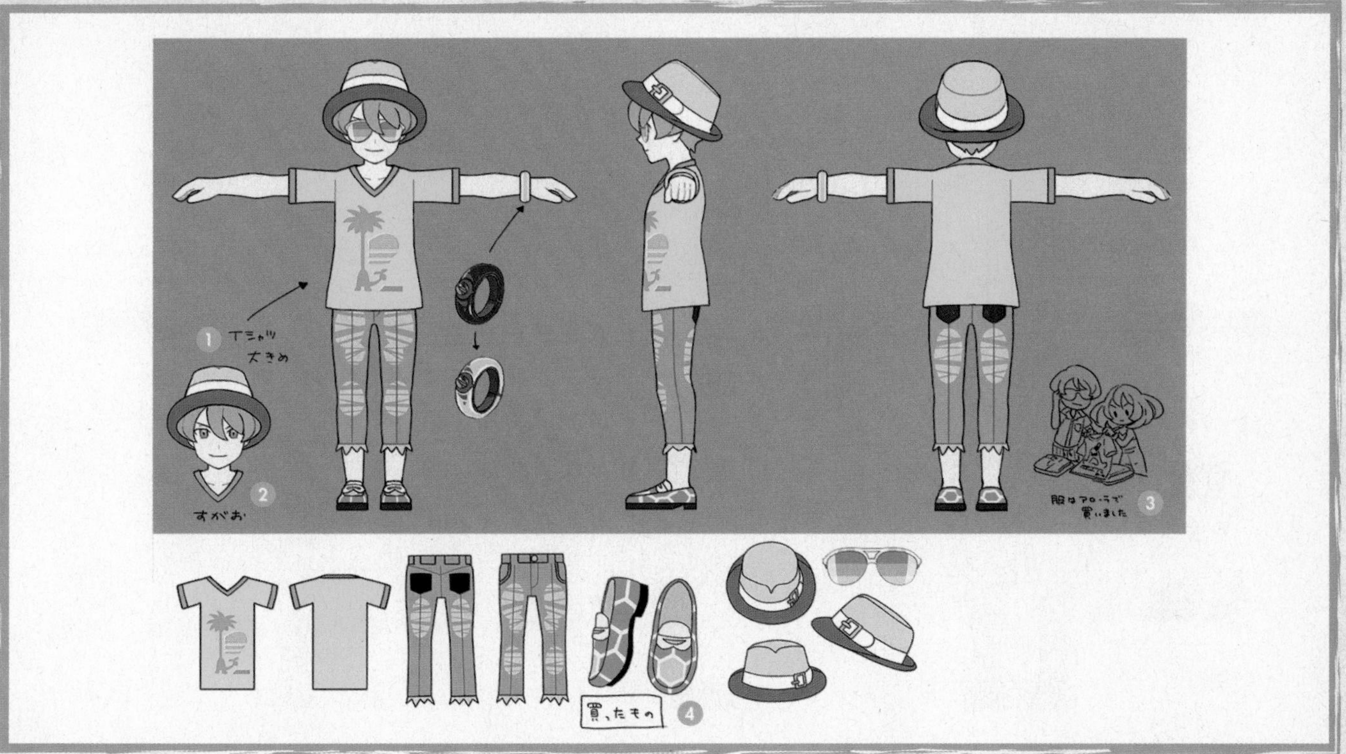

DEXIO

1. Tee is a bit baggy **2.** Without anything on **3.** Bought their clothes here in Alola **4.** What he bought

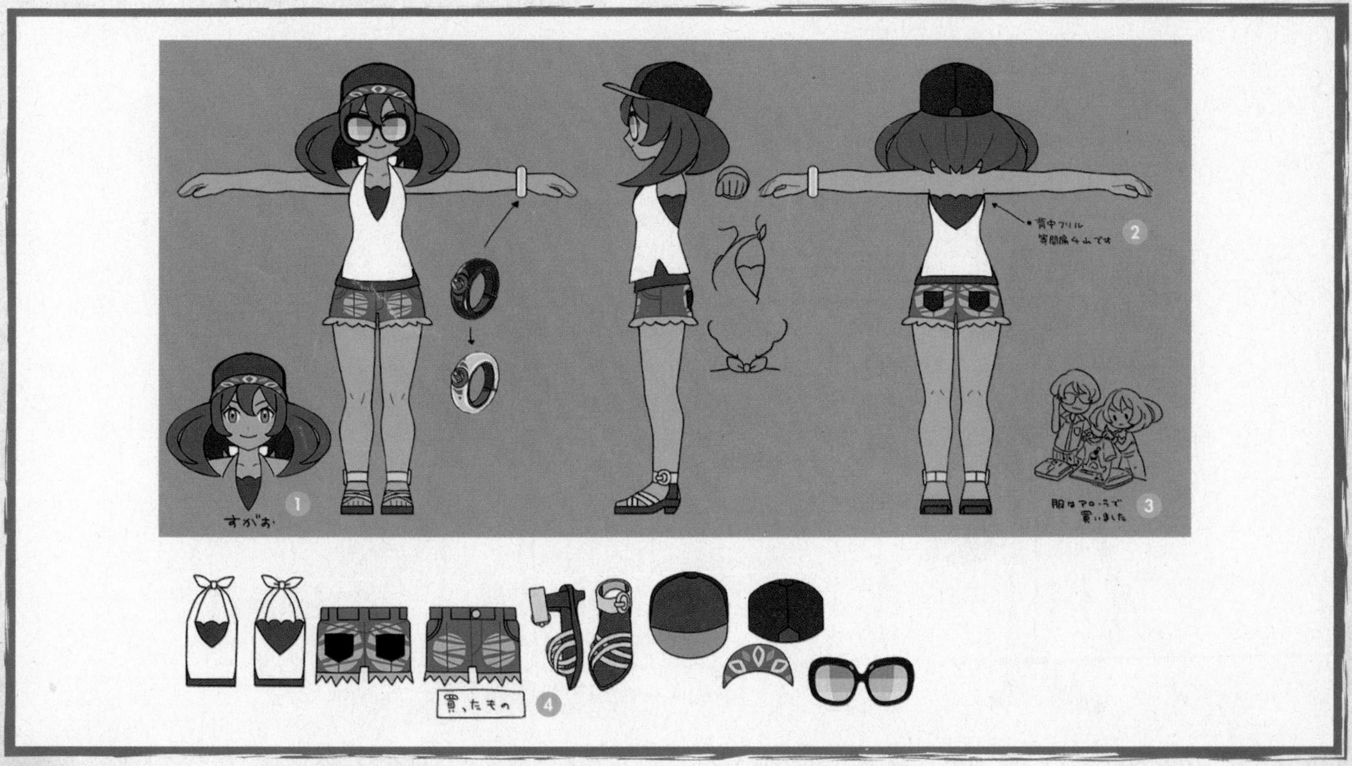

SINA

1. Without anything on **2.** Scalloped edge has four equally sized bumps **3.** Bought their clothes here in Alola **4.** What she bought

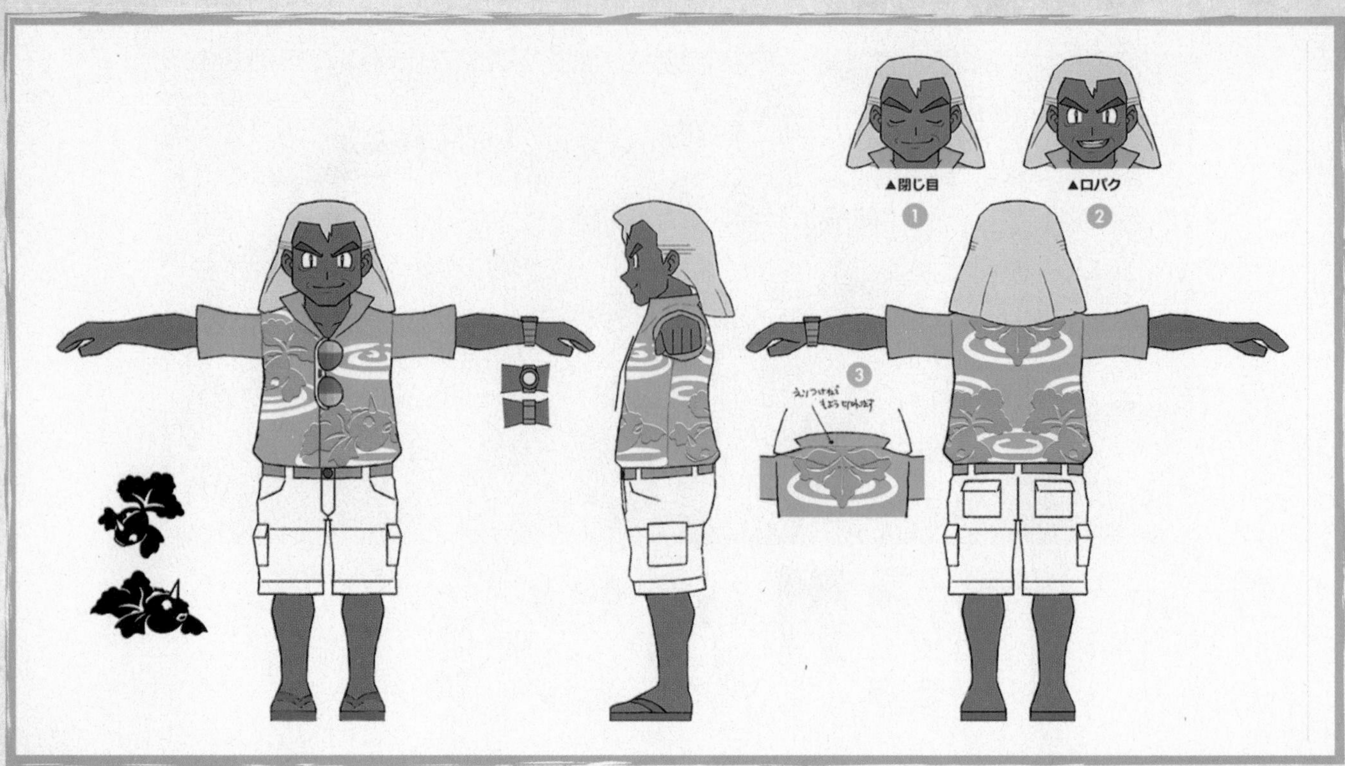

SAMSON OAK

1. Eyes closed **2.** Mouth open **3.** Pattern is cut off where the collar attaches

GRIMSLEY

1. Scarf **2.** Both ends are the same **3.** Back **4.** Kai-no-kuchi knot (shell-shaped knot) **5.** Has upswept hair that is longer at the base of the neck and has more white hairs appearing than in *Pokémon Black* and *Pokémon White Versions* **6.** Normal collar **7.** Hehehe... **8.** Eyes are more sunken than before **9.** Shoes are the same design as in *Pokémon Black* and *Pokémon White Versions* **10.** Grimsley (two years later) **11.** Still carrying a coin around with him like usual **12.** Image of the collar pattern **13.** He simply appears from somewhere and then disappears again...

RYUKI

1. Gloves (claws work as guitar picks, too) **2.** Red spikes on the shoulders, back, and legs are all the same size **3.** Choker **4.** Buckle is angled **5.** Spikes (get larger as you move out) **6.** Guitar case and speaker **7.** Spikes get bigger as you move out **8.** This eye is hidden from the front **9.** Eye color changes depending on his expression **10.** When mad **11.** Big mouth **12.** The "claws" on his chest fold over and hook around the lapels **13.** Back **14.** Full-body leather **15.** Ryuki **16.** Worries about looking baby-faced so he usually hides his eyes behind his hair **17.** Ba-baaam! **18.** This is it! **19.** Almost always pumped up to 100% **20.** Being idiotic **21.** Both he and his Pokémon are oblivious to the situation and they mess up the flow of battle

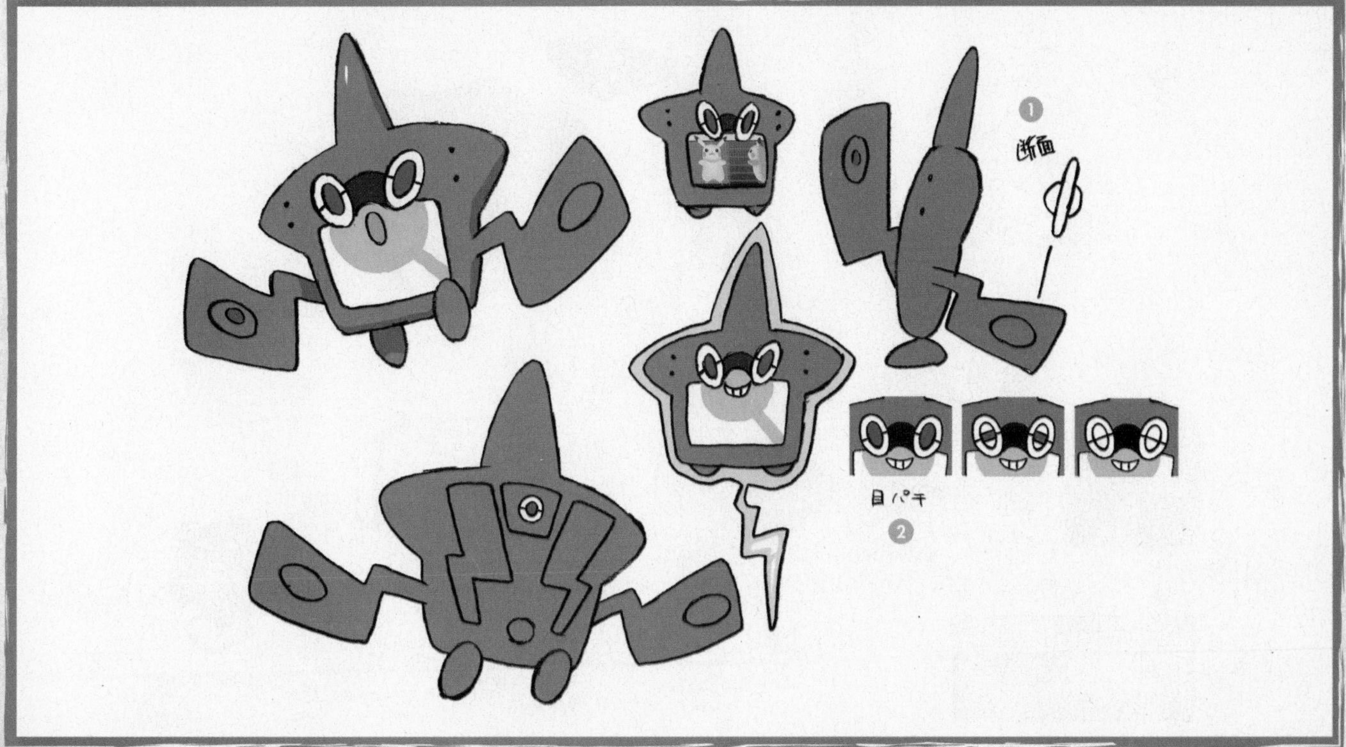

ROTOM DEX

1. Cross-section view **2.** Blinking

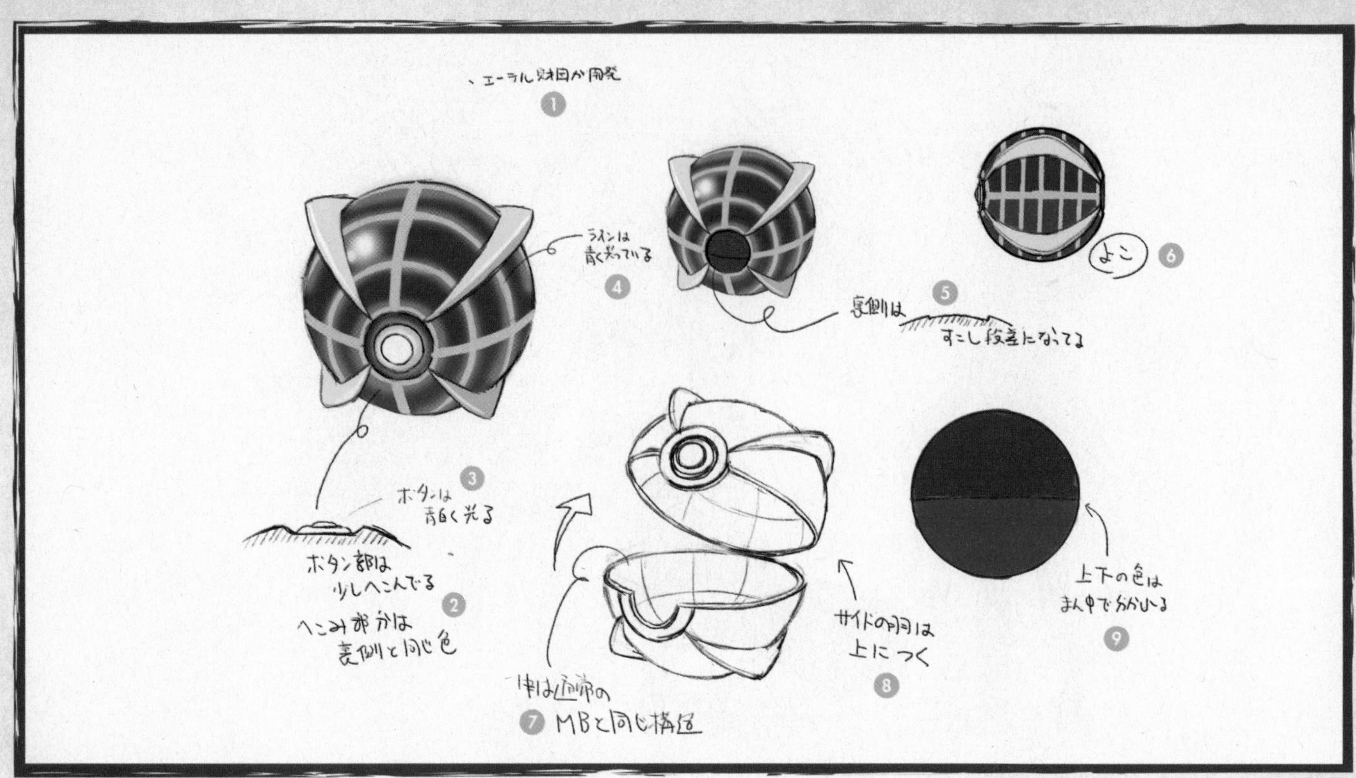

BEAST BALL

1. Developed by the Aether Foundation **2.** Button area is sunken a bit (the same color as the back) **3.** Button glows white-blue **4.** Lines glow blue **5.** Underside is like this...with a bit of a difference in height **6.** Side **7.** Inside is constructed the same way as a usual Master Ball **8.** Wings on the side attach to the top **9.** Colors of the top and bottom are split in the middle

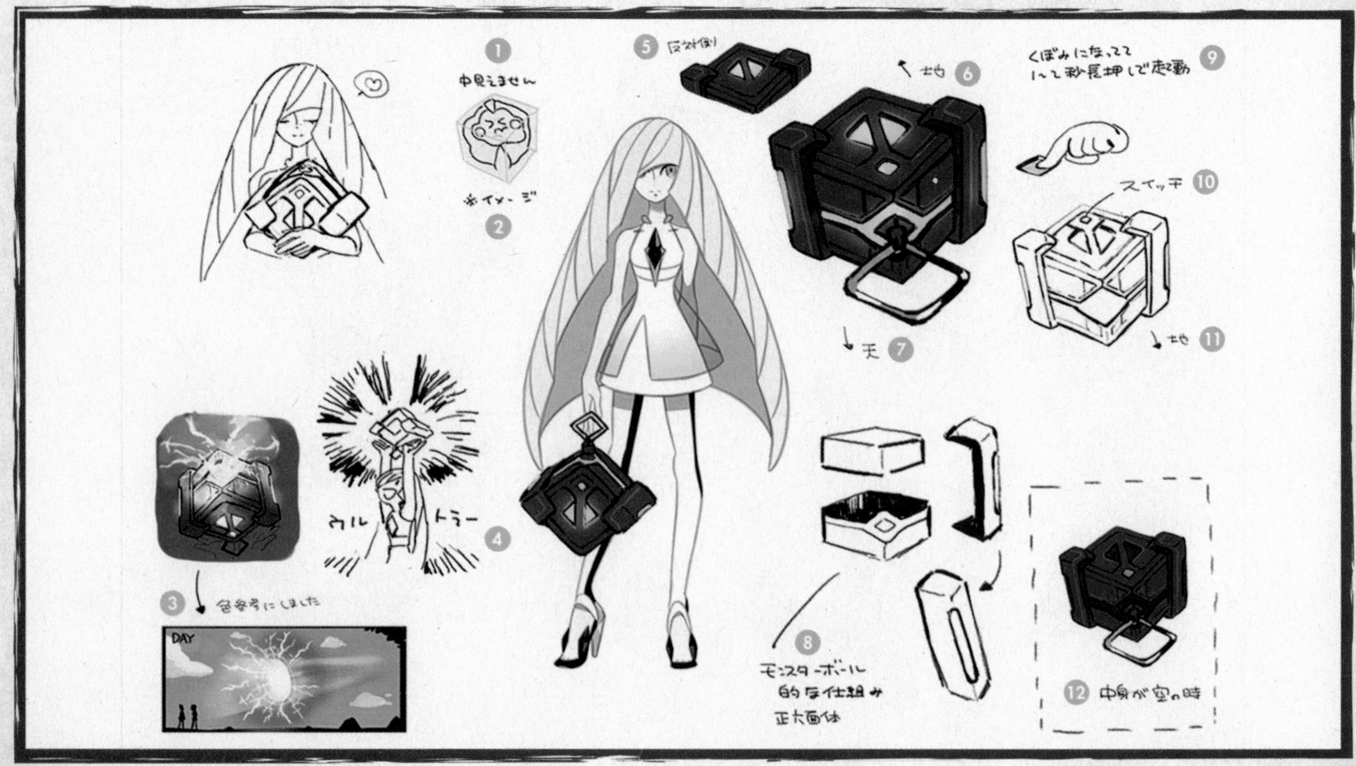

CAGE

1. Can't see inside **2.** Note: Just to illustrate **3.** Reference for the colors **4.** Ultra! **5.** Opposite side **6.** Bottom **7.** Top **8.** Poké Ball-like construction (cube shaped) **9.** Hold down the indented area for a couple of seconds to activate it **10.** Switch **11.** Bottom **12.** When it's empty

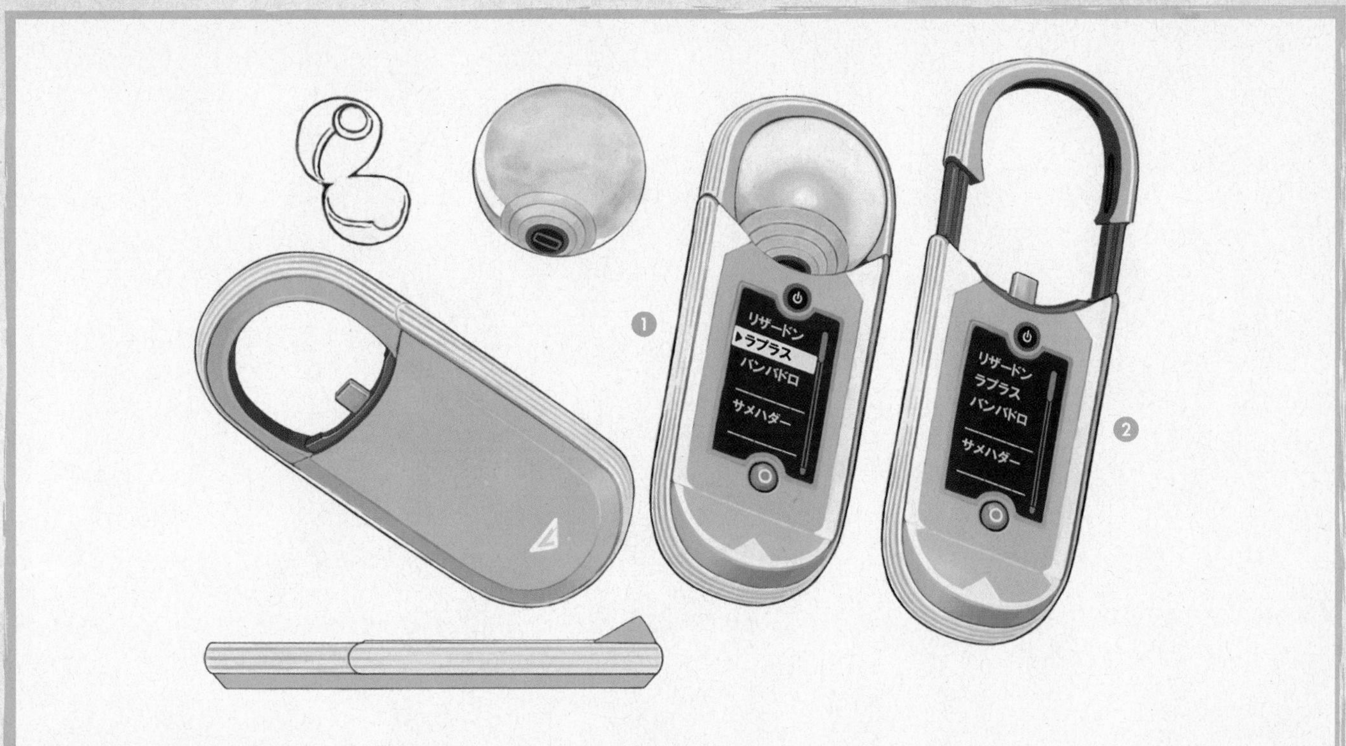

RIDE PAGER

1. Charizard ▶Lapras Mudsdale Sharpedo **2.** Charizard Lapras Mudsdale Sharpedo

RIDE POKÉMON

The Official Alola Region Strategy Guide

Table of Contents

Article Index

GETTING STARTED
BATTLE & STRATEGY
POKÉMON COLLECTING
FUN & COMMUNICATION
ADVENTURE DATA

Article Index (cont.)

Quick Location Index

How to Register in the Island Pokédexes

ALOLA REGION MAP
PONI ISLAND
Seafolk Village
Move Tutors
Restaurant
Ferry Terminal
Poni Breaker Coast
Ruins of Hope
Battle Tree
Poni Gauntlet
Altar of the Sunne / Altar of the Moone
Resolution Cave
Poni Coast
Vast Poni Canyon
Poni Meadow
Poni Wilds
Poni Plains
Poni Grove
Ancient Poni Path
Exeggutor Island
Seafolk Village
Poni Breaker Coast
Route 8
Lush Jungle
Route 5
Brooklet Hill
Paniola Ranch
Paniola Town
Route 6
Route 4
Heahea City
Diglett's Tunnel
Konikoni City
Route 9
Memorial Hill
Akala Outskirts
Po Town
Outer Cape
Route 17
Mount Hokulani
Malie Garden
Malie City
Lake of the Moone / Lake of the Sunne
Ula'ula Meadow
Route 10
Route 11
Mount Lanakila
Route 16
Haina Desert
Blush Mountain
Route 12
Route 15
Secluded Shore
Tapu Village
Route 13
Route 14
ULA'ULA ISLAND
Malie City
Apparel Shop
Salon
Malasada Shop
Restaurant
Ferry Terminal
Community Center
Haina Desert
Ruins of Abundance
Route 14
Abandoned Thrifty Megamart
Route 15
Aether House
Mount Lanakila
Move Reminder
Pokémon League
= POKÉMON CENTER
Location found in Pokémon Sun
Location found in Pokémon Moon

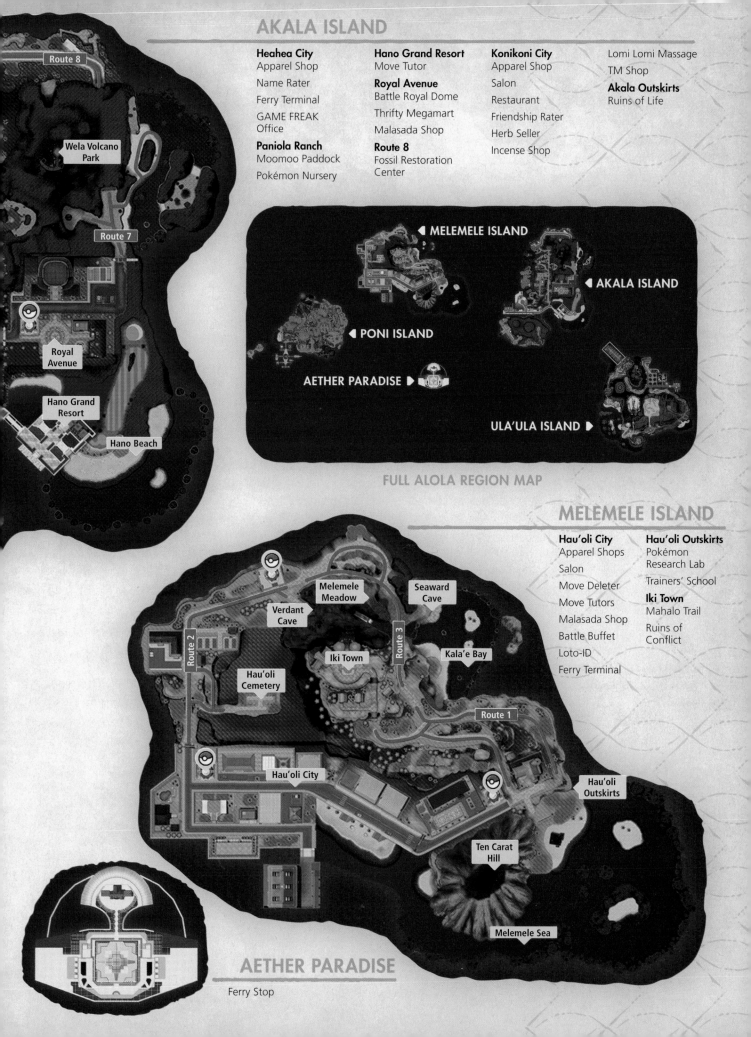

AKALA ISLAND

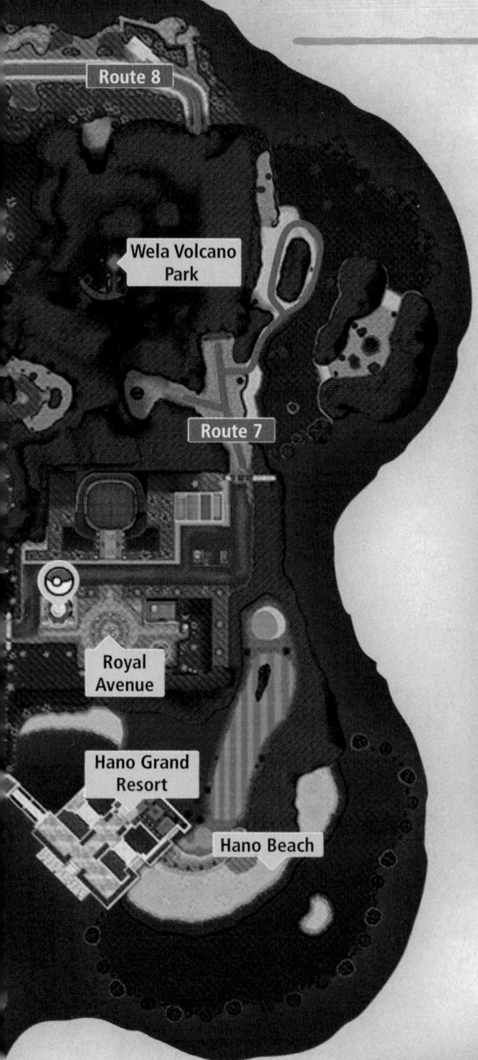

Heahea City
Apparel Shop
Name Rater
Ferry Terminal
GAME FREAK Office

Paniola Ranch
Moomoo Paddock
Pokémon Nursery

Hano Grand Resort
Move Tutor

Royal Avenue
Battle Royal Dome
Thrifty Megamart
Malasada Shop

Route 8
Fossil Restoration Center

Konikoni City
Apparel Shop
Salon
Restaurant
Friendship Rater
Herb Seller
Incense Shop
Lomi Lomi Massage
TM Shop

Akala Outskirts
Ruins of Life

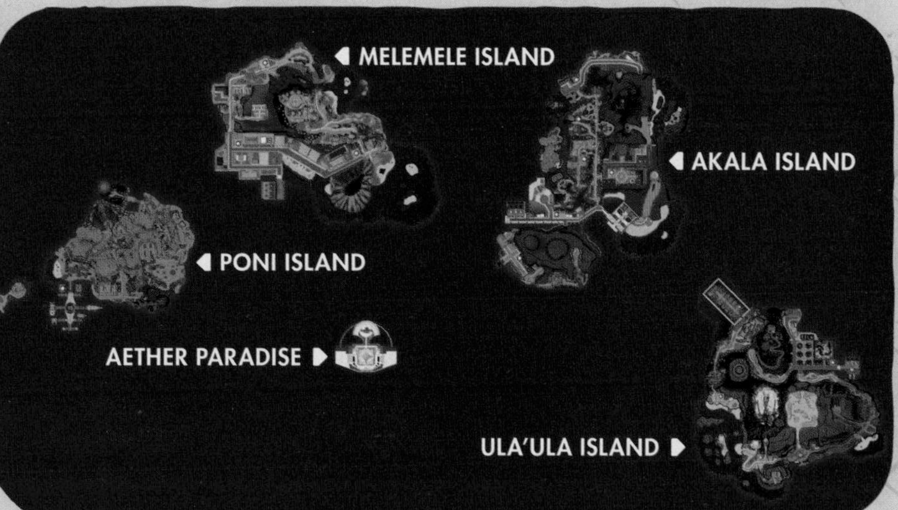

FULL ALOLA REGION MAP

MELEMELE ISLAND

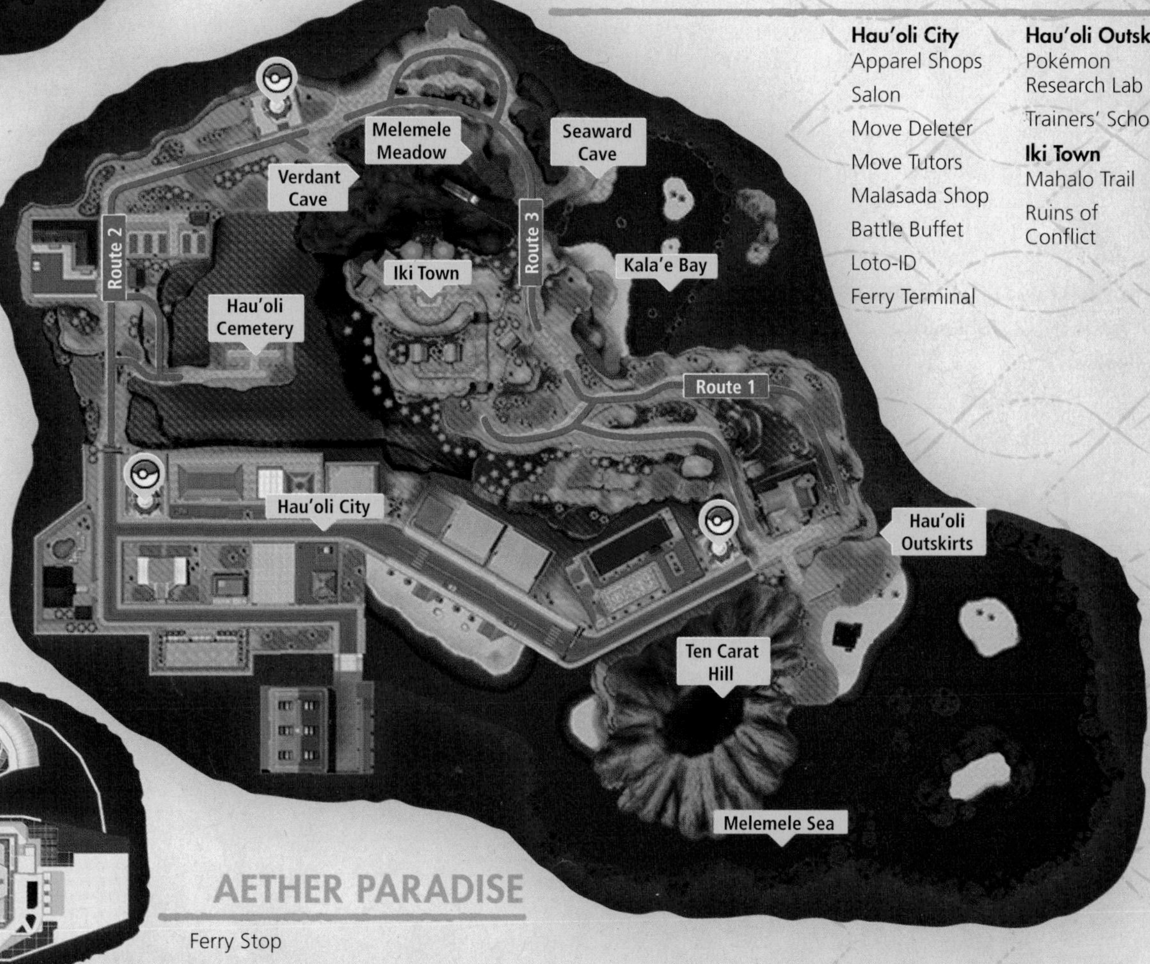

Hau'oli City
Apparel Shops
Salon
Move Deleter
Move Tutors
Malasada Shop
Battle Buffet
Loto-ID
Ferry Terminal

Hau'oli Outskirts
Pokémon Research Lab
Trainers' School

Iki Town
Mahalo Trail
Ruins of Conflict

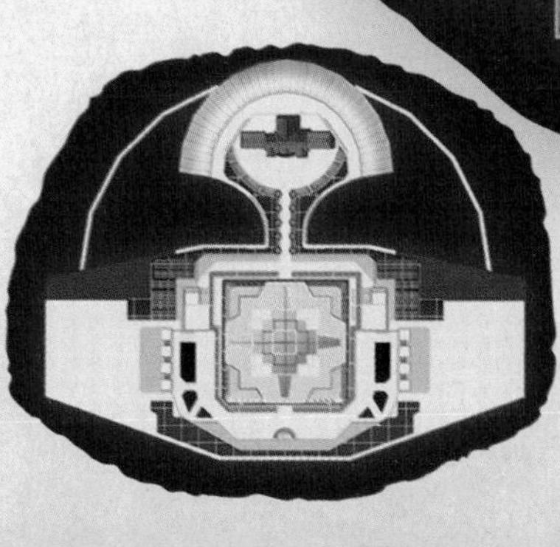

AETHER PARADISE

Ferry Stop

Welcome to the World of Pokémon!

The Pokémon world may seem very similar to the world that you and I live in, but there's one important difference: the existence of fantastic creatures known as Pokémon! Pokémon live in every corner of the world—from the depths of the sea to the peaks of the mountains, and everywhere else in between. Everyone depends on Pokémon in this world, and humans and Pokémon work closely together in their everyday life. Some ambitious people even dedicate their lives to becoming Pokémon Trainers!

What Is a Pokémon Trainer?

Pokémon Trainers are the brave men and women who venture out into the wild to catch and train Pokémon. Some do it because they want to discover every species of Pokémon hiding in the world, others do it because they simply enjoy the adventure of travel. But in the end, all Trainers must share a love for Pokémon battling, for this is how they learn to understand their Pokémon partners, as well as other people in the world around them.

Pokémon Battles

When two Trainers meet, a Pokémon battle is at hand! In a Pokémon battle, each Trainer sends out one or more Pokémon from their team to try to seize victory. If you hope to be the winner, you'll need to know all about your team's moves, as well as their strengths and weaknesses. If you hope to be the very best, you'll also need to know about each unique species of Pokémon, so that you'll know the best strategies to use no matter which sort of opponent you face.

The Ever-Increasing Number of Pokémon

New Pokémon are constantly being discovered, and many dedicated Pokémon Professors make it their lives' work to classify and describe them all. Many Trainers choose to help these noble professors in this task by traveling with a wondrous device known as a Pokédex!

A Pokédex automatically records images and basic information about every Pokémon that a Trainer encounters, whether out in the wild or during an intense Trainer battle. Succeed in catching a wild Pokémon, and your Pokédex will automatically record every known bit of information about it! Completely filling a Pokédex is a difficult goal, but many bright young Trainers aspire to catch every last Pokémon in their region. You've got your work cut out for you here in Alola, for this region has not one, but four Island Pokédexes for you to complete!

What Are Pokémon?

Pokémon are wild creatures that live in the Pokémon world. Some look rather like the animals in the world we live in, while others are as fantastical as the creatures from a dream. Pokémon Trainers seek to catch wild Pokémon and train them to be powerful allies in battle. Pokémon come in all shapes and sizes, but all Pokémon share a few common traits.

Pokémon Have Types

Rowlet

GRASS FLYING

Litten

FIRE

Popplio

WATER

Each Pokémon has one or two types. These types, like Fire and Water and Grass, interact with one another in different ways. It's like playing Rock-Paper-Scissors: Fire-type Pokémon are strong against Grass-type Pokémon, because fire can burn grass. But Fire-type Pokémon aren't very effective against Water-type Pokémon, because water puts out fire! There are 18 types in all, and each type has its own weaknesses and strengths. The full type matchup chart can be found on page 351 if you want to check it out now.

Pokémon Grow Stronger

Whenever a Pokémon participates in battle, it gains some experience. This experience is represented in Experience Points (Exp. Points). When a Pokémon gains enough Exp. Points, its level goes up. Each time a Pokémon levels up, it becomes a bit stronger. Its stats often increase, some more than others depending on your Pokémon's individual strengths. These stats—like HP (health points), Attack, Defense, and Speed—have a big effect on how your Pokémon will perform in future battles.

Pokémon Learn Moves

Each Pokémon can learn up to four moves to use in battle. This limited number means you'll have to think carefully about which moves you want your Pokémon to know. Pokémon sometimes learn moves from leveling up, and they can also be taught moves through the use of special items called TMs (p. 50). Moves can be used for attacking or for defense, but they all fall into three main categories:

Physical Moves 	Special Moves 	Status Moves 
These moves deal damage to opponents and lower their HP. They are more powerful when used by a Pokémon with a high Attack stat. They will deal less damage to a target that has a high Defense stat.	These moves deal damage to opponents and lower their HP. They are more powerful when used by a Pokémon with a high Special Attack (Sp. Atk) stat. They will deal less damage to a target that has a high Special Defense (Sp. Def) stat.	These moves affect Pokémon's status in some way other than dealing damage. They can do things like inflict status conditions (p. 49). Some boost battle stats, such as temporarily raising your Pokémon's Attack, or target an opponent's stats in some way, like lowering its Speed to make it slower.

Pokémon Have Abilities

Each Pokémon has an Ability, as well. A species of Pokémon may have two or even three possible Abilities, but each Pokémon of that species will only have one of these possible Abilities. Abilities have special effects, either during or outside of battle. Every time you catch a new Pokémon, see what its Ability can do from its Summary page (p. 27) and think of fun ways to take advantage of it!

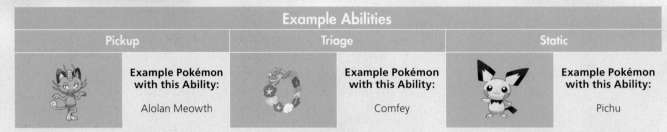

Example Abilities		
Pickup	**Triage**	**Static**
Example Pokémon with this Ability: Alolan Meowth	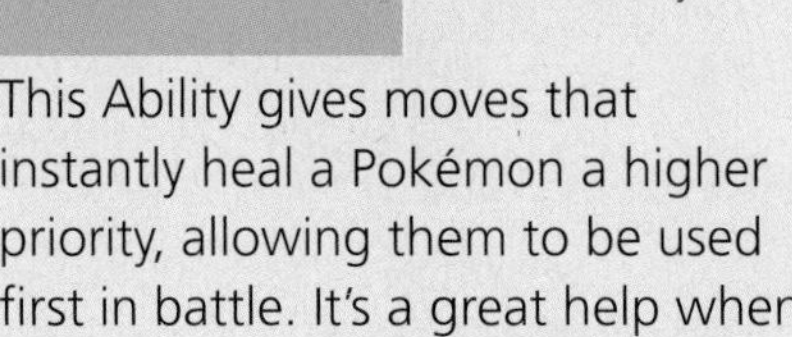 **Example Pokémon with this Ability:** Comfey	 **Example Pokémon with this Ability:** Pichu
If this Pokémon isn't holding anything (p. 47), the Pickup Ability gives it a chance of picking up an item used by an opponent in battle or finding items at the end of the battle.	This Ability gives moves that instantly heal a Pokémon a higher priority, allowing them to be used first in battle. It's a great help when your Pokémon is close to fainting!	If your Pokémon has the Static Ability and an opponent touches it in battle, then the opponent may end up with Paralysis, which can make their moves fail.

Pokémon Can Evolve

When Pokémon level up, they don't only learn new moves and increase their stats—they may also evolve! Some Pokémon never evolve, but others can evolve into several different Pokémon along their species' evolutionary chain. Leveling up isn't the only trigger for Evolution, either: sometimes Pokémon evolve when a certain item is used on them, or when you fulfill other special conditions. The Island Pokédex Pokémon List (p. 280) has more details. Enjoy the thrill of exploring Alola and seeing what new Pokémon you can obtain through Pokémon Evolution!

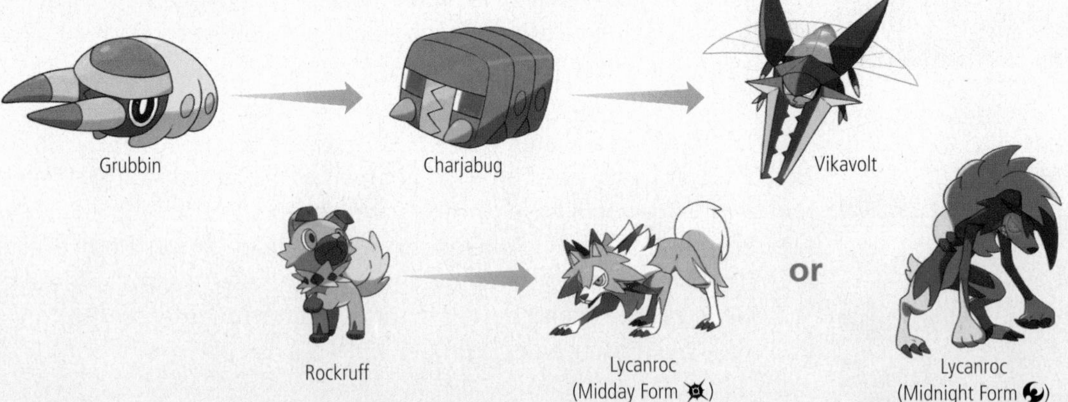

Trading Pokémon

Pokémon Trainers don't only battle with their Pokémon, they also trade them! Trading Pokémon is another way that Trainers enjoy interacting with each other and their Pokémon. You can trade Pokémon with other Trainers in several ways (p. 267) to help each other fill your Pokédexes. Trading Pokémon helps you obtain Pokémon that can only be found in one version of the game and allows you to share in the fun of both. Best of all, Pokémon you receive in a trade will grow more quickly than the Pokémon you catch in the wild!

The adventures that unfold in *Pokémon Sun* and *Pokémon Moon* are more or less the same. Both games have you exploring the exotic Alola region, and both feature similar challenges and foes. However, in the world of *Pokémon Sun*, the people of Alola revere a Legendary Pokémon known as Solgaleo, which ancient legends describe as the beast that devours the sun. Meanwhile, the myths in *Pokémon Moon* instead tell of a beast that calls the moon: the Legendary Pokémon Lunala! The Legendary Pokémon that you'll encounter in your adventure depends on the version of the game you're playing.

Solgaleo
PSYCHIC STEEL

Lunala
PSYCHIC GHOST

In addition, some of the Pokémon you'll encounter in the wilds of Alola also vary depending on the version of the game you're playing. Some Pokémon in one game won't appear in the other, but that's where trading comes in! You can easily trade Pokémon with nearby friends or with anyone around the world with an Internet connection. Learn more about that on page 267.

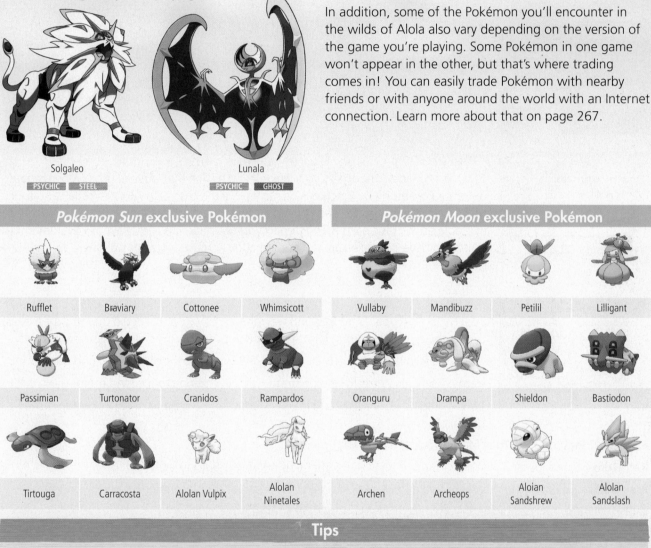

Pokémon Sun exclusive Pokémon				*Pokémon Moon* exclusive Pokémon			
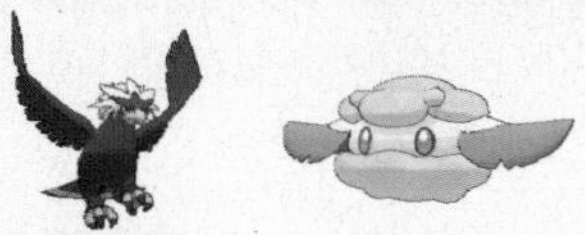							
Rufflet	Braviary	Cottonee	Whimsicott	Vullaby	Mandibuzz	Petilil	Lilligant

Passimian	Turtonator	Cranidos	Rampardos	Oranguru	Drampa	Shieldon	Bastiodon
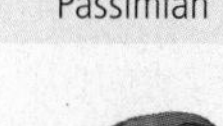							
Tirtouga	Carracosta	Alolan Vulpix	Alolan Ninetales	Archen	Archeops	Alolan Sandshrew	Alolan Sandslash

Tips

Special icons appear throughout this guide to indicate content that only appears in *Pokémon Sun* or *Pokémon Moon*. The ☀ icon means the content is only found in *Pokémon Sun*, while the ☾ icon indicates content that's only found in *Pokémon Moon*.

Time Differences

Mom
Ahhh! Can't you just feel that warmth?
The first day spent under Alola's sun!

Mom
Ahhh! Could anything be more soothing?
The first evening spent under Alola's calm moon!

The nature of time is quite different in Alola compared to other regions. If you're playing *Pokémon Sun*, when it is daytime in the real world, it will also be daytime in Alola. However, if you're playing *Pokémon Moon*, it will instead be nighttime in Alola when it's daytime in the real world. This is important, because certain Pokemon only appear during the day or night in some areas, and certain activities can only be accomplished during the day or night as well. Daytime-only activities are marked by a special icon throughout this guide (☼), while nighttime-only activities are denoted by a different icon (☽).

Menus and Options

The following pages help explain some of the screens and menus that you'll see in the game.

X Menu

This all-important menu lets you access many functions that you'll be using throughout your adventure. Press Ⓧ at any time during your journey to call up the X menu on the lower screen. It will grow to fill two pages in time, so press L or R or ✚ or ✚, or tap a blue arrow on the lower screen to change pages.

Tip

Some of the following options may not appear on your X menu at the beginning of your adventure. Don't worry, they'll unlock as you progress through the game!

Pokémon

Select "Pokémon" to view the Pokémon that are currently traveling with you in your party. Press Ⓨ or tap the "Pokémon" icon at the bottom of the lower screen, and you can swap the positions of your Pokémon. You can also drag your Pokémon around the lower screen to change its position. Press Ⓧ or press the "Held Item" icon and you can swap held items.

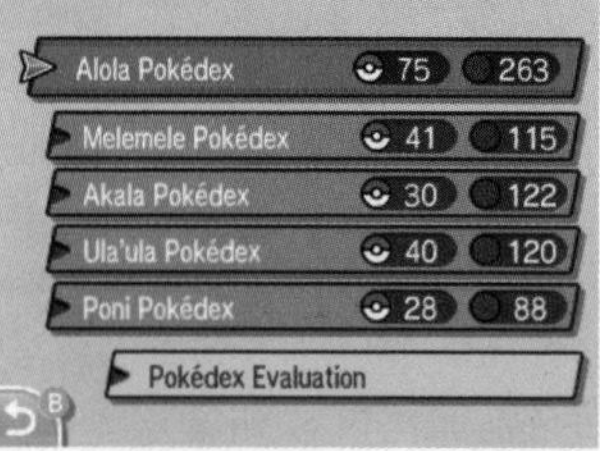

Pokédex

Choose "Pokédex" to access your Pokédex: a device that automatically records data on every Pokémon you catch or encounter. There's the main Alola Pokédex and four Island Pokédexes, one for each of Alola's four islands. The Island Pokédexes become available as you visit each island during your journey. Tap the "Pokédex Evaluation" button to have Rotom evaluate your Pokédex and give you tips on where to find new species of Pokémon.

Bag

Select "Bag" to open your Bag and view the items you've collected during your travels, or give them a good sorting with Ⓧ. Your Bag can have the following seven pockets:

Medicine: Contains items that restore HP/PP, cure status conditions, and more.

Items: Contains items for Pokémon to hold, Evolution stones, and more.

TMs: Contains Technical Machines (TMs) that can be used to teach Pokémon moves (p. 50).

Berries: Contains any Berries (p. 65) you collect on your journey.

Key Items: Contains all of the important "quest" items that you find on your journey.

Free Space: Select any item in your Bag and choose "Move to Free Space" to place it in this handy pocket.

Z-Crystals: Contains all of the Z-Crystals (p. 72) you obtain on your journey.

Save

Select "Save" to save your game. There's no auto-save feature in *Pokémon Sun* and *Pokémon Moon*, so it's up to you to save your game. Make sure to save often, and especially before you stop playing for the day or before a difficult battle!

Quick Link

Choose "Quick Link" to immediately battle or trade Pokémon with someone nearby. If you're with a friend who is also playing *Pokémon Sun* or *Pokémon Moon*, select "Quick Link" on both systems and then touch your lower screens or press Ⓐ at the same time. In a few seconds, your systems should be linked, and you can choose to trade Pokémon or have a battle!

Festival Plaza

Select "Festival Plaza" to put your adventure on hold and visit a magical place where a variety of fun communication features await (p. 299). If you have an Internet connection, you can interact with other players from around the world here whenever you want to take a little break from your main adventure.

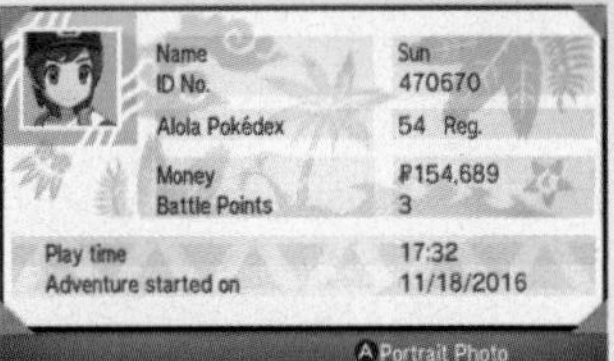

Trainer Passport

Select "Trainer Passport" to see how far you've come as a Trainer. The upper screen shows your name, Trainer ID No., current money, and more. Press Ⓐ to retake your Portrait Photo if you'd prefer a different shot. Press L or R, or ✚ or ✚, or tap a blue arrow on the lower screen, to flip through the stamp book's pages.

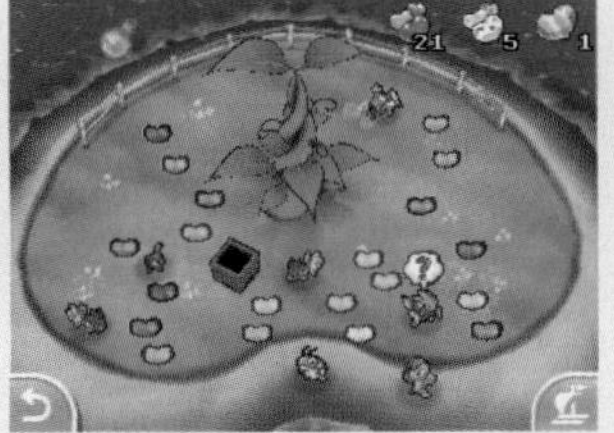

Poké Pelago

Select "Poké Pelago" on the X menu, and you'll be taken to Poké Pelago: a small group of isles created solely for the amusement of Pokémon. There's plenty to do at Poké Pelago—please see page 313 for a personal tour.

Pokémon Refresh

Choose "Pokémon Refresh" to pamper your party Pokémon in a number of ways. Page 276 contains all the details, but know that you can pet and pamper your Pokémon here, feeding them tasty Poké Beans and making sure they feel loved. A bit of affection can grant you all kinds of surprising benefits (p. 276)!

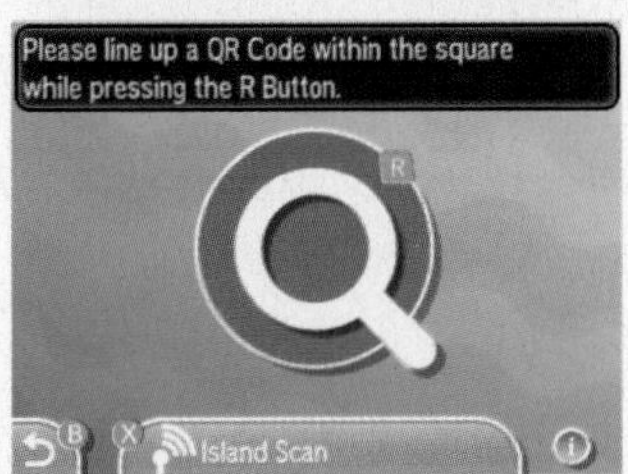

QR Scanner

Choose "QR Scanner" to fire up the QR Scanner function (p. 43). By using your system's camera function, you can scan QR Code patterns to easily register Pokémon in your Pokédex! Plus, you can earn some points for an Island Scan (p. 268)!

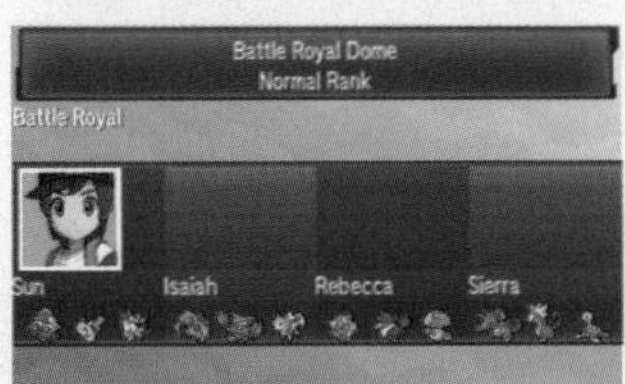

Battle Video

Select "Battle Video" to open the Vs. Recorder. Any exciting Battle Videos (p. 308) you've recorded can be watched here. You can even retry the battles in Battle Videos as mock battles (p. 308), Press Ⓧ to change the information on the upper screen, or press Ⓨ to delete multiple videos and free up space for more.

Text Speed	Normal
Battle Effects	On
Battle Style	Switch
Button Mode	Default
Party/Box	Manual

Options

Select "Options" to view and adjust a variety of gameplay options to your liking.

Text Speed: Choose from slow, normal, or fast text speeds to affect how quickly messages appear on the screen.

Battle Effects: Choose whether or not you want to see animations when Pokémon use their moves and when they're affected by status conditions.

Battle Style: By default, when you defeat a Pokémon on an opposing team, you'll be asked whether or not you want to switch your Pokémon when your opponent sends out their next team member. Change this setting to "Set" to stop being asked and always stick with your current Pokémon.

Button Mode: If you like, you can set L to function as Ⓐ for easier one-handed play.

Party/Box: By default, if your party is full when you catch a new Pokémon, you'll be asked whether to add it to your party or send it to a PC Box. Change this to "Automatic" to always send newly caught Pokémon to a PC Box when your party is full.

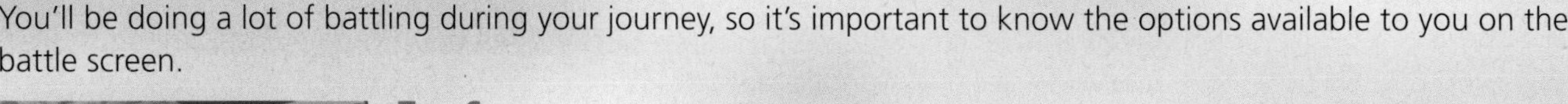

Battle Screen

You'll be doing a lot of battling during your journey, so it's important to know the options available to you on the battle screen.

Top Screen

In the top screen's top-right corner, you will find the opposing Pokémon's name, level, and HP, as well as its gender (if it has one). If you're battling a Trainer, a number of Poké Balls equal to the number of Pokémon in the Trainer's party is also displayed. The same information regarding your party is displayed in the lower-left corner of the screen.

Touch Screen

The touch screen is where you control the action during battle. It has five buttons you will need for battling Pokémon: Fight, Poké Ball, Pokémon, Bag, and Run.

> **Tip**
>
> The Poké Balls representing Pokémon may sometimes appear in different colors. A yellow Poké Ball indicates a Pokémon has a status condition, while a grayed-out Poké Ball represents a Pokémon that has fainted.

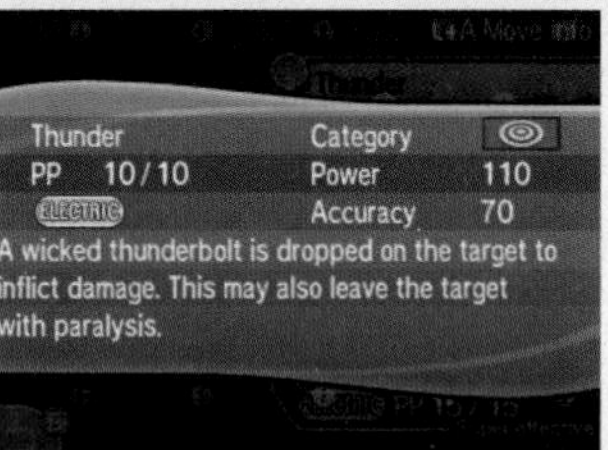

Fight

Choose "Fight" to view and unleash one of the moves your Pokémon knows. Press L + Ⓐ or tap the little icon that appears next to each move to view information about it and choose the right move for the situation.

> **Tip**
>
> If you've battled against the opposing Pokémon before, the effectiveness of your Pokémon's moves will be shown. Handy!

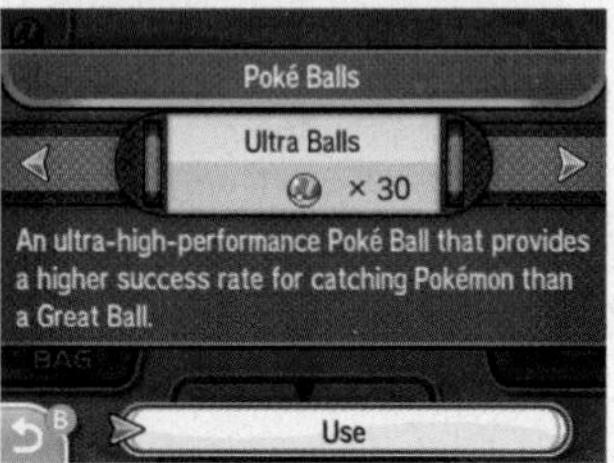

Poké Ball

During battles, a small Poké Ball icon appears in the touch screen's upper-left corner. If you're battling against a lone wild Pokémon, press Ⓨ or tap the Poké Ball icon to quickly choose a Poké Ball to throw in an effort to catch it. Press L or R, or ✚ or ✚, or tap a blue arrow to cycle through your Poké Balls, then tap "Use" or press Ⓐ to throw it. You'll learn more about catching Pokémon on pages 32 to 33.

Pokémon

Select "Pokémon" to swap in a different Pokémon; restore a Pokémon's HP or PP; view a summary of your Pokémon's stats, levels, Abilities, and held items; or check the moves that your party Pokémon currently know and their effectiveness.

Bag

Select "Bag" to access items you may need during a battle. These items are separated into four categories.

HP/PP Restore: Items that restore HP to Pokémon or PP to moves.

Status Restore: Items that can heal troublesome status conditions and their ilk.

Poké Balls: Items used to try to catch a wild Pokémon when battling one.

Battle Items: Items that help give your Pokémon a boost during battle.

Run

This is the simplest option available to you. Tap the "Run" button, and you and your party will attempt to run away. You may or may not get away safely, though, so be careful! You can't run during a battle against a Trainer.

Walkthrough

Understanding the Walkthrough

This walkthrough is filled with a variety of special elements designed to help you stay on course and get the most out of your adventure in Alola. Let's take a look at all of the various elements that appear throughout the walkthrough pages.

1 Route 1

Ride Pokémon Needed 3

2 A lush and vibrant trail, Route 1 lies along the east side of Melemele Island. It holds a few secrets that you can't explore on your first visit. It leads from Iki Town at its north end to Hau'oli Outskirts down south.

Team Recommendation 4

Tall Grass
East
Caterpie
Ledyba
Pikipek
Alolan Rattata
Spinarak
Yungoos
Near Iki Town
Caterpie
Grubbin
Ledyba
Metapod
Pichu
Pikipek
Alolan Rattata
Spinarak
Yungoos

Tall Grass
West
With Tauros Charge
Bonsly
Caterpie
Ledyba
Metapod
Munchlax
Pikipek
Alolan Rattata
Spinarak
Yungoos

frequent · average · rare · almost never · day only · night only · Pokémon Sun · Pokémon Moon

Items 5
1 Paralyze H[eal]
2 Potion
3 Poké Ball
4 Antidote
5 Potion
With Tauros Charge
6 Nest Ball
7 Nugget

1 Learn the basics of catching Pokémon

Professor Kukui stands in Route 1's tall grass, eager to teach you how to catch wild Pokémon. Pay careful attention as he sends out his Rockruff to demonstrate how to weaken wild Pokémon before throwing out his Poké Ball to catch it. The professor hands you 10 Poké Balls after his lesson, setting you up to catch wild Pokémon on your own. He also gives you five Potions so that you can heal your Pokémon during or after battle as needed.

Reward: Poké Ball ×10, Potion ×5

Route 1 31

1 Location Name

2 Location Guide

Learn a bit about the special features of various locations!

3 Ride Pokémon Needed

Check these icons to see which Ride Pokémon you need to access every area on the map and collect all available items. Note that Stoutland is only required to progress through one area (Lush Jungle), but it can also be used in many other areas to sniff out hidden items.

Tauros

Stoutland

Lapras

Mudsdale

Sharpedo

Machamp

4 Team Recommendations

This box contains information about some of the Pokémon types you might want to include in your team when tackling a particular area. Their moves will likely be supereffective against a number of the wild Pokémon you might encounter in that location.

5 Items and Shop Lists

These tables show a checklist of the items you can find by searching the area. Items found on the ground in Poké Balls are numbered on the map and can be identified using these tables. Hidden items are not labeled in the same way, but you will get a hint to where you may find a hidden item by looking for the ? icon on the map. At times, you must meet certain conditions to get an item, and those conditions are included. For cities and towns, you'll find shop tables that list the items that are sold by the clerks in the Poké Marts and other shops. In addition to text labels, the following icons are used throughout the maps in this guide:

- 1 Item
- ? Hidden Item
- 1 TM (p. 50)
- Zygarde Core/Cell (p. 91)
- Berry pile (p. 65)
- Photo Spot (p. 54)
- 1 Sub-event (p. 18)
- Fishing spot (p. 104)
- Rare fishing spot (p. 104)

6 Trainers Waiting to Challenge You

Find out where you can encounter Pokémon Trainers to battle against. The number of Poké Balls filled in below a Trainer's name tells you how many Pokémon they have, and the exact species and levels of their Pokémon are also listed to help you prepare for each battle in advance.

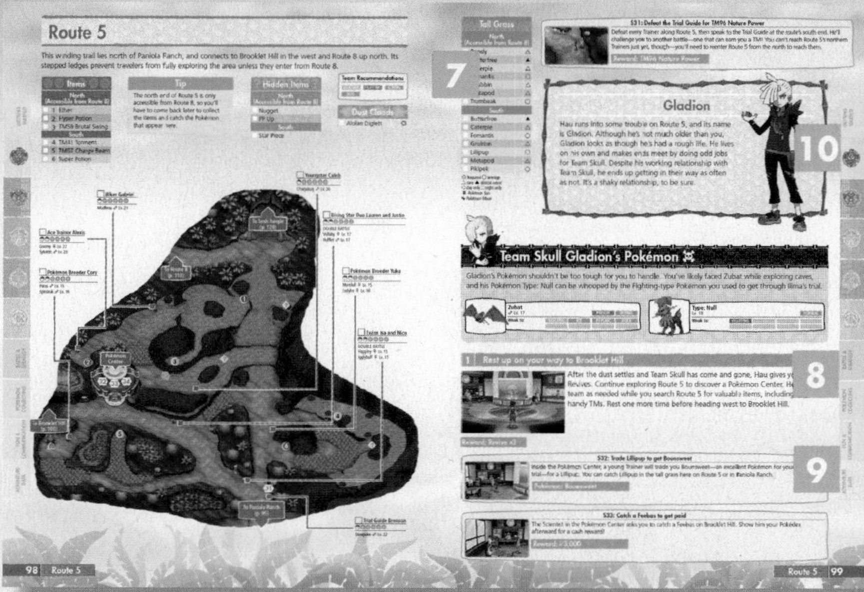

7 Pokémon Encounters

See the Pokémon that appear in the area. This information helps you complete your Pokédex. To encounter all of the Pokémon, you may sometimes need certain Ride Pokémon or have to fulfill other requirements. These will be labeled.

8 Completion Guide

What do you need to move forward? Get step-by-step descriptions of key events in each city, route, or cave. If you follow these steps in order, you'll be able to complete the main story!

9 Sub-events

Many tasks are purely optional and not required to advance through the adventure. These sub-events often have special rewards, so they're worth exploring if you have the time. Flip ahead a few pages to find the entire Sub-event List on page 18.

10 Extra Information

You want hints? Get 'em right here! Learn effective ways to use the items you receive and get behind-the-scenes stories on important characters.

11 Trial Guide Preparation

A little preparation before attempting to challenge a Trial Site will make it much easier to succeed in your trial. The information in this section helps you get ready.

12 Trial Guide Walkthrough

Get some hints on the tricks of each trial and the best ways to find your way through to the final clash against the formidable Totem Pokémon.

13 Totem Pokémon Strategies

Find out about the Totem Pokémon you'll face at the end of each trial, including their moves, weaknesses, and SOS allies. This gives you the info you need to choose the appropriate Pokémon and moves so you can target your opponent's weaknesses relentlessly!

14 Trial Rewards

Get an outline of the Z-Crystals you get for completing trials, along with any other rewards.

Tip

You'll sometimes find people in homes or places along routes that can restore your Pokémon's health. These locations are marked on each map.

Recommended Route

Below is the recommended route for your grand adventure through the Alola region. Check this guide when you want to know how much progress you've made so far, or when you're not sure where to go next.

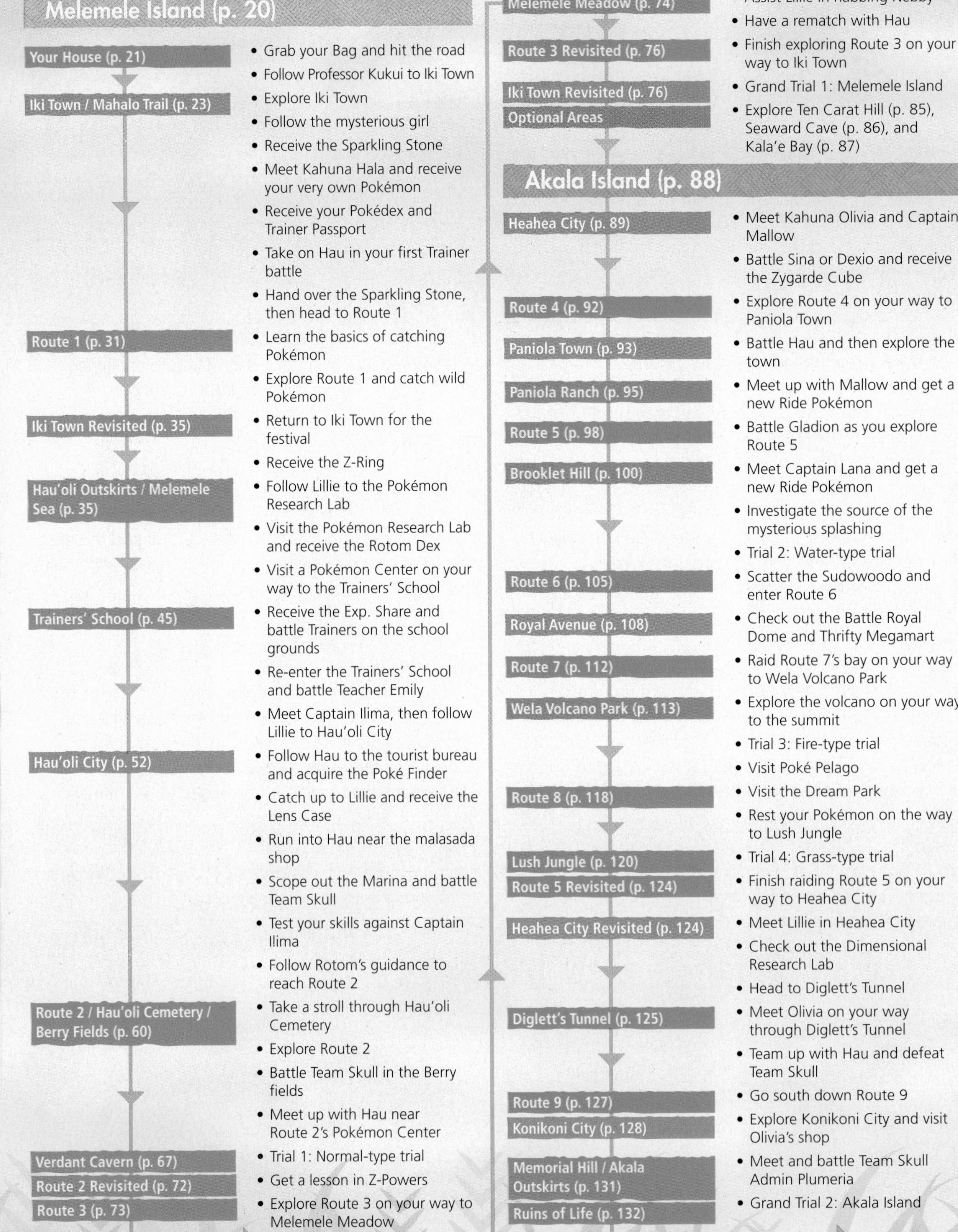

Melemele Island (p. 20)

Your House (p. 21)
- Grab your Bag and hit the road

Iki Town / Mahalo Trail (p. 23)
- Follow Professor Kukui to Iki Town
- Explore Iki Town
- Follow the mysterious girl
- Receive the Sparkling Stone
- Meet Kahuna Hala and receive your very own Pokémon
- Receive your Pokédex and Trainer Passport
- Take on Hau in your first Trainer battle
- Hand over the Sparkling Stone, then head to Route 1

Route 1 (p. 31)
- Learn the basics of catching Pokémon
- Explore Route 1 and catch wild Pokémon

Iki Town Revisited (p. 35)
- Return to Iki Town for the festival
- Receive the Z-Ring

Hau'oli Outskirts / Melemele Sea (p. 35)
- Follow Lillie to the Pokémon Research Lab
- Visit the Pokémon Research Lab and receive the Rotom Dex
- Visit a Pokémon Center on your way to the Trainers' School

Trainers' School (p. 45)
- Receive the Exp. Share and battle Trainers on the school grounds
- Re-enter the Trainers' School and battle Teacher Emily
- Meet Captain Ilima, then follow Lillie to Hau'oli City

Hau'oli City (p. 52)
- Follow Hau to the tourist bureau and acquire the Poké Finder
- Catch up to Lillie and receive the Lens Case
- Run into Hau near the malasada shop
- Scope out the Marina and battle Team Skull
- Test your skills against Captain Ilima
- Follow Rotom's guidance to reach Route 2

Route 2 / Hau'oli Cemetery / Berry Fields (p. 60)
- Take a stroll through Hau'oli Cemetery
- Explore Route 2
- Battle Team Skull in the Berry fields
- Meet up with Hau near Route 2's Pokémon Center

Verdant Cavern (p. 67)
- Trial 1: Normal-type trial

Route 2 Revisited (p. 72)
- Get a lesson in Z-Powers

Route 3 (p. 73)
- Explore Route 3 on your way to Melemele Meadow

Melemele Meadow (p. 74)
- Assist Lillie in nabbing Nebby
- Have a rematch with Hau

Route 3 Revisited (p. 76)
- Finish exploring Route 3 on your way to Iki Town

Iki Town Revisited (p. 76)
- Grand Trial 1: Melemele Island

Optional Areas
- Explore Ten Carat Hill (p. 85), Seaward Cave (p. 86), and Kala'e Bay (p. 87)

Akala Island (p. 88)

Heahea City (p. 89)
- Meet Kahuna Olivia and Captain Mallow
- Battle Sina or Dexio and receive the Zygarde Cube

Route 4 (p. 92)
- Explore Route 4 on your way to Paniola Town

Paniola Town (p. 93)
- Battle Hau and then explore the town

Paniola Ranch (p. 95)
- Meet up with Mallow and get a new Ride Pokémon

Route 5 (p. 98)
- Battle Gladion as you explore Route 5

Brooklet Hill (p. 100)
- Meet Captain Lana and get a new Ride Pokémon
- Investigate the source of the mysterious splashing
- Trial 2: Water-type trial

Route 6 (p. 105)
- Scatter the Sudowoodo and enter Route 6

Royal Avenue (p. 108)
- Check out the Battle Royal Dome and Thrifty Megamart

Route 7 (p. 112)
- Raid Route 7's bay on your way to Wela Volcano Park

Wela Volcano Park (p. 113)
- Explore the volcano on your way to the summit
- Trial 3: Fire-type trial
- Visit Poké Pelago
- Visit the Dream Park

Route 8 (p. 118)
- Rest your Pokémon on the way to Lush Jungle

Lush Jungle (p. 120)
- Trial 4: Grass-type trial

Route 5 Revisited (p. 124)
- Finish raiding Route 5 on your way to Heahea City

Heahea City Revisited (p. 124)
- Meet Lillie in Heahea City
- Check out the Dimensional Research Lab
- Head to Diglett's Tunnel

Diglett's Tunnel (p. 125)
- Meet Olivia on your way through Diglett's Tunnel
- Team up with Hau and defeat Team Skull

Route 9 (p. 127)
- Go south down Route 9

Konikoni City (p. 128)
- Explore Konikoni City and visit Olivia's shop

Memorial Hill / Akala Outskirts (p. 131)
- Meet and battle Team Skull Admin Plumeria

Ruins of Life (p. 132)
- Grand Trial 2: Akala Island

Hano Grand Resort / Hano Beach (p. 134)
- Explore the Hano Grand Resort
- Go with Branch Chief Faba to Aether Paradise

Aether Paradise (p. 139)
- Take a tour of Aether Paradise
- Witness a wormhole and battle an Ultra Beast
- Get some gifts before going to Ula'ula Island

Ula'ula Island (p. 141)

Malie City / Malie Garden (p. 142)
- Have a battle with Hau
- Meet up with Lillie and see a familiar face
- Meet Lillie and Hapu near the library
- Make a new friend on the library's second floor

Optional Areas
- Check out the Outer Cape (p. 147)

Route 10 (p. 149)
- Stop Team Skull from wrecking a bus stop
- Ride the bus to Hokulani Observatory

Mount Hokulani (p. 151)
- Meet Molayne and get tested in battle

Hokulani Observatory (p. 153)
- Trial 5: Electric-type trial

Malie City / Malie Garden Revisited (p. 156)
- Make your way back to Malie City
- Battle against Team Skull's boss
- Get a special gift from Kukui

Route 11 / Route 12 / Secluded Shore (p. 157)
- Reach Route 12 and receive a new Ride Pokémon

Optional Areas
- Pop by the Power Plant at Blush Mountain (p. 159)

Route 13 (p. 160)
- Get a warning from Gladion

Tapu Village / Route 14 (p. 161)
- Rest your Pokémon on the way to Route 15

Route 15 (p. 162)
- Clash with the kids at the Aether House
- Meet the last captain of Ula'ula Island, then battle Team Skull
- Return to Route 14 and take on the Ghost-type Pokémon trial

Abandoned Thrifty Megamart (p. 163)
- Trial 6: Ghost-type trial

Route 15 Revisited (p. 166)
- Battle Plumeria at the Aether House
- Receive a Rare Candy and a new objective
- Cross Route 15's waters atop Sharpedo

Route 16 (p. 167)
- Rest up on your way to Po Town

Ula'ula Meadow (p. 169)
- Mosey through the Meadow

Route 17 (p. 170)
- Explore Route 17 on the way to Po Town

Po Town (p. 171)
- Make your way to the Shady House

Shady House (p. 172)
- Search the Shady House for clues
- Battle Guzma in his bedroom
- Meet Nanu and Acerola, then return to Aether House

Route 15 Revisited (p. 175)
- Battle Gladion at Aether House

Malie City Revisited (p. 176)
- Grand Trial 3: Ula'ula Island

Optional Areas
- Explore Haina Desert (p. 178) and the Ruins of Abundance (p. 180)

Aether Paradise (p. 181)
- Ride the elevator up and be ready for battle
- Ride the elevator down to the secret labs
- Battle your way into Secret Lab B
- Search Secret Lab B for clues
- Have your Pokémon restored by Wicke
- Face off against a familiar foe
- Get past the Grunts and then battle Guzma
- Find Lillie and Lusamine in the mansion
- Go to the docks and shove off to Poni Island

Poni Island (p. 189)

Seafolk Village (p. 190)
- Explore Seafolk Village

Poni Wilds (p. 192)
- Make a run through Poni Wilds

Ancient Poni Path (p. 193)
- Meet Hapu and register a new Ride Pokémon

Poni Breaker Coast / Ruins of Hope (p. 195)
- Muscle through the ruins with Machamp
- Meet up with Hapu inside the ruins

Seafolk Village Revisited (p. 196)
- Speak with the chief of Seafolk Village

Exeggutor Island (p. 196)
- Search the island for the flute

Seafolk Village Revisited (p. 197)
- Prepare your team, then head for the canyon

Ancient Poni Path Revisited (p. 197)
- Receive a Z-Crystal from Plumeria
- Grand Trial 4: Poni Island

Vast Poni Canyon (p. 198)
- Make your way through the caves
- Meet Mina and receive Fairium Z
- Use a root to reach the canyon floor
- Enter the unguarded trial site
- Trial 7: Dragon-type trial

Altar of the Sunne ☼ / Altar of the Moone ☾ (p. 204)
- Summon Alola's Legendary Pokémon

Ultra Space (p. 205)
- Travel to Ultra Space
- Battle a fearsome foe

Altar of the Sunne ☼ / Altar of the Moone ☾ Revisited (p. 206)
- Battle and catch Alola's Legendary Pokémon
- Go with Nanu to Mount Lanakila

Mount Lanakila (p. 208)
- Battle Gladion at Mount Lanakila's base
- Climb Mount Lanakila
- Rest up and then battle Hau
- Meet up with Professor Kukui

Pokémon League (p. 211)
- Defeat the Elite Four and take on your final challenger

Enter the Hall of Fame
- Your adventure continues after you enter the Hall of Fame. Pack your Bag for another journey around the Alola region!

Sub-event List

Below is the complete list of every sub-event you can complete during your explorations of Alola. The numbering of the sub-events corresponds to the walkthrough, so you can easily find them if you need a bit more guidance. Refer to this list to make sure you haven't missed anything special!

No.	Location	Page	Sub-event	Conditions
1	Trainers' School	46	Get a Quick Claw in the Trainers' School	
2	Trainers' School	47	Get a Potion in the Trainers' School	
3	Hau'oli City	53	Get a Potion on the Beachfront	
4	Hau'oli City	53	Earn 10 Ultra Balls at the tourist bureau	
5	Hau'oli City	56	Get a Silk Scarf near the apparel shop	
6	Hau'oli City	56	Get ₽10,000 for catching a Drifloon in the Pokémon Center	
7	Hau'oli City	56	Get a Heal Ball outside the Pokémon Center	
8	Hau'oli City	57	Get a Lumiose Galette from Ilima's mom at Ilima's house	
9	Hau'oli City	57	Get a Revive in Hau'oli City Hall	
10	Hau'oli City	58	Get X Attack and X Defense on the pier	
11	Route 2	64	Get 2 Nest Balls in the Melemele Motel	
12	Berry Fields	65	Get a Sitrus Berry for a Persim Berry	
13	Berry Fields	65	Get a Revive from a Delibird in the Berry farmer's house	
14	Route 2	66	Trade a Spearow for a Machop in the Pokémon Center	
15	Route 2	66	Earn ₽3,000 for catching a Cutiefly in the Pokémon Center	
16	Route 3	76	Defeat all Trainers on Route 3 for a Red Card	
17	Route 3	76	Earn ₽3,000 for catching a Rockruff	
18	Route 3	76	Get a Soothe Bell from a Pokémon Breeder	
19	Hau'oli Outskirts	80	Get an Awakening from Meowth at home	
20	Hau'oli City	82	Get a Gracidea at the mall	After completing the Melemele grand trial
21	Hau'oli City	82	Get 5 Great Balls ☼ / TM48 Round ☽ at the mall	After completing the Melemele grand trial
22	Hau'oli City	84	Visit Ilima's house to battle Ilima for an Everstone	After completing the Melemele grand trial
23	Hau'oli City	84	Get a Shell Bell at City Hall	After completing the Melemele grand trial
24	Hau'oli Cemetery	84	Get TM56 Fling at night ☽	After completing the Melemele grand trial
25	Heahea City	90	Earn ₽10,000 for catching Pyukumuku in the apparel shop	
26	Heahea City	90	Get a Rare Candy from a lady	
27	Paniola Town	94	Get a Quick Ball in Kiawe's house	
28	Paniola Ranch	96	Get a Scope Lens for defeating Tauros	
29	Paniola Ranch	96	Get TM10 Hidden Power from a Breeder in the Pokémon Nursery	
30	Paniola Ranch	96	Get your first Pokémon Egg in the Pokémon Nursery	
31	Route 5	99	Defeat all Trainers on Route 5 for TM96 Nature Power	
32	Route 5	99	Trade a Lillipup for a Bounsweet in the Pokémon Center	
33	Route 5	99	Earn ₽3,000 for catching Feebas in the Pokémon Center	
34	Route 5	100	Get a Dire Hit in the Pokémon Center	
35	Hau'oli Outskirts	104	Earn a Wide Lens for helping Corsola at the beach	After getting a Fishing Rod
36	Heahea City	107	Get a Lemonade from a GAME FREAK employee	
37	Royal Avenue	110	Get Berries at the Thrifty Megamart	
38	Royal Avenue	110	Get TM44 Rest from a Hypno at the Thrifty Megamart	
39	Royal Avenue	110	Get a Lemonade from a Drifloon at the Thrifty Megamart	
40	Royal Avenue	110	Get an Effort Ribbon for a well-trained Pokémon at the dome	
41	Route 8	118	Defeat all Trainers on Route 8 for TM58 Sky Drop	
42	Route 8	119	Earn ₽5,000 for catching Stufful in the Aether Base	
43	Diglett's Tunnel	125	Defeat all Trainers in Diglett's Tunnel for a Max Revive	
44	Konikoni City	130	Have a meal and get some Heart Scales at Mallow's restaurant	
45	Konikoni City	130	Get Pikanium Z from a Pikachu lover	
46	Konikoni City	130	Trade a Zubat for a Poliwhirl at the Pokémon Center	
47	Konikoni City	130	Earn ₽5,000 for catching Passimian ☼ or Oranguru ☽	
48	Hano Beach	135	Get a Soda Pop on the beach	
49	Hano Beach	135	Get paid ₽20,000 to be a Pyukumuku chucker	

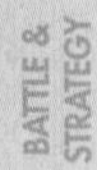

No.	Location	Page	Sub-event	Conditions
50	Hano Grand Hotel	135	Get a Metronome for a battle	
51	Hano Grand Hotel	135	Win a Double Battle for TM45 Attract	
52	Hano Grand Hotel	136	Get a Footprint Ribbon for a leveled-up Pokémon	
53	Heahea City	136	Get a Reveal Glass at the Dimensional Research Lab	After completing the Akala grand trial
54	Route 9	136	Get a Focus Band in the Route 9 Police Station	After completing the Akala grand trial
55	Konikoni City	137	Dine with Olivia at Mallow's restaurant	After completing the Akala grand trial
56	Konikoni City	137	Visit Lana's house to battle her and her sisters for a Muscle Band	After completing the Akala grand trial
57	Konikoni City	138	Visit Kiawe's house and battle him for a new battle style ☽	After completing the Akala grand trial
58	Konikoni City	138	Visit Mallow's restaurant to take her on for a new battle style ☼	After completing the Akala grand trial
59	Aether Paradise	139	Get a Stick from a staff member on 1F: Entrance	
60	Malie City	144	Have a meal and get some Heart Scales at Sushi High Roller	
61	Malie City	144	Trade a Pancham for a Happiny at Sushi High Roller	
62	Malie City	144	Earn ₽10,000 for catching Togedemaru in the apparel shop	
63	Malie City	145	Get TM76 Fly in Malie Library	
64	Malie City	145	Get a Love Ball for showing off an Alolan Persian in the library	
65	Malie City	145	Get a Strange Souvenir in the Malie Community Center	
66	Malie City	145	Get a Best Friend Ribbon for an affectionate Pokémon	
67	Malie City	145	Get weather rocks at the Malie Community Center	
68	Outer Cape	147	Get a Twisted Spoon for helping a father and son	
69	Outer Cape	147	Get a Friend Ball from Oak at the Recycling Plant	
70	Route 10	150	Find runaway Stufful for a Never-Melt Ice and ₽15,000	
71	Mount Hokulani	152	Get a Moon Ball from Oak near the Pokémon Center	
72	Mount Hokulani	152	Defeat all Trainers on Mount Hokulani for TM95 Snarl	
73	Hokulani Observatory	153	Get a Comet Shard from a staff member	
74	Malie Garden	156	Make it across Nugget Bridge for a Big Nugget	After defeating Guzma in Malie Garden
75	Route 12	158	Defeat all Trainers on Route 12 for TM77 Psych Up	
76	Blush Mountain	159	Get a Lure Ball from Oak at the Power Plant	
77	Blush Mountain	159	Get TM63 Embargo at the Power Plant ☼	
78	Route 13	160	Get TM12 Taunt in a trailer	
79	Tapu Village	161	Trade a Haunter for an Alolan Graveler in the Pokémon Center	
80	Route 15	162	Defeat all Trainers on Route 15 for a PP Max	
81	Route 16	168	Earn ₽20,000 for catching a Mimikyu in the Pokémon Center	
82	Route 16	168	Get a free Lemonade for being a café regular	After ordering a café drink five times or more
83	Ula'ula Meadow	169	Defeat all Trainers in Ula'ula Meadow for a Flame Orb	
84	Malie City	177	Get a Reaper Cloth in the Pokémon Center	After completing the Ula'ula grand trial
85	Malie Garden	177	Get an Air Balloon for a quiz ☼	After completing the Ula'ula grand trial
86	Malie City	177	Get TM21 Frustration and TM27 Return in the malasada shop ☽	After completing the Ula'ula grand trial
87	Malie City	177	Share a meal with Nanu at Sushi High Roller and get some Heart Scales	After completing the Ula'ula grand trial
88	Route 13	180	Get 3 Adrenaline Orbs for a Fresh Water at the desert entrance	After completing the Ula'ula grand trial
89	Haina Desert	180	Get Safety Goggles for some bleary eyes ☽	After completing the Ula'ula grand trial
90	Seafolk Village	190	Get a Magmarizer and Electirizer for free at the shop boat	
91	Seafolk Village	191	Get an Aerodactyl from a generous woman at the shop boat	
92	Seafolk Village	191	Have a meal and get a Heart Scale at the floating restaurant	
93	Seafolk Village	191	Get a Lucky Punch from one of the residents in a houseboat	
94	Seafolk Village	191	Get Aloraichium Z from one of the residents in a houseboat	
95	Seafolk Village	191	Trade a Granbull for a Steenee near the big central tree	
96	Poni Wilds	193	Defeat all Trainers in Poni Wilds for a Focus Sash	
97	Ancient Poni Path	194	Get an Awakening from Hapu's Meowth at Hapu's house	
98	Seafolk Village	204	Share a meal with Hapu at the floating restaurant and get some Heart Scales	After completing the Poni grand trial
99	Route 2	210	Get TM87 Swagger from Guzma's mom at Guzma's house	After the Pokémon League becomes available
100	Poni Plains	223	Defeat all Trainers in Poni Plains for TM60 Quash	
101	Poni Gauntlet	223	Trade a Bewear for a Talonflame	
102	Poni Gauntlet	223	Defeat all Trainers in Poni Gauntlet for a Bottle Cap	

Melemele Island

Welcome to Alola, Trainer! Your exciting adventure begins right here at Melemele Island—a tropical paradise that's home to happy people and exotic Pokémon. Think you've got what it takes to become an island challenge champion? Of course you do! And we're here to help you every step of the way.

1 Chat with Professor Kukui

Look at you! You've yet to set foot in Alola, and already you've received a call from the region's renowned Pokémon buff—Professor Kukui. The friendly professor requests a bit of personal info so that he can introduce you to everybody and ready your Trainer Passport. Answer Professor Kukui's questions, and you'll determine your gender, appearance, and name. Note that you can change some aspects of your appearance later in the game (eye color, hair color, and clothing), but you can't alter your name or gender. If you make a mistake, press ✚ + Ⓑ + Ⓧ simultaneously at the game's title screen to delete all of your data and start over again with a clean slate.

2 Get up and get going

After completing your chat with Professor Kukui, the scene shifts to your first day (or night) in the Alola region, and there's no time for sleeping in! Move the Circle Pad to hop out of bed, then walk through the foreground door and meet your mom in the front room. Professor Kukui soon stops by to greet you in person, and he's eager for you to meet the Island Kahuna, who lives in the next town over. Kukui says the kahuna is always happy to give adventuresome kids their very first Pokémon—so what are you waiting for?!

Kala'e Bay
(p. 87)

Your House

Pokémon Center

Pokémon Research Lab

Ten Carat Hill
(p. 85)

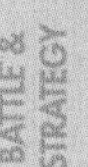

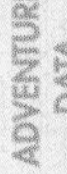

3 Grab your Bag and hit the road

Hang on, you'll need your Bag before you set off on any adventures. Return to your room (through the right background door), and search the box near your bed to find your Bag and hat. NOW you're ready for action! You return to the living room and say "bye" to your mom, then follow Professor Kukui outside.

4 Follow Professor Kukui to Iki Town

Iki Town isn't far. Follow Professor Kukui through Route 1, holding Ⓑ to dash along the dirt trail. Talk to everyone you meet for little bits of advice and info. Professor Kukui also pauses at different spots to tantalize you with tidbits about tall grass, wild Pokémon, and Pokémon battles.

Professor Kukui

A local of the Alola region, Professor Kukui yearns to prove that Alola's Trainers are as good as any others in the world. He has devoted his life to researching Pokémon moves, and he once spent time in the Kanto region—the very place from which you and your mom just moved. Professor Kukui delights in taking new Trainers under his wing, and he's always eager to provide guidance that will help them reach their full potential.

Iki Town / Mahalo Trail

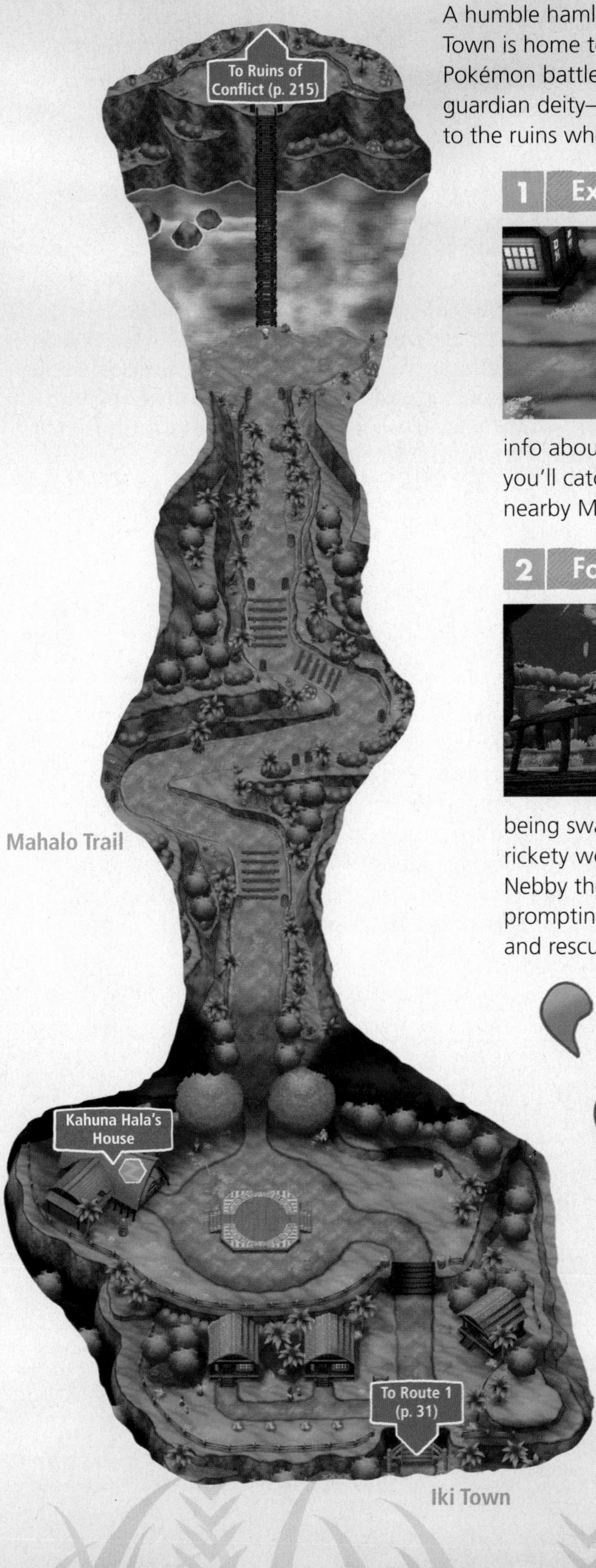

A humble hamlet nestled near the center of Melemele Island, Iki Town is home to the island's kahuna. Festivals featuring ceremonial Pokémon battles are regularly held here in honor of the island's guardian deity—Tapu Koko. Mahalo Trail leads north from the town to the ruins where Tapu Koko is said to reside.

1 Explore Iki Town

You've reached Iki Town, and Professor Kukui asks that you look around and find the local kahuna. Take a look around town, popping into each house and talking to everyone you see for more info about Alola and its Pokémon. Scale the north stairs, and you'll catch sight of a mysterious girl who begins hiking up the nearby Mahalo Trail.

2 Follow the mysterious girl

Talk to the townsfolk up north before following the mysterious girl up Mahalo Trail. Dash to the top of the winding trail to find the girl in a state of distress—her Pokémon, Nebby, is being swarmed by a flock of wild Spearow! Hurry across the rickety wooden bridge and save poor Nebby from its plight. Nebby then lets out a burst of power that shatters the bridge, prompting a powerful Pokémon to swoop down from the sky and rescue you from a nasty fall.

3 Receive the Sparkling Stone

Grateful for your help, the mysterious girl hands you a Sparkling Stone that your Pokémon savior appears to have left behind. It seems important, so you tuck it safely away in your Key Items Pocket. The girl then begs you not to tell anyone about her Pokémon and asks if you'd kindly see her back to town. Head back toward the town together with her.

Reward: Sparkling Stone

4 Meet Kahuna Hala and receive your very own Pokémon

Professor Kukui awaits you back at Iki Town, and he reveals that the mysterious girl whom you've helped is none other than his own assistant, Lillie. The great Kahuna Hala soon appears, and he's fascinated to learn that the island's guardian deity, Tapu Koko, saved you after Nebby destroyed the bridge. Seeing all of this as cause to celebrate, Kahuna Hala puts before you three young Pokémon—Rowlet, Litten, and Popplio. Whichever one you pick is yours to keep from this day forth!

Pokémon: Rowlet, Litten, or Popplio

Lillie

A mysterious girl named Lillie looks after an even more mysterious Pokémon, which she calls "Nebby." Lillie carries Nebby around in her bag instead of in a Poké Ball, and there seems to be much more to the two of them than meets the eye. Although she isn't a Trainer, Lillie possesses a love of Pokémon, and hates to see them hurt in any way. She also loves to read, and is always remembering things that she picked up from some book or another. She stays at the professor's Pokémon Research Lab and helps Kukui conduct his important research around the island.

Kahuna Hala

Kahuna Hala is one of only four kahunas in all of Alola. Each island in Alola has a kahuna, and each kahuna is chosen by their island's guardian deity, which in this case is Tapu Koko. One of the most respected figures in the Alola region, Hala is a powerful Pokémon Trainer—and he's also powerful in his own right, practicing Alolan-style sumo wrestling.

Which One Will You Choose?

Kahuna Hala presents you with three Pokémon: the Grass- and Flying-type Pokémon Rowlet, the Fire-type Pokémon Litten, and the Water-type Pokémon Popplio. This first partner Pokémon may remain with you on your entire journey, and the three Pokémon that Hala has offered you are not easily encountered. You will not find them in the wild, so this is your one and only chance unless someone trades you one. (You can learn more about trades on page 267.)

Rowlet

A Grass- and Flying-type Pokémon, Rowlet's Flying-type moves are strong against Bug-type Pokémon, which crawl all over the tall grass near your new home. Flying-type moves are also super effective against the powerful Fighting-type Pokémon you'll eventually face during your grand trial here on Melemele Island!

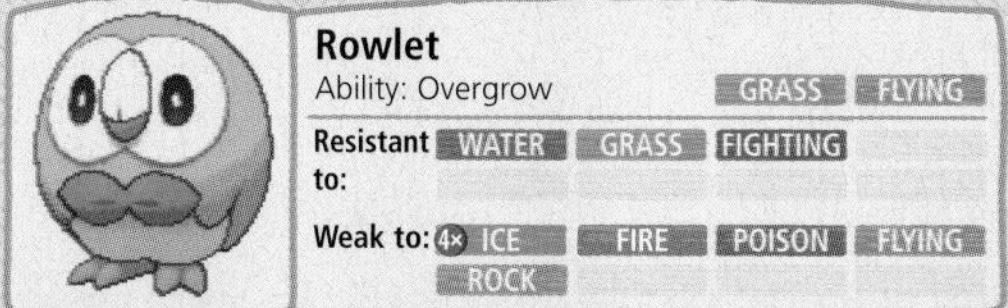

Rowlet	
Ability: Overgrow	GRASS, FLYING
Resistant to:	WATER, GRASS, FIGHTING
Weak to:	4× ICE, FIRE, POISON, FLYING, ROCK

Litten

A Fire-type Pokémon, Litten's Fire-type moves can really toast Grass- and Bug-type Pokémon. This makes Litten a solid choice for the areas you'll soon be exploring, like Route 1 and Route 2. Because Litten is a Fire type, it will take less damage from any Grass- or Bug-type moves that opponents might throw at it. Litten is a good choice if you want an easier start to your adventure.

Litten	
Ability: Blaze	FIRE
Resistant to:	FIRE, GRASS, ICE, BUG, STEEL, FAIRY
Weak to:	WATER, GROUND, ROCK

Tip

Remember that types all have their own weaknesses and strengths, as you can read about on page 232. If a Pokémon is resistant to another type, they will only take half or less of the usual damage when hit by a move of that type. But if they are weak to another type, then they will take at least double the usual damage when hit by a move of that type!

Popplio

A Water-type Pokémon, Popplio won't make a big splash until you complete Melemele Island's grand trial and shove off to Alola's second island, Akala. However, once you get to Akala Island, you'll find that Popplio's Water-type moves are quite effective against many of the indigenous Pokémon that you'll encounter. You won't encounter many other Water-type Pokémon until you're able to fish for Pokémon or travel on the water, so consider choosing Popplio if you feel like planning ahead.

Popplio	
Ability: Torrent	WATER
Resistant to:	FIRE, WATER, ICE, STEEL
Weak to:	GRASS, ELECTRIC

5 Receive your Pokédex and Trainer Passport

Now that you've got a Pokémon to care for, Professor Kukui hands you two invaluable items: a Pokédex, which automatically records data on any Pokémon you meet or catch, and your Trainer Passport, which contains all of your personal information, including your most noteworthy deeds and accomplishments around the region. Now you have everything you need to explore Alola on your own!

Reward: Pokédex, Trainer Passport

What's a Pokédex?

The Pokédex is a high-tech Trainer tool that automatically records and stores info on the Pokémon that you've seen or caught around Alola. To view its data, simply press ⓧ to open the X menu, and then select the Pokédex. You'll see that the data is split into four sub-dexes—one for each of Alola's islands. Complete each Island Pokédex in turn as you work toward completing the entire Alola Pokédex!

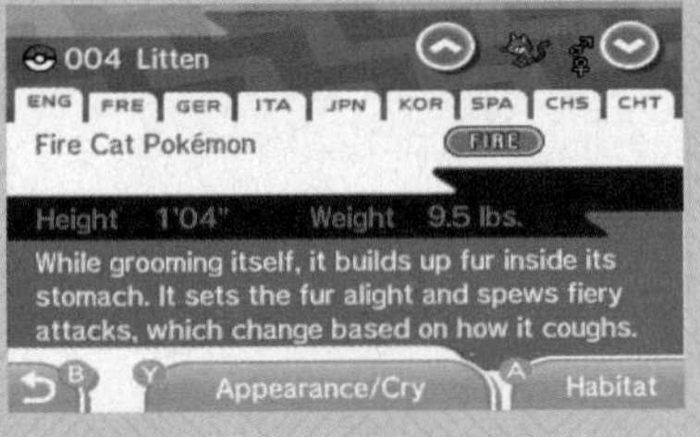

Open up an Island Pokédex and then select a registered Pokémon. All recorded data for that Pokémon will then appear, including its Category, type(s), size, and description. You can also press ⓨ to check its appearance and listen to its cry, or press ⓐ to view its known habitats. Pressing ⓧ calls up its QR Code. (More about that on page 43.)

When checking a Pokémon's appearance, press ⓨ to hear its distinct cry. Press ⓧ to see what actions it can perform on the upper screen. Rotate the image of the Pokémon using your Circle Pad, and press up or down on the +Control Pad to move through different Pokémon in your Pokédex once you've registered a few more. Pressing right or left will let you see different forms of the current Pokémon, if you've discovered any.

Select "Habitat" for a Pokémon that you've caught, and you can see where it appears in the wild. Press ⓧ or tap the numbers at the bottom of the screen to switch between Alola's islands. Press ⓨ to zoom-in on an area and see exactly where the Pokémon will appear. While you're zoomed in, the habitat icon may also change to show a sun or moon, indicating that the Pokémon will only appear during the day or night.

- Pokémon appears only at night
- Pokémon appears only during the day

Check Out Your Lower Screen

The gifts that Professor Kukui just gave you have caused a number of new options to appear on the lower screen, in addition to your Pokédex. Press ⓧ to open the X menu and check 'em out!

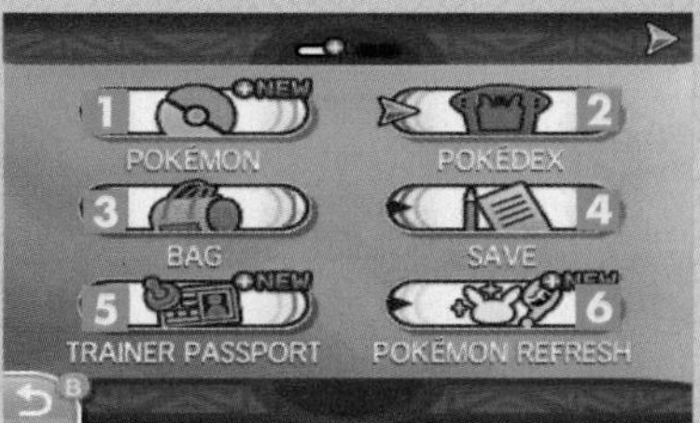

1. **Pokémon:** Check your team
2. **Pokédex:** Learn about Pokémon
3. **Bag:** Use items
4. **Save:** Save your game anytime
5. **Trainer Passport:** View your progress
6. **Pokémon Refresh:** Pamper and care for your Pokémon

Tip

To find the Options, press the small arrow at the top righthand corner of the screen or tap the Ⓡ button.

Select "Pokémon" to view the Pokémon in your current team. You can have up to six Pokémon in your team at a time. If you catch more than six, you'll have to send one to your PC Box. You can swap Pokémon in and out of your PC Box anytime by visiting a Pokémon Center (p. 40). If you have more than one Pokémon in your team, you can tap and drag your Pokémon around the lower screen to change their lineup. Just know that the Pokémon in the upper-left corner is the first one you'll send out during battle.

Select a Pokémon and choose "Summary" to call up its information. On the bottom Summary screen, you'll see the moves it knows and their types. Select any move to make its description appear on the upper screen, and tap and drag the moves to arrange them however you like. You can also see your Pokémon's Ability and learn what it does by tapping the small ⓘ icon next to it. If the Pokémon is holding an item, you can also see what item it's holding. (We'll explain more about that once you receive your first item that a Pokémon can hold.) Tap the icons up top to view further details, including the Pokémon's Nature (p. 271) and any Ribbons that it's wearing (p. 298).

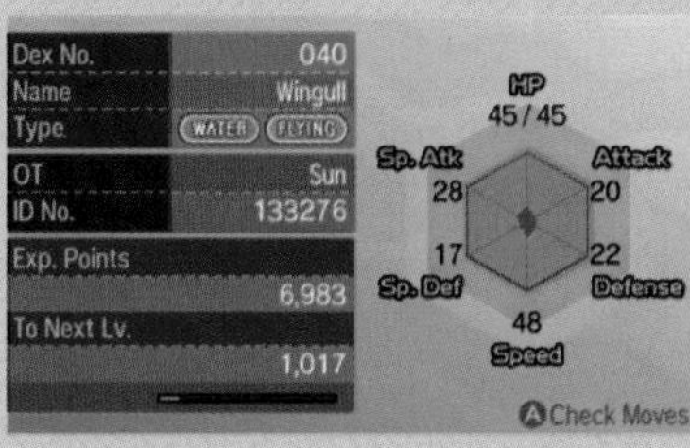

This is the upper Summary screen. See your name there beside OT? OT stands for "Original Trainer," and even if you trade a Pokémon away, you will always be listed as the OT of any Pokémon that you caught or hatched. You can see how many Exp. Points your Pokémon currently has on this screen, and how close it is to reaching its next level. The Pokémon's battle stats, such as Speed and Attack, are also shown on the right.

Select "Bag" from the X menu to check any items that you've collected. Press right or left to switch through the tabs along the top of the lower screen and view your Bag's pockets for medicine, items that you might use in battle, TMs, Berries, and Key Items that you acquire during your adventure. You'll learn more about these categories as you progress in your adventure. The pocket that's marked with a heart is a free space that you can move any items into if you want to organize them a bit differently. You may wish to place frequently used items there.

Check Out Your Lower Screen (continued)

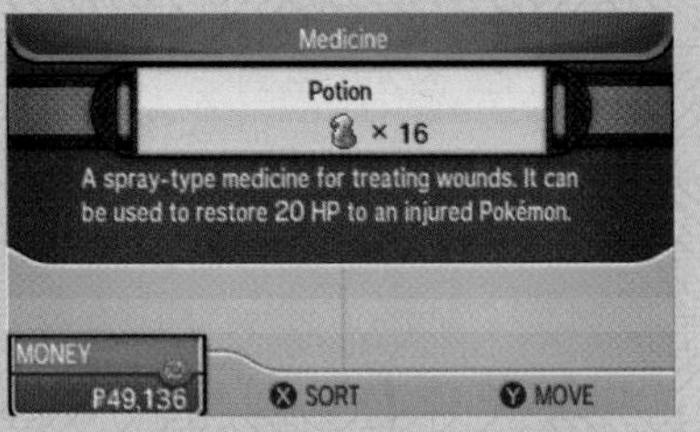

Select an item to call up a description of what it can do and how many you possess. A number of options will appear on the lower screen, such as "Use this item," "Give to Pokémon," or "Move to Free Space." Select "Cancel" or press Ⓑ if you don't want to do anything with an item. You can also press Ⓧ to sort your items using different criteria, such as when you got them or in alphabetical order.

Choose "Save" to save your game anytime. You can save your game anytime and anywhere in *Pokémon Sun* and *Pokémon Moon*, except during cinematic events and battles. There's no auto-save function in *Pokémon Sun* and *Pokémon Moon*, so remember to save often! It's especially wise to save before you begin a difficult battle, or if you think you might be heading into a challenging area. You may also want to save before attempting to catch a rare Pokémon, so that you can try again in case things don't work out!

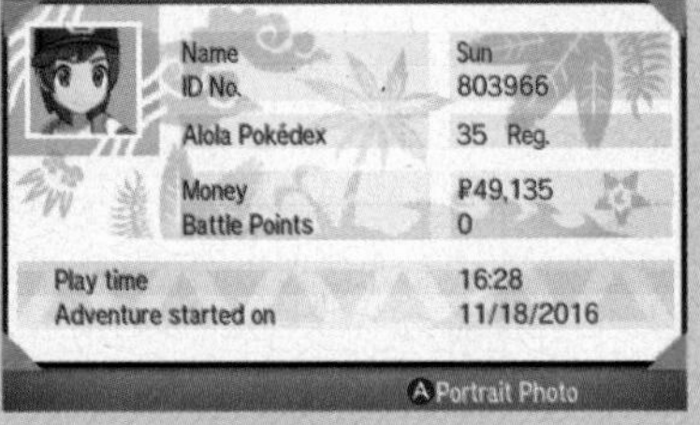

Your Trainer Passport can be viewed from the X menu as well. Here you can view your prize money, play time, and more info pertaining to your progress as a Trainer. Press Ⓐ if you'd like to retake your portrait photo. You'll also gather stamps for your passport as you explore Alola's islands, catch wild Pokémon, and more. Think you can fill your Trainer Passport full of stamps? Sure you can! And if you need a little help, just turn to page 230 to see the requirements for every last stamp.

Pokémon Refresh lets you pamper your Pokémon in a number of ways. Pet your Pokémon to increase its Enjoyment—but try not to rub it the wrong way! You can also feed your Pokémon tasty Poké Beans to increase its Fullness, provided you have some to share. Tap the top-left icon to view your Poké Beans, then drag one down to your Pokémon's mouth and hold it there until it has finished with its snack. Tap the lower-right button to view your team and see which Pokémon need the most care. (Learn more on page 276.)

Text Speed	Normal
Battle Effects	On
Battle Style	Switch
Button Mode	Default
Party/Box	Manual

Confirm

Select "Options" to view and adjust a number of game settings. Here you can increase the text speed if you want to move through dialogue more quickly, or turn off battle effects if you wish to speed up your battles. You can even change the battle style so that you won't be asked to switch Pokémon each time your opponent is about to send in a new Pokémon during battle. This last option makes battles more challenging, so only consider it if you are ready for a tougher experience!

6 Take on Hau in your first Trainer battle!

You don't get far before an excitable young man named Hau challenges you to your very first Trainer battle. Hau is Kahuna Hala's grandson, and he's eager to follow in his grandfather's footsteps. Now's your chance to show Alola what you've got! If you are a novice Trainer and need some more tips about how to navigate battles, turn the page. On page 30, you can learn all the battle basics you'll need to defeat Hau!

Hau

The grandson of Kahuna Hala, Hau has grown up under the watch of some of the strongest people in Alola. Does he have what it takes to live up to his grandfather's legacy? Only time will tell, but there's certainly no questioning the young man's heart. Hau is a cheery young boy who always has a smile for his friends and his Pokémon—and always a bit more room in his stomach for another malasada or two.

Hau's Pokémon

Have no fear during this first battle, for Hau sends out a Pokémon that's type is weak against the type of your first partner Pokémon. For instance, if you chose the Water-type Pokémon, Popplio, then Hau will send out the Fire-type Pokémon, Litten, which is weak against Water types. Simply use your Pokémon's Grass-, Fire-, or Water-type move to defeat Hau's Pokémon with ease.

If you choose Rowlet

Popplio	
♂ Lv. 5	WATER
Weak to:	GRASS, ELECTRIC

If you choose Litten

Rowlet	
♂ Lv. 5	GRASS, FLYING
Weak to:	4× ICE, FIRE, POISON, FLYING, ROCK

If you choose Popplio

Litten	
♂ Lv. 5	FIRE
Weak to:	WATER, GROUND, ROCK

Tip

Your Pokémon leveled up! Battling helps your Pokémon gain Exp. Points. When a Pokémon gains enough Exp. Points, it levels up to a new level. Each time a Pokémon levels up, its stats grow, making it more powerful. It may also learn new moves—or even evolve into a new Pokémon!

Battle Basics

It's your first battle as a Pokémon Trainer! Pokémon battles are turn-based affairs, with each Trainer choosing a move for his or her Pokémon to use each turn. After the moves have been chosen, the Pokémon's Speed stat determines which Pokémon will act first. Your goal in a battle is to make all of the other Trainer's Pokémon faint by reducing their HP to zero.

The lower screen contains all of your options in battle: 1 Pokémon, 2 Bag, 3 Fight, and 4 Run.

Pokémon: If you have more than one Pokémon on your team, you can tap this button to switch out your current Pokémon for another. Note that switching a new Pokémon into battle uses up your turn, giving your opponent an extra move against you.

Bag: You can open your Bag from within battle and choose to use healing items or battle items on your Pokémon. You can also use Poké Balls on wild Pokémon.

Fight: Tap this button to choose a move for your Pokémon to use. Moves can damage the opposing Pokémon, give the opponent some sort of negative condition, or bestow beneficial conditions to your own Pokémon. Some moves can even affect the battlefield. Your Pokémon can learn new moves as they level up by gaining experience in battle.

Run: If things aren't going so well, you can try to run from a battle against a wild Pokémon. You can't run away from battles against other Trainers, though! It seems honor demands that you stay and fight to the end.

Tip

Tap the icon next to a move to call up a description of what it does. You can also hold down L while selecting a move with Ⓐ to bring up its info.

Tip

After you've battled a particular species of Pokémon, the effectiveness of your Pokémon's moves will appear by each move when you face that species again in future battles. This is a good reason to encounter as many Pokémon as you can in the wild!

Pokémon and Move Types

On page 7, we explained that all Pokémon have types. Well, their moves have types, too! Pokémon can use many different types of moves, but if a Pokémon's type matches the type of the move that it uses, it will have 50% more power! This is often called the same-type attack bonus, and it's worth aiming for. Try to use moves that match your Pokémon's type to deal more damage in battle!

Luckily for you, Hau has chosen an opponent that is weak to your Pokémon's type. If you use an attack that shares your Pokémon's type, it will not only be super effective, but it will also get the same-type attack bonus. Victory should be yours in no time.

7 Hand over the Sparkling Stone, then head to Route 1

Pleased with your battle skill, Kahuna Hala is further wowed by the sudden shimmer of the Sparkling Stone you've stashed in your Bag. Upon learning that Tapu Koko left this mysterious item behind for you, Hala asks that you let him keep it until tomorrow evening. After handing Hala the Sparkling Stone, you return home to show your mom your Pokémon. The next day, Professor Kukui returns and ushers you back to Route 1 for a bit of training. Head out the door and go east this time to find him once again.

Route 1

Ride Pokémon Needed

A lush and vibrant trail, Route 1 lies along the east side of Melemele Island. It holds a few secrets that you can't explore on your first visit. It leads from Iki Town at its north end to Hau'oli Outskirts down south.

Team Recommendations

FIRE | FLYING | BUG

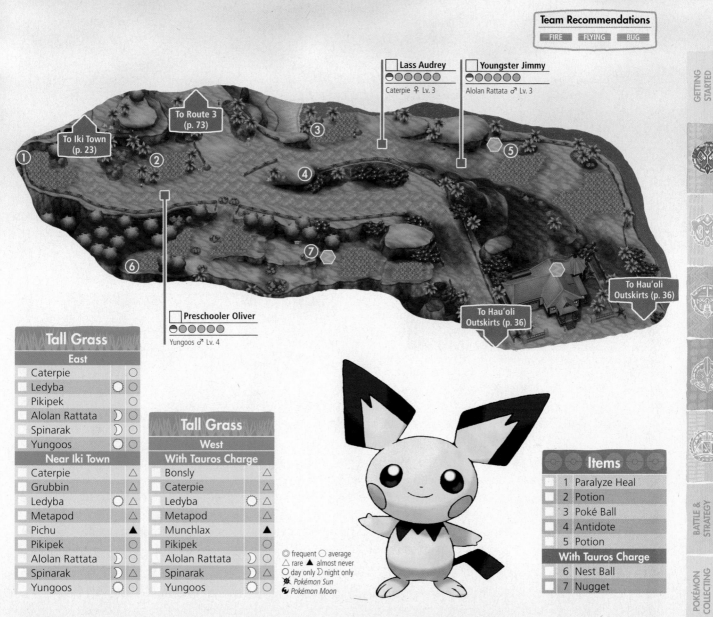

Tall Grass		
East		
Caterpie		○
Ledyba	☀	○
Pikipek		○
Alolan Rattata	☽	○
Spinarak	☽	○
Yungoos	☀	○
Near Iki Town		
Caterpie		△
Grubbin		△
Ledyba	☀	△
Metapod		△
Pichu		▲
Pikipek		○
Alolan Rattata	☽	○
Spinarak	☽	△
Yungoos	☀	○

Tall Grass		
West		
With Tauros Charge		
Bonsly		△
Caterpie		△
Ledyba	☀	△
Metapod		△
Munchlax		▲
Pikipek		○
Alolan Rattata	☽	○
Spinarak	☽	△
Yungoos	☀	○

◎ frequent ○ average
△ rare ▲ almost never
☀ day only ☽ night only
Pokémon Sun
Pokémon Moon

Items	
1	Paralyze Heal
2	Potion
3	Poké Ball
4	Antidote
5	Potion
With Tauros Charge	
6	Nest Ball
7	Nugget

1 Learn the basics of catching Pokémon

Reward: Poké Ball ×10, Potion ×5

Professor Kukui stands in Route 1's tall grass, eager to teach you how to catch wild Pokémon. Pay careful attention as he sends out his Rockruff to demonstrate how to weaken wild Pokémon before throwing out his Poké Ball to catch it. The professor hands you 10 Poké Balls after his lesson, setting you up to catch wild Pokémon on your own. He also gives you five Potions so that you can heal your Pokémon during or after battle as needed.

Catching Pokémon

You've learned how to battle with your Pokémon, but what about catching them? Finding Pokémon friends is a big part of life for a new Pokémon Trainer. You'll quickly want to get more Pokémon on your team so that you're ready for any situation. Read on to learn how to catch Pokémon and get them on your side.

Catching wild Pokémon

Wild Pokémon love nature, and their many different habitats include tall grass, caves, the desert, the water's surface, indoors, and meadows. Often you'll find that wild Pokémon leap out to attack you when you stumble across them in these kinds of areas, so always be ready for battle. In some special places, you may see a sign that a Pokémon is getting ready to ambush you, such as rustling leaves on a tree or a cloud of dust in the desert. If you get too close to these phenomena, a wild Pokémon may attack! (You can learn more on page 62.)

Main places to find Pokémon

Tall Grass

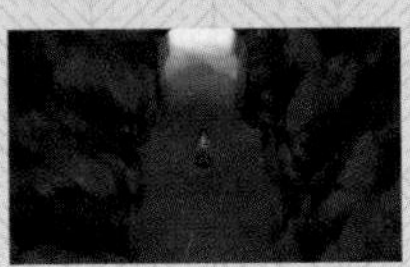
Caves

Deserts

Meadows

Water Surface

Throw Poké Balls to catch Pokémon

Encountering a Pokémon in the wild startles it, and then the battle begins. In that battle, you can try to throw a Poké Ball to catch the wild Pokémon. Poké Balls are a real technological wonder that can somehow comfortably keep any size Pokémon in their nice, portable confines. But a wild Pokémon won't just meekly hop into the Poké Ball you've thrown. Pokémon that are still full of energy are likely to escape from the Poké Ball, and the Poké Ball is lost when this happens. Also note that, when battling a Trainer, you will not be able to catch their Pokémon—that would be stealing! Use the following techniques to conserve your Poké Balls and catch Pokémon successfully.

Use the right Poké Ball

Many different kinds of Poké Ball exist, although some can only be bought in certain towns or cities. Each kind of Poké Ball performs differently, because they're each specialized for a certain use (like being used in caves or to catch water-dwelling Pokémon). You can always use a regular old Poké Ball, but try to choose a Poké Ball that's effective for the location or kind of Pokémon that you want to catch—it's a basic Pokémon-catching principle! You can learn more about the different kinds of Poké Balls from the table on page 347.

Tip

You don't even have to open your Bag to get out a Poké Ball. Just tap the Poké Ball icon on the lower screen (or press Ⓨ) during battle to select a Poké Ball to use.

Catching Pokémon (continued)

Tips for catching Pokémon

Lower its HP

Everything's easier to catch when it's weakened, and a Pokémon's HP is a measure of how weak it is. Use physical or special moves (p. 7) to attack a Pokémon and lower its HP. Every little bit that you lower a Pokémon's HP makes it that much easier to catch. When its HP bar is red, it means that the Pokémon is very weak. That's the best time to throw a Poké Ball!

Inflict status conditions

Some Pokémon moves and Abilities inflict status conditions (p. 49) on their targets. A Pokémon with a status condition, such as Paralysis, is easier to catch. Lower the target's HP and use status conditions to maximize your chances of success!

Early game Pokémon that can inflict useful status conditions:

- Caterpie can be useful to catch early on since its final Evolution, Butterfree, has multiple moves that inflict status conditions. It starts learning them at Lv. 13.
- Grubbin also learns the move Spark early on, as do its Evolutions. This move has a 30% chance of inflicting Paralysis.
- Pichu and its Evolution, Pikachu, can learn Thunder Wave, a move that inflicts Paralysis and helps you catch Pokémon more easily. Both can also have the Static Ability, which has a 30% chance of inflicting Paralysis on any Pokémon that touches it directly. (See page 247 for more on Abilities.)
- Cottonee and Cutiefly learn Stun Spore, which inflicts Paralysis, early on.

Catching a good team

Try catching Pokémon at different times of day. Some Pokémon are more active during the day, while others prefer to come out at night. You'll want to catch many different types of Pokémon in order to give yourself more options against the variety of Pokémon and Trainers you will face on your journey. Here's an example of a well-balanced team that can be formed early in the game.

- Litten FIRE: Its Fire-type moves are especially strong against all the Bug-type Pokémon that you face early in the adventure.
- Butterfree BUG FLYING: It can inflict many status conditions and has access to strong early game moves like Confusion.
- Alolan Rattata DARK NORMAL: Its Hyper Fang is one of the most powerful early moves in the game.
- Bonsly ROCK: It has access to some pretty strong Fighting- and Rock-type moves early on.
- Pichu ELECTRIC: It can evolve into Pikachu, a fast and versatile Pokémon that learns some strong Electric-type moves early.
- Cottonee GRASS FAIRY: It can inflict several useful status conditions, and Grass-type moves will help you against Water-, Ground-, and Rock-type foes.

Tip

Find more examples of balanced team structures on page 263.

Caring for Your Pokémon

Have you noticed a little icon that says "Care" appear on the lower screen after a battle? Tap it to give your Pokémon some extra TLC with Pokémon Refresh!

Pokémon Refresh isn't just fun and games—you can also use it to remove unwanted status conditions (p. 49) from your Pokémon after battles if you tap the Care icon when it appears (or press Ⓨ). For example, if your Pokémon was Poisoned or inflicted with Paralysis during battle, you can cure it using the medicine on this screen. You'll really need to rub your Pokémon to remove its icky condition—it takes time and effort to make it feel better. Regular healing items purchased at Poké Marts and the like work much faster, but it's nice to have another option in case you've run out of them.

Tip

Different Pokémon may appear in different patches of grass, and some appear more frequently than others. Refer to the Pokémon lists that accompany each map, or simply search all the natural environments thoroughly to ensure you encounter them all.

2 Explore Route 1 and catch wild Pokémon

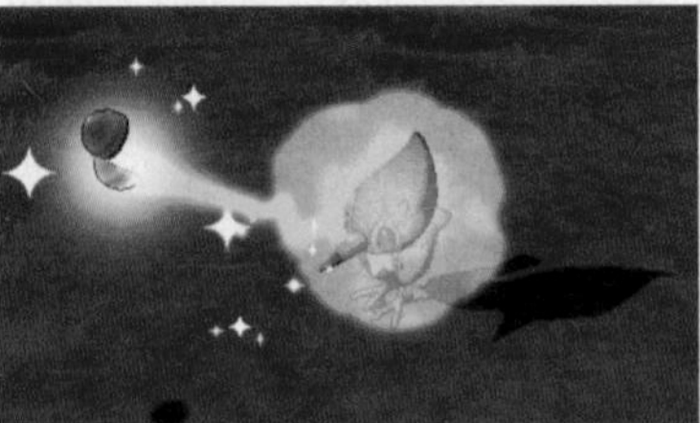

Romp through Route 1's tall grass in search of wild Pokémon. Professor Kukui taught you to weaken wild Pokémon with moves in battle before throwing a Poké Ball to catch them, but most of Route 1's wild Pokémon are low enough in level that you can catch them just by throwing a Poké Ball on your first move. See if you can catch one of each species here on Route 1!

3 Battle other Pokémon Trainers

Other Trainers are also on Route 1 looking to test their skills. If a Trainer sees you, he or she will challenge you to battle. Unlike battles against wild Pokémon, you can't run from a Trainer battle, and you also can't catch their Pokémon. But your Pokémon do earn Exp. Points from Trainer battles, and you get to pocket some prize money after the clash.

4 Find items in Poké Balls

Useful items are strewn about Route 1 as well. These are marked on Route 1's map. Some items are visible, like the one pictured here, while others are hidden and require the help of a Pokémon to find. (You can learn more about finding hidden items on page 96.)

Tip

If your Pokémon are a lot stronger than their opponents, then they won't receive many Exp. Points after a battle because it won't be any challenge for them. But if your Pokémon's levels are about the same as an opponent, then they will receive a good deal of Exp. Points. In fact, the lower your Pokémon's level is compared to the opponent's level, the more Exp. Points they will get! It's smart then to swap in your lower-leveled Pokémon so they receive more Exp. Points. Pokémon that participate in battle always gain Exp. Points afterward (unless they get knocked out), even if you swap them right back out without ever having them use a single move.

Tip

You can sneak past some Trainers if you avoid their line of sight. This is a good idea when your Pokémon are nearly out of energy and you aren't ready for more battles. Once you begin a Trainer battle, you're stuck—battle won't end until one Trainer is out of Pokémon that can fight.

Iki Town Revisited

p. 23

1 Return to Iki Town for the festival

When you've finished exploring Route 1, follow the sounds of drums to reach the festival at Iki Town. You've arrived just in time to take part in the festival's main attraction: a ceremonial battle between you and Hau in honor of the island's guardian deity, Tapu Koko. Kahuna Hala kindly restores your Pokémon to full health before the battle begins—but if you aren't quite ready for the challenge, feel free to return to Route 1 to catch more wild Pokémon and raise your Pokémon's levels.

Hau's Pokémon

Hau's first partner Pokémon has grown stronger since your first battle, and he's caught another Pokémon since then, Pichu, so he sends out two Pokémon this time. Your first partner Pokémon's type still counters Hau's, though, so you've got the upper hand. Use your best moves to hammer Hau once again!

If you choose Rowlet

Popplio
♂ Lv. 7 — WATER
Weak to: GRASS, ELECTRIC

Pichu
♂ Lv. 6 — ELECTRIC
Weak to: GROUND

If you choose Litten

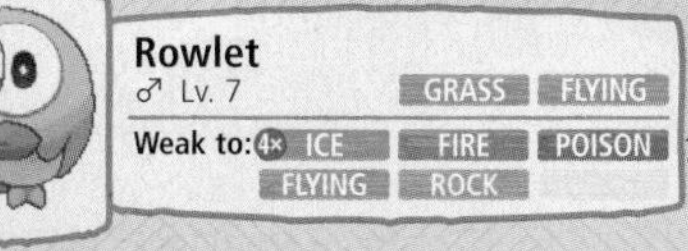

Rowlet
♂ Lv. 7 — GRASS, FLYING
Weak to: 4× ICE, FIRE, POISON, FLYING, ROCK

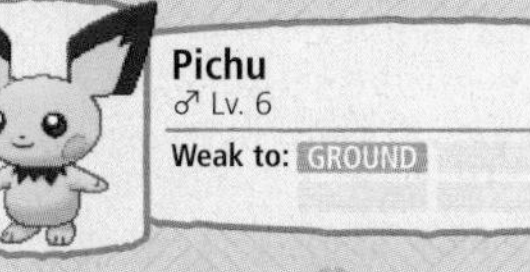

Pichu
♂ Lv. 6 — ELECTRIC
Weak to: GROUND

If you choose Popplio

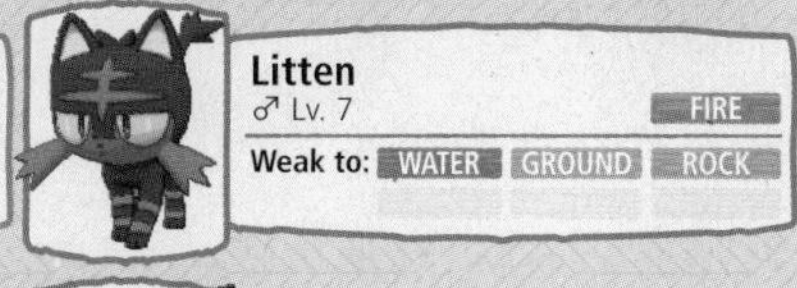

Litten
♂ Lv. 7 — FIRE
Weak to: WATER, GROUND, ROCK

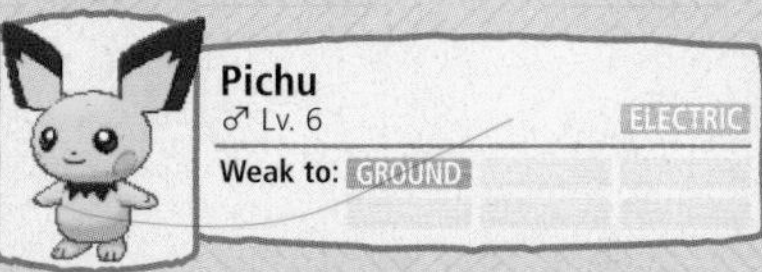

Pichu
♂ Lv. 6 — ELECTRIC
Weak to: GROUND

2 Receive the Z-Ring

Reward: Z-Ring

After your battle, Kahuna Hala hands you a special arm band called the Z-Ring. He explains that, through the use of Z-Crystals, the Z-Ring can draw out the mysterious Z-Power that lies deep within Pokémon. Many of the children in the Alola region may get Z-Rings, but yours is a bit special—he made it for you from the Sparkling Stone that you received directly from Tapu Koko. Professor Kukui goes on to say that the time has come for you to begin your island challenge, but that can wait until tomorrow. You've already had quite a day!

The Island Challenge

Dating back for generations, the island challenge is an important tradition in the Alola region. It's a rite of passage that many children choose to undergo once they turn 11. Trial-goers travel all around Alola's four islands, undertaking seven unique trials set by the islands' captains. After completing all of an island's trials, trial-goers must prove themselves to the island's kahuna. While participating in the island challenge, trial-goers will learn and grow as both people and as Trainers as they set out on the path to adulthood.

Hau'oli Outskirts / Melemele Sea

Ride Pokémon Needed  

Located between Hau'oli City and Route 1, the Hau'oli Outskirts feature several points of interest, including a Pokémon Center, the Trainers' School, the Pokémon Research Lab, Ten Carat Hill, and your humble abode. To the south and east stretches the Melemele Sea, a vast body of water that you can't soak up until later in the story.

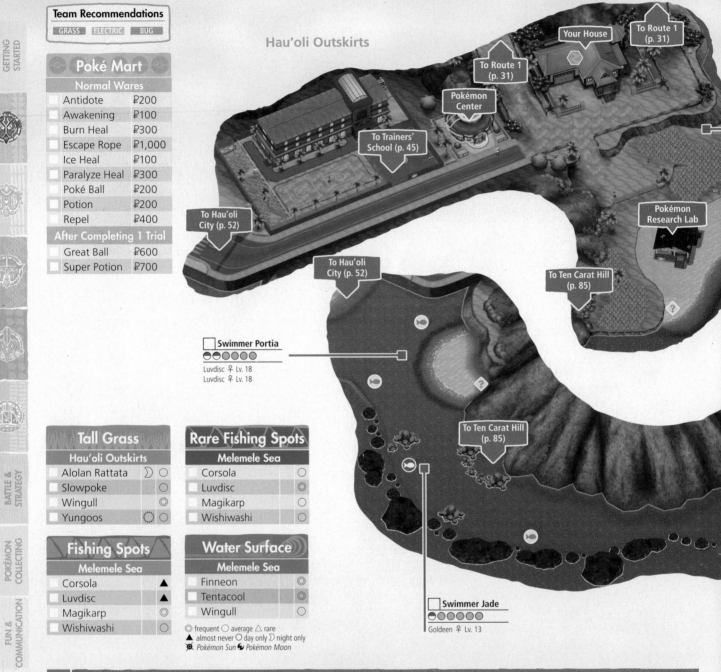

Team Recommendations

GRASS | ELECTRIC | BUG

Poké Mart	
Normal Wares	
Antidote	₽200
Awakening	₽100
Burn Heal	₽300
Escape Rope	₽1,000
Ice Heal	₽100
Paralyze Heal	₽300
Poké Ball	₽200
Potion	₽200
Repel	₽400
After Completing 1 Trial	
Great Ball	₽600
Super Potion	₽700

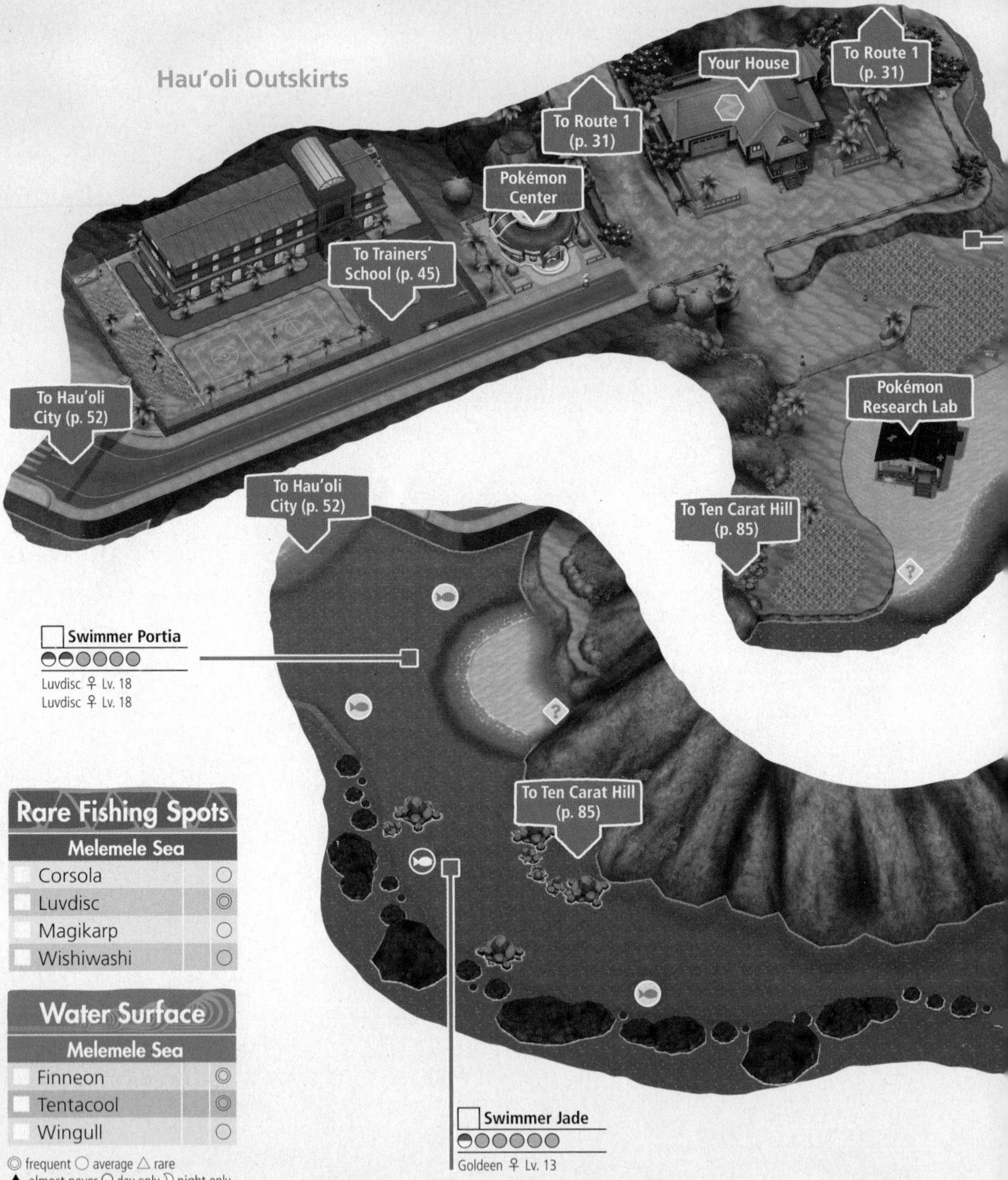

Hau'oli Outskirts

Your House
To Route 1 (p. 31)
To Route 1 (p. 31)
Pokémon Center
To Trainers' School (p. 45)
To Hau'oli City (p. 52)
To Hau'oli City (p. 52)
Pokémon Research Lab
To Ten Carat Hill (p. 85)
To Ten Carat Hill (p. 85)

Swimmer Portia
Luvdisc ♀ Lv. 18
Luvdisc ♀ Lv. 18

Swimmer Jade
Goldeen ♀ Lv. 13

Tall Grass		
Hau'oli Outskirts		
Alolan Rattata	☽	○
Slowpoke		○
Wingull		◎
Yungoos	☼	○

Rare Fishing Spots	
Melemele Sea	
Corsola	○
Luvdisc	◎
Magikarp	○
Wishiwashi	○

Fishing Spots	
Melemele Sea	
Corsola	▲
Luvdisc	▲
Magikarp	◎
Wishiwashi	○

Water Surface	
Melemele Sea	
Finneon	◎
Tentacool	◎
Wingull	○

◎ frequent ○ average △ rare
▲ almost never ☼ day only ☽ night only
Pokémon Sun *Pokémon Moon*

1 Follow Lillie to the Pokémon Research Lab

Lillie drops by your house the next day because Professor Kukui has asked her to escort you to his Pokémon Research Lab. It's not far, just head south from your house to find the Pokémon Research Lab near the beach. Before you go, your mom gives you some pocket money for your journey. Feel free to catch more wild Pokémon in the tall grass that you can trudge through along the way—new species await discovery here.

Reward: ₽30,000

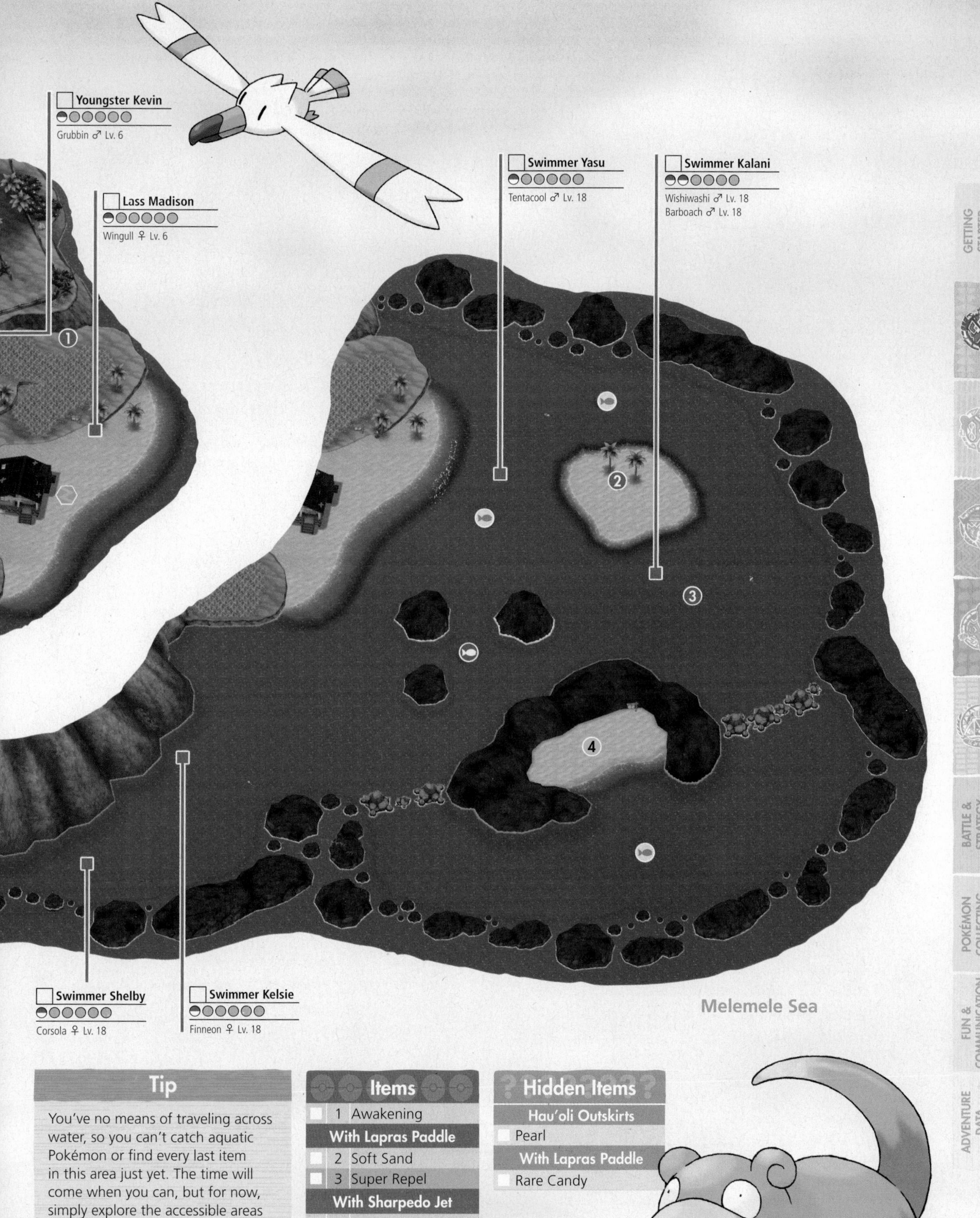

Tip

You've no means of traveling across water, so you can't catch aquatic Pokémon or find every last item in this area just yet. The time will come when you can, but for now, simply explore the accessible areas as you continue on your journey. We'll remind you to come back and explore Melemele Sea more fully when the time is right.

Items

Items
1 Awakening
With Lapras Paddle
2 Soft Sand
3 Super Repel
With Sharpedo Jet
4 TM80 Rock Slide

Hidden Items

Hidden Items
Hau'oli Outskirts
Pearl
With Lapras Paddle
Rare Candy

GETTING STARTED
BATTLE & STRATEGY
POKÉMON COLLECTING
FUN & COMMUNICATION
ADVENTURE DATA

Exploring the Landscape

Ledges

You can jump down from little ledges like this one, but they are too high for you climb back up. You'll have to work your way back around the area to return to the ledge, so search each ledge thoroughly before leaping down to lower ground.

Holes

Some areas feature small holes that you can crawl through. Press Ⓐ to crawl through these little holes and reach whatever lies on the other side.

Breakable Rocks

You'll find jagged rocks around Alola that you'll eventually be able to break with the help of a Ride Pokémon. Smashing through these rocks leads to new areas.

Ride Pokémon: Tauros

Movable Rocks

You'll also find big boulders that a certain Ride Pokémon can push around for you, moving them out of your way so you can explore the areas beyond.

Ride Pokémon: Machamp

Bodies of Water

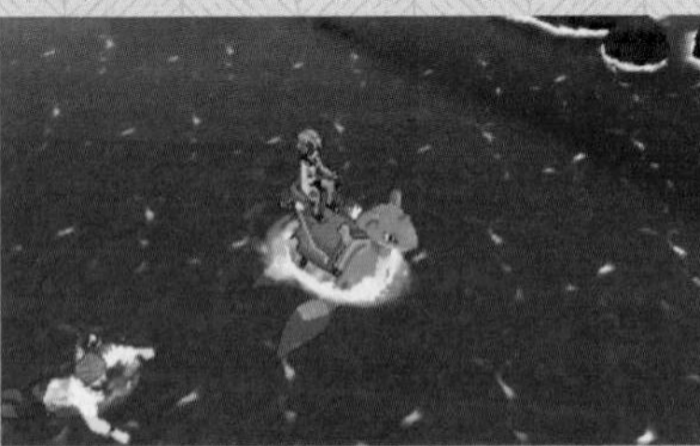

Some Ride Pokémon that you'll meet later on will help you travel across the water. Just look for gentle and sandy spots along the shore from which to shove off.

Ride Pokémon: Lapras, Sharpedo

Rocky Roads

These rough, rocky roads are impossible for you to cross on your own, but a hardy Ride Pokémon will haul you across them with no problem.

Ride Pokémon: Mudsdale

2 Visit the Pokémon Research Lab and receive the Rotom Dex

Reward: Rotom Dex

Professor Kukui is hard at work inside the Pokémon Research Lab, but he pauses to introduce you to Rotom, a Pokémon that lives inside of your Pokédex. The professor then upgrades your Pokédex, enabling Rotom to talk to you and guide you. This upgraded Rotom Dex will help you stay on course as you explore Alola! For agreeing to take on the island challenge, Kukui also hands you the island challenge amulet, signaling that your quest to become an island challenge champion has begun!

Rotom Dex

The Rotom Dex is a great ally to have at your side during your adventure. By listening to your conversations, Rotom will glean where you should go next and help you stay on course.

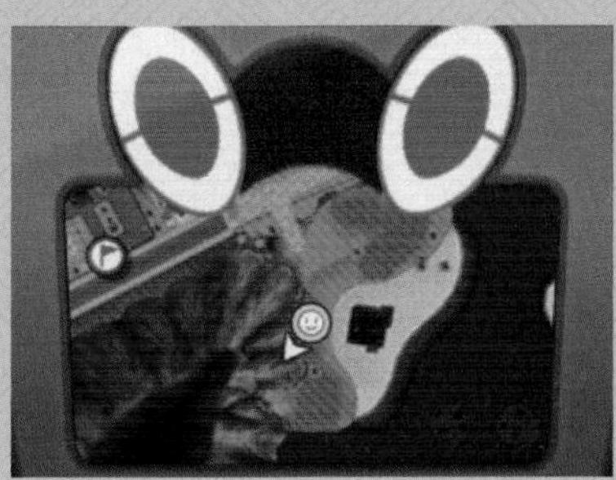

Rotom shows a map of your current surroundings as you explore. This map shows you where you are in Alola, and where you need to go next. The player icon represents your current location, while flag icon indicates the place that you need to go to continue your adventure. Tap in the center of the map, and Rotom will remind you of the current situation.

Melemele Island

Tap anywhere else on the map for a larger view of the current island, where handy Pokémon Center icons show you where to find the nearest rest stop. Move the cursor over cities and routes to see what you can find at each location on the top screen. Press R and L to switch between islands, and zoom in with Y for a closer look. Areas that you haven't yet explored will be shaded out, so try to uncover the entire map of Alola!

8%
If you wanna fill up that Alola Pokédex, it wouldn't be a bad idea to trade Pokémon with some friends, zzt-zzt!

Rotom also takes an active role in your Pokédex, evaluating it for you anytime you ask. Just open your Pokédex and then tap "Pokédex Evaluation" on the lower screen. Rotom may even give you some tips about how to make progress in completing all four of your Island Pokédexes.

3 Explore the Pokémon Research Lab, then travel westward

The Trainers' School is your next destination, but take a moment to check out the Pokémon Research Lab before you leave. Head downstairs to browse books that are filled with good info for a new Trainer to know. You can also take a peek at Lillie's loft, if you're feeling nosy. When you're ready to move on, leave the Pokémon Research Lab, go north toward your house, and then head west along the road to reach a Pokémon Center. Lillie is waiting out front for you.

Pokémon Center

Located at key points around Alola, Pokémon Centers provide vital rest stops for Trainers. Here you can rest your Pokémon to recover their HP, PP, and remove any and all status conditions they might have—all free of charge.

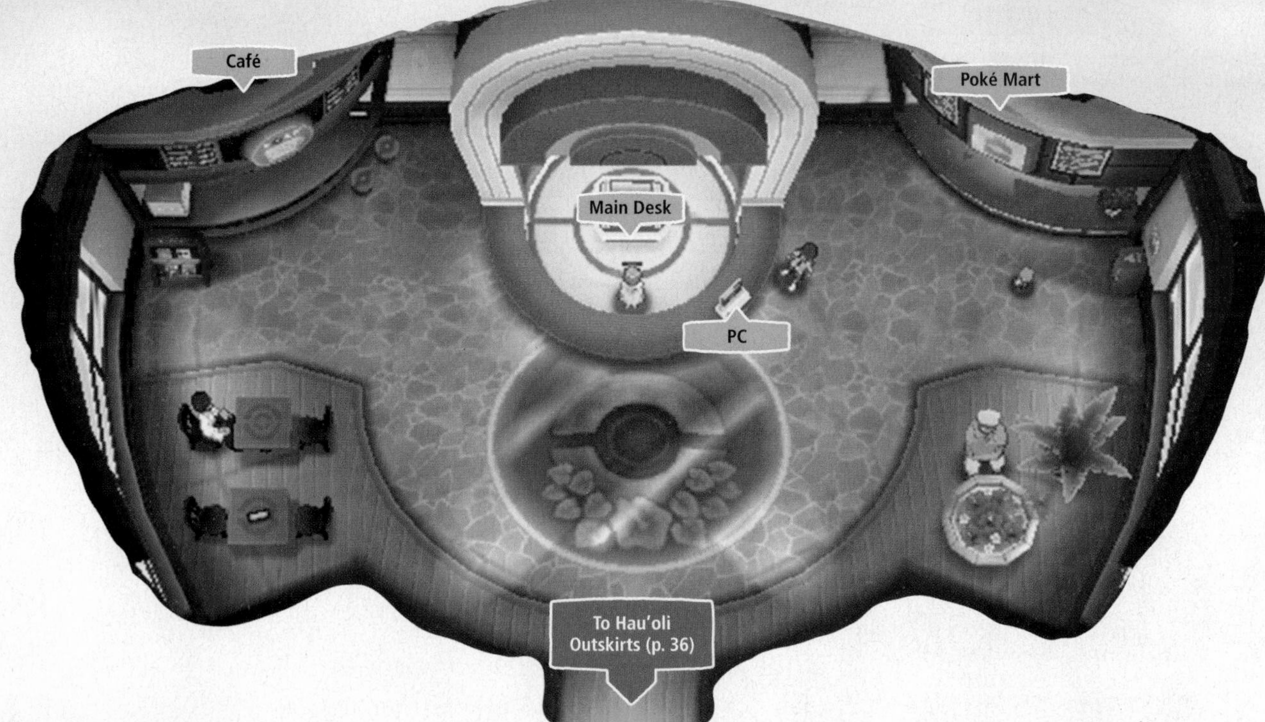

Poké Mart	
Normal Wares	
Antidote	₽200
Awakening	₽100
Burn Heal	₽300
Escape Rope	₽1,000
Ice Heal	₽100
Paralyze Heal	₽300
Poké Ball	₽200
Potion	₽200
Repel	₽400
After Completing 1 Trial	
Great Ball	₽600
Super Potion	₽700
After Completing 2 Trials	
Honey	₽300
Revive	₽200
After Completing 3 Trials	
Adrenaline Orb	₽300
Super Repel	₽700
After Completing 4 Trials	
Hyper Potion	₽1,500
Ultra Ball	₽800
After Completing 5 Trials	
Full Heal	₽400
Max Repel	₽900
After Completing 6 Trials	
Max Potion	₽2,500
After Completing 7 Trials	
Full Restore	₽3,000

Pokémon Centers

Pokémon Centers are all-important hubs for Pokémon Trainers. Here you can heal your Pokémon, organize your team, buy useful items, and even get some advice.

Main Desk

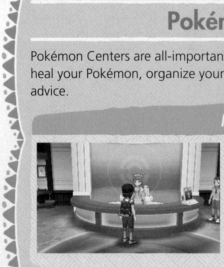

Talk to the Pokémon Center Lady at the main desk, and she can take your Pokémon and heal them for you. This service costs nothing at all and will fully restore your Pokémon's HP and PP, and remove any status conditions they may be suffering from, such as Paralysis.

Pokémon Centers (continued)

Pokérus

Oh... It looks like your Pokémon may be infected with the Pokérus.

Have you ever had the woman at the main desk tell you that your Pokémon were infected with Pokérus? Don't panic—this harmless virus can actually have a positive effect on your Pokémon. It helps their base stats (p. 272) grow more quickly from battles, and the effects last even after they have recovered from the virus. Pokérus goes away very quickly if the infected Pokémon is in your team, but it may also infect other Pokémon positioned near it in the team. However, if you move an infected Pokémon to your PC Box, the virus will stick around indefinitely. If you want more of your Pokémon to reap the benefits of the Pokérus, try to pass Pokérus along to other Pokémon in your team, and keep one infected Pokémon in your PC Box so that you can use it to spread the virus to other Pokémon in the future!

Poké Mart

The Poké Mart sells a variety of items that will help you on your adventure. Here you'll find healing items, battle items, and sometimes even TMs. You'll learn more about these items later, but remember for now that Poké Marts are your main places to shop for useful items. If a Poké Mart features two clerks, the clerk on the left will offer the standard array of Poké Mart items, while the clerk on the right will offer special items that are unique to that particular Pokémon Center. Also, note that the standard array of Poké Mart items will increase as you clear more trials on your island challenge. All of the items that are offered at any Pokémon Center are listed in the tables on the opposite page. The items which are unique to each particular Poké Mart are listed on page 350.

Café

Every Pokémon Center in Alola features a relaxing café where you can order a refreshing drink. Also, once per day, the kind baristas at these cafés will give you a special treat and some Poké Beans (p. 309) for your Pokémon. The treat that you get depends on the day, but it's always a consumable item that your Pokémon will enjoy. The baristas also sometimes give you tips that are useful for Trainers, including hints about how to tackle your upcoming trial.

Monday	Lumiose Galette	Heals all status conditions for one Pokémon
Tuesday	Rage Candy Bar	Heals all status conditions for one Pokémon.
Wednesday	Casteliacone	Heals all status conditions for one Pokémon
Thursday	Old Gateau	Heals all status conditions for one Pokémon
Friday	Shalour Sable	Heals all status conditions for one Pokémon
Saturday	Lava Cookie	Heals all status conditions for one Pokémon
Sunday	Sweet Heart	Restores 20 HP to one Pokémon

Pokémon Centers (continued)

PC

Once you've obtained more than six Pokémon, you'll have to send the extras to your PC Boxes. You can decide after you catch a Pokémon whether you want to add it to your team or send it to your Boxes. Any time that you want to rearrange which Pokémon you've got on your team, visit a Pokémon Center and use the PC to swap Pokémon in and out of your current team, which is displayed on the right.

1 Box Modes: Tap one of the icons or press Ⓧ to switch between three Box mode options. The first lets you view all of your Pokémon, the second lets you organize your Pokémon's held items, and the third lets you register your Pokémon for Battle Teams.

2 Cursor Modes: Tap one of the icons or press START to switch between three cursor modes. The first (red cursor) lets you select each Pokémon, the second (blue cursor) lets you switch Pokémon one after another, and the third (green cursor) lets you select and move groups of Pokémon.

3 View Boxes: Tap this icon to view all of your Boxes at once and quickly see which ones contain Pokémon.

4 Search: Tap this icon or press Ⓨ to search your Boxes for Pokémon based on the criteria that you input.

Select a Pokémon to view its summary when you are using a red cursor, including its stats and the moves that it knows. You may then choose to move it, change its held item, give it a mark, or even release it back into the wild if your PC is out of space. Your PC has many Boxes, however, which you can access by pressing Ⓡ or Ⓛ, so don't be in a hurry to release any Pokémon before you have to.

Tip

You can change each Box's name and wallpaper by tapping on the Box's name on the lower screen.

Marking

Some players mark their Pokémon to designate Pokémon with particularly high stats. Marking a Pokémon for the different stats that affect battle (HP, Attack, Defense, Sp. Atk, Sp. Def, and Speed) can be helpful when trying to obtain the perfect Pokémon. (You can learn more about Pokémon with naturally high stats on page 272.) But you can choose to use these marks for any purpose you'd like, and search for them using the search function that can be used by pressing Ⓨ.

Battle Teams

Battle Teams are special teams that you can create and use for special battle formats, like Link Battles (p. 305), Battle Royals (p. 111), and Online Competitions (p. 306). Pokémon can be placed in more than one Battle Team at a time, and you can change the names of your Battle Teams by tapping on their names.

New X Menu Options

New options have appeared on your X menu—had you noticed? Press Ⓧ and check 'em out when you want a bit of diversion from your main adventure.

Quick Link

This handy feature lets you immediately battle or trade Pokémon with someone nearby. If you're with a friend who is also playing *Pokémon Sun* or *Pokémon Moon*, open Quick Link from the X menu and then touch the lower screen at the same time. In a few seconds, your systems should recognize one another, and you can choose to make a trade or have a battle!

Festival Plaza

Festival Plaza is your connection to a world of fun. It's full of shops and facilities, and even visiting Trainers! If you connect to the Internet, other people playing *Pokémon Sun* and *Pokémon Moon* will pop by for a visit, even from across the world. Otherwise, you'll see people from nearby that you've passed using StreetPass. You can complete missions, earn Festival Coins, and develop your dream Festival Plaza. Turn page 299 for all the exciting details!

Battle Video

You can record Battle Videos from battles that you have using special features like Quick Link or Festival Plaza. After a battle, you will be asked if you would like to save it as a Battle Video. You can keep up to 100 Battle Videos at a time. These special videos don't just let you watch a battle again—they let you play the battle all over again! Try different moves or Pokémon and see if you would have fared better or worse against your opponent's team. They can also be swapped with others. (More about battle videos on page 308.)

QR Scanner

The QR Scanner lets you easily register Pokémon in your Pokédex by scanning QR Code patterns! Select the QR Scanner from the X menu to get started. The outer camera on your Nintendo 3DS system will then activate—line up your camera with a QR Code, then press Ⓡ or Ⓐ or press the search icon on the lower screen to capture the QR Code and see what Pokémon it brings up. Try it out on these samples and see how easy it is!

New X Menu Options (continued)

QR Scanner (continued)

To generate your own QR Code patterns for specific Pokémon, simply view a Pokémon that you have caught in your Pokédex and then press Ⓧ to display its QR Code. Your friends can then open their QR Scanner and scan the QR Code to add the Pokémon to their own Pokédex as "Seen."

Tip

The QR Scanner starts with ten scans, and it takes 2 hours to regenerate each scan. Each QR Code that you scan earns you some points, normally 10 points each. Once you accumulate 100 points, you can activate the Island Scan. Turn to page 268 if you're ready to learn more about Island Scan now.

Wonder QR Code Patterns

You can also scan QR Code patterns from sources other than *Pokémon Sun* and *Pokémon Moon*. Any QR Code that you scan from another source acts as a Wonder QR Code! Like a Wonder Trade (p. 267), you won't know which Pokémon you'll get with a Wonder QR Code until you scan it. Wonder what will appear? Start scanning QR Code patterns wherever you find them! They'll also award you points toward your next Island Scan.

Some places to find QR Code patterns:

- On signs at the mall or in shops
- In restaurants and on food wrappers
- On ads in newspapers or magazines
- On movie posters outside of theaters
- On the Internet

Be on the lookout for QR Code patterns! They're normally used to direct people to web pages where they can find more information about a topic, but they turn into something far more wondrous in the world of Pokémon.

Trainers' School

Knowledge is power, and Melemele Island's Trainers' School is the perfect place for new Trainers to learn and grow. Here you'll receive a crash-course in Pokémon battles as you take on one budding Trainer after the next.

Team Recommendations

FIRE GROUND BUG

Items

☐	1	Potion
☐	2	Antidote
☐	3	Potion
☐	4	Paralyze Heal

Hidden Items

- ☐ Great Ball
- ☐ Poké Ball

Tall Grass

Alolan Grimer	○
Magnemite	◎
Alolan Meowth	○

◎ frequent ○ average △ rare
▲ almost never ○ day only ☽ night only
Pokémon Sun *Pokémon Moon*

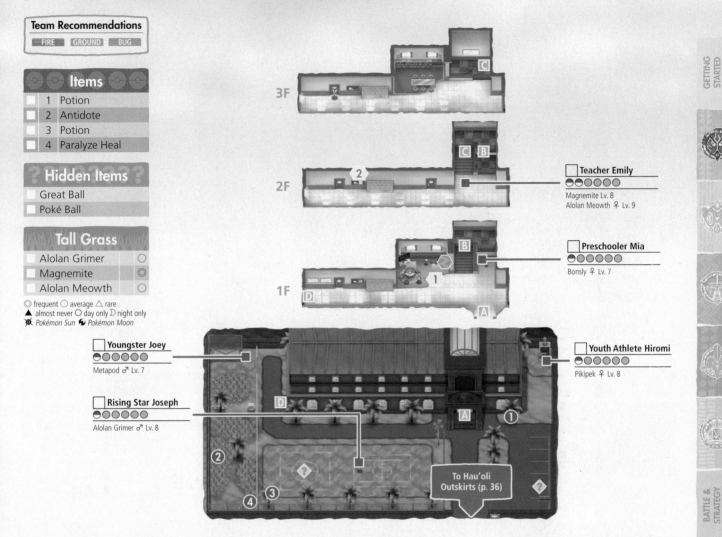

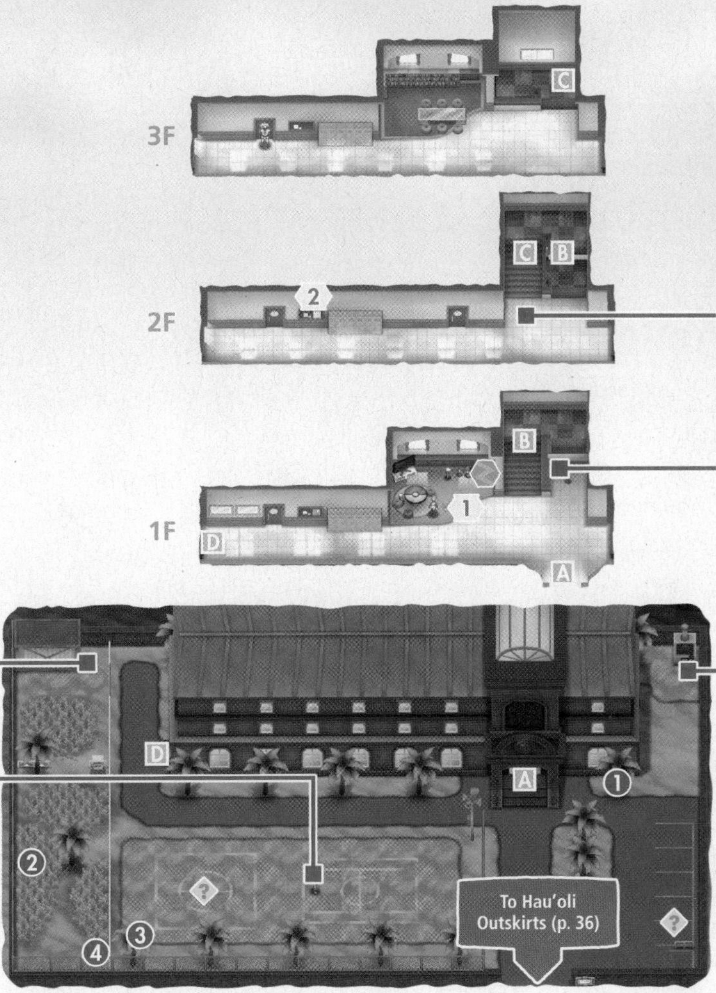

3F

2F

☐ **Teacher Emily**
Magnemite Lv. 8
Alolan Meowth ♀ Lv. 9

1F

☐ **Preschooler Mia**
Bonsly ♀ Lv. 7

☐ **Youngster Joey**
Metapod ♂ Lv. 7

☐ **Rising Star Joseph**
Alolan Grimer ♂ Lv. 8

☐ **Youth Athlete Hiromi**
Pikipek ♀ Lv. 8

To Hau'oli Outskirts (p. 36)

1 Receive the Exp. Share and explore the school grounds

An ornery Tauros blocks the road ahead, but the Trainers' School is still accessible. Go there to find Professor Kukui waiting for you. The professor challenges you to defeat four special Trainers around the school, and gives you an important item called the Exp. Share. Before entering the school, explore its grounds with the Exp. Share, battling the first two Trainers and also catching more wild Pokémon in the tall grass to the west. (Press Ⓐ to open the gate and reach the tall grass.) If your Pokémon grow weary, just talk to Lillie and she'll swiftly restore them back to full health.

Reward: Exp. Share

Tip

The Exp. Share is already turned on, so there's no need to do anything with it—Exp. Points will automatically be distributed to all Pokémon in your party from now on. This is a big advantage, but if you like, you can open your Bag and turn off the Exp. Share in the Key Items Pocket for a more challenging adventure.

Youth Athlete Hiromi's Pokémon

Hiromi stands on the school's east side, ready to do battle with her Pikipek. If you have a Pokémon with Electric-type moves, like Grubbin or Pichu, now's a good time to use it. If not, simply overwhelm her with superior numbers.

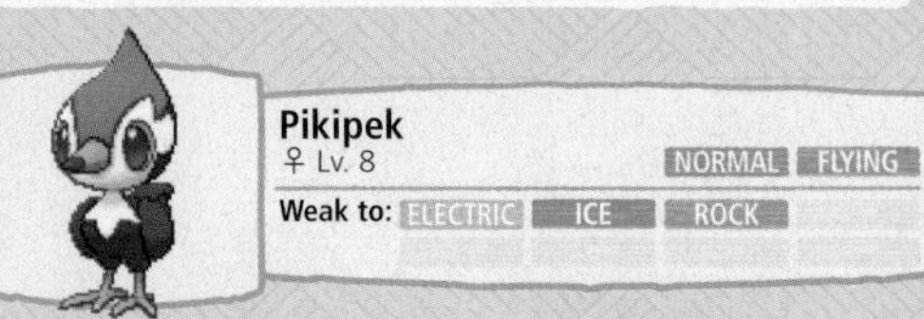

Pikipek
♀ Lv. 8
NORMAL FLYING
Weak to: ELECTRIC ICE ROCK

Youngster Joey's Pokémon

Joey stands near the tall grass beyond the gate on the school's west side. His Metapod is easy prey for Litten's Fire-type moves or Rowlet's Flying-type moves. Or use any Flying-type Pokémon you may have caught on your way here, like Wingull.

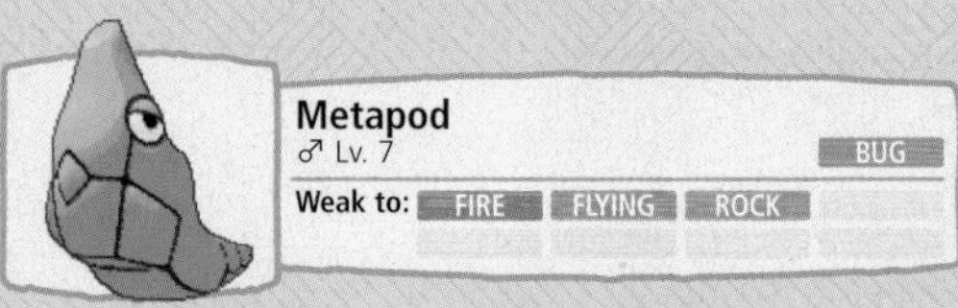

2 Enter and explore the Trainers' School

After you've beaten the two Trainers around the grounds, enter the school and battle a third Trainer under the stairs. Speak to everyone else inside the school for more pearls of wisdom.

Preschooler Mia's Pokémon

Mia's Bonsly is a prime target for Rowlet and Popplio. You also can't go wrong with Wingull, if you've managed to catch one.

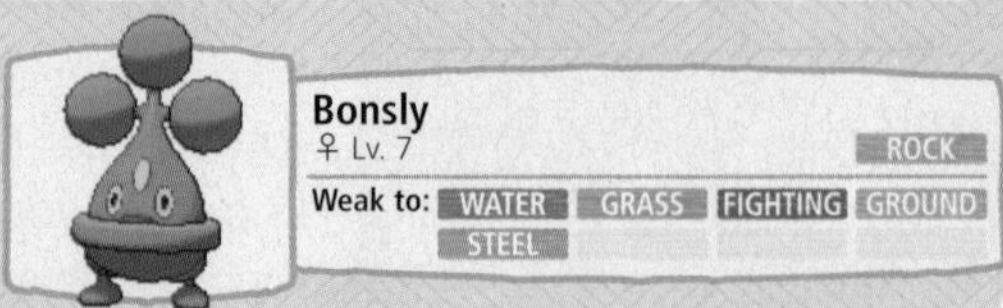

Bonsly
♀ Lv. 7
ROCK
Weak to: WATER GRASS FIGHTING GROUND STEEL

S1: Score a Quick Claw

Talk to the woman on the school's first floor to score a valuable Quick Claw.

Reward: Quick Claw

Held Items

The Quick Claw you've just received is a special item that can be held by a Pokémon to aid it in attacking first in battle. You'll find many more items like this during your adventures in Alola, but Pokémon can only hold one item at a time. Whenever you find a new item, open your Bag and see if it has any effects when held by a Pokémon. Then consider which Pokémon on your team will get the most use out of it. There are several different ways to give items to your Pokémon:

From the Pokémon page accessed from the X menu

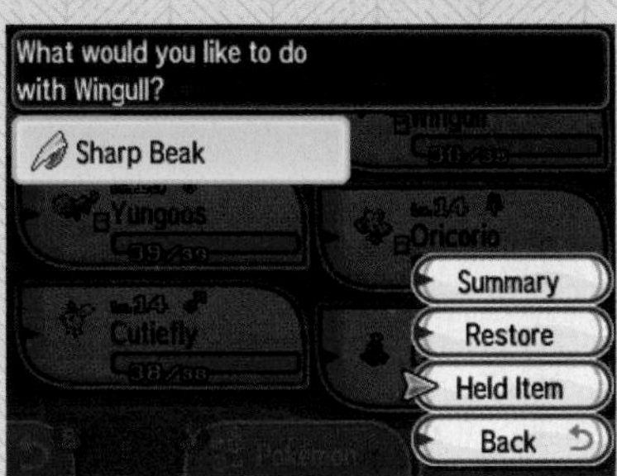

Open the X menu by pressing ⓧ and select "Pokémon." Choose a Pokémon, then select "Held Item" and choose an item from your Bag.

From your Bag

Open the X menu and select "Bag." Choose an item, and then select "Give to Pokémon."

Tip

Open your Bag and press ⓧ while viewing your items to sort them. Sort them by type, and all of the items that your Pokémon can hold will be moved to the top of the list in the Items pocket.

From your PC Boxes

Visit a Pokémon Center and use the PC. Select a Pokémon and then choose "Held Item." Alternatively, press ⓧ to switch to Held Item mode, then select any Pokémon and choose "Give."

Tip

Some wild Pokémon will already be holding an item when you catch them. Remember to check for items when you catch a new Pokémon!

S2: Get a Potion

Speak with the students in the second floor classroom to receive a free Potion.

Reward: Potion

Regional Variants

Have you noticed that the Meowth here in Alola look rather different than the one your mom brought from the Kanto region? That's because Alola is a very unique place that's given rise to so-called regional variants. While many of the Pokémon in Alola are also found in other regions, they've adapted to the Alola environment in unusual ways, gaining different appearances and different types. Be on the lookout for these regional variants as you explore this exotic region!

Meowth

Alolan Meowth

3 Challenge the last Trainer

The fourth and final Trainer awaits outside on the court, and he won't battle you until you've beaten the other three Trainers in and around the school. Head back outside and talk to Lillie to restore your Pokémon, then challenge the final Trainer. He's the toughest one of all, but the reward for beating him is great: a shiny new TM!

Reward: TM01 Work Up

Rising Star Joseph's Pokémon

Joseph's Grimer is an Alolan Grimer and it only has one weakness, which you are unlikely to be able to exploit at this point in your journey. Use Antidotes to cure your Pokémon from the effects of Grimer's Poison Gas, and try to attack Grimer with special moves instead of physical moves, as it will use Harden to raise its Defense stat. You can try using another Dark-type Pokémon, like Alolan Meowth or Alolan Rattata, to reduce the amount of damage that you take from its Dark-type Bite attack, too.

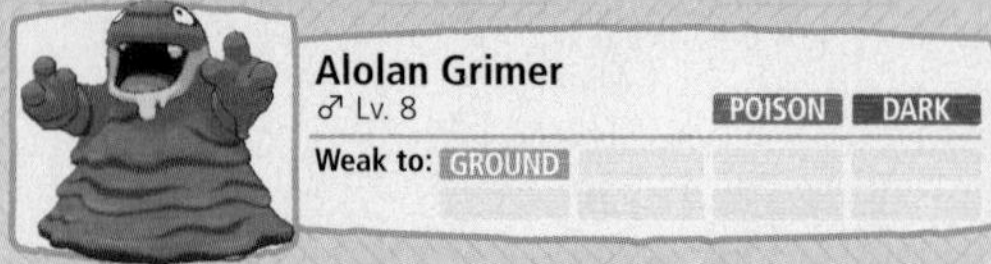

Battle Basics—Part 2

You've had a handful of Trainer battles by now, and they only get more challenging from here. Dishing out attacks and dealing damage is a good start, but let's explore some more advanced strategies that will help you when the going gets tough.

Status conditions

Some of the Trainers at the Trainers' School use Pokémon that can inflict status conditions. Some status conditions go away after a few turns, and others won't go away until they are cured. Fortunately, your Pokémon can only have one status condition at a time. During battle, an icon appears above a Pokémon's HP gauge while it is suffering under the effects of a status condition.

POISONED	**Poisoned**	Deals damage each turn. If Badly Poisoned, the damage continually increases each turn. Lasts until cured.
PARALYSIS	**Paralysis**	Speed is halved and moves sometimes fail. Lasts until cured.
ASLEEP	**Asleep**	Cannot use any moves except Sleep Talk and Snore. Lasts several turns.
BURNED	**Burned**	Power of physical moves (p. 7) is halved. Deals damage each turn. Lasts until cured.
FROZEN	**Frozen**	Cannot use moves while Frozen. Lasts several turns, but goes away if hit with a Fire-type move.

Tip

You can remove status conditions after a battle with Pokémon Refresh (p. 276). Otherwise, use a healing item, visit a Pokémon Center, or put your Pokémon in a PC Box.

Other conditions

Unlike the aforementioned status conditions, the following conditions never last longer than one battle.

Confused: Moves may fail and the Pokémon may damage itself. Lasts several turns.

Infatuation: Moves may fail. Lasts until the Pokémon that inflicted the condition is defeated or replaced in battle.

Flinching: Prevents the Pokémon from using a move that turn. Lasts only one turn.

Abilities

Pokémon Abilities can also have a big impact in battle. View a Pokémon's summary page to check its Ability, and remember to factor it in. For example, Spinarak's Insomnia prevents it from falling Asleep, while Pichu's Static could cause Paralysis in any Pokémon that touches it in battle. Abilities can have all kinds of effects, so keep them in mind as a part of your strategy.

Battle Basics—Part 2 (continued)

Items to use in battle

Use healing items, such as Potions, during battle to restore HP or PP to your Pokémon or to remove their status conditions. Use battle items, such as X Attack or X Defense, to boost one of your Pokémon's stats. Press the Bag button during battle to view all the items you can use in battle. Using items effectively can mean the difference between victory and defeat.

Tip

The daily treats that you can get in a Pokémon Center's café are great for use in battle. Many can cure all status conditions, saving you from having to buy lots of different items for every kind of status condition.

Items to use outside of battle

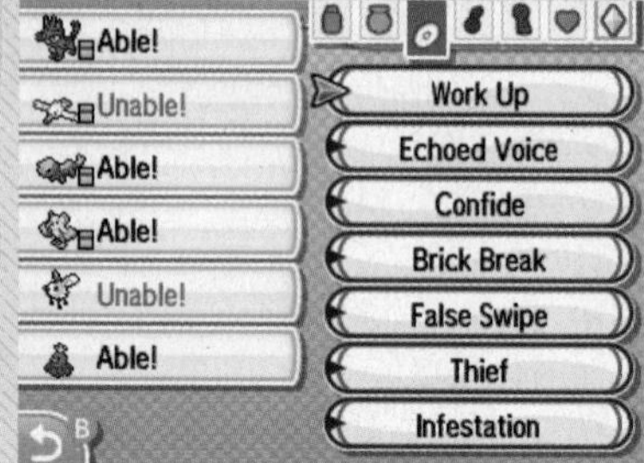

You receive your first-ever TM at the Trainers' School. A TM, or Technical Machine, is a device that can teach moves to Pokémon that they wouldn't normally learn just by leveling up. Open your Bag and choose the TM Pocket to browse your TMs. Pokémon in your current team that are able to learn the move are shown on the left. TMs can be used over and over again, and they're great for teaching Pokémon powerful moves that might surprise their opponents!

4 Battle against Teacher Emily!

Reward: Great Ball ×5

After completing the professor's challenge, you're suddenly called to the school's office. Reenter the school and go upstairs to find Teacher Emily waiting for you. She's eager to learn how you managed to beat her four top students and challenges you to one more battle. Give Teacher Emily a lesson in Pokémon battling, and she'll reward you with five shiny Great Balls.

Teacher Emily's Pokémon

Emily sends out two Pokémon, and you'll be hard pressed to capitalize on their weaknesses. Use Paralyze Heals to recover from the effects of Magnemite's Thunder Shock, and unleash Litten's Fire-type moves to defeat it quickly (if you chose Litten). Her Meowth is an Alola variant, so its type is Dark—not Normal, like the Meowth found in other regions. Counter it by sending out a Bug type that you may have caught around Route 1, such as Caterpie or Ledyba.

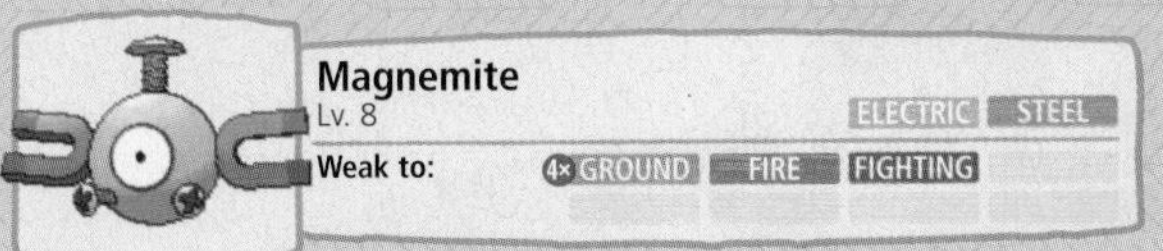

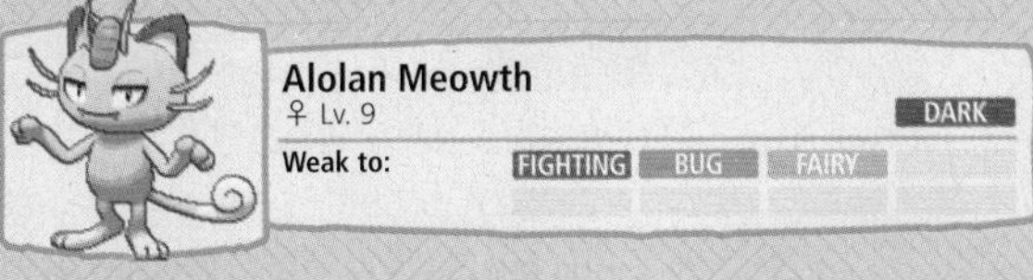

5 Meet Ilima, then follow Lillie to Hau'oli City

Professor Kukui arrives after your battle with Teacher Emily, and he introduces you to Captain Ilima, a confident young man who runs his trial in Verdant Cavern. You're already making a name for yourself in the region, and Ilima looks forward to your future challenge. You'll attempt Ilima's trial one day, but for now, simply follow Lillie into Hau'oli City, helping Kahuna Hala tame that ornery Tauros along the way.

Ilima

A gifted Trainer with a passion for Pokémon battles, Ilima is the first captain that you've met. Captains are special boys and girls who've been chosen by the kahuna of their island to help other Trainers grow and learn during their island challenges. While the captains are all great Trainers, battling them is not how you prove yourself worthy here in Alola. Instead, you must complete whatever task each captain assigns to you as his or her trial. Considering Ilima's passion for battling, though, it's safe to assume that his trial will involve Pokémon battles in some way!

Hau'oli City

Ride Pokémon Needed

Alola's largest city, Hau'oli is a bustling center of excitement and commerce. Here you'll find everything from fashion boutiques to popular eateries. The city features three districts: the Beachfront, the Shopping District, and the Marina.

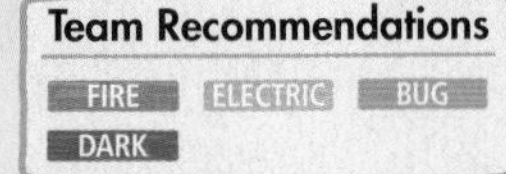

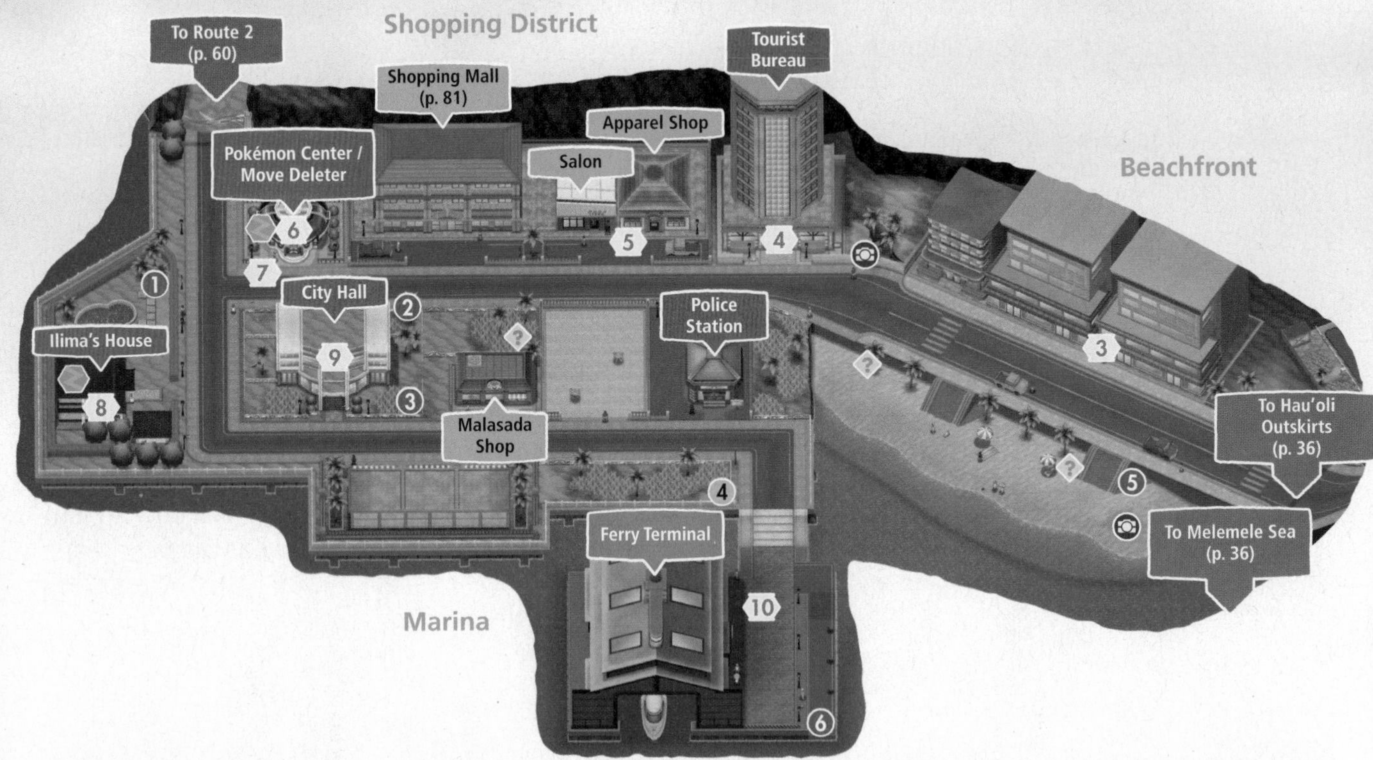

Items

Shopping District	
1	Ether
2	Revive
3	Tiny Mushroom
4	TM49 Echoed Voice
Beachfront	
5	Poké Ball
Marina	
6	Super Potion

Hidden Items

Beachfront
Fresh Water
Pearl
Shopping District
Stardust

Tall Grass

Shopping District		
Abra		○
Alolan Grimer		△
Magnemite		△
Alolan Meowth		△
Pichu		▲
Alolan Rattata	☽	○
Wingull		○
Yungoos	☼	○

Water Surface

Beachfront	
Finneon	◎
Tentacool	◎
Wingull	○

◎ frequent ○ average △ rare
▲ almost never ☼ day only ☽ night only
Pokémon Sun *Pokémon Moon*

Poké Mart

Normal Wares	
Antidote	₽200
Awakening	₽100
Burn Heal	₽300
Escape Rope	₽1,000
Ice Heal	₽100
Paralyze Heal	₽300
Poké Ball	₽200
Potion	₽200
Repel	₽400
After Completing 1 Trial	
Great Ball	₽600
Super Potion	₽700
Special Wares	
Dire Hit	₽1,000
Guard Spec.	₽1,500
X Accuracy	₽1,000
X Attack	₽1,000
X Defense	₽2,000
X Sp. Atk	₽1,000
X Sp. Def	₽2,000
X Speed	₽1,000

Malasada Shop

Item	Price
Big Malasada	₽350
Sweet Malasada	₽200

Tip

Keep an eye out for little pink gates as you explore the city—there's one right across from the tourist bureau. Open these gates to reach patches of tall grass where wild Pokémon can be caught! Note that some gates have been freshly painted and can't be opened until a bit later in the adventure.

1 Explore the Beachfront and chat with the locals

At last, you've made it to Hau'oli City! This is the largest city in the Alola region, and there are plenty of sights to see. Start chatting with people on the street—everyone here is friendly, and they have valuable advice to share. Comb the beach afterward to find more friendly faces, along with a Poké Ball.

S3: Pick up another Potion

One kind woman on the Beachfront hands you a Potion just for talking to her!

Reward: Potion

2 Follow Hau to the tourist bureau and acquire the Poké Finder

After you've fully explored the Beachfront, continue along the street to reach the Shopping District. Hau spots you here and drags you into the nearby tourist bureau, which is handing out free Poké Finders to anyone with a Rotom Dex. Now you can snap pictures of Pokémon you see during your adventure! Afterward, talk to the other receptionist who runs the Loto-ID Center to try your luck at today's drawing.

Reward: Poké Finder

Loto-ID

Located in the Hau'oli City tourist bureau, the Loto-ID Center gives you a chance to win a special prize each day at no charge. If any of your Loto Ticket numbers match your Pokémon's ID numbers, you get a prize!

1 digit match	Moomoo Milk
2 digits match	PP Up
3 digits match	PP Max
4 digits match	Rare Candy
5 digits match	Master Ball

Tip

The first number in your Pokémon's ID does not affect the Loto-ID. If the Pokémon's ID is 123456, then your Loto Ticket would need to be 23456 for you to win the grand prize.

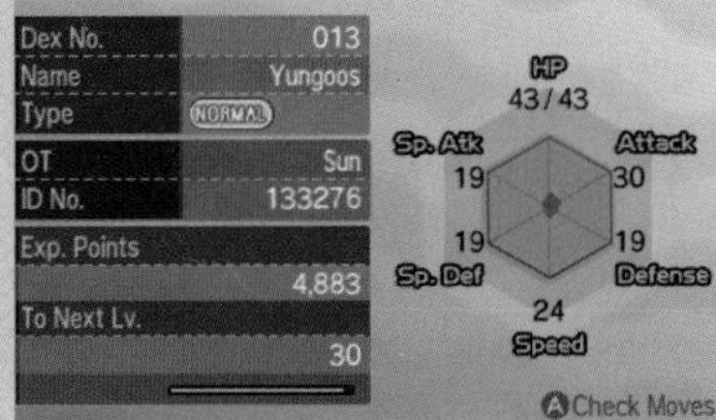

View a Pokémon's summary page to see the ID numbers of your Pokémon. Are your Pokémon's ID numbers all the same? You must not be trading Pokémon much! The ID number is based on the Pokémon's original Trainer (OT) and never changes. Trade (p. 267) a lot of Pokémon with others to get different ID numbers and improve your Loto-ID chances!

S4: Show off your Pokédex to get 10 Ultra Balls

The researcher in the tourist bureau needs a little help with his fieldwork. Show him your Pokédex with 10 Pokémon registered in it, and he'll reward your support with 10 Ultra Balls!

Reward: Ultra Ball ×10

Poké Finder

The Poké Finder is a tool that you can access thanks to your Rotom Dex. It lets you snap photos of Pokémon at special photo spots all around the Alola region. Your icon on the lower screen map changes to a camera icon when you walk near a photo spot, and you'll hear a special chime. There's one right beside the tourist bureau, in fact, so why not give it a try? Press Ⓡ to fire up your Poké Finder!

Tip

The complete list of photo spots can be found on page 314.

When using the Poké Finder, move your Nintendo 3DS around or use the Circle Pad to move the camera, and try to spot a Pokémon in the scene.

After taking your photos, you get to review them and pick one to share with the world. People will comment on your photo and give it a "thumbs-up" if they enjoyed it. To get lots of thumbs-ups, make sure that the Pokémon is facing you and in focus. Some Pokémon appear very rarely in photo spots, and people will be excited if you manage to catch them on film!

Get lots of thumbs-ups on your photos, and your Poké Finder will get upgraded. As you unlock upgraded versions of the Poké Finder, you'll be able to zoom in closer and closer to your subjects. The closer you get, the more people will like your photo! Turn to page 313 for all the details on upgrading your Poké Finder and getting rave reviews on your photos.

3 Catch up to Lillie and receive the Lens Case

You bump into Lillie just up the road from the tourist bureau. She's just come from the nearby apparel shop and hands you a nifty Lens Case before heading off to do more shopping. Female Trainers can get a Makeup Bag, too. Check out the apparel shop if you feel like updating your duds. Bop into the neighboring salon if you'd like to change your hairstyle or color.

Reward: Lens Case, Makeup Bag (girl only)

Apparel Shops and Salons

Got a passion for fashion? You're in luck, because Alola features lots of apparel shops! Each shop has a different lineup of clothes and accessories for you to try, so be sure to check 'em all. A full list of the shops and their goods can be found on pages 296–298, and two of them are right here on Melemele Island: the apparel shop in Hau'oli City's shopping district, and the high-end boutique in the nearby shopping mall (p. 81), which opens after you complete your grand trial.

Pop into an apparel shop to buy new clothes and accessories, or to simply use their fitting rooms to change into clothes that you already own. Fitting rooms also let you put in colored contacts, if you wish to change your eye color. Female Trainers can also use fitting rooms to freshen up their lipstick.

Tip

Visit the Festival Plaza to dye white apparel items, changing their color (p. 302)!

You can also visit a salon to change your haircut or color. Like apparel shops, salons are also found all around Alola: there's one here in Hau'oli City right next to the apparel shop; another in Konikoni City on Akala Island; and a third in Malie City on Ula'ula Island.

Haircuts

Boy Haircuts

Medium and layered

Medium and smooth

Caesar cut

Modern quiff

Braided cornrows

Long and tousled*

Girl Haircuts

Chin-length bob

Short and bobbed

Long and straight

Medium and wavy

Romantic tuck

Long and wavy

Cornrow braided bun

High pigtails*

Sideswept bangs

Straight bangs

No bangs

You can choose to add sideswept bangs, straight bangs, or no bangs at all to most of the girl haircuts shown here.

Hair Colors

Black

Honey blond

Dark brown

Ash brown

Caramel blond

Platinum blond

Pink brown

Wine red*

White*

*Available only after clearing the game.

Apparel Shops and Salons (continued)

Contact Colors

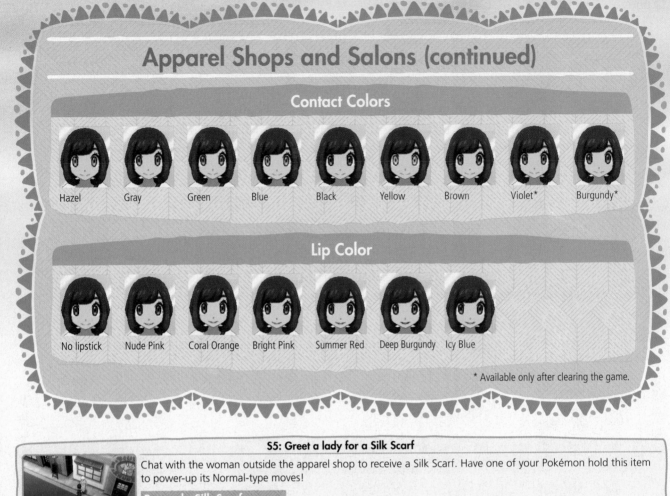

Hazel | Gray | Green | Blue | Black | Yellow | Brown | Violet* | Burgundy*

Lip Color

No lipstick | Nude Pink | Coral Orange | Bright Pink | Summer Red | Deep Burgundy | Icy Blue

* Available only after clearing the game.

S5: Greet a lady for a Silk Scarf

Chat with the woman outside the apparel shop to receive a Silk Scarf. Have one of your Pokémon hold this item to power-up its Normal-type moves!

Reward: Silk Scarf

4 Visit the Shopping District's Pokémon Center

A Pokémon Center stands farther down the street. Head inside to restore your Pokémon, which may be weary if you've been romping through the tall grass beyond the shopping district's gates. Load up on items at the Poké Mart, and be sure to talk to both clerks, as each has different goods to sell. The old man who stands near the Poké Mart is the Move Deleter—talk to him if you'd like to make your Pokémon forget their moves.

S6: Catch a Drifloon for a hefty amount of prize money

The beautiful lady inside the Pokémon Center wants you to catch a Drifloon in Hau'oli Cemetery. She'll reward you handsomely if you catch Drifloon and show her your Pokédex!

Reward: ₽10,000

S7: Say "Alola" to a tourist for a Heal Ball

Talk to the tourist outside the Pokémon Center to receive a Heal Ball. Pokémon that you catch with Heal Balls are restored to full health and any status conditions are cured, so they'll be ready for battle when they join your party.

Reward: Heal Ball

5 Hear rumors of Team Skull as you explore

Carry on down the road, and you'll suddenly overhear rumors of a band of local troublemakers called Team Skull. They sound like rough customers—here's hoping you never meet them! Keep going to find a fancy house on the left, which turns out to be Ilima's home. Around the corner you'll find Hau'oli's city hall. Feel free to enter and explore these buildings as you continue your trek through the city.

S8: Visit Ilima's house to pick up a Lumiose Galette

Stop by Ilima's house (the big one), and his mom will give you a Lumiose Galette—a rare delicacy from the Kalos region that cures all of a Pokémon's status conditions when consumed.

Reward: Lumiose Galette

S9: Speak with an old woman for a Revive

Speak to an old woman inside the city hall to receive a Revive. If one of your Pokémon faints in battle, you can use a Revive to bring it back around with half of its maximum HP.

Reward: Revive

6 Run into Hau near the malasada shop

A malasada shop lies just beyond the city hall, and your friend Hau races up to you as you approach. He's definitely excited about his malasadas, so why not see what all the buzz is about? Enter the shop to buy some tasty treats for your Pokémon. Talk to the clerk on the right if you'd like to buy a Big Malasada to take with you on your travels.

Tip

Don't miss the TM49 Echoed Voice that's tucked away in the tall grass across the street from the malasada shop. TMs can be easily identified in the field by the yellow Poké Balls that contain them.

Malasadas

A favorite snack of both the people and the Pokémon of Alola, malasadas are soft, donut-like delicacies. These delicious treats can be found in shops on all islands that have significant populations. Malasadas come in five flavors, but each store only offers a limited selection.

Location	Malasadas
Hau'oli City, Melemele Island	Sweet Malasada
Royal Avenue, Akala Island	Sour Malasada, Dry Malasada
Malie City, Ula'ula Island	Bitter Malasada, Spiced Malasada

Feeding your Pokémon malasadas makes them more affectionate toward you, and also helps fill their bellies—two important things that you can also do through Pokémon Refresh (p. 276). If your Pokémon is already full, though, it won't be able to eat any malasadas.

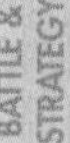

Malasadas (continued)

Your Pokémon will like some malasada flavors and dislike others. This is based on their Nature (p. 340), which you can check on the Pokémon's summary page. If they love a malasada's flavor, their affection will grow twice as fast as usual when you give them one. If they don't like a flavor, their affection will still grow—but even less than usual. The malasada will fill their bellies by the same amount, though, regardless of whether they like or dislike the flavor.

Sweet Malasada are...	Loved by Hasty, Jolly, Naive, and Timid Pokémon	Disliked by Brave, Quiet, Relaxed, and Sassy Pokémon
Sour Malasada are...	Loved by Bold, Impish, Lax, and Relaxed Pokémon	Disliked by Gentle, Hasty, Lonely, and Mild Pokémon.
Dry Malasada are...	Loved by Mild, Modest, Quiet, and Rash Pokémon	Disliked by Adamant, Careful, Impish, and Jolly Pokémon
Spiced Malasada are...	Loved by Adamant, Brave, Lonely, and Naughty Pokémon	Disliked by Bold, Calm, Modest, and Timid Pokémon
Bitter Malasada are...	Loved by Calm, Careful, Gentle, and Sassy Pokémon	Disliked by Lax, Naïve, Naughty, and Rash Pokémon

Tip

Bashful, Docile, Hardy, Quirky, and Serious Pokémon have no strong likes or dislikes, so they will react the same to all flavors.

Mythic Malasada

On rare occasions, you can also buy Mythic Malasadas at shops. These infrequent treats only appear about every month or so—don't miss your chance to buy them! Mythic Malasadas are so delicious that they are loved by all Pokémon, and they raise their affection even more than any other flavor of malasada. Get 'em while they're hot!

Tip

Tuning into any TV you find around Alola will alert you if Mythic Malasadas are currently available.

Big Malasada

You can also buy a Big Malasada once each day at each malasada shop in Alola. Big Malasadas heal all status conditions, so keep a few in your Bag at all times—just don't let Hau find them!

S10: Talk to the couple to get a pair of battle items

Before battling Team Skull, chat up the couple near the Ferry Terminal building to learn about items that enhance your Pokémon's battle prowess—and to receive two of these very useful items. Be sure to grab the Super Potion down by the dock, too.

Reward: X Attack, X Defense

7 Scope out the Marina and battle Team Skull

Hau'oli City's police station stands just past the malasada shop, and beyond that lies the Marina. Captain Ilima is enjoying the lovely weather here, but it's not long before Team Skull arrives to spoil the mood. Ilima doesn't seem concerned by the thugs—in fact, he asks that you help take care of one of them for him. Make sure your Pokémon are in good shape before taking on Team Skull!

Team Skull Grunt's Pokémon

This lowly Grunt's Zubat is no match for your team. Pound it with powerful moves, and be ready with Antidotes in case your Pokémon are Poisoned.

Zubat
♂ Lv. 8 — POISON / FLYING
Weak to: ELECTRIC, ICE, PSYCHIC, ROCK

8 Test your skills against Ilima!

Impressed by how easily you handled Team Skull, Ilima decides the time has come to see what you've got. He heals your Pokémon before challenging you to battle. The time has come to test your skills against one of Melemele's most renowned Trainers!

Captain Ilima's Pokémon

Ilima is a more challenging opponent than that goofy Team Skull Grunt. He sends out two well-trained Pokémon, and he even uses a Potion to heal one of them when its HP gets low. Be prepared for this, and don't hesitate to heal your own Pokémon if the need arises.

Yungoos
♂ Lv.9
NORMAL
Weak to:
FIGHTING
Smeargle
♂ Lv. 10
NORMAL
Weak to:
FIGHTING

9 Follow Rotom's guidance to reach Route 2

Having felt your power firsthand, Ilima is more eager than ever for you to attempt his trial. He invites you to come challenge him again at Verdant Cavern, which lies beyond Route 2. Backtrack through Hau'oli City's Shopping District, following Rotom's guidance to reach Route 2. Along the way, you'll run into Lillie and Kahuna Hala, who is still trying to wrangle that ornery Tauros. Lend Hala a hand, then rest your Pokémon at the nearby Pokémon Center before entering Route 2.

Route 2 / Hau'oli Cemetery / Berry Fields

Ride Pokémon Needed 

Running along the west side of Melemele Island, Route 2 features steep hills, tall grass, and several other Trainers who are itching for battle. This scenic route connects Hau'oli City to the south with Route 3 up north. The hallowed Hau'oli Cemetery and the fruitful Berry fields also lie off the path and to the east.

Team Recommendations

FLYING BUG GHOST DARK

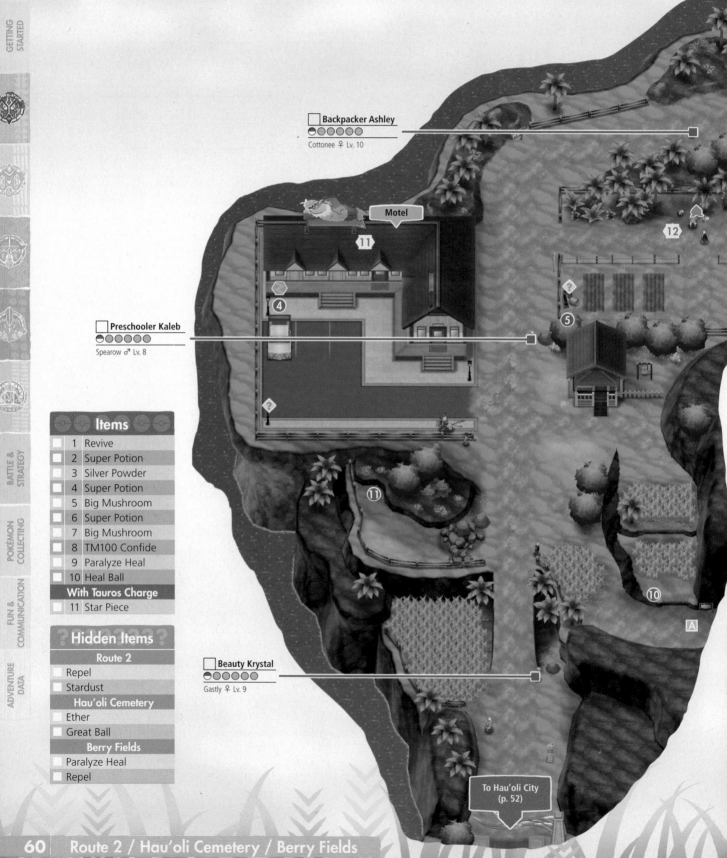

Backpacker Ashley

Cottonee ♀ Lv. 10

Motel

Preschooler Kaleb

Spearow ♂ Lv. 8

Beauty Krystal

Gastly ♀ Lv. 9

To Hau'oli City (p. 52)

Items

☐	1	Revive
☐	2	Super Potion
☐	3	Silver Powder
☐	4	Super Potion
☐	5	Big Mushroom
☐	6	Super Potion
☐	7	Big Mushroom
☐	8	TM100 Confide
☐	9	Paralyze Heal
☐	10	Heal Ball
With Tauros Charge		
☐	11	Star Piece

Hidden Items

Route 2	
☐	Repel
☐	Stardust
Hau'oli Cemetery	
☐	Ether
☐	Great Ball
Berry Fields	
☐	Paralyze Heal
☐	Repel

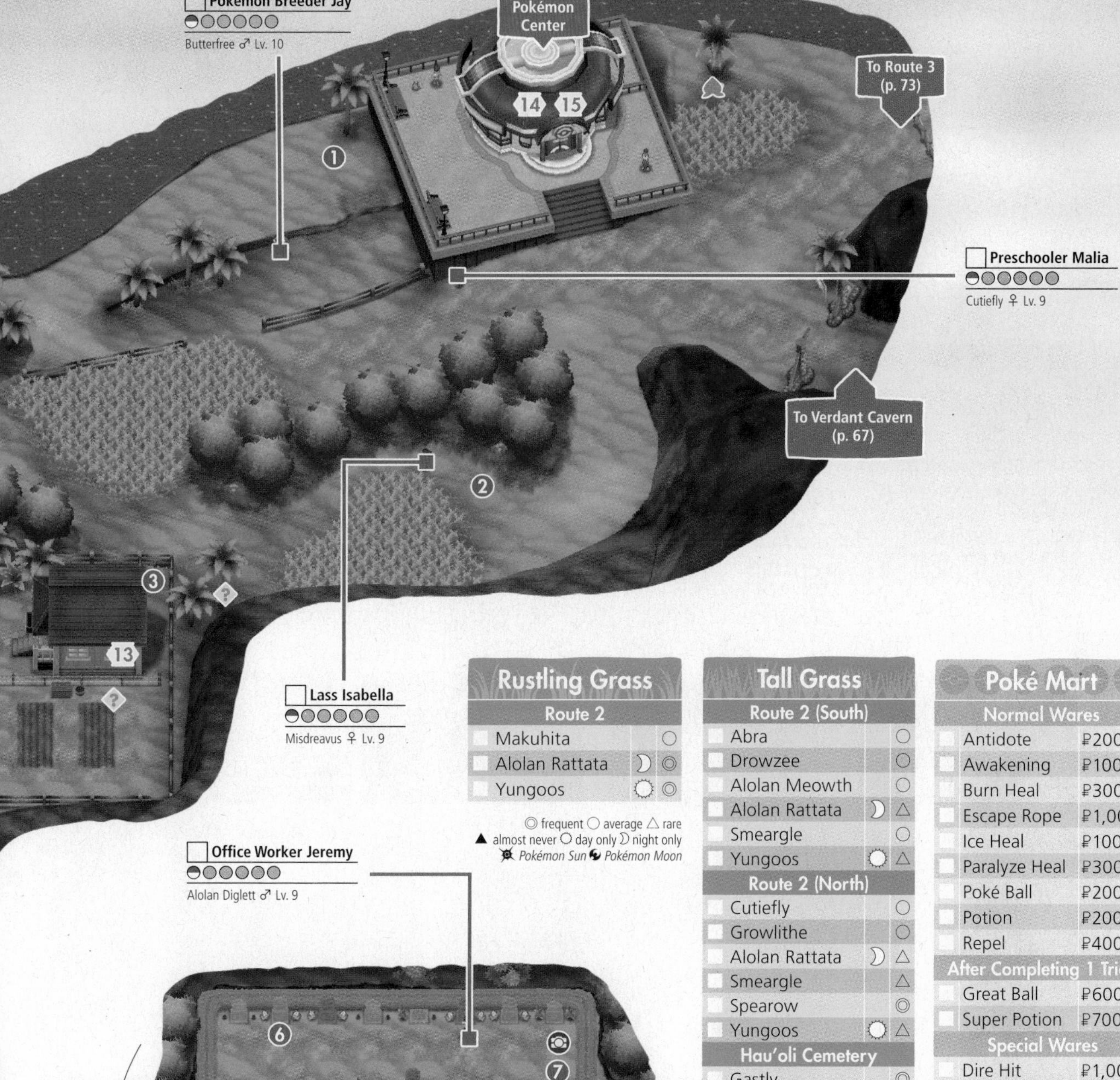

Rustling Grass

Route 2		
Makuhita		○
Alolan Rattata	☽	◎
Yungoos	☼	◎

◎ frequent ○ average △ rare ▲ almost never ☼ day only ☽ night only *Pokémon Sun* *Pokémon Moon*

Tall Grass

Route 2 (South)		
Abra		○
Drowzee		○
Alolan Meowth		○
Alolan Rattata	☽	△
Smeargle		○
Yungoos	☼	△
Route 2 (North)		
Cutiefly		○
Growlithe		○
Alolan Rattata	☽	△
Smeargle		△
Spearow		◎
Yungoos	☼	△
Hau'oli Cemetery		
Gastly		◎
Drifloon	☼	○
Misdreavus	☽	○
Zubat		○

Poké Mart

Normal Wares	
Antidote	₽200
Awakening	₽100
Burn Heal	₽300
Escape Rope	₽1,000
Ice Heal	₽100
Paralyze Heal	₽300
Poké Ball	₽200
Potion	₽200
Repel	₽400
After Completing 1 Trial	
Great Ball	₽600
Super Potion	₽700
Special Wares	
Dire Hit	₽1,000
Guard Spec.	₽1,500
Heal Ball	₽300
Luxury Ball	₽1,000
Nest Ball	₽1,000
Super Potion	₽700
X Accuracy	₽1,000
X Attack	₽1,000
X Defense	₽2,000
X Sp. Atk	₽1,000
X Sp. Def	₽2,000
X Speed	₽1,000

Tip

Run into Route 2's tall grass, and you'll be ambushed by a feisty Pokémon! It's Makuhita, a Fighting-type Pokémon that will be a handy ally to have in your upcoming trial at Verdant Cavern. Do your best to catch Makuhita without knocking it out. (Read more about ambushes on the next page.)

Ambush Encounters

Some particularly feisty Pokémon will take the initiative and spring a battle on you in the Alola region. Fortunately, there are always signs that feisty Pokémon are nearby. These Pokémon sometimes drop items after battle, so check the ground for a bit of shine after you defeat them!

Rustling grass	Rustling tree	Rustling bush	Shadows on the ground

Pokémon will rush toward you if you step into the grass. Keep your distance if you don't want a fight.	Pokémon may leap out of trees that shake and rustle as you walk by. Give them a wide berth if you want to avoid a battle.	Pokémon may leap out of bushes that shake and rustle as you walk by. Step closer if you want to engage in a battle.	Pokémon flying overhead may dive down on you for a battle. Avoid their shadows if you're tired of battles.

Dirt clouds	Sand clouds	Water splashes	Wimpod
		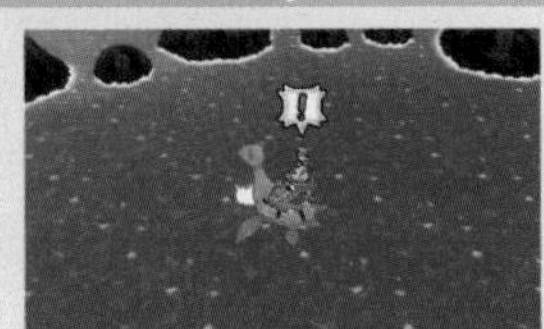	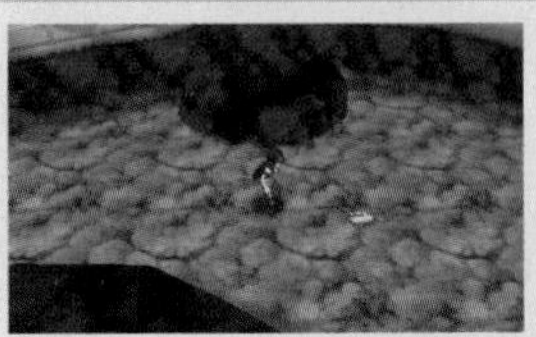
In caves, Pokémon will sometimes come rushing at you in a cloud of dust. Standing still won't fool them, but you might be able to outrun them!	On beaches and in the desert, you may see sand spitting up where a Pokémon is burrowing into the grit. Approach them for a battle.	On the water, you may see a furious splashing at times, which may hide a rare Pokémon. Seek them out when you see them!	Wimpod can sometimes be spotted on beaches—but rather than dashing toward you, they dash away! You'll have to figure out how to corner these curious Pokémon yourself.

1 Take a stroll through the cemetery

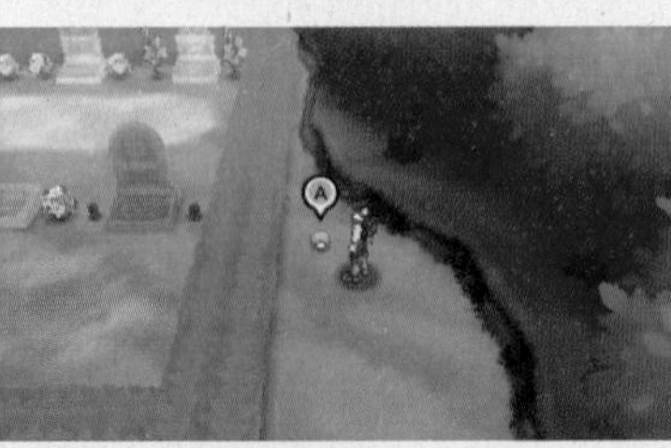

Scale Route 2's first hill and then go through the tall grass on the right to make your way to the Hau'oli Cemetery. There you'll find valuable items and wild Pokémon among the final resting spots of some of Hau'oli's former residents—and some more Trainers as well. Be sure to pick up the TM100 Confide that lies beyond more tall grass on the cemetery's right side as you explore.

Tip

If you've caught 10 or more species of Pokémon by now, you may want to show your Pokédex to the researcher back in the tourist bureau for those 10 free Ultra Balls.

Tip

If you take a moment to catch a Drifloon in Hau'oli Cemetery's tall grass during the day, you can return to Hau'oli City's Pokémon Center afterward, and show your Pokédex to the beautiful lady near the café for your ₽10,000 reward.

SOS Battles

When faced with a tough opponent, wild Pokémon will sometimes call for help. If a helper arrives, you'll suddenly find yourself in an SOS battle!

What is an SOS Battle?

SOS battles start as normal wild Pokémon encounters, but evolve into a two-on-one affair when another wild Pokémon joins the fray due to a call for help! Healthy opposing Pokémon rarely call for help, but as their HP gauge drops into the yellow and the red, an SOS battle becomes increasingly more likely. Some species of Pokémon are also more likely to call for help than others.

Tip

A Pokémon that is affected by a status condition, such as Paralysis, will not call for help, no matter how low its HP goes.

Tip

You can't aim properly if you have more than one target. If there are still two Pokémon in the battle, you won't be able to catch either. So knock out the one you don't want, then try throwing that Poké Ball!

Special helpers

The more helpers that get called into an SOS Battle, the greater the chance becomes that a special Pokémon will appear. You'll have a chance to encounter rare Pokémon that you wouldn't otherwise encounter in that area, or Pokémon that have special features, such as maximum individual strengths (p. 272) and a Hidden Ability (p. 249). If you're really lucky, an extremely rare Shiny Pokémon—which is differently colored than a normal member of its species—might appear!

Ways to increase the likelihood of an SOS Battle

Abilities

An opponent is more likely to call for help if your Pokémon has the Intimidate, Pressure, or Unnerve Ability.

Items

Using an Adrenaline Orb in battle can increase the chances that a Pokémon will call for help.

Supereffective moves

If you use a supereffective move on a helper Pokémon that your opponent just called into battle, then your original opponent is more likely to get spooked and call for help again.

Consecutive calls

If a Pokémon already called for help once, it has a greater chance of calling for help again. Try to keep your opponent from fainting so that more and more helpers will join the fray. Don't use damage-dealing moves if their health is in the red, and remember that when all of a Pokémon's moves have run out of PP, it will use Struggle. Struggle is a unique move that only appears when a Pokémon has no usable moves left, and it damages the user as well as the target. That means your opponent might knock itself out with Struggle if you aren't careful!

Tip

Some Pokémon's calls for help may invite foes instead! Murkrow sometimes target weak Carbink, just as Mareanie and Toxapex target weak Corsola. These "helpers" will attack the Pokémon that called for help, making it tough to keep the battle going!

2 Explore Route 2

Return to Route 2 and pick up the main path again to reach a house and a motel. Find a Super Potion in the motel's parking lot, and run through the tall grass near the house to reach a Heal Ball. And while the motel has a vending machine in its office, everything seems to be sold out at the moment.

Tip

Vending machines can be found in various places around Alola, and they're handy for scoring some healing items when you're out and about. You can purchase any items that they have in stock.

S11: Get some Nest Balls from a friendly traveler

Talk to the man inside the motel room to receive a couple of Nest Balls. These are useful for catching low-level Pokémon, and the man doesn't seem to need them anymore.

Reward: Nest Ball ×2

3 Battle against Team Skull in the Berry fields

Continue traveling north along Route 2 until a feisty Delibird grabs your attention. The Delibird insists that you follow it into the nearby Berry fields. Head in to find the same Team Skull Grunts causing trouble. Beat the Grunts in battle to send them packing, and the farmer will reward you with an Oran Berry. Have a look around the Berry fields afterward, making sure to snag the Silver Powder that's tucked away behind the farmer's house.

Reward: Oran Berry

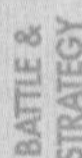

Team Skull Grunt's Pokémon

This Grunt sends out Drowzee. It's weak to Bug-, Ghost-, and Dark-type moves, so pick a supereffective attack and make quick work of it.

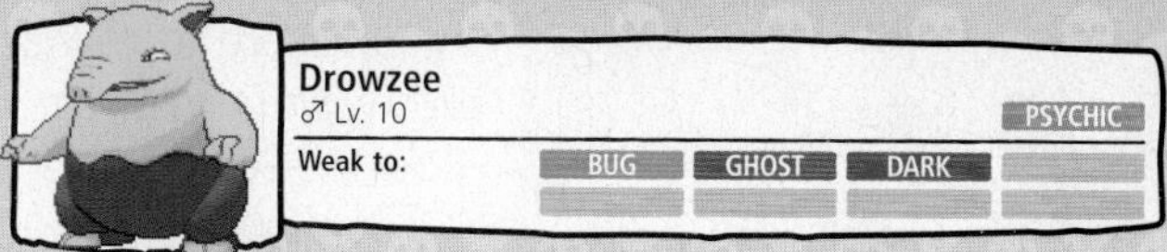

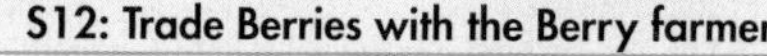

S12: Trade Berries with the Berry farmer

The Berry farmer will give you a rare Sitrus Berry if you show him a Persim Berry. Sift through the pile of Berries near the farmer and see if you can find a Persim Berry. If not, check the Berry pile that lies farther north along Route 2.

Reward: Sitrus Berry

S13: Get a Revive from a Delibird

One of the Delibird inside the Berry farmer's house will give you a valuable Revive. Don't question it—just take it!

Reward: Revive

Berries

Berries are so abundant in the Alola region that you'll find them just lying on the ground, free for the taking. Be on the lookout for palm trees with colorful piles of Berries beneath them, and harvest all the delicious Berries that you can. The maps in this guide also show the locations of every spot where Berries can be found.

Berries are quite handy, because Pokémon can use them all on their own. If you give a Pokémon a Berry to hold, it can eat it whenever it needs it in battle. Best of all, if a Pokémon eats a Berry that it is holding during battle, it won't count as a turn. Your Pokémon can therefore eat a Berry to recover HP or cure status conditions, and then attack, all in the same turn—something that it can't do if you use a healing item from your Bag.

Tip

You'll be able to grow more Berries eventually at Poké Pelago (p. 309), so you may want to hold onto any rare Berries for future harvests.

Crabrawler

Crabrawler loves Berries and sometimes it buries itself in piles of Berries to chow down. When you're collecting Berries from beneath a tree, you may sometimes get attacked by this frisky Fighting-type Pokémon!

4 Meet up with Hau near Route 2's Pokémon Center

Return to Route 2 and press onward until you meet up with Hau again. He's found a Pokémon Center (or PMC, as he calls it), and you both head inside. Hau is excited about your upcoming trial and gives you a handful of Revives that are sure to come in handy. Shop at the Poké Mart for more items that will help your Pokémon in tough battles, like Super Potions, Dire Hits, and X Speeds. Rest your Pokémon and then follow Rotom's guidance into the nearby Verdant Cavern, where Ilima's trial awaits.

Reward: Revive ×3

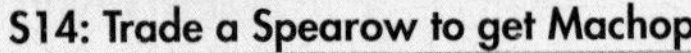

S14: Trade a Spearow to get Machop

A Lass inside the Pokémon Center really wants a Spearow, which can be found in the tall grass on Route 2. Catch one, and she'll trade you for a Machop—another Fighting-type Pokémon that will be a valuable ally in your upcoming trial.

Pokémon: Machop

S15: Show Cutiefly for a reward

The Sightseer in the Pokémon Center will pay you cold, hard cash if you show her Cutiefly's Pokédex entry. Catch a Cutiefly when you get to Route 3, then return to the Sightseer for your payment.

Reward: ₽3,000

Tip

Before your trial, take a moment to search the Berry pile near the Pokémon Center. You might startle a Crabrawler that's enjoying a snack! If this occurs, try to catch Crabrawler to add another valuable Fighting-type Pokémon to your party. And feel free to grab those Berries after the battle, too.

Trading

Trading Pokémon with other Trainers is a great way to complete your Pokédex. (Also see page 267.) Some residents of the Alola region are looking for certain Pokémon, so talk to everyone you meet on your adventure. You just might get a chance to trade a Pokémon that you've caught for a Pokémon you've been wanting!

You can trade with other Pokémon players in several ways. If a friend is playing nearby, each of you can open the X menu and choose "Quick Link" to trade.

When you're not playing close to anyone else, you can open the X menu and go to Festival Plaza if you feel like trading. Choose "Trade" on the lower screen, and you'll find three different ways to trade with people all over the world!

Link Trade: Trade with another player via local wireless communication or the Internet.

GTS: Leave a Pokémon with a request to trade for a specific Pokémon, or browse the Pokémon that other players have left and see if there are any you'd like to trade for.

Wonder Trade: Trade a Pokémon to someone somewhere in the world for a random Pokémon. Be sure you're ready to say goodbye to the Pokémon you offer up! Who knows, you may get something amazing in return.

Verdant Cavern

Ride Pokémon Needed 

Featuring steep slopes and narrow ledges, this natural cavern is an ideal site for Captain Ilima's trial. Wild Pokémon abound here, but they steer clear of Trainers until Ilima's trial conditions have been met.

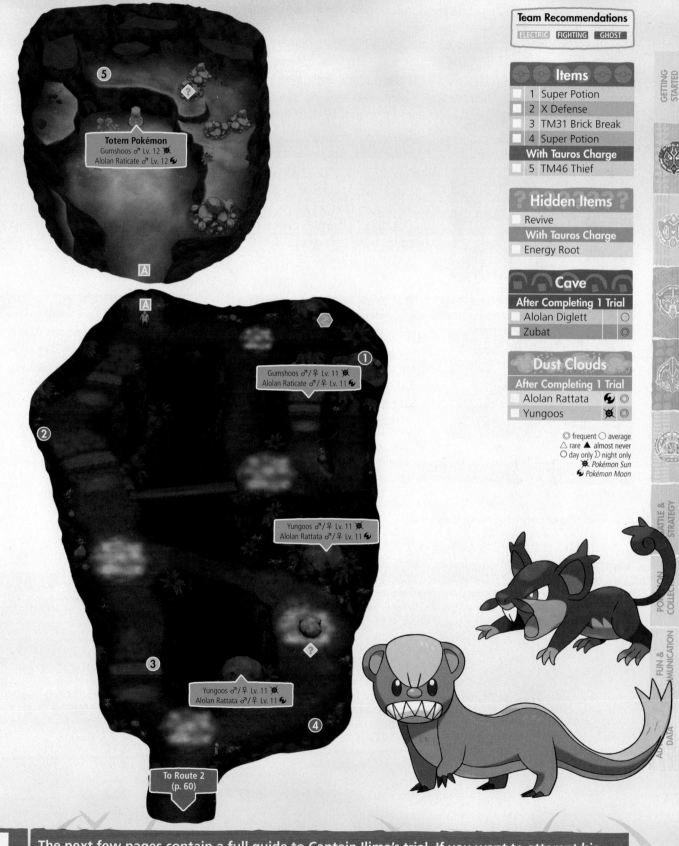

To Route 2 (p. 60)

Team Recommendations

ELECTRIC FIGHTING GHOST

Items

	1	Super Potion
	2	X Defense
	3	TM31 Brick Break
	4	Super Potion
With Tauros Charge		
	5	TM46 Thief

Hidden Items

	Revive
With Tauros Charge	
	Energy Root

Cave

After Completing 1 Trial	
Alolan Diglett	○
Zubat	◎

Dust Clouds

After Completing 1 Trial		
Alolan Rattata	*Pokémon Moon*	◎
Yungoos	*Pokémon Sun*	◎

◎ frequent ○ average
△ rare ▲ almost never
○ day only ☽ night only
Pokémon Sun
Pokémon Moon

The next few pages contain a full guide to Captain Ilima's trial. If you want to attempt his trial on your own without any spoilers, don't turn the page!

Trial Guide: Ilima's Trial

At last, the time has come for your first trial! Each captain's trial is a unique experience, but they all have one thing in common: if you give up halfway through the trial, you'll have to start over from scratch on your next attempt. Therefore, it's vital that you fully prepare yourself before entering any trial site. The other thing that all trials have in common is that you cannot catch any wild Pokémon in a trial site until you have cleared the trial and gained the captain's permission. Ilima's trial involves several Pokémon battles, so make sure you have the right team (Fighting types are best) and plenty of healing items.

Ilima's Trial Goals

- Find and defeat three Pokémon lurking inside the cavern
- Defeat the Totem Pokémon
- Retrieve the Z-Crystal from the pedestal

1 Speak with Ilima and learn about his trial

Ilima awaits you just outside of Verdant Cavern, and he's thrilled that you've come to attempt his trial. Follow Ilima into the cave, and he'll tell you all about the challenges that await you in his trial. Ilima also mentions that, although wild Pokémon live in Verdant Cavern, you can't catch any of them until you've passed his trial. Let's get to it!

2 Defeat the Yungoos / Alolan Rattata

Your first objective is to defeat three Pokémon that hide in their dens inside the cavern. If you're playing *Pokémon Sun,* the first two Pokémon you'll encounter will be Yungoos. If you're playing *Pokémon Moon*, they'll be Alolan Rattata instead. There are more than three dens in the cavern, so you gotta check 'em all! Simply approach a den and press Ⓐ to peek inside—but make sure that you're ready for battle!

Yungoos

Yungoos are your opponents in *Pokémon Sun*, and they have but one weakness: Fighting-type moves. Put your best Fighting-type Pokémon at the head of your party and dish out the damage!

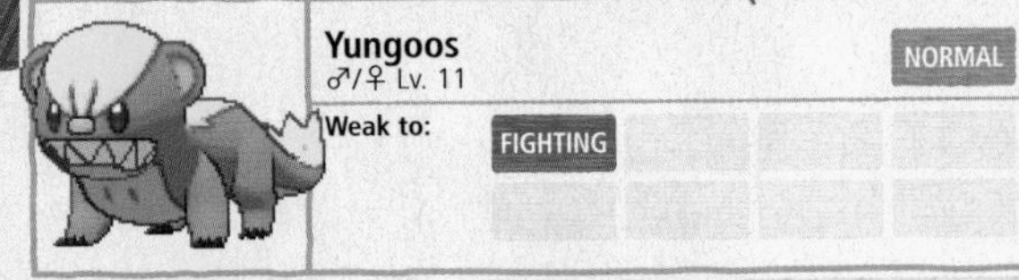

Alolan Rattata

Alolan Rattata are your opponents in *Pokémon Moon*, and they have a few weaknesses, but only one that does massive damage: Fighting-type moves. Put your best Fighting-type Pokémon at the head of your party and dish out the damage!

Tip

Did you catch Makuhita or Crabrawler back on Route 2, or trade for Machop back in Route 2's Pokémon Center? The Fighting-type moves used by these Pokémon will be super effective against both Yungoos and Alolan Rattata. Ghost-type Pokémon will also be immune to most of Yungoos and Alolan Rattata's moves, and there are plenty of Ghost types to catch back in Hau'oli Cemetery—but Ghost-type moves won't affect Yungoos or Alolan Rattata, so Fighting-type Pokémon are best for this trial.

3 Track down the third Pokémon

The first two Pokémon are easy to encounter, but the third is holed up in a den on a ledge. To reach it, go the east and press Ⓐ to crawl through a small tunnel. You'll find a Super Potion on the other side, along with the den that you were looking for—but there's no Pokémon inside. Instead, a dust cloud appears near a different den—the Pokémon has given you the slip! Track the pesky Pokémon around the cave, searching each den that it moves to.

Tip

Having a hard time against the Pokémon here in Verdant Cavern? The TM for Brick Break, a strong Fighting-type move, can be found on the cave's west side. To reach it, scale the first slope and then run down the ledges in the foreground. Use the TM afterward to teach your Pokémon the move.

4 Have a scrap with Team Skull

As you chase the Pokémon around the cave, you suddenly bump into those Team Skull numskulls again. They're set on spoiling your trial—beat one of them in battle to make them back off!

Team Skull Grunt's Pokémon

Fighting-type moves aren't very effective against Drowzee, so switch your Pokémon before beginning this battle.

Drowzee	♂ Lv. 11	PSYCHIC
Weak to:	BUG, GHOST, DARK	

5 Defeat the third Pokémon

Having suffered another humbling defeat, the Team Skull goons switch tactics and decide to hunt down the last Pokémon before you can reach it. They take up positions near two of the dens, conveniently blocking them off for you. Now you can corner the skittish Pokémon in its den! Just crawl through the small east tunnel again to reach it. Heal your party before peering into the den to begin the battle.

Gumshoos

Yungoos evolves into Gumshoos, but it still has the same weakness to Fighting-type moves. Move your Fighting types back to the head of your team before engaging this dangerous Pokémon.

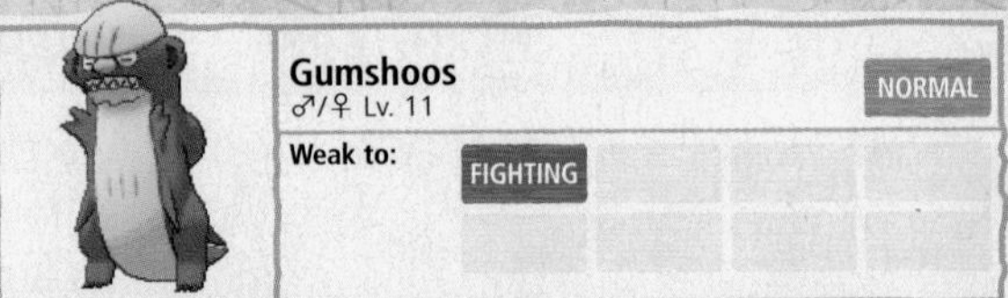

Alolan Raticate

Alolan Rattata evolves into Alolan Raticate, but it still has the same weakness to Fighting-type moves. Move your Fighting types back to the head of your team before engaging this dangerous Pokémon.

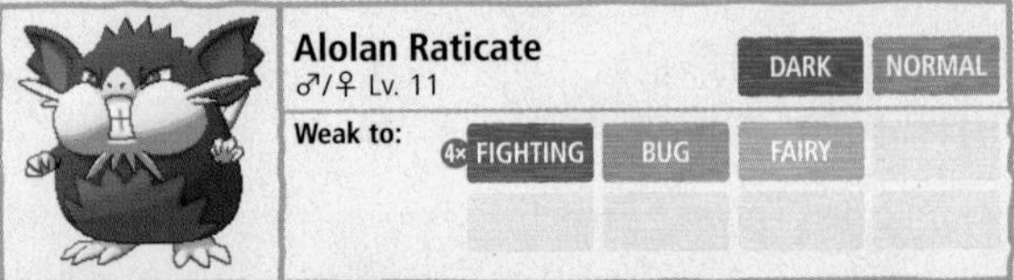

6 Delve deeper into the cave and battle the Totem Pokémon

With the three Pokémon defeated, you're able to venture deeper into the cavern. Speak to the Trial Guide near the back, and he'll let you into the cave's deepest reaches, where a glittering Z-Crystal rests atop a pedestal. Prepare your Pokémon before reaching for the Z-Crystal, for a mighty Totem Pokémon suddenly attacks! This is the true trial of Verdant Cavern. Defeat the Totem Pokémon, and the Z-Crystal will be yours!

Totem Pokémon

It's time for your first battle against a Totem Pokémon! These powerful Pokémon differ from regular wild Pokémon in several ways. First, they are surrounded by a special aura that helps boost one of their stats—for Gumshoos / Alolan Raticate, this aura boosts its Defense stat significantly, making it tough to damage with physical moves. Special moves, or moves of a supereffective type (like Fighting-type moves), are therefore your best bets in this battle.

Another trick Totem Pokémon have up their sleeves is the ability to summon allies to help them. Gumshoos will call for Yungoos, while Alolan Raticate will call in Alolan Rattata. These allies will work with the Totem Pokémon to pummel your party and divert your attacks. Do your best to defeat the Totem Pokémon quickly, or you risk being overwhelmed by their seemingly endless supply of allies!

Totem Gumshoos

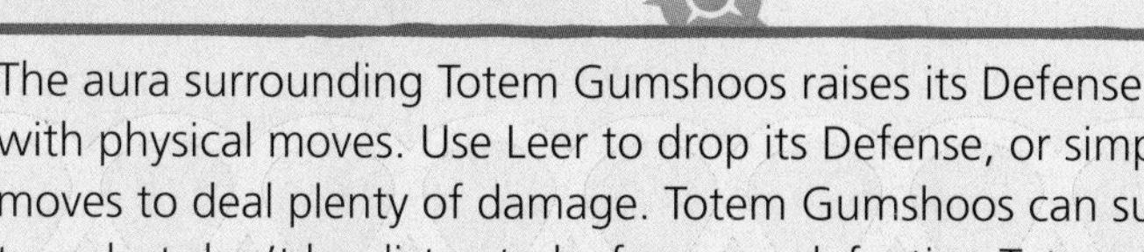

The aura surrounding Totem Gumshoos raises its Defense, making it tough to damage with physical moves. Use Leer to drop its Defense, or simply unleash Fighting-type moves to deal plenty of damage. Totem Gumshoos can summon a Yungoos ally each turn, but don't be distracted—focus on defeating Totem Gumshoos as fast as you can. It also uses Scary Face to harshly reduce your Pokémon's Speed, but this can be countered with X Speed items and the Quick Claw that you received at the Trainers' School.

Gumshoos (Totem Pokémon)
♂ Lv. 12
NORMAL
Weak to: FIGHTING

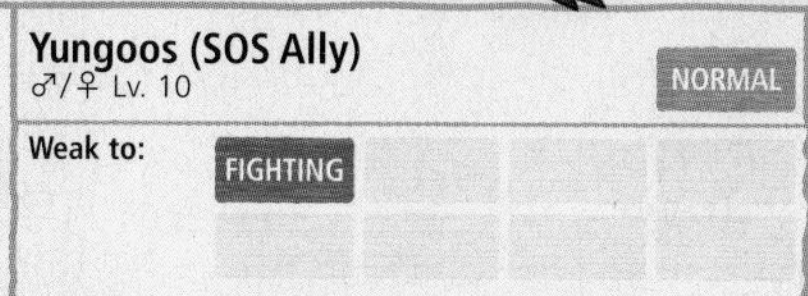

Yungoos (SOS Ally)
♂/♀ Lv. 10
NORMAL
Weak to: FIGHTING

Totem Raticate 

The aura surrounding Totem Raticate raises its Defense, making it tough to damage with physical moves. Use Leer to drop its Defense, or simply unleash Fighting-type moves to deal plenty of damage. Totem Raticate can summon an Alolan Rattata ally each turn, but don't be distracted—focus on defeating Totem Raticate as fast as you can. It also uses Scary Face to harshly reduce your Pokémon's Speed, but this can be countered with X Speed items and the Quick Claw that you received at the Trainers' School.

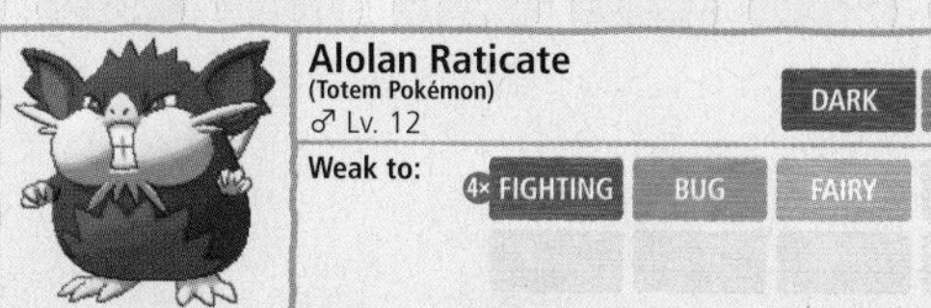

Alolan Raticate
(Totem Pokémon)
♂ Lv. 12
DARK NORMAL
Weak to: 4× FIGHTING, BUG, FAIRY

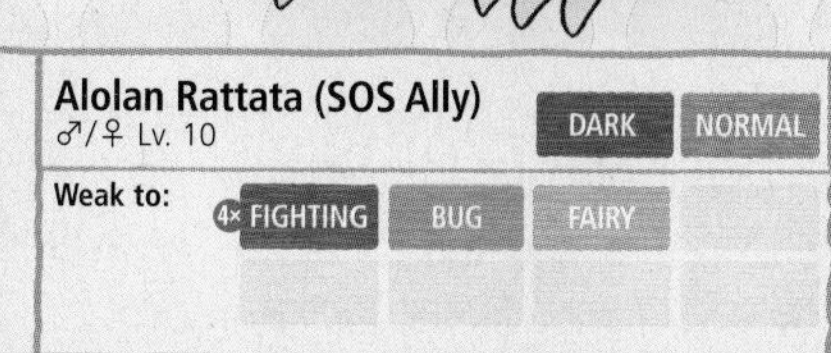

Alolan Rattata (SOS Ally)
♂/♀ Lv. 10
DARK NORMAL
Weak to: 4× FIGHTING, BUG, FAIRY

7 Obtain the Z-Crystal

Great work! You've passed Ilima's trial, and the dashing captain appears to congratulate you and instructs you to take the Z-Crystal from the pedestal, which turns out to be Normalium Z. Ilima also hands you 10 Great Balls to help you catch even more Pokémon around Alola, and he restores your Pokémon. Your trial is over, so make your way back outside to Route 2, collecting any items that you may have missed in the cave before. Just be ready to battle at any moment. Now that you've defeated the Totem Pokémon, the wild Pokémon will no longer by cowering in fear of it. And since you have cleared Ilima's trial, you're free to catch wild Pokémon here in Verdant Cavern! Refer back to the Pokémon list on page 67 to see what can be caught here.

Reward: Normalium Z, Great Ball ×10

GETTING STARTED
BATTLE & STRATEGY
POKÉMON COLLECTING
FUN & COMMUNICATION
ADVENTURE DATA

8 Get a lesson in Z-Powers

As you exit Verdant Cavern, Ilima explains the importance of captains' barricades: special checkpoints that prevent trial-goers from venturing too far out of their depth. Now that you've completed Ilima's trial and obtained the Z-Crystal, the nearby barricade opens, letting you progress into Route 3. Professor Kukui catches up to you as well and explains how to use Z-Powers. After his demonstration, Kukui recalls that he lost track of Lillie somewhere along Route 3. You'd better hurry up north and help the professor find her, but feel free to rest at Route 2's Pokémon Center first.

GETTING STARTED

BATTLE & STRATEGY

POKÉMON COLLECTING

FUN & COMMUNICATION

ADVENTURE DATA

Z-Power

Trainers that possess Z-Rings have the advantage in Alola, for they can unleash superpowerful Z-Moves! A Pokémon must be holding a Z-Crystal in order to perform a Z-Move, and Trainers can only unleash one Z-Move per battle. (See page 245 for more details.)

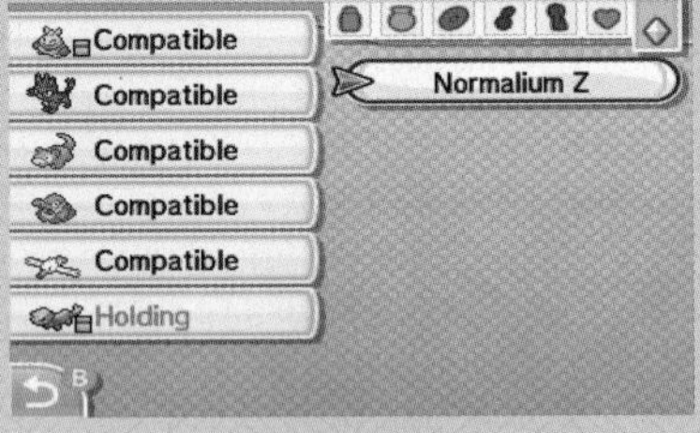

Kahuna Hala gave you a Z-Ring during the festival at Iki Town, and you've just found Normalium Z—the Normal-type Z-Crystal. This means you're all set to start using Normal-type Z-Moves! If you have a Pokémon that knows the move Tackle (or any other Normal-type move), give it Normalium Z to hold, and it will be able to use a Z-Move. Other Z-Crystals power up different types of moves, so keep a sharp lookout for Z-Crystals!

Tip

You'll get a new Z-Crystal each time you finish a trial, and there are even more to be found around Alola. Some Z-Crystals even let you to use Z-Moves that are exclusive to certain Pokémon! These Pokémon must know specific moves before they can unleash their exclusive Z-Moves, so be sure to train those Pokémon well.

Tip

Unlike other held items, one Z-Crystal can be held by multiple Pokémon. Try giving your Normalium Z to every Pokémon that can use it!

To use a Z-Move, simply tap the Z-Power button that appears on the lower screen during battle. Select the Z-Move you want to use, then sit back and watch the awesome might of Z-Power being unleashed! Remember, these moves are so powerful, and take so much energy, that they can only be used once per battle. After one of your Pokémon has used a Z-Move, none of your other Pokémon will be able to use Z-Moves for the rest of the battle. Knowing when to use a Z-Move—and which Z-Move to use—can be the key to victory!

Route 3

Ride Pokémon Needed 

Running along Melemele Island's north side, Route 3 is a sizable stretch that connects Route 2 in the northwest with Route 1 at its southeast end. Travelers must keep a sharp lookout for the shadows of overhead Pokémon that may swoop down and strike at any moment! Knowing that, you can still take in the tranquil beauty of Melemele Meadow as you explore this long, winding route.

Team Recommendations

ELECTRIC FIGHTING FLYING

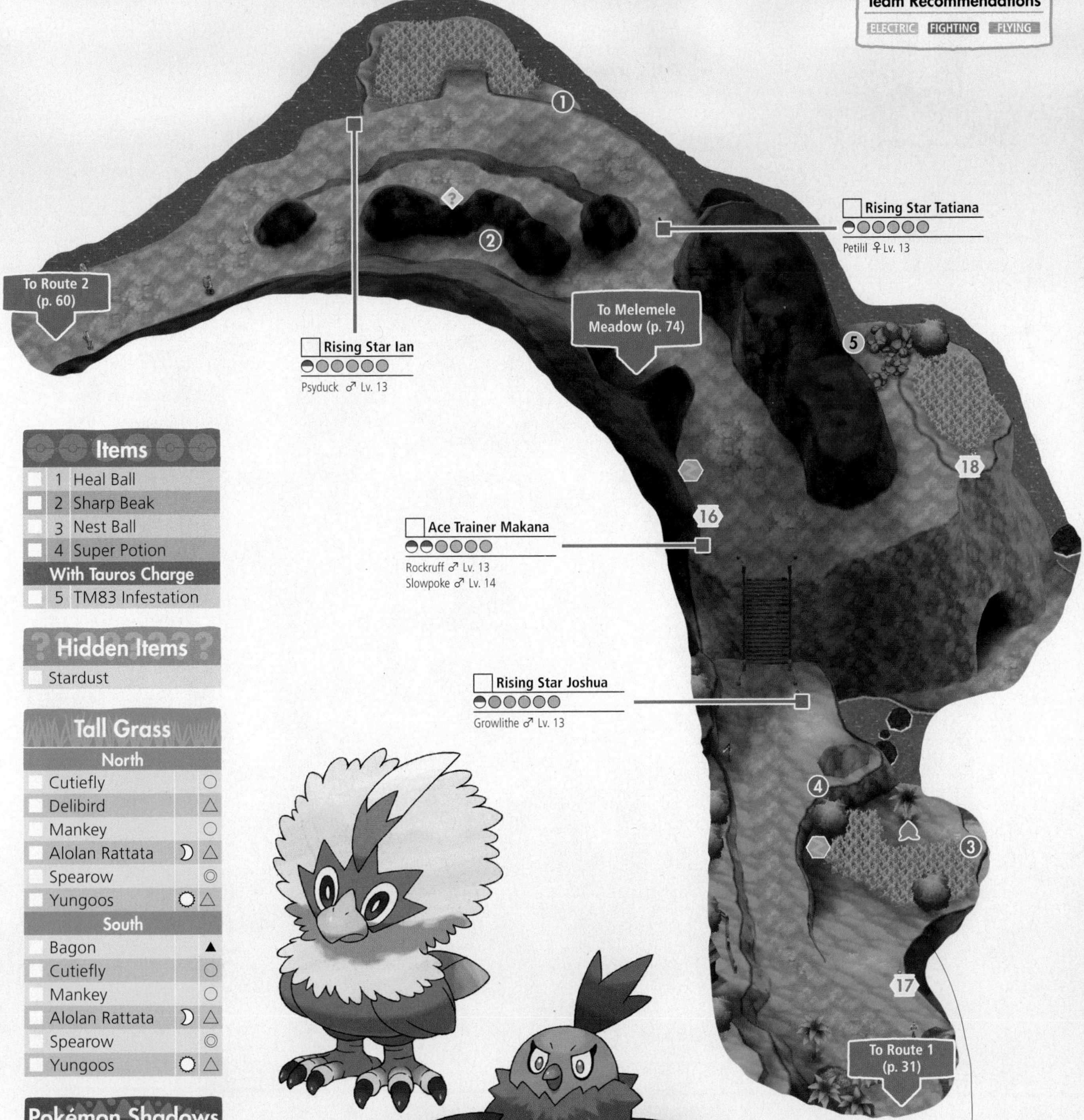

To Route 2 (p. 60)

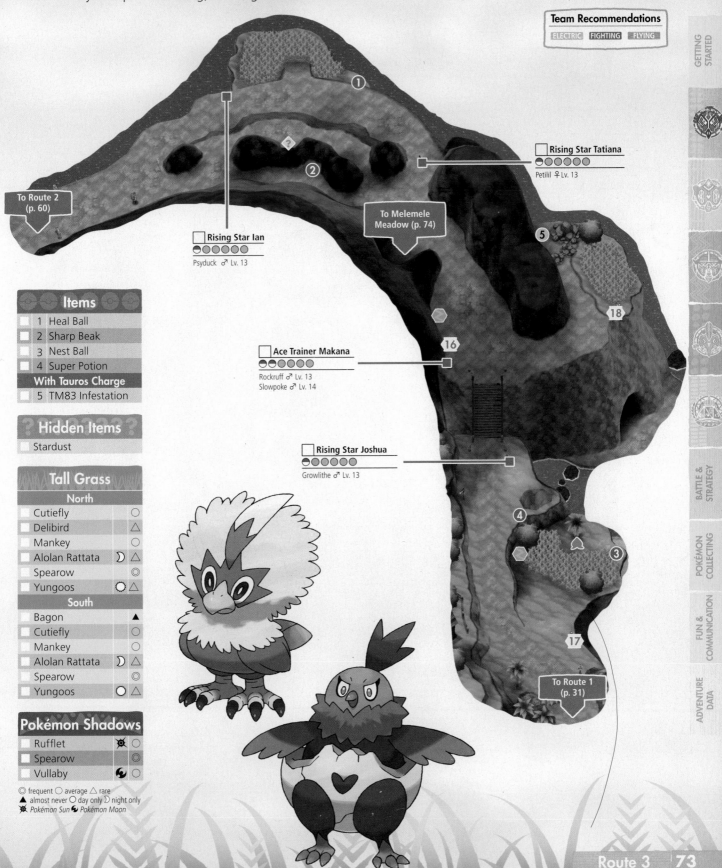

To Melemele Meadow (p. 74)

To Route 1 (p. 31)

Rising Star Ian
Psyduck ♂ Lv. 13

Rising Star Tatiana
Petilil ♀ Lv. 13

Ace Trainer Makana
Rockruff ♂ Lv. 13
Slowpoke ♂ Lv. 14

Rising Star Joshua
Growlithe ♂ Lv. 13

Items	
1	Heal Ball
2	Sharp Beak
3	Nest Ball
4	Super Potion
With Tauros Charge	
5	TM83 Infestation

Hidden Items

- Stardust

Tall Grass		
North		
Cutiefly		○
Delibird		△
Mankey		○
Alolan Rattata	☽	△
Spearow		◎
Yungoos	☼	△
South		
Bagon		▲
Cutiefly		○
Mankey		○
Alolan Rattata	☽	△
Spearow		◎
Yungoos	☼	△

Pokémon Shadows		
Rufflet	Sun	○
Spearow		◎
Vullaby	Moon	○

◎ frequent ○ average △ rare
▲ almost never ☼ day only ☽ night only
Pokémon Sun *Pokémon Moon*

1 Explore Route 3 on your way to Melemele Meadow

Professor Kukui lost Lillie somewhere along Route 3, so you'd better make a thorough search of the area. You can avoid or choose to engage the battle-ready Trainers here, but again be aware of the shadows of Pokémon that are circling overhead—for stepping into a shadow sends a wild Pokémon swooping down on you! And make sure to keep your eyes peeled for items as you follow Rotom's guidance toward Melemele Meadow.

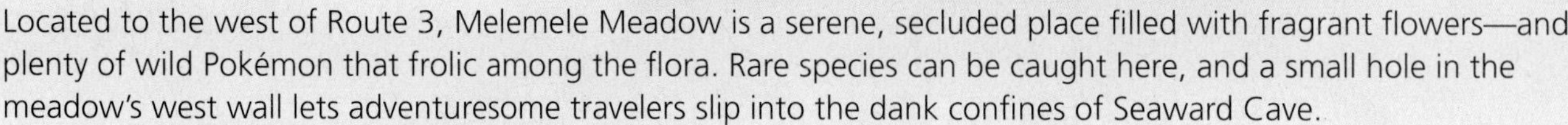

Melemele Meadow

Located to the west of Route 3, Melemele Meadow is a serene, secluded place filled with fragrant flowers—and plenty of wild Pokémon that frolic among the flora. Rare species can be caught here, and a small hole in the meadow's west wall lets adventuresome travelers slip into the dank confines of Seaward Cave.

Team Recommendations

FIRE FLYING BUG

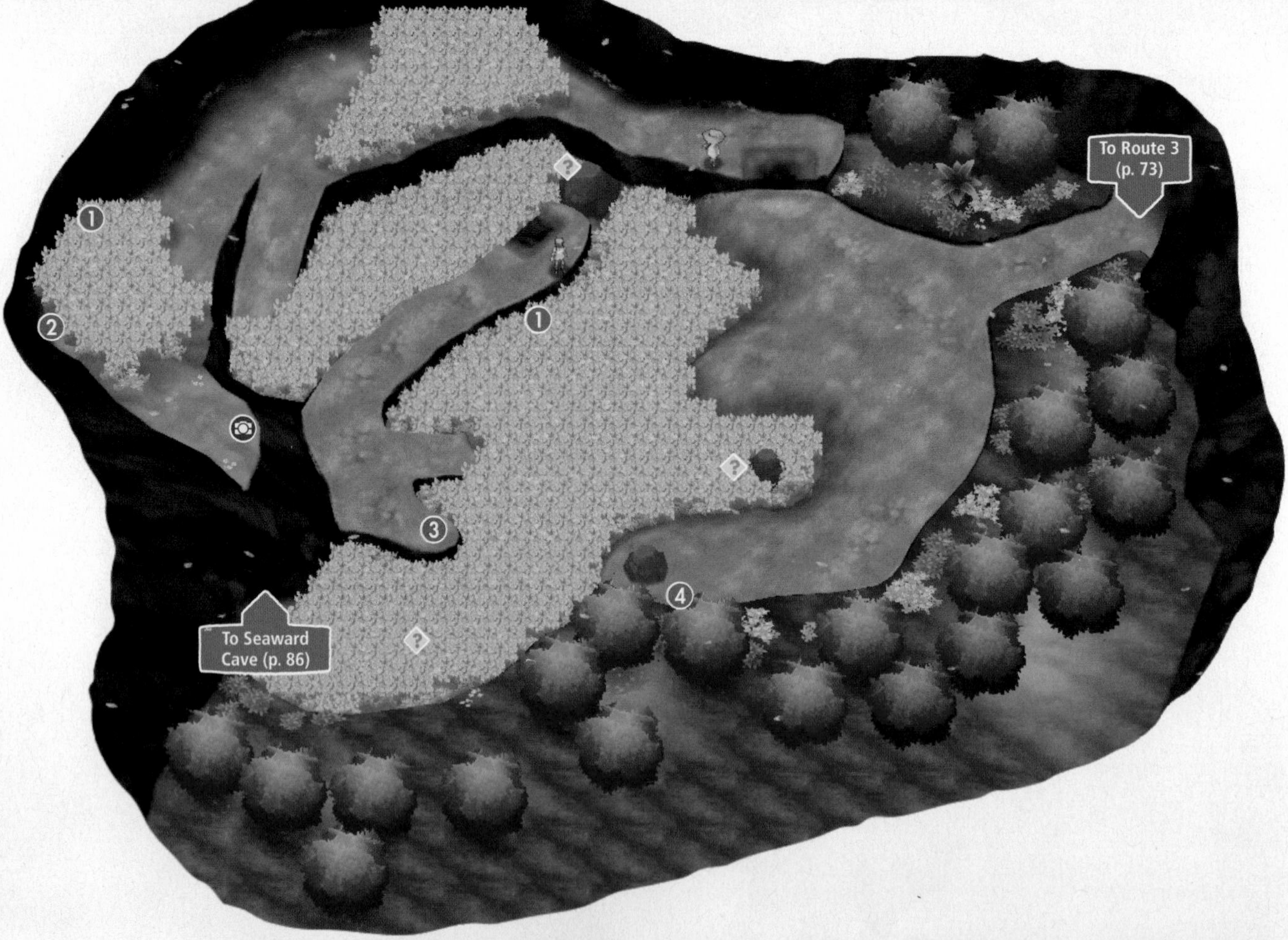

Items	
1	Yellow Nectar ×2 ☽
2	Poison Barb
3	Net Ball
4	Great Ball

Hidden Items
Honey ×3

Yellow Flowers		
Butterfree		▲
Caterpie		△
Cottonee	Sun	○
Cutiefly		○
Metapod		△
Oricorio*		○
Petilil	Moon	○

◎ frequent ○ average △ rare
▲ almost never ○ day only ☽ night only
Pokémon Sun / *Pokémon Moon*

*The form of Oricorio found in Melemele Meadow is the yellow Oricorio (Pom-Pom Style).

Tip

Did you notice the little hole in Melemele Meadow's southwest corner? You can crawl through it to reach Seaward Cave! You can't fully explore this cave at the moment, but we'll tell you all about it on page 86. Feel free to raid the cave for a few items if you like, but beware of its wild Zubat inhabitants.

1 Assist Lillie in nabbing Nebby

Lillie wasn't to be found on Route 3, but you catch up to her in the nearby Melemele Meadow. It seems that little Nebby has taken off on its own again, and Lillie needs your help to get it back. Lillie restores your Pokémon, and you can speak with her again at any time to have them restored again. Wade through the meadow's thick flower fields, battling wild Pokémon and collecting items as you head for Nebby.

2 Find Nebby, then have a battle with Hau

Nebby is hiding on the meadow's far side. Find it and bring it back to Lillie. She'll thank you and restore your Pokémon before you head back out to Route 3, where an excited Hau awaits. Hau has just completed Ilima's trial, and he's feeling like he could take on the world. There's no time to prepare, as he's ready to battle right away!

Hau's Pokémon

Hau has certainly been hard at work training his Pokémon. Their levels have increased significantly since your last battle, and his Pichu has evolved into Pikachu! Its Static Ability may leave your Pokémon with Paralysis, so be ready with Paralyze Heals or other medicines that can cure this hampering condition.

If you choose Rowlet	If you choose Litten	If you choose Popplio
Popplio ♂ Lv. 14 WATER Weak to: GRASS, ELECTRIC	 **Rowlet** ♂ Lv. 14 GRASS, FLYING Weak to: 4× ICE, FIRE, POISON, FLYING, ROCK	 **Litten** ♂ Lv. 14 FIRE Weak to: WATER, GROUND, ROCK
Pikachu ♂ Lv. 13 ELECTRIC Weak to: GROUND	**Pikachu** ♂ Lv. 13 ELECTRIC Weak to: GROUND	**Pikachu** ♂ Lv. 13 ELECTRIC Weak to: GROUND

Tip

Oricorio is one of the many colorful Pokémon found in the Alola region. It changes its appearance—and even its type—based on the nectar of the flowers upon which it feeds. Keep your eyes peeled for more Oricorio, as different Oricorio will appear around different colored flowers. And pick up any Yellow Nectar you find in Melemele Meadow. You can find Yellow Nectar wherever you spot something sparkling among the flowers at night.

Route 3 Revisited

p. 73

1 Finish searching Route 3 on your way to Iki Town

Professor Kukui appears after you wrap up your battle with Hau. He's happy to see that you've found Lillie and informs you that your next test will be to battle none other than Kahuna Hala himself, in what is known as the grand trial. Explore the rest of Route 3 on your way to Iki Town, where Hala awaits. Catch more wild Pokémon in the tall grass and battle as many Trainers as you can manage—you'll want every advantage before taking on Hala, who has a fondness for Fighting-type Pokémon.

S16: Take on a tough Trainer

Ready for a real challenge? Take on this Ace Trainer, who will only deem you worthy of battle after you've beaten every other Trainer on Route 3. If you get defeated, you can come back and try again as many times as you need to.

Reward: Red Card

S17: Show Rockruff and get a reward

The Sightseer hanging out just past the bridge on Route 3 asks you to catch him a Rockruff on Ten Carat Hill. Some prize money will be your reward, and we'll remind you later to catch one when you get there.

Reward: ₽3,000

S18: Receive a Soothe Bell from a Pokémon Breeder

The friendly Breeder on the east end of Route 3 hands you a Soothe Bell just for talking to him. Give this item to a Pokémon to hold, and the Pokémon will become friendlier (p. 130) toward you.

Reward: Soothe Bell

Tip

Remember that Sightseer back in Route 2's Pokémon Center? Catch a Cutiefly in the tall grass of Route 3, then show it to her for your cash reward!

Iki Town Revisited

p. 23

1 Return to Iki Town and take on Kahuna Hala

When you're ready to tackle your grand trial, follow Rotom's guidance to find your way back to Iki Town. Kahuna Hala and his Fighting-type Pokémon await you there, ready to give you everything they've got. Make sure you're ready for battle before approaching Hala and accepting his challenge.

Grand Trial: Island Kahuna Hala

Put your best Flying- or Ghost-type Pokémon at the head of your party before challenging Kahuna Hala. Spearow, Wingull, Zubat, and Drifloon are all excellent options at this point in your adventure. These Flying-type Pokémon will suffer less damage from Fighting-type moves, and the Flying-type moves that they can unleash will make short work of Hala's team—especially if you give your Pokémon a Sharp Beak, which boosts the power of Flying-type moves, to hold. (One can be found along Route 3 [p. 73].) Ghost-type Pokémon are also completely immune to Fighting-type moves. While Ghost-type moves are effective against Hala's Pokémon, they won't land with quite the same oomph as Flying-type moves.

Also, beware of Hala's Crabrawler, which is holding a Z-Crystal. The big kahuna will unleash his Pokémon's devastating Z-Move against you if given the chance. Crabrawler is Hala's best bet for beating you, but even it won't last long against Flying-type moves like Gust, Peck, Wing Attack, and Air Cutter. Unleash as many Flying-type moves as your Pokémon can muster, and you'll soar off with the victory!

Kahuna Hala's Pokémon

Hala's team can really crank out the damage, but they all share the same weaknesses, making them easy to counter. Fill your team with Flying types, and use X Defenses if needed to raise their Defense stats. Beware of Hala's Crabrawler—it holds a Z-Crystal and will perform a punishing Z-Move if you give it a chance to!

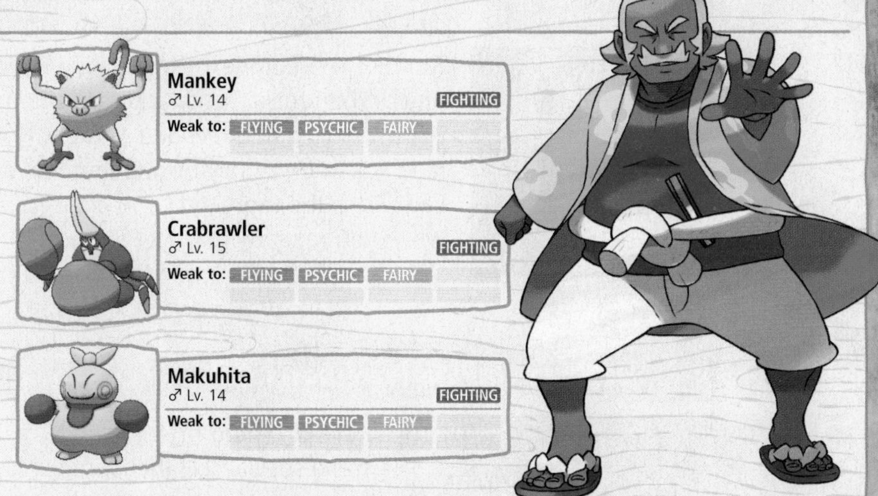

Receive a Z-Crystal, the Ride Pager, and TM54 False Swipe

Your victory comes as little surprise to Hala. There's clearly something special about you, and the big-hearted kahuna couldn't be more pleased at your success. In fact, he even hands you the same type of Z-Crystal as his Crabrawler had been holding, along with a Ride Pager. Now you can summon Ride Pokémon and explore even more of Alola! Professor Kukui shares in Hala's happiness for you, and hands you a valuable TM that will make catching wild Pokémon much easier during your travels. What a haul!

Reward: Fightinium Z, Ride Pager, TM54 False Swipe
Ride Pokémon: Tauros

False Swipe is a move that always leaves a Pokémon with 1 HP instead of knocking it out. It's perfect for plunging a wild Pokémon's HP into the red, making it easier to catch. However, this also increases the chances that a Pokémon will call for help during battle, so you'll have to work fast!

Ride Pokémon

You've received the Ride Pager and registered your first Ride Pokémon! In the Alola region, people rely on Ride Pokémon to help them navigate the islands. Ride Pokémon are specially trained Pokémon that can be called from all over the region to help you cross difficult terrain. You don't need to keep the Pokémon in your party in order to call them, and you don't need to have caught the Pokémon yourself—Ride Pokémon are separate from the Pokémon that you catch and train.

How to call a Ride Pokémon

Press Ⓨ to open the Ride Pokémon menu, then choose the Ride Pokémon you'd like to use. If a Ride Pokémon is grayed out, then you're standing in a location where they cannot be called, such as inside a building or in too narrow of a space.

Registering Ride Pokémon for quick calls

Tap the "+" icon next to your Ride Pokémon in the menu, then tap one of the four directional buttons that appear to register your Ride Pokémon to that directional button. Now you can easily call for that Ride Pokémon simply by pressing that same direction on the +Control Pad! Press the same direction again to dismiss the Ride Pokémon when you're ready to travel on foot.

Using each Ride Pokémon's skills

Ride Pokémon often have some special skill that you can use to reach new areas. For example, Tauros has Tauros Charge, which can smash certain large rocks in your path. Hold Ⓑ while riding on Tauros to perform Tauros Charge. It speeds up and smashes through rocks like they're nothing! We'll explain more about each Ride Pokémon's skills as you get them.

Tip

Riding intimidating Pokémon can decrease the likelihood that Pokémon will attack you in the wild. Riding Tauros, for example, reduces your chances of encountering wild Pokémon by about half.

Ride Pokémon (continued)

Places to visit and revisit with Tauros

Now that you have Tauros to help you, new places can be explored on Melemele Island—and new items and Pokémon can be found!

Route 1 (p. 31)

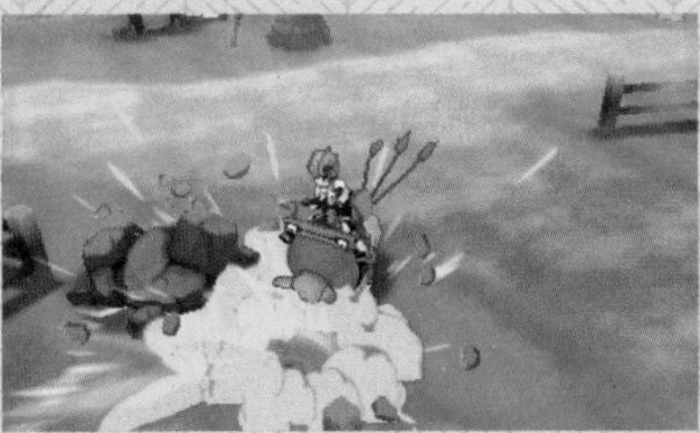

Smash through the rocks on the southwest side of Route 1 to reach the path along the side of the route.

Verdant Cavern (p. 67)

In the deepest part of Verdant Cavern, where you battled the Totem Pokémon, you can now smash some rocks to reach a TM.

Ten Carat Hill (p. 85)

Break the rocks to the west of the Pokémon Research Lab to enter and explore Ten Carat Hill.

Route 3 (p. 73)

At the east end of Route 3, you could see an item waiting for you beyond some large rocks. Charge through and claim your prize.

Route 2 (p. 60)

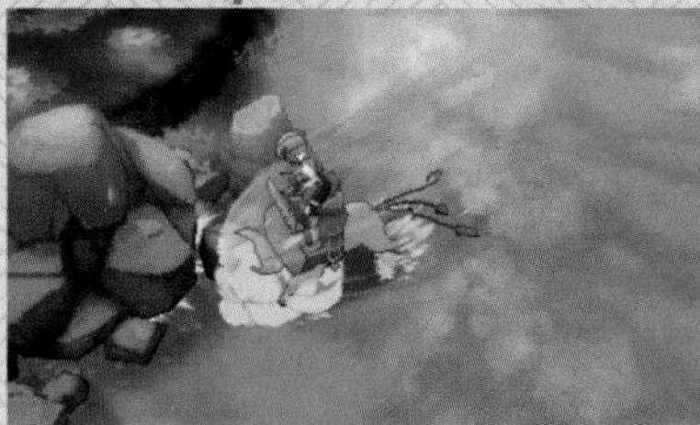

South of the motel on Route 2 is another large rock that Tauros will be able to smash for you.

Seaward Cave (p. 86)

Inside Seaward Cave, you can reach an item in a little nook that was blocked off by rocks before.

Tip

You may find items in the remnants of rocks that you smash with Tauros. If you're lucky, you may find some Stardust. If you're very, very lucky, you may find a Star Piece or even a rare Comet Shard. They can all be sold at shops for some more spending money.

Before You Leave Melemele Island

Kukui will be happy to see you to the next island, but there's still plenty to see and do around Melemele Island before you leave. Read on to explore all of the new events and areas that are open to you now that you've completed your first grand trial. When you're ready to continue with your island challenge, simply speak to Professor Kukui at Hau'oli City's Marina, and turn to page 88 to discover all that awaits you in Akala.

Tip

Feeling lucky, Trainer? Why not stop by the tourist bureau and take another crack at the Loto ID. You can play the Loto ID once each day.

S19: Head home and get some rest

It's been a while since you last saw your mom. Why not head home and see how she's doing? While you're at it, take a moment to catch some rest on your bed. You might be awakened by a surprise visitor!

Reward: Awakening

1 Pop by the mall

Our wide variety of goods and services will astound you!

Now that you've finished your grand trial, you'll find that Hau'oli City's mall is open for business. It's the big building near the Pokémon Center. Inside you'll find a plethora of posh shops, including the exclusive Gracidea apparel shop, where you'll receive a special gift just for chatting with the staff. The mall also features an antique shop, along with some Move Tutors who can teach useful moves to your Pokémon, provided they fit the criteria. Shop 'til you drop, Trainer!

Hau'oli Shopping Mall

Antiquities of the Ages

One of the mall's more mystifying shops, the antique shop sells very rare and expensive items that most Pokémon can't use. In fact, these specialty items can only be used by Pokémon that are not found in the Alola region! Unless you've visited another region before or do a lot of trading (p. 267), you probably won't have much need for the antique shop's goods.

Adamant Orb	₽10,000	Used by the Legendary Pokémon Dialga.
Lustrous Orb	₽10,000	Used by the Legendary Pokémon Palkia.
Griseous Orb	₽10,000	Used by the Legendary Pokémon Giratina.
Red Orb	₽10,000	Used by the Legendary Pokémon Groudon.
Blue Orb	₽10,000	Used by the Legendary Pokémon Kyogre.
Sky Plate / Zap Plate / Stone Plate / Iron Plate / Fist Plate / Dread Plate / Splash Plate / Pixie Plate	₽10,000 each	These plates aren't offered until you've completed three grand trials. They're primarily for the Mythical Pokémon Arceus, but other Pokémon can power up a certain type of move by holding one of them, too.

Hau'oli Shopping Mall (continued)

S20: Get a Gracidea flower for Shaymin

Talk to the clerk farthest inside at the check-out counter in the Gracidea apparel shop to get a Gracidea flower, which the Mythical Pokémon Shaymin can use to change Formes. Shaymin can't be found in Alola, but hold onto this flower just in case.

Reward: Gracidea

S21: Catch a show at the mall and then help clean up

Head to the northwest corner of the mall during the day to catch a special show. Stop by the same spot during the night to help clean up after it. Both visits sport their own rewards!

Reward: Great Ball ×5 ☀, TM48 Round ☽

Move Tutors

Yes
No
Is it all right to teach them to your Pokémon, too?

Located next to the antique shop, the mall's Move Tutors can teach some very powerful moves to some very special Pokémon.

Ultimate Moves: These can be taught to the final Evolutions of certain Grass-, Fire-, and Water-type Pokémon. See the sign in front of the shop for a complete list of Pokémon that can learn Frenzy Plant, Blast Burn, and Hydro Cannon. Please note that the Pokémon has to be friendly toward you (p. 130) to learn the move.

Battle-Combo Moves: These can be taught to any of the first partner Pokémon (and their Evolutions) that you receive in any region of the Pokémon world, as long as they're friendly toward you. They have double the power and other special effects when used together.

Battle-Combo Move Pairings	
Fire Pledge + Grass Pledge	Double power, plus a sea of fire surrounds the opponent's side for four turns, damaging all non-Fire-type Pokémon within it each turn.
Water Pledge + Fire Pledge	Double power, plus creates a rainbow over your side that increases the chances of a move's secondary effects being triggered for four turns.
Grass Pledge + Water Pledge	Double power, plus creates a swamp around the opponent's side for four turns, halving the Speed of all Pokémon on that side.

Battle Buffet

This is our super popular Take Down steak! First come, first served!

The mall also features a busy restaurant known as the Battle Buffet. This buffet-style bistro serves up various dishes—some more popular than others. Pay close attention to the dishes that the food is served on and how the chefs describe them. From that you'll be able to tell which ones will go quickly. The most delicious dishes aren't sitting out all the time, so try talking to other customers to see if they know when the good stuff is going to be served.

Like any other buffet, it's first come, first served—and other Trainers will challenge you to a Pokémon battle if you try to take a dish that they desire! If you're going after one of the more popular menu items, chances are you'll have to battle a strong Trainer before you can get a taste.

Unlike any other buffet, you can't stay at the battle buffet all day—you only have 10 turns to grab as much as you can before you sit down to eat. After you've finished your meal, the hostess will have a look at you to see how satisfied you are. Depending on how full you look, she'll give you one of four rewards: a Honey, a Big Mushroom, an HP Up, or a Max Revive. Keep in mind that it's not just how much you eat, but how delicious the dishes were. Whether you battle it out against fierce opponents to get the tastiest food possible, or fill up on a heaping helping of leftovers, is entirely up to you!

Battle Buffet Menu

- Whirlpool sushi
- Vanillite parfait
- Tamato pasta
- Eggant in chili sauce
- Hoenn ramen
- Rindo salad
- Chansey omelette
- Miltank cheese pizza
- Take Down steak

Tip

If you become a regular customer here, you get to meet a legend of the Battle Buffet after you've cleared the game!

S22: Challenge Ilima to another battle

Visit Ilima, and he'll ask if you wouldn't mind challenging him again in another battle. Defeat Ilima, and he'll reward your support with a rare Everstone.

Reward: Everstone

Tip

If this is your first time visiting Ilima's house, talk to his mom in the kitchen to score a tasty Lumiose Galette (p. 57).

GETTING STARTED

BATTLE & STRATEGY

POKÉMON COLLECTING

FUN & COMMUNICATION

ADVENTURE DATA

Captain Ilima's Pokémon

Ilima has really been training his Yungoos—so much so that it has evolved into a Gumshoos! This familiar Pokémon holds a Z-Crystal, letting Ilima unleash a devastating Z-Move at the battle's onset. Be ready to heal or switch out your first Pokémon if it suffers too much damage from this attack, and fill your team with Fighting types to finish Ilima in a blink!

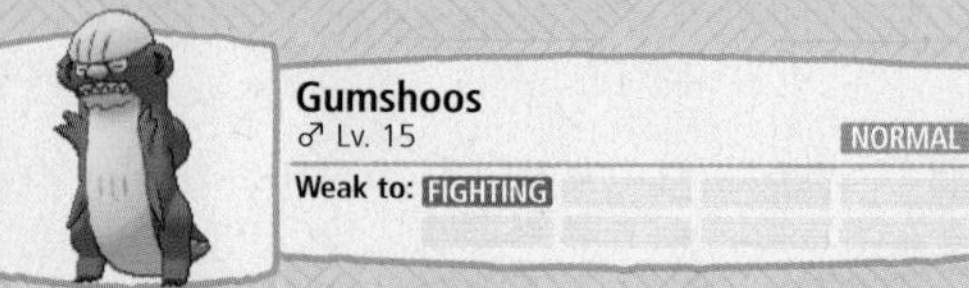

Gumshoos
♂ Lv. 15
NORMAL
Weak to: FIGHTING

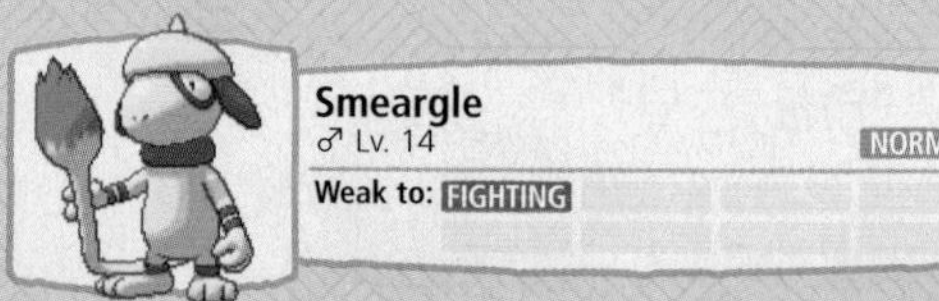

Smeargle
♂ Lv. 14
NORMAL
Weak to: FIGHTING

Tip

Give your Pokémon an Everstone to hold and it won't evolve, even when it meets all the conditions of Evolution. Pokémon that have not evolved can learn moves a bit quicker than they do when evolved, but their stats are generally lower. An Everstone can also be used when trying to find the perfect Pokémon Egg. Turn to page 288 for complete details.

S23: Visit city hall to pick up a special delivery

Stop by the city hall, and you'll arrive just in time for their regular Berry delivery. You'll also get a special treat from Delibird!

Reward: Shell Bell

Tip

Mosey into the malasada shop and talk to the clerk on the right to order up another Big Malasada to go. You can buy one of these valuable munchies each day, and their ability to heal any and all status conditions for a single Pokémon make them well worth the visit.

Tip

Now that you've completed the grand trial, you'll find that the paint has finally dried on those wet gates around Hau'oli City. Do a little exploring to discover more items beyond these gates, like the Tiny Mushroom found near the city hall and the Revive that lies across the street from the Pokémon Center.

S24: Visit Hau'oli Cemetery at night to get TM56 Fling

Visit Hau'oli Cemetery at night, and you'll meet a woman visiting her husband's grave. Listen to her story, and she'll give you TM56 Fling.

Reward: TM56 Fling

Ten Carat Hill

Ride Pokémon Needed   

Located just west of the Pokémon Research Lab, Ten Carat Hill is a sizable cavern that can only be entered by riding a Tauros through the rocks near its entrance. You couldn't have explored this place before, but you're free to do so now before shoving off to Akala Island.

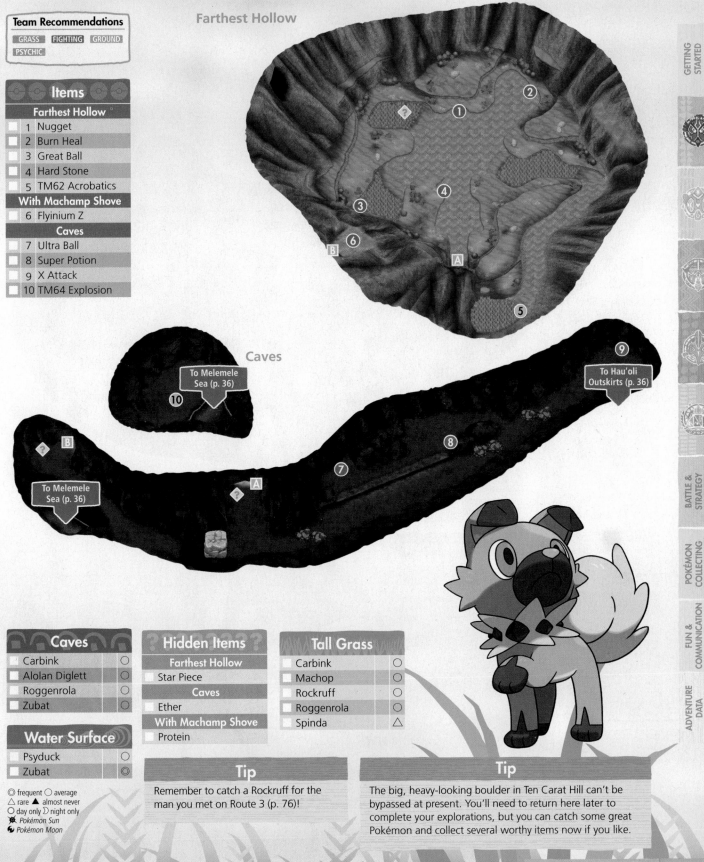

Items	
Farthest Hollow	
1	Nugget
2	Burn Heal
3	Great Ball
4	Hard Stone
5	TM62 Acrobatics
With Machamp Shove	
6	Flyinium Z
Caves	
7	Ultra Ball
8	Super Potion
9	X Attack
10	TM64 Explosion

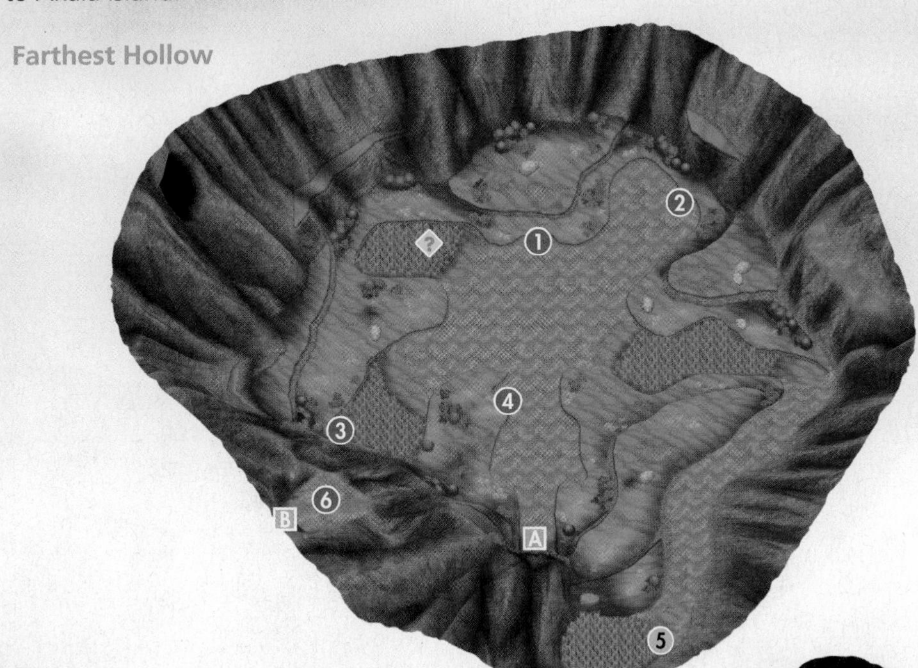

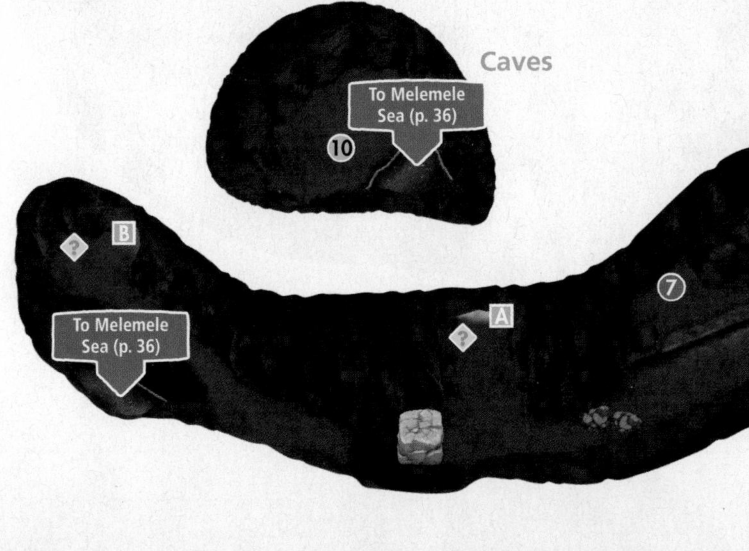

Caves	
Carbink	○
Alolan Diglett	○
Roggenrola	○
Zubat	○

Water Surface	
Psyduck	○
Zubat	◎

◎ frequent ○ average
△ rare ▲ almost never
○ day only ☽ night only
Pokémon Sun
Pokémon Moon

Hidden Items
Farthest Hollow
Star Piece
Caves
Ether
With Machamp Shove
Protein

Tall Grass	
Carbink	○
Machop	○
Rockruff	○
Roggenrola	○
Spinda	△

Tip

Remember to catch a Rockruff for the man you met on Route 3 (p. 76)!

Tip

The big, heavy-looking boulder in Ten Carat Hill can't be bypassed at present. You'll need to return here later to complete your explorations, but you can catch some great Pokémon and collect several worthy items now if you like.

Seaward Cave

Ride Pokémon Needed  

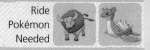

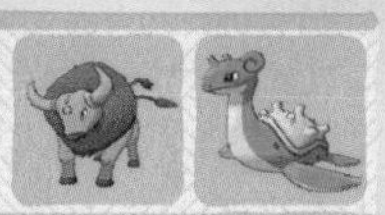

Wade through Melemele Meadow's dense flower beds and crawl through the small hole in its west wall to reach Seaward Cave—a watery cavern filled with wild Pokémon and worthwhile items. Navigate the cave to find another exit that leads out to the invigorating breezes of Kala'e Bay.

Team Recommendations

GRASS ELECTRIC FIGHTING PSYCHIC

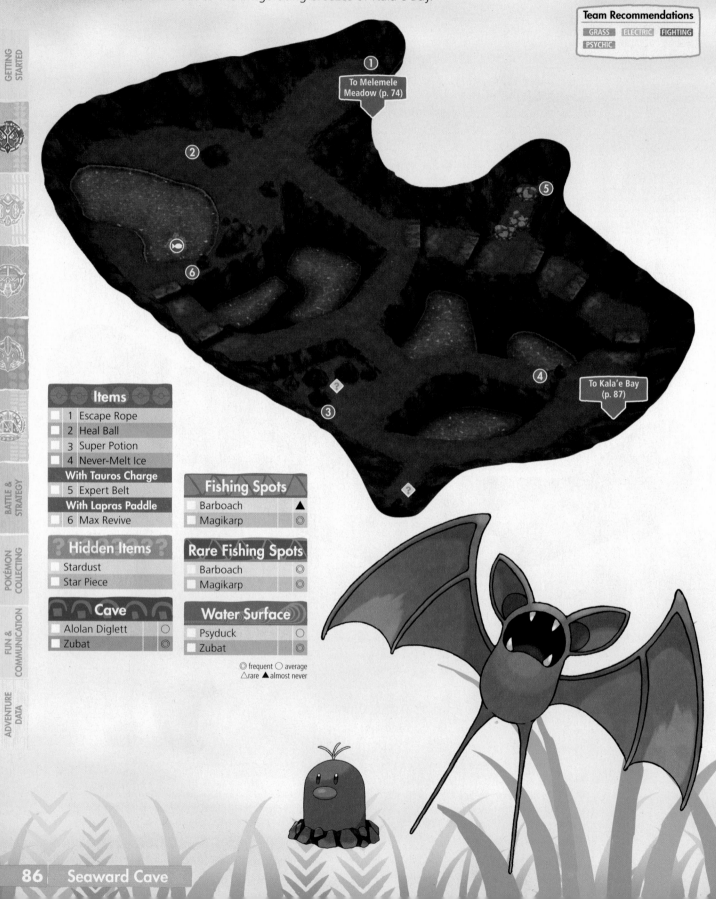

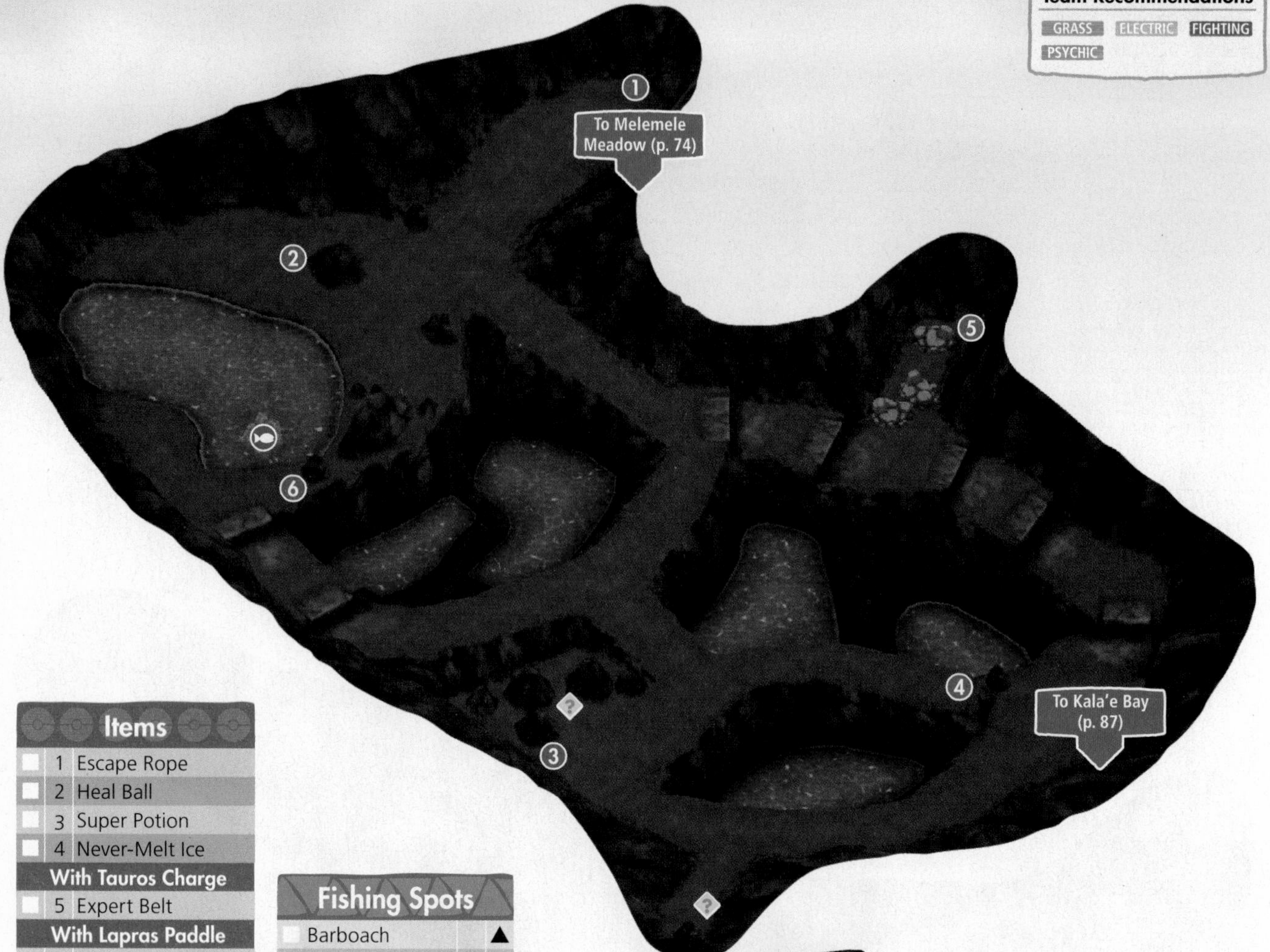

To Melemele Meadow (p. 74)

To Kala'e Bay (p. 87)

Items	
1	Escape Rope
2	Heal Ball
3	Super Potion
4	Never-Melt Ice
With Tauros Charge	
5	Expert Belt
With Lapras Paddle	
6	Max Revive

Hidden Items
Stardust
Star Piece

Cave	
Alolan Diglett	○
Zubat	◎

Fishing Spots	
Barboach	▲
Magikarp	◎

Rare Fishing Spots	
Barboach	◎
Magikarp	◎

Water Surface	
Psyduck	○
Zubat	◎

◎ frequent ○ average △ rare ▲ almost never

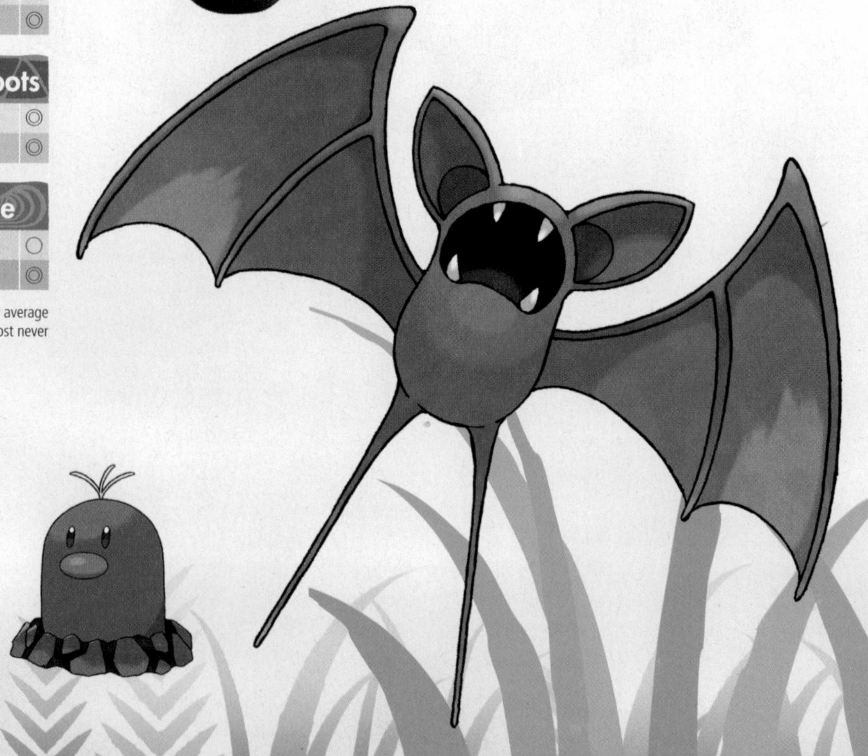

Kala'e Bay

Ride Pokémon Needed 

Pass through the Seaward Cave's south exit to reach the briny beauty of Kala'e Bay. Like Ten Carat Hill, you can't fully explore this place at present—you need a means of traveling across the water here. Still, the bay is worth a look if you've come all this way, and you can nab a free Net Ball near the shore. We'll remind you to come back here when you've got Lapras registered to your Ride Pager.

Team Recommendations

GRASS ELECTRIC FIGHTING FAIRY

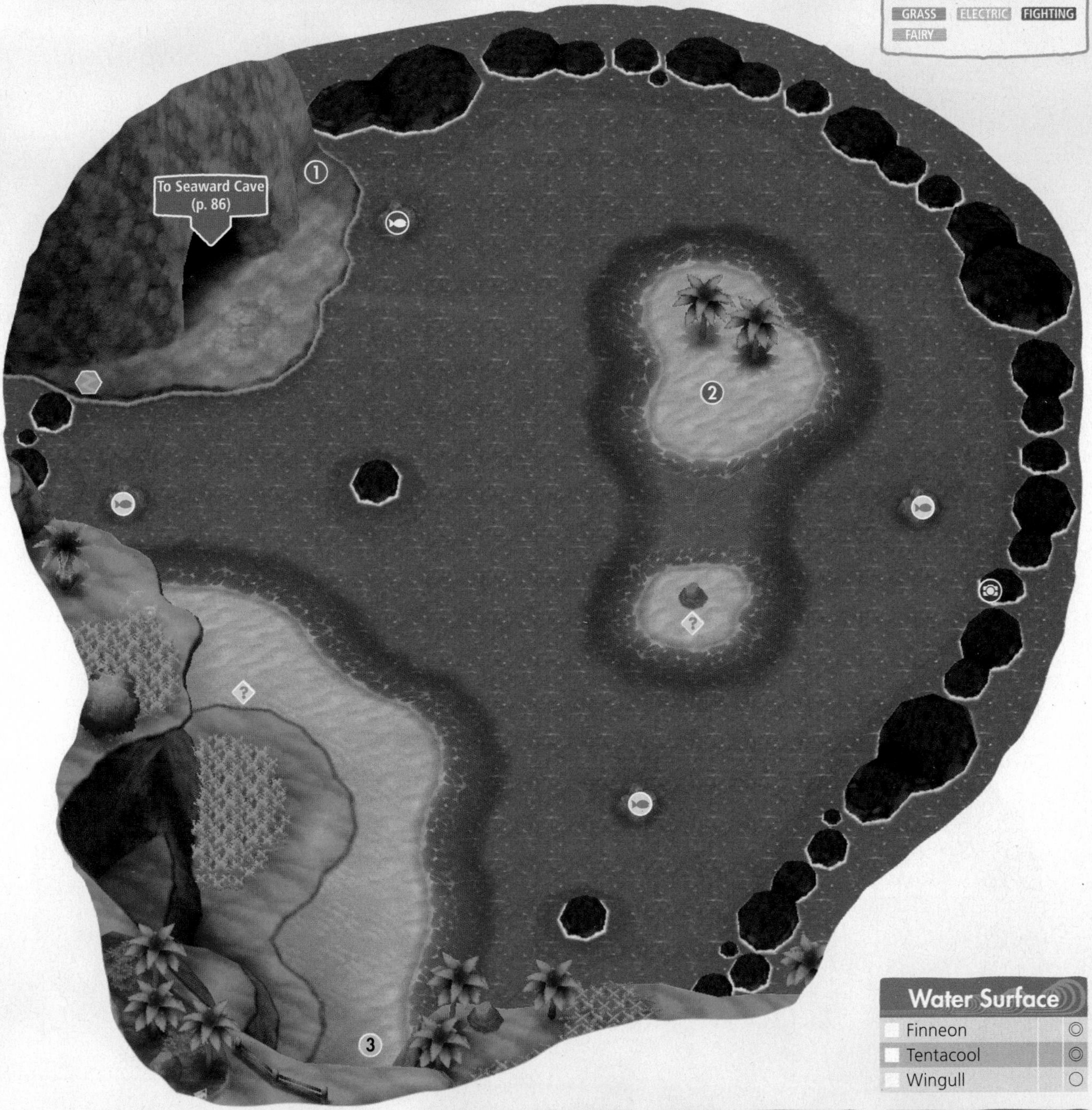

To Seaward Cave (p. 86)

1

2

3

Water Surface	
Finneon	◎
Tentacool	◎
Wingull	○

Items
1 Net Ball
With Lapras Paddle
2 Dive Ball
3 TM05 Roar

Tall Grass		
Bagon		△
Alolan Rattata	☽	○
Slowpoke		○
Wingull		◎
Yungoos	○	○

◎ frequent ○ average
△ rare ▲ almost never
○ day only ☽ night only
Pokémon Sun
Pokémon Moon

Fishing Spots	
Magikarp	◎
Shellder	▲
Wishiwashi	○

Hidden Items
With Lapras Paddle
Big Pearl
Pearl

Rare Fishing Spots	
Magikarp	◎
Shellder	○
Wishiwashi	○

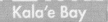

Akala Island

Having completed your grand trial at Melemele Island, the next stop in your island challenge is Akala Island: an island that hosts everything from live volcanoes to limpid pools and deep jungles. Another kahuna is in charge here, and not one, but *three* captains run trials around Akala—each one designed to test and stretch your skills a bit further than the last.

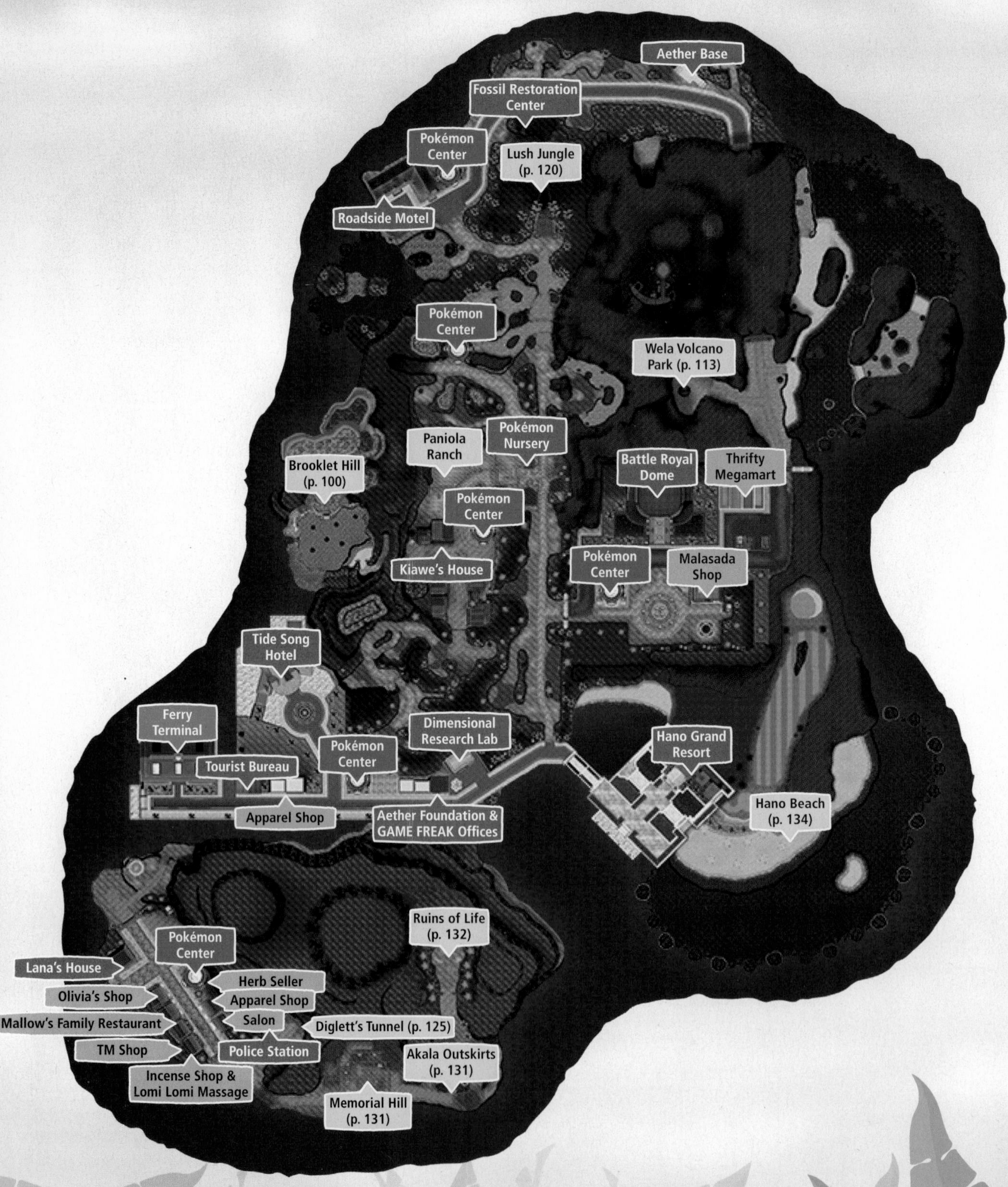

Heahea City

Akala Island's port city, Heahea, is a warm and inviting place that welcomes visitors with open arms. It hosts two of the most luxurious hotels in Alola: the Tide Song Hotel and the Hano Grand Resort. Both offer lavish accommodations to help travelers relax after their long journeys.

Items	
After Completing 2 Trials	
1	Big Mushroom

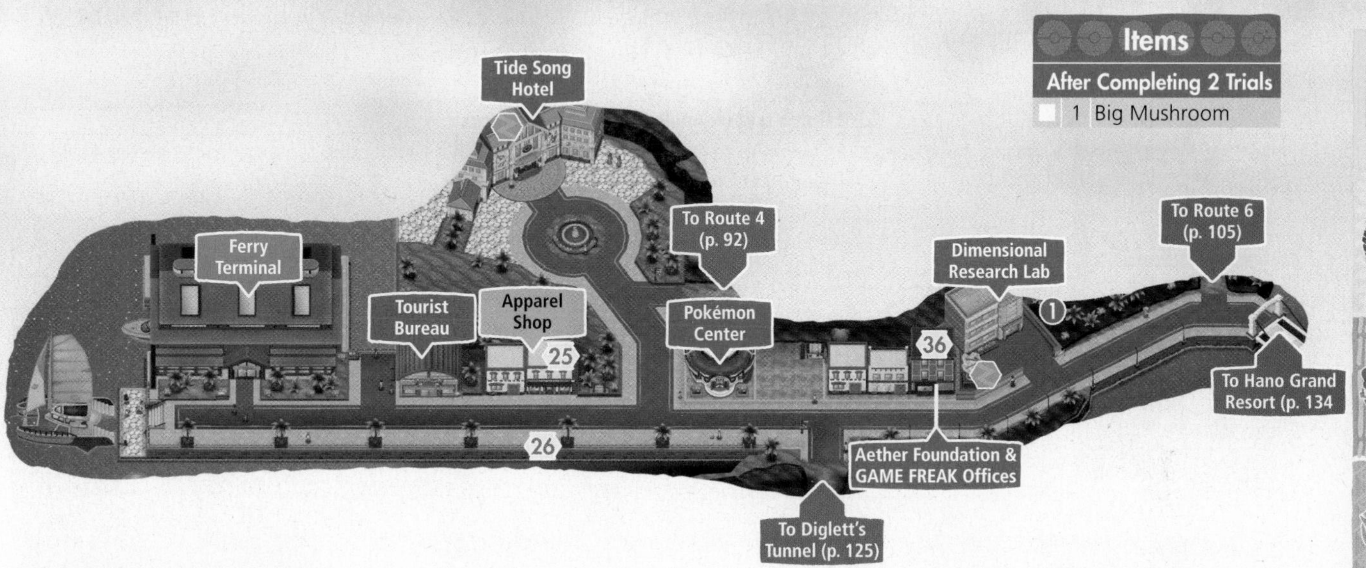

Poké Mart	
Normal Wares	
Antidote	₽200
Awakening	₽100
Burn Heal	₽300
Escape Rope	₽1,000
Great Ball	₽600
Ice Heal	₽100
Paralyze Heal	₽300
Poké Ball	₽200
Potion	₽200
Repel	₽400
Super Potion	₽700

Poké Mart	
After Completing 2 Trials	
Honey	₽300
Revive	₽2,000
After Completing 3 Trials	
Adrenaline Orb	₽300
Super Repel	₽700
After Completing 4 Trials	
Hyper Potion	₽1,500
Ultra Ball	₽800

Poké Mart	
Special Wares	
TM16 Light Screen	₽10,000
TM17 Protect	₽10,000
TM20 Safeguard	₽10,000
TM33 Reflect	₽10,000
TM70 Aurora Veil	₽30,000

Vending Machine	
Ferry Terminal	
Fresh Water	₽200

Olivia and Mallow

The kahuna of Akala Island, Olivia, may act tough but she is a kind and seasoned Trainer, and she also runs a stone shop in one of Akala's cities. She'll be waiting for you to challenge her, but your grand trial won't start for quite a while yet, as Akala Island has a total of *three* captains for you to impress—and *three* trials for you to complete. Finish all three trials to earn your right to challenge Olivia in Akala Island's grand trial!

Mallow is one of Akala Island's captains, and she's almost as passionate about Pokémon as she is about cooking and her family's restaurant. She's the first of Akala's captains that you meet, but she won't be the first captain you'll face in a trial—in fact, she'll be the last!

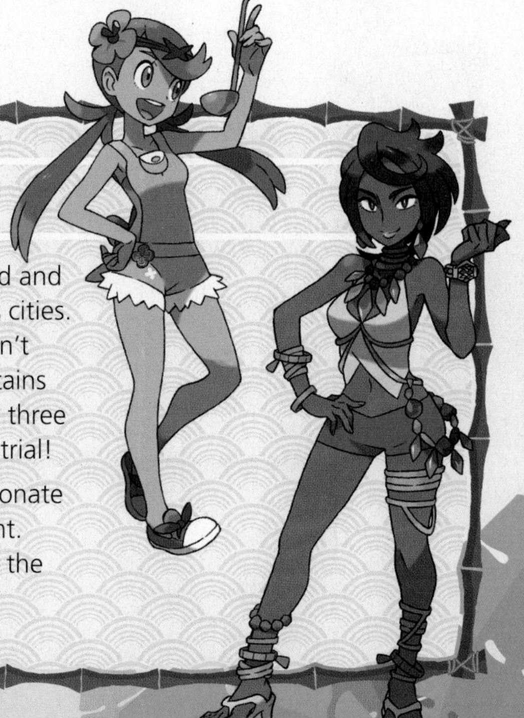

1 Meet Olivia and Mallow, then explore Heahea City

After receiving a warm welcome from Kahuna Olivia and Captain Mallow, you're free to explore Akala's port city of Heahea. Check out the ferry terminal first, where you can buy Fresh Water from a vending machine or catch a boat back to Melemele Island anytime. Meet the Name Rater in the tourist bureau next. He's the one man in Alola who can help you change your Pokémon's nicknames after they've been caught. But remember, you can't change the names of any Pokémon you receive in trades!

S25: Catch a Pyukumuku and stash some cash

A man in the apparel shop wants to send you on a little trial. Catch a Pyukumuku at Hano Beach here on Akala Island, then report back to the man for a cash reward!

Reward: ₽10,000

S26: Cross the street for a Rare Candy

Chat with the woman across the street from the apparel shop to receive a Rare Candy. Feed this sweet treat to a Pokémon to instantly raise its level by one!

Reward: Rare Candy

2 Battle Sina or Dexio and receive the Zygarde Cube

Reward: Zygarde Cube

Pop into the nearby Pokémon Center if you like, then carry on north to reach the Tide Song Hotel, where Lillie was headed when you last spoke to her. You'll run into a couple of visitors from the Kalos region along the way. If you've played *Pokémon X* or *Pokémon Y*, you may remember Sina and Dexio. They're eager to meet you—and even more eager to test your skill in battle! Battle Dexio in *Pokémon Sun* or Sina in *Pokémon Moon* to receive the Zygarde Cube after the clash. This prize will open your eyes to a new mission! Feel free to check out the nearby hotel and say hi to Lillie before continuing onto Route 4 and to Paniola Town beyond it.

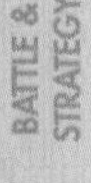

Dexio's Pokémon

Avoid using Fighting-type Pokémon in this battle, as Dexio will punish them with powerful Psychic-type moves. Favor Bug, Ghost, and Dark types instead, exploiting the shared weaknesses of Dexio's duo.

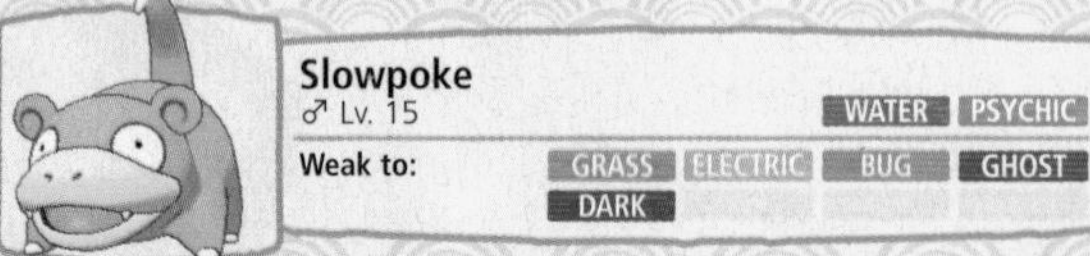

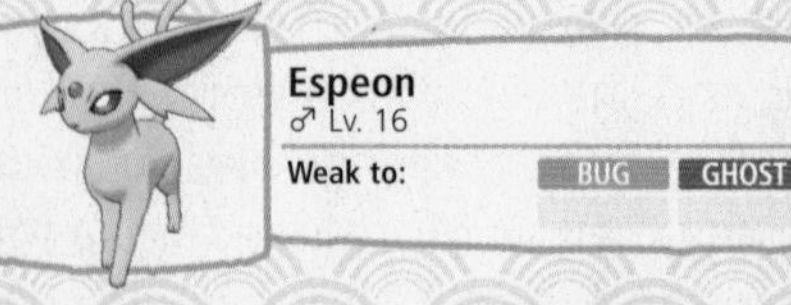

Sina's Pokémon

The Fighting-type Pokémon you trained up for Ilima's challenge may come in handy against Sina. Otherwise Fire-, Rock-, and Steel-type moves will all be super effective against both her Pokémon.

			Weak to
Delibird	♀ Lv. 15	ICE, FLYING	4× ROCK, FIRE, ELECTRIC, STEEL
Glaceon	♀ Lv. 16	ICE	FIRE, FIGHTING, ROCK, STEEL

Zygarde

Sina and Dexio are visitors from the Kalos region, which you may remember well if you played *Pokémon X* or *Pokémon Y*. A Pokémon Professor from that region, Professor Sycamore, sent them here to Alola to find out why the Legendary Pokémon Zygarde seems to have left Kalos for Alola. Lend Sina and Dexio a hand by searching for Zygarde Cores and Cells—parts that make up Zygarde's whole being—around the Alola region. Now that you've received the Zygarde Cube, you'll start spotting these sparkling pieces all over Alola—including back on Melemele Island. (Turn to page 225 for a complete listing of every Zygarde Core and Cell.)

Route 4

Connecting Heahea City to the south with Paniola Town to the north, this winding, woodsy trail features plenty of tall grass and several new species of wild Pokémon. The Trainers here seek to test themselves against passersby as they take in nature's beauty.

Team Recommendations

GRASS FIGHTING FLYING

Items	
1	Adrenaline Orb
2	Revive
3	Energy Root
4	Great Ball

Hidden Items
Big Mushroom
Dire Hit
Tiny Mushroom

Tall Grass		
Eevee		▲
Grubbin		△
Igglybuff	☼	△
Lillipup		○
Mudbray		○
Pikipek	☼	△
Pikipek	☽	○
Alolan Rattata	☽	△

◎ frequent ○ average △ rare
▲ almost never ☼ day only ☽ night only
Pokémon Sun *Pokémon Moon*

Tip

Paniola Town isn't far, but there's no need to rush. Take your time exploring Route 4 as you make your way north. Hunt for items, battle Trainers, catch wild Pokémon, and explore every nook and cranny.

Paniola Town

Surrounded by ranch land and grazing pastures, this quaint little town has the feeling of an old-timey settlement. Its wooden buildings blend right in with the surrounding forest.

Team Recommendations

GRASS ELECTRIC

Poké Mart

Item	Price
Normal Wares	
Antidote	₽200
Awakening	₽100
Burn Heal	₽300
Escape Rope	₽1,000
Great Ball	₽600
Ice Heal	₽100
Paralyze Heal	₽300
Poké Ball	₽200
Potion	₽200
Repel	₽400
Super Potion	₽700
After Completing 2 Trials	
Honey	₽300
Revive	₽2,000
After Completing 3 Trials	
Adrenaline Orb	₽300
Super Repel	₽700
After Completing 4 Trials	
Hyper Potion	₽1,500
Ultra Ball	₽800
Special Wares	
Net Ball	₽1,000
Repeat Ball	₽1,000
Timer Ball	₽1,000

Items

After Completing 2 Trials	
1	TM88 Sleep Talk

Hidden Items

- Fresh Water
- Revive

After Completing 2 Trials

- Super Repel

Fishing Spots

Pokémon	Rarity
Barboach	▲
Magikarp	◎

Rare Fishing Spots

Pokémon	Rarity
Barboach	◎
Magikarp	◎

◎ frequent ○ average △ rare
▲ almost never ○ day only ☽ night only
Pokémon Sun *Pokémon Moon*

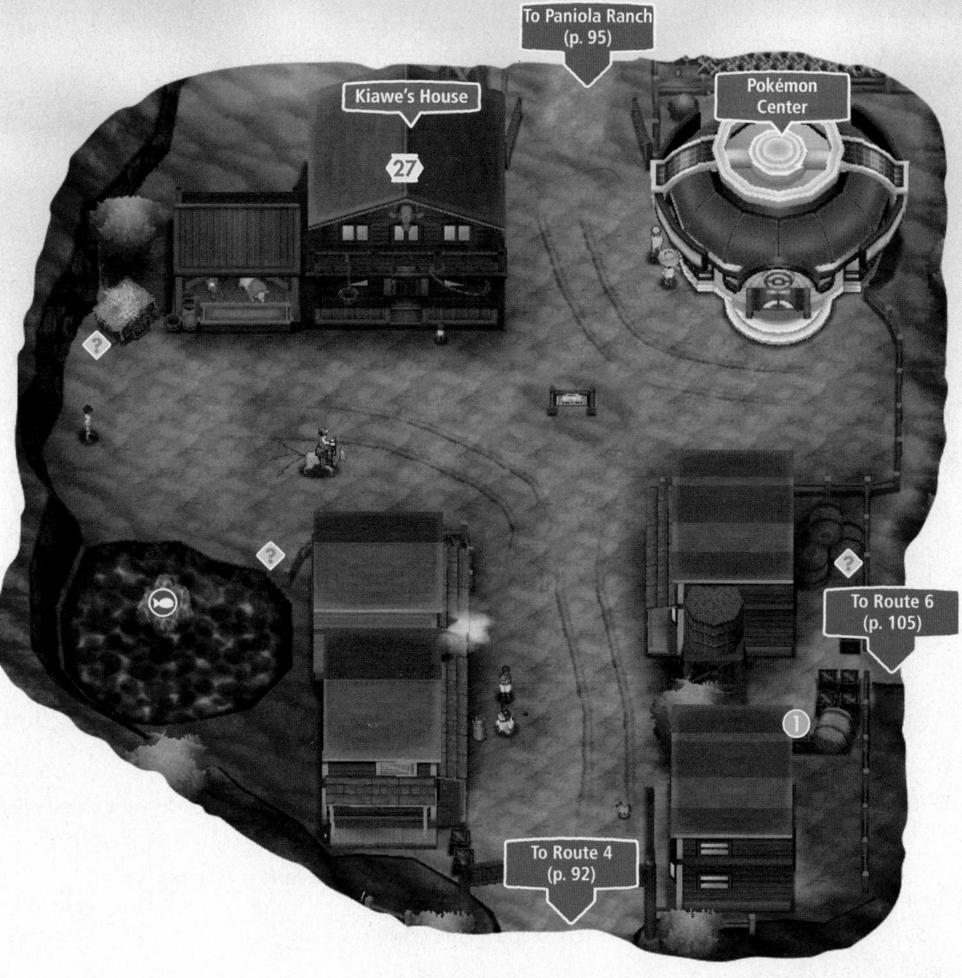

Tip

Paniola Town's fishing spot is a source of wild Pokémon. You might be able to come back and visit it soon, so remember it!

Tip

Notice those items marked on the map behind the buildings off to the east side of town? You can't reach them from here, but we'll remind you to duck into this little space from Route 6 once you get the chance to.

1 Battle Hau before exploring the town

Your buddy Hau is hanging out here in Paniola Town and, after healing your Pokémon, he quickly whisks you into another battle. Show Hau how strong you've become, and he'll reward your display with a Dire Hit. Check out the town afterward, resting at the nearby Pokémon Center and preparing your team for the difficult trek ahead. It's still a long road to your next trial site.

Reward: Dire Hit

Hau's Pokémon

Hau's first partner Pokémon has evolved since your last battle, but its type has not changed, so it still retains all of its same weaknesses. Pile on the damage with your own first partner Pokémon and end the battle with all speed—before Hau unleashes his Z-Power with his new Z-Ring!

If you choose Rowlet	If you choose Litten	If you choose Popplio
Brionne ♂ Lv. 17 — WATER Weak to: GRASS, ELECTRIC	**Dartrix** ♂ Lv. 17 — GRASS, FLYING Weak to: 4x ICE, FIRE, POISON, FLYING, ROCK	**Torracat** ♂ Lv. 17 — FIRE Weak to: WATER, GROUND, ROCK
Pikachu ♂ Lv. 16 — ELECTRIC Weak to: GROUND	**Pikachu** ♂ Lv. 16 — ELECTRIC Weak to: GROUND	**Pikachu** ♂ Lv. 16 — ELECTRIC Weak to: GROUND

S27: Grab a Quick Ball from a Magmar

Visit Captain Kiawe's house, which stands just west of the Pokémon Center. Talk to all the family's Magmar, and one Magmar will hand you a Quick Ball.

Reward: Quick Ball

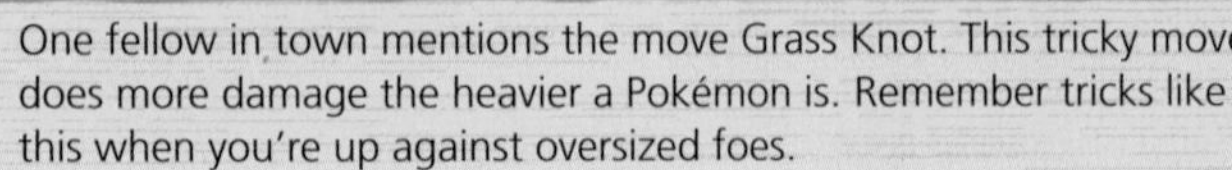

Tip

One fellow in town mentions the move Grass Knot. This tricky move does more damage the heavier a Pokémon is. Remember tricks like this when you're up against oversized foes.

Paniola Ranch / Moomoo Paddock

Stretching north of Paniola Town, this sprawling pasture offers plenty of room for Pokémon to graze. The Pokémon Nursery is located here: a place where pairs of Pokémon can play all day, and where you may possibly discover Pokémon Eggs.

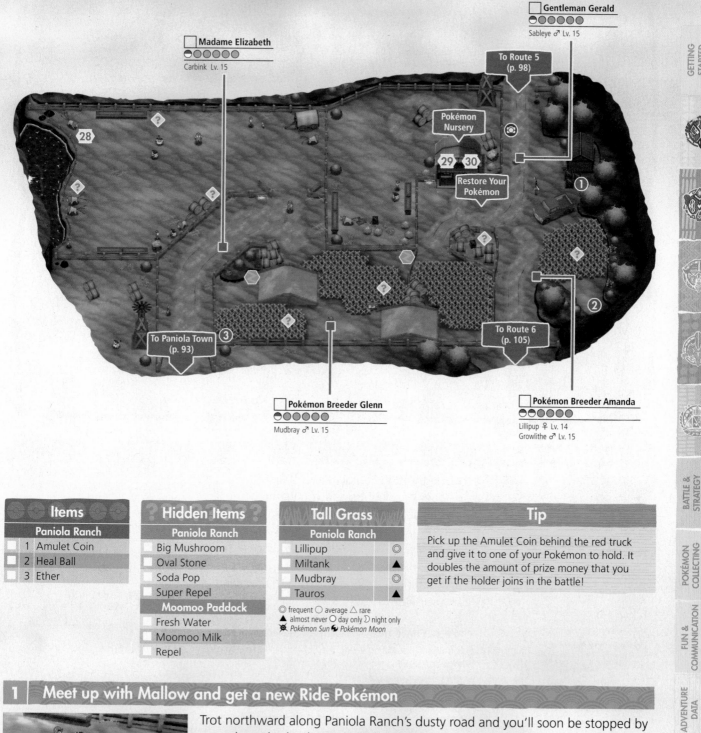

Gentleman Gerald
Sableye ♂ Lv. 15

Madame Elizabeth
Carbink Lv. 15

To Route 5 (p. 98)

Pokémon Nursery

28

29 30

Restore Your Pokémon

① ② ③

To Paniola Town (p. 93)

To Route 6 (p. 105)

Pokémon Breeder Glenn
Mudbray ♂ Lv. 15

Pokémon Breeder Amanda
Lillipup ♀ Lv. 14
Growlithe ♂ Lv. 15

GETTING STARTED

BATTLE & STRATEGY
POKÉMON COLLECTING
FUN & COMMUNICATION
ADVENTURE DATA

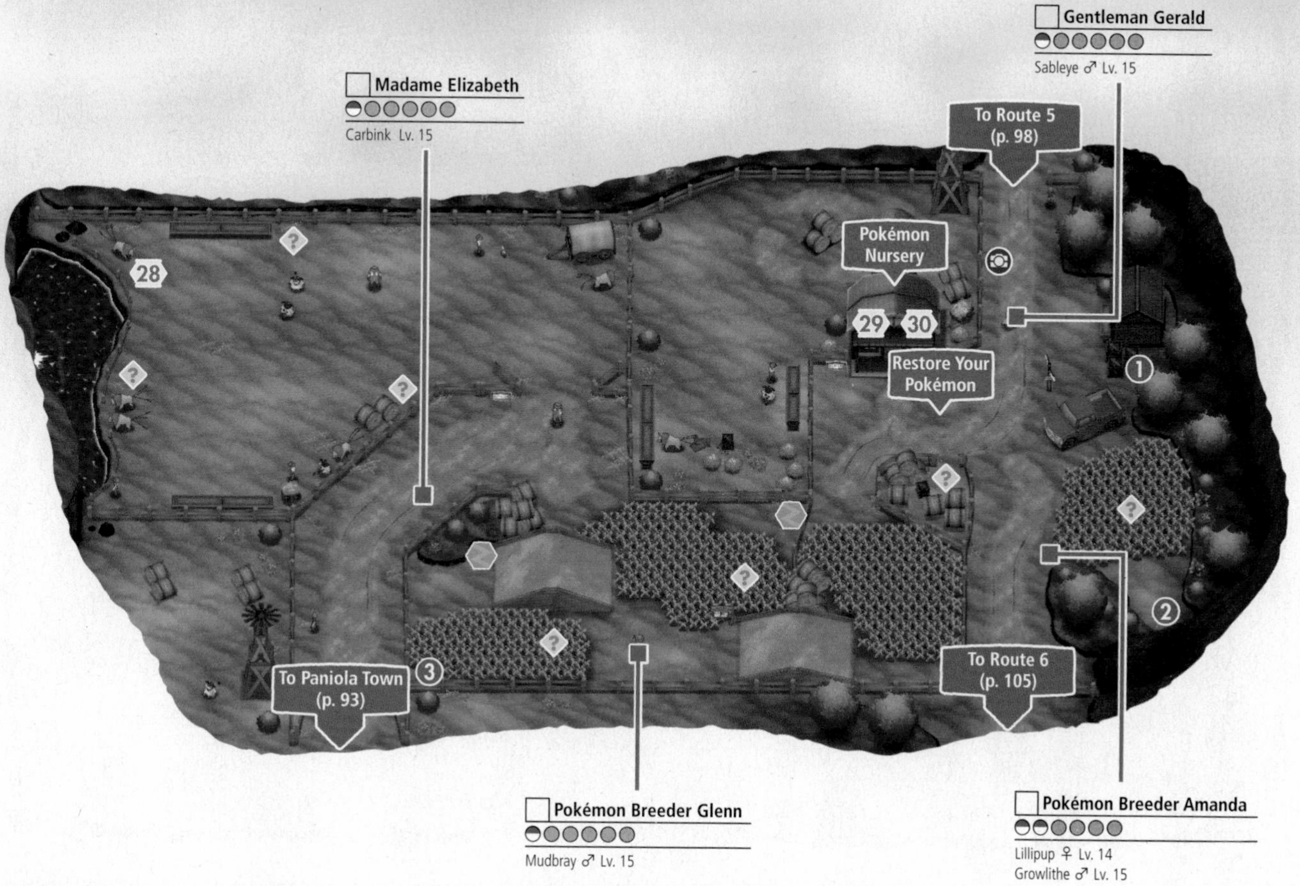

Items		
Paniola Ranch		
☐	1	Amulet Coin
☐	2	Heal Ball
☐	3	Ether

Hidden Items
Paniola Ranch
☐ Big Mushroom
☐ Oval Stone
☐ Soda Pop
☐ Super Repel
Moomoo Paddock
☐ Fresh Water
☐ Moomoo Milk
☐ Repel

Tall Grass	
Paniola Ranch	
☐ Lillipup	◎
☐ Miltank	▲
☐ Mudbray	◎
☐ Tauros	▲

◎ frequent ○ average △ rare
▲ almost never ○ day only ☽ night only
Pokémon Sun *Pokémon Moon*

Tip

Pick up the Amulet Coin behind the red truck and give it to one of your Pokémon to hold. It doubles the amount of prize money that you get if the holder joins in the battle!

1 Meet up with Mallow and get a new Ride Pokémon

Ride Pokémon: Stoutland

Trot northward along Paniola Ranch's dusty road and you'll soon be stopped by a rancher who leads you into the nearby Moomoo Paddock. Captain Mallow awaits you there, and she registers a new Ride Pokémon, Stoutland, for you in your Ride Pager. Now you can use Stoutland to sniff out hidden items! Search the ranch thoroughly as you make your way north.

S28: Battle a Tauros for a Scope Lens

Go west from the spot where you talked to Mallow and help some ranchers wrangle a rowdy Tauros. Talk to the Tauros to get things started, then beat it in battle for a reward!

Reward: Scope Lens

Stoutland Search

You got a new Ride Pokémon! Stoutland is as swift as the wind, and its strong sense of smell helps you seek out hidden items. Press Ⓨ and select Stoutland Search to start riding Stoutland—you'll be surprised at how quickly it scampers around. Hold Ⓑ while riding Stoutland and it will slow down and put its nose to the ground, sniffing for buried items in the direction in which you're moving.

As Stoutland steadily sniffs the ground, it detects any buried items within a cone-shaped area in front of it. A small blue exclamation mark appears above Stoutland's head if it gets a whiff of a hidden item, and you'll hear a plinking sound. Keep holding Ⓑ and, as you get closer to the item, Stoutland's small blue exclamation mark will turn into a big red exclamation mark and the Ride Pokémon will begin barking. Press Ⓐ at this point and you'll obtain the item that Stoutland has sniffed out. Try going back to Melemele Island and other locations, and see what Stoutland can discover!

Tip

While riding Stoutland through terrain where wild Pokémon encounters are possible (like caves or tall grass), you're only about half as likely to encounter wild Pokémon.

2 Restore your Pokémon on your way to Route 5

Wade through Paniola Ranch's first few patches of tall grass and you'll emerge near the Pokémon Nursery. Talk to the Miltank outside and it will restore your Pokémon anytime you like, free of charge. Then continue along the road, battling Trainers and sniffing out hidden items with Stoutland on your way to Route 5.

Tip

Every Pokémon has its own Hidden Power. Ask the Pokémon Breeder at the Pokémon Nursery to judge your Pokémon's hidden potential, then use that knowledge to unleash your Pokémon's Hidden Power and surprise your opponents with unexpected moves!

S29: Get TM10 Hidden Power from the Pokémon Nursery

Talk to a Pokémon Breeder standing inside the Pokémon Nursery to receive TM10 Hidden Power. This curious move's type changes depending on which Pokémon uses it.

Reward: TM10 Hidden Power

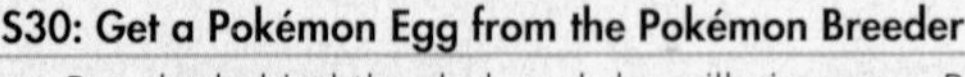

S30: Get a Pokémon Egg from the Pokémon Breeder

Talk to the Pokémon Breeder behind the desk and she will give you a Pokémon Egg. Carry the Egg around with you as part of your team, and it will eventually hatch into a Pokémon!

Reward: Pokémon Egg

Pokémon Eggs

You've received your first Pokémon Egg. Congratulations! Pokémon Eggs hatch into Pokémon, but only if they are well taken care of. To see how close an Egg is to hatching, open the X menu, select "Pokémon," then select the Egg and choose "Summary."

A mysterious Pokémon Egg that was
received from Nursery helpers
on 11/18/2016
"The Egg Watch"
What Pokémon will hatch from this Egg?
It doesn't seem close to hatching.

To help an Egg hatch, simply place it in your team and then walk around with it as you explore Alola. The longer and farther you travel while carrying the Egg as a team member, the closer it will get to hatching! Place it next to a Pokémon with the Flame Body or the Magma Armor Ability to hasten the hatching time.

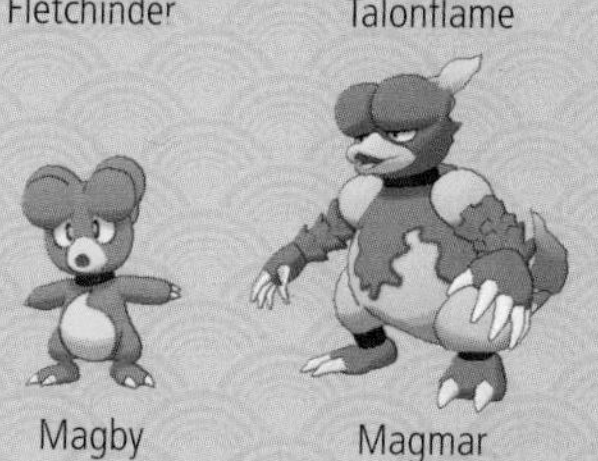

Fletchinder Talonflame

Fletchinder can be caught on Route 8 (p. 118). Both it and its Evolution, Talonflame, can have the Flame Body Ability.

Magby Magmar

Magby can be caught in Wela Volcano Park (p. 113). Magby and its Evolution, Magmar, can both have the Flame Body Ability.

Tip

Once you gain access to the Poké Pelago, you'll have another means of helping Eggs hatch more quickly. (Turn to page 312 to learn more.)

If you want to try finding an Egg of your own, here are some of the basic conditions you'll need to fulfill:

- Have at least three Pokémon either on your team or in your Boxes.
- Leave a male (♂) and a female (♀) Pokémon together at the Pokémon Nursery.
- Make sure both Pokémon are from the same Egg Group (p. 292).

After you've dropped off a pair of Pokémon, talk to the Pokémon Breeder in front of the Pokémon Nursery from time to time to see if any Eggs have been found. Running up and down the long path of Route 6 (p. 105) a few times might do the trick if nothing seems to be happening. (Route 6 becomes accessible after you complete Akala Island's first trial.)

Tip

Leave Pokémon at the Pokémon Nursery whose original Trainers hail from different countries, and you'll increase the chances of finding Eggs. You'll also increase the chances that Shiny Pokémon will hatch from any Eggs that you find! (Check page 288 for a full guide to finding Pokémon Eggs.)

Ditto

A special Pokémon, Ditto, can be left with any Pokémon at all, and help you find an Egg that hatches into that Pokémon's species. You can catch Ditto on Ula'ula Island's Mount Hokulani (p. 151).

Route 5

This winding trail lies north of Paniola Ranch, and connects to Brooklet Hill in the west and Route 8 up north. Its stepped ledges prevent travelers from fully exploring the area unless they enter from Route 8.

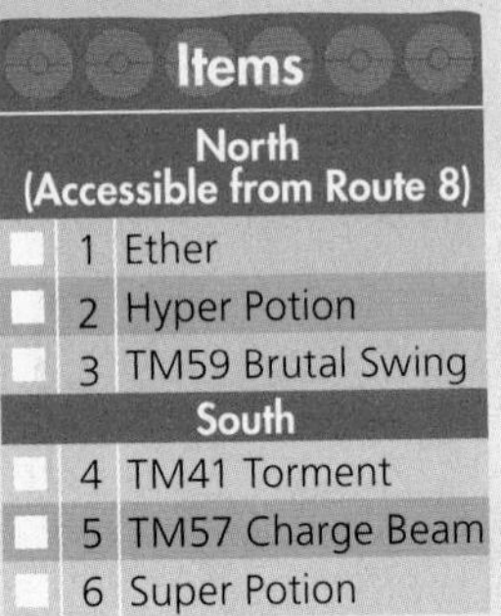

Items

North (Accessible from Route 8)		
☐	1	Ether
☐	2	Hyper Potion
☐	3	TM59 Brutal Swing
South		
☐	4	TM41 Torment
☐	5	TM57 Charge Beam
☐	6	Super Potion

Tip

The north end of Route 5 is only accessible from Route 8, so you'll have to come back later to collect the items and catch the Pokémon that appear here.

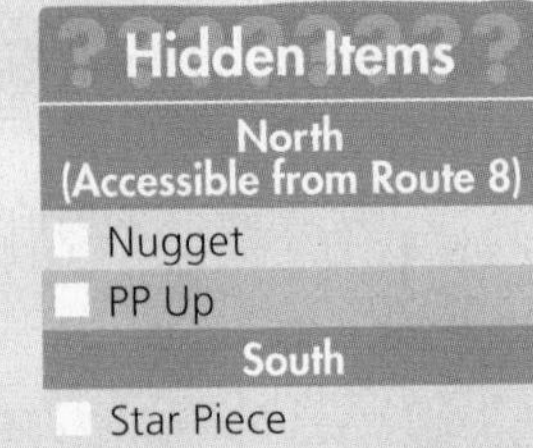

Hidden Items

	Item
North (Accessible from Route 8)	
☐	Nugget
☐	PP Up
South	
☐	Star Piece

Team Recommendations

ELECTRIC FIGHTING FLYING BUG

Dust Clouds

☐	Alolan Diglett	◎

☐ **Youngster Caleb**
Charjabug ♂ Lv. 20

☐ **Hiker Gabriel**
Mudbray ♂ Lv. 21

☐ **Rising Star Duo Lauren and Justin**
DOUBLE BATTLE
Vullaby ♀ Lv. 17
Rufflet ♂ Lv. 17

☐ **Ace Trainer Alexis**
Goomy ♀ Lv. 22
Sylveon ♂ Lv. 23

☐ **Pokémon Breeder Cory**
Paras ♂ Lv. 15
Spinarak ♂ Lv. 16

☐ **Pokémon Breeder Yuka**
Morelull ♀ Lv. 15
Ledyba ♀ Lv. 16

☐ **Twins Isa and Nico**
DOUBLE BATTLE
Happiny ♀ Lv. 15
Igglybuff ♀ Lv. 15

☐ **Trial Guide Bronson**
Slowpoke ♂ Lv. 22

To Lush Jungle (p. 120)

To Route 8 (p. 118)

Pokémon Center

32 33 34

To Brooklet Hill (p. 100)

31

To Paniola Ranch (p. 95)

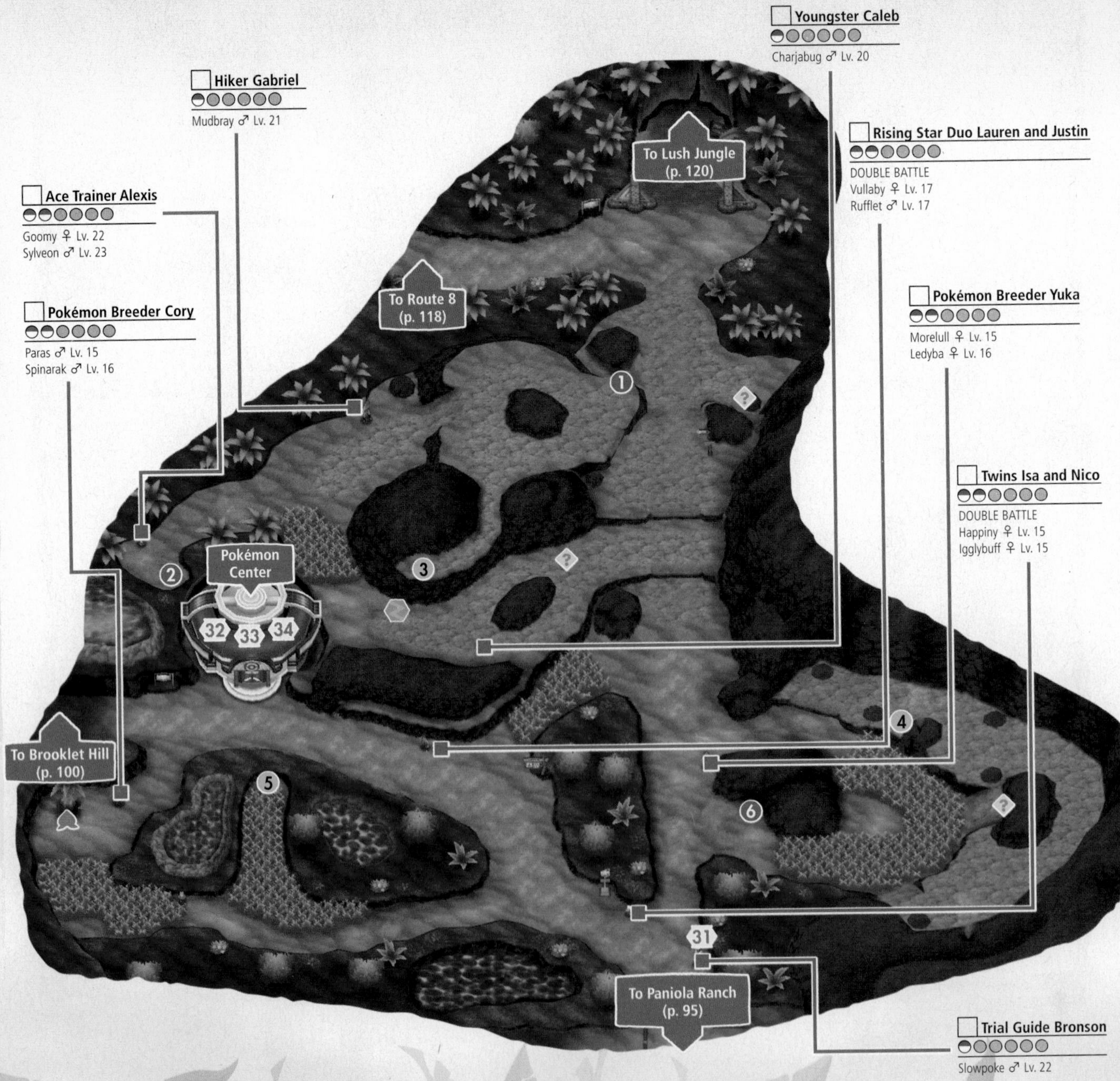

Tall Grass

North (Accessible from Route 8)	
Bonsly	△
Butterfree	▲
Caterpie	△
Fomantis	○
Grubbin	△
Metapod	△
Trumbeak	○

South	
Butterfree	▲
Caterpie	△
Fomantis	○
Grubbin	△
Lillipup	○
Metapod	△
Pikipek	○

◎ frequent ○ average
△ rare ▲ almost never
○ day only ☽ night only
Pokémon Sun
Pokémon Moon

S31: Defeat the Trial Guide for TM96 Nature Power

Defeat every Trainer along Route 5, then speak to the Trial Guide at the route's south end. He'll challenge you to another battle—one that can earn you a TM! You can't reach Route 5's northern Trainers just yet, though—you'll need to reenter Route 5 from the north to reach them.

Reward: TM96 Nature Power

Gladion

Hau runs into some trouble on Route 5, and its name is Gladion. Although he's not much older than you, Gladion looks as though he's had a rough life. He lives on his own and makes ends meet by doing odd jobs for Team Skull. Despite his working relationship with Team Skull, he ends up getting in their way as often as not. It's a shaky relationship, to be sure.

Team Skull Gladion's Pokémon ☠

Gladion's Pokémon shouldn't be too tough for you to handle. You've likely faced Zubat while exploring caves, and his Pokémon Type: Null can be whooped by the Fighting-type Pokémon you used to get through Ilima's trial.

Zubat
♂ Lv. 17 — POISON / FLYING
Weak to: ELECTRIC, ICE, PSYCHIC, ROCK

Type: Null
Lv. 18 — NORMAL
Weak to: FIGHTING

1 Rest up on your way to Brooklet Hill

After the dust settles and Team Skull has come and gone, Hau gives you three Revives. Continue exploring Route 5 to discover a Pokémon Center. Heal your team as needed while you search Route 5 for valuable items, including two handy TMs. Rest one more time before heading west to Brooklet Hill.

Reward: Revive ×3

S32: Trade Lillipup to get Bounsweet

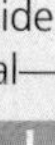

Inside the Pokémon Center, a young Trainer will trade you Bounsweet—an excellent Pokémon for your upcoming trial—for a Lillipup. You can catch Lillipup in the tall grass here on Route 5 or in Paniola Ranch.

Pokémon: Bounsweet

S33: Catch a Feebas to get paid

The Scientist in the Pokémon Center asks you to catch a Feebas on Brooklet Hill. Show him your Pokédex afterward for a cash reward!

Reward: ₽3,000

S34: Listen to a Fisherman's tale for a Dire Hit

A Fisherman in the Pokémon Center will give you a Dire Hit if you talk to him. You might use it against the Totem Pokémon!

Reward: Dire Hit

Brooklet Hill

Ride Pokémon Needed

A secluded series of hills and ponds, many of which are connected by small falls, Brooklet Hill serves as Captain Lana's trial site. Its tall grass and numerous fishing spots offer plenty of places for Trainers to catch aquatic Pokémon.

Team Recommendations: FIRE, GRASS, ELECTRIC

Items

Items
Brooklet Hill
1 Net Ball
2 X Sp. Atk
With Lapras Paddle
3 Rare Candy
4 Revive
5 TM55 Scald
Totem's Den With Lapras Paddle
6 Hyper Potion

Hidden Items

Hidden Items
Elixir
Max Repel

Fishing Spots

Brooklet Hill	
Feebas	▲
Goldeen	○
Magikarp	◎
Totem's Den	
Alomomola	▲
Magikarp	◎
Wishiwashi	○

Rare Fishing Spots

Brooklet Hill	
Feebas	▲
Goldeen	◎
Magikarp	◎
Totem's Den	
Alomomola	○
Magikarp	◎
Wishiwashi	○

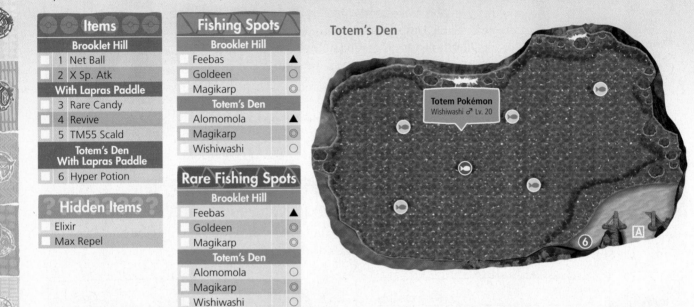

Totem's Den

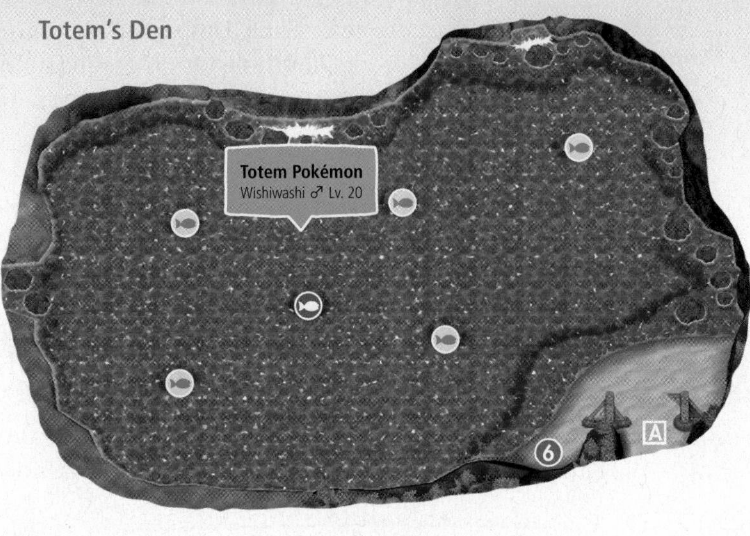

1 Meet Captain Lana and get a new Ride Pokémon

Ride Pokémon: Lapras

You bump into Captain Lana as you enter Brooklet Hill, and she asks you to help investigate some odd splashing in the nearby water. To help you, she registers Lapras to your Ride Pager. Now you can call Lapras and travel across bodies of water!

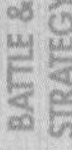

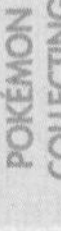

Lana

One of Akala Island's three captains, Lana loves Water-type Pokémon almost as much as she loves a good trick. Lana lives in Konikoni City with her grandmother, her parents, and two young sisters. She seems quiet at first, but the more you talk to her, the more you may notice her impish sense of humor.

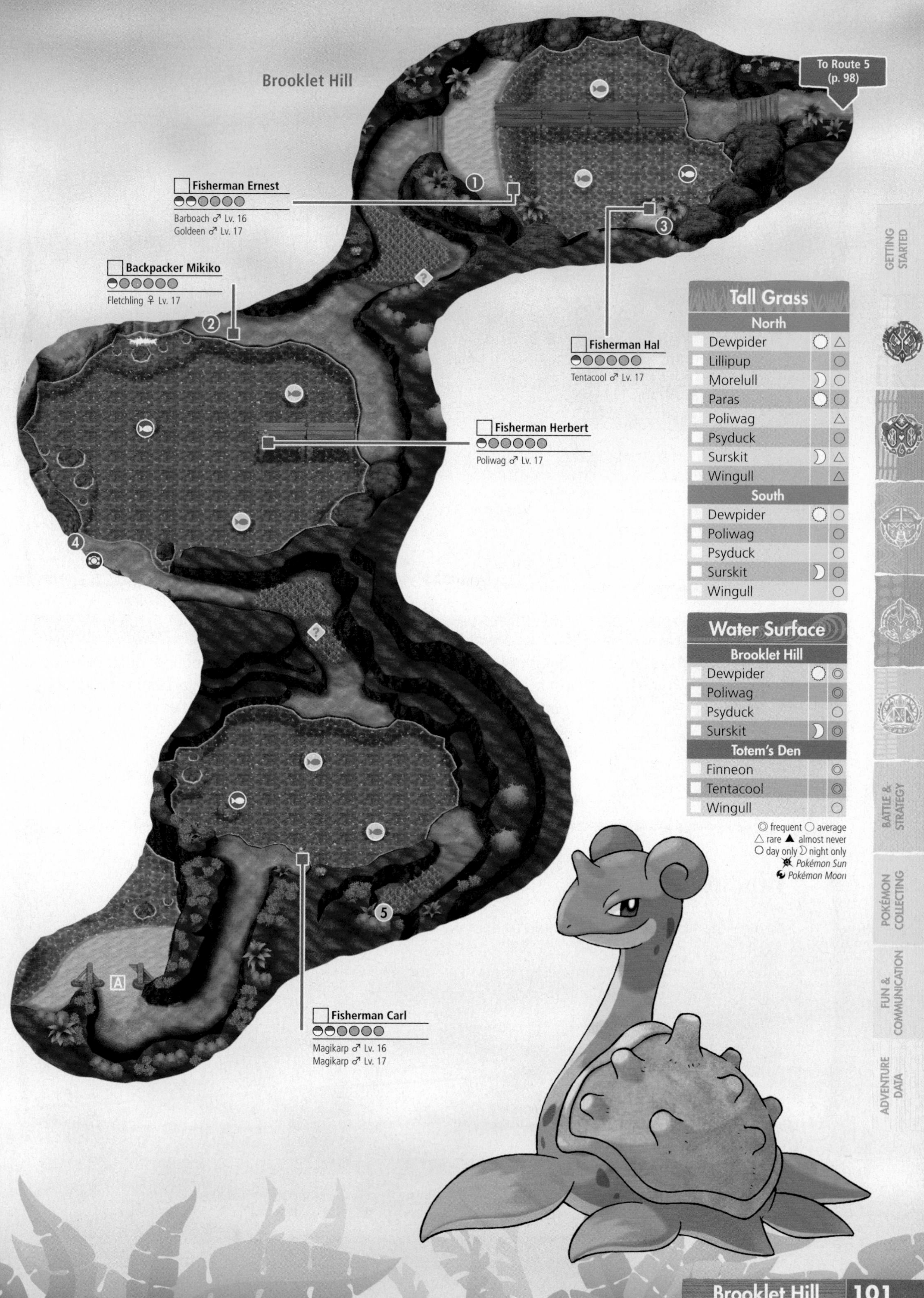

Tall Grass

North		
Dewpider	○	△
Lillipup		○
Morelull	☽	○
Paras	○	○
Poliwag		△
Psyduck		○
Surskit	☽	△
Wingull		△
South		
Dewpider	○	○
Poliwag		○
Psyduck		○
Surskit	☽	○
Wingull		○

Water Surface

Brooklet Hill		
Dewpider	○	◎
Poliwag		◎
Psyduck		○
Surskit	☽	◎
Totem's Den		
Finneon		◎
Tentacool		◎
Wingull		○

◎ frequent ○ average
△ rare ▲ almost never
○ day only ☽ night only
Pokémon Sun
Pokémon Moon

Lapras Paddle

You've got a new Ride Pokémon! Lapras loves to swim, and it can ferry you across large bodies of water, like seas, lakes, and pools in caves. Press Ⓐ when facing a body of water, or, alternatively, press Ⓨ, then select Lapras Paddle to take a comfortable ride on Lapras. If you're in a hurry, hold Ⓑ while riding Lapras to swim faster than normal. Lapras can also make some pretty tight turns—try giving the Circle Pad a few spins!

Once you get a fishing rod of your own, you'll be able to fish from Lapras's back. If you pass by a fishing spot while riding on Lapras, press Ⓐ to cast your line and see what you can catch. Be careful around bubbling fishing spots, though—you might scare away a rare Pokémon lurking there!

Tip

Now that you're able to ride Lapras, you may want to return to explore the waters of Melemele Sea (p. 36), Kala'e Bay (p. 87), and Seaward Cave (p. 86).

Tip

While riding Lapras through terrain where wild Pokémon encounters are possible (like on the surface of water), you're only about half as likely to encounter wild Pokémon.

2 Investigate the source of the splashing

Sail out on Lapras to discover the source of the splashing in Brooklet Hill. Why, it's just a little Wishiwashi! A lone Wishiwashi looks pretty harmless, but they have a tendency to call for allies if given the chance. Battles against them don't always go as you expect.

Wishiwashi

Defeating this little Wishiwashi should be short work for your Pokémon, particularly if you've trained up some Grass or Electric types. School it with Grass- and Electric-type moves to sail off with a swift victory! It's not all smooth sailing, though, as you'll have to face a second, slightly stronger Wishiwashi before you reach the fearsome Totem Pokémon.

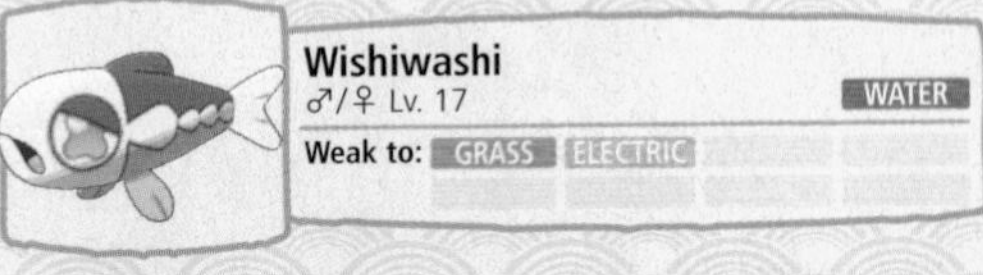

! **Clouds gather and rain begins to fall as you venture deeper into Brooklet Hill. Rain boosts the power of Water-type moves by 50% and reduces the power of Fire-type moves by 50%, so beware that Water-type opponents will start hitting harder!**

Trial Guide: Lana's Trial

Follow Lana's instructions, and your search of Brooklet Hill will lead you to a mighty Totem Pokémon. You have an advantage if you chose Rowlet as your first partner Pokémon, for Grass types are great at countering the many Water-type opponents you'll face around Brooklet Hill. Electric types can also work, as can Water types, provided they know some unusual moves.

Lana's Trial Goals

- Defeat the Totem Pokémon
- Receive the Water-type Z-Crystal

1 Battle the Totem Pokémon Wishiwashi

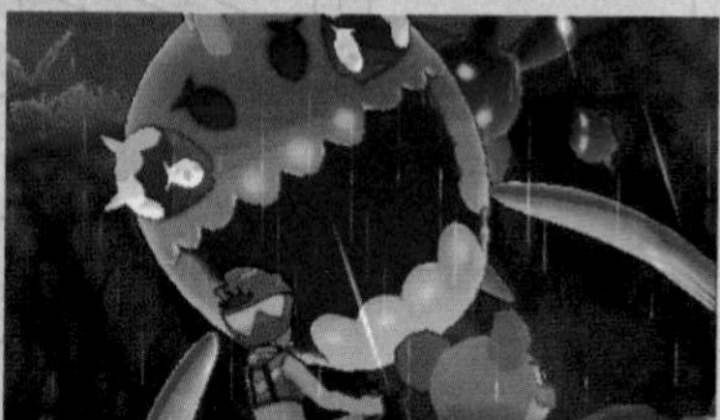

Keep following Lana, and she will lead you straight into the Totem's Den. How sneaky! Be ready for her trick, and be prepared to take on the Totem Pokémon Wishiwashi in its monstrous School Form! Defeat Totem Wishiwashi, and the Water-type Z-Crystal will be yours (among other prizes).

Reward: Waterium Z, Fishing Rod, Dive Ball ×10

Totem Wishiwashi (School Form)

This enormous Wishiwashi wastes no time making waves. Like the Totem Pokémon you faced during Ilima's Trial, Totem Wishiwashi's aura raises its Defense, helping it resist physical attacks. It also uses Soak to change your Pokémon's type to Water, negating any resistances that your Pokémon's natural type may have provided. It calls for Wishiwashi and Alomomola allies throughout the battle, and it will eat a Sitrus Berry to heal itself after it takes significant damage. Hammer Totem Wishiwashi with Grass- and Electric-type moves to inflict maximum damage, and try to inflict Paralysis or cause confusion to make it lose turns. In a pinch, use Water-type Pokémon that can unleash non-Water type moves—this will help you last through Wishiwashi's powerful Water-type attacks while countering with moves like Wingull's Air Cutter.

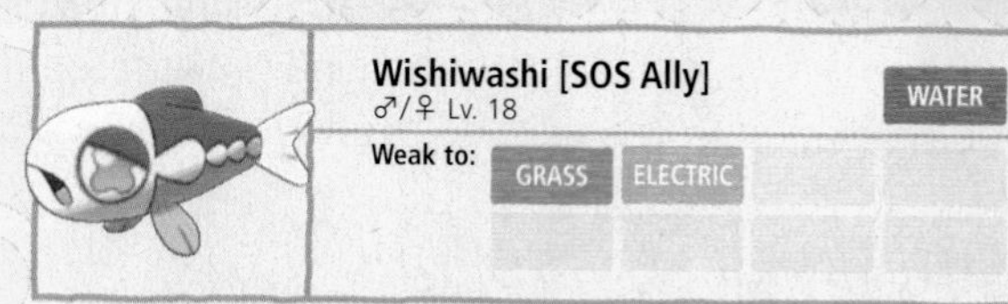

Wishiwashi [SOS Ally] WATER
♂/♀ Lv. 18
Weak to: GRASS ELECTRIC

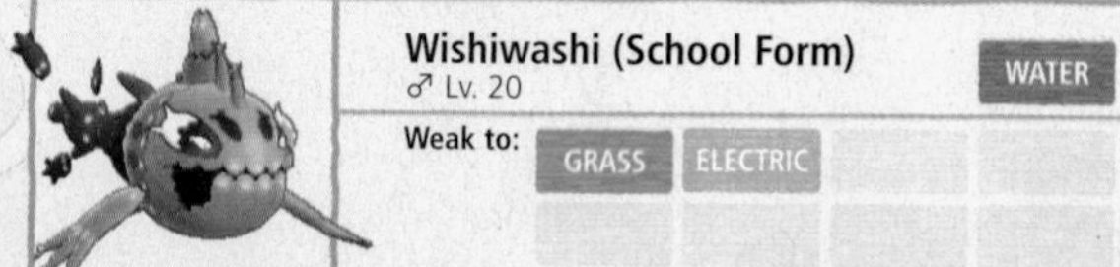

Wishiwashi (School Form) WATER
♂ Lv. 20
Weak to: GRASS ELECTRIC

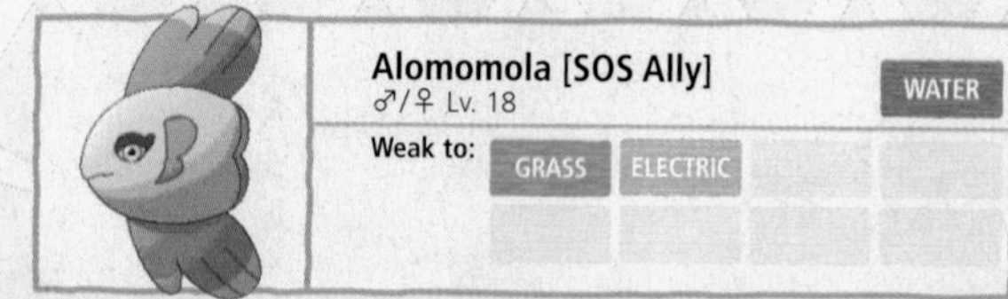

Alomomola [SOS Ally] WATER
♂/♀ Lv. 18
Weak to: GRASS ELECTRIC

Tip

Lana offers to zip you right back to the Pokémon Center after the battle. Accept her offer if your Pokémon are all tuckered out from the Totem Pokémon battle, or turn her down if you want to stay in Brooklet Hill for some fishing and additional explorations.

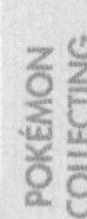

Fishing

Captain Lana hands you a Fishing Rod after you complete her trial on Akala Island. With it, you can fish from the shore or while riding on the back of Lapras. Look for piles of rocks underwater—Pokémon like to hide out in those places. In *Pokémon Sun* and *Pokémon Moon*, these are the only places where you can fish. Try fishing around Brooklet Hill, or go back and search for fishing spots you may have passed by earlier in your adventure.

When you get close to a fishing spot, press Ⓐ to cast your line. Press Ⓐ again to pull up your line the moment you see a "!" symbol appear. In *Pokémon Sun* and *Pokémon Moon*, you'll sometimes reel in items from fishing spots instead of Pokémon. At a normal fishing spot, you can get a Pearl, a Big Pearl, or a Heart Scale. At rare fishing spots, you might even get a Pearl String. If you've hooked a Pokémon instead, you'll have to battle it, or run away from it, just like any other wild Pokémon. Lana has also given you some Dive Balls, so try using those to increase your chances of catching water-dwelling Pokémon.

Tip

Place a Pokémon with the Suction Cups or Sticky Hold Ability in first position in your party to greatly boost your chances of reeling in a catch. Shellos and its Evolution Gastrodon can have the Sticky Hold Ability. Suction Cups isn't an Ability you find natively in the Alola region, but you might be able to get a Pokémon with that Ability from a trade on the GTS (p. 307). Try searching for Lileep or its Evolution Cradily because they will also provide you with a Grass-type advantage over the Water-type Pokémon you may reel in.

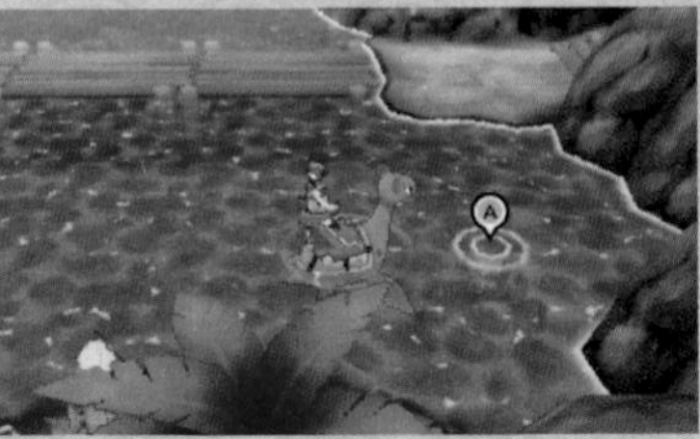

You're in luck if you see bubbles frothing up from an underwater pile of rocks, for you've just discovered a rare fishing spot! As you might expect from the name, you have a better chance to catch rare Pokémon and items. However, don't approach too quickly or get too close to a rare fishing spot, or it will suddenly become a regular fishing spot. That means no running or riding on Pokémon when you're on land! And if you're in the water, you can't be riding on a faster Ride Pokémon or swimming quickly (holding Ⓑ) with Lapras. Also, be sure not to get too close to a rare fishing spot, no matter how slowly you're going, or you will frighten off the rare Pokémon hiding there.

Tip

Remember to catch a Feebas to show to the researcher standing close to the Café in Route 5's Pokémon Center (p. 98). If you can show him its Pokédex entry, you'll earn ₽3,000.

Tip

Fishing spots that contain rare items and Pokémon are marked on your map, but that doesn't mean that they will always be a source of rare finds. You will only find rare Pokémon and items from these spots when you see bubbles frothing out of their depths. If you see no bubbles, try leaving the area once and reentering it. Perhaps your time away was long enough to lure some rare Pokémon back to the spot!

S35: Receive a Wide Lens from a Corsola Trainer

Once you receive a Fishing Rod from Lana, you can go back to Hau'oli Outskirts and speak to a Corsola in front of the Pokémon Research Lab. Its Trainer comes back from shopping and gives you a Wide Lens.

Reward: Wide Lens

Route 6

Commonly called "Straight Street," Route 6 is a linear path that connects to Paniola Ranch up north, Royal Avenue to the east, and Heahea City down south. A tiny path to the west also leads to one of Paniola Town's back alleys.

Team Recommendations

GRASS ELECTRIC FIGHTING FLYING

Items	
1	Super Potion
2	Rare Candy

Hidden Items
Carbos
X Speed

Tall Grass		
North		
Eevee		▲
Grubbin		△
Igglybuff	○	△
Lillipup		○
Mudbray		○
Pikipek	○	△
Pikipek	☽	○
Alolan Rattata	☽	△
Yungoos	○	△
South		
Eevee		▲
Grubbin		△
Igglybuff	○	△
Lillipup		○
Oricorio*		○
Pikipek	○	△
Pikipek	☽	○
Alolan Rattata	☽	△
Yungoos	○	△

◎ frequent ○ average
△ rare ▲ almost never
○ day only ☽ night only
Pokémon Sun
Pokémon Moon

*The form of Oricorio found on Route 6 is the pink Oricorio (Pa'u Style).

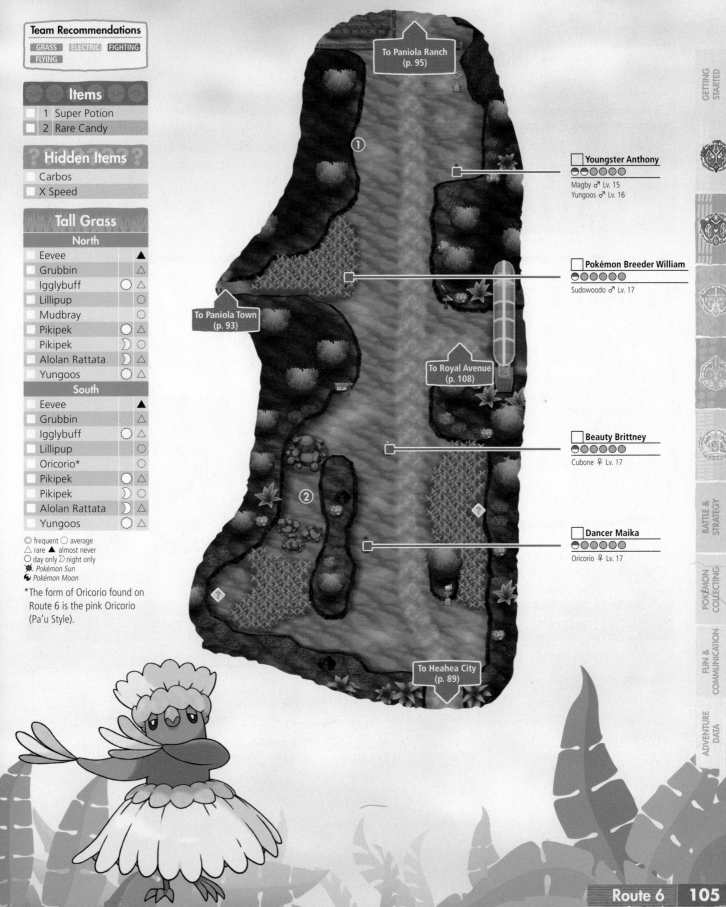

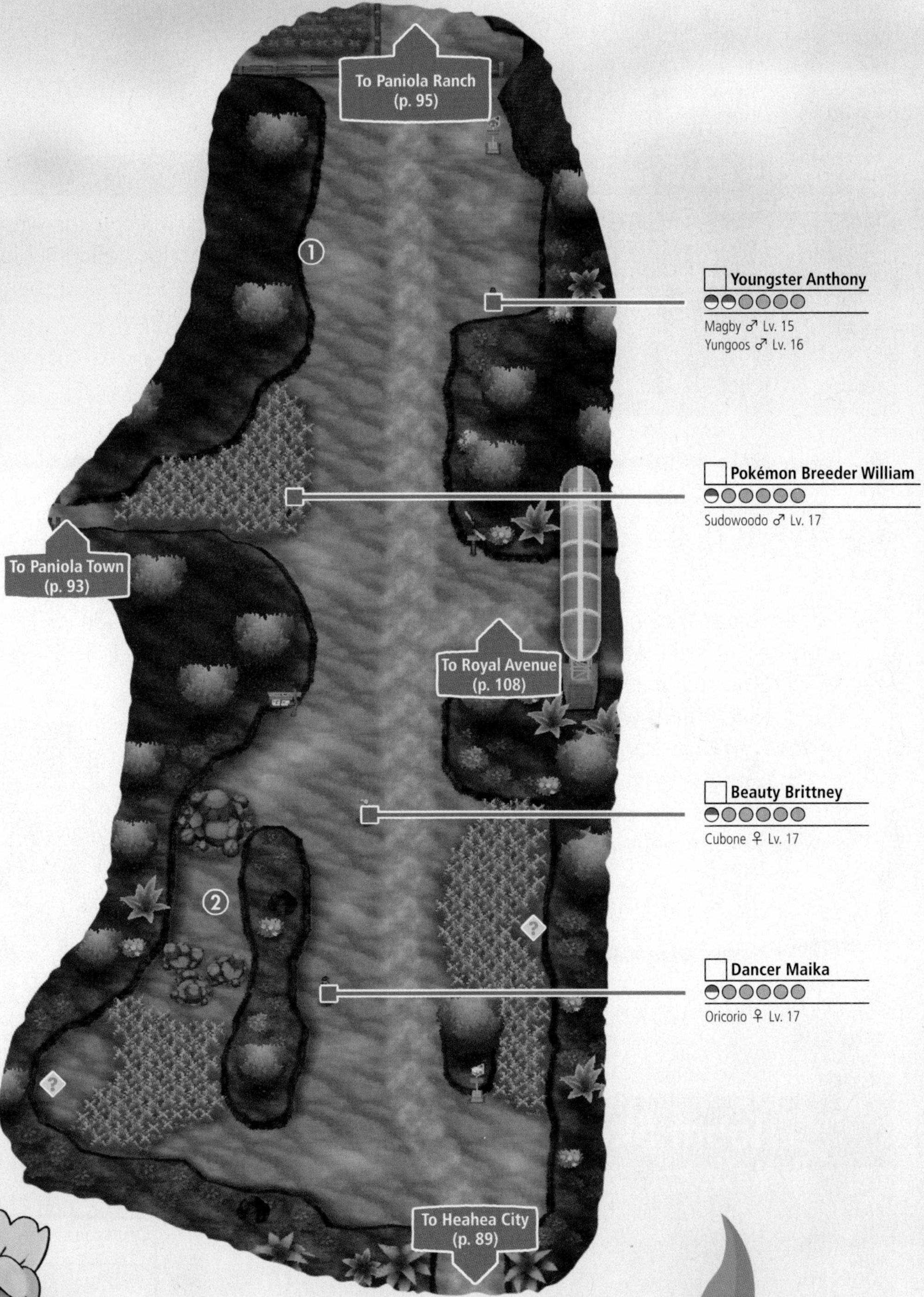

To Paniola Ranch (p. 95)
To Paniola Town (p. 93)
To Royal Avenue (p. 108)
To Heahea City (p. 89)

Youngster Anthony
Magby ♂ Lv. 15
Yungoos ♂ Lv. 16

Pokémon Breeder William
Sudowoodo ♂ Lv. 17

Beauty Brittney
Cubone ♀ Lv. 17

Dancer Maika
Oricorio ♀ Lv. 17

GETTING STARTED
BATTLE & STRATEGY
POKÉMON COLLECTING
FUN & COMMUNICATION
ADVENTURE DATA

1 Scatter the Sudowoodo and enter Route 6

Paniola Ranch's southeast trail leads to Route 6, but you'll have to do something about those pesky Sudowoodo that block the way. Fortunately, they simply run once they see your Waterium Z. You'll get a Mystic Water for helping out. Then you can head down to Route 6.

Reward: Mystic Water

2 Snatch a few items from Paniola Town

As you head south along Route 6, duck to the west and dash through the tall grass to get a TM that's technically located in Paniola Town, but couldn't be claimed before now. Collect TM88 Sleep Talk, then mount Stoutland and sniff out a Super Repel in this little nook as well.

Hapu and Mudsdale

Continue south along Route 6, and you'll soon meet Hapu and her huge Mudsdale. This little lady talks like a much older person, and she doesn't seem ruffled by anything. She demands your help in combating the Team Skull ruffians who are bothering the good citizens of Akala Island. From the sounds of things, she may not be from around these parts—her home must be very isolated if she considers the nearby Royal Avenue a big city!

Team Skull Grunt's Pokémon

This nasty Grunt has no chance this time around. Though he's raised his Drowzee a few levels, it won't pose much threat to your team. Unleash your best moves and send Team Skull packing once again.

Drowzee				
♂ Lv. 17				PSYCHIC
Weak to:	BUG	GHOST	DARK	

3 Circle back to Heahea City

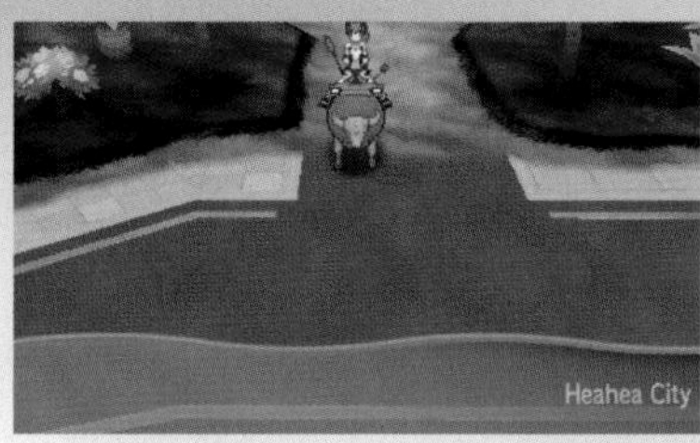

Ignore Royal Avenue for the moment and keep traveling south, smashing rocks with your Tauros to reach another item. While you're down here, why not swing back into Heahea City? Now that you're approaching from Route 6, you can see a bit more of the city than you were able to before.

Heahea City Revisited

p. 89

1 See more of the city

Stop by the third building east of the Pokémon Center, which you couldn't reach before. Inside, you'll find GAME FREAK's office and a local office of the Aether Foundation. GAME FREAK is the developer of all Pokémon main title games, like the one you're playing right now. The Aether Foundation is a Pokémon conservation group that has a branch office here in Alola. You'll probably see more of them during your island challenge.

S36: Get a Lemonade from GAME FREAK

One nice young woman in GAME FREAK's office will give you a tasty and nutritious Lemonade.

Reward: Lemonade

Tip

Return to GAME FREAK's office after you've completed your island challenge, and you can take on Morimoto in battle! He's the one responsible for designing and balancing the battle system in all the Pokémon main title games—so be ready for anything! If you win the battle against this formidable opponent, he will reward you with an Oval Charm.

Tip

As you catch more and more Pokémon, come back and show off your Pokédex to the game director at GAME FREAK. He'll reward you with a stamp if you complete an Island Pokédex and with a Shiny Charm if you manage to complete the Alola Pokédex!

Royal Avenue

If you're looking for big deals and bigger battles, then you've come to the right place! Between its Thrifty Megamart superstore and region-renowned Battle Royal Dome, Royal Avenue provides plenty of excitement for travelers of all ages.

Items	
1	HP Up
2	Ultra Ball
3	Pink Nectar ×2 ○

Hidden Items
Rare Candy
Soda Pop

Tip

You may find Pink Nectar if you examine the pink flowering shrubs in the middle of Royal Avenue when they appear to be glittering. This only seems to happen during the day, but it will happen every day, so come back to collect more if you want.

Battle Royal Dome—Interior

Clerk A
Clerk C
Clerk B
40
A

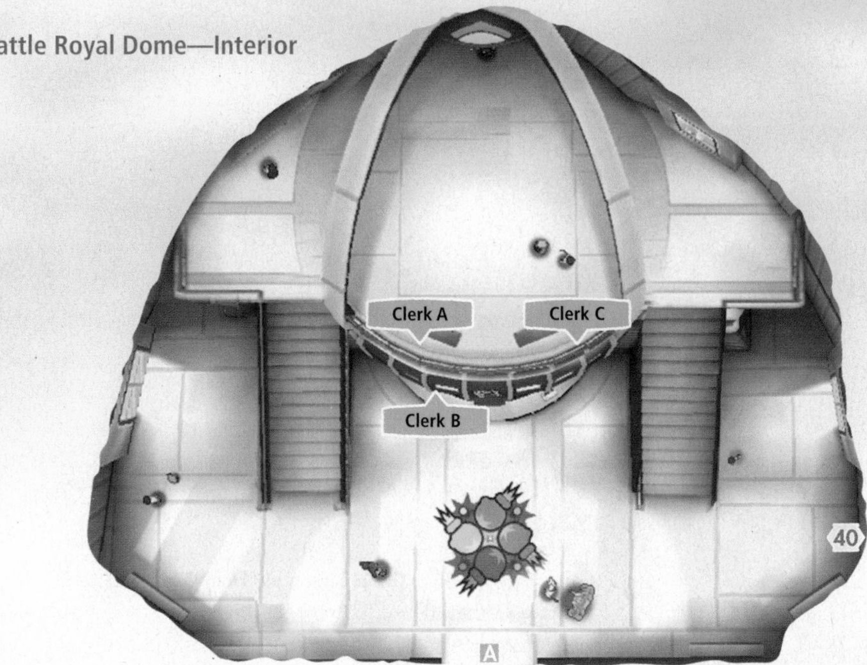

Royal Avenue

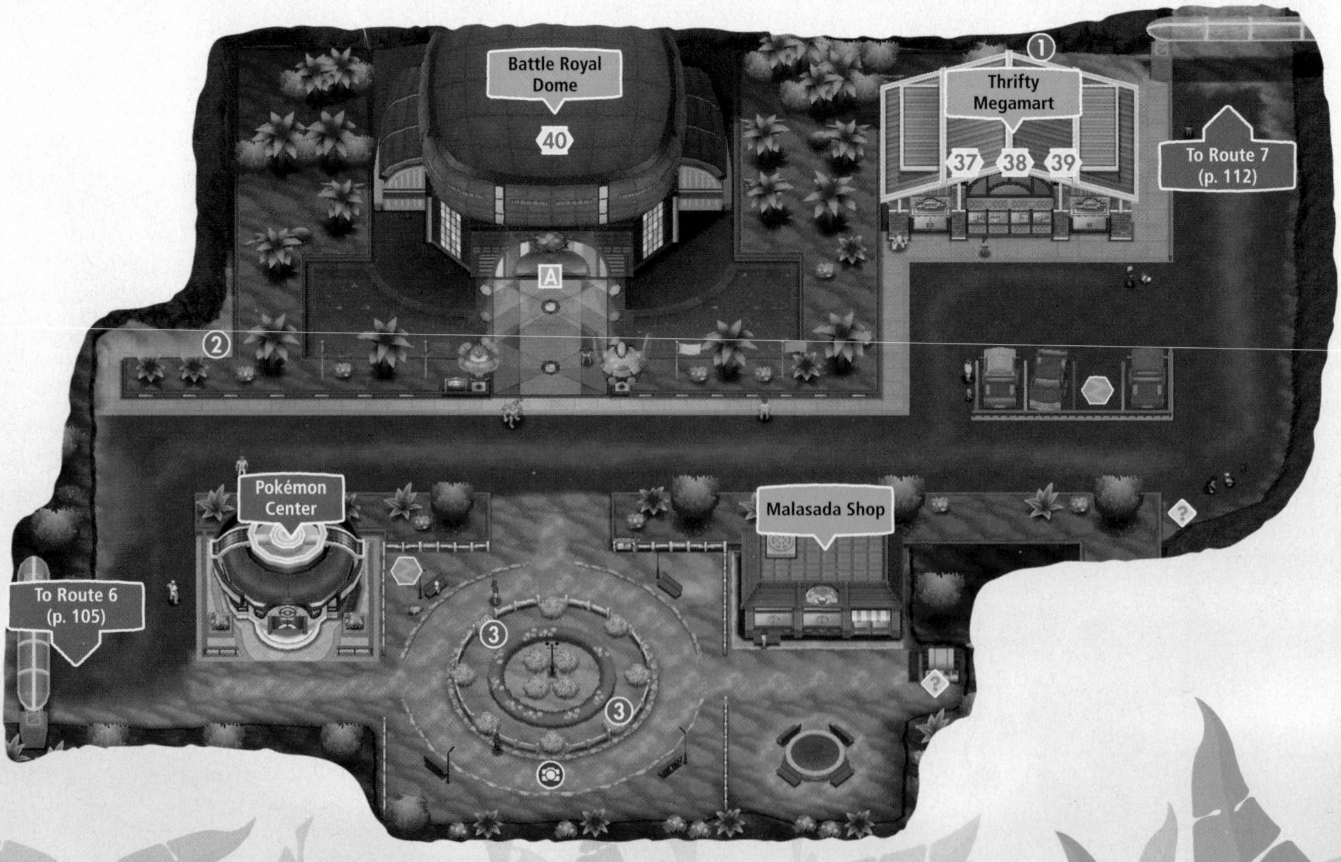

Battle Royal Dome
40
Thrifty Megamart
37
38
39
1
To Route 7 (p. 112)
A
2
Pokémon Center
Malasada Shop
To Route 6 (p. 105)
3
3

Tip

The items you buy in the Thrifty Megamart will end up costing the amounts you see here, but that is only thanks to the discount coupon that you receive in the store. The coupon will get you a refund for half the amount that you pay, but you must be able to pay up front to get the discount. So you'll need ₽600 to buy a Great Ball, but you'll get ₽300 back after your purchase!

Battle Royal Dome

Clerk A	
Ability Capsule	100 BP
Calcium	2 BP
Carbos	2 BP
HP Up	2 BP
Iron	2 BP
Protein	2 BP
Rare Candy	48 BP
Zinc	2 BP
Clerk B	
Everstone	16 BP
Power Anklet	16 BP
Power Band	16 BP
Power Belt	16 BP
Power Bracer	16 BP
Power Lens	16 BP
Power Weight	16 BP
Clerk C	
Binding Band	48 BP
Bright Powder	48 BP
Damp Rock	48 BP
Destiny Knot	48 BP
Expert Belt	48 BP
Float Stone	48 BP
Heat Rock	48 BP
Icy Rock	48 BP
Leftovers	48 BP
Metronome	48 BP
Muscle Band	48 BP
Quick Claw	48 BP
Scope Lens	48 BP
Shell Bell	48 BP
Smooth Rock	48 BP
Soothe Bell	48 BP
Wise Glasses	48 BP
Zoom Lens	48 BP

Thrifty Megamart

Clerk A	
Great Ball	₽300
Heal Ball	₽150
Nest Ball	₽500
Poké Ball	₽100
Timer Ball	₽500
Clerk B	
Antidote	₽100
Awakening	₽50
Burn Heal	₽150
Ice Heal	₽50
Paralyze Heal	₽150
Potion	₽100
Repel	₽200
Clerk C	
Strange Souvenir	₽1,500

Poké Mart

Special Wares	
TM 07 Hail	₽50,000
TM 11 Sunny Day	₽50,000
TM 18 Rain Dance	₽50,000
TM 37 Sandstorm	₽50,000

Malasada Shop

Item	Price
Big Malasada	₽350
Dry Malasada	₽200
Sour Malasada	₽200

Poké Mart

Normal Wares	
Antidote	₽200
Awakening	₽100
Burn Heal	₽300
Escape Rope	₽1,000
Great Ball	₽600
Honey	₽300
Ice Heal	₽100
Paralyze Heal	₽300
Poké Ball	₽200
Potion	₽200
Repel	₽400
Revive	₽2,000
Super Potion	₽700
After Completing 3 Trials	
Adrenaline Orb	₽300
Super Repel	₽700
After Completing 4 Trials	
Hyper Potion	₽1,500
Ultra Ball	₽800

Thrifty Megamart—Interior

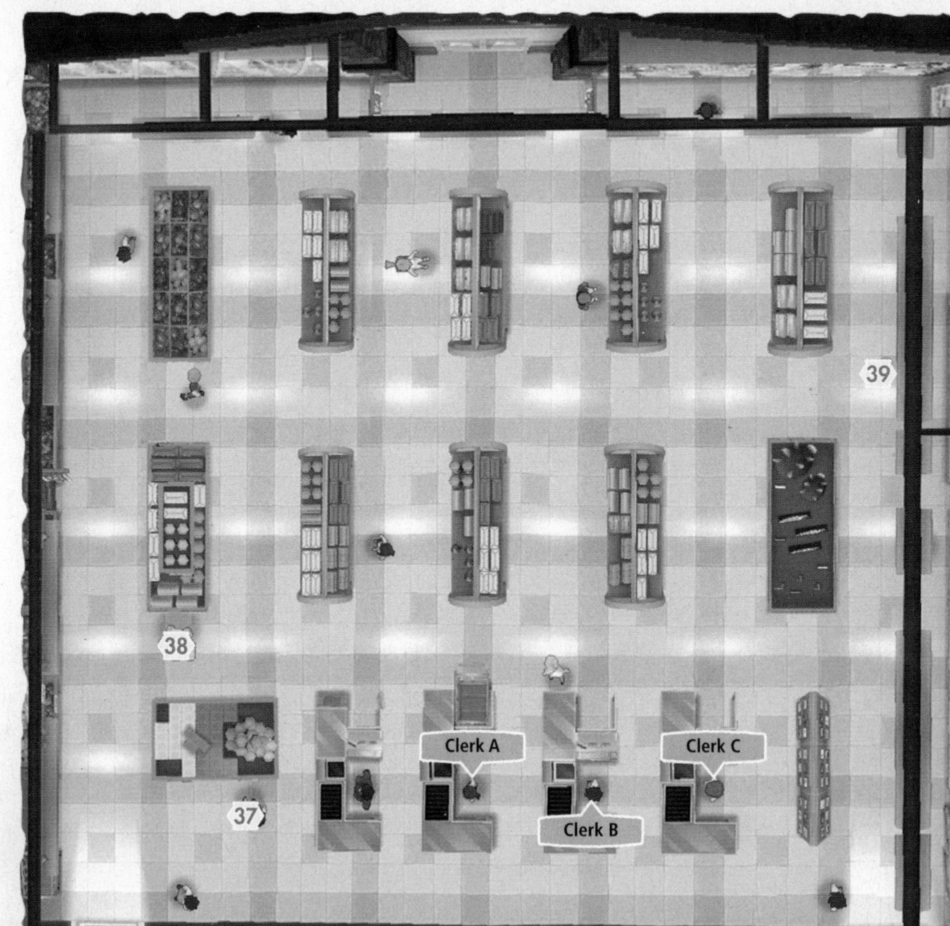

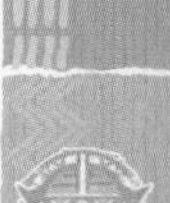

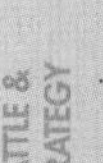
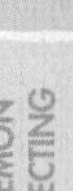

1 Explore Royal Avenue

Royal Avenue certainly lives up to its name. Rest at the Pokémon Center, then search this impressive area's every nook and cranny. Chat with everyone you meet and grab any items you find lying around, including the Pink Nectar, which can sometimes be found in the flowery bushes near the central foundation. If you have an Oricorio, this nectar will allow it to change into its Pa'u Style form!

2 Shop at the Thrifty Megamart

Grab a snack at the malasada shop and maybe pick up a Big Malasada for the road, then swing on up to the Thrifty Megamart. Each clerk has different goods for sale, so talk to them all and see what's available. With the discount coupon that a clerk gives you, you'll get a 50% rebate on anything you buy! Once you're all stocked up, head on into the Battle Royal Dome!

Tip

One of the Thrifty Megamart's cashiers hints that he'll have a challenge for you after you become the strongest Trainer in Alola. We'll remind you to come back later!

S37: Receive a Berry every day!

The clerk near the Thrifty Megamart's entrance will give you a free Berry each day, just for stopping by. Remember to visit him whenever you're nearby!

Reward: Bluk Berry, Mago Berry, Oran Berry, Pinap Berry, Rawst Berry, Sitrus Berry, or Tamato Berry

S38: Hypno offers TM44 Rest

Be generous to the Hypno in the Thrifty Megamart and you'll be rewarded with a TM!

Reward: TM44 Rest

S39: Get a Lemonade from a Drifloon

Talk to the Drifloon hanging around with its Trainer on the east side of the Thrifty Megamart to get a Lemonade.

Reward: Lemonade

S40: Collect an Effort Ribbon in the Battle Royal Dome

A lady in the Battle Royal Dome will give you a Ribbon for your Pokémon if it's really improved its stats through lots of battling and training.

Reward: Effort Ribbon

3 Experience the Battle Royal for yourself

Follow a familiar figure in the Battle Royal Dome, and you will meet the famous wrestler: the Masked Royal! He will drag you, Hau, and Gladion into a Battle Royal whether you like it or not, so go all out in this free-for-all battle style unique to the Alola region! After the battle, you'll get a chance to meet another minor Alolan celebrity: the Fire-type Captain Kiawe!

Battle Royal

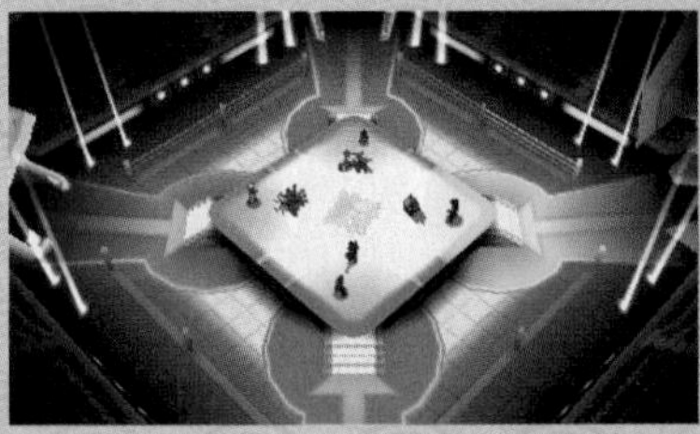

Looking for an exciting new way to battle? In a Battle Royal, four players each select a team of three Pokémon, then face off in a free-for-all from which only one player will emerge victorious! When one player's Pokémon have all fainted, the battle concludes at the end of that turn. The ranking order to decide the Battle Royal winner is then determined using the following factors:

1. Having a combination of most Pokémon left on your team and most opposing Pokémon defeated
2. Defeating more opposing Pokémon than someone else you tied with based on the above
3. Having the greatest proportion of remaining HP to max HP
4. Having the greatest total remaining HP

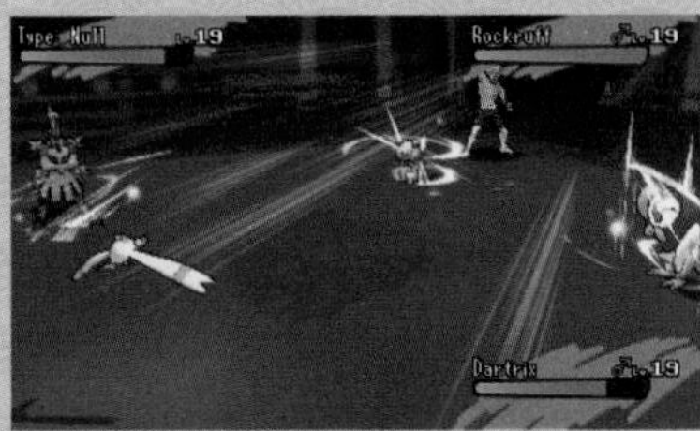

Since it's every Pokémon for itself, you'll find that some moves may work a little differently than you'd expect in a Battle Royal. For example, Helping Hand, which normally affects one ally, can be used on any of the other Pokémon in the ring. Moves like Air Cutter will still hit all of the opposing Pokémon, but their power is halved. And a move like Blizzard, which normally affects just the opposing side in battle, will now hit all of the opposing Pokémon in the ring!

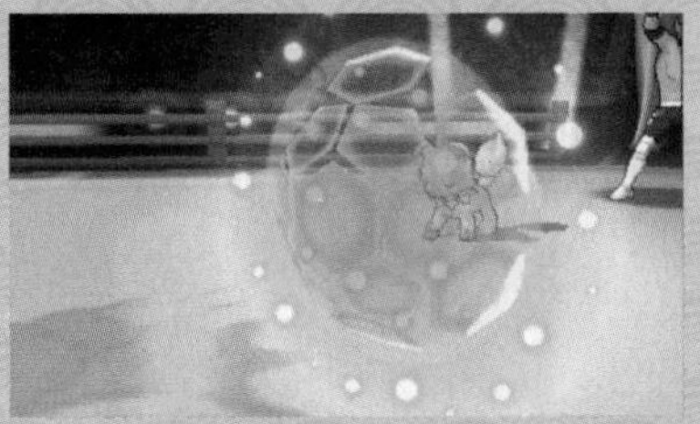

In a Battle Royal, the Speed stat still determines the Pokémon that gets to move first, with high-priority moves like Protect taking precedence. Moving first is a big advantage in a Battle Royal, for if you try to attack a Pokémon that has fainted, your Pokémon's move will fizzle and fail. And only the Pokémon that causes an opposing Pokémon to faint will be credited with a point, so it's especially important to act quickly and be the first to land the finishing blow on a weakened Pokémon.

Battle Royals can be enjoyed in the following ways:

- Visit the Battle Royal Dome and compete against three other competitors.
- Access Festival Plaza (p. 299), select "Battle" from the lower screen, then choose "Link Battle" to battle against people on your player lists.
- Access Festival Plaza, select "Battle," and then choose "Visit the Battle Spot" to battle people from around the world via the Internet.

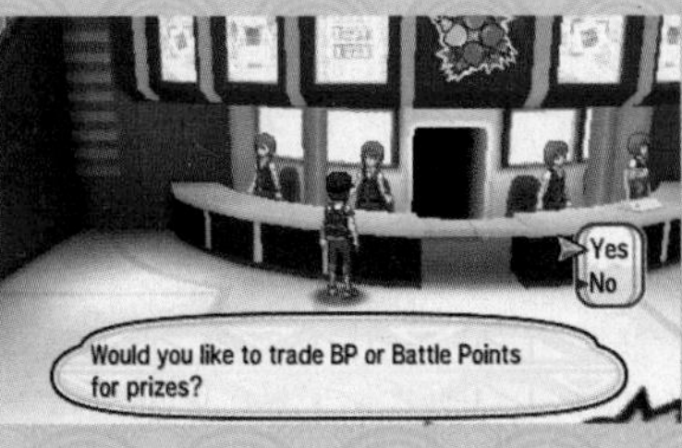

You earn Battle Points, or BP, after each Battle Royal. BP can be spent at the counter of the Battle Royal Dome and at the Battle Tree (p. 224) to buy fabulous prizes, including some pretty cool items. (See page 262 for even more details on this exciting new battle mode!)

Tip

Do really well at the Master Rank of Battle Royal, and you may get a chance to battle the mysterious Masked Royal again!

Route 7

Ride Pokémon Needed 

Featuring sandy shores and a sizable bay, this unusual route connects to Royal Avenue down south, Wela Volcano Park to the west, and Route 8 up north. A Trial Guide blocks the tunnel to Route 8, however, and won't move an inch until you've competed Kiawe's trial atop Wela Volcano.

Team Recommendations
GRASS ELECTRIC GROUND

Items	
1	Max Repel
2	Antidote
3	TM73 Thunder Wave

Fishing Spots	
Magikarp	◎
Staryu	▲
Wishiwashi	○

Rare Fishing Spots	
Magikarp	◎
Staryu	○
Wishiwashi	○

Water Surface	
Finneon	○
Pyukumuku	○
Tentacool	○
Wingull	○

Hidden Items
Net Ball
Pearl

Sand Clouds	
Alolan Diglett	◎

◎ frequent ○ average △ rare
▲ almost never ○ day only ☽ night only
Pokémon Sun *Pokémon Moon*

Swimmer Tiare
Alomomola ♀ Lv. 19

Swimmer Casey
Mareanie ♂ Lv. 19

Swimmer Vanessa
Shellder ♀ Lv. 18
Corsola ♀ Lv. 19

Swimmer Dakota
Surskit ♂ Lv. 19
Dewpider ♂ Lv. 19

To Route 8 (p. 118)
To Wela Volcano Park (p. 113)
To Royal Avenue (p. 108)

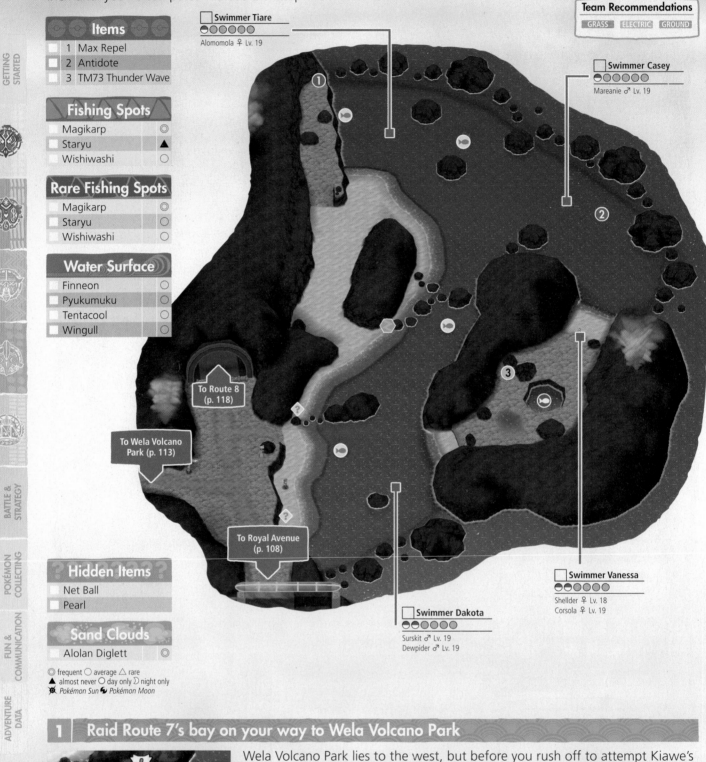

1 Raid Route 7's bay on your way to Wela Volcano Park

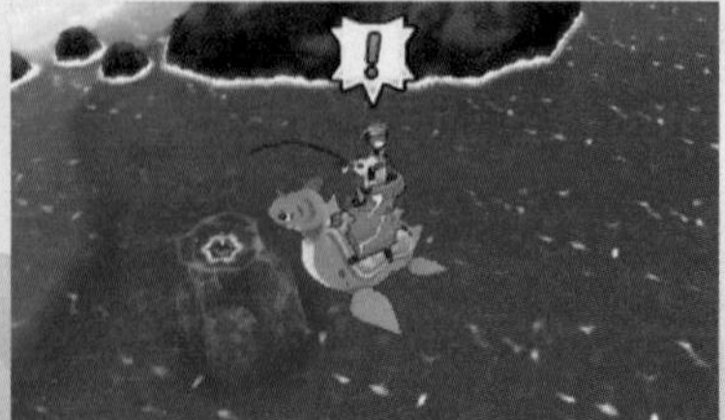

Wela Volcano Park lies to the west, but before you rush off to attempt Kiawe's trial, go east to reach a large bay here on Route 7. Use Lapras to fully explore this area, collecting valuable items in the process. This is a perfect spot to catch some Water-type Pokémon before you head up the fiery volcano to meet Kiawe's challenge.

Wela Volcano Park

Centered around a towering mountain that sizzles with excitement, Wela Volcano Park serves as the site of Captain Kiawe's trial. Reaching the summit is short work, but you're sure to break a sweat in the Totem's Den, where Kiawe really turns up the heat!

Team Recommendations

WATER GROUND ROCK DRAGON

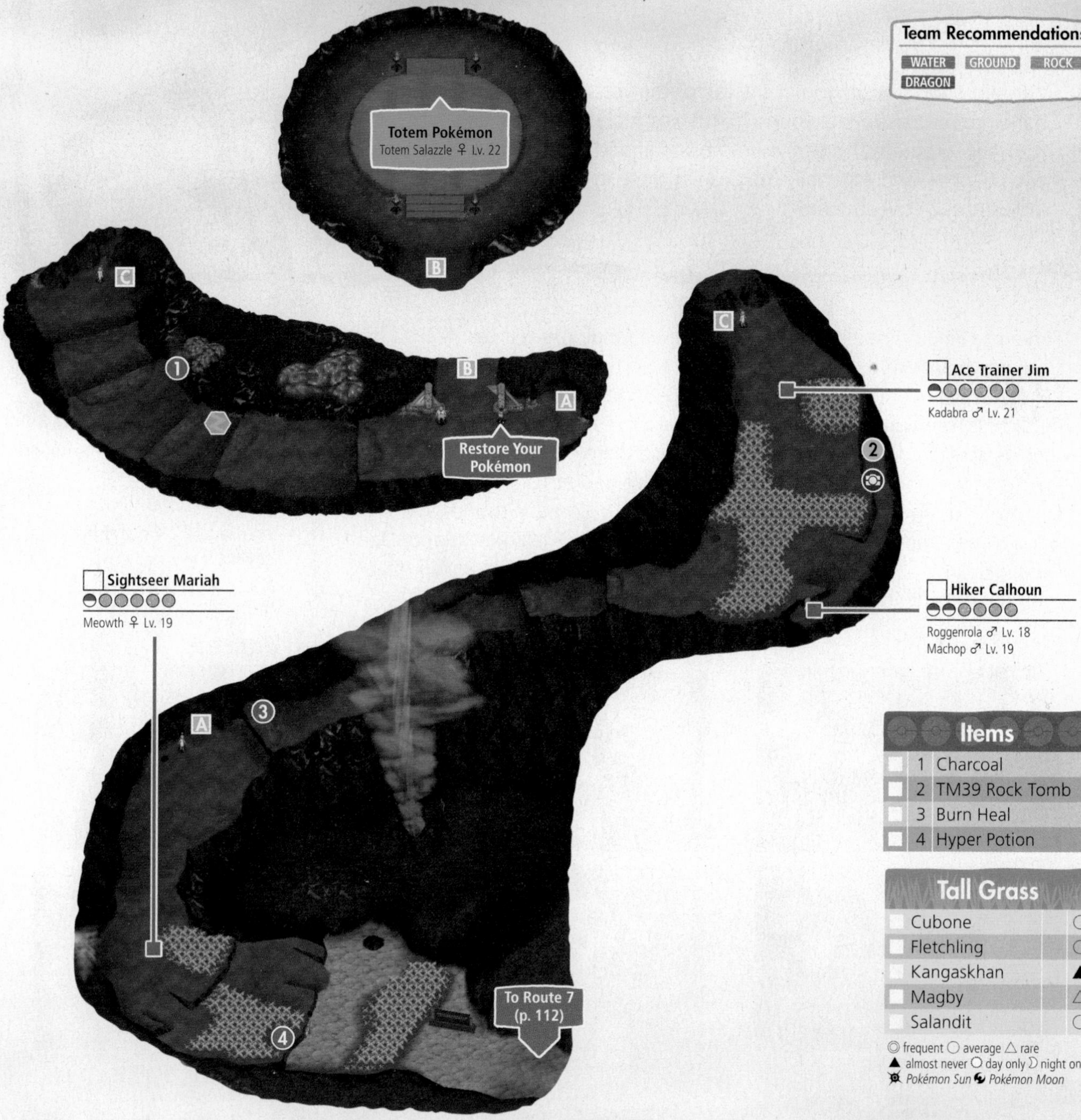

Totem Pokémon
Totem Salazzle ♀ Lv. 22

Restore Your Pokémon

Ace Trainer Jim
Kadabra ♂ Lv. 21

Hiker Calhoun
Roggenrola ♂ Lv. 18
Machop ♂ Lv. 19

Sightseer Mariah
Meowth ♀ Lv. 19

To Route 7 (p. 112)

Items	
1	Charcoal
2	TM39 Rock Tomb
3	Burn Heal
4	Hyper Potion

Tall Grass	
Cubone	○
Fletchling	○
Kangaskhan	▲
Magby	△
Salandit	○

◎ frequent ○ average △ rare
▲ almost never ○ day only ☽ night only
Pokémon Sun *Pokémon Moon*

1 Explore the volcano on your way to the summit

Battle your way to a small cave that leads you close to the summit, marked with "A" on this map. Once you pass through it, you will be right at the peak and steps away from your next trial. Talk to the Trial Guide on the right side of the gate to restore your Pokémon, then decide if you wish to go north into the Totem's Den straight away, or head west and finish exploring the volcano for more items and experience. If you head west, you will be able to explore everything that was above those unclimbable ledges at the base of the volcano.

Kiawe

Captain Kiawe awaits you at the top of the volcano. A student of fire dancing, this passionate young man takes Alola's traditional dances seriously. Kiawe incorporates his dances into his trial, and you'll have to closely watch each dance—and especially the pose at the end—to determine the subtle differences between them.

Three challenging battles await you in Kiawe's trial, the last being a showdown against a powerful Totem Pokémon! You can't restore your Pokémon between battles, so pack your Bag with plenty of potent medicines, like Super Potions and Antidotes. Fire types are your primary foes here, and you'll have an edge if you use the plethora of Water-type Pokémon you can catch on the water's surface and at fishing spots around Brooklet Hill, Route 7, and other places you've explored. Ground- and Rock-type Pokémon that can be caught in caves like Melemele Island's Ten Carat Hill are also effective. Fill your party with these types of Pokémon, then dance off with the victory!

Kiawe's Trial Goals

- Judge the differences between the Pokémon's dances
- Defeat the Totem Pokémon
- Receive the Z-Crystal from Kiawe

First dance

(Answer: the middle Marowak)

Second dance

(Answer: the Hiker)

Third dance

(Answer: all answers are correct!)

! **If you guess wrong, you'll be forced to battle an Alolan Marowak (Lv. 18) or Hiker David's Magmar (Lv. 19) before you can guess again. We've provided you the answers, though, so you shouldn't have to worry about this!**

Alolan Marowak

If you think you know Marowak, think again! Marowak are typically Ground-type Pokémon, but Marowak that hail from the Alola region are actually Fire- and Ghost-type Pokémon! Your Water-type moves will still make a splash, but in Alola, Ground and Rock types will also pack a punch.

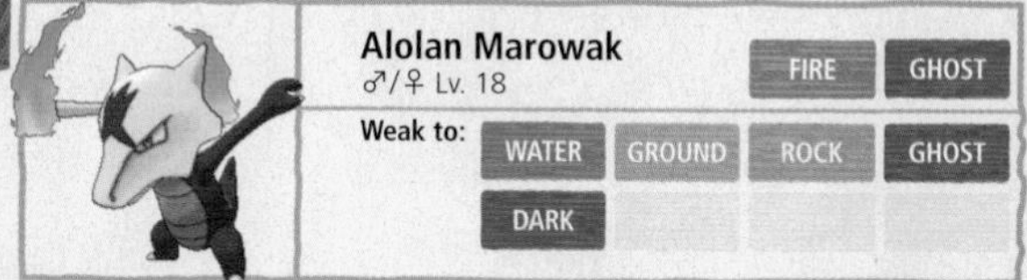

Hiker David's Pokémon

This battle is a bit more challenging, as Magmar's Fire Spin can cause your Pokémon to take damage for a few turns. Still, Water-type Pokémon should have little trouble extinguishing Magmar.

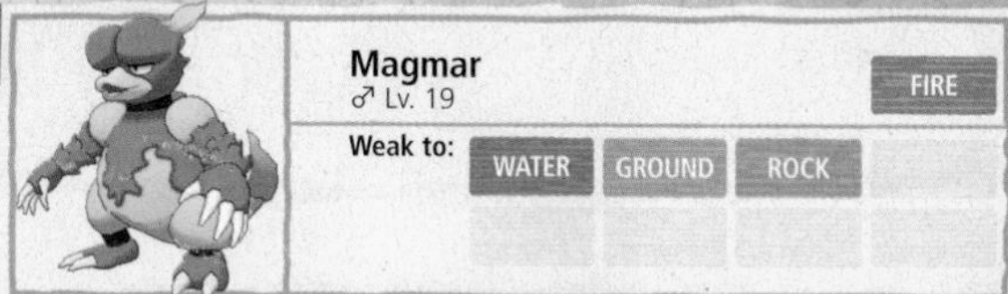

Magmar
FIRE
♂ Lv. 19
Weak to:
WATER
GROUND
ROCK

Totem Salazzle

Totem Salazzle is a tricky opponent. Its aura raises its Sp. Def, reducing damage from special moves. It uses Toxic to badly poison your Pokémon, inflicting significant damage each turn. (Cure this with Antidotes.) Salazzle also uses Torment to prevent your Pokémon from using the same move twice in a row, and its Salandit allies use Taunt, forcing your Pokémon to use only attack moves for three turns. Counter this devious combo by sending out a Pokémon that has at least two effective attack moves at its disposal.

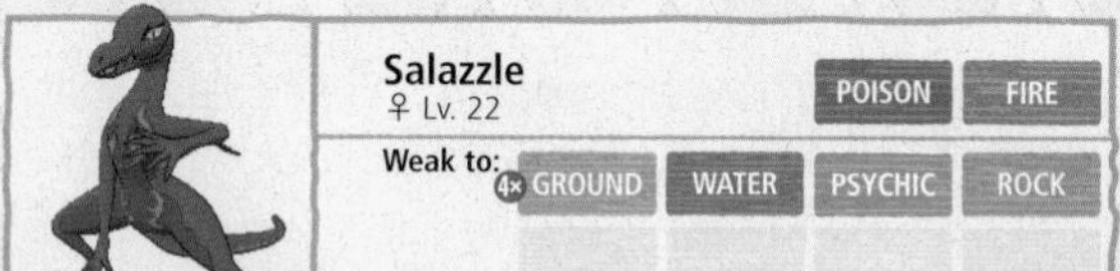

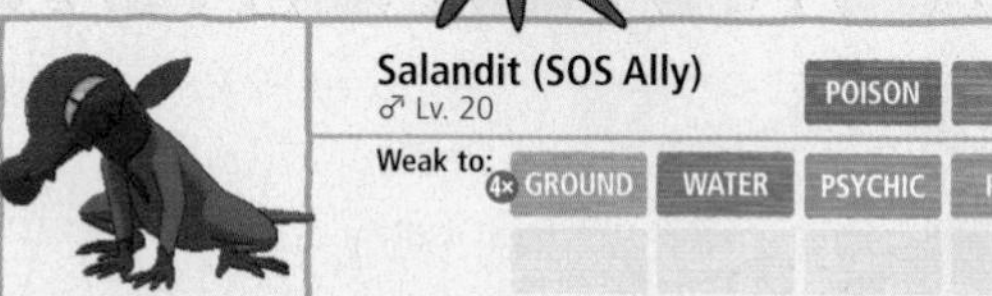

1 Receive Firium Z and a new Ride Pokémon

Reward: Firium Z, Quick Ball ×10

Ride Pokémon: Charizard

For successfully stomping out Totem Salazzle, Kiawe rewards you with the Fire-type Z-Crystal, Firium Z. He also hands you some Quick Balls and registers Charizard to your Ride Pager! With Charizard, you can swiftly fly back to locations that you've visited before. This makes getting around Alola much easier!

Charizard Glide

You got a new Ride Pokémon! Charizard can fly you to almost any location you've previously visited, helping you travel around Alola with greater haste. Press Ⓨ and select Charizard Glide, then tap any location on the lower screen map to have Charizard swoop down from the sky and fly you there (use Ⓨ to zoom in or zoom out and Ⓛ and Ⓡ to cycle through the different islands). Note that you cannot use Charizard Glide from an indoor location or an area covered by a roof.

Poké Pelago

Riding on Charizard lets you reach more than just Alola's main islands—you can now visit Poké Pelago as well! Select Poké Pelago, which has been added to your X menu, to call Charizard and fly there. If you don't see the Poké Pelago button on your X menu, tap Ⓛ or Ⓡ to check the menu's other page.

The moment you land on Poké Pelago, you're greeted by a man named Mohn, the friendly caretaker of this wondrous place. Mohn explains that Poké Pelago is a special place designed for the enjoyment of Pokémon. Any Pokémon that you deposit in your PC Boxes can come here to play, grow Berries, explore, train, and relax. And the more Pokémon you have in your Boxes, the more you can do at Poké Pelago—another good reason to catch as many new Pokémon as you can!

Start by gathering up some Poké Beans. These are the same Poké Beans that you can get as a gift once a day from Pokémon Center cafés. Your Pokémon probably enjoy eating them in Pokémon Refresh. Tap any Poké Beans that are lying on the ground around the island to pick them up. Find more Poké Beans by tapping the Poké Beanstalk that's sprouted up from the island. Poké Beans will plummet all over the island, but you can only shake loose so many at a time. Pop in at least once a day to harvest as many beans as you can!

Tip

Some beans are rarer than others and will have greater effects. Learn more about that and all of the details of navigating Poké Pelago on pages 309–312.

Isle Abeens

The first island that you visit at Poké Pelago, Isle Abeens, is the place where Pokémon come to meet, mingle, and munch on Poké Beans. Wild Pokémon may also appear here—and if they feel at home, they may even want to join your team! This is another way to get unusual Pokémon.

Poké Pelago (continued)

Isle Aplenny

You must develop this island before you can visit it. Once you do, you'll have a place where you can plant any of the Berries that you've collected around Alola. Your Pokémon can then help your Berries grow into healthy Berry plants that will provide you with even more delicious Berries!

Isle Aphun

Isle Aphun must also be developed before you can explore it. Once developed, your Pokémon can go exploring in its cave for the chance to find items. Some of them can be quite rare or valuable, and will help you on your adventure.

Isle Evelup

Develop this island, and your Pokémon can work out here to improve their base stats for battle. Several Pokémon can train at once, letting you easily boost a whole team! Base stats help boost your Pokémon's stats, like Attack and Speed, for battle. You can learn more about them beginning on page 272.

Isle Avue

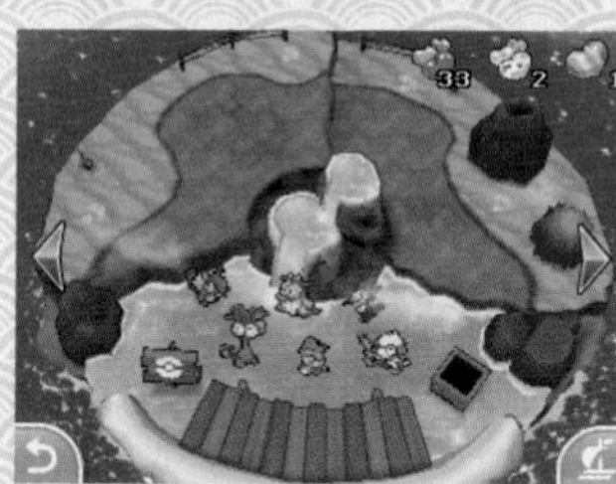

Once you've developed this island, you can leave Pokémon—and even Pokémon Eggs—here to relax and enjoy the hot springs. They'll feel more affectionate toward you after all this pampering, and your Pokémon Eggs will hatch even faster!

Remember, you can learn more specifics about each Poké Pelago island, and what you can unlock by developing them, on pages 309–312. For now, just know that you need lots of Pokémon in your Boxes, and plenty of Poké Beans, to develop islands at Poké Pelago. Keep catching Pokémon and collecting Poké Beans, and you and your Pokémon can enjoy Poké Pelago to the fullest!

Route 8

Ride Pokémon Needed  

Running along Akala Island's north end, this seaside route's fantastic views make it a popular spot for couples and Pokémon. Trainers must clear Captain Kiawe's trial atop Wela Volcano Park before they're allowed to enter this scenic stretch.

Team Recommendations

FIRE WATER ELECTRIC FIGHTING

Items

	Item
1	Big Pearl
2	Ultra Ball
3	Hyper Potion
4	Miracle Seed
5	Dive Ball
With Machamp Shove	
6	TM53 Energy Ball
With Lapras Paddle	
7	Water Stone

Hidden Items

- Adrenaline Orb
- Awakening
- Iron
- Max Repel

Vending Machine

Roadside Motel

Item	Price
Fresh Water	₽400
Soda Pop	₽600

Water Surface

Pokémon	Rate
Finneon	◎
Tentacool	◎
Wingull	○

Fishing Spots

Pokémon	Rate
Chinchou	▲
Magikarp	◎
Wishiwashi	○

Rare Fishing Spots

Pokémon	Rate
Chinchou	○
Magikarp	◎
Wishiwashi	○

Tall Grass

Pokémon		Rate
Fletchinder		△
Alolan Rattata	☽	○
Salandit		○
Stufful		▲
Trumbeak		○
Yungoos	○	○

Shore

Pokémon	Rate
Wimpod	◎

◎ Frequent ○ Average △ Rare ▲ Almost Never ○ Day only ☽ Night only *Pokémon Sun* only *Pokémon Moon* only

Poké Mart

Normal Wares

Item	Price
Adrenaline Orb	₽300
Antidote	₽200
Awakening	₽100
Burn Heal	₽300
Escape Rope	₽1,000
Great Ball	₽600
Honey	₽300
Ice Heal	₽100
Paralyze Heal	₽300
Poké Ball	₽200
Potion	₽200
Repel	₽400
Revive	₽2,000
Super Potion	₽700
Super Repel	₽700
After Completing 4 Trials	
Hyper Potion	₽1,500
Ultra Ball	₽800

Poké Mart

Special Wares

Item	Price
Dire Hit	₽1,000
Dive Ball	₽1,000
Dusk Ball	₽1,000
Guard Spec.	₽1,500
Quick Ball	₽1,000
X Accuracy	₽1,000
X Attack	₽1,000
X Defense	₽2,000
X Sp. Atk	₽1,000
X Sp. Def	₽2,000
X Speed	₽1,000

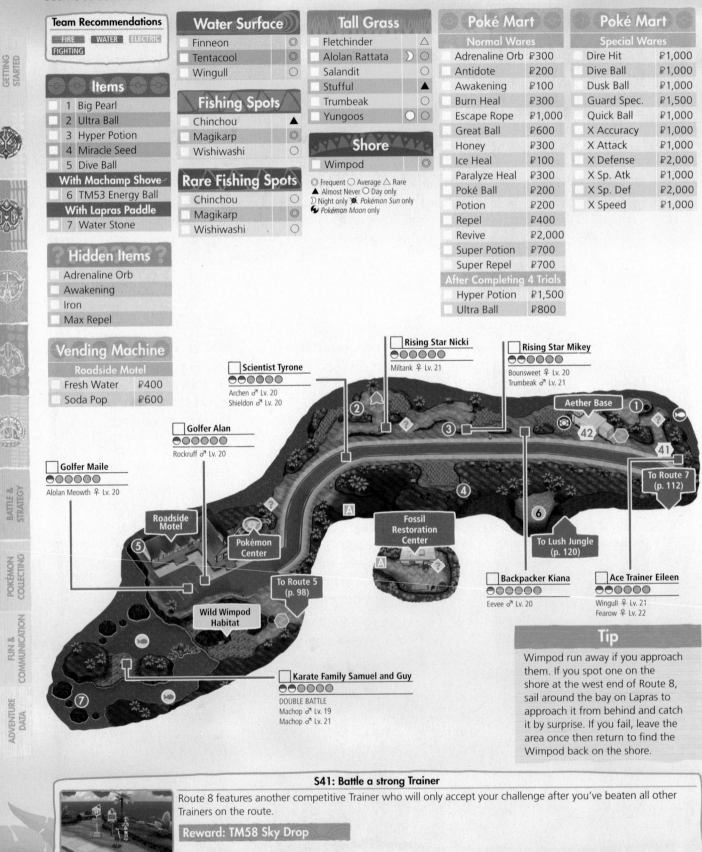

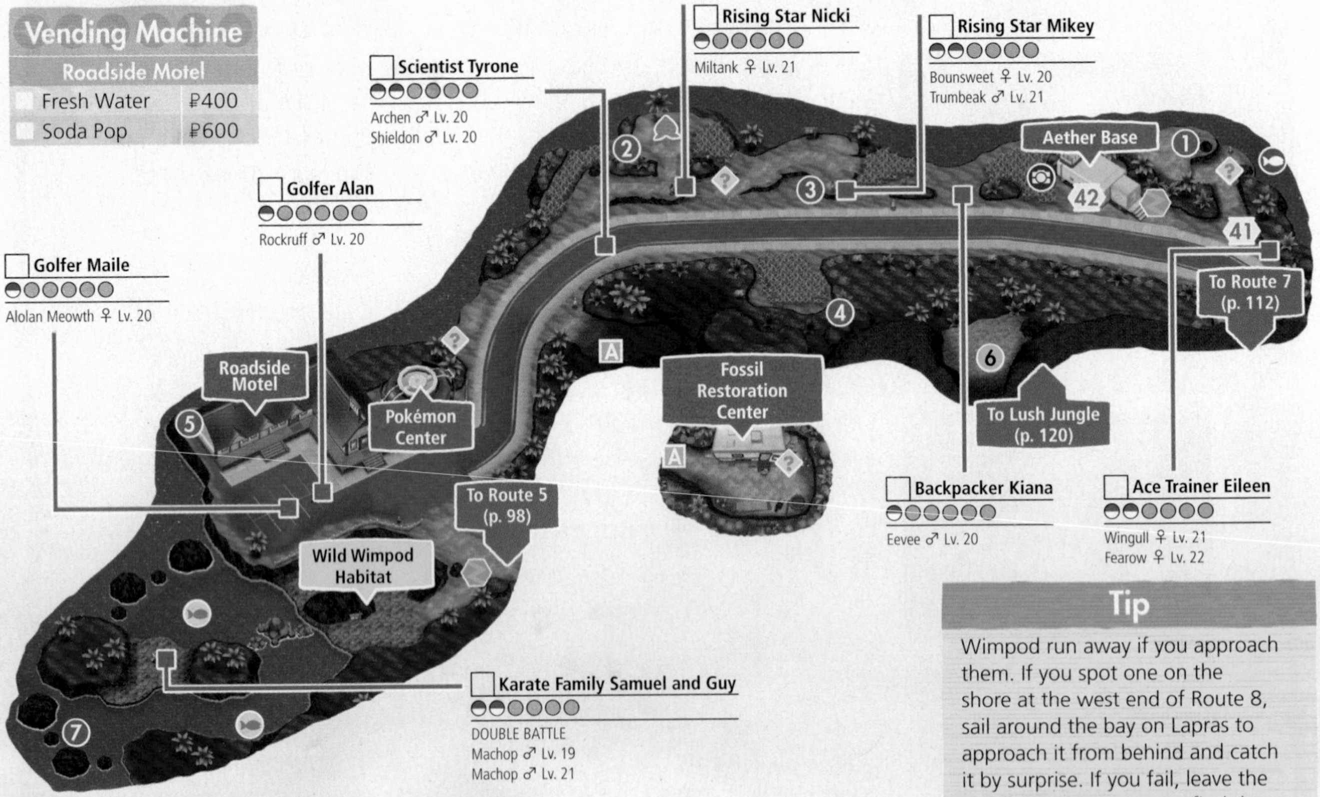

Rising Star Nicki
Miltank ♀ Lv. 21

Rising Star Mikey
Bounsweet ♀ Lv. 20
Trumbeak ♂ Lv. 21

Scientist Tyrone
Archen ♂ Lv. 20
Shieldon ♂ Lv. 20

Golfer Alan
Rockruff ♂ Lv. 20

Golfer Maile
Alolan Meowth ♀ Lv. 20

Aether Base

Roadside Motel

Pokémon Center

Fossil Restoration Center

Wild Wimpod Habitat

To Route 7 (p. 112)

To Lush Jungle (p. 120)

To Route 5 (p. 98)

Backpacker Kiana
Eevee ♂ Lv. 20

Ace Trainer Eileen
Wingull ♀ Lv. 21
Fearow ♀ Lv. 22

Karate Family Samuel and Guy
DOUBLE BATTLE
Machop ♂ Lv. 19
Machop ♂ Lv. 21

Tip

Wimpod run away if you approach them. If you spot one on the shore at the west end of Route 8, sail around the bay on Lapras to approach it from behind and catch it by surprise. If you fail, leave the area once then return to find the Wimpod back on the shore.

S41: Battle a strong Trainer

Route 8 features another competitive Trainer who will only accept your challenge after you've beaten all other Trainers on the route.

Reward: TM58 Sky Drop

S42: Catch and show Stufful

One of the staff in the Aether Base near Route 8's east end seeks information on a rare Pokémon—Stufful. Catch one in Route 8's tall grass, then show off your Pokédex to receive your payment.

Reward: ₽5,000

1 Meet Colress and receive a TM

Reward: TM43 Flame Charge

As you enter Route 8, you meet a mysterious scientist named Colress, who's visiting the Alola region. If you played *Pokémon Black 2* or *Pokémon White 2 Versions*, you may recall the pivotal role he played in those games. Colress gives you TM43 Flame Charge, which will come in handy when you get to Lush Jungle. Continue exploring Route 8's many hidden paths to find great items and Trainers to battle.

2 Visit the Dream Park

As you near Route 8's western end, follow a small side trail that leads east to a sheltered facility known as the Dream Park. Its humble appearance may not match its intriguing name, but the work they do here is indeed a dream—for here at the Dream Park, they restore old Fossils into real, living Pokémon!

Fossils

Located along Route 8, the Dream Park lets you restore the Fossils of ancient Pokémon back into living, breathing creatures. Visit Olivia's shop in Konikoni City (p. 128) to purchase Fossils for ₽7,000 apiece, then bring them to the Dream Park if you want the Pokémon that can be restored from the genetic material each Fossil contains.

3 Rest your Pokémon on the way to Lush Jungle

Take a break at the Pokémon Center to rest and restore your team. If you like, swing by the nearby Roadside Motel to see a familiar, unpleasant face. Finish your explorations of Route 8, then head east to reach the north end of Route 5 (p. 98), which you couldn't explore before. Raid Route 5 if you like, then head north into Lush Jungle—the site of your final trial here on Akala Island!

Lush Jungle

Ride Pokémon Needed   

Filled with tall grass and crawling with wild Pokémon, Lush Jungle is an excellent place to forage for delicious ingredients. It's located just north of Route 5 and serves as the site of Captain Mallow's trial.

Team Recommendations

FIRE · ELECTRIC · POISON · FLYING · BUG

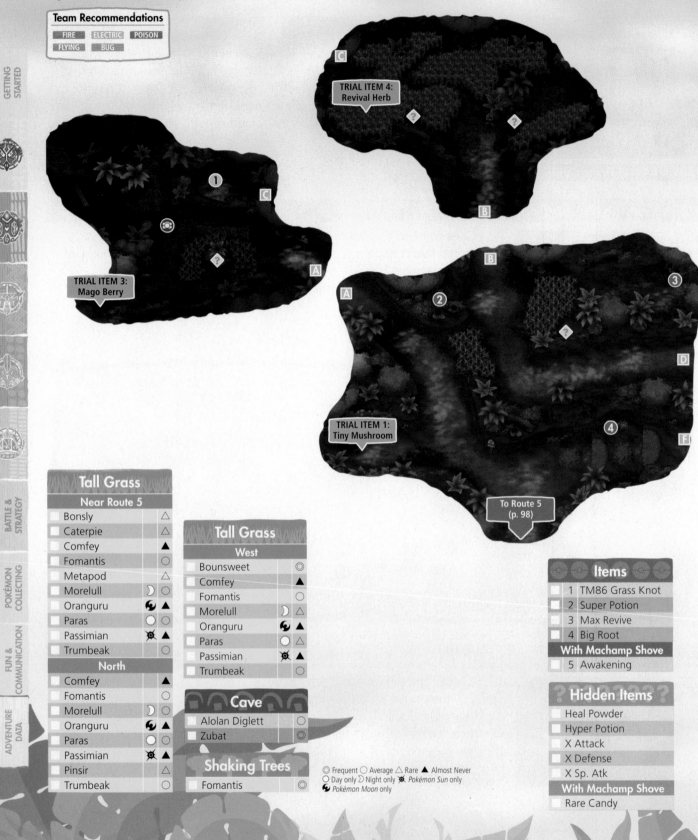

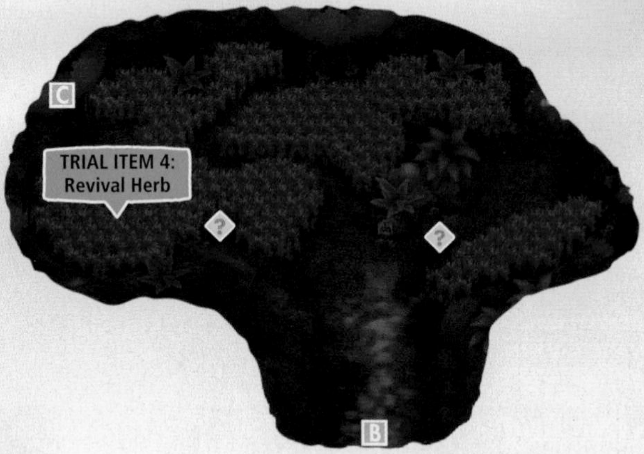

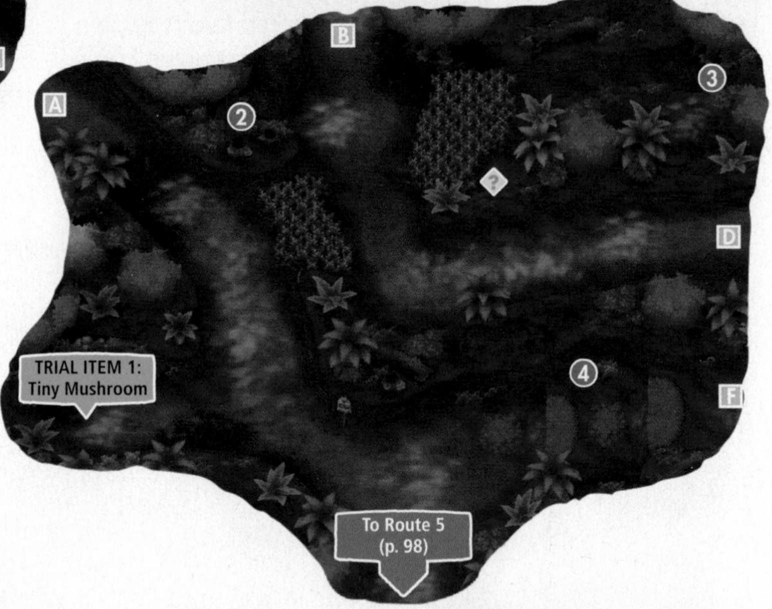

TRIAL ITEM 4: Revival Herb

TRIAL ITEM 3: Mago Berry

TRIAL ITEM 1: Tiny Mushroom

To Route 5 (p. 98)

Tall Grass

Near Route 5		
Bonsly		△
Caterpie		△
Comfey		▲
Fomantis		○
Metapod		△
Morelull	Night only	○
Oranguru	*Pokémon Moon* only	▲
Paras	Day only	○
Passimian	*Pokémon Sun* only	▲
Trumbeak		○

North		
Comfey		▲
Fomantis		○
Morelull	Night only	○
Oranguru	*Pokémon Moon* only	▲
Paras	Day only	○
Passimian	*Pokémon Sun* only	▲
Pinsir		△
Trumbeak		○

Tall Grass

West		
Bounsweet		◎
Comfey		▲
Fomantis		○
Morelull	Night only	△
Oranguru	*Pokémon Moon* only	▲
Paras	Day only	△
Passimian	*Pokémon Sun* only	▲
Trumbeak		○

Cave

Pokémon	Rate
Alolan Diglett	○
Zubat	◎

Shaking Trees

Pokémon	Rate
Fomantis	◎

◎ Frequent ○ Average △ Rare ▲ Almost Never
Day only · Night only · *Pokémon Sun* only
Pokémon Moon only

Items

1	TM86 Grass Knot
2	Super Potion
3	Max Revive
4	Big Root
With Machamp Shove	
5	Awakening

Hidden Items

Item
Heal Powder
Hyper Potion
X Attack
X Defense
X Sp. Atk
With Machamp Shove
Rare Candy

Special SOS Allies

Lush Jungle is one of the few places in Alola where weather conditions can affect the species of Pokémon allies that appear when wild Pokémon call for help (p. 63). If it's raining in Lush Jungle, Castform and Goomy might appear as SOS allies!

Weather	SOS allies
Rain	Castform (Rainy Form), Goomy, Politoed, Poliwhirl, Poliwrath, Sliggoo
Hail	Castform (Snowy Form), Vanillish, Vanillite
Sandstorm	Castform (Sunny Form), Gabite

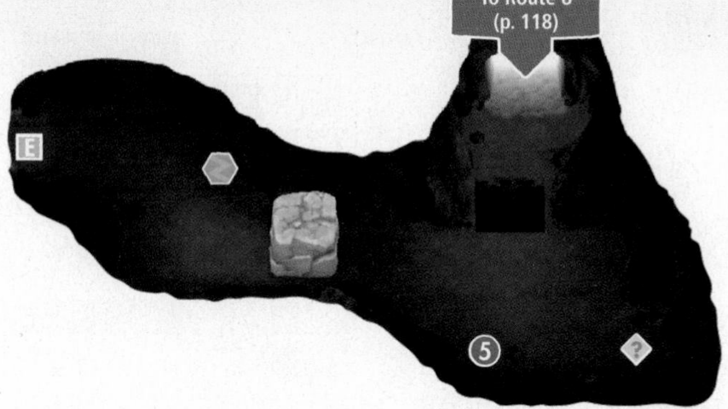

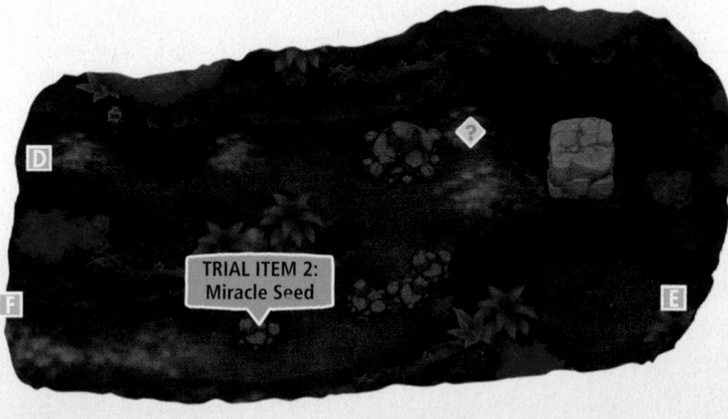

Tip

Notice the large moss-covered boulder in the northeast corner of this area? If you catch a Pokémon called Eevee (found on Route 6, p. 105) and it levels up near this boulder, it will evolve into a Grass-type Pokémon called Leafeon!

Tip

Before leaving Lush Jungle, try to catch a Passimian or an Oranguru. You'll soon meet someone who'll reward you for this important research!

1 Meet up with Mallow and learn of her trial

Reward: Forage Bag

Captain Mallow stands just inside of Lush Jungle, and she's eager for your help. Mallow asks that you gather a number of special ingredients from around Lush Jungle, as part of her trial. She hands you a Forage Bag to help you carry everything and hints that you'll need Stoutland's help to sniff out some of the ingredients. Let the hunt begin!

Trial Guide: Mallow's Trial

Take one part scavenger hunt and three parts battle, mix it all together—and you've got Mallow's trial! With the help of Stoutland, you'll be sniffing out ingredients all over Lush Jungle. Each ingredient you grab moves you closer to concocting a delicious dish that the jungle's Totem Pokémon can't resist. You'll be battling a variety of Grass-type Pokémon in the process, so pack your party full of Fire, Flying, and Bug types to gain every advantage.

1 Track down the Tiny Mushroom

Head left to the first branch in the path and spot some mushrooms growing on a log (use Stoutland to sniff them out). Choose the Tiny Mushroom that Mallow wanted, but look out—you'll get more than you bargained for!

Mallow's Trial Goals

- Find the four ingredients: Tiny Mushroom, Miracle Seed, Mago Berry, and Revival Herb
- Defeat the Totem Pokémon
- Receive the Z-Crystal from Captain Mallow

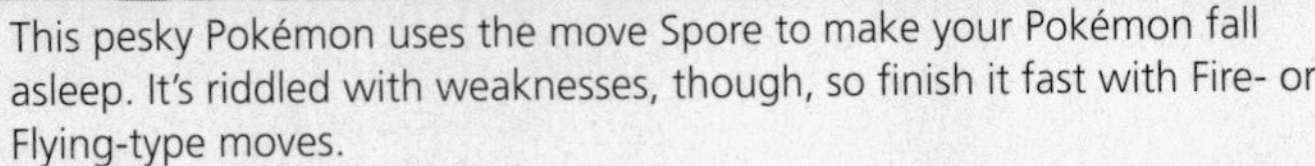

Parasect

This pesky Pokémon uses the move Spore to make your Pokémon fall asleep. It's riddled with weaknesses, though, so finish it fast with Fire- or Flying-type moves.

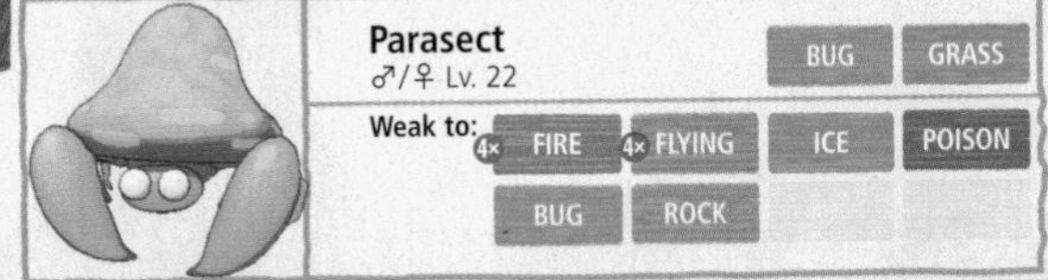

Parasect ♂/♀ Lv. 22 — BUG, GRASS

Weak to: 4× FIRE, 4× FLYING, ICE, POISON, BUG, ROCK

Shiinotic

Shiinotic can sap your Pokémon's HP with Mega Drain, while also restoring itself with Ingrain if you let it. Take care of it before it can set the situation up against you.

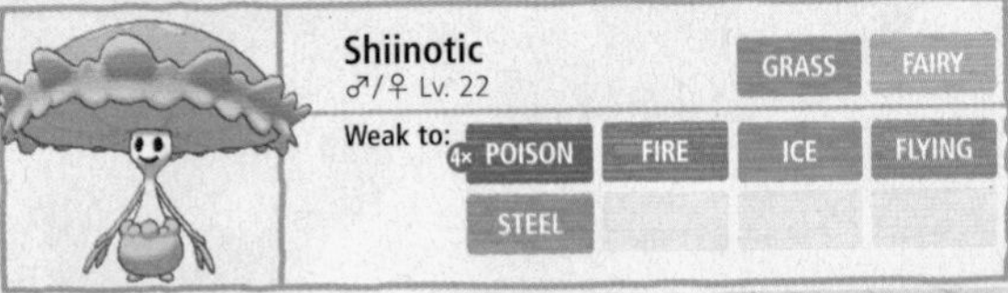

Shiinotic ♂/♀ Lv. 22 — GRASS, FAIRY

Weak to: 4× POISON, FIRE, ICE, FLYING, STEEL

2 Sniff out the Miracle Seed

Continue north, then go east through some tall grass to reach D. Head up the incline that follows to find some big rocks for Tauros to smash. Charge through the rocks, then nose through the debris with Stoutland to find Mallow's second ingredient: a Miracle Seed. Don't worry—nothing leaps out to battle you this time!

Tips

See that big, square boulder at the east end of the path? It's just like the one you might have seen back in Ten Carat Hill. When you get a Ride Pokémon that can push heavy boulders around (p. 38), return to these locations and discover what lies beyond!

3 Make off with the Mago Berry

Hop down the southern ledges, nabbing a Big Root as you go. Go north along the main path afterward, and when it forks, veer to the west through A to reach a small dead end with a tree that won't stop shaking. Defeat the Fomantis that hops out at you, then search beneath the tree to find Mallow's Mago Berry.

Fomantis

This little Pokémon uses Growth to boost its Attack and Sp. Atk, so don't give it a chance to power up. Target its many weaknesses with powerful moves, flattening Fomantis as fast as you can.

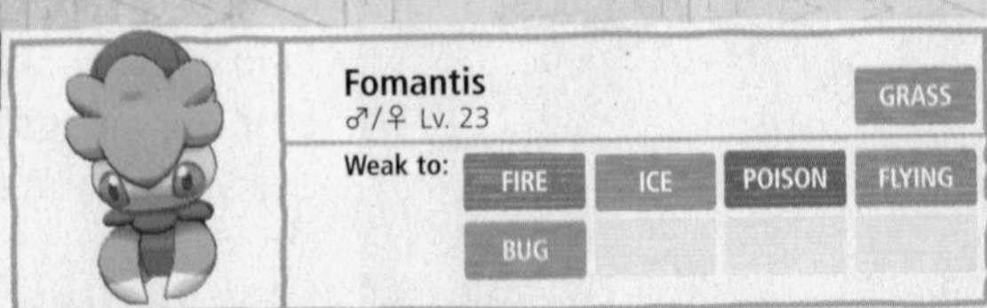

Fomantis ♂/♀ Lv. 23 — GRASS

Weak to: FIRE, ICE, POISON, FLYING, BUG

4 Uproot the Revival Herb

Return to the main path once more, and this time veer east at the fork to reach another dead end up north that's filled with tall grass. Sniff around with Stoutland to find several suspicious patches of grass—the Revival Herb grows to the west, at the spot where the tall grass is a bit shorter. Crawl through the small nearby hole to reach TM86 Grass Knot, then snatch up your Revival Herb and battle another Fomantis that ambushes you.

5 Help Mallow cook up some trouble

After you've found all four ingredients, return to the jungle's entrance and help Mallow create her culinary masterpiece. Captains Lana and Kiawe also join in the fun, supplying everything you need to make a meal worthy of a Totem Pokémon. Pound and mash all those ingredients to make the Mallow Special—a fragrant dish that draws out Totem Lurantis!

Totem Lurantis

Totem Lurantis's aura raises its Speed stat sharply. It attacks with X-Scissor and Razor Leaf, two powerful moves that aren't very effective against Fire types. It also uses Synthesis to heal, so don't think the battle's over when its HP gets low. Totem Lurantis can call for either Castform or Trumbeak as an ally. Castform uses Sunny Day, changing its type to Fire so that it takes less damage from Fire-type moves. Lurantis can also unleash a two-turn attack, Solar Blade.

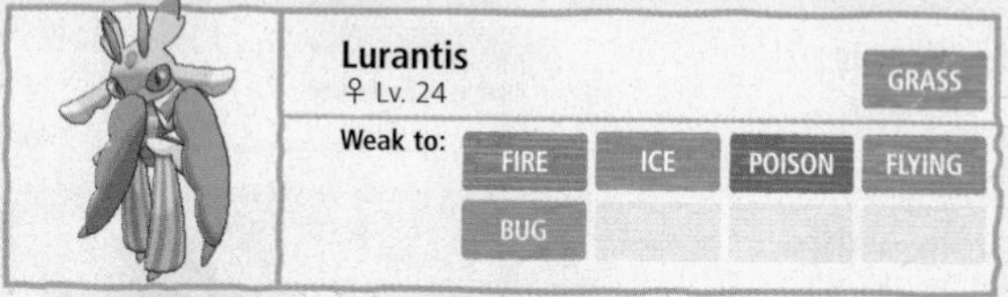

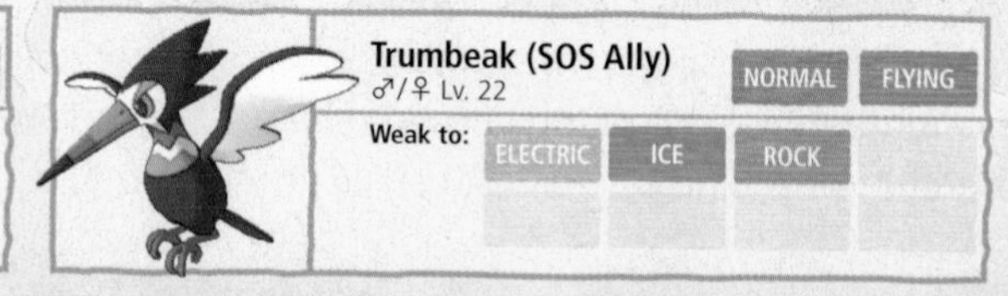

Trumbeak (SOS Ally)
♂/♀ Lv. 22
NORMAL
FLYING
Weak to:
ELECTRIC
ICE
ROCK

6 Receive the Grass Z-Crystal

Amazed at how you bested her trial, Mallow hands you Grassium Z and some Nest Balls. Professor Kukui also appears to congratulate you, hand you a TM, and invite you to visit the Dimensional Research Lab in Heahea City. Make your way south to Heahea City when you're ready to move on.

Reward: Grassium Z, Nest Ball ×10, TM67 Smart Strike

Route 5 / Route 4 / Heahea City Revisited

p. 98

1 Finish raiding Route 5 on your way to Heahea City

You could call Charizard and fly straight to Heahea City, but if you didn't already, take a moment to explore Route 5's (p. 98) northern half, which you couldn't reach before due to the route's many ledges. Check the little dens for wild Pokémon—or valuable items. Pick up any other items you find on the ground, battle some Trainers, nab another Zygarde Cell, then carry on to Paniola Ranch and then Heahea City, battling the competitive Trainer at Route 5's south end along the way.

Tip

If you explore the north end of Route 5 and defeat all the Trainers there, you'll finally be able to take on the tough Trainer at its south end who was waiting for you to beat everyone else first.

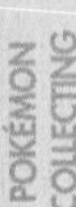

2 Meet Lillie in Heahea City

Head for the Dimensional Research Lab when you reach Heahea City, and you'll find Lillie outside, pretending to be a Trainer. Perhaps you're opening her eyes to the possibilities of Pokémon training? Enter the building after your chat (and after picking up another Zygarde Cell and a Big Mushroom outside), and take the elevator upstairs.

Burnet

Sorry, ladies—Professor Kukui is spoken for! His wife is Professor Burnet, a brilliant researcher whom you might recognize from *Pokémon Dream Radar*, where she was investigating a dimensional space known as the Interdream Zone. Her strong background in the studies of different dimensions has brought her to Alola, where local tales of so-called Ultra Wormholes appearing in the sky have piqued her interest. It's said that fearsome creatures appear from these Ultra Wormholes—the dreaded Ultra Beasts! Intent on unraveling the mystery surrounding Ultra Wormholes, Professor Burnet has set up the Dimensional Research Lab, where she and her colleagues work at studying and recording the known relationships between Pokémon and different dimensions.

Kukui
And she's also my wife!

3 Check out the lab, then head to Diglett's Tunnel

Chat with Burnet and the Dimensional Research Lab's staff and read the books on the shelves for more information. One researcher mentions a man named Mohn... Isn't that the man who runs the Poké Pelago? Talk to Lillie to learn more about her past, then speak with Professor Kukui, who's excited about your upcoming grand trial. Kukui advises you to head south through Diglett's Tunnel next.

Diglett's Tunnel

Ride Pokémon Needed  

Built by the might of many Diglett, this sizable passage connects Heahea City with Route 9 and Konikoni City. Recent troubles in the tunnel have made it a dangerous place for inexperienced Trainers to explore.

Items	Hidden Items	Cave		Dust Clouds	
1 Fire Stone	Escape Rope	Alolan Diglett	○	Alolan Diglett	◎
2 Dusk Ball	Nugget	Zubat	◎		
3 Hyper Potion	X Attack				

Team Recommendations
WATER ELECTRIC ICE GROUND

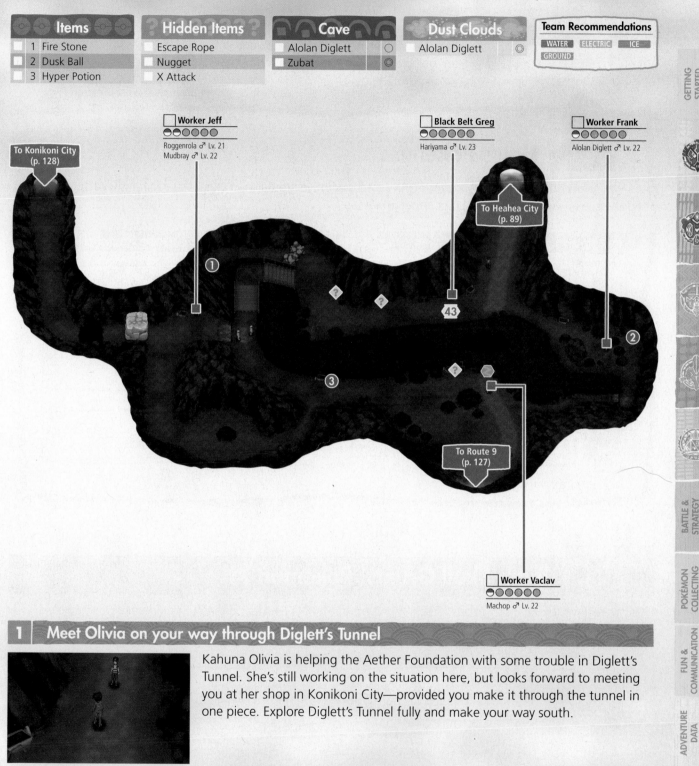

Worker Jeff
Roggenrola ♂ Lv. 21
Mudbray ♂ Lv. 22

Black Belt Greg
Hariyama ♂ Lv. 23

Worker Frank
Alolan Diglett ♂ Lv. 22

Worker Vaclav
Machop ♂ Lv. 22

To Konikoni City (p. 128)
To Heahea City (p. 89)
To Route 9 (p. 127)

1 2 3 43

1 Meet Olivia on your way through Diglett's Tunnel

Kahuna Olivia is helping the Aether Foundation with some trouble in Diglett's Tunnel. She's still working on the situation here, but looks forward to meeting you at her shop in Konikoni City—provided you make it through the tunnel in one piece. Explore Diglett's Tunnel fully and make your way south.

S43: Battle another tough Trainer

Confront another competitive Trainer in this tunnel who will only take you on after you defeat all the other Trainers to be found.

Reward: Max Revive

GETTING STARTED

BATTLE & STRATEGY
POKÉMON COLLECTING
FUN & COMMUNICATION
ADVENTURE DATA

2 Team up with Hau and defeat Team Skull

Those troublesome Team Skull Grunts lurk near the tunnel's south exit. They intend to gang up on you, but Hau arrives just in time to lend you a hand. Beat Team Skull with Hau's help in a Double Battle to send them scrambling off. Hau rewards you after the battle with a Max Ether to help keep your team going as you press onward into Route 9.

Reward: Max Ether

Tip

Diglett's Tunnel features another one of those strange square boulders. That means there's more to explore here after you gain the ability to push them around (p. 38).

Hau's Pokémon

Hau sends out Pikachu first, and primarily attacks with Electro Ball and Quick Attack. If his Pikachu faints, Hau will send out his first partner Pokémon.

If you choose Rowlet

Pokémon	Level	Type	Weak to
Brionne	♂ Lv. 24	WATER	GRASS, ELECTRIC
Pikachu	♂ Lv. 23	ELECTRIC	GROUND
Eevee	♂ Lv. 23	NORMAL	FIGHTING

If you choose Litten

Pokémon	Level	Type	Weak to
Dartrix	♂ Lv. 24	GRASS, FLYING	4× ICE, FIRE, POISON, FLYING, ROCK
Pikachu	♂ Lv. 23	ELECTRIC	GROUND
Eevee	♂ Lv. 23	NORMAL	FIGHTING

If you choose Popplio

Pokémon	Level	Type	Weak to
Torracat	♂ Lv. 24	FIRE	WATER, GROUND, ROCK
Pikachu	♂ Lv. 23	ELECTRIC	GROUND
Eevee	♂ Lv. 23	NORMAL	FIGHTING

Team Skull Grunts' Pokémon

You've recently battled the species of Pokémon sent out by the Grunts, so there's nothing new to see here. Since this is a Double Battle, try to damage both Grunts' Pokémon at once with moves that affect all opposing Pokémon, like Air Cutter and Bulldoze.

Pokémon	Level	Type	Weak to
Salandit	♂ Lv. 22	POISON, FIRE	4× GROUND, WATER, PSYCHIC, ROCK
Fomantis	♀ Lv. 22	GRASS	FIRE, ICE, POISON, FLYING, BUG

Route 9

Short and sweet, Route 9 connects Diglett's Tunnel and Memorial Hill to the nearby Konikoni City.

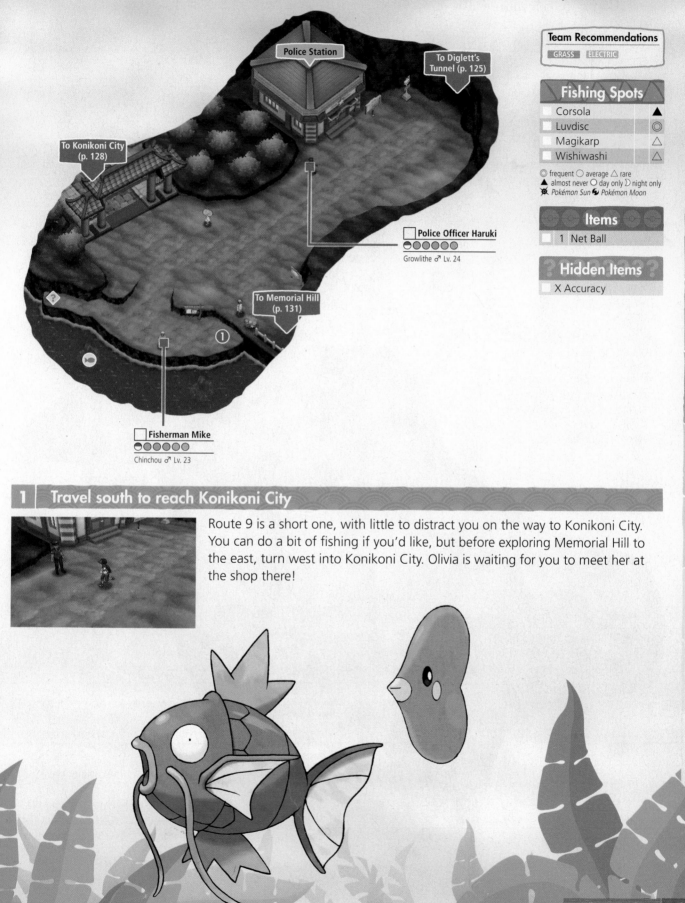

Police Station

To Diglett's Tunnel (p. 125)

To Konikoni City (p. 128)

To Memorial Hill (p. 131)

①

Police Officer Haruki
Growlithe ♂ Lv. 24

Fisherman Mike
Chinchou ♂ Lv. 23

Team Recommendations

Fishing Spots	
Corsola	▲
Luvdisc	◎
Magikarp	△
Wishiwashi	△

◎ frequent ○ average △ rare
▲ almost never ☼ day only ☽ night only
Pokémon Sun *Pokémon Moon*

Items	
1	Net Ball

Hidden Items
X Accuracy

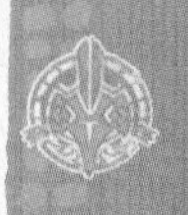

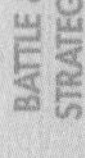

1 Travel south to reach Konikoni City

Route 9 is a short one, with little to distract you on the way to Konikoni City. You can do a bit of fishing if you'd like, but before exploring Memorial Hill to the east, turn west into Konikoni City. Olivia is waiting for you to meet her at the shop there!

Konikoni City

Ride Pokémon Needed

Konikoni City is a small yet bustling port town that's filled with specialty shops and vendors. Take time to browse and stock up on curious and useful items like TMs, Evolution stones, fossils, herbs, and incense.

Poké Mart

Normal Wares	
Adrenaline Orb	₽300
Antidote	₽200
Awakening	₽100
Burn Heal	₽300
Escape Rope	₽1,000
Great Ball	₽600
Honey	₽300
Hyper Potion	₽1,500
Ice Heal	₽100
Paralyze Heal	₽300
Poké Ball	₽200
Potion	₽200
Repel	₽400
Revive	₽2,000
Super Potion	₽700
Super Repel	₽700
Ultra Ball	₽800

TM Shop

Item	Price
TM08 Bulk Up	₽10,000
TM09 Venoshock	₽10,000
TM32 Double Team	₽10,000
TM47 Low Sweep	₽10,000
TM65 Shadow Claw	₽10,000
TM82 Dragon Tail	₽10,000

Olivia's Jewelry Shop

Younger Clerk	
Fire Stone	₽3,000
Leaf Stone	₽3,000
Thunder Stone	₽3,000
Water Stone	₽3,000
Older Clerk	
Armor Fossil	₽7,000
Cover Fossil	₽7,000
Plume Fossil	₽7,000
Skull Fossil	₽7,000

Herb Seller

Item	Price
Energy Powder	₽500
Energy Root	₽1,200
Heal Powder	₽300
Revival Herb	₽2,800

Incense Shop

Item	Price
Full Incense	₽5,000
Lax Incense	₽5,000
Luck Incense	₽11,000
Odd Incense	₽2,000
Pure Incense	₽6,000
Rock Incense	₽2,000
Rose Incense	₽2,000
Sea Incense	₽2,000
Wave Incense	₽2,000

Items

1	Eviolite
With Machamp Shove	
2	TM61 Will-O-Wisp

Hidden Items

With Machamp Shove
Big Pearl

Tip

Konikoni City has a whole shop dedicated to TMs. Check it out if you're in the market for some wicked moves for your upcoming trials.

Tip

Check out Olivia's studio flat upstairs from her shop and find a Zygarde Core in the kitchen!

1 Explore Konikoni City and visit Olivia's shop

Stroll down Route 9 and turn right to find Konikoni City: a bustling market town with plenty of shops to explore. Stop by each shop and stall as you make your way through town, and maybe even swing by the salon and apparel shop to freshen up your look. Visit Olivia's shop to discover a letter she left with her Probopass. You'll get an item from it and instructions to meet Olivia at the nearby Ruins of Life.

Reward: Max Potion

Incense

Incenses are useful items that bestow special effects to the Pokémon that hold them. Some can power up certain types of moves, while others have special effects outside of battle. Incenses can even help you find special Pokémon Eggs (p. 288) if you give them to certain Pokémon to hold when you leave them at the Pokémon Nursery (p. 95).

Incense	Effect
Full Incense	Makes the holder move later in battle. / Give to a Snorlax to find a Munchlax Egg.
Lax Incense	May cause attacks to miss the holder. / Give to a **Wobbuffet** to find a Wynaut Egg.
Luck Incense	Doubles any prize money received if the holder joins a battle. / Give to a Chansey or Blissey to find a Happiny Egg.
Odd Incense	Boosts the power of Psychic-type moves. / Give to a **Mr. Mime** to find a Mime Jr. Egg.
Pure Incense	Helps keep wild Pokémon away if the holder is the head of the party. / Give to a **Chimecho** to find a Chingling.
Rock Incense	Boosts the power of Rock-type moves. / Give to a Sudowoodo to find a Bonsly Egg.
Rose Incense	Boosts the power of Grass-type moves. / Give to a **Roselia** or **Roserade** to find a Budew Egg.
Sea Incense	Boosts the power of Water-type moves. / Give to a **Marill** or **Azumarill** to find an Azurill Egg.
Wave Incense	Boosts the power of Water-type moves. / Give to a **Mantine** to find a Mantyke Egg.

* Pokémon in **bold** can be obtained from another game by using *Pokémon Bank* (p. 316) or by receiving them in a trade (p. 306).

Olivia's Jewelry Shop

Olivia's isn't just Akala Island's kahuna—she's also the owner of a prominent jewelry shop here in Konikoni City. Each of her shop's clerks has special items to sell. The lady in front of the cash register sells Evolution stones. These special stones can make certain species of Pokémon evolve. To make one of the Pokémon in the list below evolve, simply use an appropriate stone on the Pokémon. It will instantly evolve!

Item	Price	Pokémon that evolve with the stone
Fire Stone	₽3,000	Growlithe, **Vulpix***, Eevee, **Pansear****
Leaf Stone	₽3,000	Exeggcute, **Gloom**, **Weepinbell**, **Nuzleaf**, **Pansage**
Thunder Stone	₽3,000	Pikachu, Eevee, **Eelektrik**
Water Stone	₽3,000	Shellder, Poliwhirl, Staryu, Eevee, **Lombre**, **Panpour**

*Alolan Vulpix needs an Ice Stone to evolve into Alolan Ninetales.

Pokémon in **bold can be obtained by transferring them from another game using *Pokémon Bank* (p. 316) or by receiving them in a trade (p. 306).

If you're playing as a female character, then another clerk stands to the right of the cashier. She sells the items listed on page 297. Sorry, boys, her special accessories are only for girls! But the older woman sells Fossils to anyone as long as they are in stock. After you've bought one, bring it to Dream Park on Route 8 (p. 119) to have it restored into a living Pokémon!

Lomi Lomi Massage

Alola is all about good times and pampering, and there's no better way to pamper your Pokémon than a lomi lomi massage! Speak to the lady next to the incense vendor in Konikoni City, and she'll give your lead Pokémon a free massage, but only once per day. Massages make your Pokémon feel more friendly toward you, and friendly Pokémon may have special benefits.

Friendly Pokémon May Evolve

Many species of Pokémon evolve when they level up while they're on friendly terms with you. The following Pokémon can be obtained in Alola, and they each evolve when they level up with high friendship:

Chansey, Cleffa, Golbat, Igglybuff, Munchlax, Pichu, Riolu*, and Type: Null

*Riolu evolves with high friendship during the daytime.

Friendly Pokémon May Learn Moves

If certain Pokémon are friendly toward you, they can learn special moves, including battle-combo moves, the strongest Dragon-type move, and the ultimate moves for final Evolutions of your first partner Pokémon. Visit the Move Tutors in Hau'oli City's shopping mall (p. 81) when your Pokémon are ready to learn these moves.

Tip

Curious if your Pokémon is friendly toward you? Speak with the lady near the TM Shop here in Konikoni City—she has a knack for detecting friendship. And be careful using the herbs that are sold here, too. They may heal your Pokémon in a pinch, but they lower their friendship, too!

S44: Fill up on Heart Scales

Stop in at Mallow's family restaurant for a meal. Whatever you order is sure to be scrumptious, and you'll get a little after-meal treat: some Heart Scales!

Reward: Heart Scale ×2

S45: Procure Pikanium Z

Talk to the woman near the crowd of Pikachu at the far end of town, and she'll hand you a piece of Pikanium Z. It's a special Z-Crystal that's just for Pikachu! Talk to the woman again, and she'll offer to teach your Pikachu a powerful move known as Volt Tackle. Teach Pikachu this move, and you'll be able to use its exclusive Z-Move!

Reward: Pikanium Z

S46: Trade for Poliwhirl

Inside Konikoni City's Pokémon Center, you can trade for a Poliwhirl if you have a Zubat to share. Poliwhirl can evolve into two different Pokémon: Poliwrath or Politoed (p. 284). If you don't have a Zubat to trade, go to nearby Memorial Hill and catch one.

Pokémon: Poliwhirl

S47: Divulge some data

Catch a Passimian or an Oranguru back in Lush Jungle, then help out another Aether Foundation employee here in the Konikoni City Pokémon Center by showing him its Pokédex data.

Reward: ₽5,000

Memorial Hill / Akala Outskirts / Ruins of Life

Ride Pokémon Needed 

A maze-like graveyard, Memorial Hill is a sacred place where Akala's ancestors have been laid to rest. To the east lies the Akala Outskirts: a small area that borders the shore and leads to the Ruins of Life.

Items

Akala Outskirts
1 TM28 Leech Life
Memorial Hill
2 Spell Tag
3 Dusk Ball
4 Hyper Potion
5 Cleanse Tag

Hidden Items

Akala Outskirts
Big Mushroom
Tiny Mushroom 2
Memorial Hill
Revival Herb
Super Repel
Adrenaline Orb
Heal Powder

Tall Grass

Akala Outskirts	
Gumshoos	day only ○ average
Nosepass	△ rare
Alolan Raticate	night only ○ average
Stufful	▲ almost never
Wingull	◎ frequent
Memorial Hill	
Gastly	◎ frequent
Phantump	○ average
Zubat	○ average

Fishing Spots

Akala Outskirts	
Chinchou	▲
Magikarp	◎
Wishiwashi	○

◎ frequent ○ average
△ rare ▲ almost never
○ day only ☽ night only

Team Recommendations

ELECTRIC FIGHTING PSYCHIC DARK

Rare Fishing Spots

Akala Outskirts	
Chinchou	○
Magikarp	◎
Wishiwashi	○

Gentleman Smith
Umbreon ♂ Lv. 23

Punk Girl Melissa
Ariados ♀ Lv. 23

Preschooler Liam
Jigglypuff ♀ Lv. 21
Ledian ♂ Lv. 22

Madame Sayuri
Comfey ♀ Lv. 23

Black Belt Kenji
Hariyama ♂ Lv. 24

Fisherman Vernon
Staryu Lv. 23
Gyarados ♂ Lv. 23

Akala Outskirts

To Ruins of Life (p. 132)

To Route 9 (p. 127)

Memorial Hill

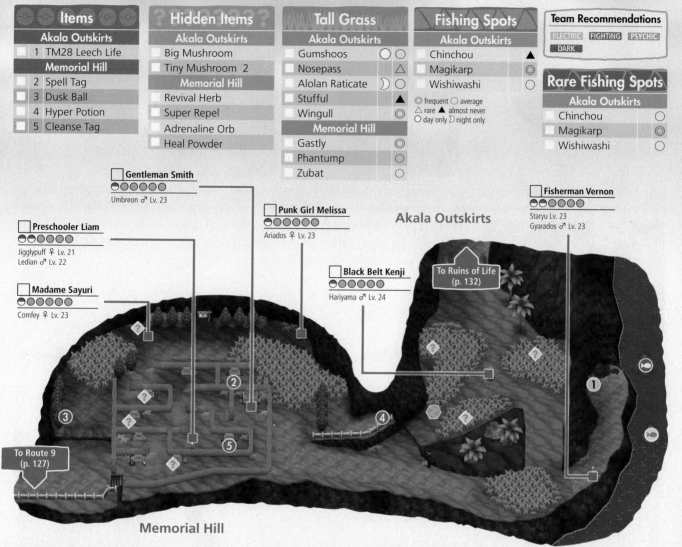

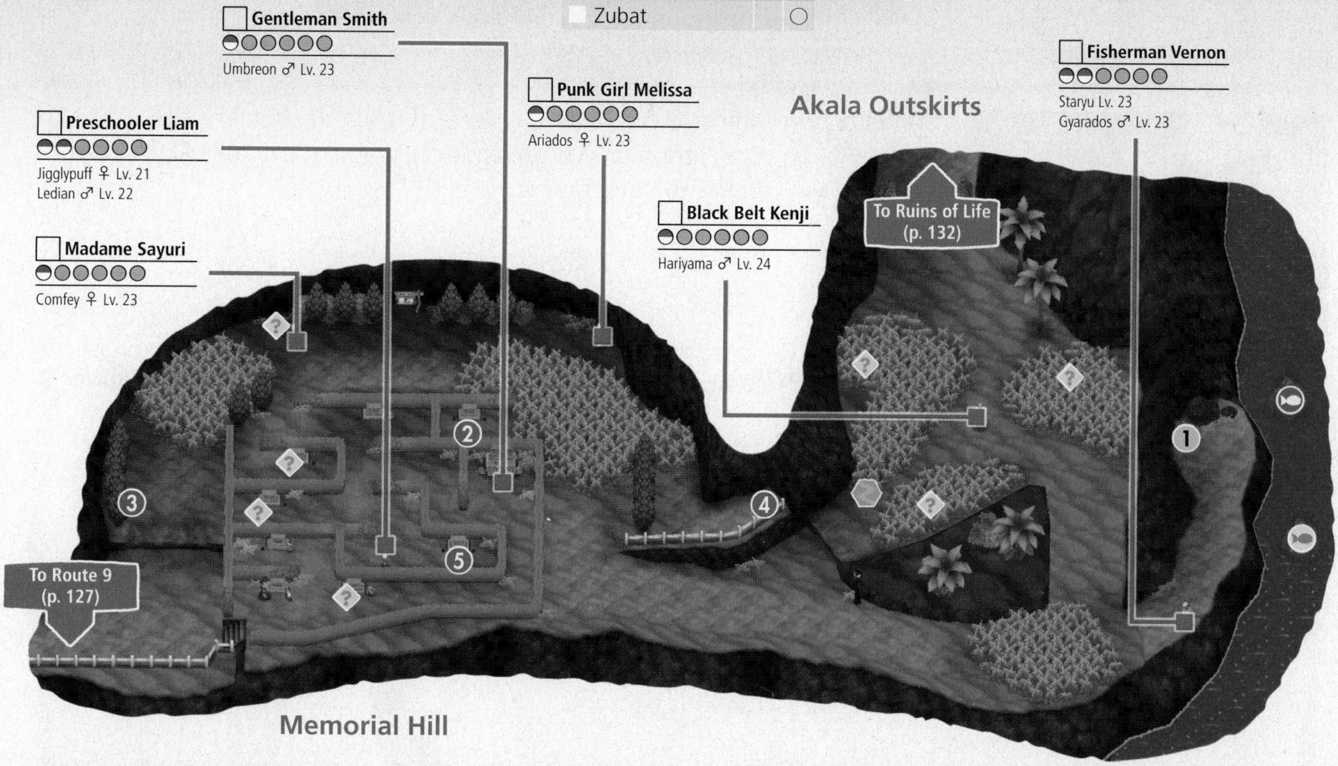

1 Battle Team Skull

Make your way through Memorial Hill, collecting items and battling the Trainers who have come to pay their respects to their ancestors. As you near the Akala Outskirts, you stumble upon some Aether Foundation members who are about to tussle with Team Skull. Lend them a hand, and the mysterious man with green glasses from the Aether Foundation will invite you to meet him at the Hano Grand Resort later. Sounds too good to pass up!

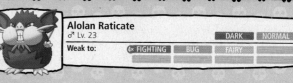

Team Skull Grunt's Pokémon

This Grunt sends out Alolan Raticate, and it can inflict some serious damage with its Hyper Fang. Light it up with Fighting-type moves to end the battle fast.

Alolan Raticate
♂ Lv. 23
DARK NORMAL
Weak to: 4× FIGHTING, BUG, FAIRY

Ruins of Life

2 Meet and battle Team Skull Admin Plumeria

Continue north through the Akala Outskirts to reach the Ruins of Life. Just before you get there, though, you are ambushed again! It's Team Skull again, but someone you haven't met before.

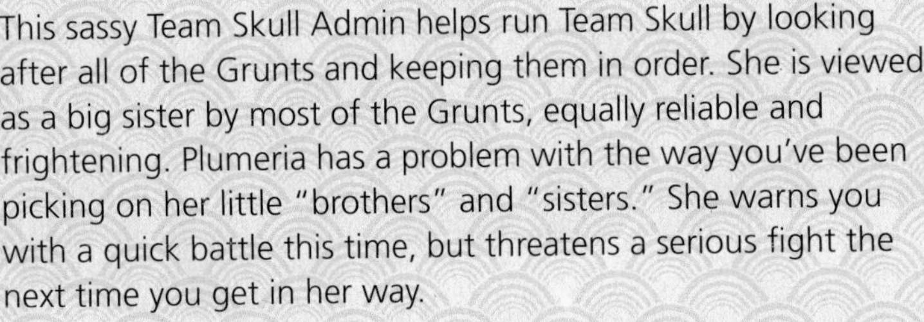

Plumeria

This sassy Team Skull Admin helps run Team Skull by looking after all of the Grunts and keeping them in order. She is viewed as a big sister by most of the Grunts, equally reliable and frightening. Plumeria has a problem with the way you've been picking on her little "brothers" and "sisters." She warns you with a quick battle this time, but threatens a serious fight the next time you get in her way.

Team Skull Admin Plumeria's Pokémon

Plumeria's Golbat uses Confuse Ray, and her Salandit uses Poison Gas, so be prepared to cure these conditions. Try to exploit their common weaknesses by using Psychic- and Rock-type moves.

Golbat ♀ Lv. 25	POISON	FLYING		
Weak to:	ELECTRIC	ICE	PSYCHIC	ROCK

Salandit ♀ Lv. 26	POISON	FIRE		
Weak to:	4× GROUND	WATER	PSYCHIC	ROCK

Be prepared, because continuing ahead to the Ruins of Life will pit you in battle against Kahuna Olivia! Your Pokémon will be healed for you before the battle, but be sure you've got the right team together to take on this grand trial.

Grand Trial: Island Kahuna Olivia

Like Kahuna Hala, all of Olivia's Pokémon are of the same type—in Olivia's case, they're all Rock-type Pokémon. Her team is therefore easy to counter, provided you've brought the appropriate Pokémon to exploit their many shared weaknesses. Targeting their weaknesses is key, for Rock-type Pokémon are quite resilient, even when struck by supereffective moves.

Alolan Diglett, which can be caught in—surprise!—Diglett's Tunnel, is excellent against Olivia, especially if it has evolved into a formidable Dugtrio. The Ground-type moves these Pokémon can unleash, like Sand Tomb and Mud Bomb, are super effective against Olivia's whole team, and many of the moves used by Olivia's Pokémon won't be very effective against them. Fighting-type Pokémon also enjoy these same advantages against Olivia's team, and you can give them Fightinium Z to unleash a powerful Z-Move.

Kahuna Olivia's Pokémon

Olivia's Nosepass attacks with Rock Slide, and her Boldore uses Headbutt—two moves that aren't very effective against Diglett. Her Nosepass may also paralyze your Pokémon with Thunder Wave—it can be a real shock to even any Water types you might have brought along. Her Lycanroc's Bite deals normal damage, however, and is perhaps the greatest threat you face in this battle. Olivia has a single Super Potion to use, so expect her to restore one of her Pokémon's HP during the clash. Heal your Pokémon as needed, and don't relent until the kahuna's whole team has been reduced to rubble!

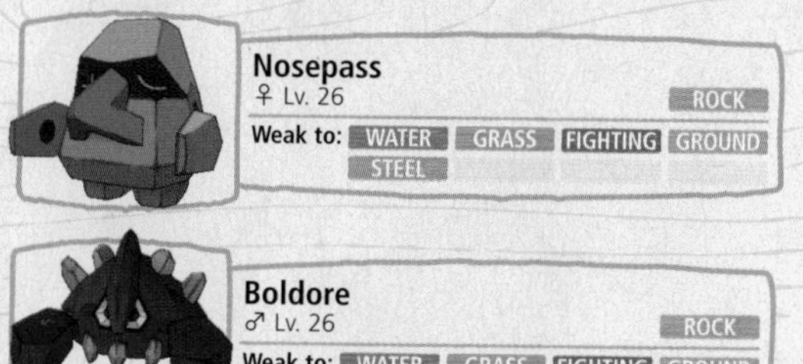

Nosepass
♀ Lv. 26
ROCK
Weak to: WATER GRASS FIGHTING GROUND STEEL
Boldore
♂ Lv. 26
ROCK
Weak to: WATER GRASS FIGHTING GROUND STEEL

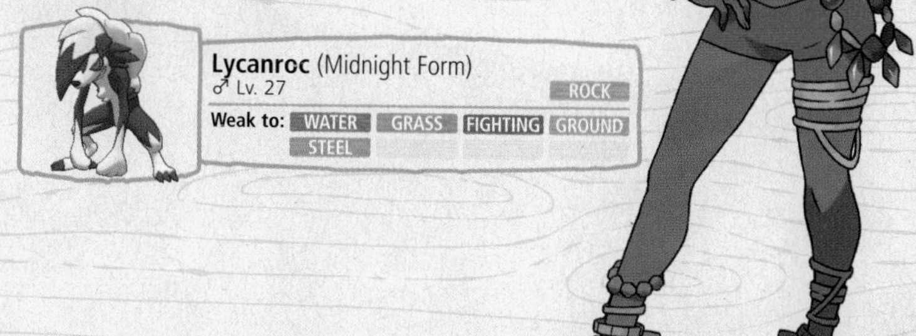

Lycanroc (Midnight Form)
♂ Lv. 27
ROCK
Weak to: WATER GRASS FIGHTING GROUND STEEL

Receive a Z-Crystal, then head for Hano

Reward: Rockium Z

You've completed your grand trial here on Akala Island, and Olivia rewards your show of strength with the Rock-type Z-Crystal, Rockium Z. Hau soon arrives with news that he's also received an invitation from the mysterious man from the Aether Foundation, whom you met just before your battle with Plumeria. Since more of those pesky big boulders prevent you from exploring the Ruins of Life, the Hano Grand Resort is your next stop: run or fly back to Heahea City, then head east to check it out! There's definitely something special about this place, though, so you'll have to return here later.

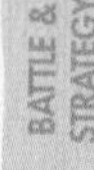

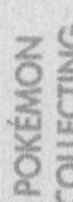

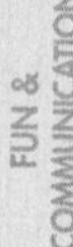

Hano Grand Resort / Hano Beach

Ride Pokémon Needed

The grandest resort in all of Alola, Hano attracts wealthy and famous vacationers from regions near and far. The place is so popular that its rooms are booked a full year in advance.

Items	
1	Pearl String
2	Black Glasses
3	Dive Ball
4	Antidote

Hidden Items
Heart Scale ×2
Pearl ×3
Soda Pop

Water Splashes	
Tentacool	◎

Water Surface	
Finneon	○
Pyukumuku	○
Tentacool	○
Wingull	○

Sand Clouds	
Sandygast	○
Staryu	◎

◎ frequent ○ average △ rare ▲ almost never ☼ day only ☽ night only *Pokémon Sun* *Pokémon Moon*

Team Recommendations

GRASS ELECTRIC

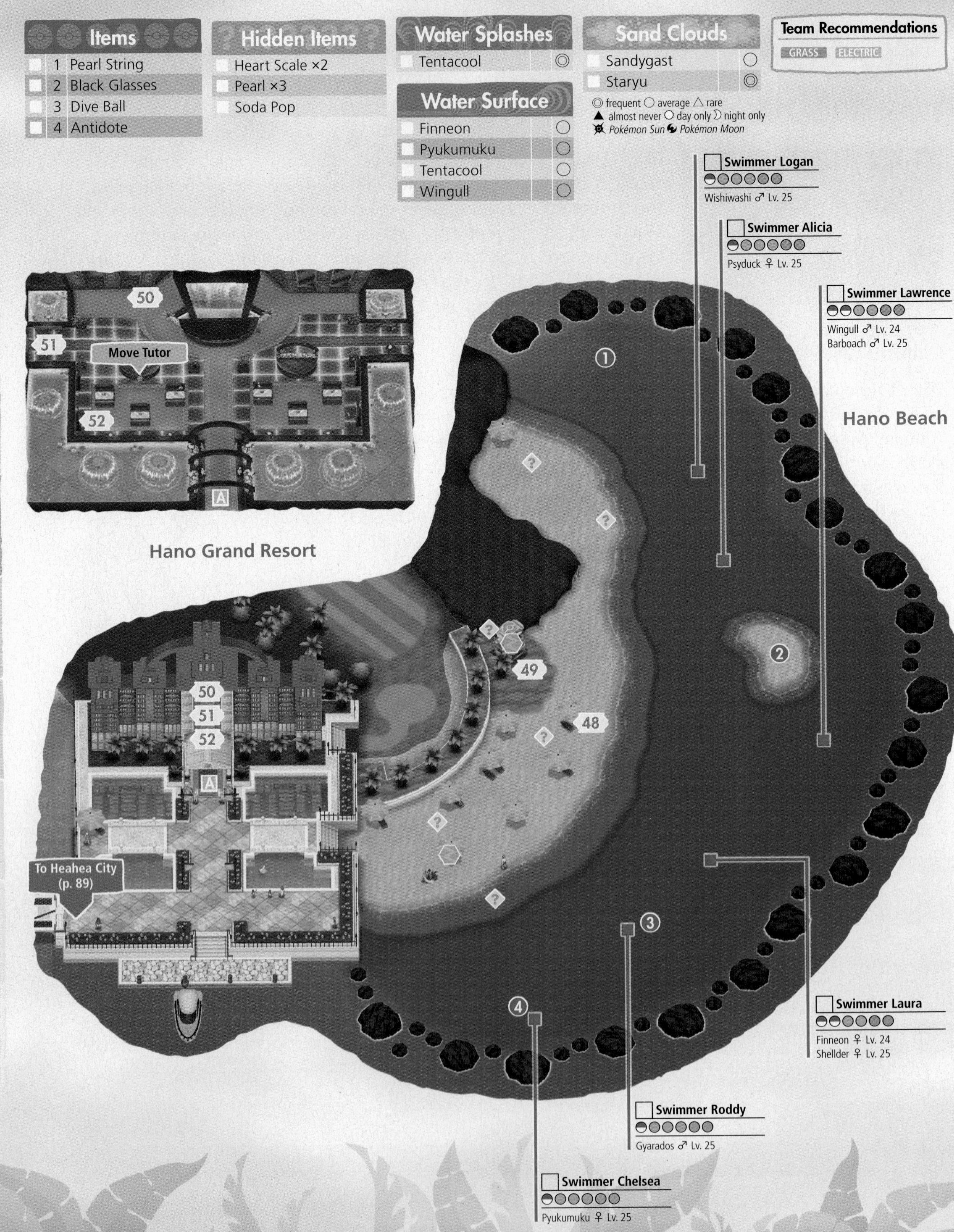

1 Explore the Hano Grand Resort

Have a look around the Hano Grand Resort's impressive grounds before heading into the hotel itself. You can also swim across the bay and battle Trainers, or explore the far end of the beach to find some Pokémon burrowed in the sand.

S48: Suck down a Soda Pop

One generous lady on the beach will give you a cool, refreshing Soda Pop.

Reward: Soda Pop

S49: Do some side work

Talk to the hotel bellhop near the lifeguard station if you're looking for some side work as a Pyukumuku chucker. The pay is great! If you can't find all the Pyukumuku to chuck back in the sea, keep an eye on the shore where the waves come crashing in—they sometimes hide in the shallows.

Reward: ₽20,000

Tip

If you catch a Pyukumuku of your own, remember to show its Pokédex entry to the man you met in Heahea City's apparel shop for a cash reward of ₽10,000!

Tip

All sorts of items have sunk to the bottom of the bay here at Hano, so hop on Lapras and scan the water thoroughly. Just watch out for signs of furious splashing, for you may be ambushed by wild Pokémon!

2 Meet Faba inside the hotel

The mysterious man with green glasses from the Aether Foundation awaits inside the hotel. This time, he introduces himself as Faba. He offers to take you to the famed Aether Paradise (p. 139), but there are still a number of things to do around Akala Island. Say "Yes" if you wish to continue with the story, or "No" if you'd like to continue exploring Akala. Faba will still be waiting for you here whenever you're ready to move on.

S50: Face the Future

At the back of the hotel's lobby, a man who calls himself Future will give you a Metronome if you battle him.

Reward: Metronome

S51: Help out Machamp

Try to save a poor Machamp caddy from some overzealous golfers, and you'll end up with a Double Battle on your hands—and a TM, if you're victorious!

Reward: TM45 Attract

Tip

If you have Keldeo or Meloetta in your team, talk to the gentleman next to Meowth. He can teach either Pokémon a special move—Sacred Sword to Keldeo and Relic Song to Meloetta. Keldeo changes into Resolute Form after learning Sacred Sword. Meloetta changes temporarily into its Pirouette Forme when it uses Relic Song during a battle.

S52: Receive a Ribbon

Show the Pokémon Breeder in the lobby's southwest corner a Pokémon that has leveled up by 30 or more levels since you first met it, and he'll hand it a nifty Footprint Ribbon.

Reward: Footprint Ribbon

Before You Leave Akala Island

The excitement of Aether Paradise beckons, but there's still more to do around Akala Island. Read on if you're up for some profitable ventures, or skip to page 139 to find out what awaits you at Aether Paradise.

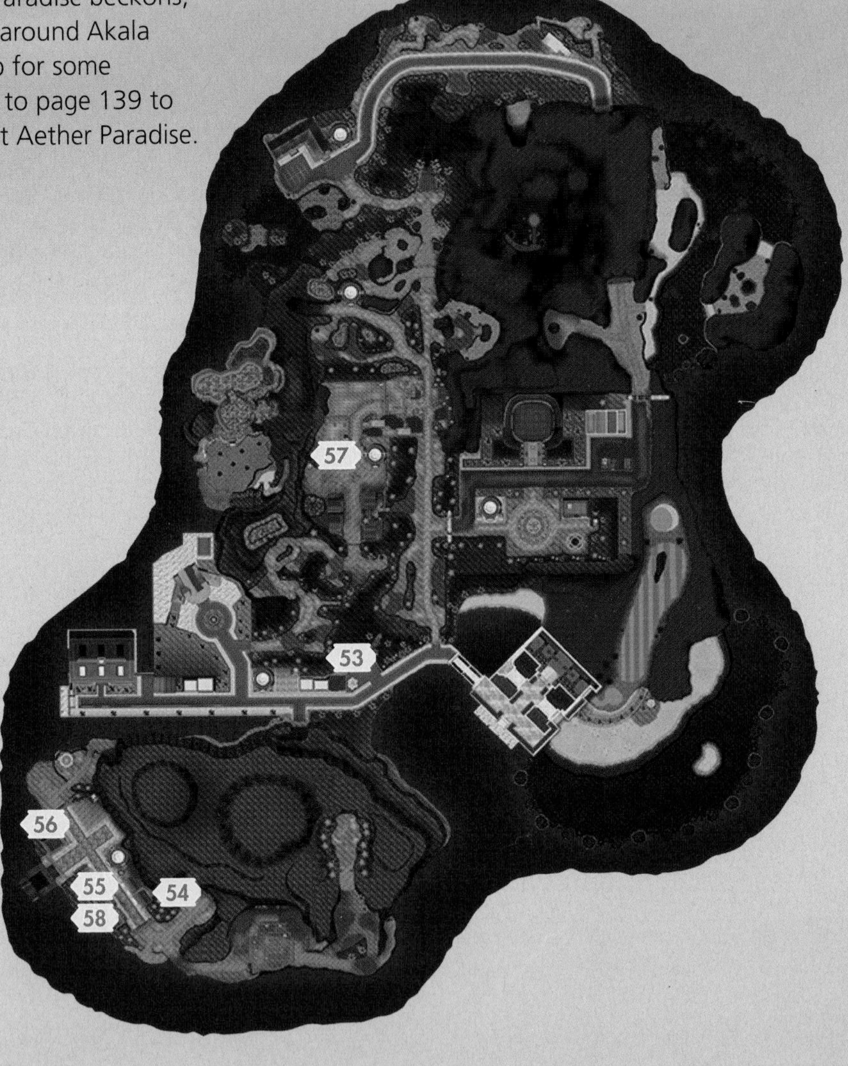

57

53

56

55

54

58

S53: Get a Reveal Glass

Head to Heahea City and pay Professor Burnet a visit at the Dimensional Research Lab. She'll give you a Reveal Glass as a reward for defeating Olivia. It's an item for the Legendary Pokémon Thundurus, Landorus, and Tornadus.

Reward: Reveal Glass

S54: Lock down a Focus Band

Pop by the police station on Route 9 to find the front desk officer a bit more eager to see you. Keep chatting with him, and he'll confide in you the truth about him and his Pokémon partner—and send you off with a Focus Band!

Reward: Focus Band

S55: Eat a special meal and get Heart Scales for dessert

Order the special Z-set meal from Mallow's family restaurant in Konikoni City, and you'll dine with company! Olivia will appear and treat you to a meal on her. She'll even give you her Heart Scales after you've eaten!

Reward: Heart Scale ×4

S56: Battle Captain Lana

Swing by Lana's house in Konikoni City and let yourself into her bedroom. Lana isn't around, but her two little sisters, Harper and Sarah, will challenge you to a Double Battle. Like Lana, they prefer to use Water-type Pokémon, so be prepared. Lana arrives afterward and, at her sisters' insistence, challenges you to another battle—one that's quite a bit more challenging! Defeat Lana to receive a special gift.

Reward: Muscle Band

Twins Harper and Sarah's Pokémon

Since this is a Double Battle, the first two Pokémon in your team are sent out to battle side-by-side against the twins. Prepare your party accordingly before accepting the battle, and try to use moves that affect all opposing Pokémon at once (p. 260).

Luvdisc
♀ Lv. 24 — WATER
Weak to: GRASS, ELECTRIC

Corsola
♀ Lv. 24 — WATER, ROCK
Weak to: 4× GRASS, ELECTRIC, FIGHTING, GROUND

Captain Lana's Pokémon

Lana's team share similar weaknesses, but they also have some surprises in store. Chinchou has the Volt Absorb Ability, so Electric-type moves won't affect it. Araquanid is holding a Z-Crystal, letting Lana unleash a mighty Z-Move. Lana also has medicines to use at her discretion. Pick your Pokémon carefully for this challenging clash!

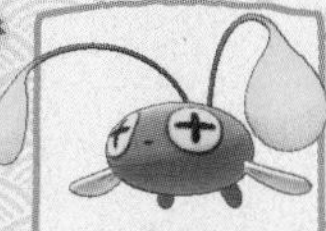

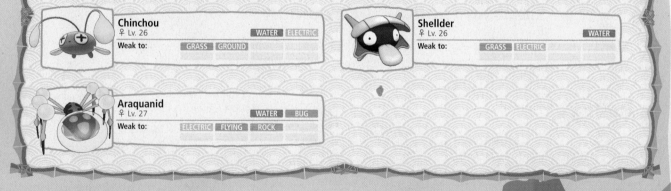

Chinchou
♀ Lv. 26 — WATER, ELECTRIC
Weak to: GRASS, GROUND

Shellder
♀ Lv. 26 — WATER
Weak to: GRASS, ELECTRIC

Araquanid
♀ Lv. 27 — WATER, BUG
Weak to: ELECTRIC, FLYING, ROCK

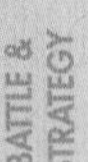

S57: Battle Captain Kiawe

If it's nighttime, stop by Kiawe's house in Paniola Town and visit the room next to his bedroom upstairs. He has to run to his part-time job, so follow him to the Thrifty Megamart on Royal Avenue. After he gets some disheartening news there, he wants an intense battle against you to help pump him back up again. Give him and his Fire-type team a battle worth remembering!

Captain Kiawe's Pokémon

Kiawe's Fire types can quickly toast your team if given the chance. Use Water- and Rock-type Pokémon to reduce the effectiveness of their moves, and inflict maximum damage with supereffective attacks of the same types or of Ground type.

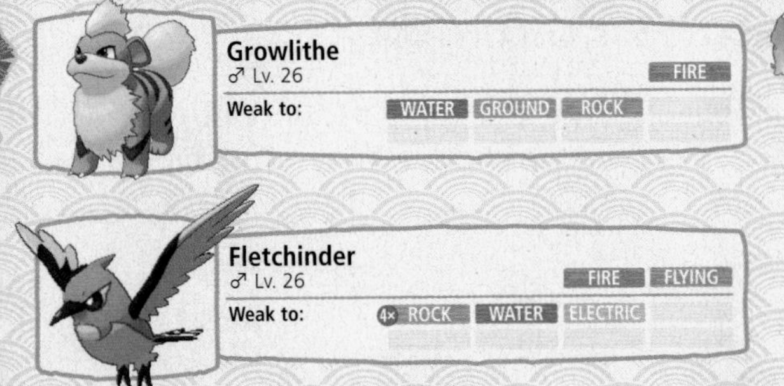

Growlithe
♂ Lv. 26
Type: FIRE
Weak to: WATER, GROUND, ROCK

Alolan Marowak
♂ Lv. 27
Type: FIRE, GHOST
Weak to: WATER, GROUND, ROCK, GHOST, DARK

Fletchinder
♂ Lv. 26
Type: FIRE, FLYING
Weak to: 4× ROCK, WATER, ELECTRIC

S58: Battle Captain Mallow

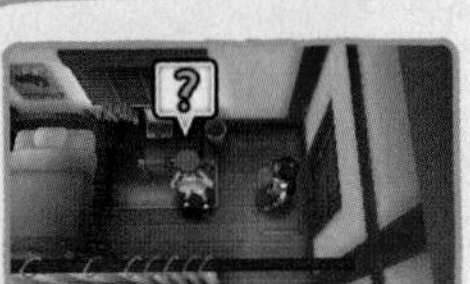

If it's daytime, stop by Mallow's family's restaurant in Konikoni City and go upstairs to find her in the room she shares with her siblings. She'll challenge you to a battle and a bit of a treasure hunt, too. Find Mallow in Lush Jungle by finding a Wimpod and talking to it. Then it's time for a Grass-powered battle!

Captain Mallow's Pokémon

Mallow's Pokémon are no pushovers, but just look at all those shared weaknesses. Fire- and Flying-type moves should help you cut them down in short order.

Phantump
♀ Lv. 26
Type: GHOST, GRASS
Weak to: FIRE, ICE, FLYING, GHOST, DARK

Steenee
♀ Lv. 27
Type: GRASS
Weak to: FIRE, ICE, POISON, FLYING, BUG

Shiinotic
♀ Lv. 26
Type: GRASS, FAIRY
Weak to: 4× POISON, FIRE, ICE, FLYING, STEEL

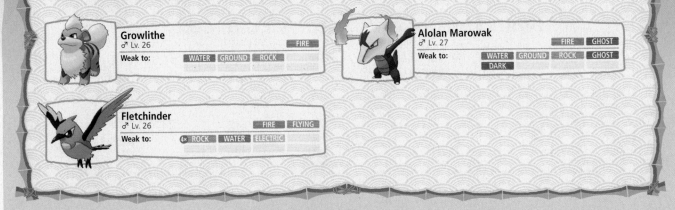

Aether Paradise

A very large floating structure, Aether Paradise could arguably be considered Alola's fifth island.

Team Recommendations

WATER GROUND PSYCHIC STEEL

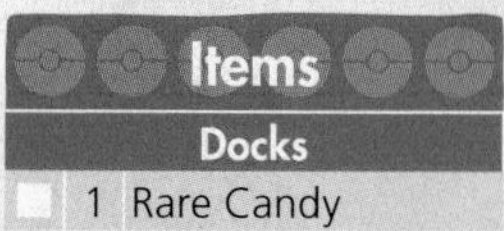

Items

Docks	
1	Rare Candy

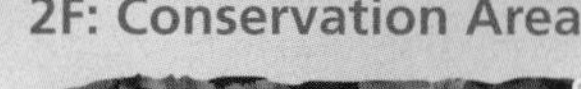

2F: Conservation Area

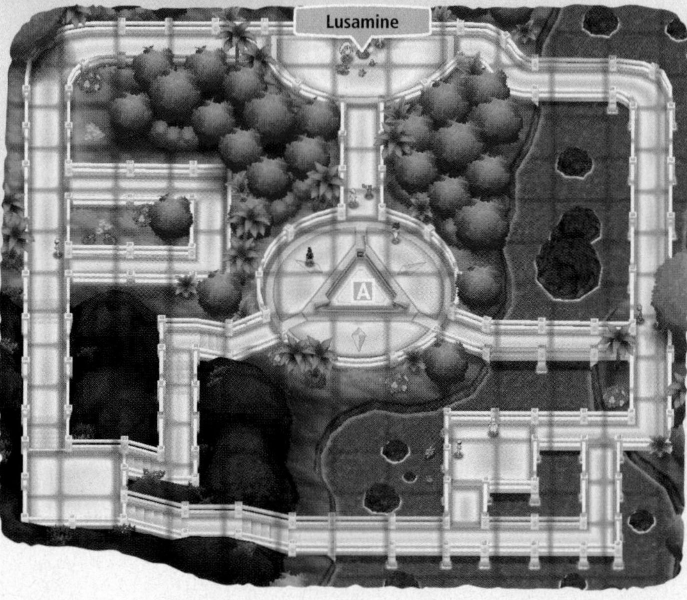

1F: Entrance

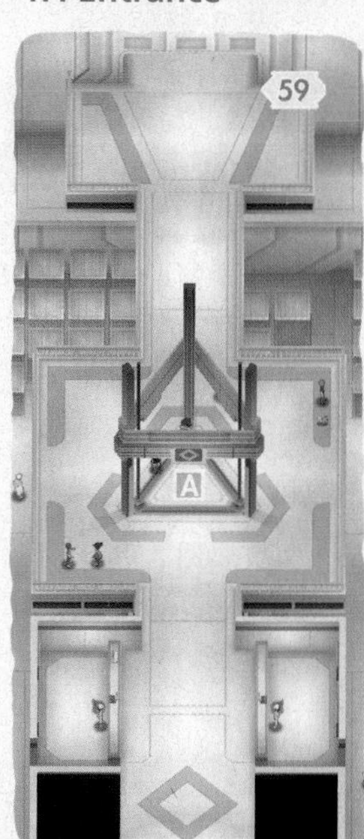

B1F: Docks

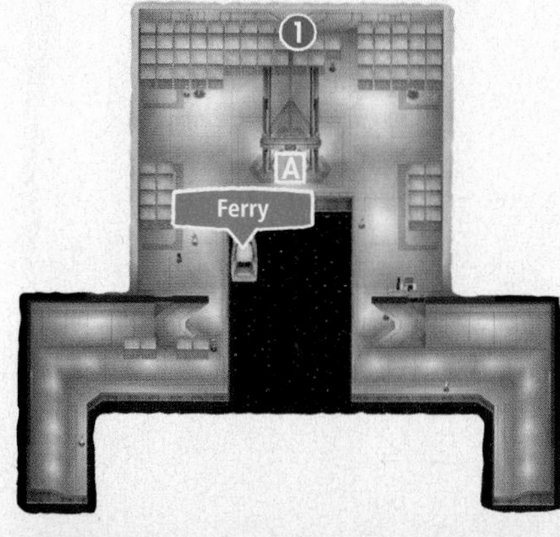

B2F: Elevator Hall

1 Take a tour of Aether Paradise

What an amazing place! Branch Chief Faba introduces you to Vice-Chief Wicke and then quickly disappears, claiming to have important business with the Aether Foundation's president. Wicke takes you on a tour of the facility's different floors, eventually leaving you to explore the conservation area. Find the president, Lusamine, at the north end.

S59: Get a Stick

Before looking for Lusamine in the conservation area, you can take the elevators to explore other floors if you'd like. There is not much to see on B2F at this point, but you can find an item on B1F. You can also get a Stick if you talk to the Aether Employee on the right side of the passage to the north on 1F.

Reward: Stick

Wicke, Faba, and Lusamine

A large and complex organization, the Aether Foundation is run by several important people. Vice-Chief Wicke is a kind woman and very friendly to both you and Hau, while Branch Chief Faba seems more impressed with himself than anything else around him. President Lusamine is something else entirely: she has a commanding presence, despite looking far more youthful than her age. It's clear that Lusamine is in charge of the foundation, and she has lofty goals for the protection of Pokémon. Perhaps you'll be able to aid her somehow in the future.

2 Witness a wormhole and battle an Ultra Beast

Your conversation with President Lusamine is cut short by a sudden tremor and a blinding flash of light. An Ultra Wormhole appears! They really do exist! A strange creature emerges—could it be one of the so-called Ultra Beasts? Whatever it is, you've got to fight it!

???

Much like a Totem Pokémon, this formidable opponent has a persistent aura that raises its Defense sharply. It blasts your Pokémon with Venoshock for heavy damage, so keep your Grass and Fairy types out of the fight. Its Ability, Beast Boost, causes its Sp. Def to rise each time it knocks out one of your Pokémon. Fortunately, this dangerous opponent flees after several turns.

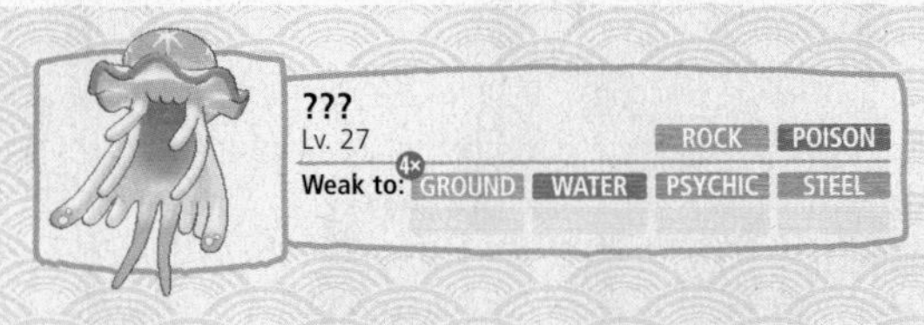

3 Get some gifts before going to Ula'ula Island

Wicke escorts you and Hau out of Aether Paradise after the threat has passed. Before booking you a ferry to Ula'ula Island, she gives you each a souvenir: some Big Malasadas for Hau and TM29 Psychic for you. It's been quite an experience here at Aether Paradise, but the time has come to continue with your island challenge. Enjoy your trip over the sea!

Reward: TM29 Psychic

Ula'ula Island

Two islands down, two to go! Your next stop is Alola's third island—Ula'ula Island. Your island challenge continues here, with fresh, new trials to overcome. Of course, there's also that small matter of the Ultra Wormhole that you witnessed back at Aether Paradise and the mighty Ultra Beast that emerged. Perhaps your explorations of Ula'ula will uncover more clues into this amazing occurrence and what it could mean for the future of Alola.

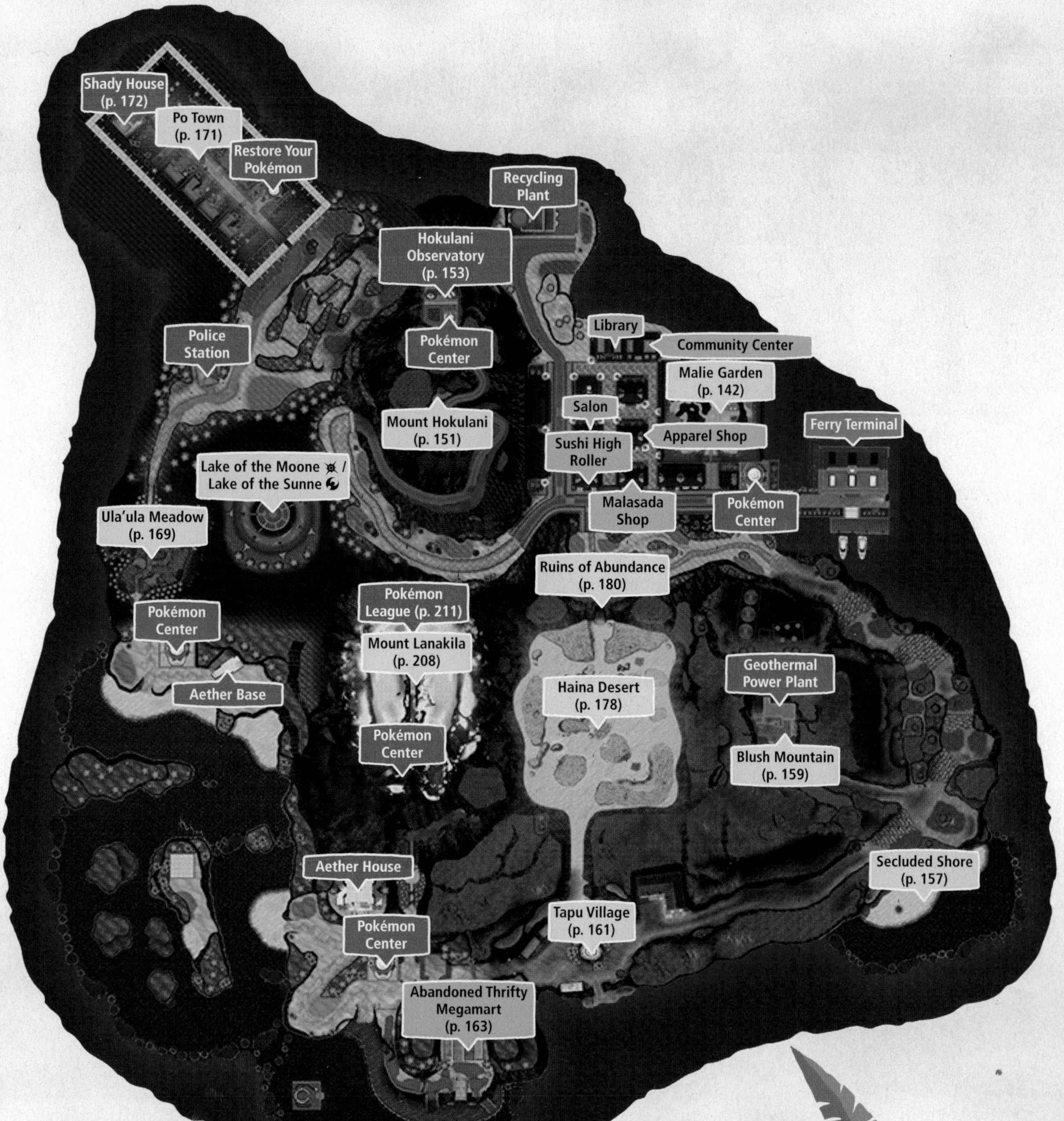

Shady House (p. 172)
Po Town (p. 171)
Restore Your Pokémon
Recycling Plant
Hokulani Observatory (p. 153)
Police Station
Pokémon Center
Library
Community Center
Malie Garden (p. 142)
Salon
Mount Hokulani (p. 151)
Apparel Shop
Ferry Terminal
Sushi High Roller
Lake of the Moone / Lake of the Sunne
Malasada Shop
Pokémon Center
Ula'ula Meadow (p. 169)
Ruins of Abundance (p. 180)
Pokémon League (p. 211)
Pokémon Center
Mount Lanakila (p. 208)
Geothermal Power Plant
Haina Desert (p. 178)
Aether Base
Pokémon Center
Blush Mountain (p. 159)
Secluded Shore (p. 157)
Aether House
Tapu Village (p. 161)
Pokémon Center
Abandoned Thrifty Megamart (p. 163)

Malie City / Malie Garden

Ula'ula Island's port city Malie is known around Alola for its large, tranquil garden. The city's impressive architecture is quite distinctive and clearly influenced by Eastern design.

Team Recommendations
FIRE ELECTRIC FLYING

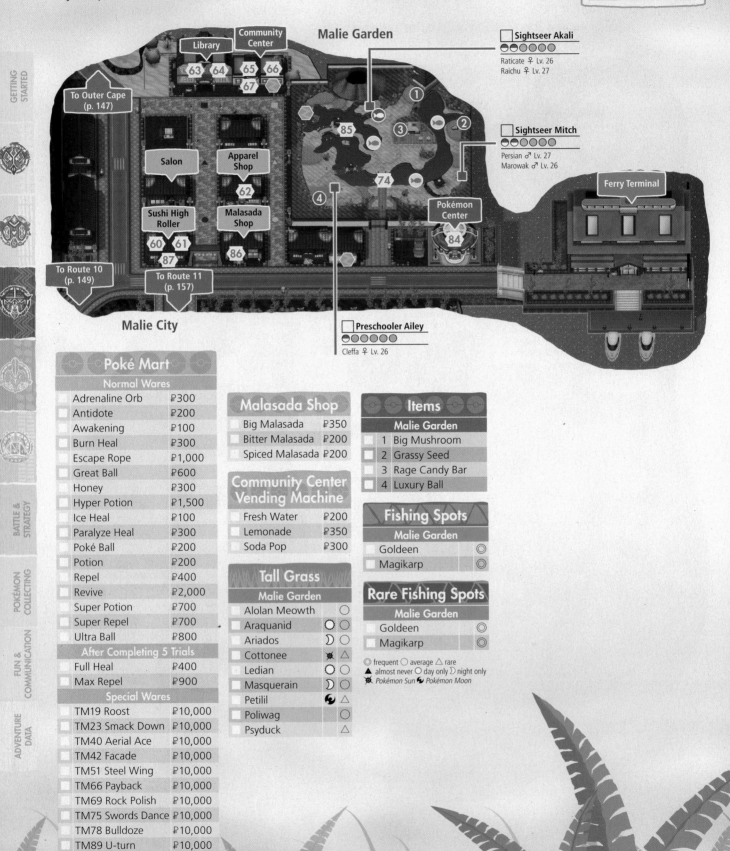

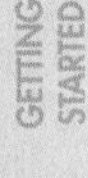
GETTING STARTED

BATTLE & STRATEGY
POKÉMON COLLECTING
FUN & COMMUNICATION
ADVENTURE DATA

Malie Garden

Library 63 64
Community Center 65 66 67
Salon
Apparel Shop 62
Sushi High Roller 60 61 87
Malasada Shop 86
Pokémon Center 84
Ferry Terminal
85 74
1 2 3 4

To Outer Cape (p. 147)
To Route 10 (p. 149)
To Route 11 (p. 157)

Malie City

Sightseer Akali
Raticate ♀ Lv. 26
Raichu ♀ Lv. 27

Sightseer Mitch
Persian ♂ Lv. 27
Marowak ♂ Lv. 26

Preschooler Ailey
Cleffa ♀ Lv. 26

Poké Mart

Normal Wares	
Adrenaline Orb	₽300
Antidote	₽200
Awakening	₽100
Burn Heal	₽300
Escape Rope	₽1,000
Great Ball	₽600
Honey	₽300
Hyper Potion	₽1,500
Ice Heal	₽100
Paralyze Heal	₽300
Poké Ball	₽200
Potion	₽200
Repel	₽400
Revive	₽2,000
Super Potion	₽700
Super Repel	₽700
Ultra Ball	₽800
After Completing 5 Trials	
Full Heal	₽400
Max Repel	₽900
Special Wares	
TM19 Roost	₽10,000
TM23 Smack Down	₽10,000
TM40 Aerial Ace	₽10,000
TM42 Facade	₽10,000
TM51 Steel Wing	₽10,000
TM66 Payback	₽10,000
TM69 Rock Polish	₽10,000
TM75 Swords Dance	₽10,000
TM78 Bulldoze	₽10,000
TM89 U-turn	₽10,000

Malasada Shop

Big Malasada	₽350
Bitter Malasada	₽200
Spiced Malasada	₽200

Community Center Vending Machine

Fresh Water	₽200
Lemonade	₽350
Soda Pop	₽300

Tall Grass

Malie Garden		
Alolan Meowth		○
Araquanid	☼	○
Ariados	☽	○
Cottonee	Sun	△
Ledian	☼	○
Masquerain	☽	○
Petilil	Moon	△
Poliwag		○
Psyduck		△

Items

Malie Garden	
1	Big Mushroom
2	Grassy Seed
3	Rage Candy Bar
4	Luxury Ball

Fishing Spots

Malie Garden	
Goldeen	◎
Magikarp	◎

Rare Fishing Spots

Malie Garden	
Goldeen	◎
Magikarp	◎

◎ frequent ○ average △ rare
▲ almost never ☼ day only ☽ night only
Sun *Pokémon Sun* Moon *Pokémon Moon*

Tip

Depending on the weather, different Pokémon may appear when wild Pokémon call for SOS allies in battle. Politoed, Poliwhirl, and Poliwrath may appear when it's raining in Malie Garden, as well as Castform. It rains around Malie every evening before night falls.

1 Have a battle with Hau at Ula'ula Island

Hau
I've got an idea, Sun!
Let's have a battle!
Sure
Why?

Here you are: Ula'ula Island! Hau suggests that you mark your arrival with a battle—one that will help his team get a good, deep breath of that fresh Ula'ula air. He won't take no for an answer, either!

Hau's Pokémon

Hau's been busy since your last battle. His Pikachu has evolved into the Alola form of Raichu—Alolan Raichu—gaining the Psychic type and all of the benefits and weaknesses that come along with it. He's also evolved his Eevee into a Pokémon that complements his first partner Pokémon by balancing out its weaknesses. Switch out your Pokémon as needed to counter Hau's, and make good use of items and Z-Power to give your team the edge.

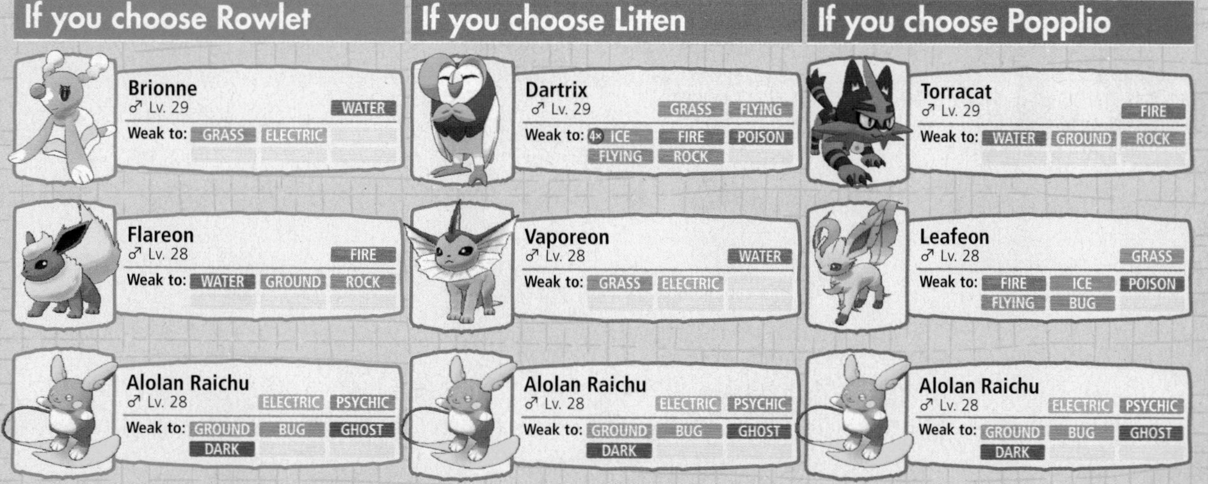

If you choose Rowlet	If you choose Litten	If you choose Popplio
Brionne ♂ Lv. 29 — WATER Weak to: GRASS, ELECTRIC	**Dartrix** ♂ Lv. 29 — GRASS, FLYING Weak to: 4× ICE, FIRE, POISON, FLYING, ROCK	**Torracat** ♂ Lv. 29 — FIRE Weak to: WATER, GROUND, ROCK
Flareon ♂ Lv. 28 — FIRE Weak to: WATER, GROUND, ROCK	**Vaporeon** ♂ Lv. 28 — WATER Weak to: GRASS, ELECTRIC	**Leafeon** ♂ Lv. 28 — GRASS Weak to: FIRE, ICE, POISON, FLYING, BUG
Alolan Raichu ♂ Lv. 28 — ELECTRIC, PSYCHIC Weak to: GROUND, BUG, GHOST, DARK	**Alolan Raichu** ♂ Lv. 28 — ELECTRIC, PSYCHIC Weak to: GROUND, BUG, GHOST, DARK	**Alolan Raichu** ♂ Lv. 28 — ELECTRIC, PSYCHIC Weak to: GROUND, BUG, GHOST, DARK

2 Rest your Pokémon, then explore Malie Garden

Pop into Malie City's Pokémon Center to rest your team, then head north into Malie Garden. This elegant area is actually home to quite a few passionate Trainers. Explore its every corner, and maybe catch some new Pokémon before you meet Professor Kukui at the tea house. He's shocked to learn of your recent encounter with the Ultra Beast. The professor says you can catch a bus to your next island challenge trial on Route 10.

3 Meet up with Lillie and see a familiar face

Leave the garden after your chat with Kukui and go west to find Lillie standing in the road. She's heading for Malie Library and would appreciate your help in finding a certain book there. Stroll a bit farther down the road, and you'll meet another friendly person with a familiar face.

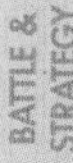

Samson Oak

Is that the renowned Professor Samuel Oak of the Kanto region?! Nope. It's his cousin, Samson Oak! This spry researcher is visiting the Alola region to learn more about the regional variants that are found only in Alola. He spends most of his time poring over books at Malie City's library and welcomes any help he can get with his studies.

S60: Scoop up some Heart Scales

Stop in at the Sushi High Roller restaurant for a hot meal and some Heart Scales. Each meal costs ₽4,000, but the four Heart Scales you receive help lessen the blow to your wallet.

Reward: Heart Scale ×4

S61: Trade for Happiny

A woman in the Sushi High Roller restaurant will happily trade you her Happiny, provided you're willing to part with a Pancham.

Pokémon: Happiny

Furfrou

A popular Pokémon in the Kalos region, Furfrou can be uniquely groomed into 10 different styles (including natural form). The stylist in Malie City's salon is just itching to trim Furfrou hair, but Furfrou don't live in Alola. Don't be discouraged, though—you can get Furfrou through the GTS (p. 307). The style goes back to normal after a few days.

Natural Form

Heart Trim

Star Trim

Diamond Trim

La Reine Trim

Kabuki Trim

Pharoah Trim

Debutante Trim

Matron Trim

Dandy Trim

S62: Catch and show Togedemaru

A man in the apparel shop is in love with Togedemaru and asks you to catch one and show him its Pokédex entry. You can catch Togedemaru near the power plant on Blush Mountain (p. 159), then return here for your reward.

Reward: ₽10,000

4 Meet Lillie and Hapu near the library

Meet Lillie in front of the library, and you'll soon have lots more company! Hapu and Mudsdale show up and introduce themselves. Hapu offers to help see Lillie to the ruins anytime, but for now Lillie has her sights fixed on the library. You can follow her upstairs, or take a bit of time to check out a few more things around the city.

S63: Talk about TMs

A tourist sitting downstairs in the library is surprised to learn that HMs aren't used in Alola. She rewards your informative chat with a TM for Fly.

Reward: TM76 Fly

S64: Evolve an Alolan Meowth to show off an Alolan Persian

Samson Oak stands in the back corner of the library. Show him an Alolan Persian, and he'll hand you a lovely surprise.

Reward: Love Ball

S65: Score a Strange Souvenir

Step out of the library for a moment and visit the community center next door. Talk to a gentleman in the lobby for a curious little gift.

Reward: Strange Souvenir

S66: Receive a Ribbon

A little girl in the community center's lobby can tell how affectionate your lead Pokémon is toward you. If you've played a lot with it in Pokémon Refresh (p. 276) or fed it a lot of malasadas (p. 57–58), it'll get a Ribbon!

Reward: Best Friends Ribbon

S67: Rock a quiz

Pop into the community center's classroom, the first door to the right, and take a quiz that teaches you how certain rocks can affect the weather. After the quiz, the teacher will generously give you four special stones that can prolong certain weather conditions in battle.

Reward: Damp Rock, Heat Rock, Icy Rock, Smooth Rock

Flea Market

Malie City's community center features a flea market, where savvy shoppers search for steals. Speak to the girl on the right to browse her selection of rare fashion items. Talk to the boy on the left, and he'll tell you that he's found a Shiny Stone or Dusk Stone, but he doesn't know what to do with it. Come back after completing Ula'ula Island's grand trial, and he'll offer to sell you his stone for ₽3,000.

Weather Effects

The weather is usually beautiful in Alola—it's just one of the region's many charms. However, certain places in Alola feature special weather conditions that can have a dramatic impact on battle. You can also choose to use Pokémon that can summon whatever weather condition they like, either by using moves or through Abilities.

Major Effects of Weather in Battle	
Hail	Damages all Pokémon that are not Ice type every turn.
Sandstorm	Damages all Pokémon that are not Rock, Ground, or Steel type every turn. Also boosts the Sp. Def of Rock-type Pokémon.
Harsh Sunlight	Boosts the power of Fire-type moves and lowers the power of Water-type moves.
Rain	Boosts the power of Water-type moves and lowers the power of Fire-type moves.
Extremely Harsh Sunlight	Boosts the power of Fire-type moves and protects Pokémon from Water-type moves.
Heavy Rain	Boosts the power of Water-type moves and protects Pokémon from Fire-type moves.

Make Your Own Weather	
Hail	Snow Warning Ability (ex. Vanilluxe) or Hail move
Sandstorm	Sand Stream Ability (ex. Gigalith) or Sandstorm move
Harsh Sunlight	Drought Ability (ex. Torkoal) or Sunny Day move
Rain	Drizzle Ability (ex. Pelipper) or Rain Dance move
Clear weather	Cloud Nine Ability (ex. Psyduck/Golduck)

Tip

Some Abilities can give Pokémon great benefits from the weather. For example, Leaf Guard prevents status conditions in sunny weather, while Sand Veil boosts the Pokémon's evasion in a sandstorm. Rain Dish will cause a Pokémon to recover HP during rain. Consider your Pokémon's Abilities whenever weather is a factor.

5 Make a new friend on the library's second floor

Follow Lillie up to the library's second floor. There you meet a friendly girl named Acerola who helps Lillie find the book that she's after. The old tome provides a poetic telling of Alola's Legendary Pokémon, Solgaleo or Lunala. Acerola and Lillie have much to discuss, so leave them to their research and either head north to Outer Cape (an optional area) or southwest to Route 10 (p. 149).

Acerola

A kind yet mysterious girl, Acerola is the last living member of a family who once ruled the Alola region. She now lives in a special home for children and Pokémon who have no one else to care for them. She knows much about Alola's history and is an invaluable resource to Lillie in unraveling the secrets of the past.

Outer Cape

Located just north of Malie City, this small cape features a big recycling plant, where all of Alola's refuse is consumed by Muk and Grimer. The wild Poison-type Pokémon found here seem to be drawn to the plant's potent aroma.

Team Recommendations

FIGHTING GROUND

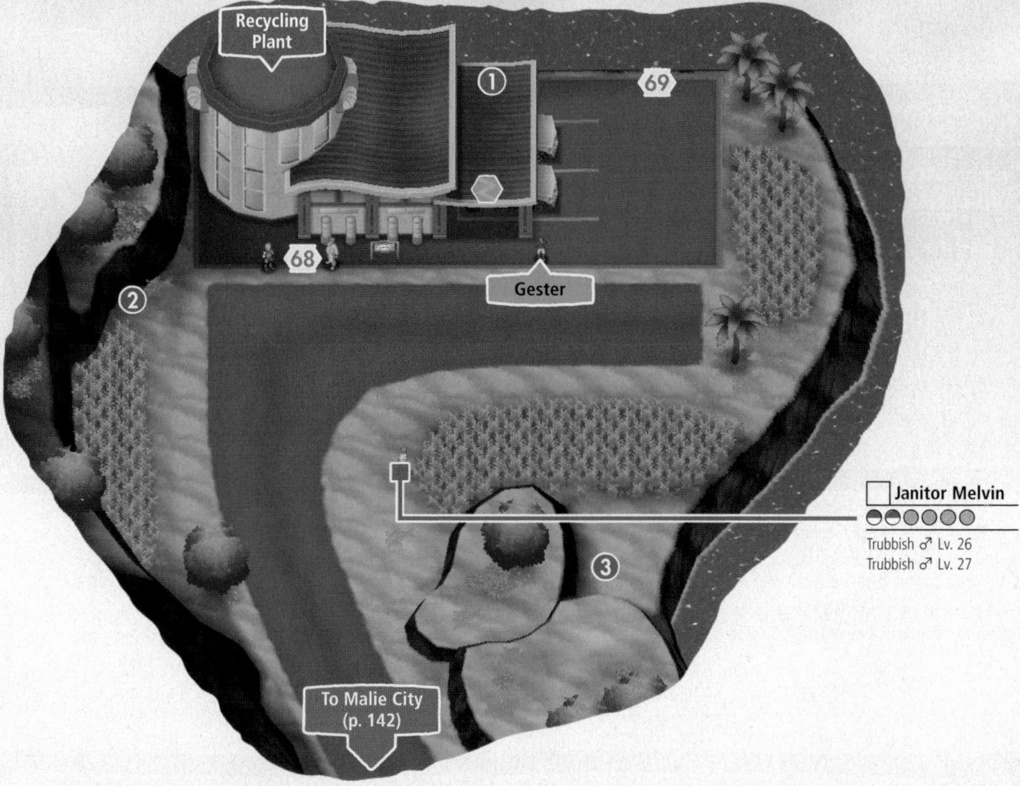

(p. 142)

Janitor Melvin

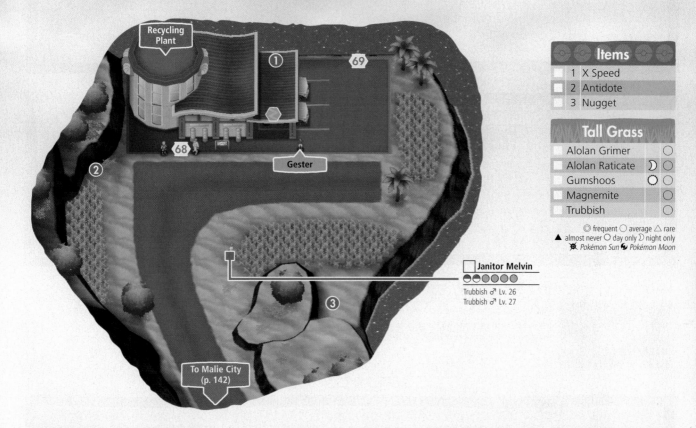

Trubbish ♂ Lv. 26
Trubbish ♂ Lv. 27

Items

1	X Speed
2	Antidote
3	Nugget

Tall Grass

Alolan Grimer		○
Alolan Raticate	☽	○
Gumshoos	○	○
Magnemite		○
Trubbish		○

◎ frequent ○ average △ rare
▲ almost never ○ day only ☽ night only
Pokémon Sun *Pokémon Moon*

1 Check out the Outer Cape (Optional)

It's not necessary to visit the Outer Cape, but it sure is fun! Here you can find some new Pokémon and items, learn about how Alola's refuse is processed, and meet several interesting characters who enjoy life on the edge of Ula'ula Island.

S68: Score a Twisted Spoon

Get caught up in some family drama at the Recycling Plant! You'll have a couple of exciting battles and walk off with a Twisted Spoon. If you want to know what you'll be up against, turn the page to check out this father and son's lineup.

Reward: Twisted Spoon

GETTING STARTED
BATTLE & STRATEGY
POKÉMON COLLECTING
FUN & COMMUNICATION
ADVENTURE DATA

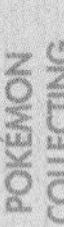

Janitor Shawn's Pokémon

You're first challenged by Janitor Shawn. Use a Ground-type Pokémon, like the Diglett you may have caught back in Diglett's Tunnel, to mash his Alolan Muk in short order.

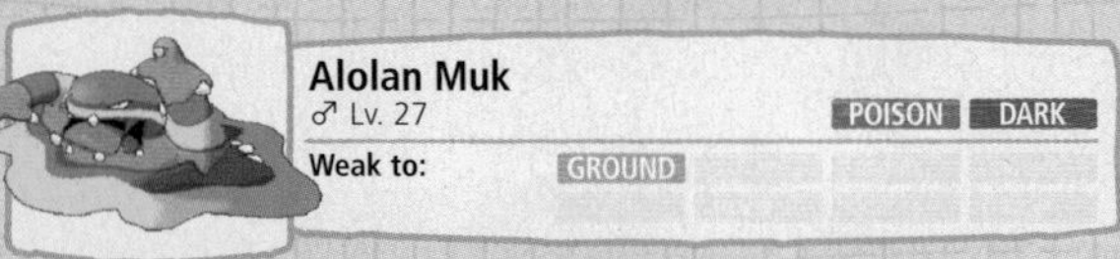

Ace Trainer Chase's Pokémon

Shawn's son Chase is a bit more of a challenge. Still, his Alolan Grimer shares the same weakness to Ground-type moves, so use the same approach to end the fight fast.

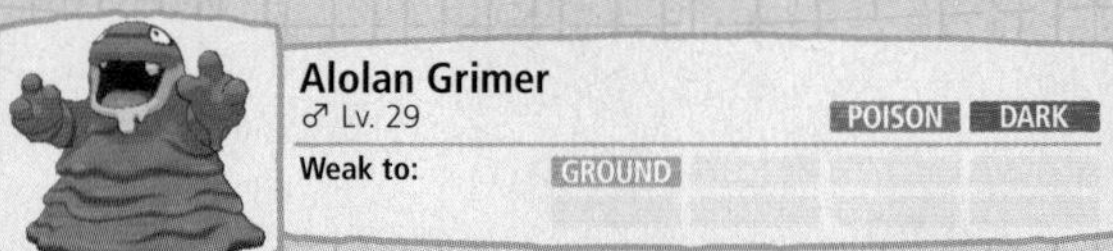

S69: Get a Friend Ball

Talk to Oak, who has somehow beaten you here. He'll hand you a Friend Ball, along with some knowledge.

Reward: Friend Ball

Gester

Next to the Recycling Plant stands an elderly gentleman named Gester. Talk to him, and he'll teach you a new battle style—meaning a cool new way to throw a Poké Ball and pose during battles! Aside from your normal battle style, Gester can teach you the following styles.

Style	Requirement
Elegant style	Gester will teach you this style right away
Girlish style	Visit Lana's house and complete the sub-event (p. 137)
Left-handed style	Visit Ilima's house and complete the sub-event (p. 84)
Reverent style	Visit the house of Kiawe ☀ or Mallow ☾ and complete the sub-event (p. 138)
Smug style	Defeat Gladion at the base of Mount Lanakila (p. 209)
Passionate style	Win 50 battles in a row at the Battle Tree (p. 224)
Idol style	Achieve the highest rank in Battle Royal (p. 111)

Normal Elegant Girlish Left-Handed Reverent Smug Passionate Idol

Route 10

Running southwest of Malie City, Route 10 is a straightforward trail that leads up into the peaks of Mount Hokulani. Its bushy trees have enticed many bird Pokémon to nest here.

Team Recommendations

FIRE ELECTRIC FLYING ROCK

Items	
1	X Accuracy
2	Paralyze Heal

Shaking Trees	
Fearow	◎
Skarmory	○

Hidden Items
Lemonade
Tiny Mushroom

Tall Grass		
Ariados	night only	○
Fearow		○
Gumshoos	day only	○
Ledian	day only	○
Pancham		△
Alolan Raticate	night only	○
Skarmory		△

◎ frequent ○ average
△ rare ▲ almost never
day only night only
Pokémon Sun
Pokémon Moon

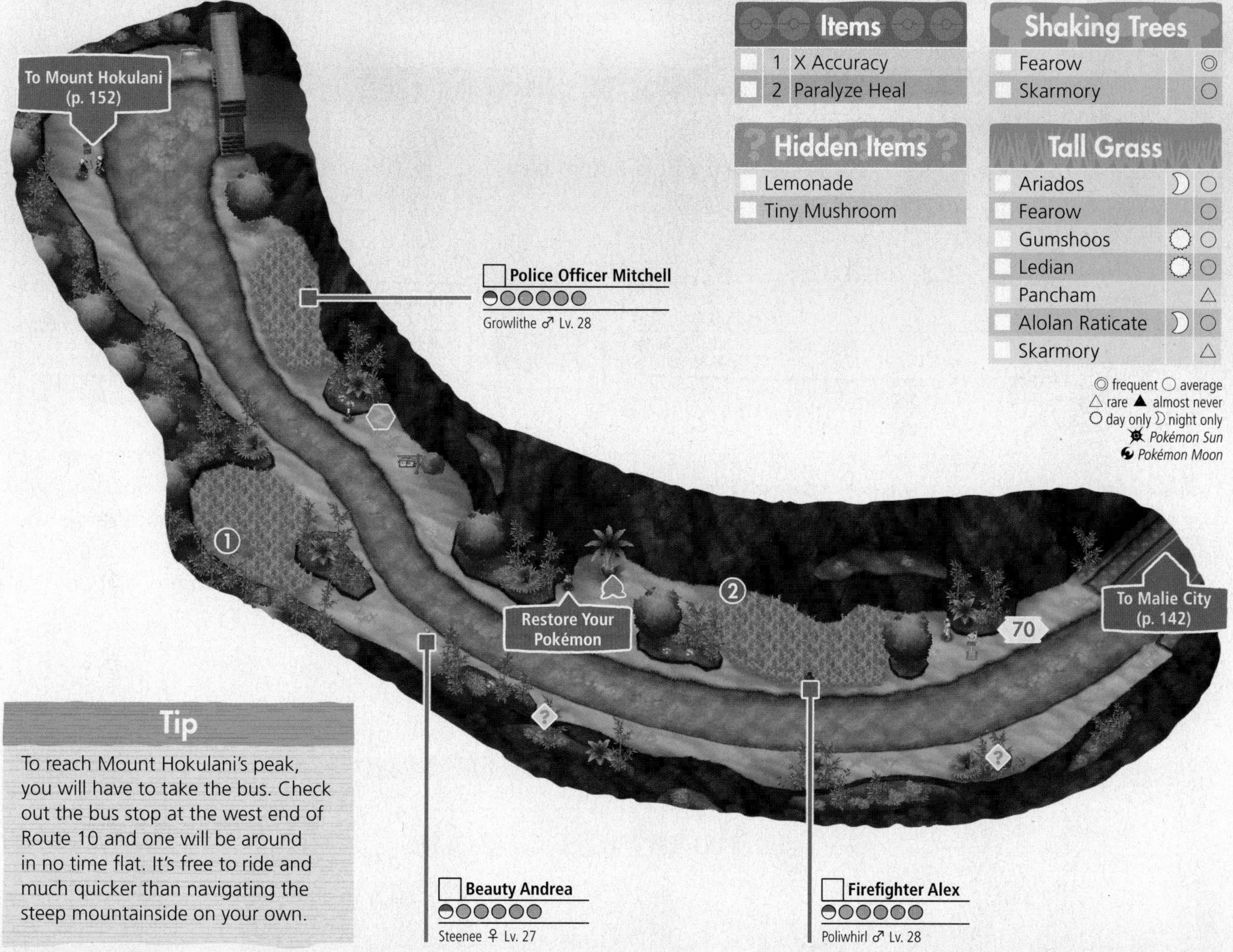

To Mount Hokulani (p. 152)

Police Officer Mitchell
Growlithe ♂ Lv. 28

Restore Your Pokémon

To Malie City (p. 142)

Beauty Andrea
Steenee ♀ Lv. 27

Firefighter Alex
Poliwhirl ♂ Lv. 28

Tip

To reach Mount Hokulani's peak, you will have to take the bus. Check out the bus stop at the west end of Route 10 and one will be around in no time flat. It's free to ride and much quicker than navigating the steep mountainside on your own.

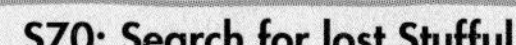

S70: Search for lost Stufful

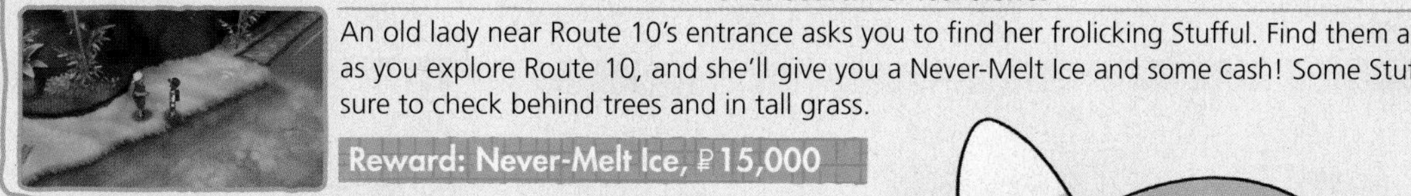

An old lady near Route 10's entrance asks you to find her frolicking Stufful. Find them and send them back to her as you explore Route 10, and she'll give you a Never-Melt Ice and some cash! Some Stufful are well hidden, so be sure to check behind trees and in tall grass.

Reward: Never-Melt Ice, ₽15,000

1 Stop Team Skull from wrecking a bus stop

Watch out for shaky trees as you explore Route 10, for bird Pokémon just love to get the drop on unsuspecting Trainers. Reach the end of the stretch to find Team Skull up to no good once again. This time, they're trying to steal a bus stop sign—and they don't take kindly to being interrupted!

Team Skull Grunts' Pokémon

Both Grunts battle you in turn, so you face two Single Battles back-to-back. The first Grunt sends out Golbat, which uses Confuse Ray to confuse your Pokémon. The second Grunt's Alolan Raticate is a heavy-hitter, but you can eradicate it with Fighting-type moves.

Pokémon	Level	Type	Weak to
Golbat	♂ Lv. 27	POISON, FLYING	ELECTRIC, ICE, PSYCHIC, ROCK
Alolan Raticate	♂ Lv. 27	DARK, NORMAL	4× FIGHTING, BUG, FAIRY

2 Ride the bus to Hokulani Observatory

Kukui catches up to you after Team Skull flees the scene. Check out the nearby bus stop and the bus will arrive in no time, ready to whisk you up the road to Hokulani Observatory! There, Kukui dishes about his dream: the formation of a Pokémon League right here in Alola!

The Pokémon League

An organization that exists in many regions of the Pokémon world, the Pokémon League helps Trainers grow and compete. It serves as a means of determining the strongest Trainer in the region—the Pokémon League Champion! To become a Champion, a Trainer must typically defeat four of the strongest Trainers in the region—a quartet known as the Elite Four. Defeating the Elite Four in a series of battles earns you the right to battle the current Champion for a chance to take his or her title!

Mount Hokulani

Rising up from Route 10, Mount Hokulani towers over Malie City. It's the second tallest peak in all of Alola, making it an ideal spot for stargazing.

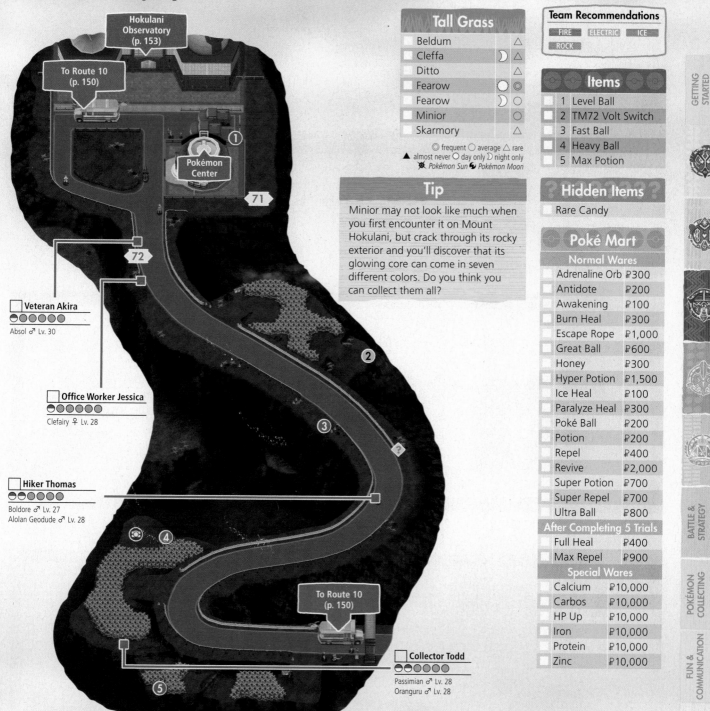

Hokulani Observatory (p. 153)

To Route 10 (p. 150)

Pokémon Center

71

72

Veteran Akira
Absol ♂ Lv. 30

Office Worker Jessica
Clefairy ♀ Lv. 28

Hiker Thomas
Boldore ♂ Lv. 27
Alolan Geodude ♂ Lv. 28

To Route 10 (p. 150)

Collector Todd
Passimian ♂ Lv. 28
Oranguru ♂ Lv. 28

Tall Grass

Pokémon	Time	Rarity
Beldum		△
Cleffa	☽	△
Ditto		△
Fearow	○	◎
Fearow	☽	○
Minior		○
Skarmory		△

◎ frequent ○ average △ rare ▲ almost never ○ day only ☽ night only *Pokémon Sun* *Pokémon Moon*

Tip

Minior may not look like much when you first encounter it on Mount Hokulani, but crack through its rocky exterior and you'll discover that its glowing core can come in seven different colors. Do you think you can collect them all?

Team Recommendations

FIRE ELECTRIC ICE ROCK

Items

1	Level Ball
2	TM72 Volt Switch
3	Fast Ball
4	Heavy Ball
5	Max Potion

Hidden Items

- Rare Candy

Poké Mart

Normal Wares	
Adrenaline Orb	₽300
Antidote	₽200
Awakening	₽100
Burn Heal	₽300
Escape Rope	₽1,000
Great Ball	₽600
Honey	₽300
Hyper Potion	₽1,500
Ice Heal	₽100
Paralyze Heal	₽300
Poké Ball	₽200
Potion	₽200
Repel	₽400
Revive	₽2,000
Super Potion	₽700
Super Repel	₽700
Ultra Ball	₽800
After Completing 5 Trials	
Full Heal	₽400
Max Repel	₽900
Special Wares	
Calcium	₽10,000
Carbos	₽10,000
HP Up	₽10,000
Iron	₽10,000
Protein	₽10,000
Zinc	₽10,000

1 Explore Mount Hokulani for fun and profit

Hokulani Observatory is the site of your next trial. If you think your Pokémon need a bit more training, or if you'd just like to explore a bit more before heading indoors, set off down the road of Mount Hokulani. You can catch a bus back down to Route 10 if you like, but for now, simply explore the peak, popping into the Pokémon Center to rest your team as needed.

S71: Make off with a Moon Ball

Your friend Samson Oak is taking in the view behind the Pokémon Center. He sure does get around! Chat with Oak to learn about Minior and score a Moon Ball.

Reward: Moon Ball

S72: Challenge a tough Trainer

A veteran Trainer near the top of the mountain will only battle you after you've defeated every other Trainer on Mount Hokulani. Beat him for a TM!

Reward: TM95 Snarl

2 Meet Molayne and get tested in battle

When you're ready to attempt your next trial, head for the observatory's front door. A friendly man named Molayne stands just outside, and after catching up a bit with Kukui, he challenges you to a battle to show him what you've got.

Molayne

A friendly scientist, Molayne monitors the sky and the stars up at Hokulani Observatory. He and Professor Kukui go way back. In fact, the two completed their island challenges together when they were kids, just like you and Hau. Although he's a seasoned Trainer, Molayne is not the captain of your upcoming trial—he merely prefers to test Trainers and ensure they're prepared for the trial ahead.

Molayne's Pokémon

Molayne has a soft spot for Steel-type Pokémon, and this gives you a big advantage. If possible, send out a seasoned Pokémon that can exploit his team's shared weakness to Fire-type moves. You'll find Fire-type Pokémon to be a big help during your upcoming trial as well.

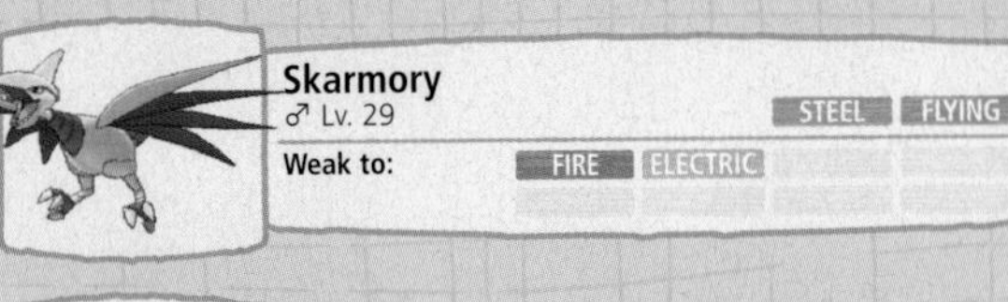

Skarmory
♂ Lv. 29
STEEL FLYING
Weak to: FIRE ELECTRIC

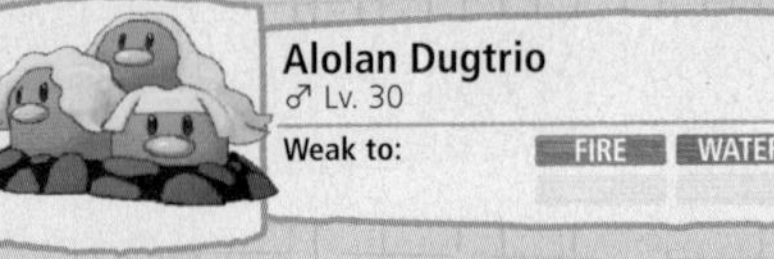

Alolan Dugtrio
♂ Lv. 30
GROUND STEEL
Weak to: FIRE WATER FIGHTING GROUND

Metang
Lv. 29
STEEL PSYCHIC
Weak to: FIRE GROUND GHOST DARK

Hokulani Observatory

Perched on the peak of Mount Hokulani, this impressive facility was built to study the stars. It also serves as the site of Sophocles's trial, which has some shocking surprises in store.

Team Recommendations

FIRE FLYING ROCK

S73: Claim a Comet Shard

Chat with the man at the observatory's front desk to receive a Comet Shard for stopping by.

Reward: Comet Shard

Sophocles

Molayne's cousin, Sophocles, is one of Alola's seven captains. He's also the genius behind Festival Plaza, which you may have been using to interact with other players during your journey (p. 299). Sophocles isn't very confident in his abilities as a captain, but he thinks he can quickly summon his trial's Totem Pokémon with his latest invention: the Ping Totem Pokémon 2.0!

Sadly, Sophocles's little experiment ends up blowing the observatory's breakers, plunging the entire place into darkness. You'll have to override the security system to get the lights back on!

Trial Guide: Sophocles's Trial

Your fifth trial is short and sweet, especially if you've trained strong Fire-type Pokémon, which are plentiful around Wela Volcano Park. You face a straightforward series of battles against Bug-type Pokémon here, all of which share weaknesses to Fire- and Rock-type moves. One of your opponents is also weak to Flying-type moves, but avoid using Flying-type Pokémon in this trial, for many of these Bug-type foes can unleash Electric-type moves like Spark, which are super effective against Flying types. Their Electric-type moves can paralyze your Pokémon as well, so come prepared with plenty of Paralyze Heals and other potent medicines.

Sophocles's Trial Goals

- Reset the breakers and restore the power
- Defeat the Totem Pokémon
- Receive the Z-Crystal

1 Answer the first security question

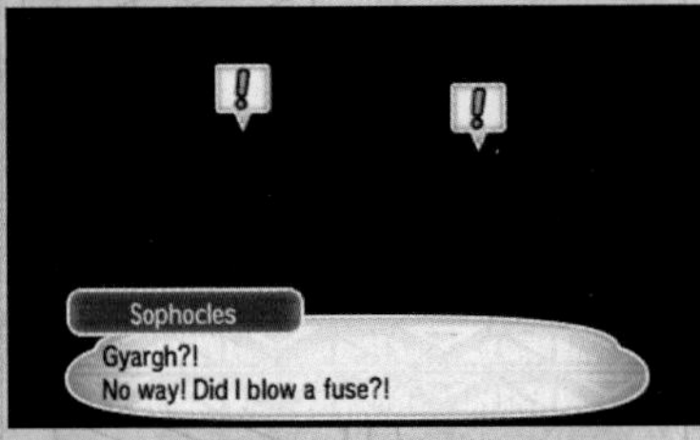

Sophocles's machine blows the observatory's breakers, plunging the place into pitch darkness. The security system activates, demanding that you answer a quiz to open the door. Turn up your volume and listen carefully to the sound that plays, then give your answer as to what the sound means. Guess wrong, and poor Sophocles will get a nasty shock! Guess correctly, and a wild Pokémon will emerge from the door and attack you!

Grubbin

The first Pokémon you face is just a little Grubbin. You shouldn't have any trouble squashing this teensy bug!

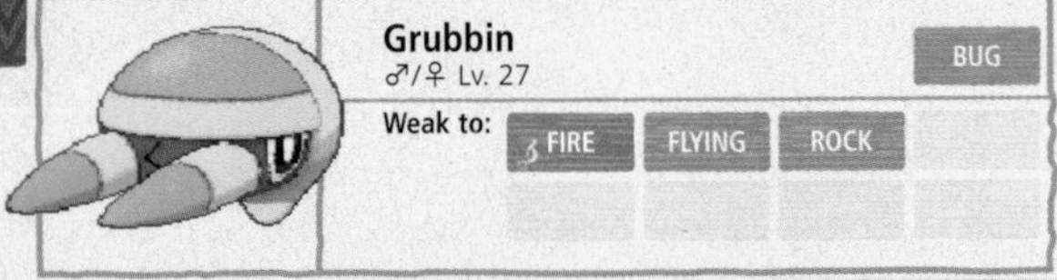

Grubbin	BUG
♂/♀ Lv. 27	
Weak to:	FIRE, FLYING, ROCK

2 Answer the second security question

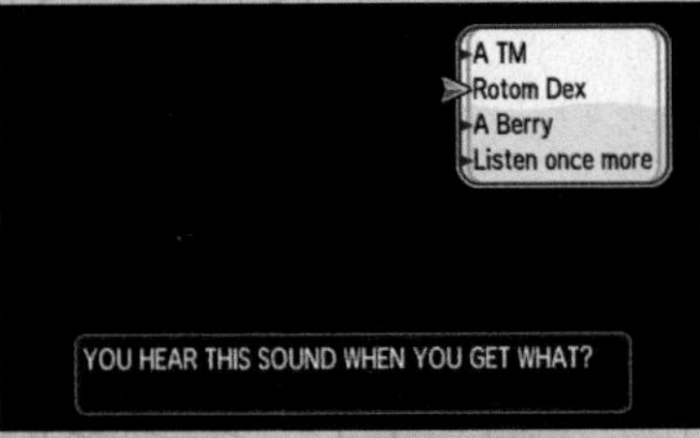

Sophocles is slow to react after your battle, and the security door slams shut. Oh no! Guess you'll have to answer another question. Listen carefully to the sound that plays, then give your answer. Another wild Pokémon emerges from the door and attacks when you guess correctly.

Charjabug

Aw, it's so cute! Charjabug shares most of the same weaknesses as Grubbin, so you should be in good shape to squash it, too.

Charjabug	BUG, ELECTRIC
♂/♀ Lv. 27	
Weak to:	FIRE, ROCK

3 Answer the third security question

Sophocles slips up again, allowing the security door to slam shut once more. What a goof! There's nothing else for it: answer another security question, and be ready to battle another Charjabug when you guess the right answer.

4 Answer the fourth security question

The third time is not the charm for Sophocles, who fails to stop the door from closing once more. Could he be doing it on purpose? No matter. Answer the fourth security question to open the door again—and be ready for a shocking battle against the Totem Pokémon!

Totem Vikavolt

Although it's far more powerful than the Bug types you've been bashing, Totem Vikavolt shares their same weaknesses, making it relatively easy prey. Its aura raises all of its stats, and it can use Charge to raise its Sp. Def even more. Charge also boosts the power of its next Electric-type attack, so don't let your Pokémon's HP dip too low. Vikavolt's ally Charjabug can attack with Thunder Wave, an Electric-type move that paralyzes your Pokémon. While your Pokémon will likely have Paralysis during this battle, you may not want to waste turns curing them. Depending on how the battle unfolds, it may be better to simply punish Vikavolt with supereffective blows.

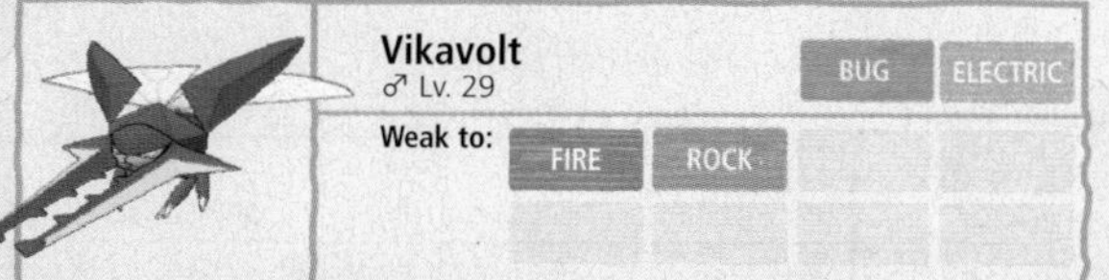

Vikavolt	BUG	ELECTRIC
♂ Lv. 29		
Weak to:	FIRE	ROCK

Charjabug (SOS Ally)	BUG	ELECTRIC
♂/♀ Lv. 27–28		
Weak to:	FIRE	ROCK

5 Receive your trial rewards

Happy to have the power restored, Sophocles hands you an Electrium Z. His cousin, Molayne, parts with a Steelium Z, and then asks you to return a familiar looking mask to Professor Kukui. It's a strange request, but sure, why not!

Reward: Electrium Z, Steelium Z, Professor's Mask

p. 142

1 Make your way back to Malie City

Catch a bus back down the mountain—there's a stop near the observatory and another at the far end of the road. Rush back through Route 10 and return to Malie City. Or you could call Charizard and fly straight back to Malie in a blink. Either way, you'll find more than you bargained for when you arrive in Malie Garden when the boss of all Team Skull suddenly appears, and battle soon erupts!

Guzma

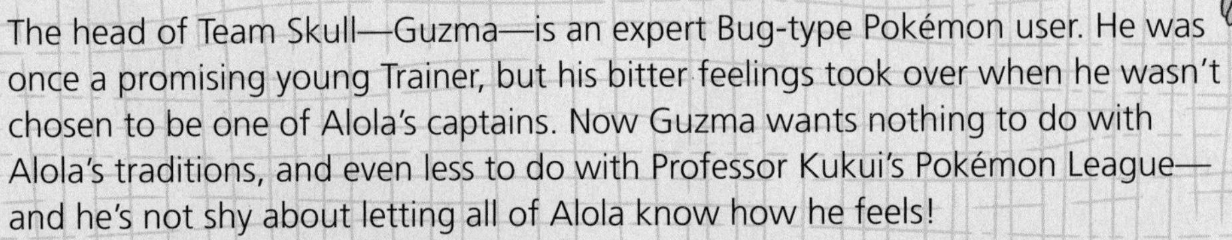

The head of Team Skull—Guzma—is an expert Bug-type Pokémon user. He was once a promising young Trainer, but his bitter feelings took over when he wasn't chosen to be one of Alola's captains. Now Guzma wants nothing to do with Alola's traditions, and even less to do with Professor Kukui's Pokémon League—and he's not shy about letting all of Alola know how he feels!

Team Skull Boss Guzma's Pokémon

An expert Bug-type user, Guzma sends out Golisopod and Ariados. Counter these big, bad Bug types with a strong Flying-type Pokémon like Pelipper, and you'll have little trouble getting past Guzma. Avoid using Fire- or Rock-type Pokémon if you can, for Golisopod may exploit their weakness to Water-type moves.

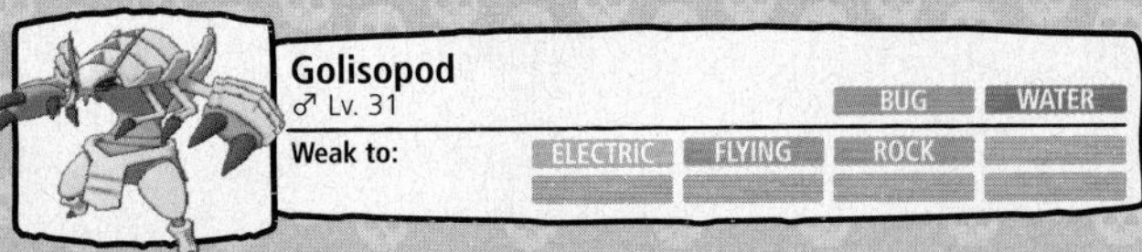

Golisopod	♂ Lv. 31	BUG	WATER
Weak to:	ELECTRIC	FLYING	ROCK

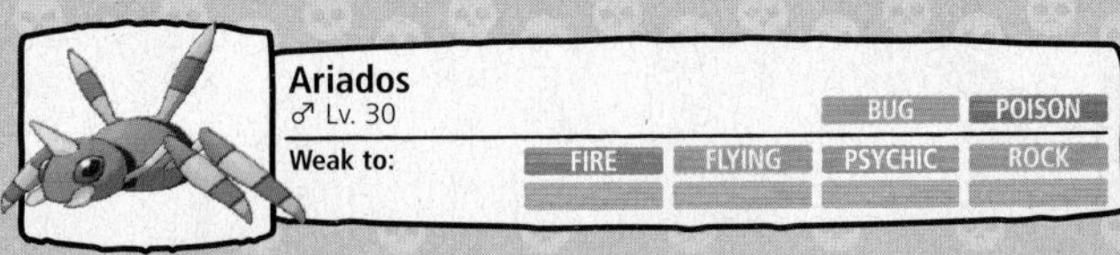

Ariados	♂ Lv. 30	BUG	POISON
Weak to:	FIRE	FLYING	PSYCHIC	ROCK

2 Get a special gift from Kukui

After Team Skull slithers off, Kukui remembers to give you something important: the Z-Crystal for your very first partner Pokémon! If you chose Rowlet, you'll get Decidium Z. If you chose Litten, you'll receive Incinium Z, and if you chose Popplio, you'll score Primarium Z. Lillie and Acerola arrive soon after, and Acerola says that your next trial lies beyond Route 11. Let's get a move on!

Reward: Decidium Z, Incinium Z, or Primarium Z

S74: Cross "Nugget Bridge"

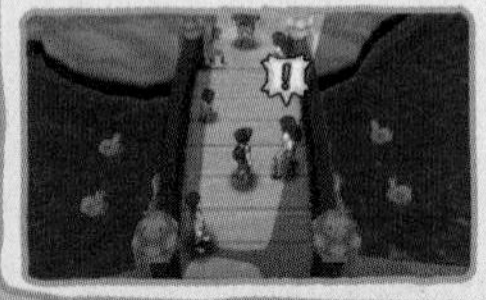

Leave Malie Garden and then return to find five new Trainers on the bridge. Beat them all to receive a big prize! If you also defeat the Veteran at the end of the bridge, you will leave with a little more prize money!

Reward: Big Nugget

Route 11 / Route 12 / Secluded Shore

Ride Pokémon Needed  

Together, these routes connect Malie City to Ula'ula Island's eastern mountains. Route 11 is easily traversed, but travelers must mount a Mudsdale to maneuver through Route 12's rocky road.

Team Recommendations

FIRE, ELECTRIC, FIGHTING, GROUND, FLYING, ROCK

Route 11

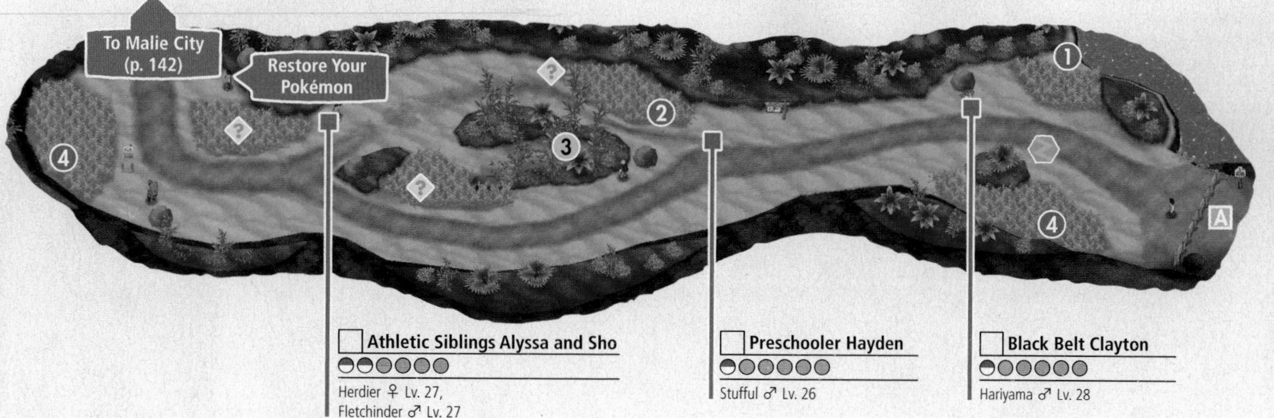

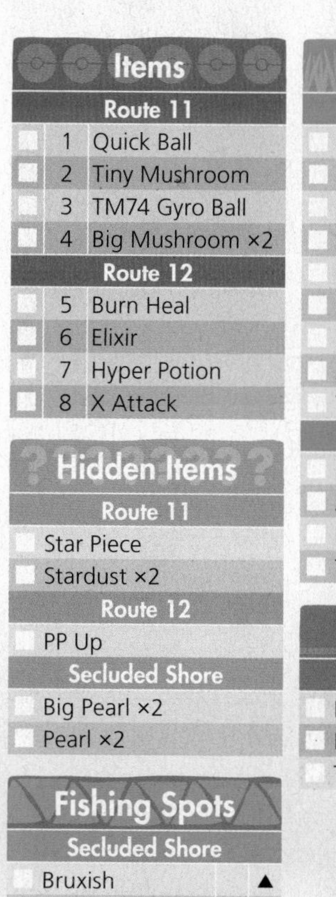

Items

	Item
Route 11	
1	Quick Ball
2	Tiny Mushroom
3	TM74 Gyro Ball
4	Big Mushroom ×2
Route 12	
5	Burn Heal
6	Elixir
7	Hyper Potion
8	X Attack

Hidden Items

Hidden Items
Route 11
Star Piece
Stardust ×2
Route 12
PP Up
Secluded Shore
Big Pearl ×2
Pearl ×2

Fishing Spots

Secluded Shore	
Bruxish	▲
Magikarp	◎
Wishiwashi	○

Rare Fishing Spots

Secluded Shore	
Bruxish	○
Magikarp	◎
Wishiwashi	○

◎ frequent ○ average △ rare
▲ almost never ○ day only ☽ night only
Pokémon Sun *Pokémon Moon*

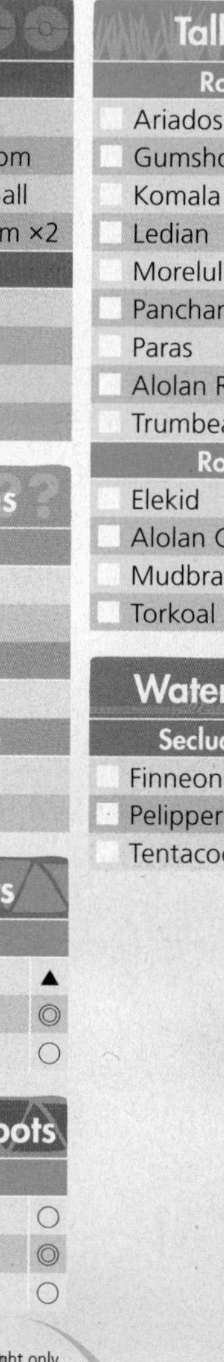

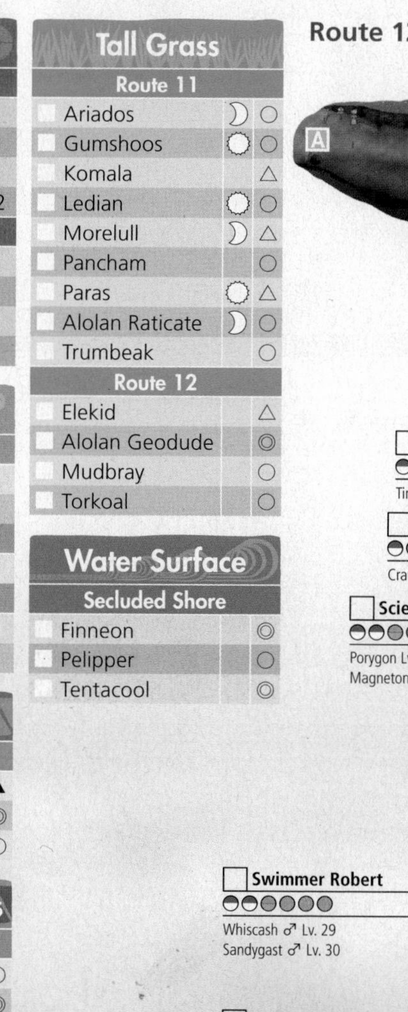

Tall Grass

Pokémon	Time	Rate
Route 11		
Ariados	☽	○
Gumshoos	○	○
Komala		△
Ledian	○	○
Morelull	☽	△
Pancham		○
Paras	○	△
Alolan Raticate	☽	○
Trumbeak		○
Route 12		
Elekid		△
Alolan Geodude		◎
Mudbray		○
Torkoal		○

Water Surface

Secluded Shore	
Finneon	◎
Pelipper	○
Tentacool	◎

Route 12 and Secluded Shore

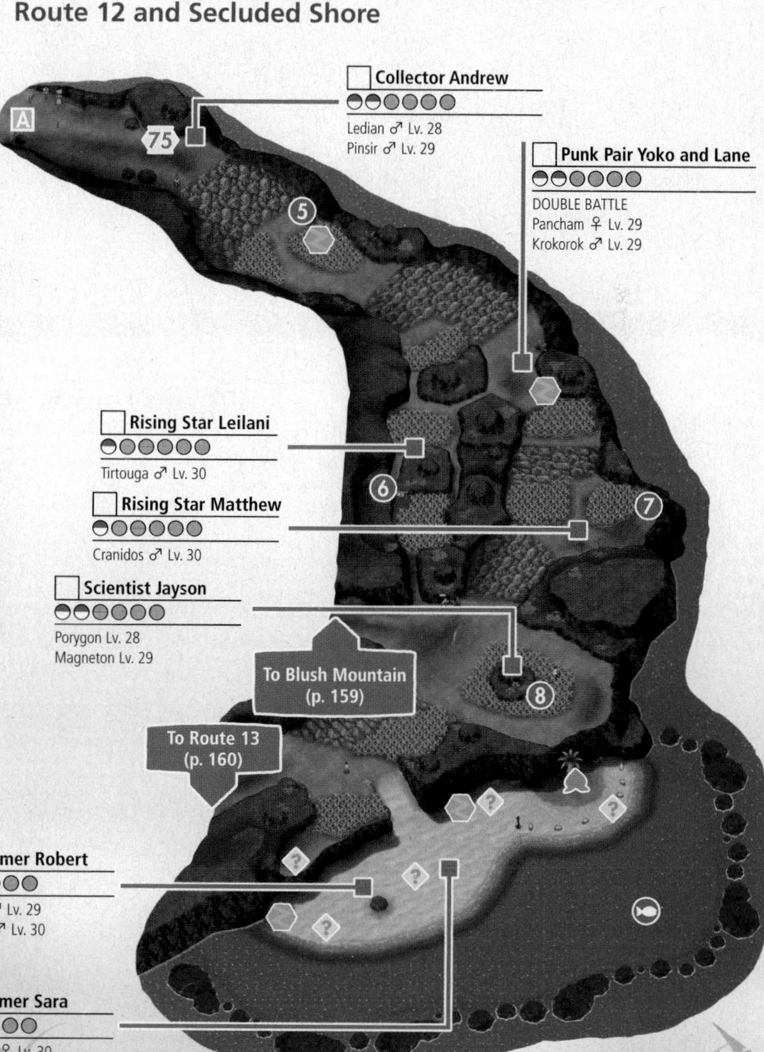

1 Reach Route 12 and receive a new Ride Pokémon

Travel through the short Route 11, speaking with the Trial Guide at its east end to open the captain's barricade. Pass through to reach Route 12, where your friend Hapu catches up to you once again. This time, Hapu registers her partner—Mudsdale—to your Ride Pager. Now you've got what you need to navigate through Route 12!

Ride Pokémon: Mudsdale

Mudsdale Gallop

You got a new Ride Pokémon! Mudsdale can help you cross rough, rocky paths that no other Pokémon can travel, including parts of Route 12. Press Ⓨ and select Mudsdale Gallop to mount Mudsdale, then move the Circle Pad in any direction to steer Mudsdale and hold Ⓑ to gallop. Note that you cannot call for Mudsdale while indoors or in narrow areas, and you can't get down from Mudsdale while crossing rough, rocky terrain.

Tip

You're 1/3 less likely to encounter wild Pokémon while riding Mudsdale through terrain in which wild Pokémon encounters can occur (such as tall grass).

S75: Tackle a tough Trainer

The "Kahuna of Route 12" will battle you—but only after you've beaten every other Trainer on Route 12!

Reward: TM77 Psych Up

2 Explore Route 12 and the Secluded Shore

There's plenty to see and do now that you can ride Mudsdale. Trot along Route 12, swinging down to the Secluded Shore to sniff out some hidden goodies. Battle more Trainers, catch more Pokémon, and claim more items as you explore with Mudsdale and Stoutland. If your Pokémon aren't too tuckered out, head west to explore Blush Mountain as well for a chance to catch some rare Pokémon. Remember: you can fly back to Malie City's Pokémon Center and rest your team any time you like. Then make your way down south to Route 13 next (p. 160).

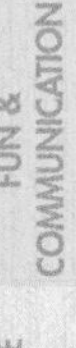

Blush Mountain

Rising up to the west of Route 12, Blush Mountain is home to Alola's Geothermal Power Plant. Visitors are welcome to tour the plant and learn how the steam of the nearby volcano is processed into energy that powers the entire region.

Team Recommendations

WATER GROUND ROCK

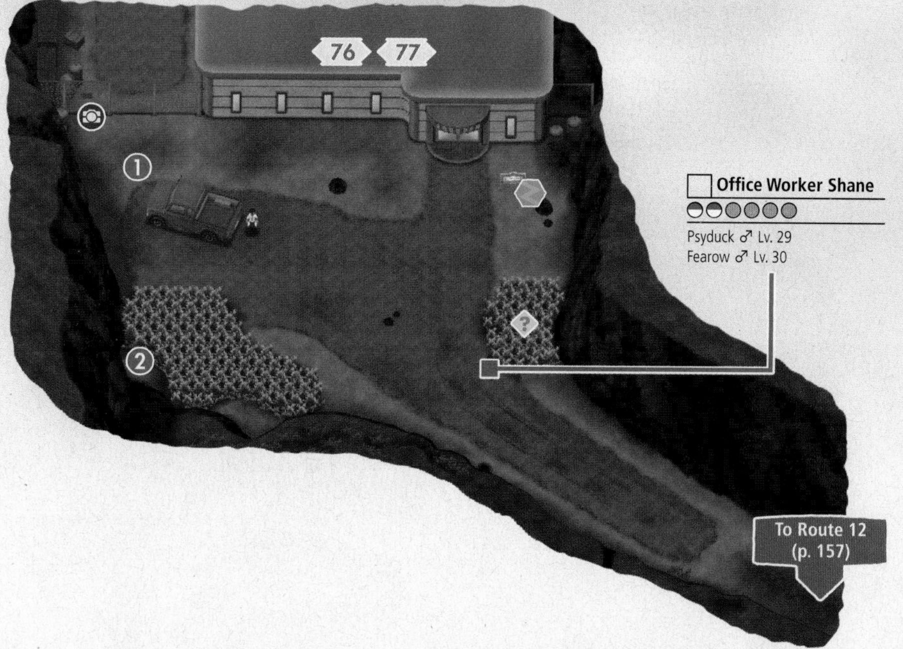

Items

	Items
1	Timer Ball
2	Sun Stone

Hidden Items

- Zinc

Tall Grass

Pokémon	Version	Frequency
Charjabug		△
Elekid		△
Alolan Geodude		○
Mudbray		○
Togedemaru		△
Torkoal	Pokémon Sun	△
Torkoal	Pokémon Moon	○
Turtonator	Pokémon Sun	△

◎ frequent ○ average △ rare ▲ almost never ○ day only ☽ night only ☀ *Pokémon Sun* ☾ *Pokémon Moon*

1 Pop by the Power Plant (Optional)

You don't have to make this little detour into Blush Mountain, but it's worth checking out if you aren't in a rush. You can catch some more Pokémon here, find a few more items, and learn all about the Geothermal Power Plant, which turns the steam produced by the nearby volcano into clean energy for almost the whole island.

Tip

Remember to catch a Togedemaru for that fanatic back in Malie City's apparel shop (p. 142). He'll pay you top dollar for its Pokédex data!

S76: Score a Lure Ball

Meet up with your friend Oak once again inside the geothermal plant. He'll teach you a bit about Alola's volcanoes and Diglett and hand you a Lure Ball before departing.

Reward: Lure Ball

S77: Get a shocking TM

Visit the Geothermal Power Plant during the day and talk to the scientist with the power-hungry Magnemite. You'll get a TM after receiving a small shock.

Reward: TM63 Embargo

Route 13

Running along the island's south edge, Route 13 links Ula'ula's eastern mountains with its southernmost settlement, Tapu Village. To the north lies Haina Desert (which leads to the Ruins of Abundance): a sweltering place that can't be entered until the Ghost-type trial has been completed.

Team Recommendations
GRASS ELECTRIC

Items	
1	Moon Stone
2	Guard Spec.

Vending Machine	
Motel	
Fresh Water	₽400
Lemonade	₽700
Soda Pop	₽600

Fishing Spots	
Bruxish	▲
Magikarp	◎
Wishiwashi	○

Rare Fishing Spots	
Bruxish	○
Magikarp	◎
Wishiwashi	○

◎ frequent ○ average △ rare
▲ almost never ☼ day only ☽ night only
Pokémon Sun Pokémon Moon

1 Get a warning from Gladion

Hau is waiting for you on Route 13 and hands you a Max Potion, but your happy reunion is suddenly interrupted by Gladion, who appears with an ominous warning. It seems that Team Skull is also looking for Cosmog, the little Pokémon that Lillie calls "Nebby." Lillie is not a Trainer, so she would have no way to fight the thugs off if they find her.

Reward: Max Potion

S78: Take off with TM12 Taunt

Talk to a punk in the trailer closest to Haina Desert entrance and accept his battle challenge! It actually won't be much of a challenge, as the punk backs out and hands you TM12 Taunt for your trouble.

Reward: TM12 Taunt

Tip

Haina Desert lies to the north, but you can't explore it until you've completed your next trial. Keep moving west into Tapu Village and Route 14 for now.

Tapu Village / Route 14

Ride Pokémon Needed 

A small settlement perched near Ula'ula's south shore, Tapu Village is best known for its abandoned Thrifty Megamart: a spacious superstore that was razed by the island's guardian deity, Tapu Bulu. And down on the shore, you can explore Route 14 and its shockingly black sand.

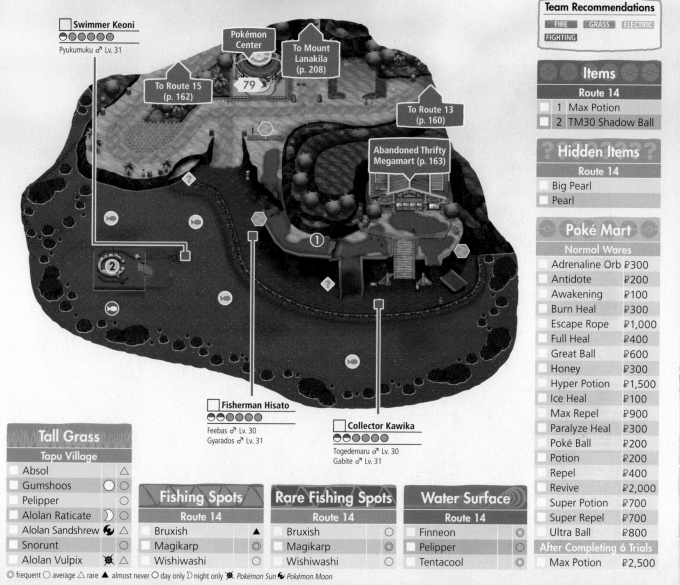

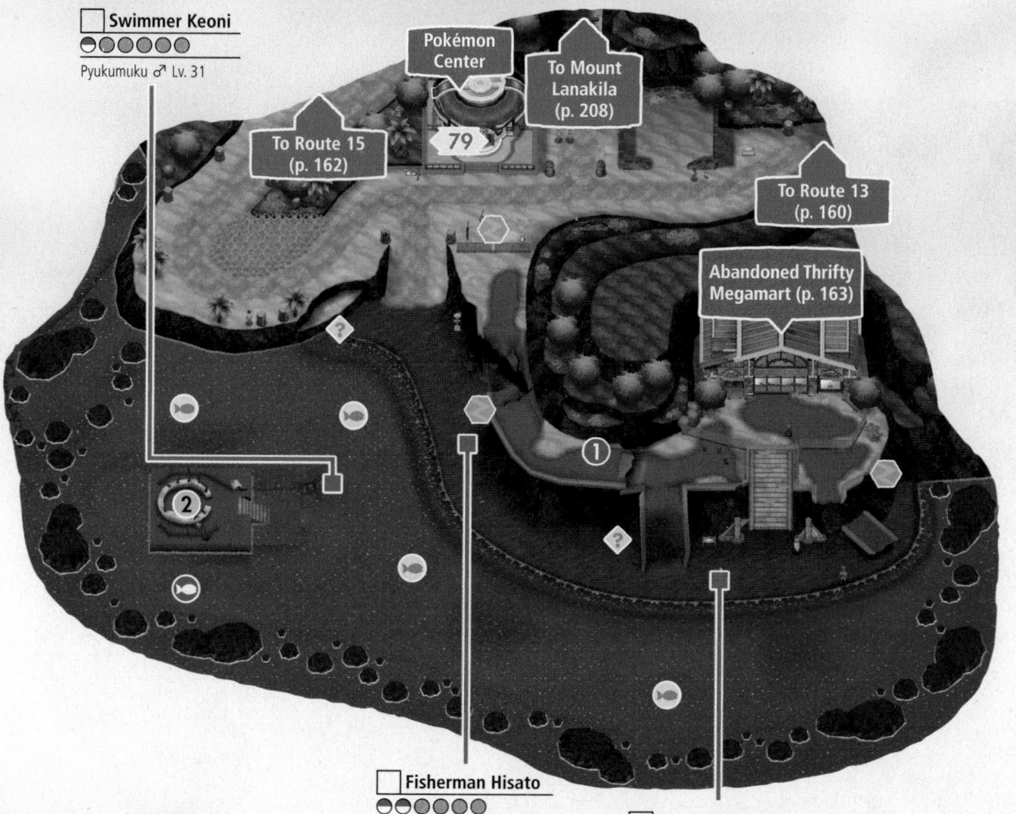

Pokémon Center

To Mount Lanakila (p. 208)

To Route 15 (p. 162)

To Route 13 (p. 160)

Abandoned Thrifty Megamart (p. 163)

79

Swimmer Keoni
Pyukumuku ♂ Lv. 31

Fisherman Hisato
Feebas ♂ Lv. 30
Gyarados ♂ Lv. 31

Collector Kawika
Togedemaru ♂ Lv. 30
Gabite ♂ Lv. 31

Team Recommendations

FIRE GRASS ELECTRIC FIGHTING

Items

Route 14		
	1	Max Potion
	2	TM30 Shadow Ball

Hidden Items

Route 14	
	Big Pearl
	Pearl

Poké Mart

Normal Wares	
Adrenaline Orb	₽300
Antidote	₽200
Awakening	₽100
Burn Heal	₽300
Escape Rope	₽1,000
Full Heal	₽400
Great Ball	₽600
Honey	₽300
Hyper Potion	₽1,500
Ice Heal	₽100
Max Repel	₽900
Paralyze Heal	₽300
Poké Ball	₽200
Potion	₽200
Repel	₽400
Revive	₽2,000
Super Potion	₽700
Super Repel	₽700
Ultra Ball	₽800
After Completing 6 Trials	
Max Potion	₽2,500

Tall Grass

Tapu Village		
Absol		△
Gumshoos	○ (day only)	○
Pelipper		○
Alolan Raticate	☽ (night only)	○
Alolan Sandshrew	Pokémon Moon	△
Snorunt		○
Alolan Vulpix	Pokémon Sun	△

Fishing Spots

Route 14	
Bruxish	▲
Magikarp	◎
Wishiwashi	○

Rare Fishing Spots

Route 14	
Bruxish	○
Magikarp	◎
Wishiwashi	○

Water Surface

Route 14	
Finneon	◎
Pelipper	○
Tentacool	◎

◎ frequent ○ average △ rare ▲ almost never ○ day only ☽ night only *Pokémon Sun* *Pokémon Moon*

1 Rest your Pokémon on the way to Route 15

Finally, a place to rest! After chatting with Hau about the new Pokémon League that Professor Kukui is building atop Mount Lanakila, swing into the Pokémon Center and give your team some well-deserved downtime. Take a spin through Tapu Village afterward, and head south to comb the black sands of Route 14's shore. When you're ready, follow the road west from Tapu Village to reach Route 15.

S79: Trade for Alolan Graveler

A Hiker in the Pokémon Center wants to trade you his Alolan Graveler for a Haunter. You can catch one at the abandoned Thrifty Megamart after you've completed the trial there (p. 163). Your new Alolan Graveler will immediately evolve into an Alolan Golem, as it can only do so via trade!

Pokémon: Alolan Graveler

Route 15

Ride Pokémon Needed

An aquatic route that runs along Ula'ula's southwest shore, Route 15 is home to the Aether House: a special place for children who have no one to care for them. This route's huge waterways can only be fully explored with the aid of the speedy Ride Pokémon Sharpedo.

Team Recommendations

ELECTRIC FIGHTING

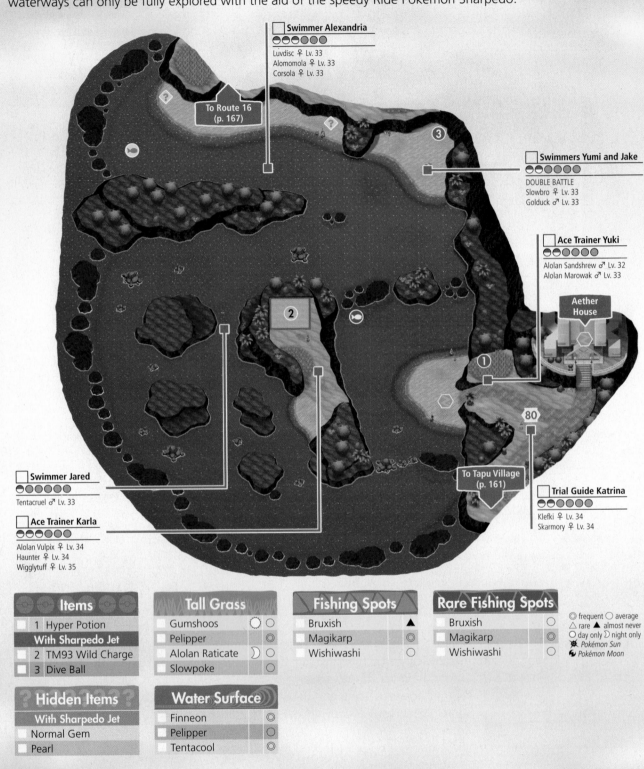

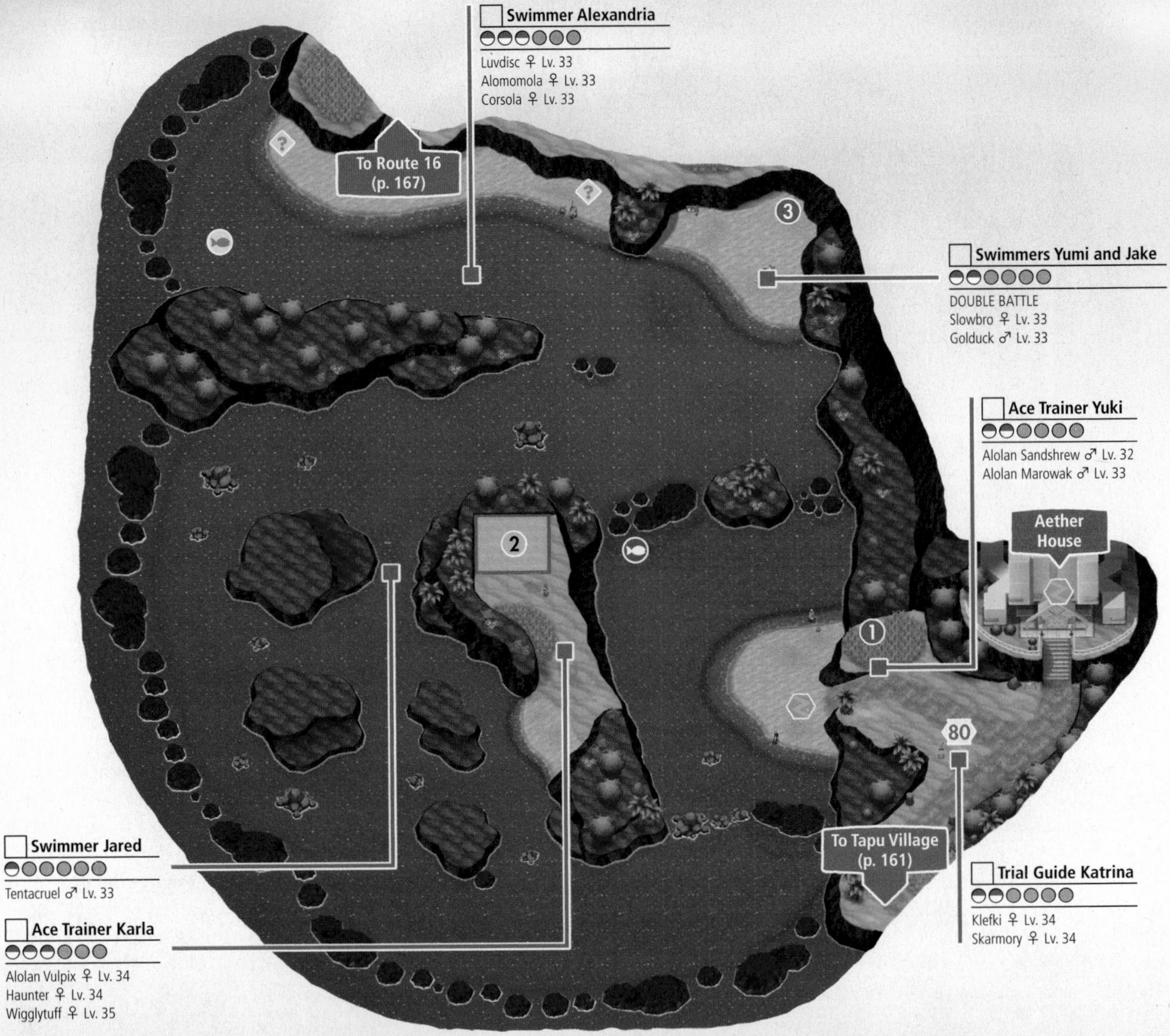

Items	
1	Hyper Potion
With Sharpedo Jet	
2	TM93 Wild Charge
3	Dive Ball

Tall Grass		
Gumshoos	day only	average
Pelipper		frequent
Alolan Raticate	night only	average
Slowpoke		average

Fishing Spots	
Bruxish	almost never
Magikarp	frequent
Wishiwashi	average

Rare Fishing Spots	
Bruxish	average
Magikarp	frequent
Wishiwashi	average

◎ frequent ○ average △ rare ▲ almost never ○ day only ☽ night only *Pokémon Sun* *Pokémon Moon*

Hidden Items
With Sharpedo Jet
Normal Gem
Pearl

Water Surface	
Finneon	frequent
Pelipper	average
Tentacool	frequent

S80: Battle a strong Trainer

A Trial Guide at the start of Route 15 will test your skill in battle, but only after you've beaten all the other Trainers on Route 15. You'll need a new Ride Pokémon in order to reach all of Route 15's Trainers.

Reward: PP Max

1 Clash with the kids at the Aether House

As you enter Route 15, you catch sight of the Aether House, which is the home of your new friend Acerola from Malie City. Explore the route if you like, then head into the Aether House, where Hau joins you. Careful, though: seeing you as a stranger, the Aether House children suddenly swarm and drag you into battle to protect their home!

Tip

Check the Aether House's rooms to find a Zygarde Cell in a corner. How did that get here?

2 Meet Captain Acerola, then battle Team Skull

After the battle, Acerola appears with a bombshell: she's the captain in charge of your next trial! Acerola will guide you back to Route 14, where the Ghost-type trial awaits. You run into trouble as you step outside, however: it's another Team Skull Grunt and he's harassing poor Lillie! He has a single Drowzee, and you should be more than up to defeating this Psychic-type Pokémon with its weaknesses to Bug-, Ghost-, and Dark-type moves.

3 Return to Route 14 and take on Acerola's trial

Lillie thanks you with a handful of Luxury Balls, which she hopes will help you on your island challenge. Acerola invites Lillie to rest at the Aether House while she guides you back to her trial. Head south, returning to Tapu Village, and rest your Pokémon before continuing south onto Route 14's black sand beach. Climb the stairs at the beach's far end to arrive at the abandoned Thrifty Megamart—the site of the Ghost-type trial!

Reward: Luxury Ball ×5

Abandoned Thrifty Megamart

Once an oasis of steals and savings, this rundown superstore is now stocked with all sorts of spooky Pokémon. Angered at seeing such a superficial shop built upon its sacred ground, Tapu Bulu ravaged the Thrifty Megamart, which now serves as the site of the Ghost-type trial.

Interior

After Completing 6 Trials	
Golbat	◎
Haunter	◎
Klefki	△
Mimikyu	▲

◎ frequent ○ average
△ rare ▲ almost never
○ day only ☽ night only
Pokémon Sun
Pokémon Moon

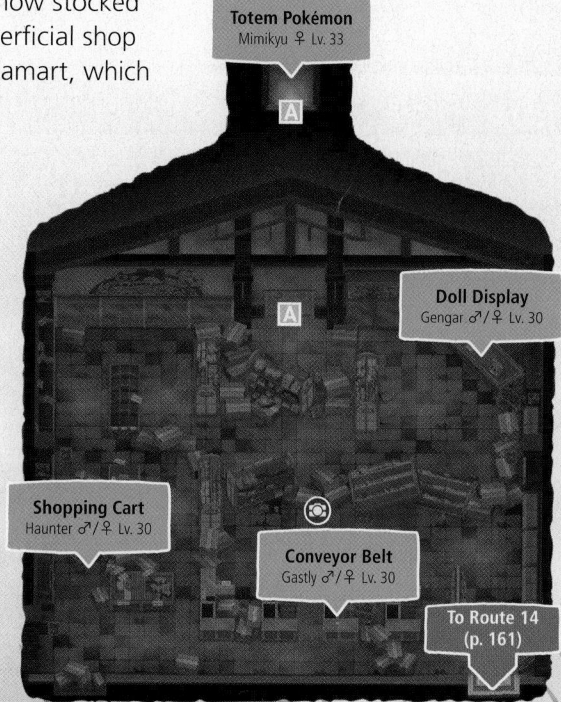

GETTING STARTED

BATTLE & STRATEGY
POKÉMON COLLECTING
FUN & COMMUNICATION
ADVENTURE DATA

This hair-raising trial has you busting a number of Ghost-type Pokémon that are haunting the abandoned Thrifty Megamart. You'll be battling a variety of Ghost-type foes as you explore the spooky store, so pack your team with plenty of Dark-type Pokémon, like Absol (conveniently found in Tapu Village) and Alolan Meowth (found in Malie Garden, among other places). Claim TM30 Shadow Ball from Route 14 as well, and you can teach these Dark-type Pokémon a powerful Ghost-type move that's sure to help you succeed.

Acerola's Trial Goals:

- Catch Ghost-type Pokémon with a special Poké Finder
- Defeat the Totem Pokémon
- Receive the Z-Crystal

Dark-type Pokémon are great until you reach the Totem Pokémon. It uses a powerful Fairy-type move that's super effective against Dark types, so you'll need a backup plan. Steel-type Pokémon and moves are super effective against the Totem. Try using a Skarmory that can be caught on Route 10 or an Alolan Diglett found in Diglett's Tunnel.

GETTING STARTED

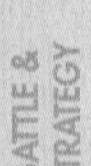

BATTLE & STRATEGY
POKÉMON COLLECTING
FUN & COMMUNICATION
ADVENTURE DATA

1 Check the conveyor belt

As you approach the trial site, Acerola updates your Poké Finder with a special function to help you spot the unseen in her trial. Gather your courage and enter the shop, then search for signs that suggest the presence of Ghost-type Pokémon. First up is the conveyor belt that suddenly starts moving—check it out with your Poké Finder, but be prepared for a ghastly surprise!

Gastly

What's this? Your enhanced Poké Finder has revealed a Ghost-type Pokémon! You may have battled Gastly before around Hau'oli Cemetery—perhaps you've even caught one. It sure looks scary, but it's no match for the Dark-type Pokémon you've (hopefully) brought with you into this trial.

Gastly ♂/♀ Lv. 30 — GHOST / POISON

Weak to: PSYCHIC, GHOST, DARK

2 Scrutinize a shopping cart

Drat! That wasn't the Totem Pokémon! Well, at least you know your Poké Finder works. Take a deep breath and then continue to explore this eerie store. When you spot a shopping cart moving all on its own, fire up the Poké Finder and snap a shot of Haunter!

Haunter

Haunter shares all of Gastly's weaknesses, making it easy prey for your chosen Pokémon. Send it to rest with a slew of supereffective moves. Note that Haunter has the Levitate Ability, however, so Ground-type moves won't work on it.

Haunter ♂/♀ Lv. 30 — GHOST / POISON

Weak to: PSYCHIC, GHOST, DARK

3 Scope out floating dolls

No sign of the Totem Pokémon yet, but you do catch a fleeting glimpse of a fleeing Pikachu...or is it? Follow it to the back of the store, where a rack of dolls suddenly starts moving. Whip out your Poké Finder, take your time, and get a pic of Gengar!

Gengar

Another Ghost- and Poison-type Pokémon, Gengar should be short work for your team—assuming you came prepared with plenty of Dark-type Pokémon. Its Shadow Ball is quite powerful, so don't give it too many chances to strike.

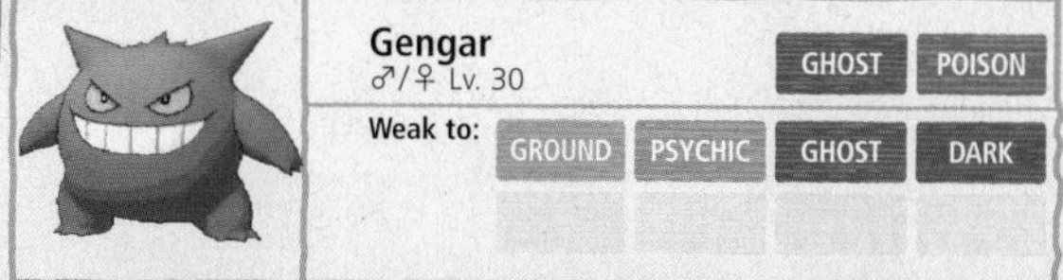

4 Pursue "Pikachu" into the back room

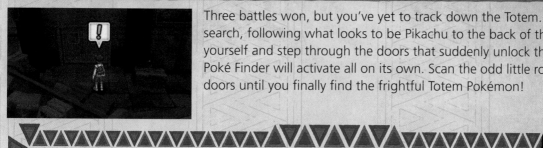

Three battles won, but you've yet to track down the Totem. Continue your search, following what looks to be Pikachu to the back of the store. Brace yourself and step through the doors that suddenly unlock themselves, and your Poké Finder will activate all on its own. Scan the odd little room beyond the doors until you finally find the frightful Totem Pokémon!

Totem Mimikyu

Totem Mimikyu forces you to change your tactics—or pay the ultimate price. Its aura raises all of its stats, and its Disguise Ability effectively nullifies your first attack. It primarily strikes with Play Rough—a powerful Fairy-type move that will dice up your Dark-type Pokémon in seconds. Steel types are ideal for countering this tough opponent.

Totem Mimikyu can also use Mimic to learn your Pokémon's moves—a very bad thing if you've decided to send out Ghost types loaded with strong Ghost-type moves. Its Gengar SOS ally has the Cursed Body Ability, which may disable a move used against it, so don't battle Gengar with any moves you're relying on to defeat Totem Mimikyu.

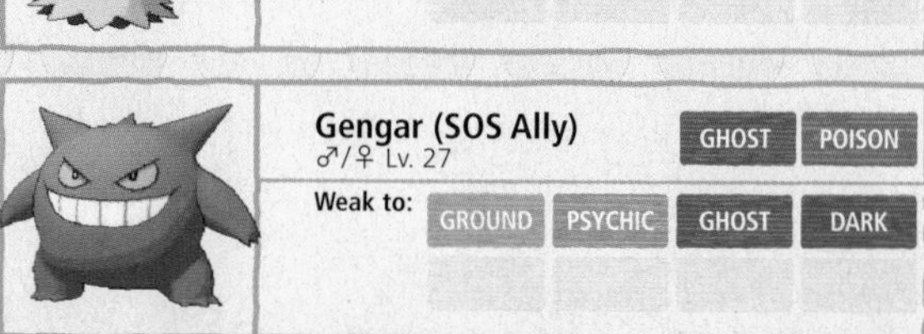

5 Receive the Z-Crystal, then return to Route 15

For completing her frightening trial, Acerola gives you Ghostium Z and some Dusk Balls—and perhaps some goose bumps as well, when she tells you that there's no small room at the back of the store. Creepy! You're probably ready to head back to Route 15, making a pit stop at the Pokémon Center in Tapu Village along the way.

Reward: Ghostium Z, Dusk Ball ×10

Tip

If your nerves aren't wrecked yet, consider reentering the abandoned Thrifty Megamart and using your newfound Dusk Balls to catch some of those ghastly Ghost types. Nab a Haunter and you can trade with that Hiker waiting in Tapu Village's Pokémon Center (p. 161). You can also score another reward later on if you catch a Mimikyu.

Route 15 Revisited

p. 162

1 Battle Plumeria at the Aether House

What's this? Team Skull is skulking around the Aether House again, and they're not interested in answering any questions. Be prepared, as Plumeria immediately pulls you into battle!

Team Skull Admin Plumeria's Pokémon

Plumeria doesn't hold anything back this time. Her Golbat tries to mix up your Pokémon with its Confuse Ray and poison them with its Poison Fang. Her Salazzle can also poison your Pokémon with a potent dose of Toxic, so keep your Grass- and Fairy-type Pokémon well away from the fray.

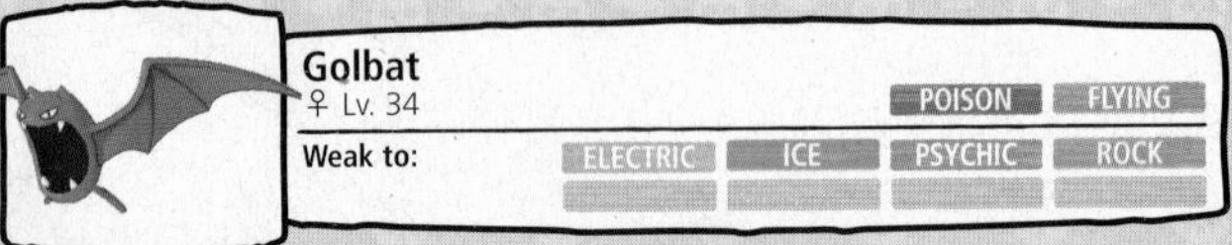

Golbat ♀ Lv. 34	POISON	FLYING		
Weak to:	ELECTRIC	ICE	PSYCHIC	ROCK

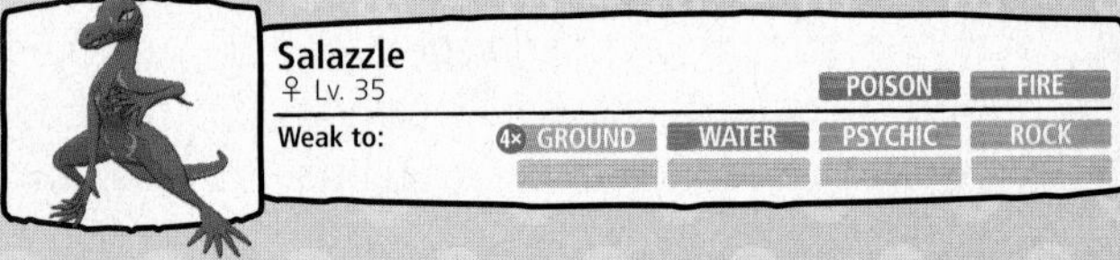

Salazzle ♀ Lv. 35	POISON	FIRE		
Weak to:	4× GROUND	WATER	PSYCHIC	ROCK

2 Receive a Rare Candy and a new objective

Reward: Rare Candy

Plumeria may have lost the battle, but she's not about to give up. She and her beloved Grunts have stolen a Pokémon from the Aether House, and you'll have to come to their base in Po Town alone if you want to get it back. The poor little Trainer who lost her Pokémon gives you a Rare Candy, along with a desperate plea that you save her precious friend.

3 Cross Route 15's waters atop Sharpedo

Ride Pokémon: Sharpedo

Po Town lies beyond Route 15, so you'll need a way to cross the route's rocky waters. Luckily, someone on the beach is able to help you: Grimsley. A member of the Unova region's Elite Four, he is soaking up Alola's rays on the shore. Talk to him, and he'll happily register Sharpedo to your Ride Pager. Now you can ride Sharpedo and explore all of Route 15's waterways on your way to Po Town!

Sharpedo Jet

You got a new Ride Pokémon! Like Lapras, Sharpedo helps you cross large bodies of water. Stand near the water's edge, press Ⓨ, and select Sharpedo Jet to start riding Sharpedo. Use the Circle Pad to steer Sharpedo, and hold Ⓑ to use Sharpedo Jet. This causes Sharpedo to swim faster—so fast that it can smash right through certain rocks that block your way over the water.

Tip

You're 2/3 less likely to encounter wild Pokémon while riding Sharpedo across terrain where encounters with wild Pokémon can occur (such as the water's surface).

Tip

Now that you can ride Sharpedo, consider revisiting the Melemele Sea (p. 36). Smash through the rocks in the water with Sharpedo to reach new items, including TM80 Rock Slide! You can also enter Ten Carat Hill (p. 85) from the water and claim TM64 Explosion.

Tip

Now that you have Sharpedo, you can fully explore Route 15 (p. 162). Beat all of its Trainers, then take on the tough Trial Guide at Route 15's south entrance for a special reward!

Route 16

This short route connects Route 15 with Ula'ula Meadow. Its Pokémon Center provides a place for travelers to recuperate as they jaunt along Ula'ula's west shore.

Team Recommendations
ELECTRIC FIGHTING

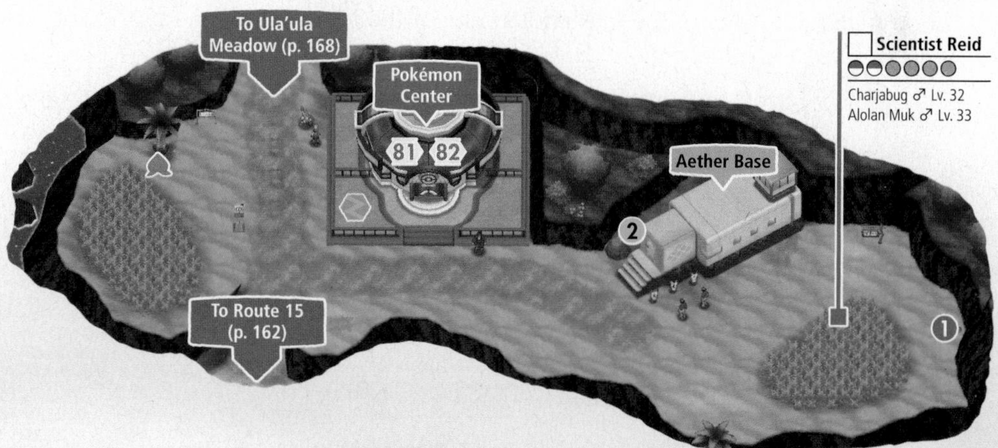

Tall Grass

Pokémon		
Gumshoos	○	○
Pelipper		◎
Alolan Raticate	☽	○
Slowpoke		○

◎ frequent ○ average △ rare ▲ almost never ○ day only ☽ night only
Pokémon Sun *Pokémon Moon*

Items

	Item
1	PP Up
2	TM81 X-Scissor

Poké Mart

Normal Wares	
Adrenaline Orb	₽300
Antidote	₽200
Awakening	₽100
Burn Heal	₽300
Escape Rope	₽1,000
Full Heal	₽400
Great Ball	₽600
Honey	₽300
Hyper Potion	₽1,500
Ice Heal	₽100
Max Potion	₽2,500
Max Repel	₽900
Paralyze Heal	₽300
Poké Ball	₽200
Potion	₽200
Repel	₽400
Revive	₽2,000
Super Potion	₽700
Super Repel	₽700
Ultra Ball	₽800

1 Make a pit stop on your way to Po Town

Route 16 is short and sweet. Catch your breath at the Pokémon Center, and make sure to purchase any items you think you'll need for the looming Po Town showdown. Explore the route thoroughly, and when you're ready to advance, follow the trail north into Ula'ula Meadow.

S81: Catch and show Mimikyu

Inside the Pokémon Center, an Aether Foundation employee will reward you if you show her Mimikyu's Pokédex data. Catch Mimikyu at the abandoned Thrifty Megamart (p. 163), then return here for your reward!

Reward: ₽20,000

S82: Get a cool Lemonade

If you've ordered a drink five times or more at cafés, speak to the lady sitting near the café. She'll give you a Lemonade.

Reward: Lemonade

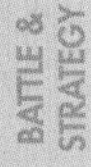

Tip

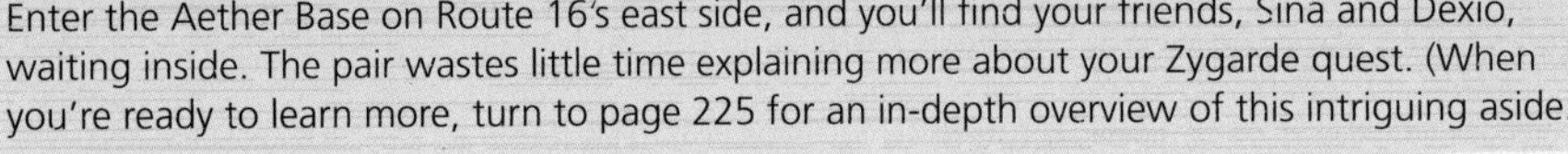

Enter the Aether Base on Route 16's east side, and you'll find your friends, Sina and Dexio, waiting inside. The pair wastes little time explaining more about your Zygarde quest. (When you're ready to learn more, turn to page 225 for an in-depth overview of this intriguing aside.)

Tip

Crawl under the Aether Base to reach a TM tucked behind the trailer: TM81 X-Scissor!

Ula'ula Meadow

Filled with dense fog, fragrant flowers, and feisty Trainers, Ula'ula Meadow is an interesting place to explore. It lies between Route 16 and Route 17, and also connects to the mysterious Lake of the Moone (Pokémon Sun) / Lake of the Sunne (Pokémon Moon) to the northeast.

Team Recommendations

FIRE POISON FLYING ROCK

	Items
1	Red Nectar ×2
2	Adrenaline Orb
3	X Sp. Def
4	Repeat Ball

Tall Grass		
Ariados	night only	average
Cottonee	Pokémon Sun	average
Ledian	day only	average
Oricorio*		average
Petilil	Pokémon Moon	average
Ribombee		average

*The form of Oricorio found in Ula'ula Meadow is the red Oricorio (Baile Style).

Red Flowers		
Ariados	night only	average
Cottonee	Pokémon Sun	average
Ledian	day only	average
Oricorio*		average
Petilil	Pokémon Moon	average
Ribombee		average

◎ frequent ○ average △ rare ▲ almost never ○ day only ☽ night only (Sun icon) Pokémon Sun (Moon icon) Pokémon Moon

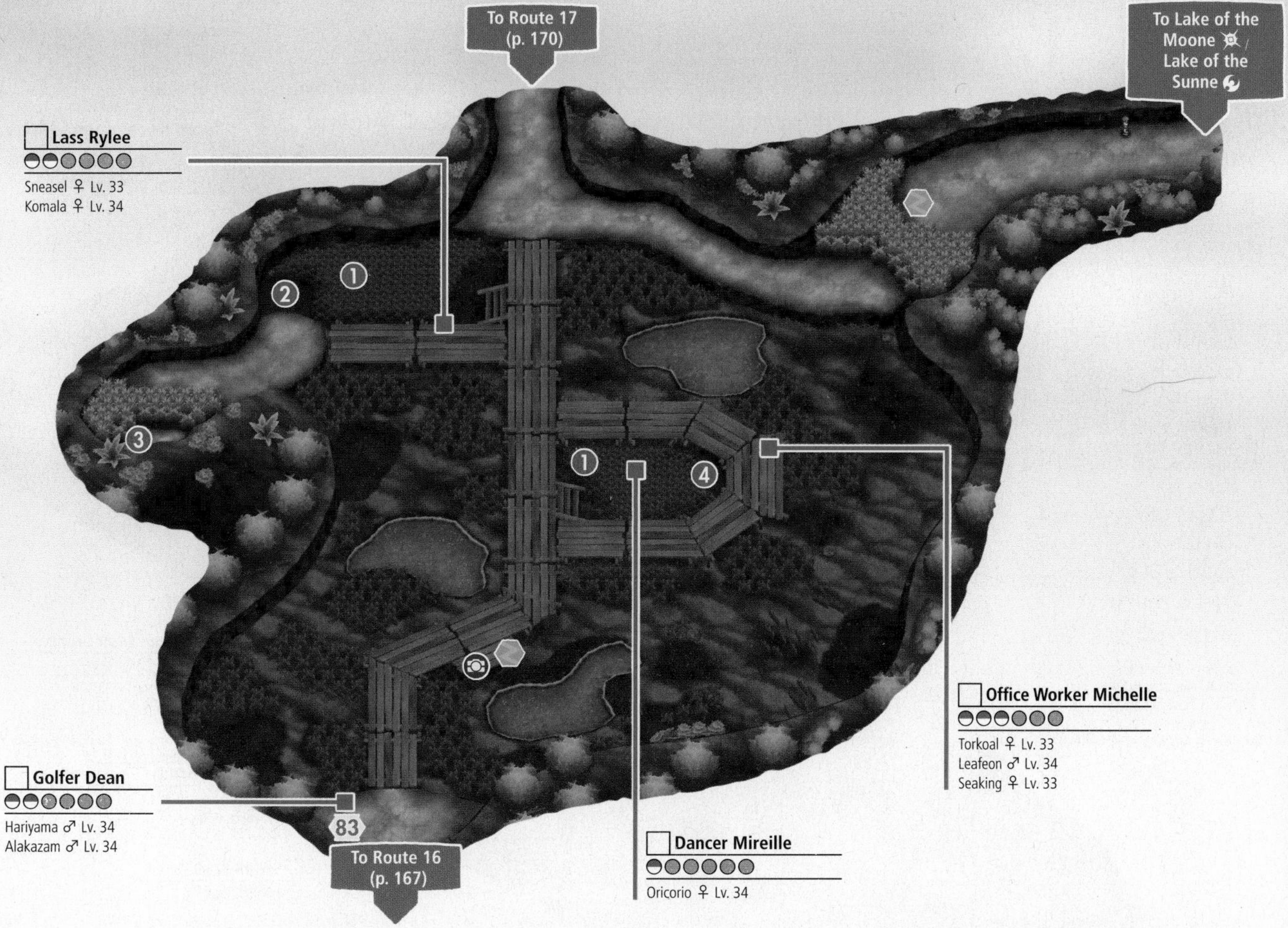

To Route 17 (p. 170)

To Lake of the Moone / Lake of the Sunne

Lass Rylee
Sneasel ♀ Lv. 33
Komala ♀ Lv. 34

Office Worker Michelle
Torkoal ♀ Lv. 33
Leafeon ♂ Lv. 34
Seaking ♀ Lv. 33

Golfer Dean
Hariyama ♂ Lv. 34
Alakazam ♂ Lv. 34

83

To Route 16 (p. 167)

Dancer Mireille
Oricorio ♀ Lv. 34

1 Mosey through the meadow

My, what a mystical place! There's plenty to see and do in this spacious meadow, so take your time and stop to smell the dramatic flowers here. Route 17 lies up north, and beyond it, Po Town—but there's no need to rush. Give the meadow a good going over before you press onward to Route 17.

S83: Challenge a tough Trainer

Defeat all of Ula'ula Meadow's Trainers for a chance to take on the golfer near the entrance. The battle won't be easy, but the reward is worth the effort!

Reward: Flame Orb

Tip

Search any sparkling flowers you see in the meadow to nab some Red Nectar for Oricorio.

Tip

Head northeast and you can reach the lonely Lake of the Moone / Lake of the Sunne. There's not much to see there now, but you can pick up a TM and admire the splendor of the past. Once you've proven yourself worthy as a Champion of Alola, there may be more to find in these ancient ruins. You'll have to experiment quite a bit to find what hides here, but the prize that awaits you is more than worth the trouble!

Route 17

Ride Pokémon Needed

This rugged route runs from Ula'ula Meadow to Po Town, home of Team Skull. A gang of Grunts watches over the road, eager to beat up on unsuspecting travelers.

Team Recommendations

ELECTRIC ICE GROUND FIGHTING ROCK

Tall Grass

Green		
Ariados	☽	○
Fearow		○
Gumshoos	☼	○
Ledian	☼	○
Pancham		○
Alolan Raticate	☽	○
Brown		
Fearow		○
Alolan Graveler		○
Gumshoos	☼	○
Pancham		△
Alolan Raticate	☽	○
Skarmory		△

◎ frequent ○ average
△ rare ▲ almost never
☼ day only ☽ night only
Pokémon Sun
Pokémon Moon

Items

1	Full Heal
2	Lemonade
3	TM84 Poison Jab

Hidden Items

- Dire Hit
- X Attack

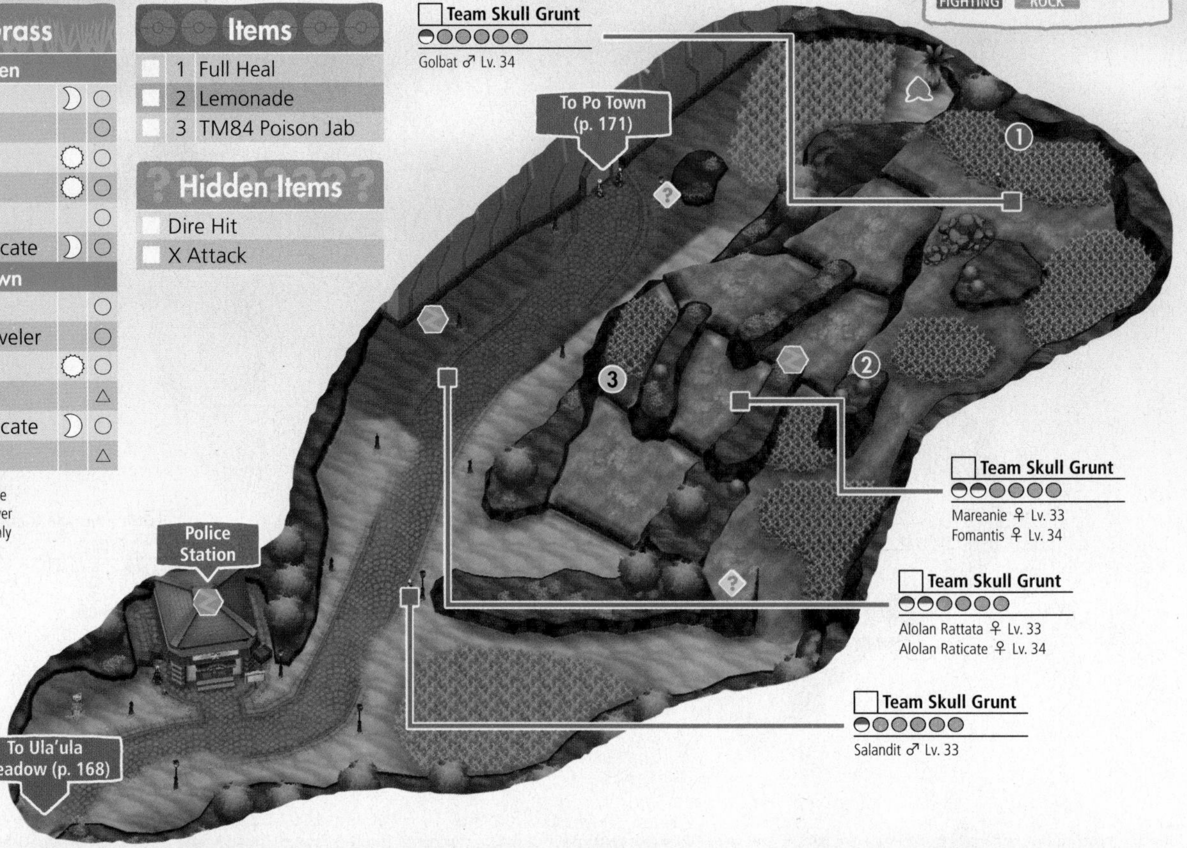

Team Skull Grunt
Golbat ♂ Lv. 34

Team Skull Grunt
Mareanie ♀ Lv. 33
Fomantis ♀ Lv. 34

Team Skull Grunt
Alolan Rattata ♀ Lv. 33
Alolan Raticate ♀ Lv. 34

Team Skull Grunt
Salandit ♂ Lv. 33

To Po Town (p. 171)

Police Station

To Ula'ula Meadow (p. 168)

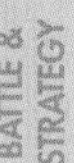
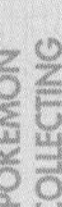

Tip

Some special Pokémon may appear when wild Pokémon call for SOS allies in battle on Route 17, due to the weather. Castform (Rainy Form) and Goomy may appear when it is raining, and it is always raining here. Don't forget that rain will also have some effects in battle. (Read about weather effects in battle on page 146.)

1 Explore Route 17 on the way to Po Town

Route 17 isn't the most cheerful place in Alola, but it's the only road to Po Town. Search the strange old police station to find a Zygarde Core among a multitude of Alolan Meowth. Battle or avoid Team Skull Grunts as you scale the east mountain in search of items and new species of Pokémon. Po Town's imposing gate lies up north, but you'll need to defeat two more Grunts in a Double Battle to clear the way.

Team Skull Grunts' Pokémon

Getting into Po Town isn't easy, because Grunts guard the gate. This is a Double Battle, so you'll be sending out your team's first two Pokémon. Before approaching the Grunts, arrange your team so that the twosome you use can counter the Grunts' pair.

Nanu

This mysterious, dour man shows up shortly after your Double Battle with an ominous warning: those who enter Po Town must be prepared to live as Team Skull, or to battle against them. Assure Nanu that you're ready for the challenge, and he'll let you into Po Town. Team Skull obviously listens to Nanu, but he doesn't exactly seem to be on their side. Aren't those police shields on his shirt? Who is this odd fellow, anyway?

Po Town

This once-fine city is now covered with grime, graffiti, and Team Skull Grunts. It is anything but inviting, and there's no getting through here without a fight!

Items

☐	1	Ice Stone
☐	2	Smoke Ball
☐	3	Rare Candy
☐	4	Max Repel

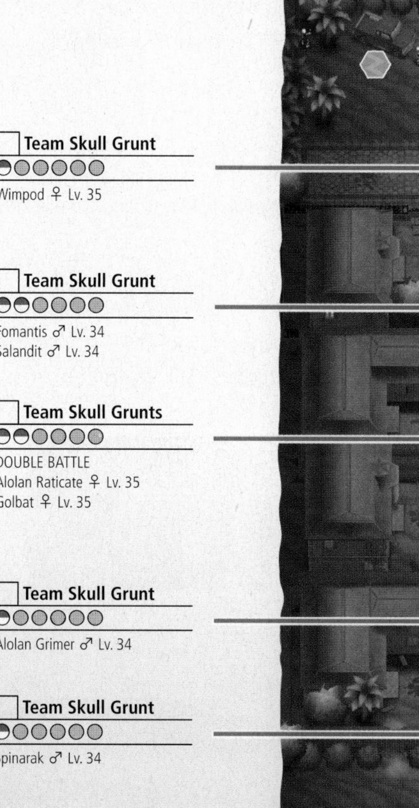

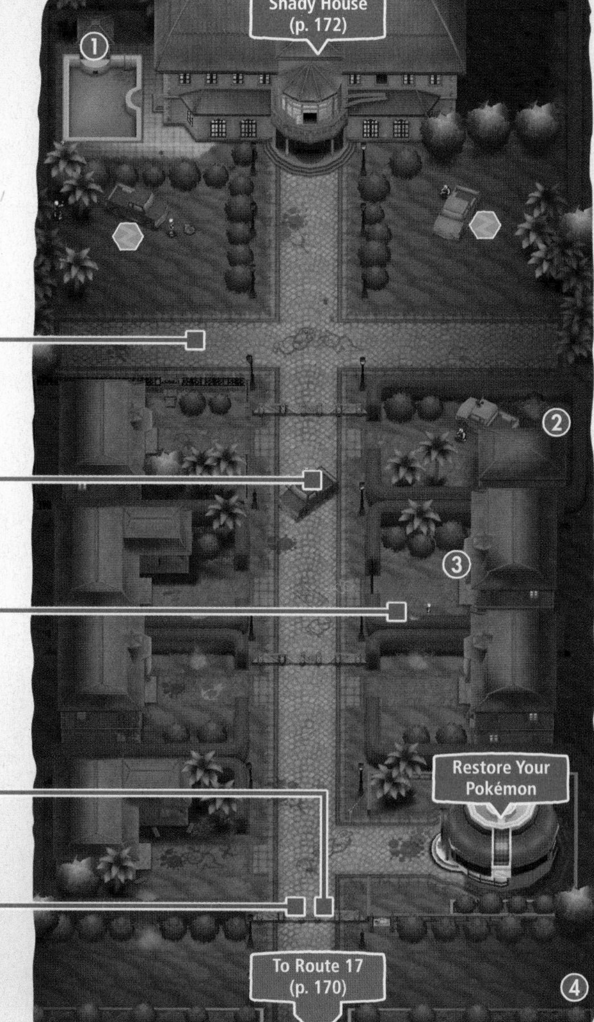

1 Find a way past the barricade

Wow, what a dump! Team Skull has really done a number on this place, and they've even erected a barricade that blocks off the main road. Sneak past by heading west and crawling through a small hole in the hedge, but beware: two Grunts who thought they'd outsmarted you will force you to battle them, one at a time. Mind the rain, which will lower the effectiveness of Fire-type moves!

Team Skull Grunts' Pokémon

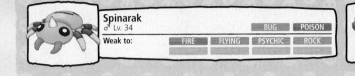

The two Grunts battle you one after the other, so you must endure two Single Battles in a row. Luckily, the battles aren't too tough. Beware of their Pokémon's penchant for poisoning yours, and use moves with high accuracy against Alolan Grimer, which uses Minimize to sharply raise its evasiveness.

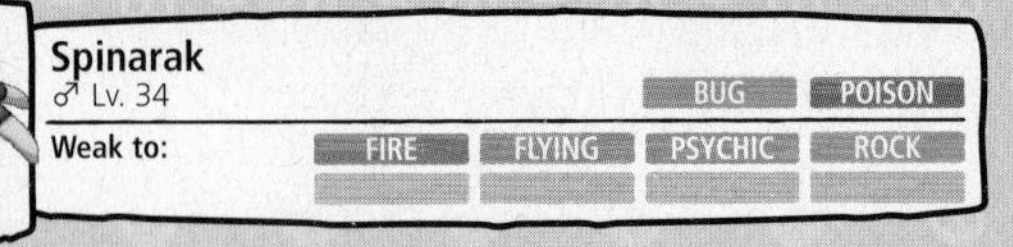

Alolan Grimer
♂ Lv. 34
POISON DARK
Weak to: GROUND

Tip

Stop by Po Town's half-destroyed Pokémon Center if your team needs some healing. The Grunts inside are so desperate for money that they'll heal your team—for a price. There's no hope of using the PC or buying goods at the Poké Mart, because the Grunts haven't been able to pay their power bill in months!

2 Make your way to the Shady House

More barricades block your progress through Po Town. Search for additional holes in the hedges and crawl through them to sneak through the rundown town. Avoid or seek out Trainers as you make your way north. Press onward until you reach a large mansion known as the Shady House.

Shady House

True to its name, the Shady House is filled with shady characters—namely Team Skull Grunts. Guzma, the bug Pokémon-loving boss of Team Skull, holds court in his bedroom on the second floor.

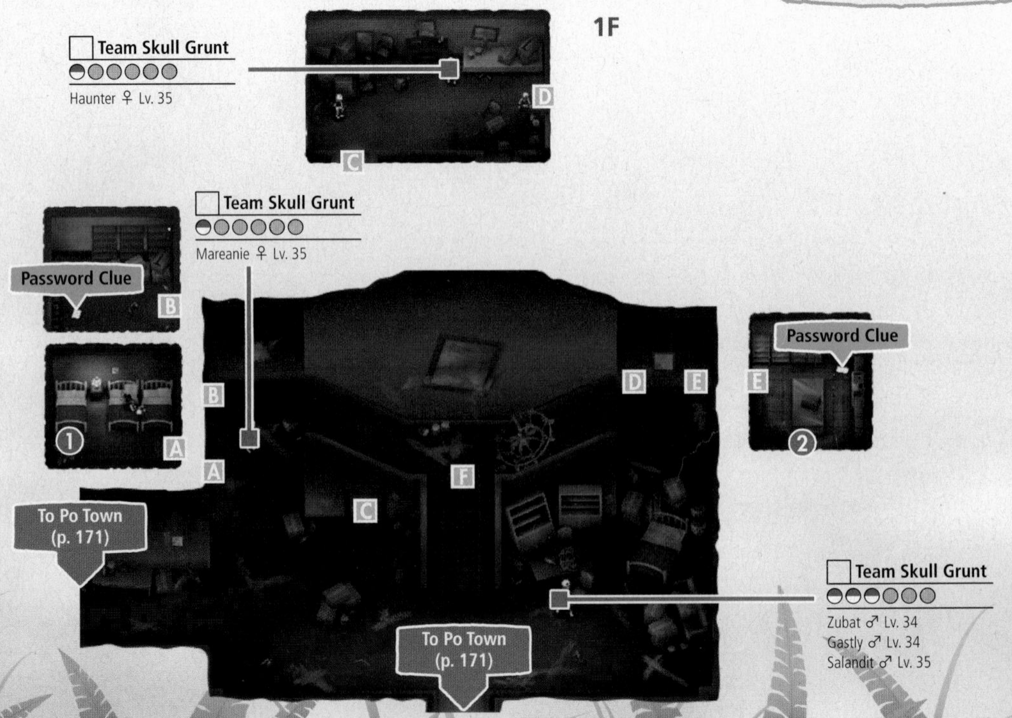

Items

☐	1	Max Revive
☐	2	Heal Powder
☐	3	TM36 Sludge Bomb
☐	4	Iron
☐	5	Escape Rope

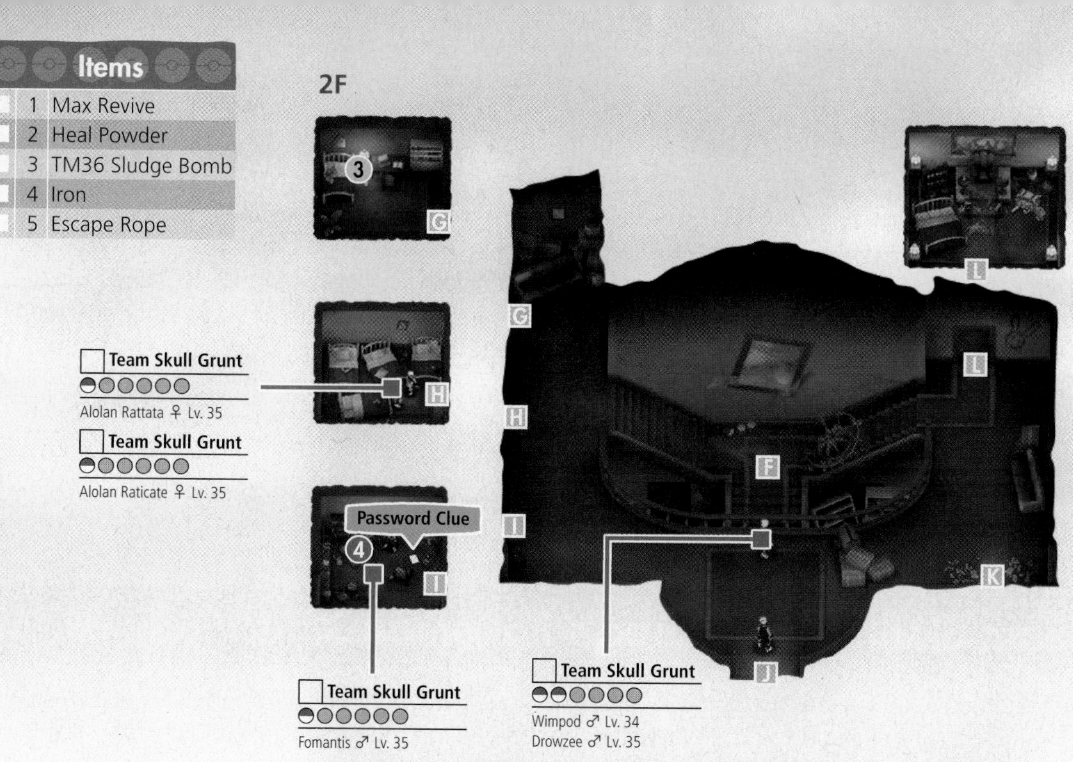

1 Search the Shady House for clues

Getting to Guzma isn't easy, because the Shady House is packed full of Grunts ready to pick a fight. Take them on as you visit each room, scouring the rooms for items and clues to the passwords you'll soon need on the second floor.

2 Get past the guard on the second floor

The guard on the second floor is waiting for your answer to three questions: which move does Master Guzma like best, which Pokémon does Master Guzma like best, and which drink does Master Guzma like best. If you failed to find the clues or you simply can't seem to get past the guard, turn the page for the answers.

Feeling stuck? If you need a little help, here are the answers to the Team Skull Quiz: Beat Up, Golisopod, and Tapu Cocoa. And remember that a Team Skull member is no yes-man, so when you are asked if you're sure about the answers, reply with a firm "No!"

3 Battle Guzma in his bedroom

Once you've gotten past the guard, work your way around the Shady House's balcony to reach Guzma's room. Team Skull's big bad boss waits for you within, and he's not about to give up the Yungoos his goons stole from the Aether House without a fight!

Team Skull Boss Guzma's Pokémon

A strong Bug-type Pokémon user, Guzma sends out Golisopod and Ariados. His Golisopod uses Swords Dance to sharply raise its Attack, then lashes out with a Water-type move—Razor Shell—to deal waves of physical damage. Keep your Fire, Ground, and Rock types well away from Golisopod. Guzma's Ariados uses Sucker Punch to catch you off guard. It's a Dark-type move, so don't send out any Psychic or Ghost types if you can avoid it.

Pokémon	Level	Type	Weak to
Golisopod	♂ Lv. 37	BUG, WATER	ELECTRIC, FLYING, ROCK
Ariados	♂ Lv. 36	BUG, POISON	FIRE, FLYING, PSYCHIC, ROCK

4 Grab Guzma's Z-Crystal before you go

Having suffered a humiliating defeat, Guzma bugs out and orders his nearby goon to return Yungoos to you. The brute then storms off, leaving you alone in his room. Search the nearby glittering chest to claim the Bug-type Z-Crystal, Buginium Z!

Reward: Buginium Z

Tip

Guzma's chair looks pretty cozy, hey? Take a load off and see what happens!

5 Meet Nanu and Acerola, then return to Aether House

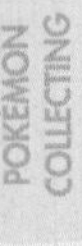

You've got what you came for, so make tracks back outside. You're met by the mysterious Nanu, who restores your Pokémon's health for you. He's difficult to read, but Nanu seems pleased that Team Skull has been humbled. Acerola soon arrives, thanks you for rescuing Yungoos, and urges you to meet her back at the Aether House. Head back the way you came or fly directly to Tapu Village and then head for Route 15.

Tip

Although they aren't related, Acerola uses the word "uncle" when speaking to Nanu. Like "cousin," "uncle" is a term of affection used in the Alola region, so it's clear that Acerola knows and trusts Nanu, even though he still seems very odd.

Crisis at the Aether House!

1 Battle Gladion at the Aether House

Disaster has struck Aether House! Though the children are happy to have Yungoos back, Hau reports that stealing the little Pokémon was merely a distraction. While you were off being oh so heroic, Team Skull slithered back to kidnap poor Lillie and Cosmog! As if things weren't bad enough, Gladion suddenly storms in, furious to learn that Lillie had Cosmog all along. There's no talking him down—battle is at hand!

Team Skull Gladion's Pokémon

How does this bully even know Lillie, anyway?! No matter, his Pokémon are your focus now.

You've seen his Golbat many times before. Bring it down, then send out a strong Fighting-type Pokémon to finish off the rest of Gladion's gang.

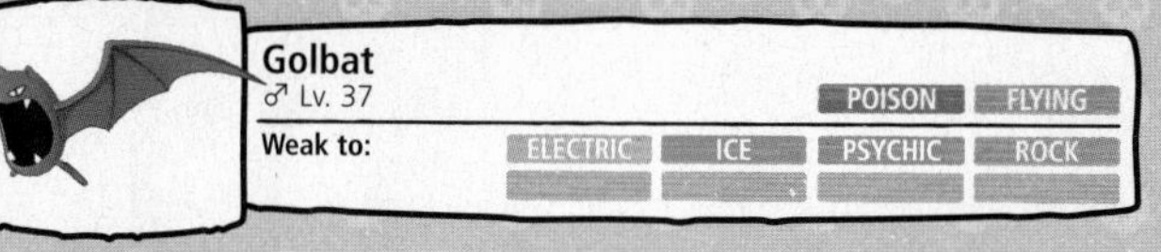

Golbat
♂ Lv. 37
POISON FLYING
Weak to: ELECTRIC, ICE, PSYCHIC, ROCK

Type: Null
Lv. 38
NORMAL
Weak to: FIGHTING

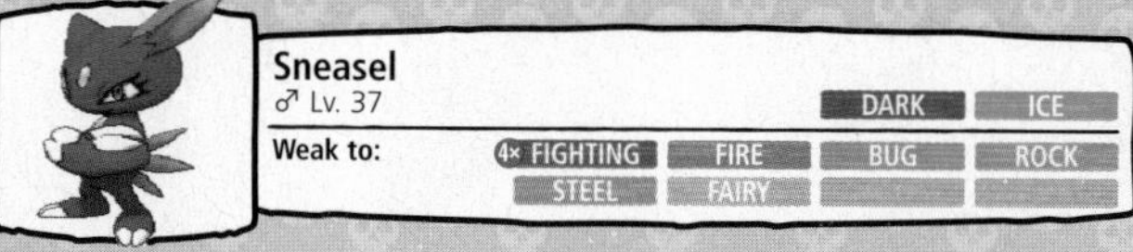

Sneasel
♂ Lv. 37
DARK ICE
Weak to: 4× FIGHTING, FIRE, BUG, ROCK, STEEL, FAIRY

2 Go along with Gladion

Gathering his emotions, Gladion apologizes for his outburst, but insists that you come with him to find Lillie and Cosmog. Agree, and he'll take you straight to Malie City's ferry terminal. Say no if you'd rather wrap up some loose ends around Ula'ula before racing to Lillie's rescue.

3 Battle Kahuna Nanu at the ferry terminal

Agree to go with Gladion, and you'll be in for another surprise: Nanu appears at the ferry terminal and reveals that he is, in fact, the kahuna of Ula'ula Island! You couldn't have known this, for Nanu certainly hasn't been acting very kahuna-like. He hasn't been appointing captains, or even lifting a finger to stop Team Skull from running wild on his island. Granting you your grand trial is the one kahuna-like thing Nanu seems willing to do. Accept his challenge to start the showdown!

Grand Trial: Island Kahuna Nanu

In keeping with his brooding demeanor, Nanu favors Dark-type Pokémon. His Sableye has but one weakness, while his Krokorok and Alolan Persian share several. Fairy types are ideal for countering his whole team, as all three of his Pokémon are weak to Fairy-type moves. You can also find success by sending out strong Fighting- and Bug-type Pokémon, which two of his three Pokémon are also weak to.

Kahuna Nanu's Pokémon

Dark-type Pokémon, is it? See if you can send out a Fairy type to tackle Sableye and, if possible, use a Flying-type Pokémon against Krokorok to negate its devastating Earthquake attack. Krokorok also uses Swagger to sharply raise your Pokémon's Attack stat while simultaneously inflicting them with confusion. Be ready with Big Malasadas or other cure-alls to heal this.

Pokémon	Gender / Level	Type	Weak to
Sableye	♀ Lv. 38	DARK, GHOST	FAIRY
Krokorok	♂ Lv. 38	GROUND, DARK	WATER, GRASS, ICE, FIGHTING, BUG, FAIRY
Alolan Persian	♀ Lv. 39	DARK	FIGHTING, BUG, FAIRY

Receive a Z-Crystal before shoving off

Reward: Darkinium Z

Impressed by your show of strength, Nanu restores your Pokémon and hands you the Dark-type Z-Crystal—Darkinium Z. He then departs and Hau arrives, eager to be off to Lillie's rescue. Gladion believes the search should start at Aether Paradise, though only he seems to know why.

After Beating Kahuna Nanu (Optional)

New optional ventures are open to you now that you've beaten Alola's third kahuna. If you'd like to pursue them now, return to Malie City (p. 142) immediately after arriving at the Aether Foundation, and refer to the following pages. If you'd rather race to Lillie's rescue, feel free to do so, and return to this section anytime you like.

S84: Claim a Reaper Cloth

Stop by Malie City's Pokémon Center and talk to the little girl with Mimikyu. She'll give you a Reaper Cloth that she no longer has any use for.

Reward: Reaper Cloth

S85: Take a ponderous quiz

Talk to a girl near Malie Garden's northwest bench during the day and answer her quiz about the pond's shape. (Hint: it's shaped like Gyarados.) You'll drift off with a nifty gift!

Reward: Air Balloon

S86: Get two gifts

Visit the Malie City's Malasada Shop at night and talk to Oranguru. Accept its gift, and you'll get another one when a Police Officer suddenly shows up!

Reward: TM21 Frustration, TM27 Return

S87: Grab a bite with Ula'ula's high roller

Visit the restaurant Sushi High Roller in Malie City, and you may get a surprise. Order up the Z-Kaiseki: Ronin Set, and Kahuna Nanu will arrive! You've ordered the old fellow's favorite dish, and Nanu graciously treats you to a meal on him. He even hands you his Heart Scales at the end of the banquet before sauntering off.

Reward: Heart Scale ×8

Plates Have Appeared!

Now that you've defeated Kahuna Nanu, new hidden items can be found on Melemele Island! These special plates can boost the power of certain types of moves, and they aren't shown on previous maps, so you'll need to sniff them out with Stoutland. Here's what and where you can find:

Hau'oli Outskirts: Mind Plate

Hau'oli Outskirts: Earth Plate

Trainers' School: Flame Plate

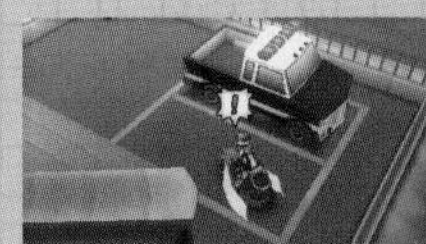

Hau'oli City Shopping District: Draco Plate

Hau'oli City Shopping District: Toxic Plate

Hau'oli City Shopping District: Meadow Plate

Hau'oli City Shopping District: Insect Plate

Hau'oli City Beachfront: Icicle Plate

Hau'oli Cemetery: Spooky Plate

Haina Desert / Ruins of Abundance

Ride Pokémon Needed

Located north of Route 13, Haina Desert is a treacherous and confounding place that you may choose to explore now that you've defeated Nanu. Many secrets hide within its shifting sands, but unwary travelers can easily lose their way in the dunes.

Team Recommendations

WATER | GRASS | ICE

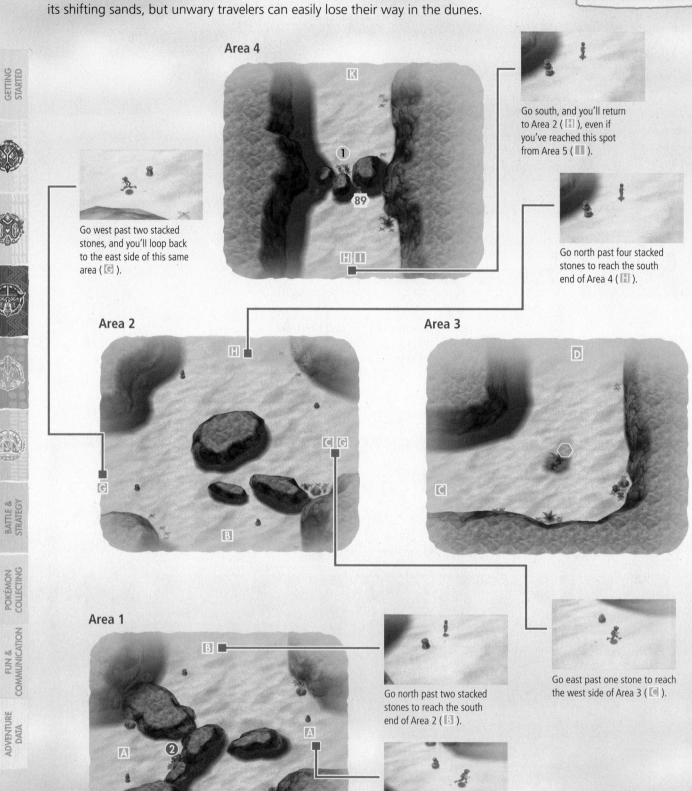

Area 4

K
1
89
H I

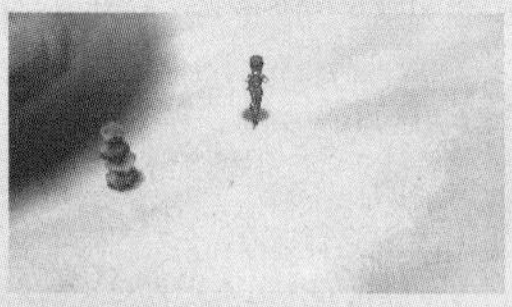

Go south, and you'll return to Area 2 (H), even if you've reached this spot from Area 5 (I).

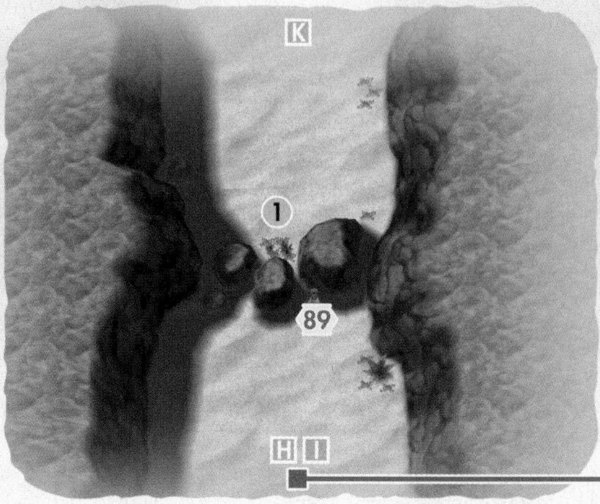

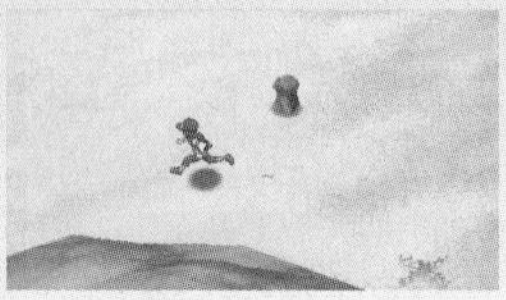

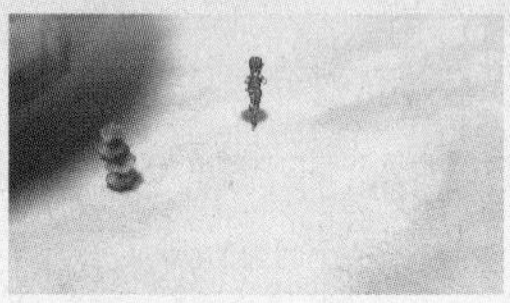

Go west past two stacked stones, and you'll loop back to the east side of this same area (G).

Go north past four stacked stones to reach the south end of Area 4 (H).

Area 2

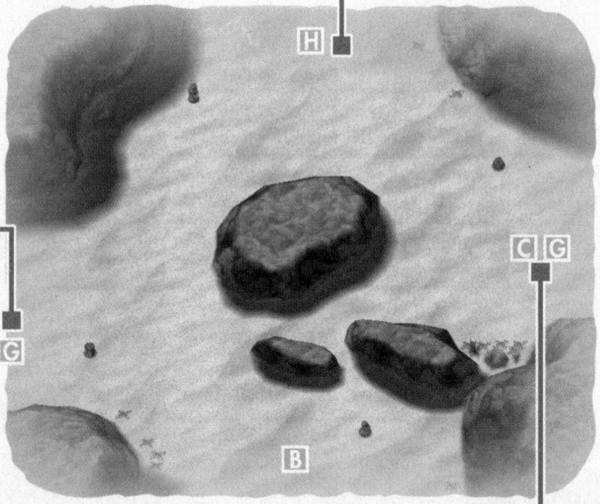

H
C G
G
B

Area 3

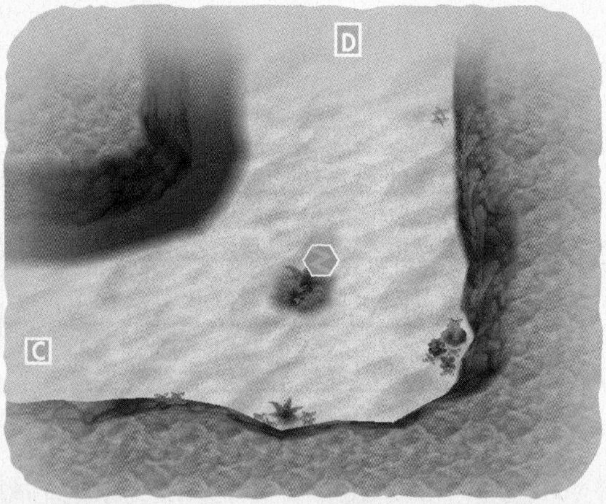

D
C

Go east past one stone to reach the west side of Area 3 (C).

Area 1

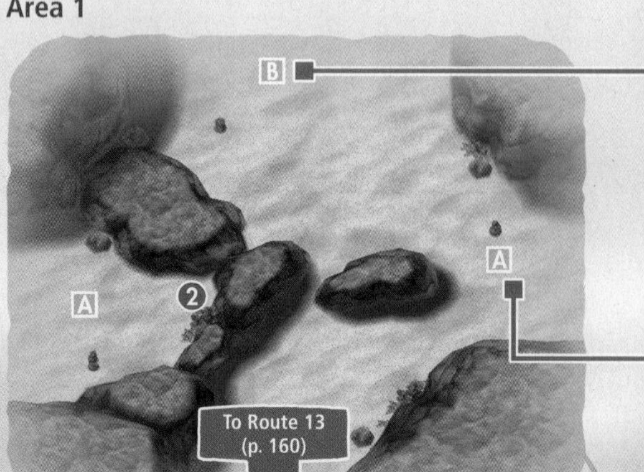

Go north past two stacked stones to reach the south end of Area 2 (B).

Go east past three stacked stones to reach the west side of this same area (A).

Area 8

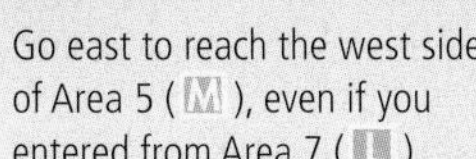

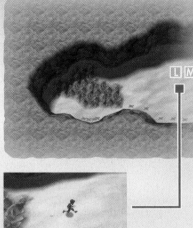

Go east to reach the west side of Area 5 (M), even if you entered from Area 7 (L).

Sand Clouds	
Alolan Dugtrio	○
Sandile	◎
Trapinch	△

Desert	
Alolan Dugtrio	○
Sandile	◎

Items	
1	TM85 Dream Eater
2	Max Elixir
3	Psychium Z
4	Comet Shard

◎ frequent ○ average
△ rare ▲ almost never
day only night only

Area 6

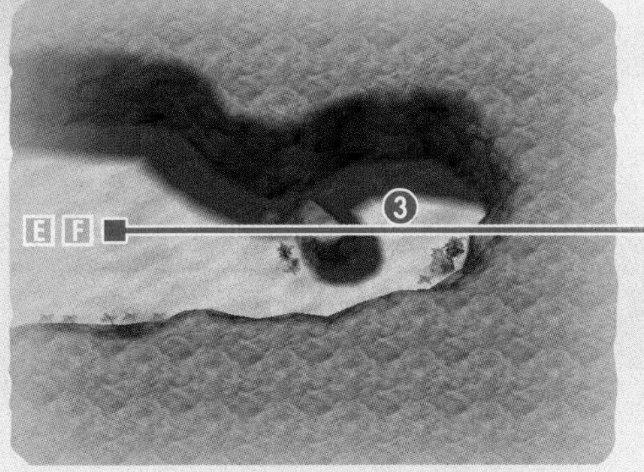

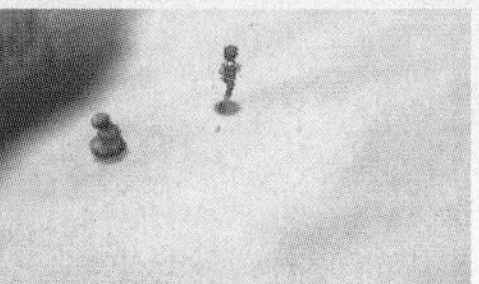

Go west, and you'll end up on the east side of Area 7 (F), even if you entered from Area 5 (E).

Area 7

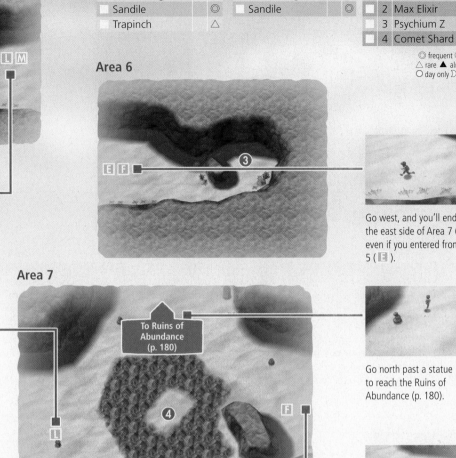

Go west past two stones to reach Area 8 (L).

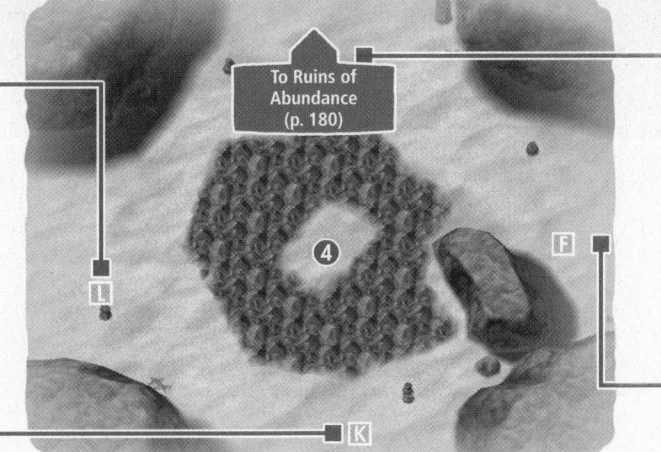

Go north past a statue to reach the Ruins of Abundance (p. 180).

Go east past one stone to reach Area 6 (F).

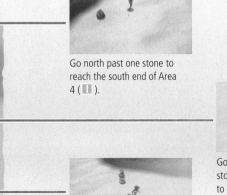

Go south past four stacked stones to reach the north end of Area 4 (K).

Area 5

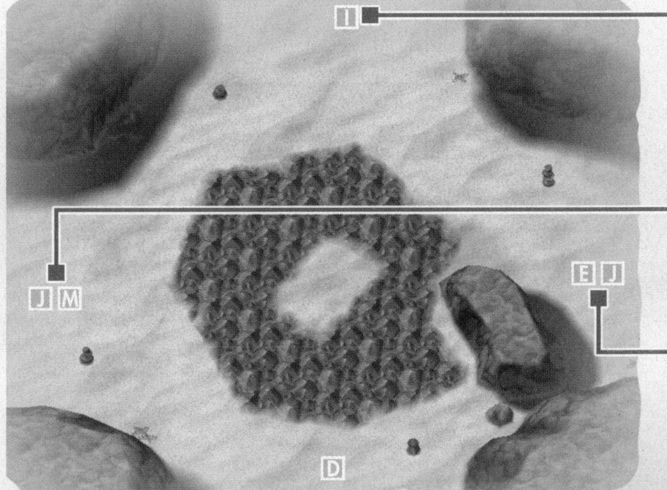

Go north past one stone to reach the south end of Area 4 (I).

Go west past three stacked stones, and you'll loop back to the east side of this same area (J).

Go east past four stacked stones to reach Area 6 (E).

Tip

Depending on the weather, different Pokémon may appear when wild Pokémon call for SOS allies in battle. When a sandstorm is raging, Castform (Sunny Form) and Gabite might jump into a battle.

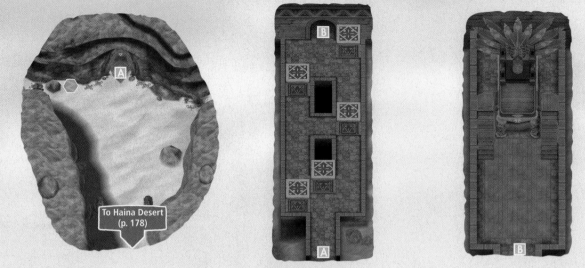

Ruins of Abundance

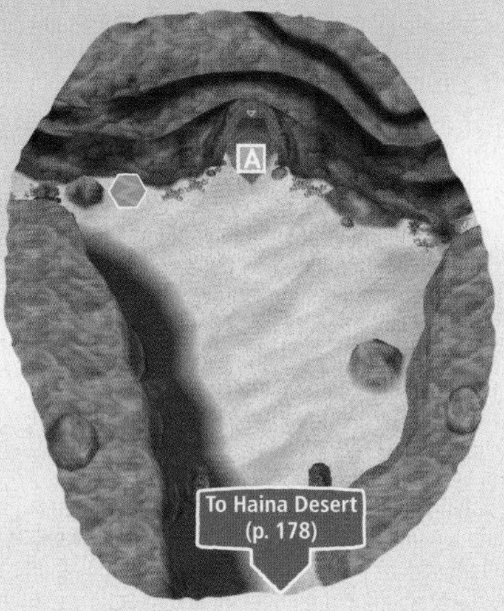

To Haina Desert (p. 178)

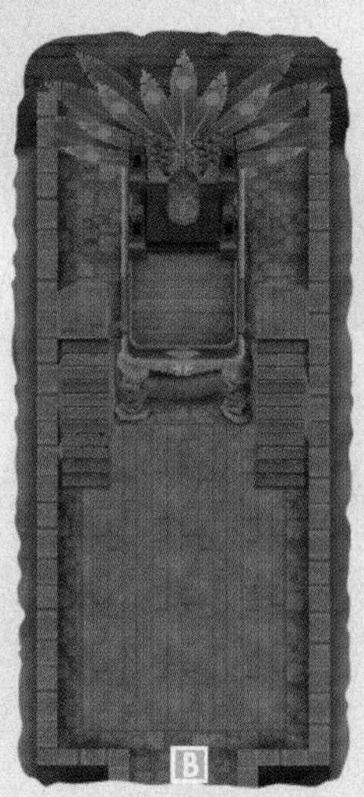

Tip

The old man near the desert's entrance says that the secret of the desert is 2-1-4-3. This pattern relates to the number of stacked stones you see near the desert's connecting paths, and following it will lead you to all of Haina Desert's most important parts—though there's more to explore if you like. Look for the stacked stones and count the number of stones in each stack to crack the code.

First, head north past two stones, then go east past one stone. The next area will have no stones, so dash right through it. In the next area, following a rocky patch, head past a stack of four stones to the east to reach a Z-Crystal. Leave that area, and you will come out at point F. It may look like you are back in Area 5, but you've actually arrived in Area 7—though the two are nearly identical! Then go north past one stone and a stone statue like the ones you saw outside the Ruins of Conflict. You'll have arrived right in front of the Ruins of Abundance!

S88: Give and receive

Take pity on the thirsty Trial Guide at the entrance to the desert back on Route 13, and give her a Fresh Water in exchange for some gifts.

Reward: Adrenaline Orb ×3

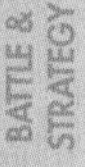

Tip

When you backtrack to the previous area after claiming the Psychium Z, you'll actually appear at F. It looks just like the previous area, but close observation reveals that a Comet Shard has mysteriously appeared in the midst of the central rocky patch that only Mudsdale can help you cross. Go south from there into K, and you'll get another surprise: you're now able to reach TM85 Dream Eater!

Tip

After taking the Psychium Z and backtracking to F, go north to reach the Ruins of Abundance. There's not much to do there at the moment, but you can claim a Zygarde Cell if you like.

S89: Get Safety Goggles

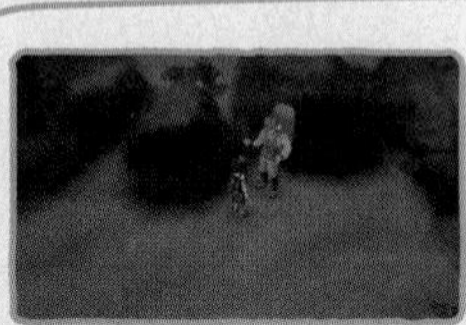

Enter the desert at night, and go north through B and H to reach a Hiker. Tell him that your Pokémon's eyes are "looking pretty bleary," and he'll hand you some protective Safety Goggles.

Reward: Safety Goggles

Aether Paradise

Gladion believes your search for Lillie should begin at Aether Paradise. His reasons for this are unclear, but it's as good a place to start as any. If you are ever overwhelmed and want to regroup back on one of Alola's other islands, check out the ship you sailed in on to get a ride away from Aether Paradise.

Team Recommendations

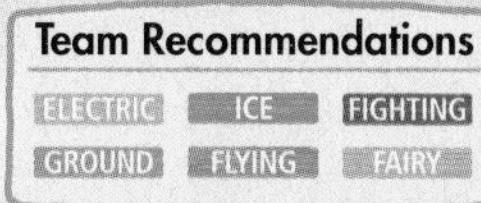

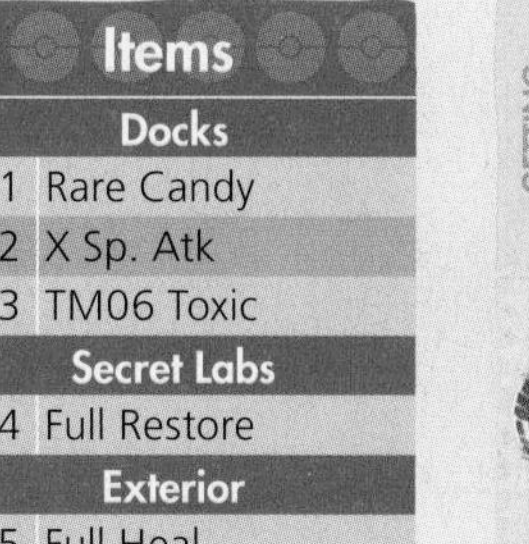

Items

	#	Item
Docks		
☐	1	Rare Candy
☐	2	X Sp. Atk
☐	3	TM06 Toxic
Secret Labs		
☐	4	Full Restore
Exterior		
☐	5	Full Heal
☐	6	Hyper Potion

B1F: Docks

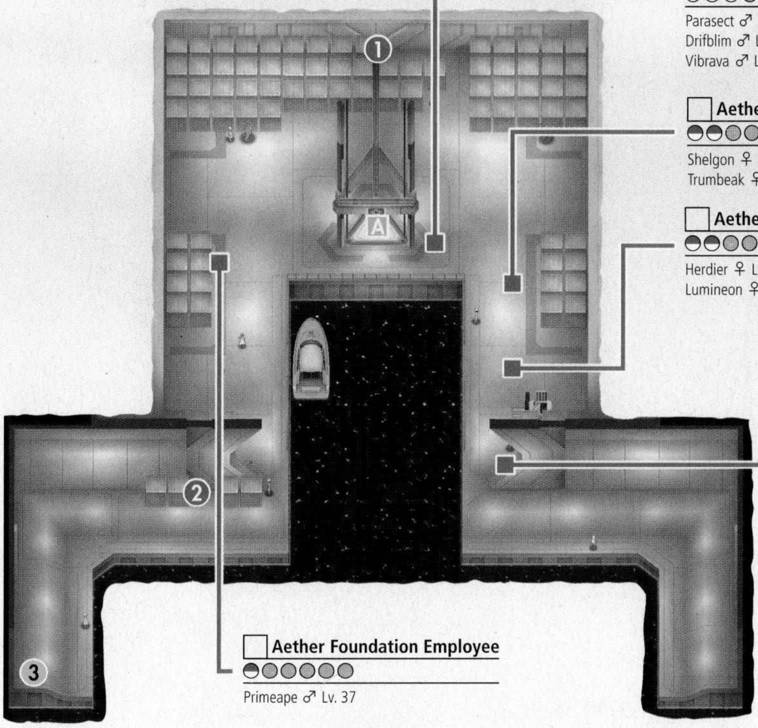

☐ Aether Foundation Employee
Parasect ♂ Lv. 36
Drifblim ♂ Lv. 36
Vibrava ♂ Lv. 37

☐ Aether Foundation Employee
Shelgon ♀ Lv. 37
Trumbeak ♀ Lv. 36

☐ Aether Foundation Employee
Herdier ♀ Lv. 36
Lumineon ♀ Lv. 37

☐ Aether Foundation Employee
Alolan Dugtrio ♂ Lv. 37
Sliggoo ♂ Lv. 37

☐ Aether Foundation Employee
Primeape ♂ Lv. 37

B2F: Elevator Hall

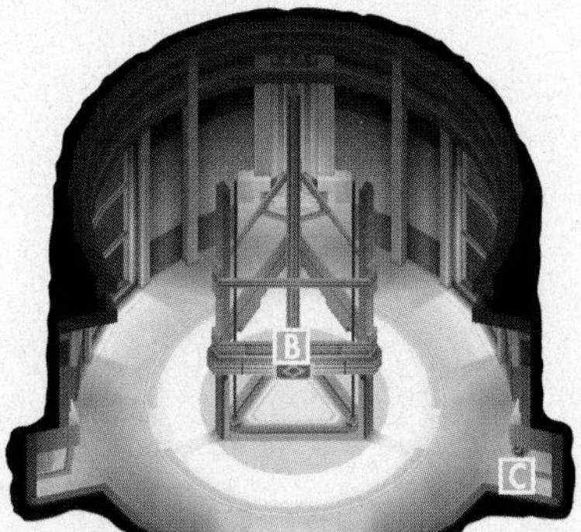

B2F: Lab Area

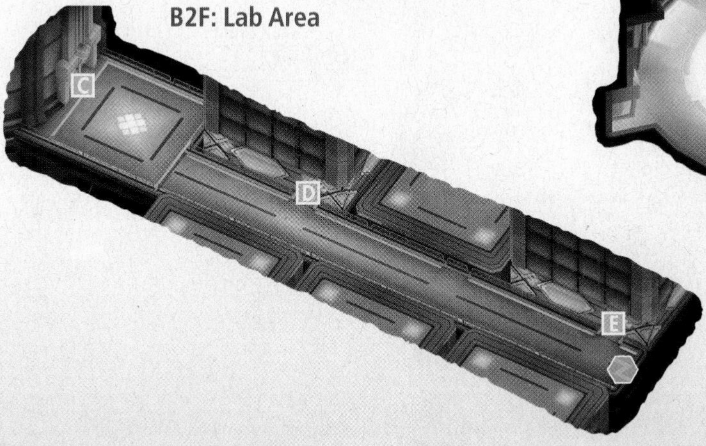

1F: Entrance

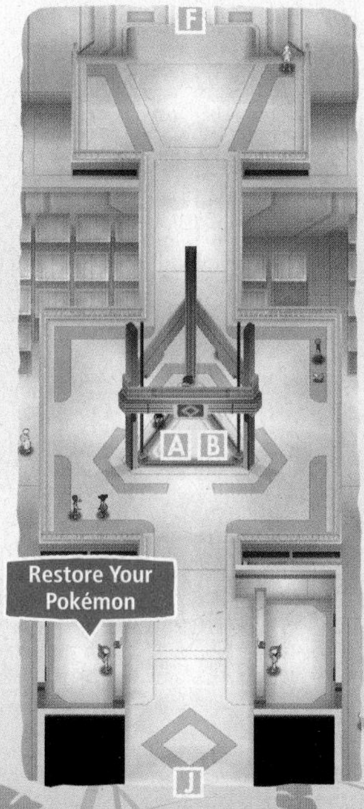

Restore Your Pokémon

Secret Lab A

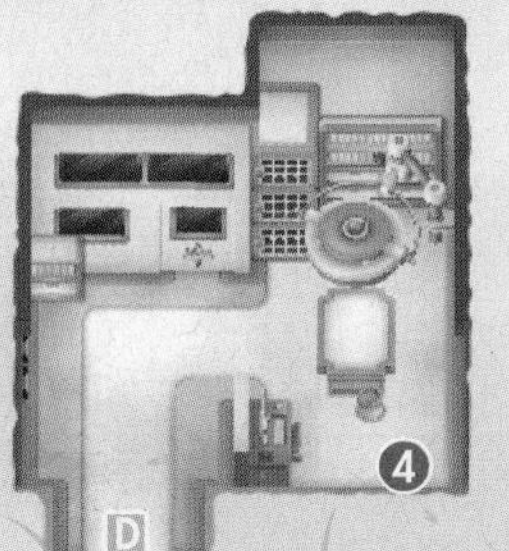

Secret Lab B

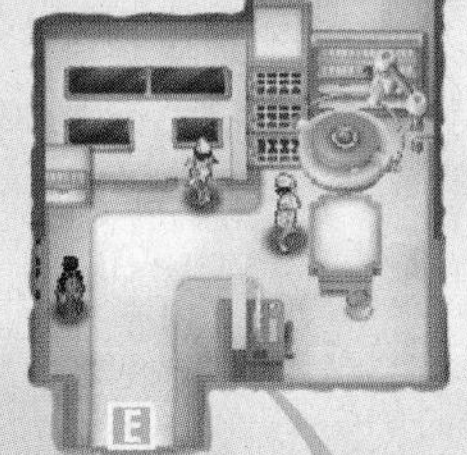

GETTING STARTED

BATTLE & STRATEGY
POKÉMON COLLECTING
FUN & COMMUNICATION

ADVENTURE DATA

GETTING STARTED
BATTLE & STRATEGY
POKÉMON COLLECTING
FUN & COMMUNICATION
ADVENTURE DATA

Lusamine's Mansion: Lusamine's Room

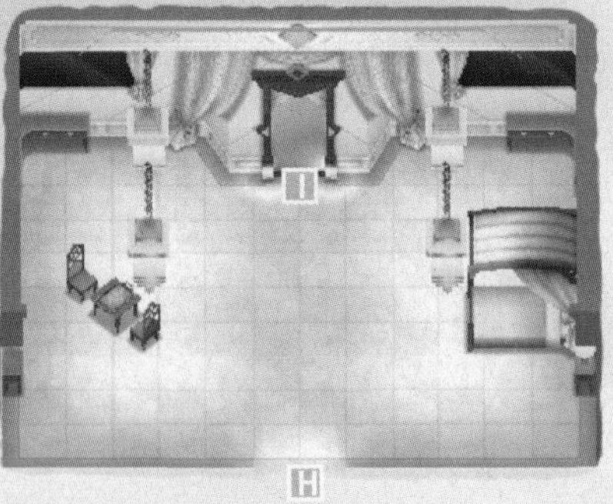

I
H

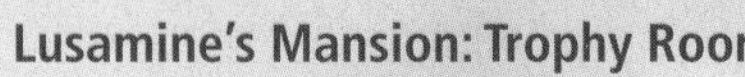

Lusamine's Mansion: Trophy Room

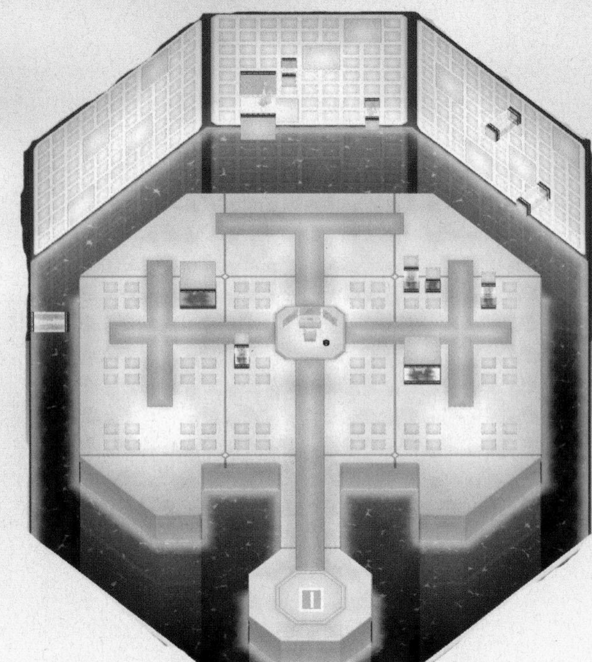

Lusamine's Mansion: Entry Room

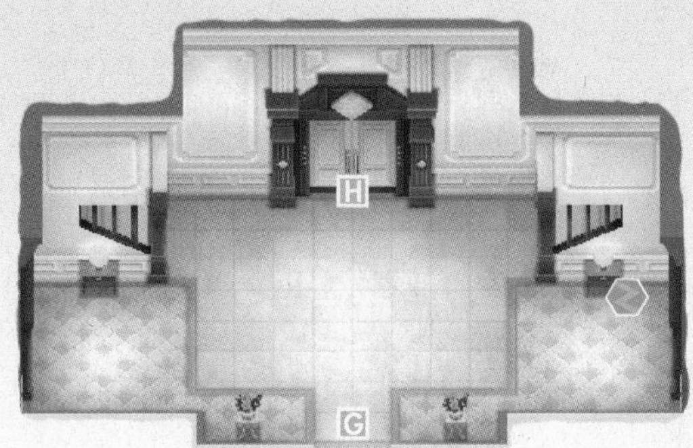

Exterior

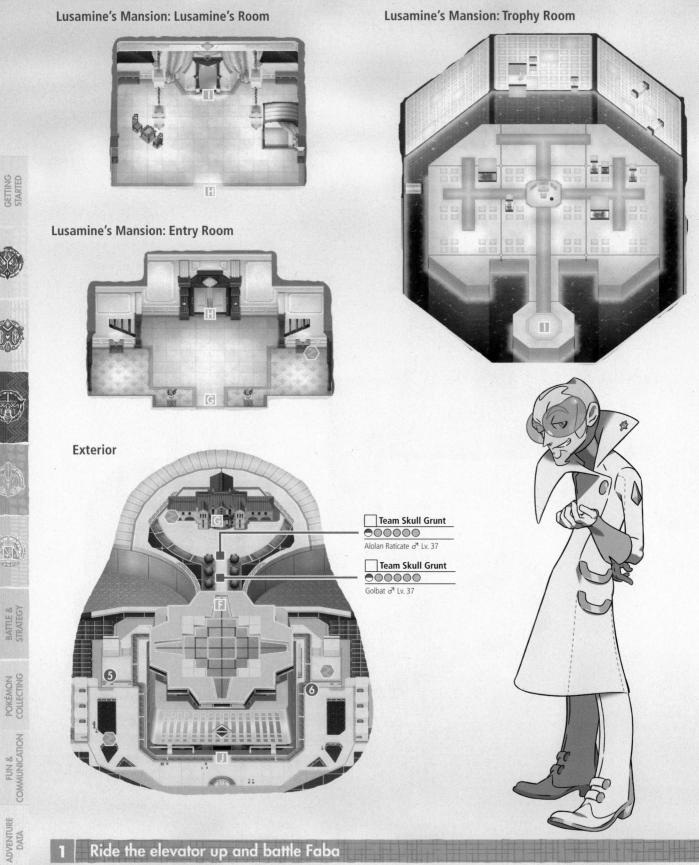

Team Skull Grunt
Alolan Raticate ♂ Lv. 37

Team Skull Grunt
Golbat ♂ Lv. 37

F
5
6
J

1 Ride the elevator up and battle Faba

Aether Paradise's employees are on high alert, so don't expect a warm welcome this time around. Proceed through the facility's spacious docks, dodging or battling the patrolling staff. Ride the elevator up to the higher floors with Gladion and Hau, and you'll run straight into a battle with Branch Chief Faba!

Branch Chief Faba's Pokémon

The Aether Foundation's overconfident Branch Chief sends out just one Pokémon: Hypno. It uses Hypnosis to make your Pokémon fall asleep and lashes out with Psychic, but it should be no match for your well-trained team.

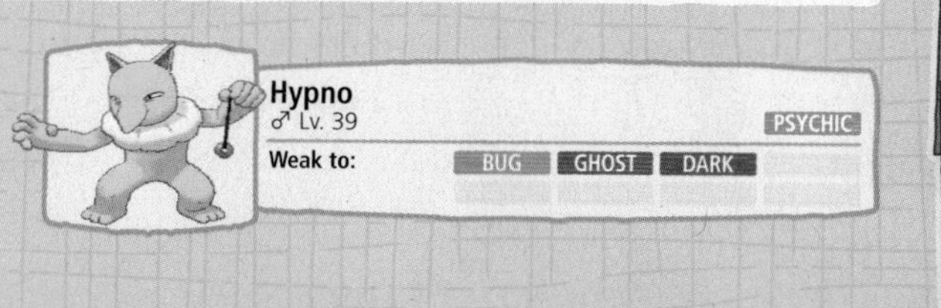

Hypno
♂ Lv. 39
PSYCHIC
Weak to:
BUG
GHOST
DARK

2 Ride the elevator down to the secret labs

Beaten, Faba has little choice but to program the elevator to let you access the lower floors. If you're ready to go at once, agree to Gladion's suggestion that you head straight down.

Tip

Answer "No" when Gladion asks if you're ready to ride the elevator, and you'll be free to head south to find a friendly Aether employee who'll promptly heal your Pokémon. You can also use the nearby PC to rearrange your team if you like.

3 Battle your way to Secret Lab B

The lower floors feature secret labs, and Gladion asks you and Hau to investigate the furthest one down the hall: Secret Lab B. After Hau hooks you up with a Max Revive, head through the nearby door to reach a long hall that's guarded by Aether employees. They're not pleased to see you in their secret labs, and battle soon breaks out.

Reward: Max Revive

Aether Foundation Employees' Pokémon

The three Aether employees battle you one at a time, so you face a series of Single Battles. The first employee's Alolan Muk uses Knock Off to slap away your Pokémon's held items—pound it with Ground-type moves to reclaim your goods. The second employee's Magneton uses Mirror Shot to potentially lower your Pokémon's accuracy, and the third employee's Porygon2 can use Recover to heal during the battle. Be prepared for these tricks!

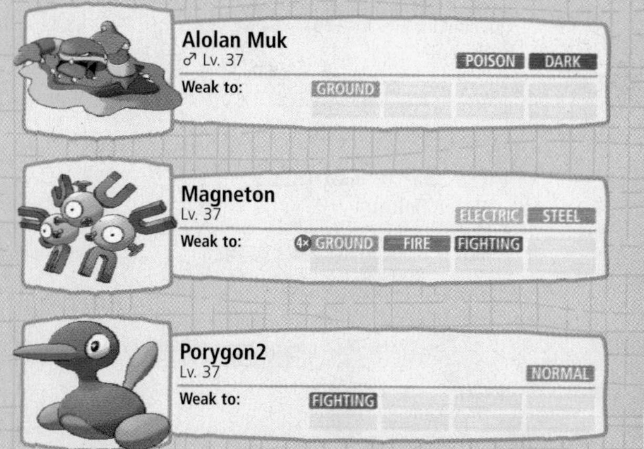

Alolan Muk
♂ Lv. 37
POISON
DARK
Weak to:
GROUND
Magneton
Lv. 37
ELECTRIC
STEEL
Weak to:
4× GROUND
FIRE
FIGHTING
Porygon2
Lv. 37
NORMAL
Weak to:
FIGHTING

GETTING STARTED

BATTLE & STRATEGY

POKÉMON COLLECTING

FUN & COMMUNICATION

ADVENTURE DATA

4 Face more Aether employees in Secret Lab B

After defeating all three Aether employees, continue on to the Secret Labs. Talk to Gladion outside Secret Lab A to learn more about his history with his Pokémon—Type: Null—then continue down to Secret Lab B. The employees there aren't happy to have kids mucking about in their research, and you're drawn into battle once again.

Aether Foundation Employees' Pokémon

Hau has your back during this Multi Battle, so the odds are in your favor. His Alolan Raichu's Psychic-type moves will make short work of Machoke, so focus your attacks on Vanillish to end the battle with all speed.

Pokémon	Gender / Level	Type	Weak to
Machoke	♂ Lv. 37	FIGHTING	FLYING, PSYCHIC, FAIRY
Vanillish	♀ Lv. 37	ICE	FIRE, FIGHTING, ROCK, STEEL

Hau's Pokémon

Hau has three Pokémon at his disposal, and he sends out his Alolan Raichu first. Hau will send out another Pokémon if Raichu faints—and you may be surprised to see him send out the final Evolution of his first partner Pokémon!

If you choose Rowlet

Pokémon	Gender / Level	Type	Weak to
Primarina	♂ Lv. 39	WATER, FAIRY	GRASS, ELECTRIC, POISON
Flareon	♂ Lv. 38	FIRE	WATER, GROUND, ROCK
Alolan Raichu	♂ Lv. 38	ELECTRIC, PSYCHIC	GROUND, BUG, GHOST, DARK

If you choose Litten

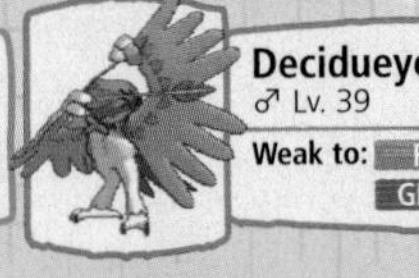

Pokémon	Gender / Level	Type	Weak to
Decidueye	♂ Lv. 39	GRASS, GHOST	FIRE, ICE, FLYING, GHOST, DARK
Vaporeon	♂ Lv. 38	WATER	GRASS, ELECTRIC
Alolan Raichu	♂ Lv. 38	ELECTRIC, PSYCHIC	GROUND, BUG, GHOST, DARK

If you choose Popplio

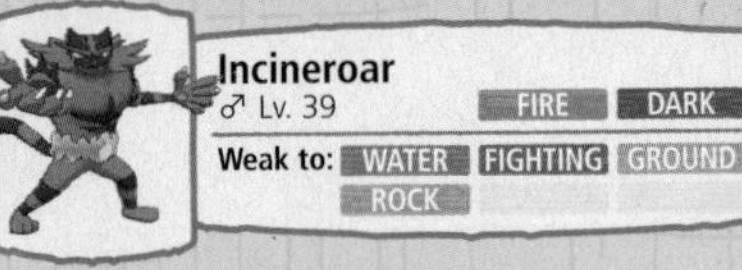

Pokémon	Gender / Level	Type	Weak to
Incineroar	♂ Lv. 39	FIRE, DARK	WATER, FIGHTING, GROUND, ROCK
Leafeon	♂ Lv. 38	GRASS	FIRE, ICE, POISON, FLYING, BUG
Alolan Raichu	♂ Lv. 38	ELECTRIC, PSYCHIC	GROUND, BUG, GHOST, DARK

5 Search Secret Lab B for clues

The Aether employees flee after the battle, leaving you and Hau to raid their lab. Hau's and your Pokémon are healed after this battle, so you are ready for whatever comes next! Check the bookshelf and computer to discover their presumptions about Lillie's little companion, Cosmog. Report back to Gladion afterward, then return to the elevator and ride up to 1F: Entrance, where Faba has arranged a special "welcome" for you.

Tip

After talking to Gladion in the hall, slip into Secret Lab A to find a Full Restore. You can also check the bookshelf and computer for more insights into the Aether Foundation's troubling research.

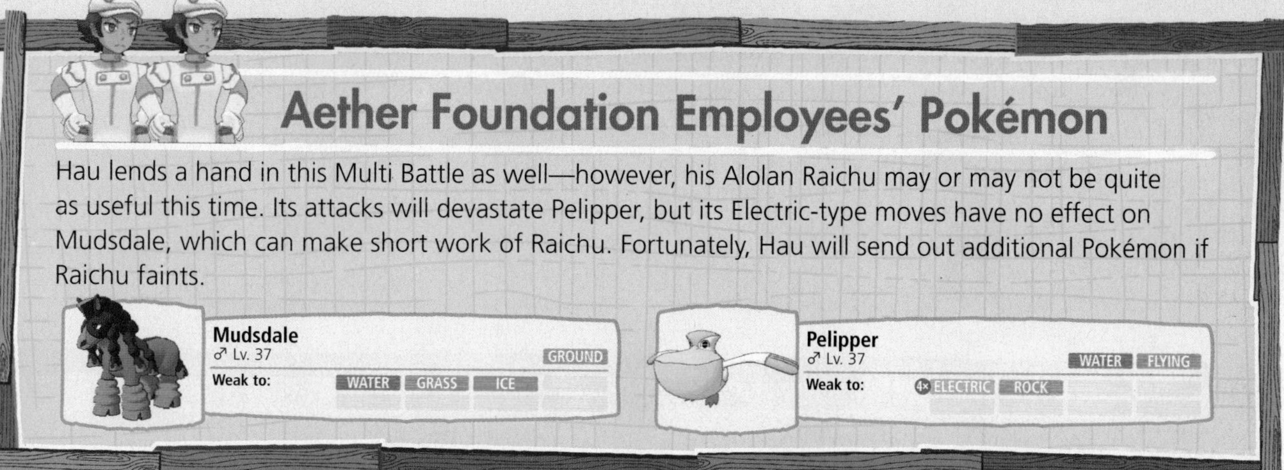

Aether Foundation Employees' Pokémon

Hau lends a hand in this Multi Battle as well—however, his Alolan Raichu may or may not be quite as useful this time. Its attacks will devastate Pelipper, but its Electric-type moves have no effect on Mudsdale, which can make short work of Raichu. Fortunately, Hau will send out additional Pokémon if Raichu faints.

Pokémon	Level	Type	Weak to
Mudsdale	♂ Lv. 37	GROUND	WATER, GRASS, ICE
Pelipper	♂ Lv. 37	WATER, FLYING	4× ELECTRIC, ROCK

6 Have your Pokémon restored by Wicke

Your former Aether Paradise tour guide—Wicke—arrives shortly after your battle. Unlike her boss Faba, she's not trying to get in your way. In fact, she heals your Pokémon and gives you a clue on how to find Lillie—she believes she is with the president. Run from her straight into a Branch Chief blockade!

Aether Foundation Employees' Pokémon

Faba stands his ground just beyond the elevator, sending two Aether employees against you. Gladion has your back during this Multi Battle, and he sends out Golbat. (Turn the page for more details about Gladion's Pokémon team.) Beware of the opposing Electabuzz, which uses Discharge to zap all surrounding Pokémon. Keep Water- and Flying-type Pokémon out of the fight.

Pokémon	Level	Type	Weak to
Magmar	♂ Lv. 38	FIRE	WATER, GROUND, ROCK
Electabuzz	♂ Lv. 38	ELECTRIC	GROUND

Team Skull Gladion's Pokémon

Gladion's Golbat won't last long against the opposing Electabuzz's Discharge blasts. Fortunately, the troubled young man also has his trusty Type: Null to send out if his Golbat faints.

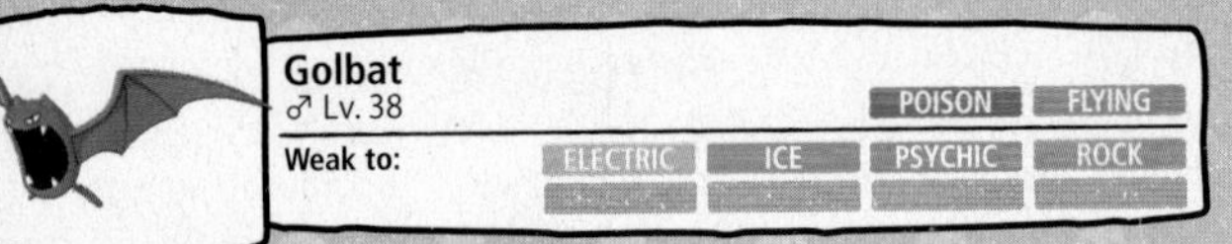

Golbat
♂ Lv. 38
POISON FLYING
Weak to: ELECTRIC ICE PSYCHIC ROCK

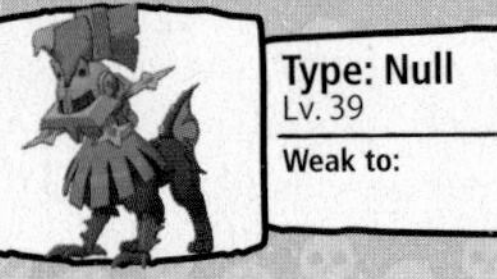

Type: Null
Lv. 39
NORMAL
Weak to: FIGHTING

7 Face off against Faba again

Undeterred by his underlings' defeat, Branch Chief Faba stands ready to stop your advance. With an Aether employee by his side, Faba forces you and Hau into another Multi Battle. (Turn back to page 184 if you need a reminder of which Pokémon are on Hau's team.) Defeat Faba so you can continue your search for Lillie!

Aether Foundation Employee's Pokémon

The Aether employee's lone Ledian is the least of your worries. Wipe it out with a Rock-type move so you and Hau can focus on Faba.

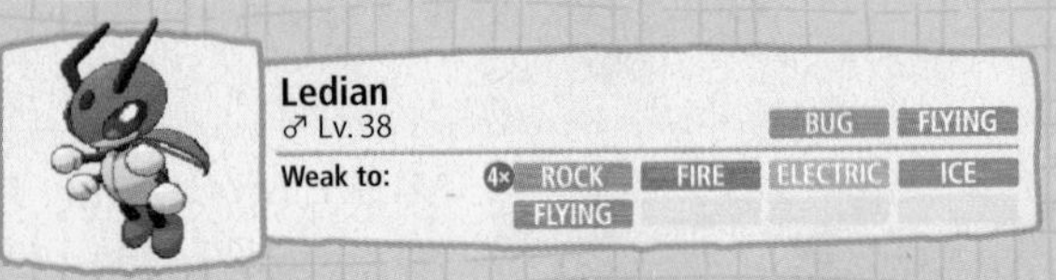

Ledian
♂ Lv. 38
BUG FLYING
Weak to: 4× ROCK FIRE ELECTRIC ICE FLYING

Branch Chief Faba's Pokémon

Faba doesn't hold back in this battle. He has three Pokémon to use, but you and Hau can double-team each one after you've knocked out his Aether employee ally. Smash Ledian fast, then focus your attacks on Faba's unfortunate team of Psychic types, which share similar weaknesses. Hau sends out the same Pokémon as he did during your previous battle down in Secret Lab B, and his Alolan Raichu's Electric-type moves are sure to be useful against Faba's crew.

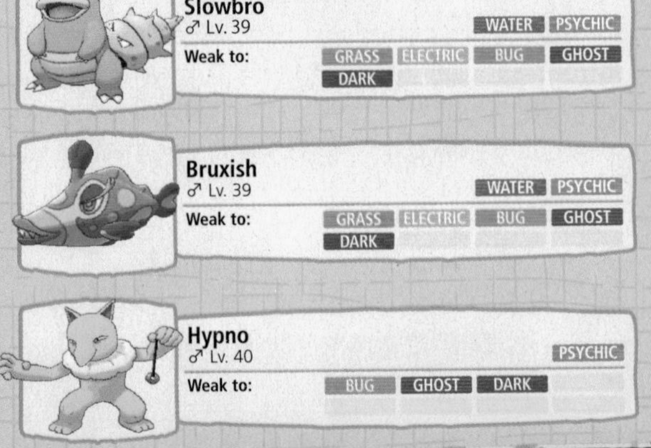

Slowbro
♂ Lv. 39
WATER PSYCHIC
Weak to: GRASS ELECTRIC BUG GHOST DARK

Bruxish
♂ Lv. 39
WATER PSYCHIC
Weak to: GRASS ELECTRIC BUG GHOST DARK

Hypno
♂ Lv. 40
PSYCHIC
Weak to: BUG GHOST DARK

8 Get past the Grunts and then battle Guzma

Proceed through the north door after defeating Faba, and you'll find yourself in the courtyard outside of President Lusamine's mansion. Battle through a gang of Team Skull Grunts to reach their big, bad boss: Guzma. He's already flattened Gladion, and he's still hungry for battle!

Before battling the Grunts, run west and then south to find a Full Heal. Go east and then south to track down a Zygarde Cell. Grab another Zygarde Cell by going west after defeating Guzma.

Team Skull Boss Guzma's Pokémon

Guzma's team has doubled in size since your Shady House showdown, and his Pokémon have grown even stronger. His Golisopod's First Impression move is so powerful it can wipe out one of your Pokémon in a single shot, and his other Pokémon also pack a tremendous punch. Targeting his team's weaknesses is therefore vital, as is speed—you don't want Guzma's gang going first. Items like the Quick Claw can help your Pokémon move first, and you can also feed your Pokémon Carbos to help their Speed stat increase more quickly when they level up. Don't react to Guzma—strike first, strike hard, and put down his Pokémon as fast as you can!

Pokémon	Level	Type	Weak to
Golisopod	♂ Lv. 41	BUG, WATER	ELECTRIC, FLYING, ROCK
Pinsir	♂ Lv. 40	BUG	FIRE, FLYING, ROCK
Masquerain	♂ Lv. 40	BUG, FLYING	4× ROCK, FIRE, ELECTRIC, ICE, FLYING
Ariados	♂ Lv. 40	BUG, POISON	FIRE, FLYING, PSYCHIC, ROCK

9 Meet Lillie and Lusamine in the mansion

Having suffered another defeat, Guzma has no choice but to step aside. Race into the mansion ahead and find a Zygarde Cell in the entry room. Enter the next room to find Lillie in a heated discussion with Lusamine. Their relationship is far more complicated than you knew, and you still have to rescue Nebby. Step onto the warp panel and join Lusamine in her trophy room, where Hau and Gladion soon catch up to you. Watch as a series of dramatic events unfold, culminating in a battle against the Aether Foundation's imposing president.

Aether President Lusamine's Pokémon

Lusamine must be stopped! Her team is well-rounded, however, so you must switch out your Pokémon to exploit her team's weaknesses. Beware that her Clefable uses Moonblast, a Fairy-type move that can lower your Pokémon's Sp. Atk. Pound Clefable with physical moves if this occurs. Her Milotic uses Safeguard to protect her team from status conditions and it also deals waves of damage with Hydro Pump. Mismagius unleashes Mystical Fire to harm your Pokémon and lower their Sp. Atk, while Bewear lets loose with devastating Fighting-type moves like Hammer Arm. Lilligant uses Stun Spore to inflict your Pokémon with Paralysis—be ready to heal them with Paralyze Heals or other medicines.

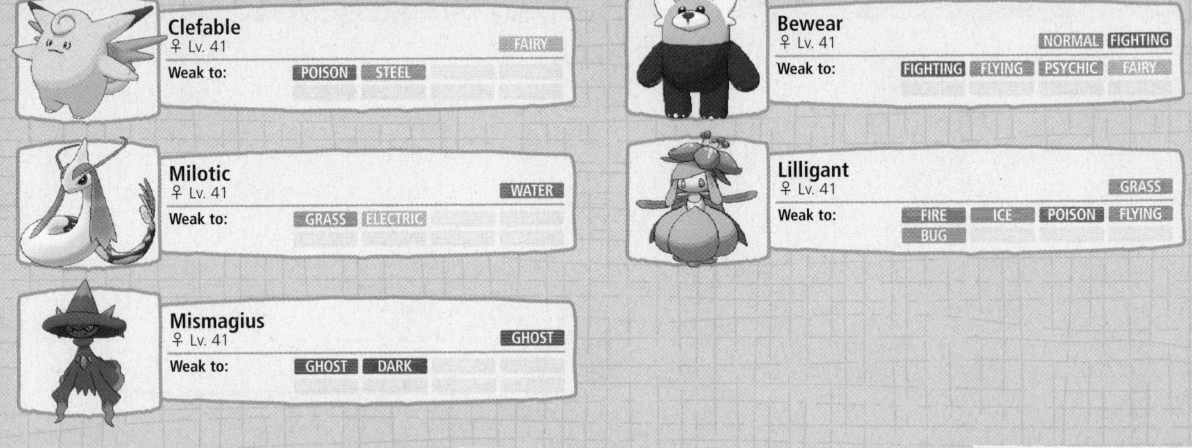

Clefable
♀ Lv. 41
FAIRY
Weak to: POISON STEEL
Bewear
♀ Lv. 41
NORMAL FIGHTING
Weak to: FIGHTING FLYING PSYCHIC FAIRY
Milotic
♀ Lv. 41
WATER
Weak to: GRASS ELECTRIC
Lilligant
♀ Lv. 41
GRASS
Weak to: FIRE ICE POISON FLYING BUG
Mismagius
♀ Lv. 41
GHOST
Weak to: GHOST DARK

10 Go to the docks and shove off to Poni Island

Lusamine and Guzma vanish after the battle, finally giving you a chance to rest. When you're ready, leave the mansion to find Lillie waiting outside. Gladion soon arrives and entrusts Lillie with the Moon Flute / Sun Flute before handing you a precious Master Ball. There's little else to accomplish here at Aether Paradise, so the time has come to set off to Poni Island. Go south and take the elevator down to B1F: Docks and speak to Gladion to be on your way.

Reward: Master Ball

Tip

Aether Paradise holds many items of value. If you rushed through to Lillie's rescue, consider giving the compound a more thorough search before you go.

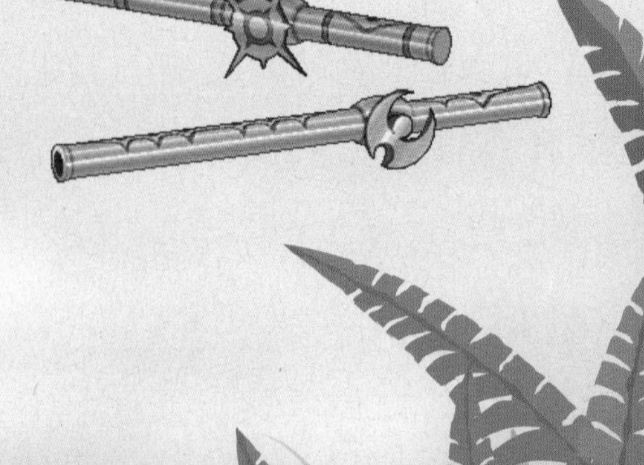

Poni Island

Welcome to Poni Island! Few people live on Alola's fourth island, but there's lots of nature here to explore—and plenty of new Pokémon species to register to your Pokédex. Recent events have been quite disturbing, but that's no reason to slack off on your island challenge. Explore the wilds of Poni Island on your way to your final trial!

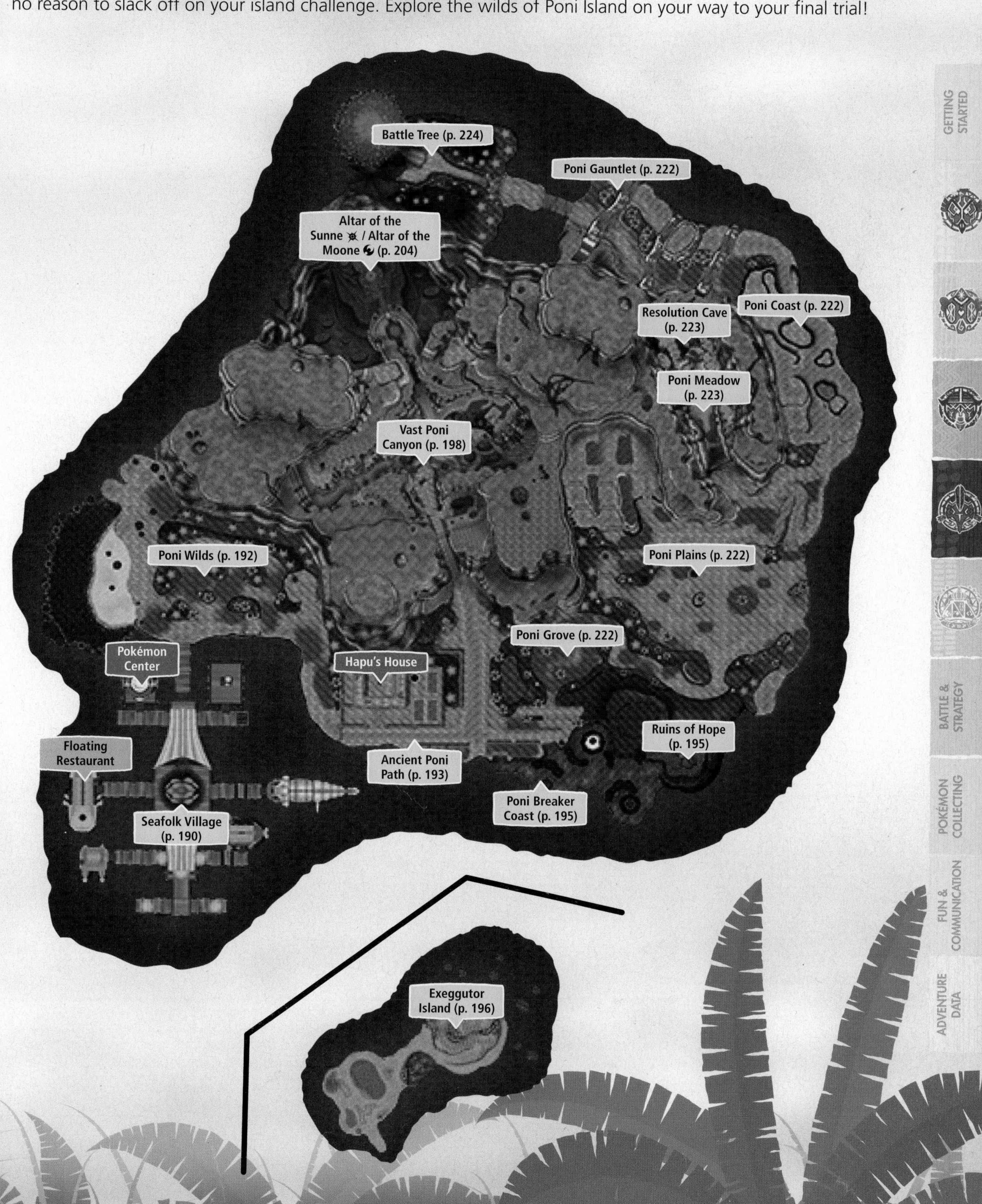

Seafolk Village

This humble village is home to a handful of happy mariners. The seafolk who live here have spent years searching out new wonders among the endless briny blue.

Team Recommendations

GRASS ELECTRIC

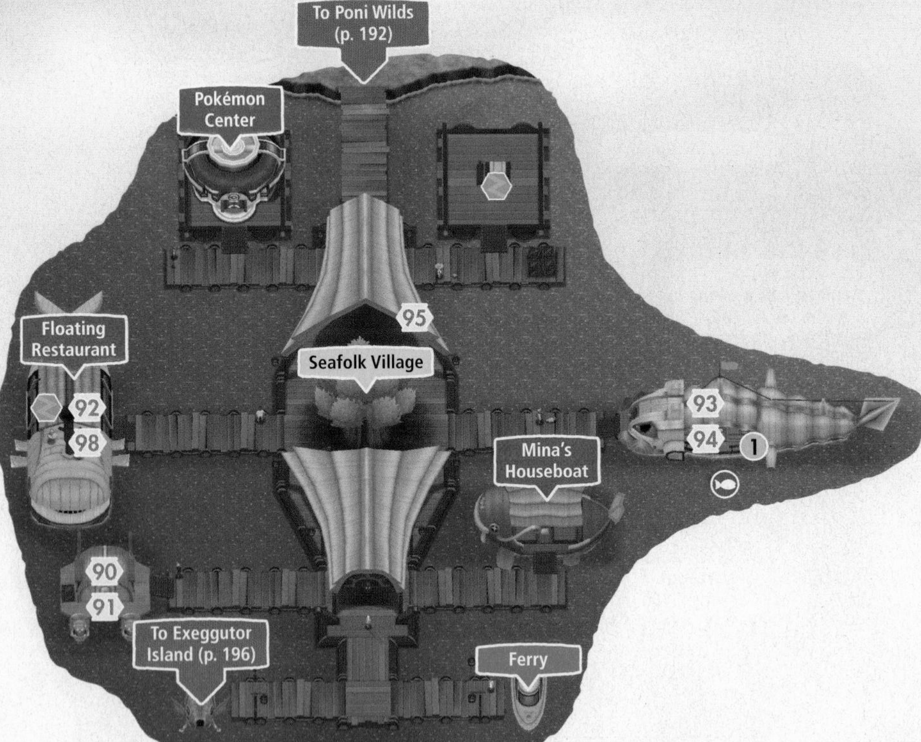

Poké Mart	
Normal Wares	
Adrenaline Orb	₽300
Antidote	₽200
Awakening	₽100
Burn Heal	₽300
Escape Rope	₽1,000
Full Heal	₽400
Great Ball	₽600
Honey	₽300
Hyper Potion	₽1,500
Ice Heal	₽100
Max Potion	₽2,500
Max Repel	₽900
Paralyze Heal	₽300
Poké Ball	₽200
Potion	₽200
Repel	₽400
Revive	₽2,000
Super Potion	₽700
Super Repel	₽700
Ultra Ball	₽800
After Completing 7 Trials	
Full Restore	₽3,000
Special Wares	
TM04 Calm Mind	₽10,000
TM14 Blizzard	₽30,000
TM15 Hyper Beam	₽50,000
TM22 Solar Beam	₽10,000
TM25 Thunder	₽30,000
TM34 Sludge Wave	₽10,000
TM38 Fire Blast	₽30,000
TM52 Focus Blast	₽30,000
TM68 Giga Impact	₽50,000
TM71 Stone Edge	₽30,000

Items	
1	TM91 Flash Cannon

Fishing Spots	
Dhelmise	▲
Magikarp	◎
Wailmer	○

Rare Fishing Spots	
Dhelmise	△
Magikarp	◎
Wailmer	◎

◎ frequent ○ average △ rare ▲ almost never ○ day only ☽ night only ☀ *Pokémon Sun* ☾ *Pokémon Moon*

1 Say "Alola" to Seafolk Village

Welcome to Seafolk Village, a whole town of floating houseboats! Run north to find Lillie, and you'll soon meet the seafolk's friendly chief as well. He greets you and tells you to find Hapu if you need help locating the kahuna of Poni Island. Who knew Hapu lived here? It'll be good to see your friend again.

S90: Stop by the shop boat

Visit the southwest floating houseboat to find a shop that isn't quite open for business. Still, you'll get a Magmarizer and Electirizer just for stopping by. These rare items are needed for Magmar and Electabuzz to evolve.

Reward: Magmarizer, Electirizer

S91: Acquire Aerodactyl

Talk to the girl in the shop's corner afterward, and agree to take her Fossil Pokémon, Aerodactyl. Just like that, you've found a new Pokémon!

Pokémon: Aerodactyl

S92: Have a Heart Scale

Head into Seafolk Village's floating restaurant for a hot meal and a Heart Scale. Check under one of the tables for a Zygarde Cell as well!

Reward: Heart Scale

S93: Get a Lucky Punch

The girl in the houseboat across from the restaurant asks if you're a lucky person. Answer "Yes" or "No" to receive a Lucky Punch!

Reward: Lucky Punch

S94: Score Aloraichium Z

In the same houseboat, show the woman on the opposite couch an Alolan Raichu. She'll reward you with Alolan Raichu's exclusive Z-Crystal!

Reward: Aloraichium Z

Tip

After claiming your Lucky Punch and Aloraichium Z, step out through the houseboat's south door to reach a fishing spot and TM91 Flash Cannon!

S95: Trade for Steenee

Past the village's big central tree, a woman is willing to trade her Steenee for a Granbull. You can catch Granbull at many locations around Poni Island, including the nearby Poni Wilds.

Pokémon: Steenee

Tip

The Ace Trainer in the Pokémon Center can teach Draco Meteor to your Pokémon, while an old man can teach Dragon Ascent. Only the Legendary Pokémon Rayquaza can learn Dragon Ascent, but any Dragon-type Pokémon can learn Draco Meteor as long as the Pokémon is completely friendly (p. 130) toward you.

Poni Wilds

Ride Pokémon Needed

One need not venture far from Seafolk Village to reach Poni Island's untamed wilds. Powerful Pokémon and tenacious Trainers abound in this spacious field.

Team Recommendations

GRASS ELECTRIC FIGHTING
POISON GROUND BUG

Items

	Items
1	Dusk Stone
2	Max Repel
3	Max Potion
4	Pearl String
5	Rare Candy

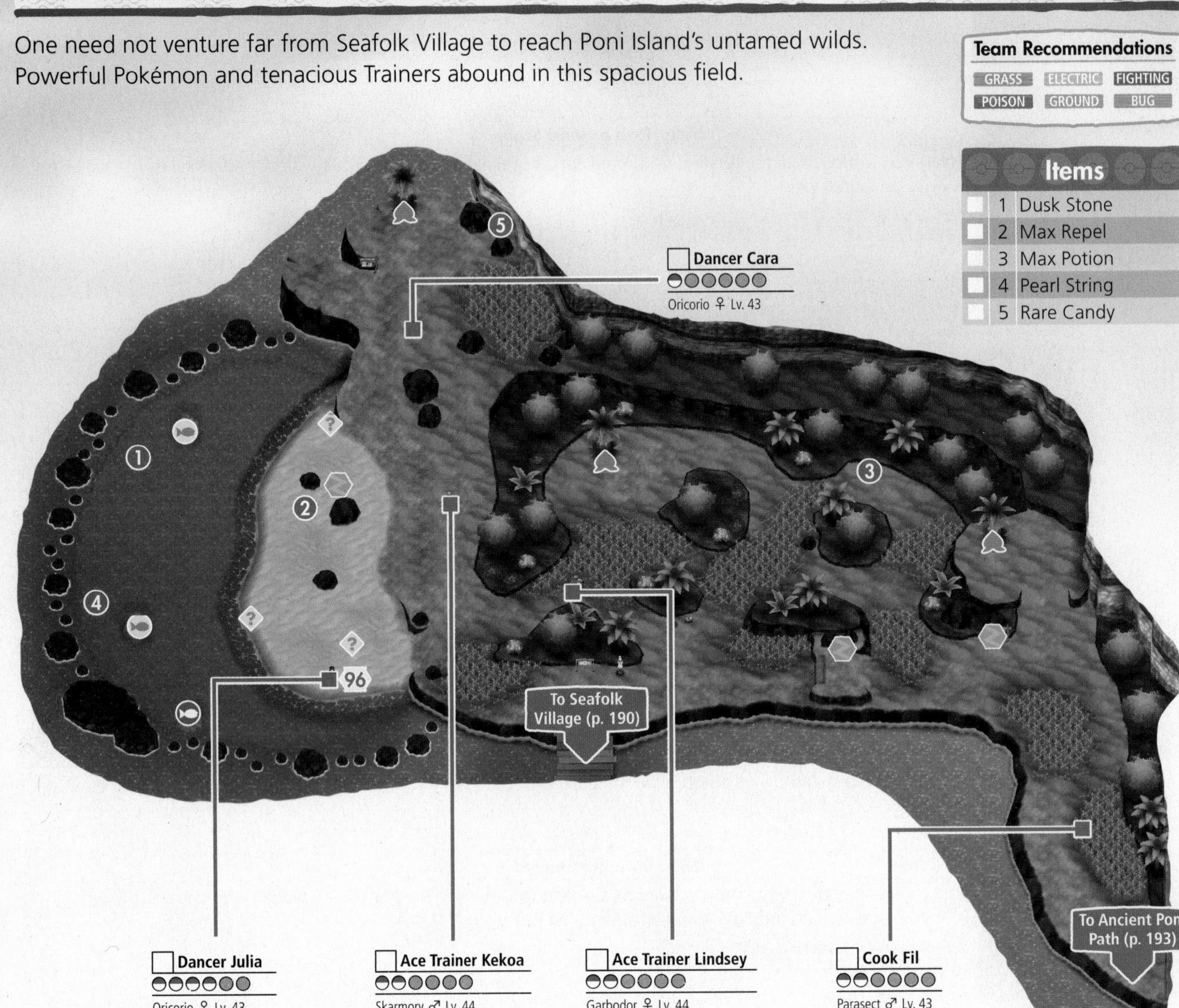

Hidden Items
Big Pearl
Pearl
Repeat Ball

Tall Grass		
Exeggcute		△
Gastrodon		△
Granbull		○
Gumshoos	○ (day only)	○
Pelipper		○
Alolan Raticate	☽	○

Water Surface	
Gastrodon	○
Lapras	▲
Lumineon	○
Pelipper	○
Tentacruel	○

Fishing Spots	
Magikarp	◎
Relicanth	▲
Wailmer	○

Rare Fishing Spots	
Magikarp	◎
Relicanth	△
Wailmer	◎

Splashing Water	
Wailmer	◎
Wailord	△

Shore	
Wimpod	◎

◎ frequent ○ average △ rare
▲ almost never ○ day only ☽ night only
Pokémon Sun *Pokémon Moon*

Tip

Remember: Wimpod is skittish and flees when it sees you, just like the Wimpod you may have seen on Route 8. You've got to be quick and corner it if you wish to battle and catch it! If Wimpod gives you the slip, leave the area and return for another chance at tracking it down.

1 Make a run through Poni Wilds

A large wilderness lies just north of Seafolk Village and it's filled with strong Trainers who strive to be the best. You won't find Hapu here, but you'll discover lots of items and Berries and new species of Pokémon. Search the wilds from one end to the other, then head east to reach the Ancient Poni Path.

S96: Battle a tough Trainer

The dancing woman on the beach will battle you if you beat every other Trainer in the Poni Wilds. Her Pokémon tend to hang on with their Focus Sash—a valuable item that will become yours if you emerge victorious!

Reward: Focus Sash

Tip

Remember to catch a Granbull and trade it to the woman near the big tree in Seafolk Village for her Steenee!

Ancient Poni Path

Located near the heart of Poni Island, this old path connects the Poni Wilds to the Vast Poni Canyon and Poni Breaker Coast. A few people and Pokémon make their homes in the ruins here, but not many.

Team Recommendations

Tall Grass		
Exeggcute		△
Gastrodon		△
Granbull		○
Gumshoos	○	○
Pelipper		○
Alolan Raticate	☽	○

◎ frequent ○ average
△ rare ▲ almost never
○ day only ☽ night only
Pokémon Sun
Pokémon Moon

Items	
1	Shiny Stone
2	Adrenaline Orb
3	TM79 Frost Breath

Hidden Items
PP Up
Revival Herb

Collector Raymond

Turtonator ♂ Lv. 43
Drampa ♂ Lv. 43

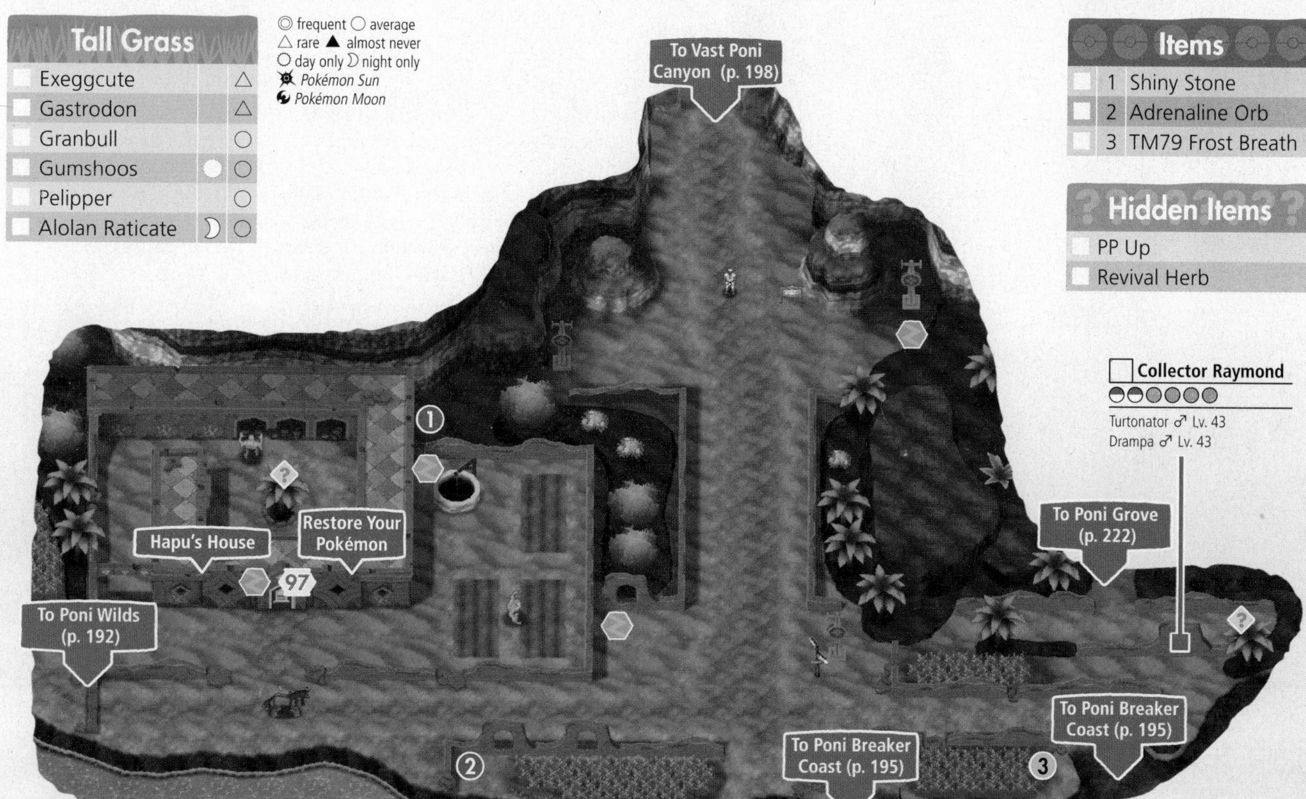

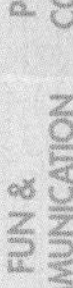

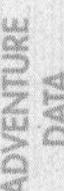

1 Meet Hapu and register a new Ride Pokémon

You find your friend Hapu here on the Ancient Poni Path. Surprisingly, she informs you that Poni Island has no kahuna. How could that be?! Hapu then invites you to meet her at the nearby Ruins of Hope. Her grandmother arrives after Hapu leaves, and kindly registers Machamp to your Ride Pager, saying that you'll need its help to navigate the ruins. Give the Ancient Poni Path a thorough search before proceeding east into Poni Breaker Coast.

Ride Pokémon: Machamp

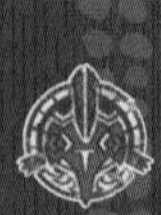

Machamp Shove

You got a new Ride Pokémon! Machamp has the power it takes to push large, square boulders around. You've likely seen such boulders in places like Ten Carat Hill and Diglett's Tunnel. Whenever you see one, press Ⓨ and select Machamp Shove to start riding Machamp, then hold Ⓑ to use Machamp Shove and move those big boulders around! Try shoving them into square holes to forge new paths through certain areas. Note that you cannot ride Machamp in certain indoor locations or in narrow areas.

Tip

Unlike other Ride Pokémon, riding Machamp doesn't affect your odds of encountering wild Pokémon—you'll encounter them at the same rate as you would when traveling on foot.

Tip

Now that you can ride Machamp, you can use its strength to fully explore previous areas that featured big, square boulders. Consider revisiting Ten Carat Hill (p. 85), Lush Jungle (p. 120), and Diglett's Tunnel (p. 125) to reach a variety of valuables, including Flyinium Z, TM53 Energy Ball, and TM61 Will-O-Wisp (respectively).

Tip

If your Pokémon are weary, enter Hapu's house and talk to her Miltank—it'll restore your team back up to snuff. Check Hapu's bedroom afterward to find a Zygarde Core!

S97: Receive an Awakening from Hapu's Alolan Meowth

Catch some rest on Hapu's bed, and you'll be awoken by her Alolan Meowth. It has a special gift for you!

Reward: Awakening

Poni Breaker Coast / Ruins of Hope

Ride Pokémon Needed 

Easily identified by its dark soil, Poni Island's southern coast is a barren place where few Trainers dare venture. The mysterious and ancient Ruins of Hope are located here.

Team Recommendations
GRASS ELECTRIC

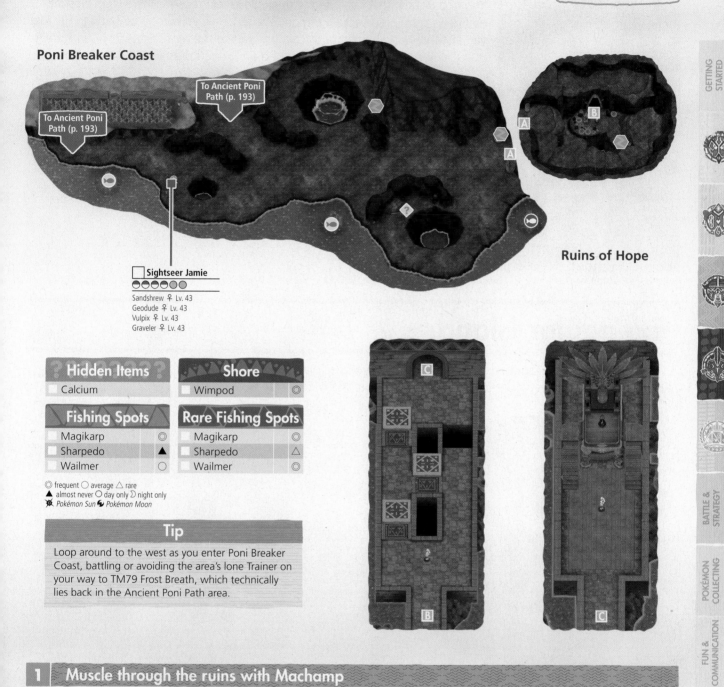

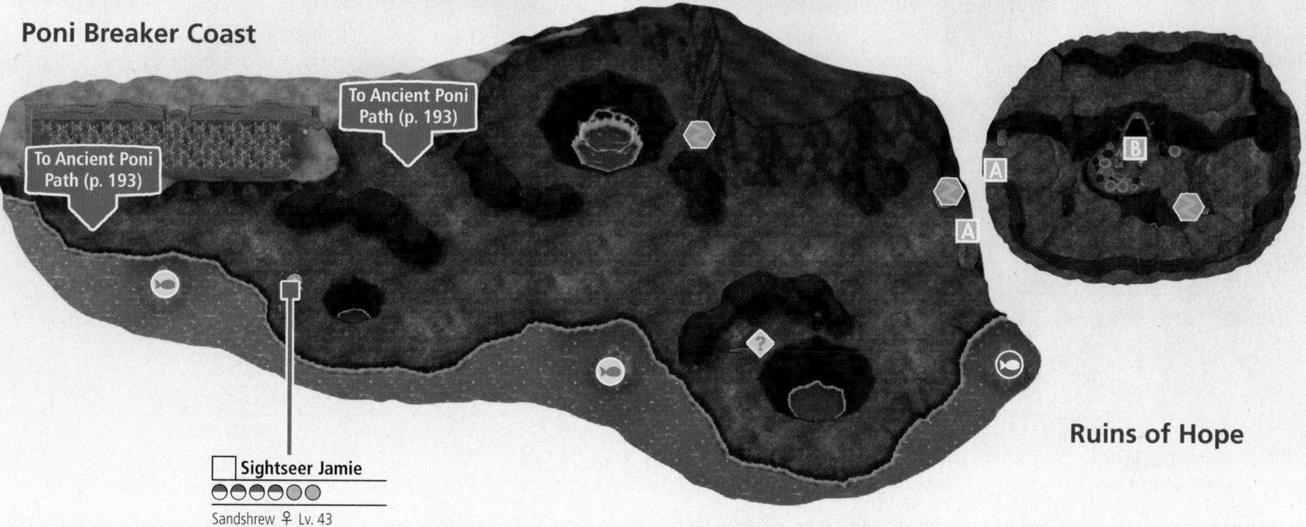

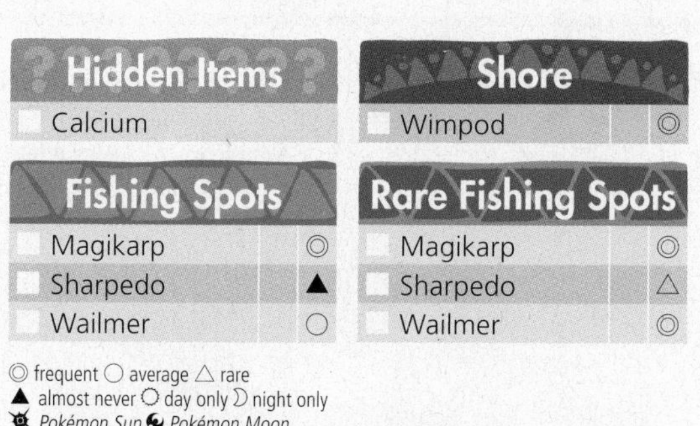

Hidden Items
Calcium

Shore	
Wimpod	◎

Fishing Spots	
Magikarp	◎
Sharpedo	▲
Wailmer	○

Rare Fishing Spots	
Magikarp	◎
Sharpedo	△
Wailmer	◎

◎ frequent ○ average △ rare
▲ almost never ☼ day only ☽ night only
Pokémon Sun *Pokémon Moon*

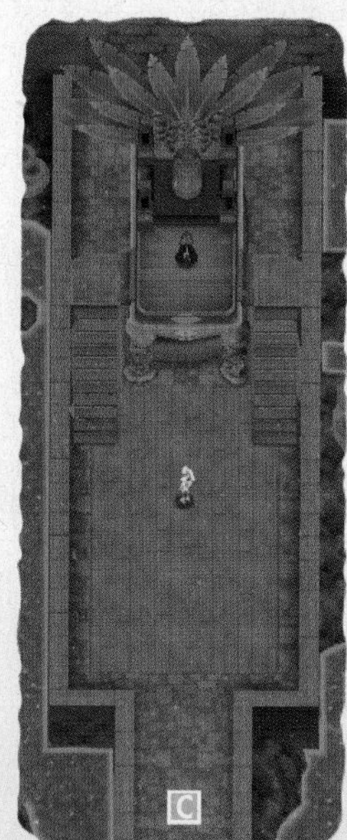

Tip

Loop around to the west as you enter Poni Breaker Coast, battling or avoiding the area's lone Trainer on your way to TM79 Frost Breath, which technically lies back in the Ancient Poni Path area.

1 Muscle through the ruins with Machamp

Cruise through Poni Breaker Coast on your way to the Ruins of Hope, where Machamp gets a chance to flex his muscles. Ride Machamp and hold Ⓑ to shove the ruins' big stone blocks out of your way. Push the southwest block all the way north first, so that you can reach the block in the middle of the two paths. Push the middle block to the east, then circle back around and shove it north and into the hole.

Tip

If you make a mistake with Machamp, simply exit the ruins and enter again to find the blocks back where they started.

2 Meet up with Hapu inside the ruins

You find Hapu in the heart of the ruins. She's just received Tapu Fini's blessing and been appointed kahuna of Poni Island! Relax, you won't be battling her just yet. Instead, Hapu hints that the counterpart to the Moon Flute (Sun) / Sun Flute (Moon) that Gladion gave to Lillie can be found on Exeggutor Island.

3 Speak with the chief of Seafolk Village

Exeggutor Island is too far to reach by way of Lapras or Sharpedo. You need a ship! Return to Seafolk Village, calling for Charizard if you like. Rest at the Pokémon Center, then talk to the village chief down by the dock. He'll happily ferry you to your destination on his trusty vessel, the *S.S. Magikarp*.

Exeggutor Island

As one might expect, Exeggutor Island is home to many wild Alolan Exeggutor. Legends also say it's the last resting place of the mystical Sun Flute (Sun) / Moon Flute (Moon).

Team Recommendations

FIRE, GRASS, ELECTRIC, ICE, POISON, FLYING

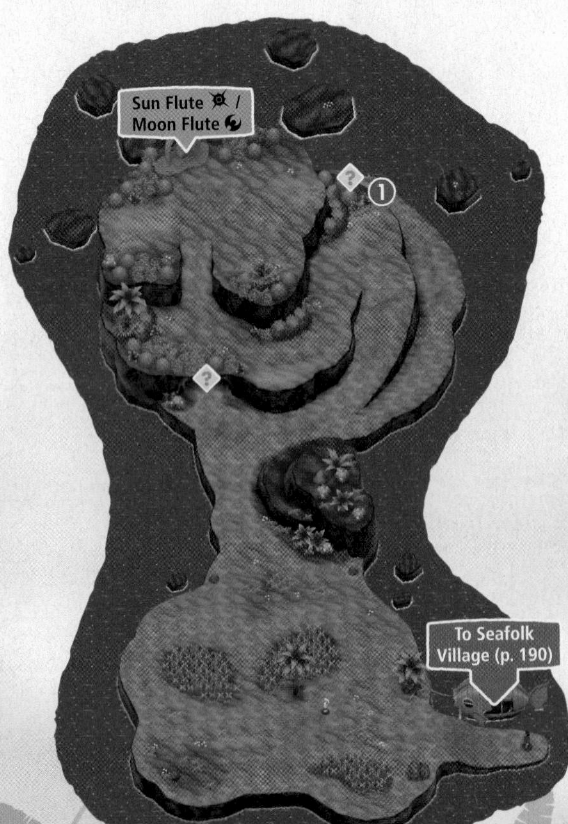

Items
1 Prism Scale

Hidden Items
Big Pearl
Heart Scale

Tall Grass	
Exeggcute	◎
Alolan Exeggutor	○
Gastrodon	△
Pelipper	○

◎ frequent ○ average △ rare
▲ almost never ○ day only ☽ night only
(Sun) *Pokémon Sun* (Moon) *Pokémon Moon*

Tip

Depending on the weather, different Pokémon may appear when wild Pokémon call for SOS allies in battle. When it rains, Castform (Rainy Form) and Sliggoo may appear in battles.

Tip

If the going gets rough, speak to the chief to return to Poni Island at any time.

1 Search the island for the flute

It's not long before you discover how Exeggutor Island got its name. Defeat the wild Alolan Exeggutor that ambushes you, and prepare to battle more of its kind if you tread through the tall grass as you make your way north. Despite some rainy weather, you should have little problem finding the precious flute. It rests on a pedestal at the island's north end. When you find it in *Pokémon Moon*, the Moon Flute will look a little different than what you see on the left, but the location is the same!

2 Prepare your team, then head for the canyon

With the flute in hand, your next destination is Vast Poni Canyon. A long and difficult trek awaits you there, so be sure your team is well-balanced and ready to go. Make a pit stop at Seafolk Village's Pokémon Center to pack your Bag full of medicines and Repels, then return to Hapu's house on the Ancient Poni Path. Go north to reach the canyon's entrance, where trouble in the form of Team Skull awaits you!

Team Skull Grunt's Pokémon

The first Grunt you face sends out a lone Fomantis. It should be short work for your seasoned team.

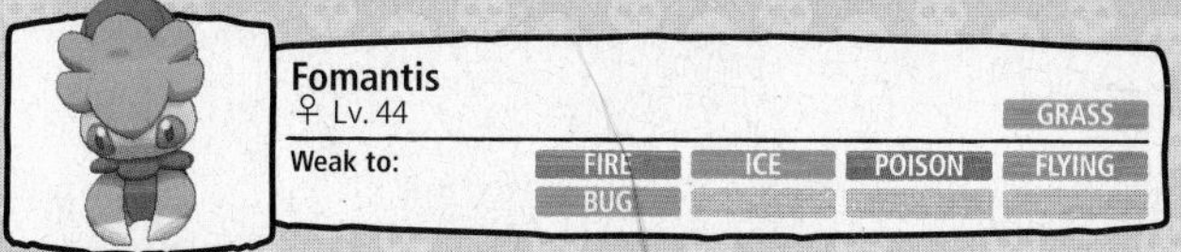

Team Skull Grunt's Pokémon

Backed by his whole crew of homeboys, the second Grunt goes all out, sending out a whopping five Pokémon. Switch out your Pokémon throughout the battle to capitalize on the opposing team's weaknesses. Get past this Grunt's gang to clear the way forward into the canyon.

3 Receive a Z Crystal from Plumeria

Team Skull Admin Plumeria appears after the smoke clears, but she isn't here to fight. Instead, she admires your conviction and apologizes for her recent behavior. Plumeria can't help you through the canyon ahead, but she can send you on your way with one last gift, and the hope that you'll somehow find a way to save Guzma. Lillie kindly heals your team, so you can continue your journey to Vast Poni Canyon.

Reward: Poisonium Z

Vast Poni Canyon

Ride Pokémon Needed

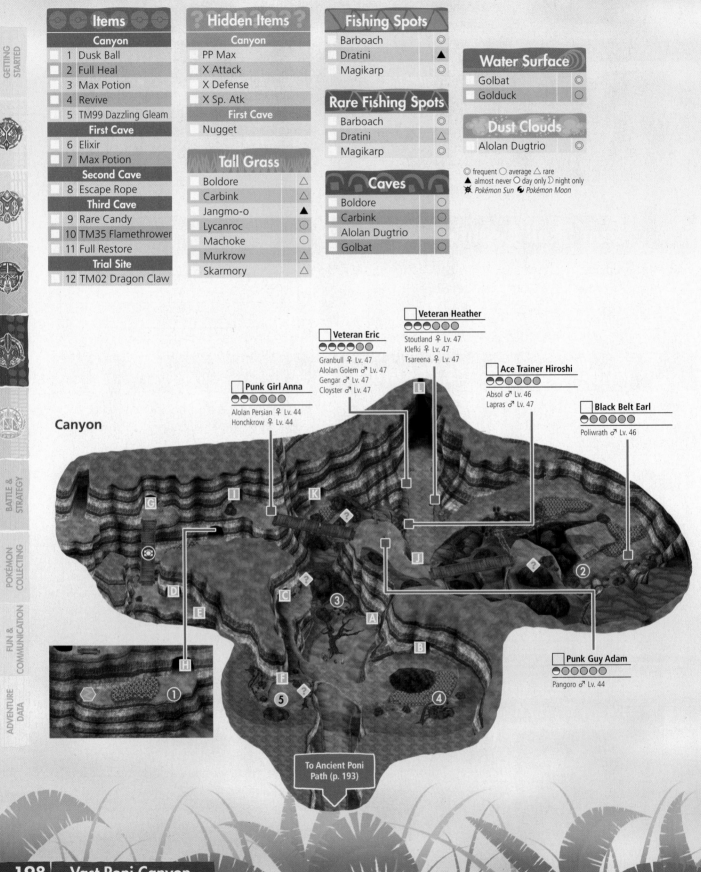

Located in the heart of Poni Island, this massive valley puts even the most powerful Trainers to the test. Somewhere among its caves and chasms lies the altar where the Sun and Moon Flutes must be played to summon Alola's Legendary Pokémon.

Team Recommendations

WATER · GRASS · FIGHTING · GROUND · FLYING · PSYCHIC

GETTING STARTED

BATTLE & STRATEGY
POKÉMON COLLECTING
FUN & COMMUNICATION
ADVENTURE DATA

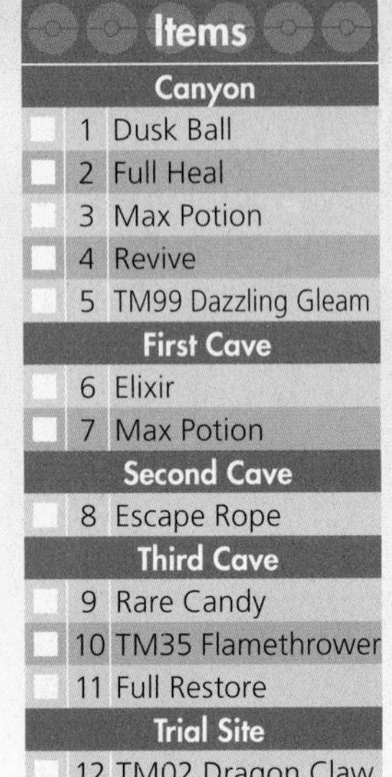

Items

Canyon	
1	Dusk Ball
2	Full Heal
3	Max Potion
4	Revive
5	TM99 Dazzling Gleam
First Cave	
6	Elixir
7	Max Potion
Second Cave	
8	Escape Rope
Third Cave	
9	Rare Candy
10	TM35 Flamethrower
11	Full Restore
Trial Site	
12	TM02 Dragon Claw

Hidden Items

Item
Canyon
PP Max
X Attack
X Defense
X Sp. Atk
First Cave
Nugget

Tall Grass

Pokémon	Rate
Boldore	△
Carbink	△
Jangmo-o	▲
Lycanroc	○
Machoke	○
Murkrow	△
Skarmory	△

Fishing Spots

Pokémon	Rate
Barboach	◎
Dratini	▲
Magikarp	◎

Rare Fishing Spots

Pokémon	Rate
Barboach	◎
Dratini	△
Magikarp	◎

Caves

Pokémon	Rate
Boldore	○
Carbink	○
Alolan Dugtrio	○
Golbat	○

Water Surface

Pokémon	Rate
Golbat	◎
Golduck	○

Dust Clouds

Pokémon	Rate
Alolan Dugtrio	◎

◎ frequent ○ average △ rare
▲ almost never ○ day only ☽ night only
Pokémon Sun *Pokémon Moon*

Canyon

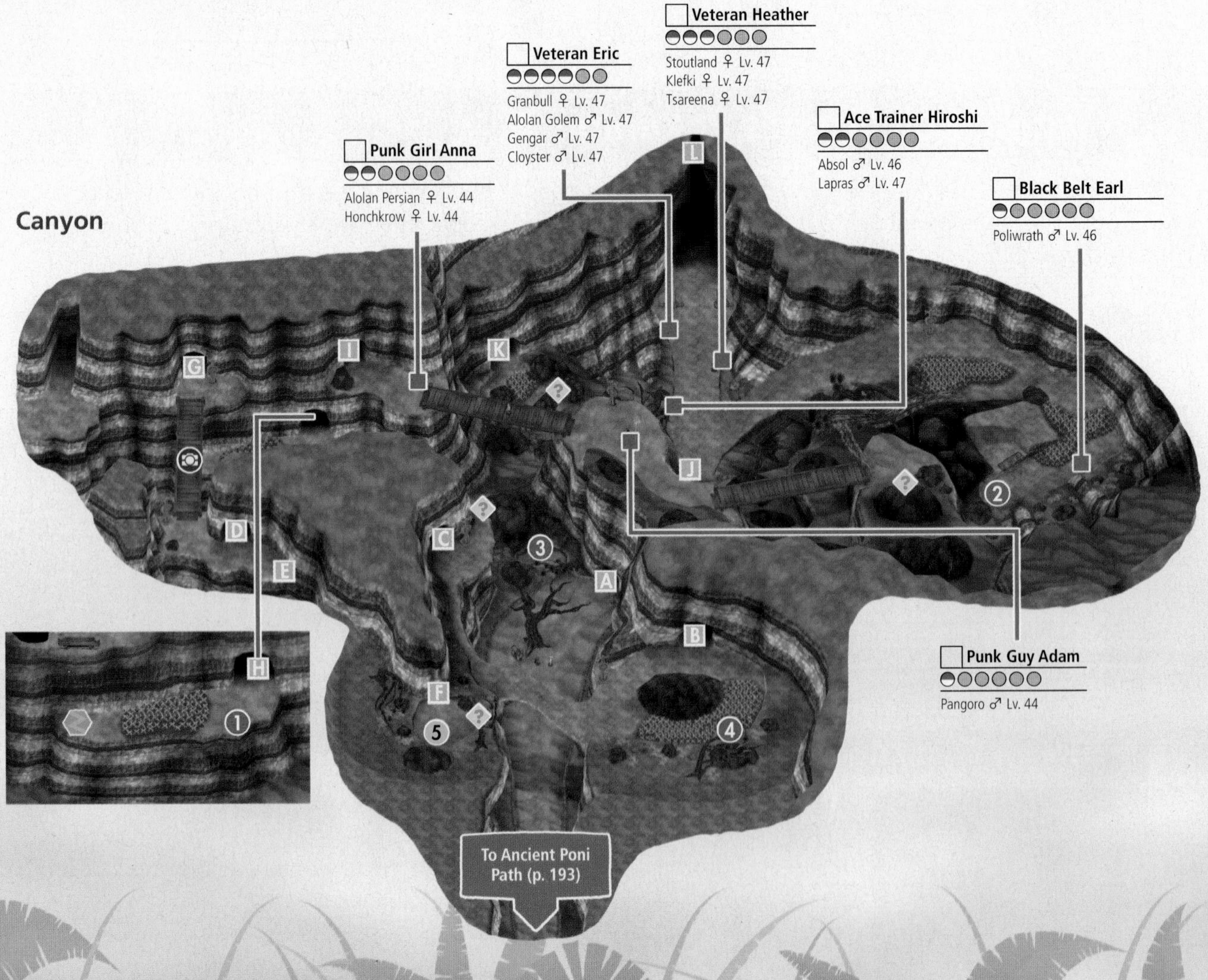

Veteran Heather
Stoutland ♀ Lv. 47
Klefki ♀ Lv. 47
Tsareena ♀ Lv. 47

Veteran Eric
Granbull ♀ Lv. 47
Alolan Golem ♂ Lv. 47
Gengar ♂ Lv. 47
Cloyster ♂ Lv. 47

Ace Trainer Hiroshi
Absol ♂ Lv. 46
Lapras ♂ Lv. 47

Punk Girl Anna
Alolan Persian ♀ Lv. 44
Honchkrow ♀ Lv. 44

Black Belt Earl
Poliwrath ♂ Lv. 46

Punk Guy Adam
Pangoro ♂ Lv. 44

A B C D E F G H I J K L

① ② ③ ④ ⑤

To Ancient Poni Path (p. 193)

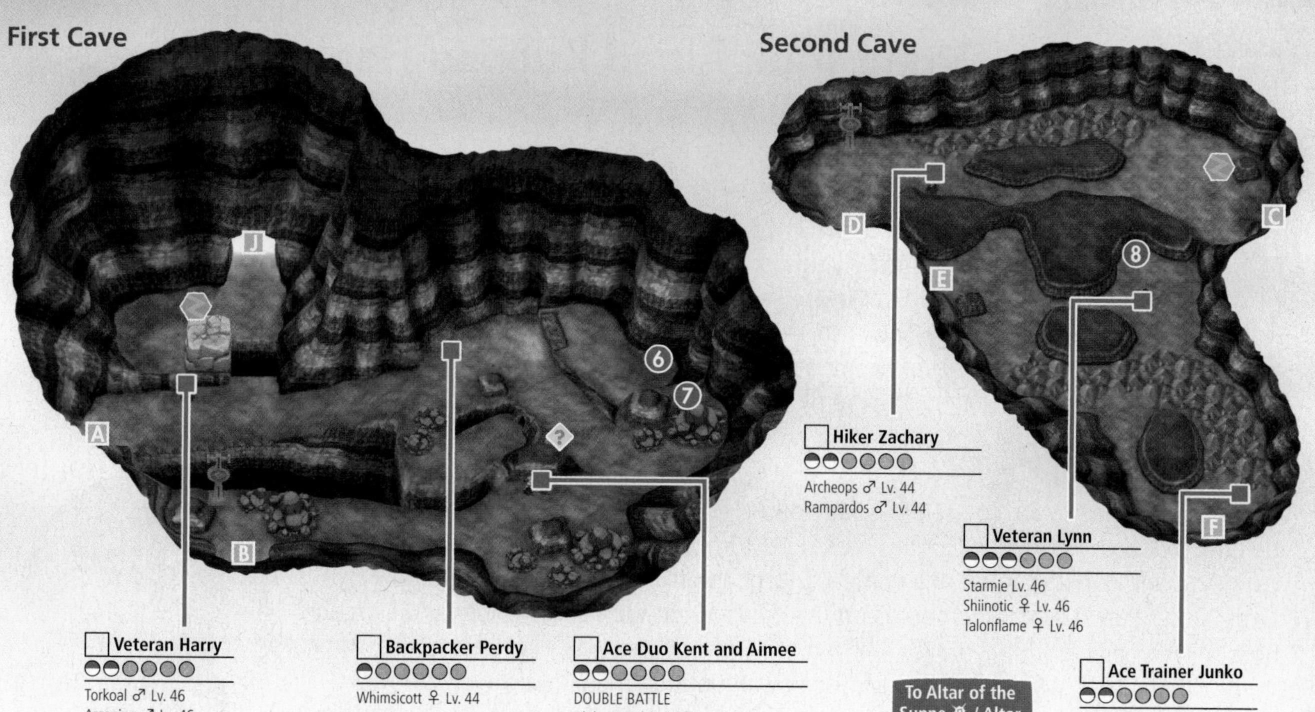

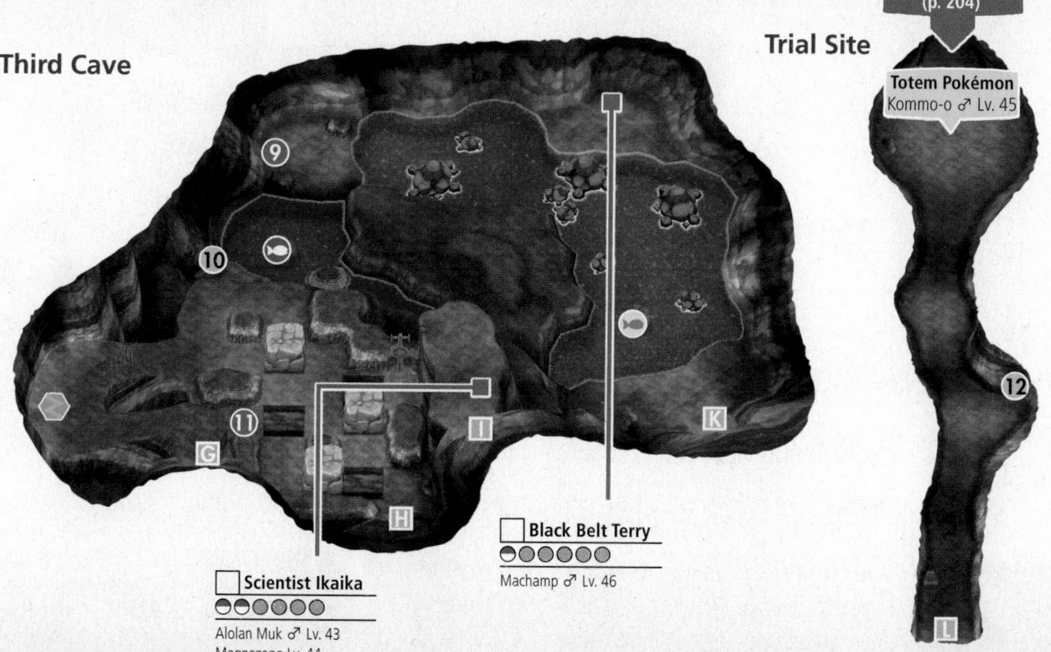

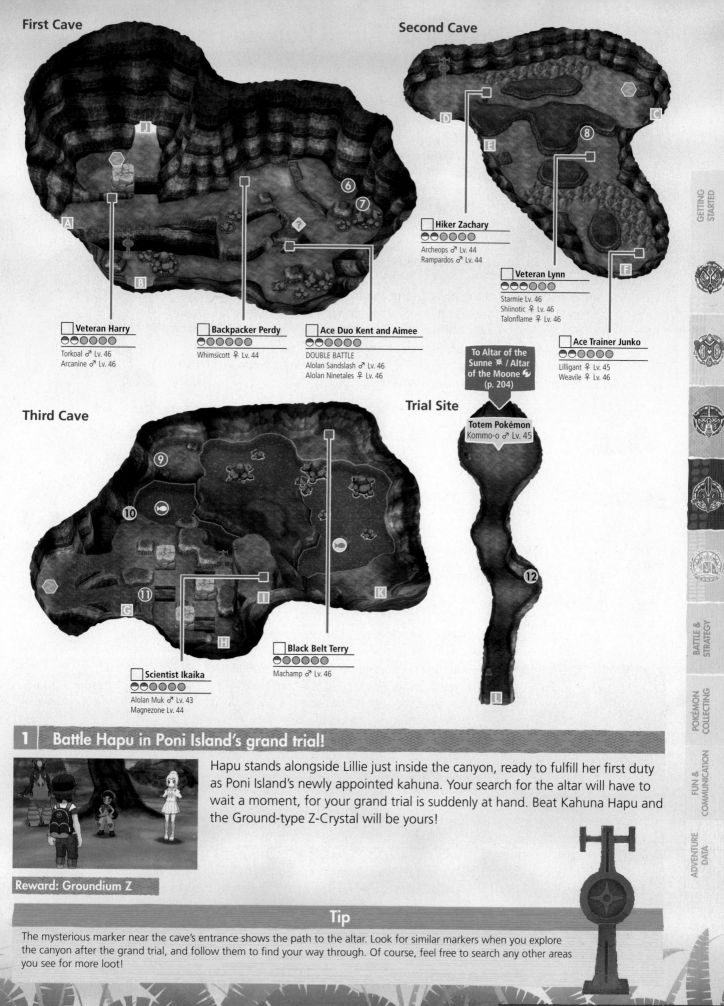

1 Battle Hapu in Poni Island's grand trial!

Hapu stands alongside Lillie just inside the canyon, ready to fulfill her first duty as Poni Island's newly appointed kahuna. Your search for the altar will have to wait a moment, for your grand trial is suddenly at hand. Beat Kahuna Hapu and the Ground-type Z-Crystal will be yours!

Reward: Groundium Z

Tip

The mysterious marker near the cave's entrance shows the path to the altar. Look for similar markers when you explore the canyon after the grand trial, and follow them to find your way through. Of course, feel free to search any other areas you see for more loot!

Grand Trial: Island Kahuna Hapu

As you may have guessed from her traveling companion, Mudsdale, Hapu has a soft spot for Ground-type Pokémon. This means that Water-, Grass-, Ice-, and Flying-type Pokémon are your best bets to send out against her. Try using Grass-type Pokémon that know HP-stealing moves, such as Giga Drain—they'll inflict supereffective damage while also recovering HP each turn. Flying-type Pokémon, or Bug- and Grass-type Pokémon like Parasect, are excellent, as they're highly resistant to Ground-type moves.

Kahuna Hapu's Pokémon

Hapu has a Hyper Potion to use at her discretion, so don't expect her weary Pokémon to be easy pickings. Her Alolan Dugtrio uses Sandstorm to create the sandstorm weather condition and damage your Pokémon each turn, and it also tries to get the drop on you with Sucker Punch. Her Flygon pours on the punishment with Earth Power and Dragon Breath—two strong special moves that can really wreck your day. Her Gastrodon can heal itself with Recover, while her trusty Mudsdale can unleash the Ground-type Z-Power—Tectonic Rage—for earth-shattering amounts of mayhem. Stand your ground with Flying- or Grass-type Pokémon, and you're sure to emerge victorious!

Alolan Dugtrio
♀ Lv. 47
GROUND STEEL
Weak to: FIRE WATER FIGHTING GROUND
Mudsdale
♂ Lv. 48
GROUND
Weak to: WATER GRASS ICE
Flygon
♂ Lv. 47
GROUND DRAGON
Weak to: 4× ICE DRAGON FAIRY
Gastrodon
♀ Lv. 47
WATER GROUND
Weak to: 4× GRASS

2 Crash through the first cave

Your grand trial is complete, but the real test is yet to come. Grab the Max Revive that Lillie gives you, and allow her to heal your Pokémon before entering the nearby cave. Make your way through with Tauros's help, battling tough Trainers and collecting items as you climb ever upward to the cave's high exit.

Reward: Max Revive

Tip

Before heading into the first cave, there's one more valuable item to nab. Do you see the big roots just a bit north of the entrance to the cave? Crawl under them by pressing Ⓐ while standing beside them, and you can reach a Max Potion!

3 Cut through the second cave

Back outside, you find yourself on the high ground. Go east to nab a Revive from the nearby tall grass, then cross a land bridge to reach another cave. You can't explore much of this one on your first trip through, so simply head for its exit, returning outside.

Tip

Go east and spot a little hole as you exit the second cave. Crawl through the hole to reenter the cave and complete your explorations with Mudsdale's help. Inch through another small hole at the cave's south end to reach TM99 Dazzling Gleam that lies outside. Backtrack through the cave afterward and continue your trek through the canyon.

4 Muscle through the third cave

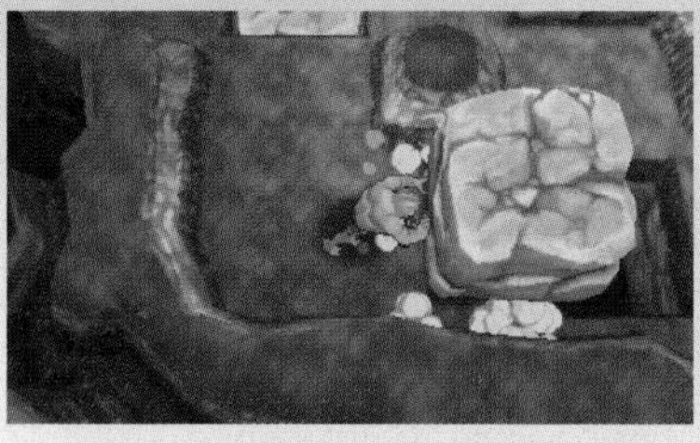

Lillie catches up to you as you near a frightfully long bridge. After gathering her courage and crossing it, she kindly heals your Pokémon. Enter the cave that follows, and use Machamp's ample might to push a large square boulder south until it drops into a hole and get a Full Restore. Push the southern boulder east afterward, slotting it into another hole. Shove the third and final boulder north, then climb the nearby ladder and exit the cave to meet a colorful new character on a bridge who gives you the Fairy-type Z-Crystal.

Reward: Fairium Z

Tip

Before climbing the ladder, pass through the cave's south exit to reach a little ledge with a Dusk Ball and Zygarde Cell.

Mina

A free spirit with a passion for painting, Mina is the final captain for your island challenge. Rather than pinning herself down to a specific trial site, Mina prefers to wander the region in search of fresh inspiration for her art. You can tell she's friendly right away, for she gives you Fairium Z without so much as a fight!

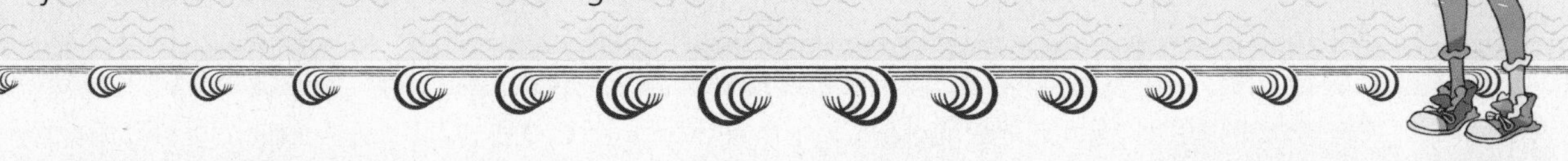

5 Use a root to reach the canyon floor

Continue across the bridge after Mina leaves, then run down a huge root to return to the canyon floor. Go east to reach a Full Heal and battle a Black Belt if you like, then head west to find a row of Trainers up north. Before heading north through the Trainers, go south to reach a new area back in the first cave. Shove a boulder into a hole with Machamp, and you'll create a shortcut back to the canyon's entrance. Fly back to Seafolk Village to rest your team if you want, or return to the canyon and head north, battling through the row of Trainers.

Tip

After shoving the boulder back in the first cave, check the nearby ground to find a Zygarde Cell that was hiding behind it!

Tip

Before battling the Trainers up north, crawl through the roots to the west and re-enter the third cave to explore its ground level for a Rare Candy and TM35 Flamethrower.

6 Enter the unguarded trial site

Beyond the row of Trainers lies an open Captain's Gate. Strangely, no one is guarding it. Allow Lillie to restore your Pokémon, then pass through the open gate to reach a vacant trial site. Perhaps it was abandoned by some former captain? Whatever its origins, you must explore the site and defeat the Totem Pokémon to advance in your island challenge!

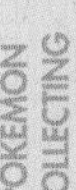

Trial Guide: Deserted Trial

Your final trial is quite unusual. With no captain around to run it, you're free to explore the trial site on your own. Somewhere inside lurks the Totem Pokémon, but you must battle through a few ambush encounters to reach it. Dragon-type Pokémon oppose you here, but don't rely too heavily on Fairy-type Pokémon, even though they're immune to Dragon-type moves. Fairy types are easy prey for the trial's Totem Pokémon, which unleashes a devastating Steel-type move that's super effective against Ice- and Fairy-type Pokémon. Favor Flying and Psychic types instead: Pelipper's strong defense and Flying-type moves make it an ideal candidate, and it can be caught in the nearby Poni Wilds.

Trial Goals

- Search the abandoned trial site
- Defeat the Totem Pokémon
- Retrieve the Z-Crystal from the pedestal

1 Explore the trial site

This trial site is quiet—too quiet. There's no captain here to guide you, but the stone tablet in the entrance confirms that you're in the right place. Gather your courage and begin your search for the Totem Pokémon. Ensure that your party is ready to battle against Dragon-type Pokémon, because you'll be facing several on your trip to the Totem Pokémon.

2 Get ambushed by wild Pokémon

It's not long before you're drawn into battle. Without warning, a wild Pokémon suddenly swoops down on you from above! You haven't stepped into its shadow—this wild Jangmo-o simply gets the drop on you. Defeat Jangmo-o and then Hakamo-o, which also ambushes you a bit farther down the passage.

Jangmo-o

You're first ambushed by Jangmo-o, a Dragon-type Pokémon that shouldn't be too much trouble. Surprise it with supereffective attacks and continue your search for the Totem Pokémon.

Jangmo-o	DRAGON
♂/♀ Lv. 40	
Weak to:	ICE, DRAGON, FAIRY

Tip

After defeating Jangmo-o, grab TM02 Dragon Claw that's tucked away in a nearby nook.

Hakamo-o

The second ambusher is Hakamo-o. It is a Dragon- and Fighting-type Pokémon, making it highly vulnerable to Fairy-type moves. Defeat Hakamo-o to clear the way to the Z-Crystal pedestal you can see in the distance.

Hakamo-o	DRAGON, FIGHTING
♂/♀ Lv. 40	
Weak to:	4× FAIRY, ICE, FLYING, PSYCHIC, DRAGON

GETTING STARTED

BATTLE & STRATEGY

POKÉMON COLLECTING

FUN & COMMUNICATION

ADVENTURE DATA

3 | Defeat the Totem Pokémon!

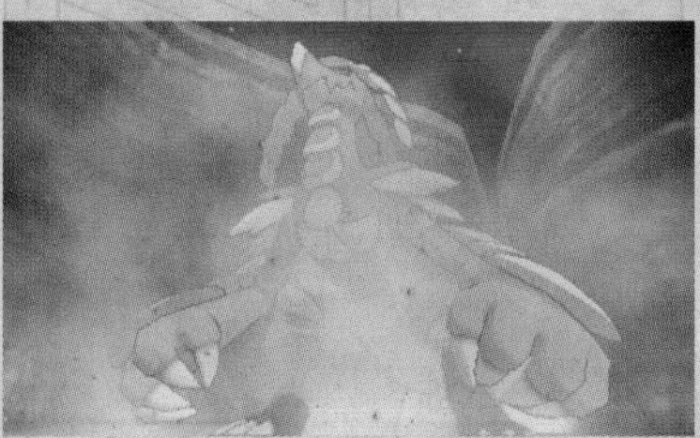

After you've defeated Hakamo-o, the Z-Crystal is within your grasp. Ensure that your team is ready for battle, then approach the pedestal and reach for the Z-Crystal. A massive Pokémon slams down from above and lets out a thunderous roar, which echoes throughout the cavern—your clash with Totem Kommo-o is at hand!

Totem Kommo-o

This imposing Totem Pokémon is one tough customer. Its aura raises all of its stats, and it commonly uses Protect—a defensive move that lets the Totem Pokémon evade your moves, but with an increasingly greater chance of failing each time it's used in a row. Totem Kommo-o lashes out with Clanging Scales and Flash Cannon, two powerful moves that can shock unprepared trial-goers. Clanging Scales is a strong Dragon-type move that will devastate your Dragon-type Pokémon, while Flash Cannon is an incredible Steel-type move that will shred through Fairy and Ice types in short order. Avoid sending out Ice-, Dragon- or Fairy-type Pokémon against Totem Kommo-o, even though it's highly vulnerable to those types of moves. Favor Flying- and Psychic-type Pokémon instead, as they'll serve you best in this grueling battle.

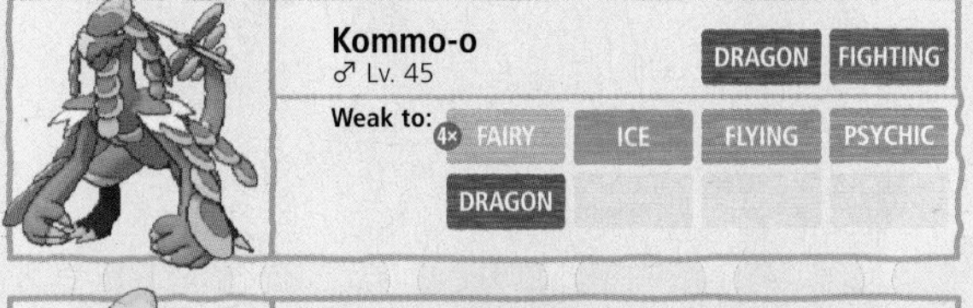

Kommo-o	DRAGON	FIGHTING
♂ Lv. 45		
Weak to:	4× FAIRY, ICE, FLYING, PSYCHIC, DRAGON	

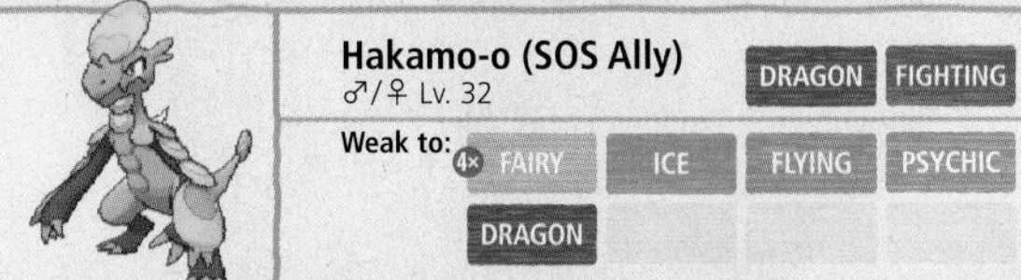

Hakamo-o (SOS Ally)	DRAGON	FIGHTING
♂/♀ Lv. 32		
Weak to:	4× FAIRY, ICE, FLYING, PSYCHIC, DRAGON	

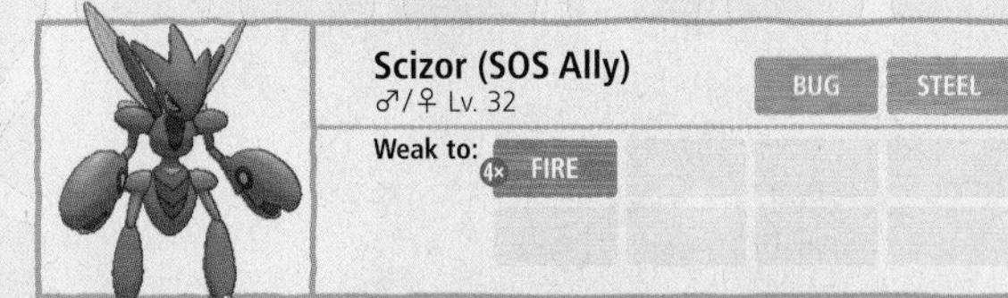

Scizor (SOS Ally)	BUG	STEEL
♂/♀ Lv. 32		
Weak to:	4× FIRE	

4 | Claim the Dragonium Z

You obtained a Dragon-type Z-Crystal.
The Dragonium Z is yours!

Once you have defeated the fearsome Kommo-o and its allies in battle, the Dragonium Z is yours to claim. Grab it from the pedestal and you can give it to any Pokémon that know Dragon-type moves to use their Z-Power to the fullest.

Seafolk Village Revisited

p. 190

S98: Have a meal with Hapu

If you're exhausted after the trial, head to Seafolk Village before heading to the altar. Rest your Pokémon and stock up items at the Pokémon Center. Also, swing by the floating restaurant, and order the Zumongous Z-Noodles. You'll get a surprise visit from your friend, Hapu! Poni's new kahuna has brought along her appetite, and she's kind enough to spring for your feast. As if that weren't enough, she also hands you her Heart Scales after the meal!

Reward: Heart Scale ×2

Altar of the Sunne / Altar of the Moone

Located just beyond the Vast Poni Canyon, this ancient ruin's countless steps stretch up to a mysterious altar. Legends say that two mystical flutes must be played there to summon Alola's Legendary Pokémon, Solgaleo / Lunala.

Altar of the Sunne

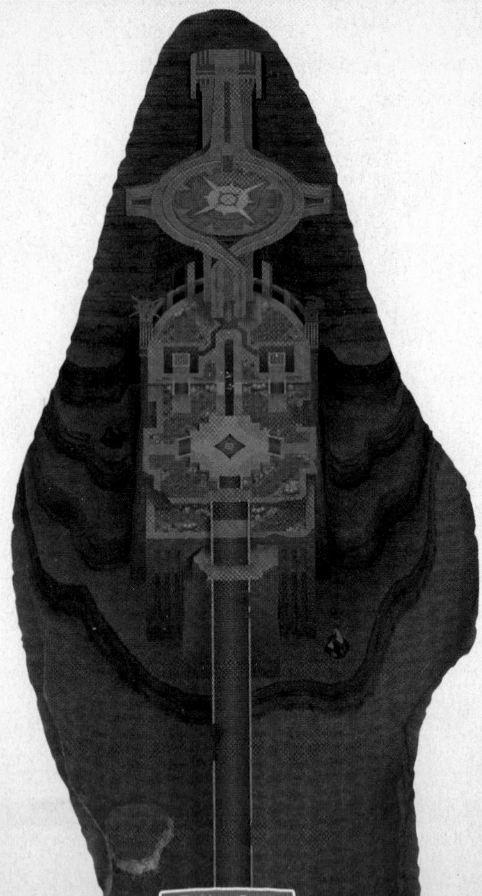

Altar of the Moone

1 Summon Alola's Legendary Pokémon!

Proceed through the exit beyond the Z-Crystal pedestal to meet up with Lillie and Hapu at the foot of an impossibly long set of stairs. The Altar of the Sunne / Altar of the Moone lies at the top, and there isn't a moment to lose. Sprint up to the altar after Lillie heals your Pokémon, then take your place and play your flute in sync with Lillie. If you are playing *Pokémon Moon*, you will play the Moon Flute, which appears a bit different than the Sun Flute you see on the left.

2 Travel to Ultra Space

The flutes' mystical melody activates the altar, unleashing incredible power. Drawn to the immense energy, Nebby zips to the source and evolves, becoming the Legendary Pokémon! You've been traveling with it all along! At Lillie's insistence, the Legendary Pokémon tears open a portal and whisks you away to a mysterious new dimension.

Ultra Space

The air hangs heavy in this beautiful yet bizarre dimension, which the Ultra Beasts call home. Little is known about this mysterious, otherworldly realm.

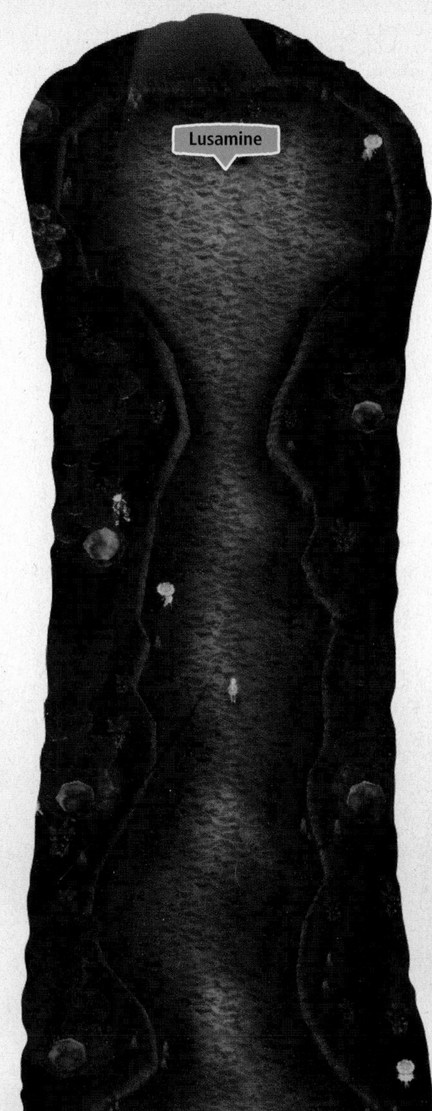

1 Explore Ultra Space

What an unusual place! Could Lillie's mother really be here? It doesn't take long for you to find out. Go north to bump into Guzma, who has troubling news of Lusamine. The Aether Foundation's obsessed president awaits farther ahead, and even Lillie can't believe her mother's words when she reveals her true feelings and desires. The conversation quickly devolves into a shocking confrontation.

Aether President Lusamine's Pokémon

Lillie's mother must be stopped! Unfortunately, it won't be easy. Her Pokémon share few weaknesses, and each has a unique aura that raises one of its stats—you'll need a well-balanced team that can capitalize on every advantage. Clefable lashes out with Moonblast, and also raises its Defense and Sp. Def with Cosmic Power—use Poison- or Steel-type moves to deal it supereffective damage. Milotic blasts you with Hydro Pump, heals itself with Recover, and also uses Safeguard to shield Lusamine's team from status conditions for five turns. Unleash strong Grass-type moves, like Giga Drain, to gain the edge. Mismagius often moves first due to its Speed-boosting aura, and it strikes with Shadow Ball and Power Gem. Counter it with a sturdy Pokémon that can soak up damage and respond with supereffective moves. Bewear uses Baby-Doll Eyes to lower your Pokémon's Attack, and bashes your team with big Normal- and Fighting-type moves—send out a strong Flying-type Pokémon like Pelipper to gain the upper hand. Last but not least, Lilligant saps your Pokémon's HP with Leech Seed, recovering its own HP in the process. Torch it with Fire-type moves to ensure its defeat.

Clefable
♀ Lv. 50
FAIRY
Weak to: POISON STEEL
Bewear
♀ Lv. 50
NORMAL FIGHTING
Weak to: FIGHTING FLYING PSYCHIC FAIRY
Milotic
♀ Lv. 50
WATER
Weak to: GRASS ELECTRIC
Lilligant
♀ Lv. 50
GRASS
Weak to: FIRE ICE POISON FLYING BUG
Mismagius
♀ Lv. 50
GHOST
Weak to: GHOST DARK

Altar of the Sunne / Altar of the Moone Revisited

p. 204

1 Battle and catch Alola's Legendary Pokémon!

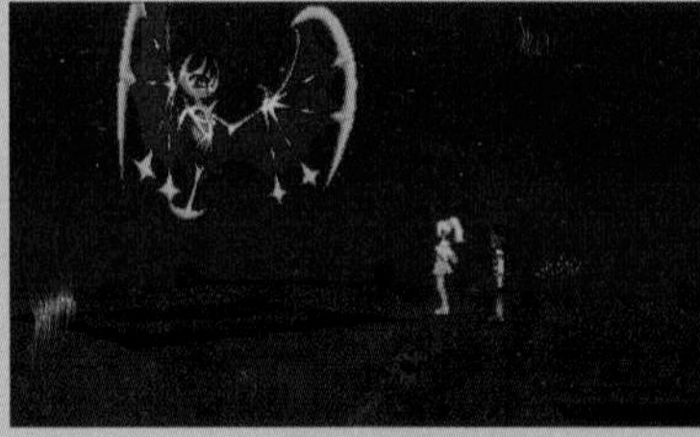

Beaten, Lusamine collapses from exhaustion. The Legendary Pokémon swiftly whisks everyone back to Alola. After making sure that her mother is all right, Lillie determines that the Legendary Pokémon would like to continue its journey by your side. Battle against Solgaleo / Lunala and give it a Poké Ball to call home!

Tip

Catching the Legendary Pokémon is short work if you've still got the Master Ball that Gladion handed you back at Aether Paradise. Simply throw it on your first turn to catch Solgaleo / Lunala right away—Master Balls never fail! However, you may wish to save the Master Ball for future catches. You can keep trying to catch Solgaleo / Lunala until you succeed, but other exceptional Pokémon you've yet to encounter aren't as willing to stick around if you fail.

Legendary Pokémon: Solgaleo

If you'd rather not use your Master Ball, you'll have to battle and weaken Solgaleo before you can catch it. Prepare your team accordingly, potentially using TM54 False Swipe to teach one of your Pokémon a move that'll help it lower the Legendary Pokémon down to 1 HP. Solgaleo can soak up plenty of damage, so don't be shy about using supereffective moves at first. As its HP dips into the yellow and red, switch to moves that deal less damage, and try to gauge how much HP each attack is taking off its health bar. Start throwing Poké Balls when Solgaleo's health is as low as you can comfortably bring it without landing the final blow.

If you're still having trouble, try using moves like Lick or Stun Spore to inflict Paralysis, or Yawn or Sleep Powder to inflict the Asleep status condition. If the battle drags on, consider using a Timer Ball, which becomes more effective the longer the battle lasts. You'll have to try again if you accidentally defeat it, for the Legendary Pokémon must be caught!

Solgaleo
Lv. 55 — PSYCHIC | STEEL
Weak to: FIRE | GROUND | GHOST | DARK

Legendary Pokémon: Lunala

If you'd rather not use your Master Ball, you'll have to battle and weaken Lunala before you can catch it. Prepare your team accordingly, but remember that you may not be able to utilize TM54 False Swipe since one of Lunala's types is Ghost, unless your Pokémon can also use Foresight. If you started your adventure with Rowlet, consider yourself lucky. It and its Evolutions are able to learn both of these moves. However, Dark-type moves should be particularly effective against Lunala.

If you're still having trouble, try using moves like Lick or Stun Spore to inflict Paralysis, or Yawn or Sleep Powder to inflict the Asleep status condition. If the battle drags on, consider using a Timer Ball, which becomes more effective the longer the battle lasts. You'll have to try again if you accidentally defeat it, for the Legendary Pokémon must be caught!

Lunala
Lv. 55 — PSYCHIC | GHOST
Weak to: 4× GHOST | 4× DARK

2 Go with Nanu to Mount Lanakila

Kahuna Nanu arrives shortly after your battle with Alola's Legendary Pokémon. Now that you've defeated all four kahunas and ended the threat posed by Lusamine, the time has come for you to complete your island challenge! Agree to go with Nanu, and he'll take you directly to Mount Lanakila in a flash. There's no rush, however, so feel free to decline Nanu's offer if you'd prefer to do more exploring around Alola.

Mount Lanakila

Towering over Tapu Village, Mount Lanakila is the tallest peak in the region. Trial-goers must make the long and arduous trek to the summit to challenge Alola's newly founded Pokémon League.

Team Recommendations

FIRE | ELECTRIC | FIGHTING

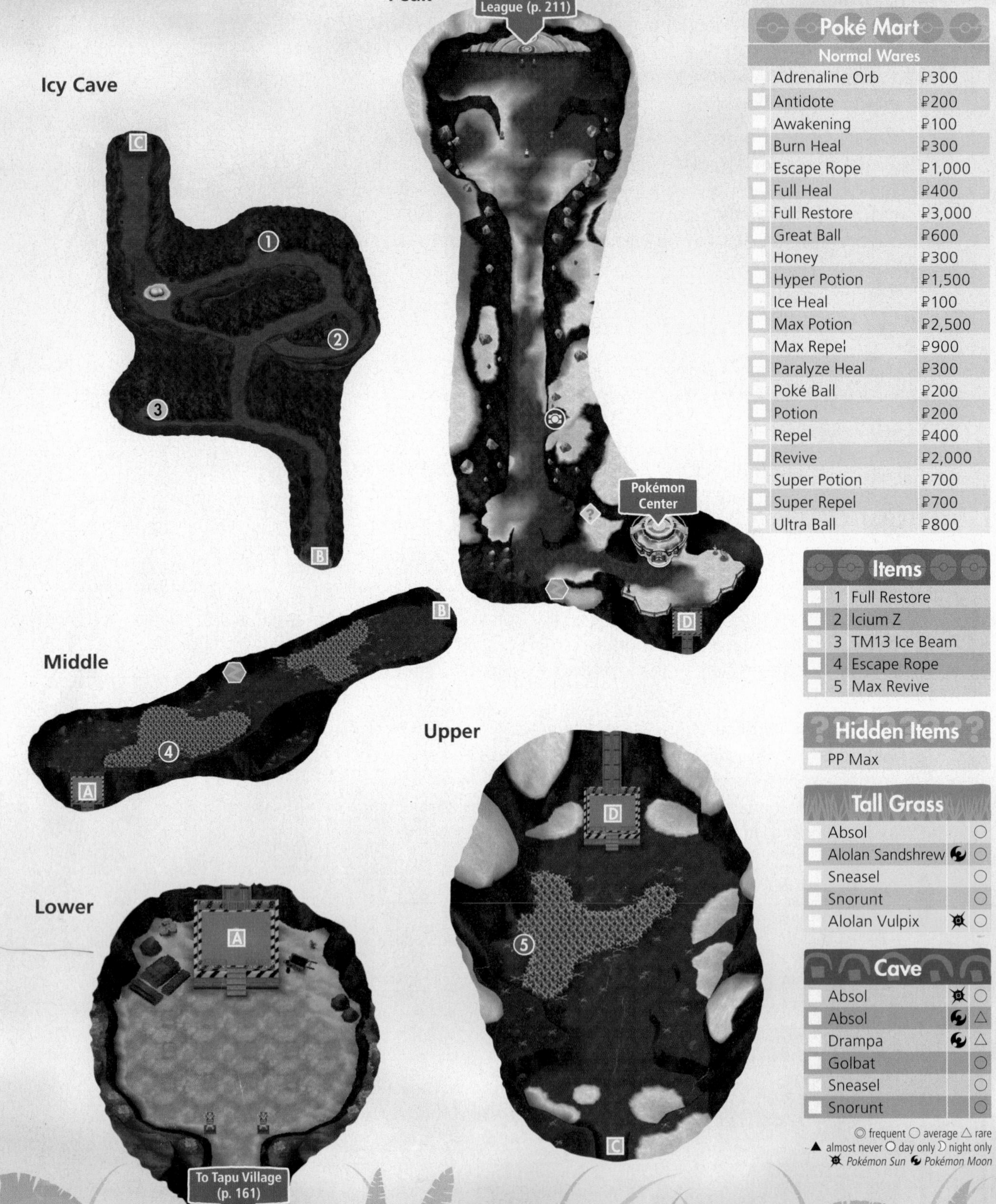

Poké Mart

Normal Wares	
Adrenaline Orb	₽300
Antidote	₽200
Awakening	₽100
Burn Heal	₽300
Escape Rope	₽1,000
Full Heal	₽400
Full Restore	₽3,000
Great Ball	₽600
Honey	₽300
Hyper Potion	₽1,500
Ice Heal	₽100
Max Potion	₽2,500
Max Repel	₽900
Paralyze Heal	₽300
Poké Ball	₽200
Potion	₽200
Repel	₽400
Revive	₽2,000
Super Potion	₽700
Super Repel	₽700
Ultra Ball	₽800

Items

1	Full Restore
2	Icium Z
3	TM13 Ice Beam
4	Escape Rope
5	Max Revive

Hidden Items

- PP Max

Tall Grass

Pokémon	Version	Rate
Absol		○
Alolan Sandshrew	Pokémon Moon	○
Sneasel		○
Snorunt		○
Alolan Vulpix	Pokémon Sun	○

Cave

Pokémon	Version	Rate
Absol	Pokémon Sun	○
Absol	Pokémon Moon	△
Drampa	Pokémon Moon	△
Golbat		○
Sneasel		○
Snorunt		○

◎ frequent ○ average △ rare ▲ almost never ○ day only ☽ night only *Pokémon Sun* *Pokémon Moon*

Tip

Depending on the weather, different Pokémon may appear when wild Pokémon call for SOS allies in battle. When it's hailing, Castform (Snowy Form) or Vanillish may appear.

1 Battle Gladion at Lanakila's base

A more-or-less friendly face greets you at the base of Mount Lanakila. It's Gladion, and he wants to thank you for helping Lillie rescue their mother. Gladion's fresh out of Master Balls, but he can offer you an intense battle—and a Max Elixir, if you manage to beat him at his best!

Reward: Max Elixir

Gladion's Pokémon

Gladion sure has a strange way of saying "Thank you." He's got a Z-Ring, and his Lucario is holding a Z-Crystal, letting it unleash a devastating Z-Move if you don't defeat it fast. His Golbat has also evolved into Crobat, and his Type: Null has evolved into Silvally, a unique Pokémon whose type will match up favorably (for Gladion) against the first partner Pokémon you picked. Fighting-type moves will help you beat down Gladion's team, but keep your Dark-type Pokémon away from the fray, for many of Gladion's team's moves are super effective against Dark types.

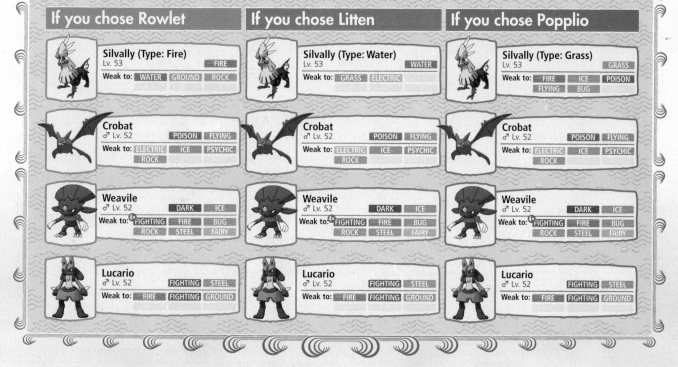

If you chose Rowlet

Pokémon	Level	Type	Weak to
Silvally (Type: Fire)	Lv. 53	FIRE	WATER, GROUND, ROCK
Crobat	♂ Lv. 52	POISON, FLYING	ELECTRIC, ICE, PSYCHIC, ROCK
Weavile	♂ Lv. 52	DARK, ICE	FIGHTING (4×), FIRE, BUG, ROCK, STEEL, FAIRY
Lucario	♂ Lv. 52	FIGHTING, STEEL	FIRE, FIGHTING, GROUND

If you chose Litten

Pokémon	Level	Type	Weak to
Silvally (Type: Water)	Lv. 53	WATER	GRASS, ELECTRIC
Crobat	♂ Lv. 52	POISON, FLYING	ELECTRIC, ICE, PSYCHIC, ROCK
Weavile	♂ Lv. 52	DARK, ICE	FIGHTING (4×), FIRE, BUG, ROCK, STEEL, FAIRY
Lucario	♂ Lv. 52	FIGHTING, STEEL	FIRE, FIGHTING, GROUND

If you chose Popplio

Pokémon	Level	Type	Weak to
Silvally (Type: Grass)	Lv. 53	GRASS	FIRE, ICE, POISON, FLYING, BUG
Crobat	♂ Lv. 52	POISON, FLYING	ELECTRIC, ICE, PSYCHIC, ROCK
Weavile	♂ Lv. 52	DARK, ICE	FIGHTING (4×), FIRE, BUG, ROCK, STEEL, FAIRY
Lucario	♂ Lv. 52	FIGHTING, STEEL	FIRE, FIGHTING, GROUND

2 Climb Mount Lanakila

Ride the lift after Gladion departs to reach Lanakila's first rocky path. Battle your way through the wild Pokémon that live in the tall grass as you head for a large ice cave. Navigate the ice cave's frigid tunnels as you head for its northern exit.

Tip

Notice the large, snowy boulder in the ice cave's northwest corner? If you catch an Eevee, found on Route 6 (p. 105), and it levels up near this boulder, it will evolve into an Ice-type Pokémon called Glaceon!

3 Rest up and then battle Hau

After passing through the ice cave, ride another lift up to the welcome sight of a Pokémon Center. Rest up and buy any last-minute items for your ultimate trial. Head north toward the Pokémon League, and you'll be stopped by your good friend, Hau. Show Hau just how strong you've become, and beat him to earn the right to challenge the Pokémon League first!

Reward: Max Revive ×3

Hau's Pokémon

Hau has come quite a ways since your first battle back in Iki Town. All of his Pokémon are much stronger now, and his first partner Pokémon has fully evolved into its final form. He's also added a fourth member to his team—Komala—a Normal-type Pokémon that has the Comatose Ability, making it be able to attack while sleeping. As with your previous battles with Hau, your first partner Pokémon can easily counter his—but beware of his first partner Pokémon's potential to unleash a powerful Z-Move. Also, be sure to pull back your first partner Pokémon when Hau sends out his Flareon, Vaporeon, or Leafeon to counter it.

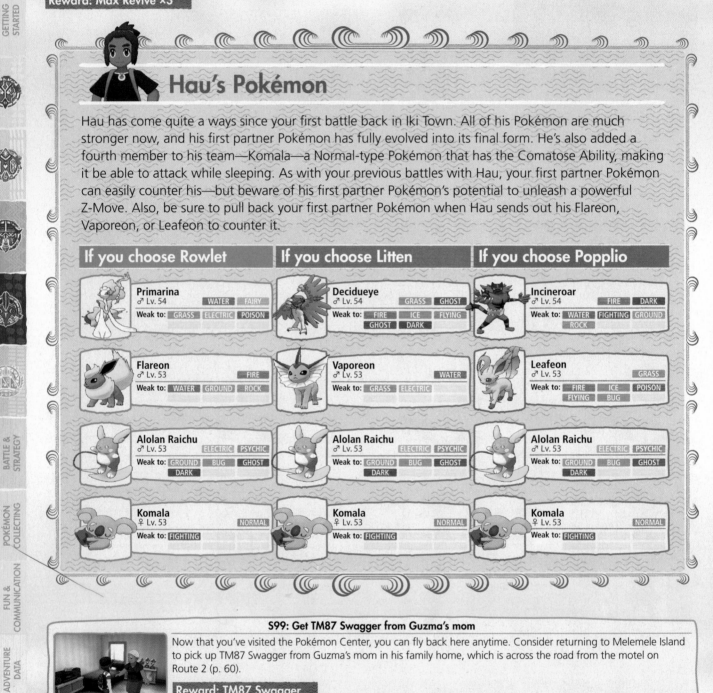

If you choose Rowlet

Pokémon	Level	Type	Weak to
Primarina	♂ Lv. 54	WATER, FAIRY	GRASS, ELECTRIC, POISON
Flareon	♂ Lv. 53	FIRE	WATER, GROUND, ROCK
Alolan Raichu	♂ Lv. 53	ELECTRIC, PSYCHIC	GROUND, BUG, GHOST, DARK
Komala	♀ Lv. 53	NORMAL	FIGHTING

If you choose Litten

Pokémon	Level	Type	Weak to
Decidueye	♂ Lv. 54	GRASS, GHOST	FIRE, ICE, FLYING, GHOST, DARK
Vaporeon	♂ Lv. 53	WATER	GRASS, ELECTRIC
Alolan Raichu	♂ Lv. 53	ELECTRIC, PSYCHIC	GROUND, BUG, GHOST, DARK
Komala	♀ Lv. 53	NORMAL	FIGHTING

If you choose Popplio

Pokémon	Level	Type	Weak to
Incineroar	♂ Lv. 54	FIRE, DARK	WATER, FIGHTING, GROUND, ROCK
Leafeon	♂ Lv. 53	GRASS	FIRE, ICE, POISON, FLYING, BUG
Alolan Raichu	♂ Lv. 53	ELECTRIC, PSYCHIC	GROUND, BUG, GHOST, DARK
Komala	♀ Lv. 53	NORMAL	FIGHTING

S99: Get TM87 Swagger from Guzma's mom

Now that you've visited the Pokémon Center, you can fly back here anytime. Consider returning to Melemele Island to pick up TM87 Swagger from Guzma's mom in his family home, which is across the road from the motel on Route 2 (p. 60).

Reward: TM87 Swagger

Tip

Madam Memorial, an old woman found inside Mount Lanakila's Pokémon Center, can remind your Pokémon of any moves they've forgotten as they were growing, including moves that you chose to not have them learn. If you want to make any changes to your Pokémon's moves, now's the time! She doesn't work for free, though—you must trade her a Heart Scale for each move you want your Pokémon to recall. Get Heart Scales by dining at restaurants, like the one in Konikoni City (p. 128), Malie City (p. 142), and Seafolk Village (p. 190).

4 Meet up with Professor Kukui

Kukui awaits you at the peak of Mount Lanakila, eager to welcome you to the Pokémon League he helped to found here in Alola. Gushing like a proud parent, Kukui fondly recalls his own attempt at becoming Champion of the Kanto region. Rousing himself out of his trip down memory lane, Kukui informs you that you'd better be prepared before setting foot inside the Pokémon League—for once you enter, there's no turning back!

Pokémon League

A newly founded facility built high atop Mount Lanakila, the Pokémon League is the place where Alolan trial-goers gather for their ultimate test. Powerful Trainers known as the Elite Four must be bested here before an epic showdown against the region's strongest Trainer.

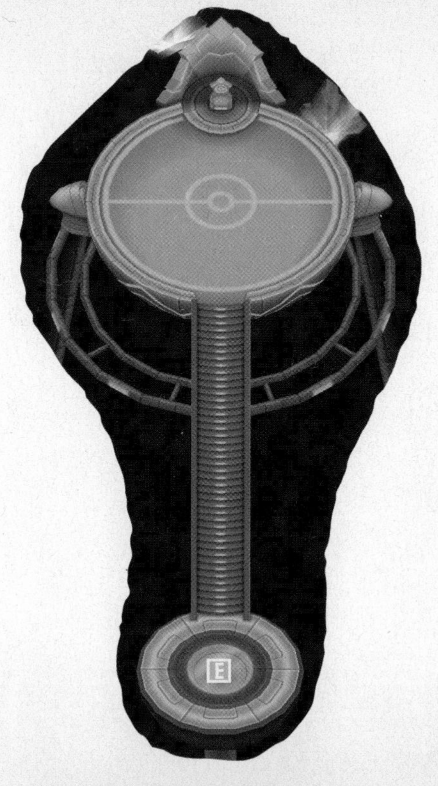

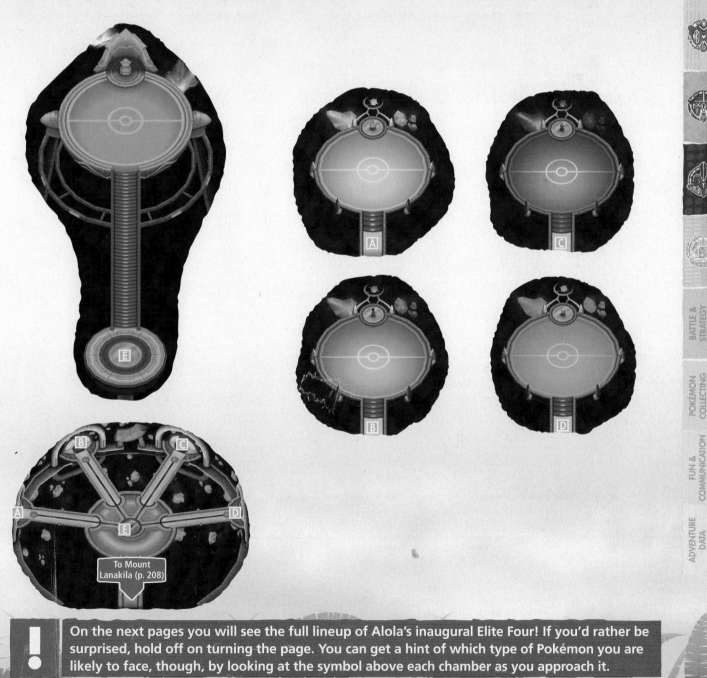

On the next pages you will see the full lineup of Alola's inaugural Elite Four! If you'd rather be surprised, hold off on turning the page. You can get a hint of which type of Pokémon you are likely to face, though, by looking at the symbol above each chamber as you approach it.

Elite Four Hala's Pokémon A

A mighty Fighting-type Pokémon user, Hala holds nothing back in your epic battle here at the Pokémon League. His team has grown much stronger since your first kahuna clash back on Melemele Island, and Hala still has a fondness for Fighting types, so keep your Normal-, Ice-, Rock-, Dark-, and Steel-type Pokémon well out of harm's way. Hala's team share many weaknesses, making it relatively easy to counter if you've come prepared. Strong Flying-, Psychic-, or Fairy-type Pokémon will serve you well in this battle, as will defensive items such as X Defense. Pelipper's high defense and Flying-type moves make it a good counter to Hala's horde, and you also can't go wrong with the Legendary Pokémon you recently caught at the Altar of the Sunne ☀ / Altar of the Moone ☾—its Psychic-type moves will tear through Hala's team.

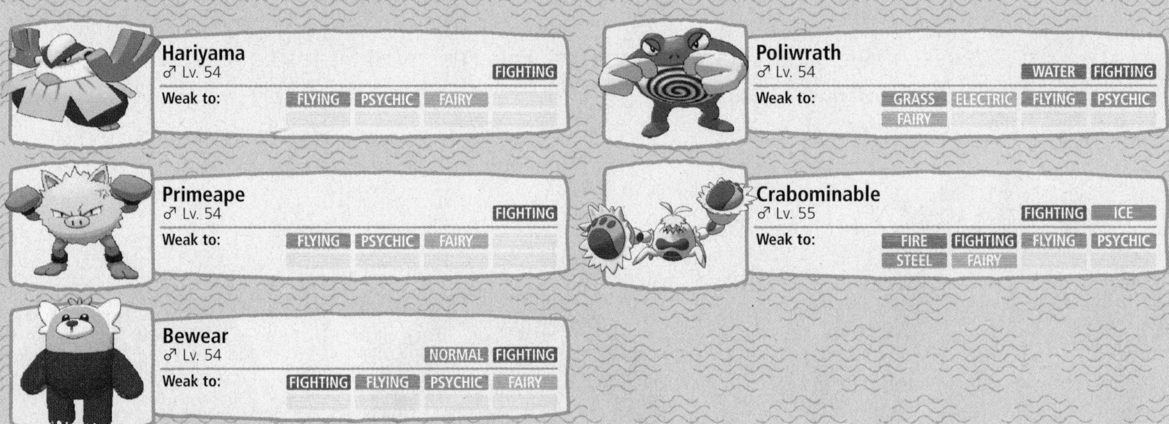

Pokémon	Gender / Level	Type	Weak to
Hariyama	♂ Lv. 54	FIGHTING	FLYING, PSYCHIC, FAIRY
Poliwrath	♂ Lv. 54	WATER, FIGHTING	GRASS, ELECTRIC, FLYING, PSYCHIC, FAIRY
Primeape	♂ Lv. 54	FIGHTING	FLYING, PSYCHIC, FAIRY
Crabominable	♂ Lv. 55	FIGHTING, ICE	FIRE, FIGHTING, FLYING, PSYCHIC, STEEL, FAIRY

Pokémon	Gender / Level	Type	Weak to
Bewear	♂ Lv. 54	NORMAL, FIGHTING	FIGHTING, FLYING, PSYCHIC, FAIRY

Elite Four Olivia's Pokémon B

Another of Alola's kahunas, Olivia, is also a member of the Elite Four. Like Hala, her team has grown far stronger since your kahuna battle back on Akala Island. Olivia retains her favoritism toward rugged Rock-type Pokémon, and her team is very tough and resilient. Exploiting their common weaknesses is vital, especially any 4× weaknesses you see. Still, don't expect to knock out her Pokémon with single blows. Carbink uses Reflect to raise the team's Defense for five turns, while Probopass's Sturdy Ability lets it survive an attack that would normally knock it out (but only if its HP is full). Olivia also has Full Restores to use at any moment to heal any of her Pokémon's status conditions and bring it back to full health. Use items like X Defense in combination with medicines to help your team endure this grueling battle.

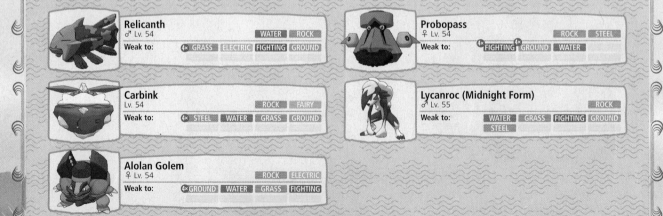

Pokémon	Gender / Level	Type	Weak to
Relicanth	♂ Lv. 54	WATER, ROCK	4× GRASS, ELECTRIC, FIGHTING, GROUND
Probopass	♀ Lv. 54	ROCK, STEEL	4× FIGHTING, 4× GROUND, WATER
Carbink	Lv. 54	ROCK, FAIRY	4× STEEL, WATER, GRASS, GROUND
Lycanroc (Midnight Form)	♂ Lv. 55	ROCK	WATER, GRASS, FIGHTING, GROUND, STEEL
Alolan Golem	♀ Lv. 54	ROCK, ELECTRIC	4× GROUND, WATER, GRASS, FIGHTING

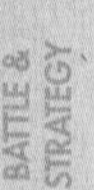

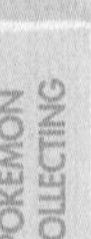

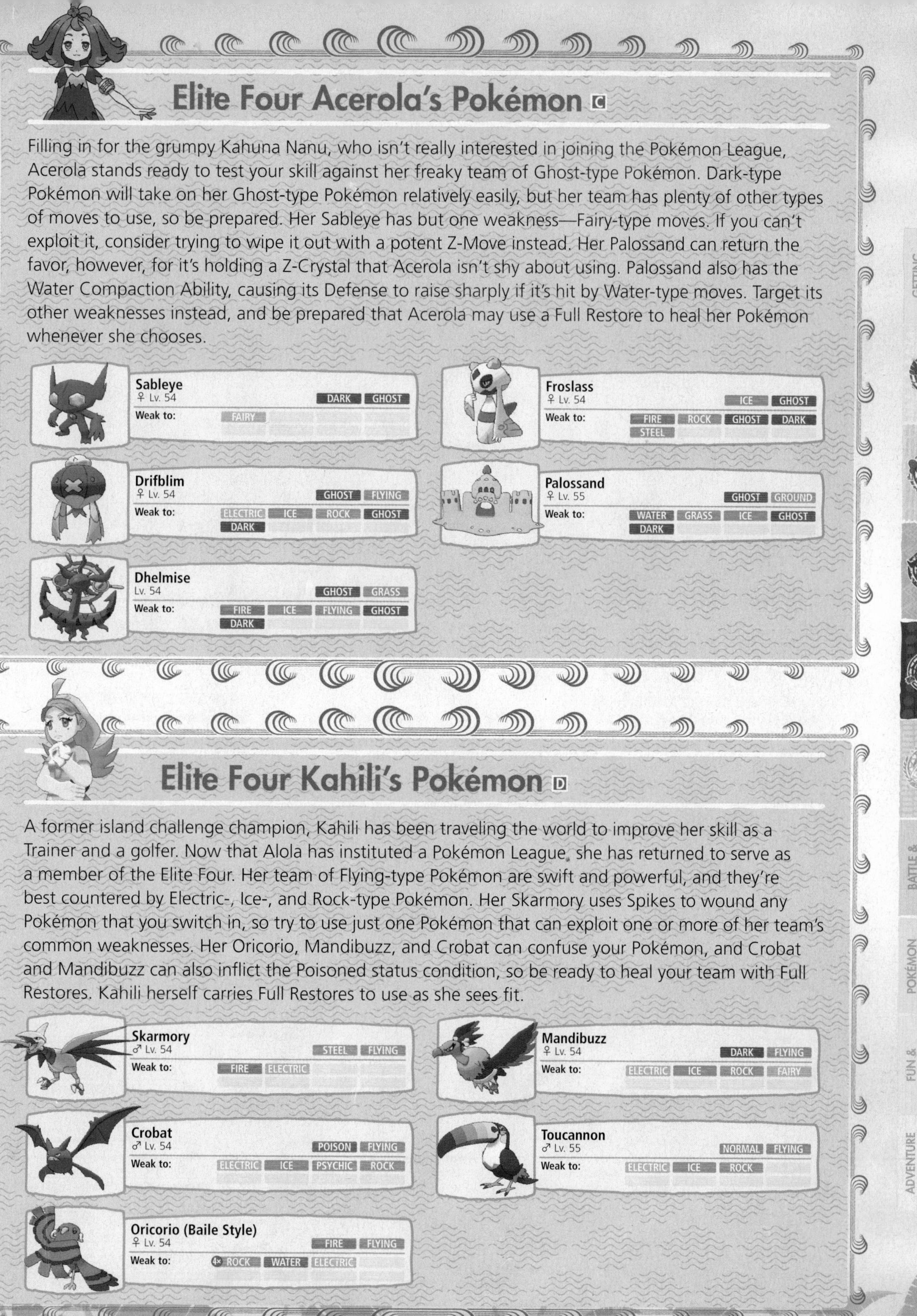

Elite Four Acerola's Pokémon C

Filling in for the grumpy Kahuna Nanu, who isn't really interested in joining the Pokémon League, Acerola stands ready to test your skill against her freaky team of Ghost-type Pokémon. Dark-type Pokémon will take on her Ghost-type Pokémon relatively easily, but her team has plenty of other types of moves to use, so be prepared. Her Sableye has but one weakness—Fairy-type moves. If you can't exploit it, consider trying to wipe it out with a potent Z-Move instead. Her Palossand can return the favor, however, for it's holding a Z-Crystal that Acerola isn't shy about using. Palossand also has the Water Compaction Ability, causing its Defense to raise sharply if it's hit by Water-type moves. Target its other weaknesses instead, and be prepared that Acerola may use a Full Restore to heal her Pokémon whenever she chooses.

Sableye
♀ Lv. 54 — DARK, GHOST
Weak to: FAIRY

Froslass
♀ Lv. 54 — ICE, GHOST
Weak to: FIRE, ROCK, GHOST, DARK, STEEL

Drifblim
♀ Lv. 54 — GHOST, FLYING
Weak to: ELECTRIC, ICE, ROCK, GHOST, DARK

Palossand
♀ Lv. 55 — GHOST, GROUND
Weak to: WATER, GRASS, ICE, GHOST, DARK

Dhelmise
Lv. 54 — GHOST, GRASS
Weak to: FIRE, ICE, FLYING, GHOST, DARK

Elite Four Kahili's Pokémon D

A former island challenge champion, Kahili has been traveling the world to improve her skill as a Trainer and a golfer. Now that Alola has instituted a Pokémon League, she has returned to serve as a member of the Elite Four. Her team of Flying-type Pokémon are swift and powerful, and they're best countered by Electric-, Ice-, and Rock-type Pokémon. Her Skarmory uses Spikes to wound any Pokémon that you switch in, so try to use just one Pokémon that can exploit one or more of her team's common weaknesses. Her Oricorio, Mandibuzz, and Crobat can confuse your Pokémon, and Crobat and Mandibuzz can also inflict the Poisoned status condition, so be ready to heal your team with Full Restores. Kahili herself carries Full Restores to use as she sees fit.

Skarmory
♂ Lv. 54 — STEEL, FLYING
Weak to: FIRE, ELECTRIC

Mandibuzz
♀ Lv. 54 — DARK, FLYING
Weak to: ELECTRIC, ICE, ROCK, FAIRY

Crobat
♂ Lv. 54 — POISON, FLYING
Weak to: ELECTRIC, ICE, PSYCHIC, ROCK

Toucannon
♂ Lv. 55 — NORMAL, FLYING
Weak to: ELECTRIC, ICE, ROCK

Oricorio (Baile Style)
♀ Lv. 54 — FIRE, FLYING
Weak to: 4× ROCK, WATER, ELECTRIC

Pokémon Professor Kukui's Pokémon

Defeating the Elite Four earns you the right to challenge the Pokémon League's chief enthusiast, Professor Kukui. The stakes couldn't be higher, for the victor will be crowned Alola's very first Pokémon League Champion! Conquering Kukui won't be easy, though. He has a full team of six Pokémon, one of which is a direct counter to your first partner Pokémon. That same counter Pokémon will be holding a Z-Crystal, letting Kukui clobber you with a devastating Z-Move at any time of his choosing. Kukui also carries Full Restores to heal his team and remove any status conditions you might try to inflict. In short, he's the toughest test you've faced up to this point!

Kukui sends out Lycanroc first, which uses Stealth Rock to damage any Pokémon that you switch in throughout the battle. This is troublesome, for you'll need to do plenty of Pokémon swapping to counter Kukui's well-rounded team. His Magnezone has the Sturdy Ability to compensate for its 4× weakness to Ground-type moves, so don't expect to defeat it in one shot. And expect Kukui to heal it back up with a Full Restore if you try. Still, this can be a good way to force Kukui to burn through his stock of Full Restores—keep hitting Magnezone with Ground-type attacks to potentially force Kukui's hand.

Kukui's Alolan Ninetales uses Safeguard to shield its team from status conditions for five turns, and his Braviary uses Tailwind to double his team's Speed stat for four turns. A Quick Claw can help your Pokémon move first, but you may wish to simply wipe out Braviary with a Z-Move the moment it appears. Braviary is a dangerous opponent, for it often moves first and can devastate your Pokémon with its powerful Brave Bird move.

If you're struggling against Kukui, try playing a more patient and defensive game, relying on items to gain the advantage. Send out a stalwart Pokémon to soak up damage, then use Max Revives to restore any Pokémon that may have fainted. Once your team is in better shape, strike back at Kukui with more aggressive tactics. Repeat this as necessary until you've taught the professor a lesson he'll never forget!

If you choose Rowlet

Pokémon	Gender / Level	Type	Weak to
 Incineroar	♂ Lv. 58	FIRE, DARK	WATER, FIGHTING, GROUND, ROCK
 Lycanroc (Midday Form)	♂ Lv. 57	ROCK	WATER, GRASS, FIGHTING, GROUND, STEEL
 Alolan Ninetales	♀ Lv. 56	ICE, FAIRY	4× STEEL, FIRE, POISON, ROCK
 Braviary	♂ Lv. 56	NORMAL, FLYING	ELECTRIC, ICE, ROCK
 Magnezone	Lv. 56	ELECTRIC, STEEL	4× GROUND, FIRE, FIGHTING
 Snorlax	♂ Lv. 56	NORMAL	FIGHTING

If you choose Litten

Pokémon	Gender / Level	Type	Weak to
 Primarina	♀ Lv. 58	WATER, FAIRY	GRASS, ELECTRIC, POISON
 Lycanroc (Midday Form)	♂ Lv. 57	ROCK	WATER, GRASS, FIGHTING, GROUND, STEEL
 Alolan Ninetales	♀ Lv. 56	ICE, FAIRY	4× STEEL, FIRE, POISON, ROCK
 Braviary	♂ Lv. 56	NORMAL, FLYING	ELECTRIC, ICE, ROCK
 Magnezone	Lv. 56	ELECTRIC, STEEL	4× GROUND, FIRE, FIGHTING
 Snorlax	♂ Lv. 56	NORMAL	FIGHTING

If you choose Popplio

Pokémon	Gender / Level	Type	Weak to
 Decidueye	♂ Lv. 58	GRASS, GHOST	FIRE, ICE, FLYING, GHOST, DARK
 Lycanroc (Midday Form)	♂ Lv. 57	ROCK	WATER, GRASS, FIGHTING, GROUND, STEEL
 Alolan Ninetales	♀ Lv. 56	ICE, FAIRY	4× STEEL, FIRE, POISON, ROCK
 Braviary	♂ Lv. 56	NORMAL, FLYING	ELECTRIC, ICE, ROCK
 Magnezone	Lv. 56	ELECTRIC, STEEL	4× GROUND, FIRE, FIGHTING
 Snorlax	♂ Lv. 56	NORMAL	FIGHTING

Congratulations!

You've done it! The Elite Four have fallen, and Professor Kukui has been crushed. None are left to stand against you. Enjoy your moment with your team of trustworthy and loyal Pokémon. You couldn't have done it without their help, yet here you stand: Alola's first-ever Champion!

You've had a lot of help along the way, and all of the friends you've made during your island challenge are eager to celebrate your amazing achievement. A festival in your honor is thrown at Iki Town, and everyone's there to share in your victory. It couldn't be a happier time for the good people of Alola!

Wanting to congratulate you personally, your good friend Lillie pulls you away from the excitement. She then suggests you visit the nearby Ruins of Conflict. The bridge has been rebuilt, so you can finally pay your respects to Melemele Island's guardian deity, Tapu Koko!

Deep within the Ruins of Conflict, you find Tapu Koko's humble shrine. Lillie thanks the great guardian deity for all it has done, then invites you to do the same. She then heals your Pokémon. Reaching out and touching the statue, you feel a great power awaken within your Z-Ring. The great Tapu Koko appears before you, and battle is suddenly at hand!

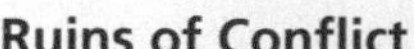

Ruins of Conflict

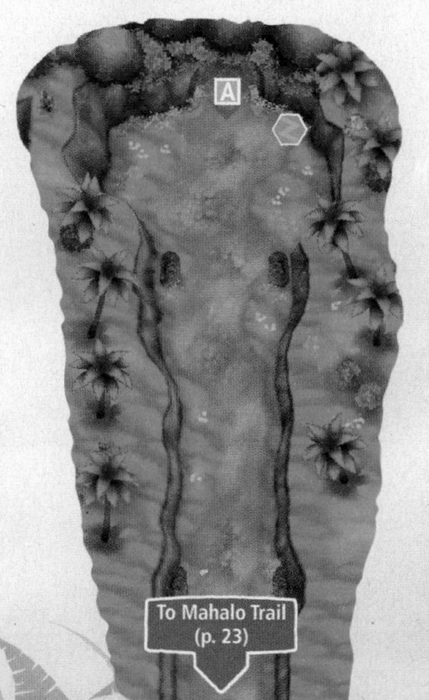

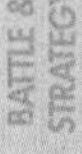
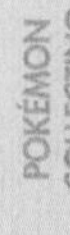
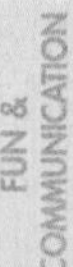

1 Catch Tapu Koko!

It isn't clear why Tapu Koko has appeared before you, but you've no choice but to battle it. Don't simply defeat Tapu Koko—try to catch it in a Poké Ball! You can't save before the battle, so be very careful not to make Tapu Koko faint. Whittle down its health instead, and try to inflict status conditions to make it easier prey. Whether or not you manage to catch Tapu Koko, you'll receive a piece of Tapunium Z—a special Z-Crystal that allows any guardian deity to unleash its Z-Power!

Reward: Tapunium Z

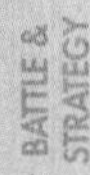

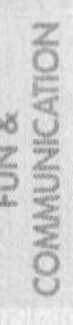

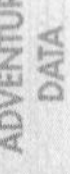

Tip

Still have that Master Ball that Gladion gave you back at Aether Paradise? Throw it to catch Tapu Koko in a snap!

Tip

Don't worry if you fail to catch Tapu Koko—you'll be able to come back and try again later. It reappears if you prove yourself worthy by once again defeating all challengers at the Pokémon League and keeping your seat as Champion!

Tapu Koko

This is it—your big chance to catch one of Alola's guardian deities! Tapu Koko has the Electric Surge Ability, which creates the Electric Terrain battle condition as Tapu Koko enters battle. This condition boosts the power of Electric-type moves for five turns—a big advantage for Melemele Island's guardian. Tapu Koko also uses Agility to sharply raise its Speed stat, all but ensuring it will act first each turn. It attacks with Nature's Madness, a Fairy-type move, along with Electro Ball and Discharge, two powerful Electric-type moves that are even more potent while Electric Terrain is in play. Nullify the bulk of Tapu Koko's offense by sending out a Ground-type Pokémon, but be careful not to defeat the guardian deity with Ground-type moves. Wear it down with other moves that aren't super effective instead, and try to inflict status conditions to increase your odds of catching it.

Tapu Koko
Lv. 60

ELECTRIC | FAIRY

Weak to: POISON | GROUND

After Becoming Champion

You've completed your island challenge and etched your name into Alola's history books as the region's first-ever Pokémon League Champion—but your time in this wondrous tropical region isn't over yet! Many new adventures are available to you now that you've become Champion. Read on for a taste of all the exciting escapades that await!

Things for a Champion to Do in Alola

Melemele Island

- ❑ Get Z-Crystals from Hau for the other two first partner Pokémon you could have chosen.
- ❑ Find an Electric Seed near the newly repaired bridge.
- ❑ Visit Guzma's house on Route 2 and battle Guzma for a Dawn Stone.
- ❑ Swing by the Pokémon Research Lab for TM90 Substitute—and a peek at Lillie's diary!
- ❑ If your Pokédex is nearing completion, get a Lucky Egg at the Pokémon Research Lab as well.
- ❑ Battle the principal of the Trainers' School for a King's Rock.
- ❑ Explore Seaward Cave (p. 86), Kala'e Bay (p. 87), Melemele Sea (p. 36), and Ten Carat Hill (p. 85) if you missed any of them.
- ❑ Master the Battle Buffet in the Hau'oli City Shopping Mall and meet the buffet queen!
- ❑ Have your Pokémon hyper trained in Hau'oli City Shopping Mall.

Akala Island

- ❑ Visit Kiawe's home in Paniola Town to get a Protector from his dad.
- ❑ Battle Morimoto at GAME FREAK's office in Heahea City for an Oval Charm.
- ❑ Get special stamps from the game director at GAME FREAK's office for each island Pokédex you complete!
- ❑ Meet Elite Four Kahili at Hano Grand Hotel and score TM92 Trick Room.
- ❑ Talk to the cashier near the entrance of the Thrifty Megamart and beat all the Eevee users in Alola for an Eevium Z.
- ❑ Meet Colress on Route 8 to receive a variety of drives for a Pokémon called Genesect.
- ❑ Visit Mallow's family restaurant in Konikoni City for several gifts.
- ❑ Master Battle Royals at the Battle Royal Dome on Royal Avenue (p. 108).

Ula'ula Island

- ❑ Master all of the battle styles that Gester can teach you at the Outer Cape.
- ❑ Purchase a Skull Tank in the Po Town Pokémon Center.
- ❑ Assemble Zygarde at the Aether Base on Route 16.
- ❑ Get a Porygon and an Up-Grade at the Aether House on Route 15.
- ❑ Explore Haina Desert (p. 178) if you haven't before. Show the old man Solrock or Lunatone to receive a reward!

Poni Island

- ❑ Meet Dexio and Sina on the Ancient Poni Path to learn about Mega Evolution and receive the Key Stone and Alakazite from Dexio!
- ❑ Defeat Swimmer Girls in a Double Battle to get TM94 Surf and TM98 Waterfall on Poni Breaker Coast.
- ❑ Explore the entire east half of Poni Island, which was not accessible before (p. 222)!
- ❑ Hatch a lot of Pokémon Eggs and have the Ace Trainer in front of the Battle Tree upgrade your PC Boxes to have the Judge function added.
- ❑ Bring Solgaleo or Lunala to the Altar of the Sunne / Altar of the Moone at night / during the day to visit a reversed world!
- ❑ Defeat the Sightseer in the Seafolk Village Pokémon Center and receive 6 Nuggets!

Aether Paradise

- ❑ Get Type: Null and various memory drives from Gladion in the 2F: Conservation area.
- ❑ Defeat Faba to get a Dubious Disc in the 1F: Entrance.
- ❑ Receive two Big Malasadas from Wicke and the DNA Splicers, Prison Bottle, and Soul Dew from an Aether Foundation Employee in the B2F: Lab area.

All over Alola

- ❑ Make sure you've collected all 100 Zygarde Cells and Cores (p. 225), and check out all the Poké Finder spots (p. 313).
- ❑ Review the sub-event list (p. 18–19) to make sure you've completed every last quest!

Catching Alola's Guardian Deities

Now that you've become Champion, you're able to battle the mighty guardian deities that keep watch over Alola's islands. Each guardian deity resides in the ancient ruins found on each island. Pass through these ruins with Machamp's help, then touch the statue in the final chamber to begin the battle! But remember to save first, as these rare Pokémon are hard to catch and won't reappear until you've proven your worth by defending your Championship at the Pokémon League (p. 211).

Tapu Koko Ruins of Conflict (p. 215)

ELECTRIC FAIRY

The feisty Tapu Koko flies too fast for the eye to follow, confusing its enemies. It has a terribly short temper, but it forgets what made it angry right away. This guardian deity of Melemele is brimming with curiosity and loves battle—whether watching it or taking part in it. It resides within the Ruins of Conflict on Melemele Island. If you failed to catch Tapu Koko when you became Champion, defend your Pokémon League title and then return to the Ruins of Conflict to try again. (You can find strategy information back on page 216.)

Tapu Lele Ruins of Life (p. 132)

PSYCHIC FAIRY

It is said that those touched by Tapu Lele's glowing scales are immediately returned to good health. It gathers energy from the fragrant aroma of flowers. Despite the tales of its healing effects, though, this guardian deity of Akala is said to be guilelessly cruel. Tape Lele has the Psychic Surge Ability, which creates the Psychic Terrain battle condition as it enters battle. This condition protects Pokémon on the ground from priority moves used against them for five turns. Psychic Terrain also boosts the power of Psychic-type moves for its duration, making Tapu Lele's Extrasensory move very dangerous. Although Dark-type Pokémon are immune to Psychic-type moves, keep your Dark types away from the fray, because Tapu Lele also lashes out with Nature's Madness and Moonblast: two Fairy-type moves that are super effective against Dark-type Pokémon. Tapu Lele also uses Flatter to confuse your Pokémon and raise their Sp. Atk, so be ready to counter with curatives such as Big Malasadas, Full Heals, and Full Restores.

Tapu Bulu Ruins of Abundance (p. 180)

GRASS FAIRY

Tapu Bulu is said to be a lazy creature, but when the time calls for battle, it charges ahead with its large horns. Tapu Bulu also pulls up large trees and swings them about. It causes vegetation to grow and absorbs energy from them. Tapu Bulu has the Grassy Surge Ability, which creates the Grassy Terrain battle condition as it enters battle. This condition causes Pokémon on the ground to recover a little HP each turn for five turns. Grassy Terrain also boosts the power of Grass-type moves for its duration. Like its fellow guardian deities, Tapu Bulu uses Nature's Madness to halve your Pokémon's HP. It also uses Skull Bash, a two-turn Normal-type move that increases Tapu Bulu's Defense on the first turn, and then causes Tapu Bulu to lash out for damage on the second. Another attack is Zen Headbutt, a strong Psychic-type move with a chance to make your Pokémon flinch and fail to act.

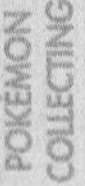

Tapu Fini Ruins of Hope (p. 195)

WATER FAIRY

Tapu Fini is both purifying and dangerous. This guardian can control water, and people say it can even create pure water that washes away any uncleanness. Deriving its energy from ocean currents, Tapu Fini confuses its enemies with a thick fog that can cause them to defeat themselves. Tapu Fini has the Misty Surge Ability, which creates the Misty Terrain battle condition as it enters battle. While this condition is active, Pokémon on the ground won't get any status conditions for five turns. Misty Terrain also halves the damage from Dragon-type moves for its duration, but Tapu Fini is immune to Dragon-type moves, so this shouldn't be much of a factor for you. Tapu Fini can cut your Pokémon's HP in half with Nature's Madness, and wash them away with Muddy Water, a strong Water-type move that can reduce your Pokémon's accuracy. Tapu Fini also uses Aqua Ring to recover some HP each turn. Play a largely defensive battle until Misty Terrain wears off, then look to inflict status conditions on Tapu Fini and catch it once its HP is low.

Defending Your Champion Title

You've worked hard to become Alola's first-ever Champion—now you get to defend your title! Fly back to the Pokémon League on Ula'ula Island and defeat the Elite Four once more. Then return to the Champion's room and claim your throne once you are ready to face your first challenger: Hau! Every time you beat the Pokémon League, one of the following Trainers will challenge you and they all come ready to fight. Save your game as you progress through the Pokémon League in case things don't go your way!

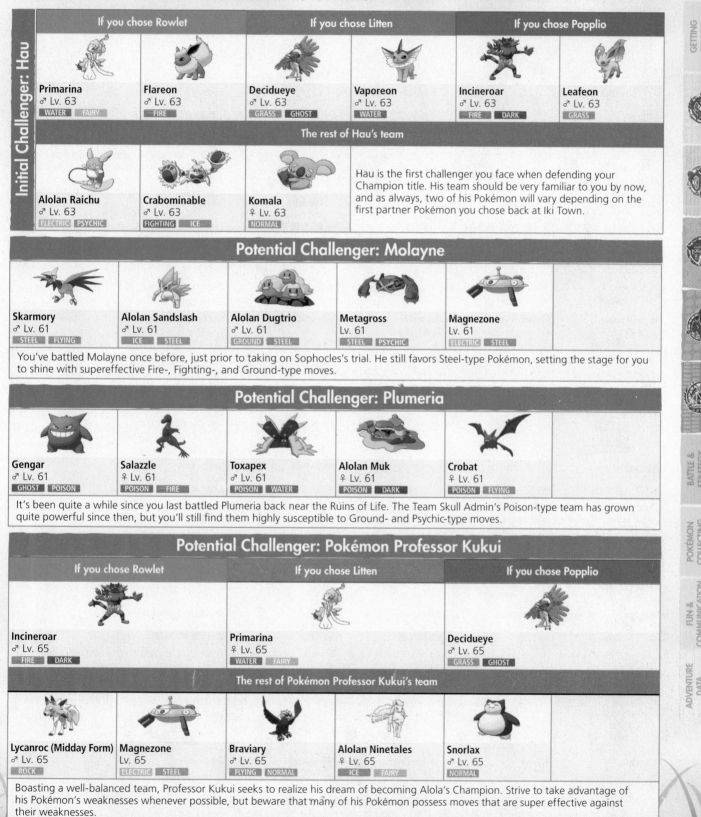

Initial Challenger: Hau

If you chose Rowlet		If you chose Litten		If you chose Popplio	
Primarina ♂ Lv. 63 WATER FAIRY	 **Flareon** ♂ Lv. 63 FIRE	 **Decidueye** ♂ Lv. 63 GRASS GHOST	 **Vaporeon** ♂ Lv. 63 WATER	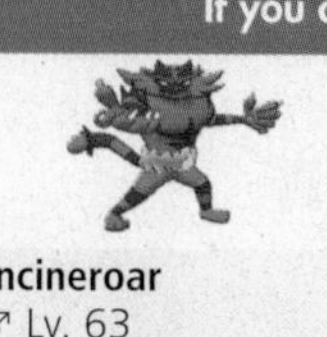 **Incineroar** ♂ Lv. 63 FIRE DARK	 **Leafeon** ♂ Lv. 63 GRASS

The rest of Hau's team			
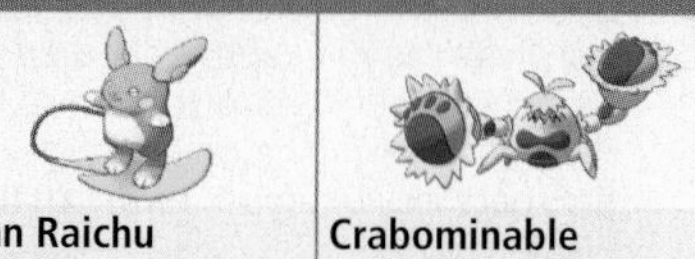 **Alolan Raichu** ♂ Lv. 63 ELECTRIC PSYCHIC	**Crabominable** ♂ Lv. 63 FIGHTING ICE	 **Komala** ♀ Lv. 63 NORMAL	Hau is the first challenger you face when defending your Champion title. His team should be very familiar to you by now, and as always, two of his Pokémon will vary depending on the first partner Pokémon you chose back at Iki Town.

Potential Challenger: Molayne

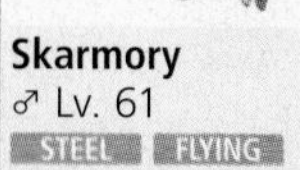 **Skarmory** ♂ Lv. 61 STEEL FLYING	 **Alolan Sandslash** ♂ Lv. 61 ICE STEEL	 **Alolan Dugtrio** ♂ Lv. 61 GROUND STEEL	 **Metagross** Lv. 61 STEEL PSYCHIC	 **Magnezone** Lv. 61 ELECTRIC STEEL

You've battled Molayne once before, just prior to taking on Sophocles's trial. He still favors Steel-type Pokémon, setting the stage for you to shine with supereffective Fire-, Fighting-, and Ground-type moves.

Potential Challenger: Plumeria

 **Gengar** ♂ Lv. 61 GHOST POISON	 **Salazzle** ♀ Lv. 61 POISON FIRE	 **Toxapex** ♂ Lv. 61 POISON WATER	 **Alolan Muk** ♀ Lv. 61 POISON DARK	 **Crobat** ♀ Lv. 61 POISON FLYING

It's been quite a while since you last battled Plumeria back near the Ruins of Life. The Team Skull Admin's Poison-type team has grown quite powerful since then, but you'll still find them highly susceptible to Ground- and Psychic-type moves.

Potential Challenger: Pokémon Professor Kukui

If you chose Rowlet	If you chose Litten	If you chose Popplio
 **Incineroar** ♂ Lv. 65 FIRE DARK	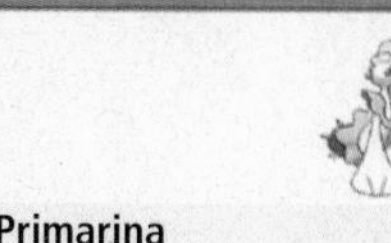 **Primarina** ♀ Lv. 65 WATER FAIRY	 **Decidueye** ♂ Lv. 65 GRASS GHOST

The rest of Pokémon Professor Kukui's team				
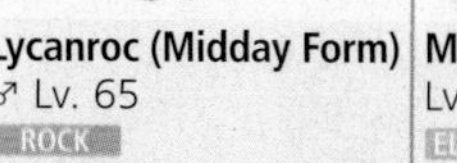 **Lycanroc (Midday Form)** ♂ Lv. 65 ROCK	 **Magnezone** Lv. 65 ELECTRIC STEEL	**Braviary** ♂ Lv. 65 FLYING NORMAL	 **Alolan Ninetales** ♀ Lv. 65 ICE FAIRY	 **Snorlax** ♂ Lv. 65 NORMAL

Boasting a well-balanced team, Professor Kukui seeks to realize his dream of becoming Alola's Champion. Strive to take advantage of his Pokémon's weaknesses whenever possible, but beware that many of his Pokémon possess moves that are super effective against their weaknesses.

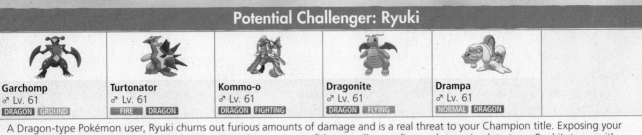

Potential Challenger: Ryuki

 Garchomp	 Turtonator	 Kommo-o	 Dragonite	Drampa
♂ Lv. 61	♂ Lv. 61	♂ Lv. 61	♂ Lv. 61	♂ Lv. 61
DRAGON GROUND	FIRE DRAGON	DRAGON FIGHTING	DRAGON FLYING	NORMAL DRAGON

A Dragon-type Pokémon user, Ryuki churns out furious amounts of damage and is a real threat to your Champion title. Exposing your Dragon-type Pokémon to Ryuki's horde is unwise unless you're confident you'll move first each turn. Look to tame Ryuki's team with fast-acting Fairy-type Pokémon instead.

Potential Challenger: Gladion

If you chose Rowlet	If you chose Litten	If you chose Popplio
Silvally (Type: Fire)	Silvally (Type: Water)	Silvally (Type: Grass)
Lv. 63	Lv. 63	Lv. 63
FIRE	WATER	GRASS

The rest of Gladion's team

Crobat	Lucario	Porygon-Z	Weavile
♂ Lv. 63	♂ Lv. 63	Lv. 63	♂ Lv. 63
POISON FLYING	FIGHTING STEEL	NORMAL	DARK ICE

A game changer, Gladion's team is well balanced and not easily beaten. Like Hau, his Silvally's type varies depending on the first partner Pokémon you chose. But unlike Hau, its type will be one that counters your first partner Pokémon, rather than one it is weak to.

Potential Challenger: Captain Sophocles

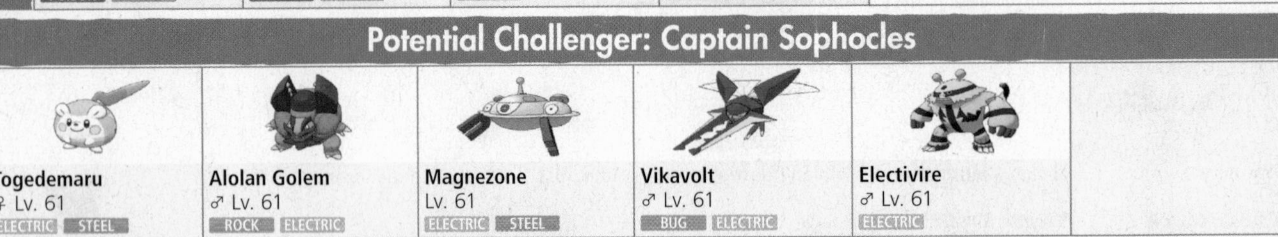

Togedemaru	Alolan Golem	Magnezone	Vikavolt	Electivire
♀ Lv. 61	♂ Lv. 61	Lv. 61	♂ Lv. 61	♂ Lv. 61
ELECTRIC STEEL	ROCK ELECTRIC	ELECTRIC STEEL	BUG ELECTRIC	ELECTRIC

Young and ambitious, Sophocles seeks to supplant you as Alola's Champion. His Electric-type team is prepared to counter your Ground-type Pokémon, so be ready to exploit their other common weaknesses, of which there are many.

Potential Challenger: Island Kahuna Hapu

Alolan Dugtrio	Krookodile	Flygon	Mudsdale	Gastrodon
♀ Lv. 63	♂ Lv. 63	♂ Lv. 63	♂ Lv. 63	♀ Lv. 63
GROUND STEEL	GROUND DARK	GROUND DRAGON	GROUND	WATER GROUND

Not satisfied with her status as Poni Island's new kahuna, Hapu has her sights set on your Champion crown. Her tough team of Ground-type Pokémon are good at downing Flying-type Pokémon, so don't think you can take her out simply by taking to the skies.

Potential Challenger: Youngster Tristan

Emolga	Magmortar	Sharpedo	Tauros	Alolan Exeggutor
♂ Lv. 59	♂ Lv. 59	♂ Lv. 59	♂ Lv. 59	♂ Lv. 59
ELECTRIC FLYING	FIRE	WATER DARK	NORMAL	GRASS DRAGON

Though his Pokémon's levels are a bit lower than other potential challengers, Youngster Tristan nonetheless grasps the value of a well-rounded team. Switch out your Pokémon as needed to stay one step ahead of him.

Potential Challenger: Aether Branch Chief Faba

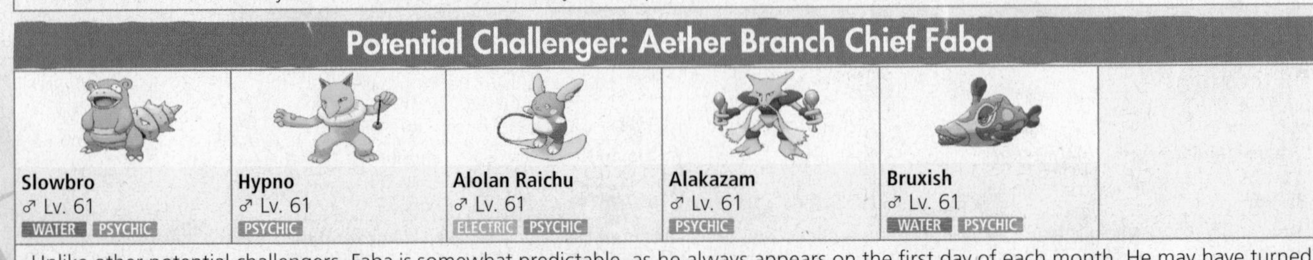

Slowbro	Hypno	Alolan Raichu	Alakazam	Bruxish
♂ Lv. 61	♂ Lv. 61	♂ Lv. 61	♂ Lv. 61	♂ Lv. 61
WATER PSYCHIC	PSYCHIC	ELECTRIC PSYCHIC	PSYCHIC	WATER PSYCHIC

Unlike other potential challengers, Faba is somewhat predictable, as he always appears on the first day of each month. He may have turned over a new leaf since Lusamine's defeat, but Faba's fondness for Psychic-type Pokémon will never change.

Looker Episode

The day after you become Champion, a mysterious old man hands you an Enigmatic Card just outside of your house. Check it in your Bag for a curious message: your presence is requested at the Roadside Motel on Route 8. Going there kicks off a series of adventures involving a well-known member of the International Police, some familiar old faces, and mind-boggling foes!

Reward: Enigmatic Card

Recommended Route

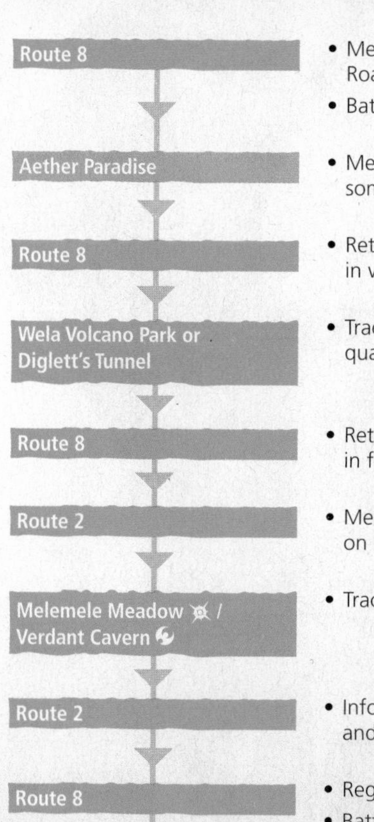

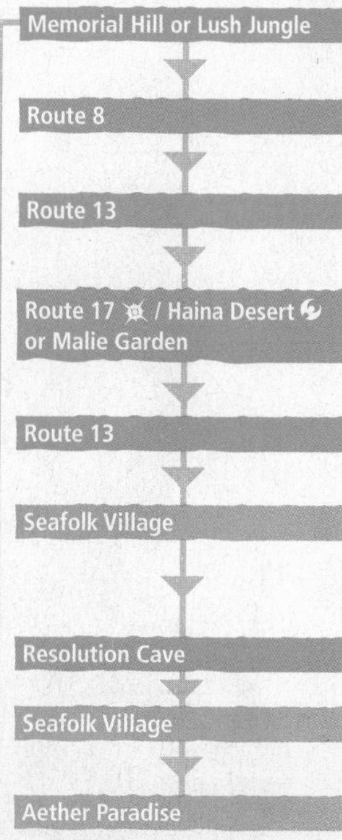

Route 8	• Meet Looker and Anabel at the Roadside Motel • Battle against Anabel
Aether Paradise	• Meet Wicke on B2F to receive some assistance
Route 8	• Return to the motel and check in with Looker
Wela Volcano Park or Diglett's Tunnel	• Track down and catch your quarry
Route 8	• Return to the motel and report in for an update
Route 2	• Meet the task force at the motel on Route 2
Melemele Meadow ☀ / Verdant Cavern ☾	• Track down your quarry
Route 2	• Inform Looker of your success and get some news
Route 8	• Regroup at the Roadside Motel • Battle against Captain Mina
Memorial Hill or Lush Jungle	• Track down and catch your quarry
Route 8	• Return to the motel and update Looker
Route 13	• Meet the task force at the motel on Route 13
Route 17 ☀ / Haina Desert ☾ or Malie Garden	• Track down your next quarry
Route 13	• Inform Looker of your success and hear the latest news
Seafolk Village	• Meet the task force at the floating restaurant • Battle against Kahuna Nanu
Resolution Cave	• Battle and catch your last target
Seafolk Village	• Return to the floating restaurant to report your success
Aether Paradise	• Thank Wicke in the B2F Lab area • Learn of a possible sighting somewhere on Melemele Island • Receive your payment from the International Police • Case closed!

Poni's Eastern Reaches

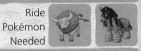

Ride Pokémon Needed

Now that you've become Champion, you're able to explore all of Poni Island's eastern reaches. Poni Grove is the gateway to these new lands. Nestled near the Ancient Poni Path's northeast corner, Poni Grove may only be entered and explored by the strongest Trainers. From there, you will be able to reach Poni Plains, Poni Coast, and the intimidating Poni Gauntlet.

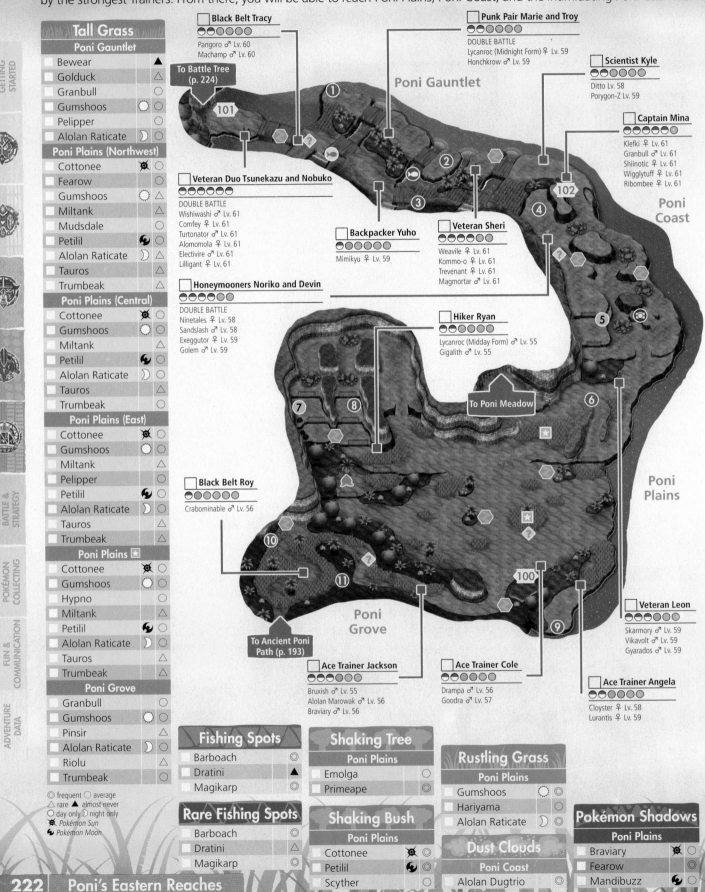

Tall Grass

Poni Gauntlet		
Bewear		▲
Golduck		△
Granbull		○
Gumshoos	☼	○
Pelipper		○
Alolan Raticate	☽	○
Poni Plains (Northwest)		
Cottonee	(Sun)	○
Fearow		○
Gumshoos	☼	△
Miltank		△
Mudsdale		○
Petilil	(Moon)	○
Alolan Raticate	☽	△
Tauros		△
Trumbeak		△
Poni Plains (Central)		
Cottonee	(Sun)	○
Gumshoos	☼	○
Miltank		△
Petilil	(Moon)	○
Alolan Raticate	☽	○
Tauros		△
Trumbeak		○
Poni Plains (East)		
Cottonee	(Sun)	○
Gumshoos	☼	○
Miltank		△
Pelipper		○
Petilil	(Moon)	○
Alolan Raticate	☽	○
Tauros		△
Trumbeak		△
Poni Plains ★		
Cottonee	(Sun)	○
Gumshoos	☼	○
Hypno		○
Miltank		△
Petilil	(Moon)	○
Alolan Raticate	☽	○
Tauros		△
Trumbeak		△
Poni Grove		
Granbull		○
Gumshoos	☼	○
Pinsir		△
Alolan Raticate	☽	○
Riolu		△
Trumbeak		○

◎ frequent ○ average
△ rare ▲ almost never
☼ day only ☽ night only
(Sun) *Pokémon Sun*
(Moon) *Pokémon Moon*

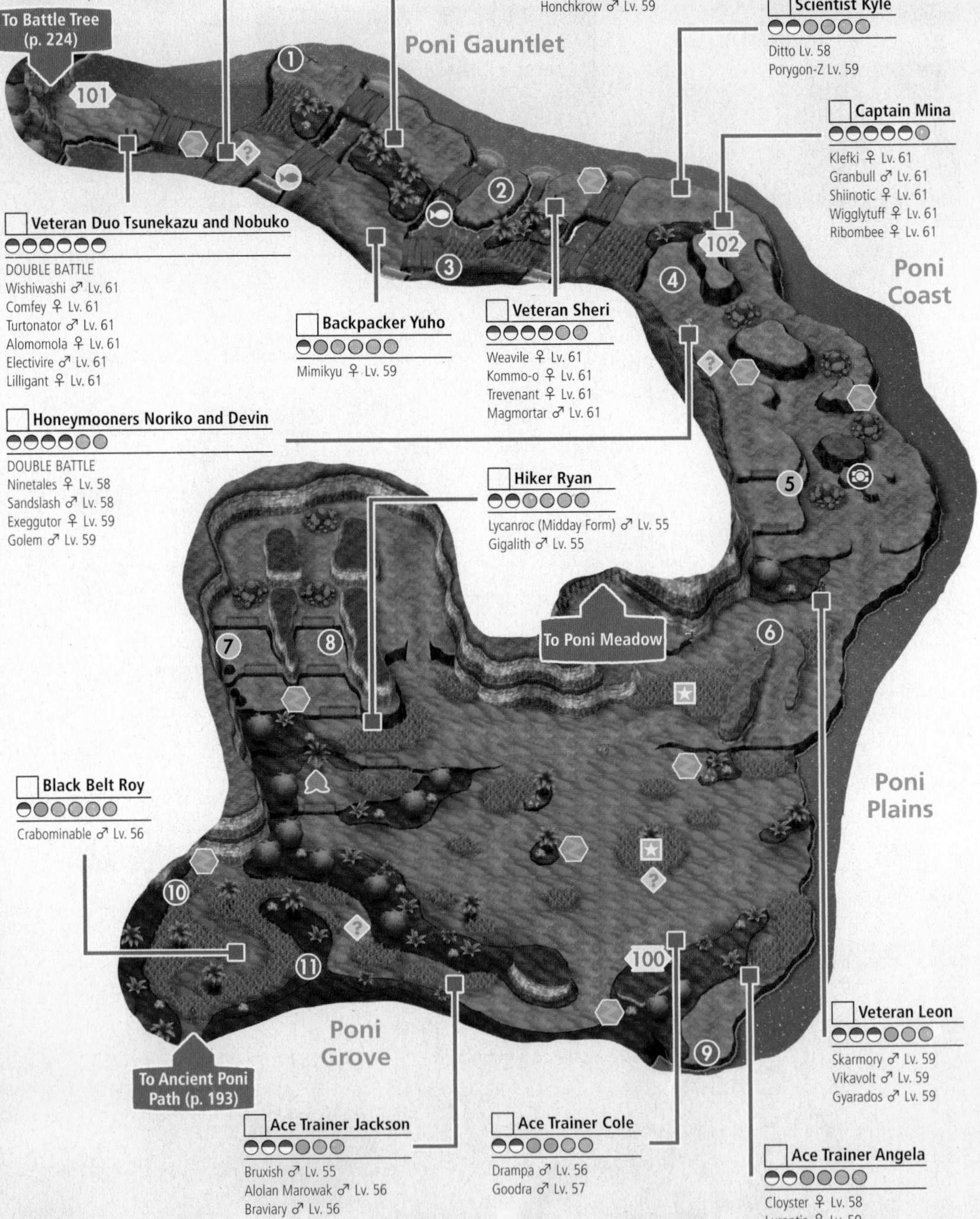

To Battle Tree (p. 224)

Black Belt Tracy

Pangoro ♂ Lv. 60
Machamp ♂ Lv. 60

Punk Pair Marie and Troy

DOUBLE BATTLE
Lycanroc (Midnight Form) ♀ Lv. 59
Honchkrow ♂ Lv. 59

Poni Gauntlet

Scientist Kyle

Ditto Lv. 58
Porygon-Z Lv. 59

Captain Mina

Klefki ♀ Lv. 61
Granbull ♂ Lv. 61
Shiinotic ♀ Lv. 61
Wigglytuff ♀ Lv. 61
Ribombee ♀ Lv. 61

Veteran Duo Tsunekazu and Nobuko

DOUBLE BATTLE
Wishiwashi ♂ Lv. 61
Comfey ♀ Lv. 61
Turtonator ♂ Lv. 61
Alomomola ♀ Lv. 61
Electivire ♂ Lv. 61
Lilligant ♀ Lv. 61

Backpacker Yuho

Mimikyu ♀ Lv. 59

Veteran Sheri

Weavile ♀ Lv. 61
Kommo-o ♀ Lv. 61
Trevenant ♀ Lv. 61
Magmortar ♂ Lv. 61

Poni Coast

Honeymooners Noriko and Devin

DOUBLE BATTLE
Ninetales ♀ Lv. 58
Sandslash ♂ Lv. 58
Exeggutor ♀ Lv. 59
Golem ♂ Lv. 59

Hiker Ryan

Lycanroc (Midday Form) ♂ Lv. 55
Gigalith ♂ Lv. 55

To Poni Meadow

Poni Plains

Black Belt Roy

Crabominable ♂ Lv. 56

Poni Grove

To Ancient Poni Path (p. 193)

Veteran Leon

Skarmory ♂ Lv. 59
Vikavolt ♂ Lv. 59
Gyarados ♂ Lv. 59

Ace Trainer Jackson

Bruxish ♂ Lv. 55
Alolan Marowak ♂ Lv. 56
Braviary ♂ Lv. 56

Ace Trainer Cole

Drampa ♂ Lv. 56
Goodra ♂ Lv. 57

Ace Trainer Angela

Cloyster ♀ Lv. 58
Lurantis ♀ Lv. 59

Fishing Spots

Pokémon		
Barboach		◎
Dratini		▲
Magikarp		◎

Rare Fishing Spots

Pokémon		
Barboach		◎
Dratini		△
Magikarp		◎

Shaking Tree

Poni Plains		
Emolga		○
Primeape		◎

Shaking Bush

Poni Plains		
Cottonee	(Sun)	◎
Petilil	(Moon)	◎
Scyther		○

Rustling Grass

Poni Plains		
Gumshoos	☼	◎
Hariyama		○
Alolan Raticate	☽	◎

Dust Clouds

Poni Coast		
Alolan Dugtrio		◎

Pokémon Shadows

Poni Plains		
Braviary	(Sun)	○
Fearow		◎
Mandibuzz	(Moon)	○

Items

	Item
Poni Gauntlet	
1	Misty Seed
2	Big Pearl
3	Guard Spec.
Poni Coast	
4	Comet Shard
5	TM97 Dark Pulse
Poni Plains	
6	X Defense
7	TM24 Thunderbolt
8	Star Piece
9	Carbos
Poni Grove	
10	X Sp. Atk
11	Max Potion
Poni Meadow	
12	Power Herb
13	TM50 Overheat
14	Purple Nectar ×2
15	Honey
Resolution Cave	
16	Elixir
17	TM26 Earthquake
18	Terrain Extender
19	Adrenaline Orb
20	Life Orb
21	Light Ball

Hidden Items

Hidden Items
Poni Gauntlet
Max Elixir
Poni Coast
Max Revive
Poni Plains
PP Max
Poni Grove
Max Ether
Resolution Cave
HP Up
Big Nugget

Poni Meadow

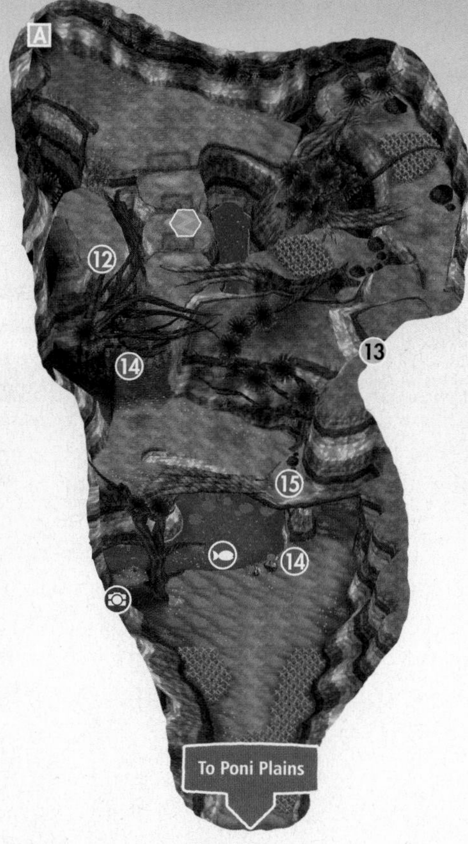

Resolution Cave: Exterior

Hiker Travis
Alolan Dugtrio ♂ Lv. 56
Mudsdale ♂ Lv. 57

Backpacker Maria
Emolga ♀ Lv. 57

Resolution Cave: Interior

Tall Grass

Poni Meadow		
Cottonee	[icon]	◎
Oricorio*		○
Petilil	[icon]	◎
Ribombee		○

*The form of Oricorio found in Poni Meadow is the purple Oricorio (Sensu Style).

Cave

Resolution Cave	
Alolan Dugtrio	○
Golbat	◎

S100: Battle a Tough Trainer

Defeat every Trainer around Poni Plains for a chance to battle against Ace Trainer Cole, who stands near the area's south end. The battle won't be easy, but victory comes with great reward!

Reward: TM60 Quash

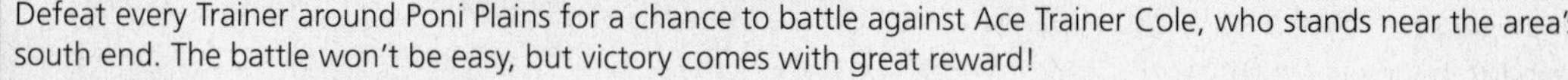

S101: Trade for Talonflame

The Punk Guy near the Battle Tree's entrance would like to trade you his Talonflame in exchange for your Bewear. Catch Bewear in the tall grass on Route 15 if need be, then talk to the Punk Guy to make the trade!

Reward: Talonflame

S102: Battle Captain Mina!

Mina, the artsy girl you met on the bridge in the Vast Poni Canyon, stands near the Poni Gauntlet's entrance. Beat every other Trainer in the area, and she'll give you a masterpiece of a battle against her team of Fairy-type Pokémon.

Reward: Bottle Cap

Battle Tree

Located just beyond the Poni Gauntlet, the Battle Tree is a special place where powerful Trainers gather to put their skills to the ultimate test. Your goal at the Battle Tree is simple: win as many battles as you can in a row without losing. It may sound easy, but the more wins you rack up, the tougher your opponents will become!

Rada
Yes
No
Are you OK with this Trainer?

Rules and Restrictions

First, a few ground rules for taking on the Battle Tree! Pokémon above Lv. 50 will be set to Lv. 50 and your Pokémon must all differ from one another in species and held items. Legendary and Mythical Pokémon can't take part in the battles, and you can't use items from your Bag either. If you're ready for this challenge, you can choose to take part in Single Battles, Double Battles, or Multi Battles. (See page 258 for more on battle formats.)

Battle Ranks

Each battle format features two ranks: Normal Rank and Super Rank. Win 19 battles in a row in the Normal Rank, and you'll face off against a boss (or a team of two bosses, in the case of Multi Battles) that you may remember. Defeat these Battle Legends in your 20th Normal Rank battle to unlock the Super Rank for that format!

Battle Points

Your Pokémon don't receive Exp. Points when at the Battle Tree. Instead, you earn Battle Points (BP) each time you win a battle here. BP can be exchanged for prizes at the counters found here at the Battle Tree and at the Battle Royal Dome (p. 109). BP can also be spent to scout Trainers (read on to learn more). As your win streak increases, so too does the amount of BP you receive with each win.

Multi Battle Teammates

After winning a Single or Double Battle, you'll have the option to "scout" the Trainer you've just beaten for 10 BP. Once scouted, you can team up with that Trainer and his or her two favorite Pokémon in future Multi Battles! Reach Super Rank, and you'll start to encounter familiar Trainers from *Pokémon Sun* and *Pokémon Moon* and past Pokémon games. With the exception of a few notable "Battle Legends," these Trainers can also be registered via the scout system, so consider saving some of your hard-earned BP to scout these special allies! Or you can always team up with a friend by speaking with the receptionist at the Battle Tree.

Taking a Break

The Battle Tree is an intense place, and you'll probably need a break from all the action at some point. After each battle, you have the option to put your Battle Tree challenge on hold, save your progress, and then return later and resume your win streak right where you left off. Just don't turn off your Nintendo 3DS system without saving, or your win streak will be at an end!

Battle Tree Prizes

Left Attendant	
King's Rock	32 BP
Deep Sea Tooth	32 BP
Deep Sea Scale	32 BP
Dragon Scale	32 BP
Up-Grade	32 BP
Dubious Disc	32 BP
Protector	32 BP
Electirizer	32 BP
Magmarizer	32 BP
Reaper Cloth	32 BP
Whipped Dream	32 BP
Sachet	32 BP
Middle Attendant	
Toxic Orb	16 BP
Flame Orb	16 BP
Iron Ball	16 BP
Ring Target	16 BP
White Herb	24 BP
Mental Herb	24 BP
Power Herb	24 BP
Focus Sash	32 BP
Air Balloon	32 BP
Red Card	32 BP
Eject Button	32 BP
Weakness Policy	32 BP
Choice Band	48 BP
Choice Specs	48 BP
Choice Scarf	48 BP
Life Orb	48 BP
Rocky Helmet	48 BP
Assault Vest	48 BP
Safety Goggles	48 BP
Terrain Extender	48 BP
Protective Pads	48 BP

Right Attendant	
Gengarite	64 BP
Scizorite	64 BP
Pinsirite	64 BP
Aerodactylite	64 BP
Lucarionite	64 BP
Kangaskhanite	64 BP
Gyaradosite	64 BP
Absolite	64 BP
Alakazite	64 BP
Garchompite	64 BP
Sablenite	64 BP
Metagrossite	64 BP
Sharpedonite	64 BP
Slowbronite	64 BP
Glalitite	64 BP
Salamencite	64 BP

Win Streak Prizes

Visit the Battle Tree each day, because you may get prizes based on your best win streak from the previous day. Talk to the receptionist to see what your hard work has earned you!

Win Streak Prizes	
5 straight wins	Moomoo Milk
10 straight wins	PP Up
20 straight wins	Rare Candy
30 straight wins	Bottle Cap
40 straight wins	PP Max
50 straight wins	Ability Capsule
100 straight wins	Lansat Berry
200 straight wins	Starf Berry

Assembling Zygarde

Using the Reassembly Unit on Route 16 (p. 167), you can form the mighty Pokémon Zygarde from the Zygarde Cores and Cells you've collected around Alola—or separate a Zygarde back into its individual Cores and Cells.

Zygarde Formes

10% Forme

This is the Forme that Zygarde assumes when it gathers 10% of its Cells. Its HP is half of 50% Forme's HP, and its stats are inferior to those of the other Formes except for its Speed stat, which is highest among the three Formes. A 10% Forme Zygarde with the Power Construct Ability transforms into its Complete Forme when its HP falls to half or less in battle.

10% Forme Zygarde (Aura Break Ability)	Assemble using Zygarde Cube with 10 Cells/Cores
10% Forme Zygarde (Power Construct Ability)	Change Formes using a unified Zygarde

GETTING STARTED

50% Forme

Until recently, this was the only known Forme of Zygarde. In actuality, this Forme only has 50% of the Cells in its structure. A 50% Forme Zygarde with the Power Construct Ability transforms into its Complete Forme when its HP drops to half or less in battle.

50% Forme Zygarde (Aura Break Ability)	Assemble using a Zygarde Cube with 50 Cells/Cores
50% Forme Zygarde (Power Construct Ability)	Assemble using a Zygarde Cube with 100 Cells/Cores or a 10% Forme Zygarde + 90 Cells/Cores or a 50% Forme Zygarde + 50 Cells/Cores

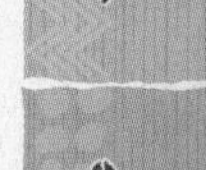

Complete Forme

A Zygarde with the Power Construct Ability assumes this perfect Forme when the HP of its 10% Forme or 50% Forme falls to half or less during battle. Its HP is twice as high as that of 50% Forme.

> Want a Zygarde with a particular Nature? Put a Pokémon with the Synchronize Ability at the head of your team before assembling Zygarde, and the assembled Zygarde will have the same Nature as the lead Pokémon!

Unified Zygarde

Once you've collected all 100 Cells and Cores, and used the Reassembly Unit to assemble Zygarde with the Power Construct Ability, you will have created the unified Zygarde, which can change its Forme using the Zygarde Cube. Open your Bag, go to the Key Items Pocket, select "Zygarde Cube," select the Zygarde in the Forme you want to change, and then select "Change Forme." You'll then be able to switch between Zygarde's 10% Forme and its 50% Forme. Note that changing to Zygarde Complete Forme only occurs during battle.

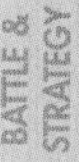

BATTLE & STRATEGY

POKÉMON COLLECTING

FUN & COMMUNICATION

ADVENTURE DATA

Zygarde Core and Cell Locations

Each Zygarde Core contains a move that Zygarde can learn, and three of these moves are exclusive to this Pokémon. To teach Zygarde a move after you have found a Core, open your Bag, go to the Key Items Pocket, and select "Zygarde Cube." Then choose the Zygarde you want to teach a new move to from your team, and select "Learn Move."

Zygarde Cores

Location	Move the Core retains
Your house (p. 36)	Extreme Speed
Hala's house (p. 23)	Thousand Arrows
Olivia's house (p. 128)	Dragon Dance
Route 9 Police Station (p. 170)	Thousand Waves
Hapu's house (p. 193)	Core Enforcer

GETTING STARTED
BATTLE & STRATEGY
POKÉMON COLLECTING
FUN & COMMUNICATION
ADVENTURE DATA

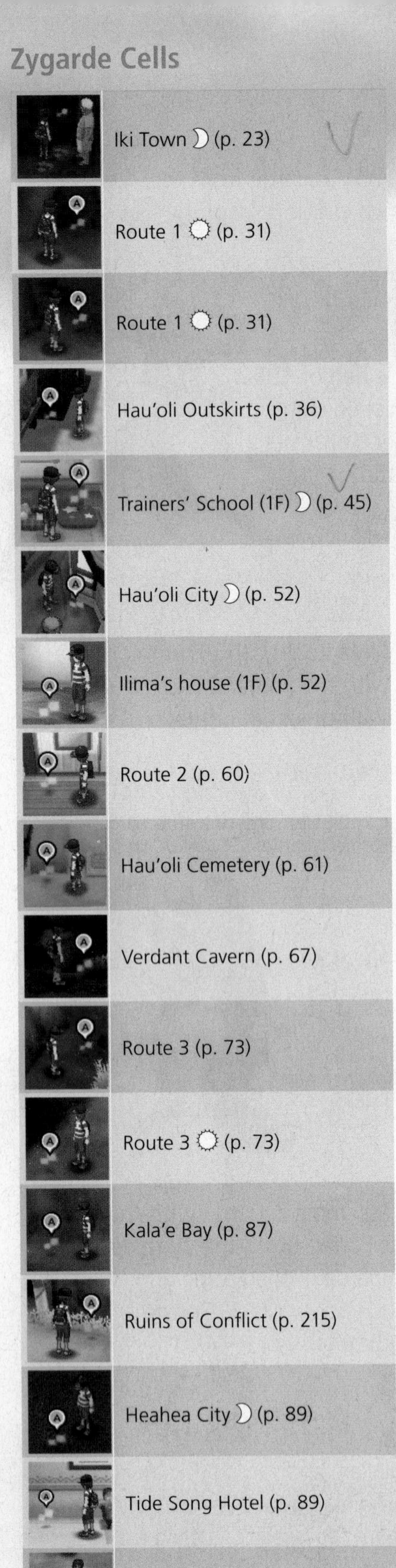

Iki Town ☽ (p. 23)
Route 1 ☼ (p. 31)
Route 1 ☼ (p. 31)
Hau'oli Outskirts (p. 36)
Trainers' School (1F) ☽ (p. 45)
Hau'oli City ☽ (p. 52)
Ilima's house (1F) (p. 52)
Route 2 (p. 60)
Hau'oli Cemetery (p. 61)
Verdant Cavern (p. 67)
Route 3 (p. 73)
Route 3 ☼ (p. 73)
Kala'e Bay (p. 87)
Ruins of Conflict (p. 215)
Heahea City ☽ (p. 89)
Tide Song Hotel (p. 89)
Route 4 (p. 92)
Paniola Ranch ☼ (p. 95)

Paniola Ranch ☽ (p. 95)
Route 5 (p. 98)
Royal Avenue ☼ (p. 108)
Royal Avenue ☽ (p. 108)
Route 7 (p. 112)
Wela Volcano Park (p. 113)
Route 8 (p. 118)
Route 8 ☼ (p. 118)
Lush Jungle (p. 121)
Diglett's Tunnel (p. 125)
Akala Outskirts (p. 131)
Konikoni City ☽ (p. 128)
Hano Beach (p. 134)
Hano Beach ☼ (p. 134)
Malie City ☼ (p. 142)
Malie Community Center ☽ (p. 142)
Malie Garden (p. 142)
Outer Cape ☼ (p. 147)
Route 10 ☼ (p. 149)

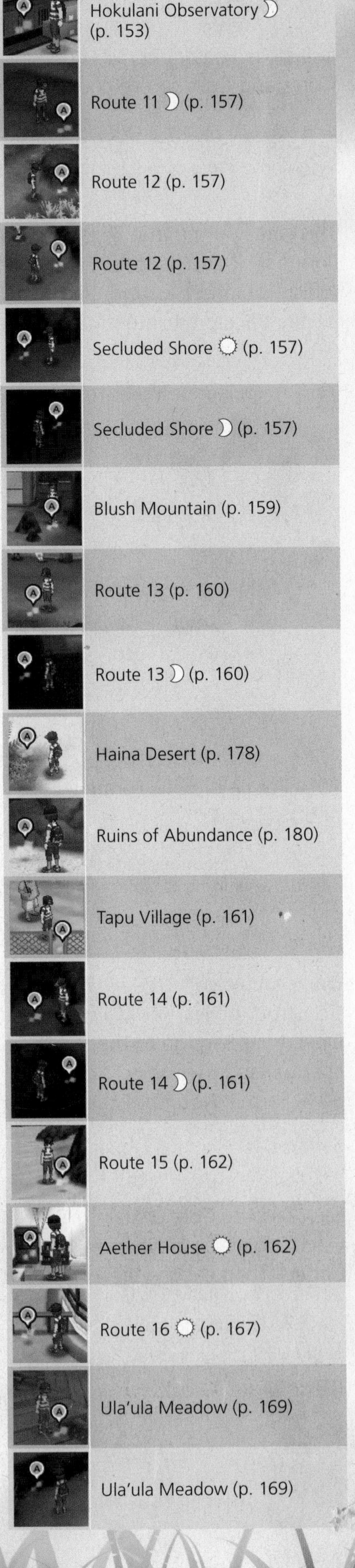

Hokulani Observatory ☽ (p. 153)
Route 11 ☽ (p. 157)
Route 12 (p. 157)
Route 12 (p. 157)
Secluded Shore ☼ (p. 157)
Secluded Shore ☽ (p. 157)
Blush Mountain (p. 159)
Route 13 (p. 160)
Route 13 ☽ (p. 160)
Haina Desert (p. 178)
Ruins of Abundance (p. 180)
Tapu Village (p. 161)
Route 14 (p. 161)
Route 14 ☽ (p. 161)
Route 15 (p. 162)
Aether House ☼ (p. 162)
Route 16 ☼ (p. 167)
Ula'ula Meadow (p. 169)
Ula'ula Meadow (p. 169)

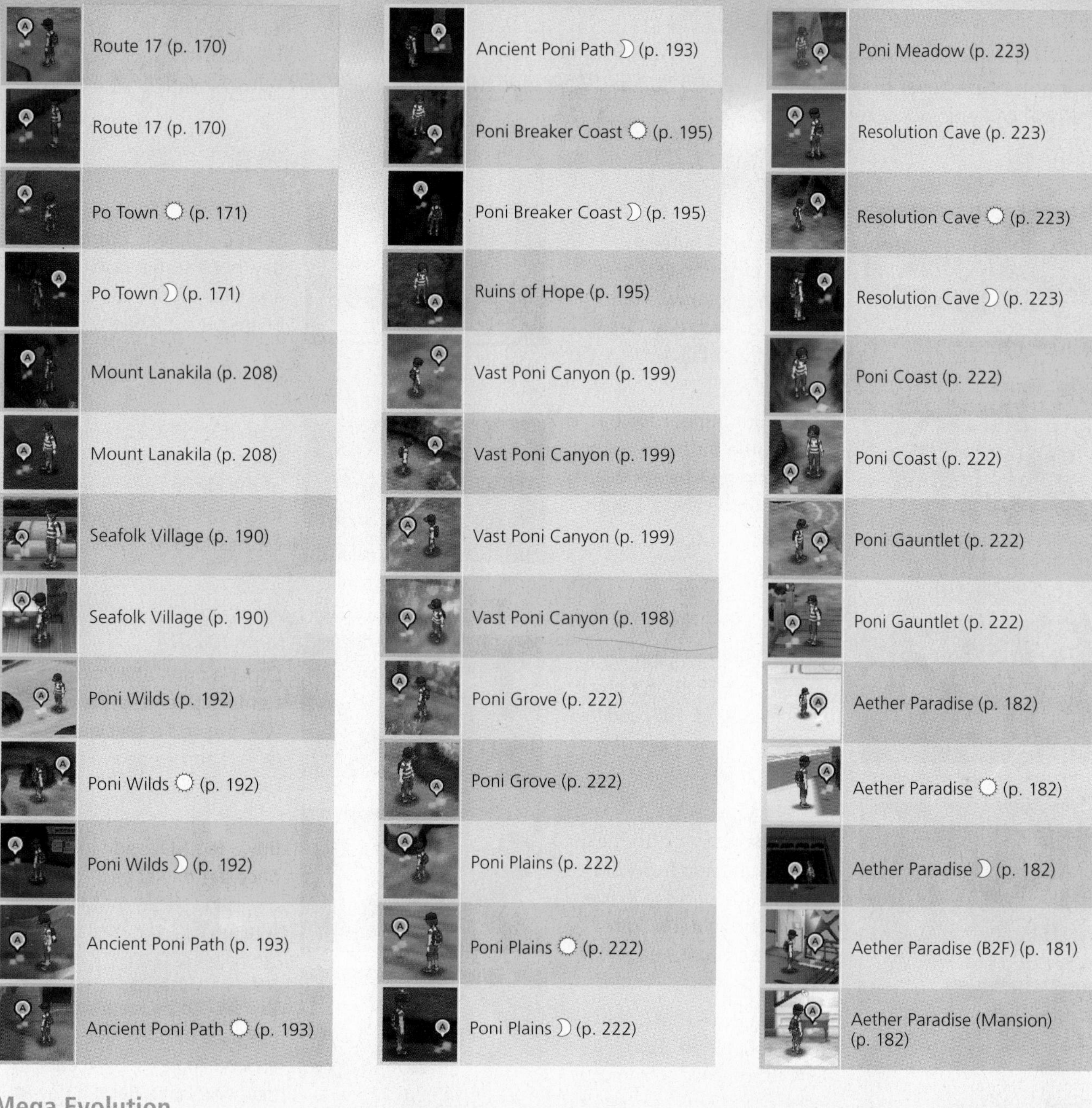

Mega Evolution

Battle Dexio on the Ancient Poni Path after becoming Champion to feel the power of Mega Evolution! It is an Evolution beyond all typical Evolutions and has some astounding effects: potentially changing a Pokémon's stats, Ability, and type, as well as its appearance. With the Key Stone Dexio gave you for your Z-Ring, you can try it for yourself! To Mega Evolve, a Pokémon must be holding its specific Mega Stone (much like a Pokémon holds a Z-Crystal to use Z-Moves) and only certain Pokémon are capable of Mega Evolving. Collect the right stones and the right Pokémon, then head into battle! If your Pokémon is holding its Mega Stone, the Mega Evolution button should appear on the lower screen during battle. Select it and then a move to Mega Evolve your Pokémon—but just like Z-Moves, Mega Evolution can only be used once per battle!

You can purchase Mega Stones in exchange for BP at the Battle Tree. You can also get four particular stones—Blastoisinite, Charizardite X, Charizardite Y, and Venusaurite—by defeating Red in the Battle Tree (p. 224).

Things to Do Daily

Your adventure never truly ends in *Pokémon Sun* and *Pokémon Moon*. Each new day brings a variety of activities that you can enjoy on a regular basis.

Melemele Activities

Play the loto

Visit the tourist bureau in Hau'oli City and talk to the receptionist to draw a Loto Ticket once each day. (See page 53 for details.)

Fill up on battle

Satisfy your hunger for battle at the Battle Buffet in Hau'oli City Shopping Mall (p. 83). You can battle there once per day.

Akala Activities

Challenge Morimoto

Once you're Champion, you can visit GAME FREAK's office in Heahea City (p. 107) and take on Morimoto once per day.

Get a massage

Talk to the lady next to the incense vendor in Konikoni City (p. 130), and she'll give your Pokémon a free lomi lomi massage once each day.

Earn some cash

Work as a Pyukumuku chucker on Hano Beach (p. 135) anytime you need to line your pockets. You can complete this job once a day.

Poni Activities

Reap rewards from the Battle Tree

Earn daily rewards from the Battle Tree based on your performance from the previous day (p. 224).

Poké Pelago Activities

Give and receive Beans

Send out a Bean Bottle each day, hope to get one in return, and shake loose some Poké Beans on Isle Abeens (p. 310).

Festival Plaza Activities

Get your tickets

Chat with the woman in front of the castle to receive three free Festival Tickets each day for missions (p. 304).

Anywhere Activities

Visit a café

Order a drink at a Pokémon Center's Café and the barista will give you a special treat (p. 41) and some Poké Beans once per day.

Serve up a malasada

Buy a Big Malasada (p. 58) once per day at each of the malasada shops on Melemele, Akala, and Ula'ula Islands.

Bag some Berries

Berries can be harvested from the base of Berry trees all around Alola (p. 349) each day. And get a Berry a day at the Thrifty Megamart (p. 110)!

Use the QR Scanner

Use your QR Scanner (p. 43) each day in search of new Pokédex data. You earn one QR Code scan every two hours, until you reach the maximum of 10 scans.

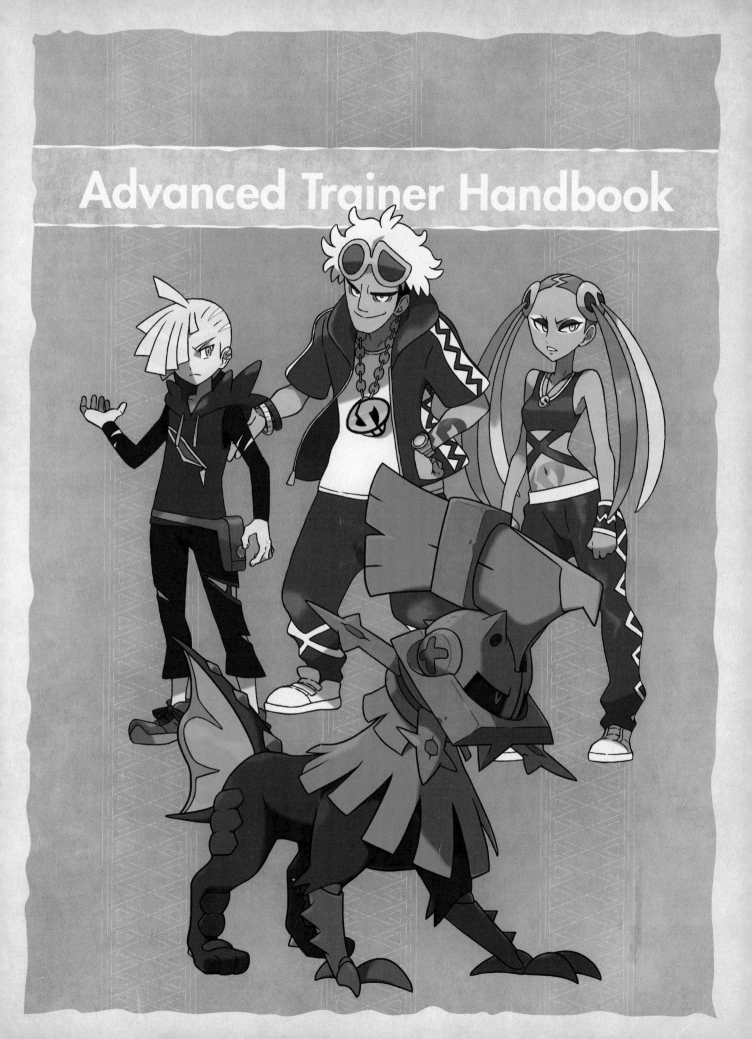

Advanced Trainer Handbook

Advanced Trainer Handbook

Welcome to the Advanced Trainer Handbook! This section is dedicated to helping players who've mastered the basics step up their game and learn what it takes to rank among the very best Pokémon Trainers in the world.

Tip

You've clearly mastered the basics by this point—or have you? If you feel the need to brush up on fundamentals, review the introductory sections at the beginning of this book (p. 7). You can also turn to any of the articles covering specific game features in the walkthrough. A complete list of them can be found on page 3.

Complete Your Trainer Passport!

Each time you complete a noteworthy goal in *Pokémon Sun* and *Pokémon Moon*, a special stamp is added to your Trainer Passport. Use the following table to obtain all 15 stamps!

How to Obtain: Get your Trainer Passport

Official Pokémon Trainer

How to Obtain: Clear the grand trial on Melemele Island (p. 77)

Note: With this stamp, all Pokémon up to Lv. 35 will obey your every command.

Melemele Trial Completion

How to Obtain: Clear the grand trial on Akala Island (p. 133)

Note: With this stamp, all Pokémon up to Lv. 50 will obey your every command.

Akala Trial Completion

How to Obtain: Clear the grand trial on Ula'ula Island (p. 176)

Note: With this stamp, all Pokémon up to Lv. 65 will obey your every command.

Ula'ula Trial Completion

How to Obtain: Clear the grand trial on Poni Island (p. 200)

Note: With this stamp, all Pokémon up to Lv. 80 will obey your every command.

Poni Trial Completion

How to Obtain: Become the first Champion of Alola and complete the island challenge (p. 211)

Note: With this stamp, all Pokémon will obey your every command.

Island Challenge Completion

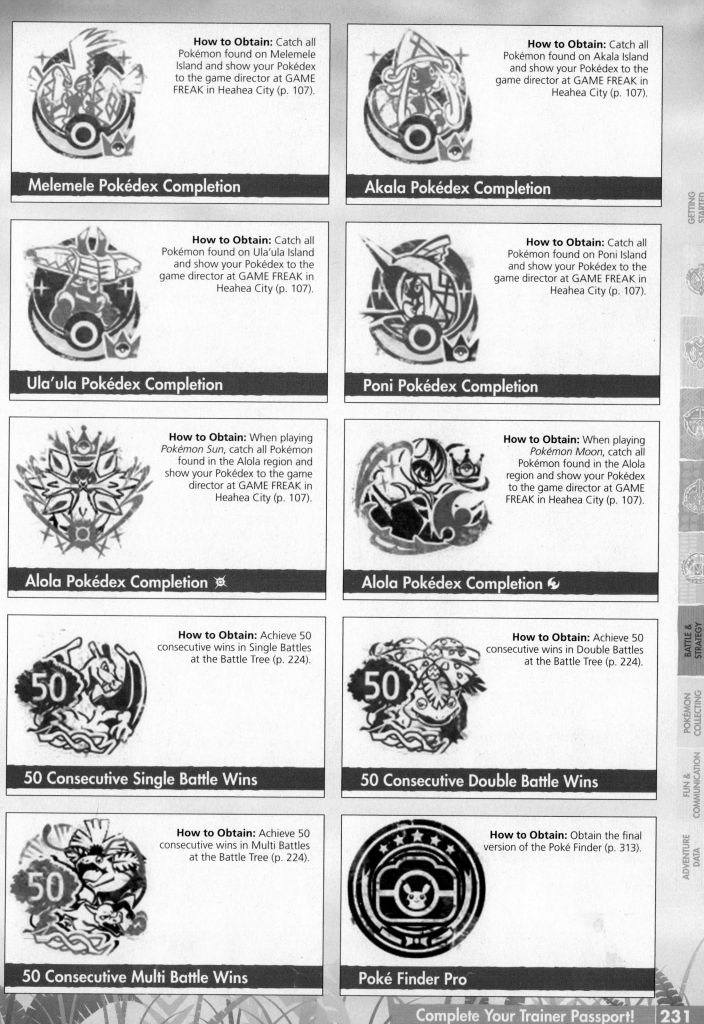

How to Obtain: Catch all Pokémon found on Melemele Island and show your Pokédex to the game director at GAME FREAK in Heahea City (p. 107).

Melemele Pokédex Completion

How to Obtain: Catch all Pokémon found on Akala Island and show your Pokédex to the game director at GAME FREAK in Heahea City (p. 107).

Akala Pokédex Completion

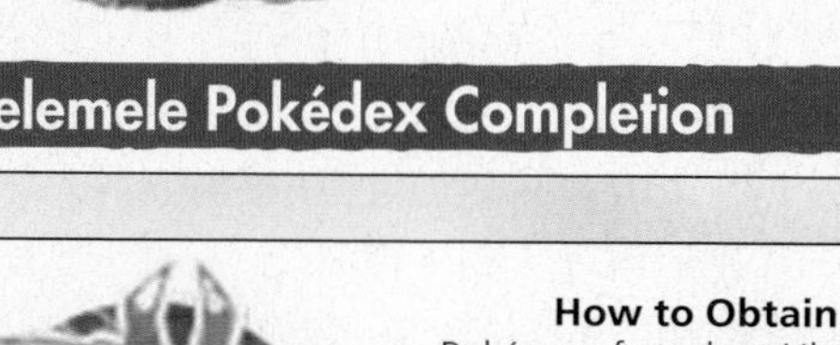

How to Obtain: Catch all Pokémon found on Ula'ula Island and show your Pokédex to the game director at GAME FREAK in Heahea City (p. 107).

Ula'ula Pokédex Completion

How to Obtain: Catch all Pokémon found on Poni Island and show your Pokédex to the game director at GAME FREAK in Heahea City (p. 107).

Poni Pokédex Completion

How to Obtain: When playing *Pokémon Sun*, catch all Pokémon found in the Alola region and show your Pokédex to the game director at GAME FREAK in Heahea City (p. 107).

Alola Pokédex Completion ☼

How to Obtain: When playing *Pokémon Moon*, catch all Pokémon found in the Alola region and show your Pokédex to the game director at GAME FREAK in Heahea City (p. 107).

Alola Pokédex Completion ☾

How to Obtain: Achieve 50 consecutive wins in Single Battles at the Battle Tree (p. 224).

50 Consecutive Single Battle Wins

How to Obtain: Achieve 50 consecutive wins in Double Battles at the Battle Tree (p. 224).

50 Consecutive Double Battle Wins

How to Obtain: Achieve 50 consecutive wins in Multi Battles at the Battle Tree (p. 224).

50 Consecutive Multi Battle Wins

How to Obtain: Obtain the final version of the Poké Finder (p. 313).

Poké Finder Pro

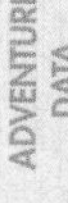

Become an Expert of Pokémon Battling!

You've learned a lot about the basics of Pokémon battles—now it's time to become an expert Pokémon battler! The following pages detail the most intricate points of Pokémon battling, helping you gain every possible advantage. More general information can be found in previous sections, including:

The most basic of basics. The absolute beginning for any new Trainer (p. 7).

The battle menu options and how battle unfolds (p. 30).

Status conditions and using items for battle (p. 49).

Z-Moves and how to use Z-Power in battle (p. 72).

Weather conditions and how they affect Pokémon battles (p. 146).

Mastering Type Matchups

You can check the types of Pokémon that you have on your team or in your PC Boxes from their Summary screens (p. 27). Pokémon that you've encountered already in Alola can be checked from your Pokédex (p. 26). Pokémon that are new to you can be found in the Pokémon List that begins on page 280, which lists the types and possible Abilities of the Pokémon you can encounter in the wild in Alola.

Type matchup chart

Attacking Pokémon's Move Type \ Defending Pokémon's Type	Normal	Fire	Water	Grass	Electric	Ice	Fighting	Poison	Ground	Flying	Psychic	Bug	Rock	Ghost	Dragon	Dark	Steel	Fairy
Normal													▲	×			▲	
Fire		▲	▲	●		●						●	▲		▲		●	
Water		●	▲	▲					●				●		▲			
Grass		▲	●	▲				▲	●	▲		▲	●		▲		▲	
Electric			●	▲	▲				×	●					▲			
Ice		▲	▲	●		▲			●	●					●		▲	
Fighting	●					●		▲		▲	▲	▲	●	×		●	●	▲
Poison				●				▲	▲				▲	▲			×	●
Ground		●		▲	●			●		×		▲	●				●	
Flying				●	▲		●					●	▲				▲	
Psychic							●	●			▲					×	▲	
Bug		▲		●			▲	▲		▲	●			▲		●	▲	▲
Rock		●				●	▲		▲	●		●					▲	
Ghost	×										●			●		▲		
Dragon															●		▲	×
Dark							▲				●			●		▲		▲
Steel		▲	▲		▲	●							●				▲	●
Fairy		▲					●	▲							●	●	▲	

Using the type matchup chart—a copy of which can be easily referenced anytime on the last page of this book—you can check each Pokémon type to see what other types it's weak to, and which types it's able to resist and take less damage from. There are many relationships to remember, so keep a copy of this chart handy for battles against new opponents. Making connections to everyday life is another good way to remember type matchups—for example, Electric-type moves have no effect on Ground-type Pokémon. Not so surprising if you know that the ground can absorb huge amounts of electricity, which is why most households' electrical systems are connected to a grounding rod sunk in the soil!

Move effectiveness

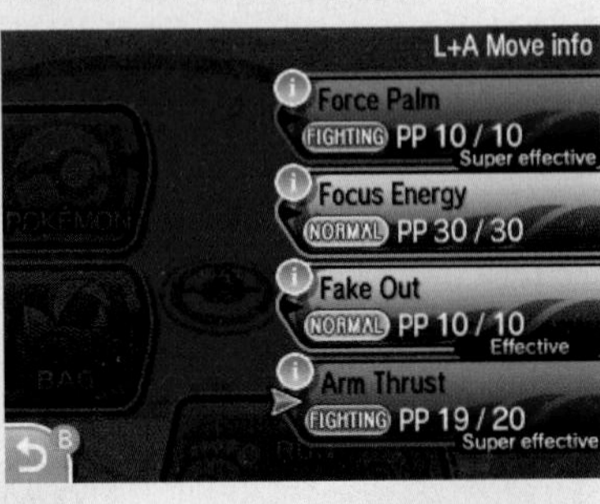

Luckily, you don't have to memorize every type matchup if you're a diligent battler. Once you've battled a particular species of Pokémon, you'll be able to see how effective your moves are against Pokémon of the same species in future battles. This is a great reason to dive into tall grass, venture through caves, and explore other environments where you can encounter wild Pokémon (p. 32). Encountering as many Pokémon as possible not only helps you reach the lofty goal of completing your Pokédexes (p. 278), it also gives you a huge advantage in battle!

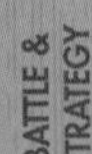

Dealing supereffective damage

When looking at type matchups, remember that a Pokémon's weakness refers to the type of the move used against it, not the type of the Pokémon using the move. For example: Popplio is a Water-type Pokémon, so it's weak to both Grass- and Electric-type moves. This means Popplio will take supereffective damage from Grass- and Electric-type moves, regardless of the type of Pokémon that uses them. If a Fire-type Pokémon such as Litten knows a Grass-type move and uses it against Popplio, it will still deal supereffective damage, even though Litten's type is Fire. When it comes to dealing supereffective damage, the type of the attacking Pokémon does not matter, only the type of the move that it uses. In the example below, Litten knows Hidden Power, and the move type happens to be Grass.

Litten FIRE

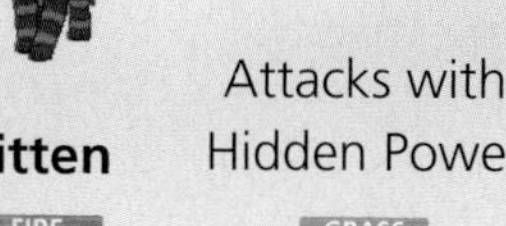

Attacks with Hidden Power GRASS

Popplio WATER = 2× damage!

So, even though Popplio is weak to Grass-type moves, a Grass-type Pokémon using a Normal-type move would not deal supereffective damage to Popplio, because Popplio is not weak to Normal-type moves. However, if that same Grass-type Pokémon uses a Grass-type move against Popplio, then it will deal supereffective damage, multiplied by 150% thanks to the same-type attack bonus (p. 30).

Rowlet GRASS FLYING

Attacks with Tackle NORMAL

Popplio WATER = Normal damage

Rowlet GRASS FLYING

Attacks with Leafage GRASS

Popplio WATER = 3× damage!

Pokémon with two types

What happens when Pokémon have more than one type? In these cases, the strengths and weaknesses of both its types are combined, sometimes canceling each other out, and other times making the Pokémon extremely vulnerable to certain types of moves. For example, Rowlet is a Grass- and Flying-type Pokémon, and both of these types are weak to Ice-type moves. So, an Ice-type move used against Rowlet will deal 4× the regular damage, not just 2×!

It's not all bad news for Rowlet, though, because Grass- and Flying-type Pokémon are also resistant to Grass-type moves. Usually a Grass-type move would do only half its regular damage to either a Grass- or Flying-type Pokémon. But on a Grass- and Flying-type Pokémon like Rowlet, the double resistance means that Grass-type moves will only deal Rowlet 25% of their regular damage.

Popplio WATER

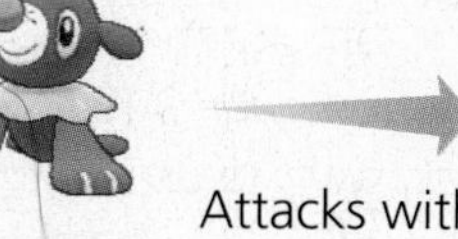

Attacks with Ice Beam ICE

Rowlet GRASS FLYING = 4× damage!

Popplio WATER

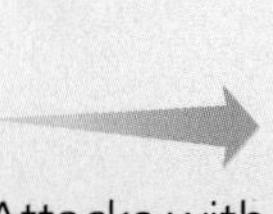

Attacks with Hidden Power GRASS

Rowlet GRASS FLYING = 25% damage

Abilities that affect damage

Lapras's
Water Absorb
Lapras's HP was restored.

There are some ways that type matchups can be manipulated, though. First of all, some Abilities can protect Pokémon from taking supereffective damage from a type of move that they're normally weak to. Other Abilities can make them entirely immune to attacks of certain types, or even help them power up. Here are some Abilities to watch out for.

Filter: Reduces the power of any supereffective attacks taken by the Pokémon.

Flash Fire: Powers up the Pokémon's own Fire-type moves when hit by a Fire-type move instead of taking damage.

Levitate: Makes the Pokémon immune to all Ground-type moves.

Lightning Rod: Boosts Sp. Atk stat when hit by an Electric-type move instead of taking damage.

Motor Drive: Boosts Speed stat when hit by an Electric-type move instead of taking damage.

Prism Armor: Reduces the power of any supereffective attacks taken by the Pokémon.

Sap Sipper: Boosts Attack stat when hit by a Grass-type move instead of taking damage.

Solid Rock: Reduces the power of any supereffective attacks taken by the Pokémon.

Storm Drain: Boosts Sp. Atk stat when hit by a Water-type move instead of taking damage.

Thick Fat: Halves the damage taken from Fire- and Ice-type moves.

Volt Absorb: Restores HP when hit by an Electric-type move instead of taking damage.

Water Absorb: Restores HP when hit by a Water-type move instead of taking damage.

Held items that reduce supereffective damage

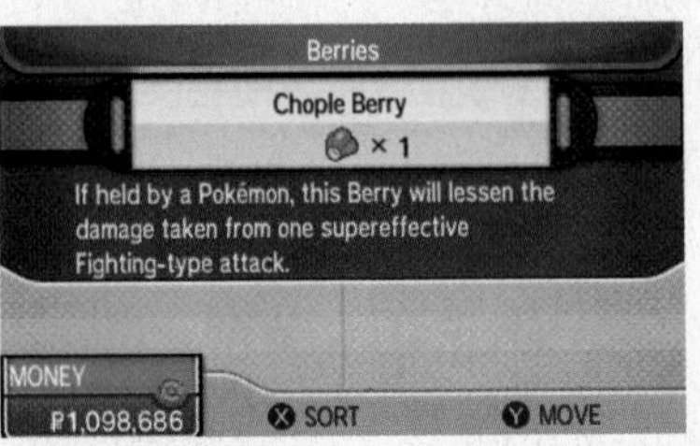
Berries
Chople Berry
× 1
If held by a Pokémon, this Berry will lessen the damage taken from one supereffective Fighting-type attack.
MONEY
₽1,098,686
SORT
MOVE

Some tricky opponents may also have their Pokémon hold items, like the Berries below, that can reduce supereffective damage. Like all other Berries, these Berries can only be used once, and they disappear after they're consumed. But Berries can really surprise you when you thought you were about to knock out an opponent with a supereffective attack! Check out the Berry tables beginning on page 348 to learn where you can find these Berries, then grow some of your own to use in Poké Pelago (p. 309).

Berry	Reduces supereffective damage from
Chilan Berry	Normal-type moves*
Occa Berry	Fire-type moves
Passho Berry	Water-type moves
Rindo Berry	Grass-type moves
Wacan Berry	Electric-type moves
Yache Berry	Ice-type moves
Chople Berry	Fighting-type moves
Kebia Berry	Poison-type moves
Shuca Berry	Ground-type moves

Berry	Reduces supereffective damage from
Coba Berry	Flying-type moves
Payapa Berry	Psychic-type moves
Tanga Berry	Bug-type moves
Charti Berry	Rock-type moves
Kasib Berry	Ghost-type moves
Haban Berry	Dragon-type moves
Colbur Berry	Dark-type moves
Babiri Berry	Steel-type moves
Roseli Berry	Fairy-type moves

*Normal-type moves do not deal supereffective damage, but this Berry reduces damage taken from Normal-type moves.

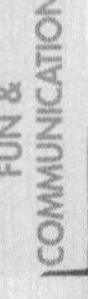
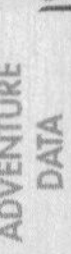

Held items that increase damage

Items
Black Glasses
× 1
An item to be held by a Pokémon. A pair of shady-looking glasses that boost the power of Dark-type moves.
MONEY ₽1,098,686 SORT MOVE

On the other hand, some held items (p. 47) can boost the effectiveness of certain types of moves. Having your Pokémon hold one of these items is a sound strategy, but these items only boost the power of their corresponding moves by 20%. You may therefore wish to consider whether another held item will be more useful to your team (p. 250). Turn to the items lists beginning on page 341 to learn how to obtain these special items.

Held Item	Type of move it boosts
Silk Scarf	Normal-type moves
Charcoal, Flame Plate	Fire-type moves
Mystic Water, Sea Incense, Splash Plate, Wave Incense	Water-type moves
Meadow Plate, Miracle Seed, Rose Incense	Grass-type moves
Magnet, Zap Plate	Electric-type moves
Icicle Plate, Never-Melt Ice	Ice-type moves
Black Belt, Fist Plate	Fighting-type moves
Poison Barb, Toxic Plate	Poison-type moves
Earth Plate, Soft Sand	Ground-type moves
Sharp Beak, Sky Plate	Flying-type moves
Mind Plate, Odd Incense, Twisted Spoon	Psychic-type moves
Insect Plate, Silver Powder	Bug-type moves
Hard Stone, Rock Incense, Stone Plate	Rock-type moves
Spell Tag, Spooky Plate	Ghost-type moves
Draco Plate, Dragon Fang	Dragon-type moves
Black Glasses, Dread Plate	Dark-type moves
Iron Plate, Metal Coat	Steel-type moves
Pixie Plate	Fairy-type moves

Tip

Plates, like the Flame Plate and Toxic Plate mentioned in the table above, can be found as hidden items on Melemele Island after you've beaten the kahuna of Ula'ula Island (p. 177). Sniff them out with Stoutland and add some oomph to your moves!

Type immunities

Gastly
It doesn't affect the wild Gastly...

In addition to determining a Pokémon's weaknesses and resistances to moves, some Pokémon types also feature special immunities. For example, a Pokémon's type may make it completely immune to certain status conditions or types of moves. Consider these immunities carefully when going up against tricky opponents.

*Types usually don't have effects on status moves, but Thunder Wave won't work against Ground-type Pokémon.

Ineffective status conditions and moves depending on type

Type	Effect
Fire	• Immune to the Burned condition
Grass	• Immune to Leech Seed • Immune to powder and spore moves
Electric	• Immune to the Paralysis condition
Ice	• Immune to the Frozen condition • Take no damage from hail • Immune to Sheer Cold
Poison	• Immune to the Poisoned and Badly Poisoned conditions, even when switched in with Toxic Spikes in play • Nullify Toxic Spikes so no other Pokémon will be Poisoned when switching in. (Note: if the Poison-type Pokémon is also a Flying type, has the Levitate Ability, or holds an Air Balloon, this nullifying effect will not occur.)
Ground	• Immune to Thunder Wave* • Take no damage from sandstorms
Flying	• Cannot be damaged by Spikes when switching in • Cannot be afflicted with a Poisoned or Badly Poisoned condition due to switching in with Toxic Spikes in play
Rock	• Take no damage from sandstorms • Sp. Def goes up in a sandstorm
Ghost	• Cannot be affected by moves and Abilities that prevent Pokémon from fleeing from battle
Dark	• Immune to the effect of status moves used by Pokémon with the Prankster Ability
Steel	• Take no damage from sandstorms • Immune to the Poisoned and Badly Poisoned conditions, even when switched in with Toxic Spikes in play

So how effective are your moves against other Pokémon? Let's review, using everything that you've learned about type matchups, same-type attack bonuses, Abilities, held items, and immunities.

Type immunity

When the target's type is immune to the move's type, the move does no damage at all.

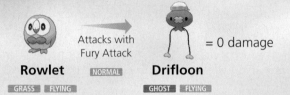

Rowlet

GRASS FLYING

Attacks with Fury Attack

NORMAL

Drifloon

GHOST FLYING

= 0 damage

Type resistance

When the target is resistant to the move's type, the move does half its normal damage.

Rowlet

GRASS FLYING

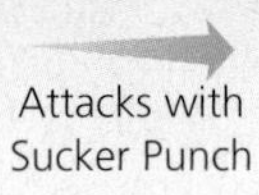

Attacks with Sucker Punch

DARK

Alolan Meowth

DARK

= 50% damage

Same-type attack bonus vs. type resistance

When a Pokémon uses moves of its same type but the target is resistant to that type, those moves do only half the boosted 150% damage.

Rowlet

GRASS FLYING

Attacks with Leafage

GRASS

Litten

FIRE

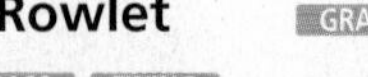

= 75% damage

Type weakness

When the target is weak to the move's type, the move does double its normal damage.

Rowlet

GRASS FLYING

Attacks with Sucker Punch

DARK

Drifloon

GHOST FLYING

= 200% damage

Two-type weakness + same-type attack bonus

When both of the target's types are weak to the move's type, and the move's type is the same as the attacking Pokémon's type, the move does 6× its normal damage

Rowlet

GRASS FLYING

Attacks with Leafage

GRASS

Corsola

WATER ROCK

= 600% damage

Ability immunity/boost

When the target's Ability gives it immunity, the move does no damage and the target may get a boost.

Rowlet

GRASS FLYING

Attacks with Leafage

GRASS

Sliggoo

Sap Sipper Ability

= 0 damage + Atk ↑

Same-type attack bonus

When Pokémon attack with moves that match its type, those moves do 50% more damage.

Rowlet

GRASS FLYING

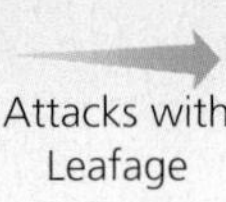

Attacks with Leafage

GRASS

Pichu

ELECTRIC

= 150% damage

No weakness, bonus, or resistance

When the target is neither weak nor resistant to a move's type, and the attacking Pokémon's type doesn't match its move's type, the move does its normal damage.

Rowlet

GRASS FLYING

Attacks with Fury Attack

NORMAL

Popplio

WATER

= 100% damage

Two-type weakness

When both of the target's types are weak to the move's type, the move does 4× its normal damage

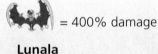

Rowlet

GRASS FLYING

Attacks with Sucker Punch

DARK

Lunala

PSYCHIC GHOST

= 400% damage

Two-type weakness + same-type attack bonus + held item

When both of the target's types are weak to the move's type, and the move's type is the same as the attacking Pokémon's type, and the attacking Pokémon is holding a type-enhancing item, the move does over 7× its normal damage

Rowlet

GRASS FLYING

+

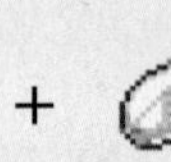

Miracle Seed

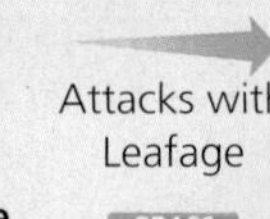

Attacks with Leafage

GRASS

Corsola

WATER ROCK

= 720% damage

As you can see, type matchups are extremely important in the world of Pokémon. They can determine if a Pokémon's move with, say, a base power of 20, deals a mere 10 damage or a whopping 144—or even no damage at all! Notice that the same-type attack bonus doesn't generally make up for a poor type matchup, unless the move's power is so great that it's still stronger than your Pokémon's other moves, even at 75% strength!

Become a Move Expert

Most Pokémon can learn dozens of different moves by leveling up, using TMs (p. 50), and through other means. Let's explore the various ways your Pokémon can learn moves.

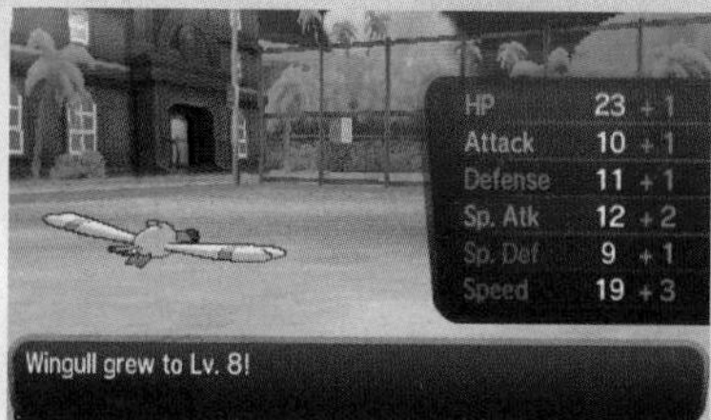

Leveling up

Pokémon often learn new moves just by leveling up. Every few levels, you may find that your Pokémon has the chance to learn a new move. Read the new move's description and decide whether it's worth replacing one of your Pokémon's older moves with it.

Example: Primeape
Final Gambit

Primeape can learn this move when it reaches Lv. 57.

Evolving

Some Pokémon also have the chance to learn new moves when they evolve. These are often moves that the Pokémon's next Evolution might have learned in the wild, but doesn't otherwise learn by leveling up. Through Evolution, you'll have one more chance to teach your Pokémon these useful moves!

Example: Hakamo-o
Clanging Scales

When Hakamo-o evolves into Kommo-o at Lv. 45, it can learn Clanging Scales, Kommo-o's signature move.

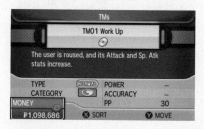

TMs

Technical Machines (TMs) can be used over and over to teach powerful moves to many different Pokémon. There are 100 TMs in the Alola region—think you can find them all? The list on page 334 will help you if you're missing any. Some are found in the field, some are given to you by people you meet, and others can be bought at shops (p. 350).

Example: Trumbeak
Roost

Buy TM19 Roost at Malie City's Poké Mart and use it to teach Trumbeak the move Roost.

Madam Memorial

Madam Memorial is a Move Reminder: a special individual with the ability to help Pokémon relearn moves they've forgotten or moves they chose not to learn when they had the chance. She can even help them learn moves that they haven't yet learned from previous levels! Madam Memorial can be found in the Pokémon Center on Mount Lanakila (p. 208), and she'll help you in exchange for Heart Scales. Get Heart Scales by dining in Alola's restaurants, fishing (p. 104), visiting Festival Plaza (p. 299), catching wild Luvdisc, or through the use of a high-level Pokémon with the Pickup Ability.

Example: Scizor
Bullet Punch

Bullet Punch is a move that a Scizor may know by default. If you catch or evolve a Scizor that doesn't know it, Madam Memorial can help your Scizor remember it!

Move Tutors

The Move Tutors in Hau'oli City's shopping mall (p. 82), Hano Grand Resort (p. 134), and Seafolk Village (p. 190) can help certain Pokémon learn special moves. Other than Draco Meteor, which any Dragon-type Pokémon with high friendship can learn, these moves can only be learned by specific species of Pokémon. Check them out in the tables beginning on the next page if you think you've got the right Pokémon for the job!

Alola Region Move Tutors		
Tutor Location	**Move Name**	**Pokémon That Can Learn It**
Hau'oli City Shopping Mall	Frenzy Plant	Venusaur, Meganium, Sceptile, Torterra, Serperior, Chesnaught, Decidueye (max friendship required)
Hau'oli City Shopping Mall	Blast Burn	Charizard, Typhlosion, Blaziken, Infernape, Emboar, Delphox, Incineroar (max friendship required)
Hau'oli City Shopping Mall	Hydro Cannon	Blastoise, Feraligatr, Swampert, Empoleon, Samurott, Greninja, Primarina (max friendship required)
Hau'oli City Shopping Mall	Grass Pledge	Bulbasaur, Ivysaur, Venusaur, Chikorita, Bayleef, Meganium, Treecko, Grovyle, Sceptile, Turtwig, Grotle, Torterra, Snivy, Servine, Serperior, Pansage, Simisage, Chespin, Quilladin, Chesnaught, Rowlet, Dartrix, Decidueye
Hau'oli City Shopping Mall	Fire Pledge	Charmander, Charmeleon, Charizard, Cyndaquil, Quilava, Typhlosion, Torchic, Combusken, Blaziken, Chimchar, Monferno, Infernape, Tepig, Pignite, Emboar, Pansear, Simisear, Fennekin, Braixen, Delphox, Litten, Torracat, Incineroar
Hau'oli City Shopping Mall	Water Pledge	Squirtle, Wartortle, Blastoise, Totodile, Croconaw, Feraligatr, Mudkip, Marshtomp, Swampert, Piplup, Prinplup, Empoleon, Oshawott, Dewott, Samurott, Panpour, Simipour, Froakie, Frogadier, Greninja, Popplio, Brionne, Primarina
Hano Grand Resort	Secret Sword	Keldeo
Hano Grand Resort	Relic Song	Meloetta
Seafolk Village	Draco Meteor	Any Dragon-type Pokémon with high friendship
Seafolk Village	Dragon Ascent	Rayquaza

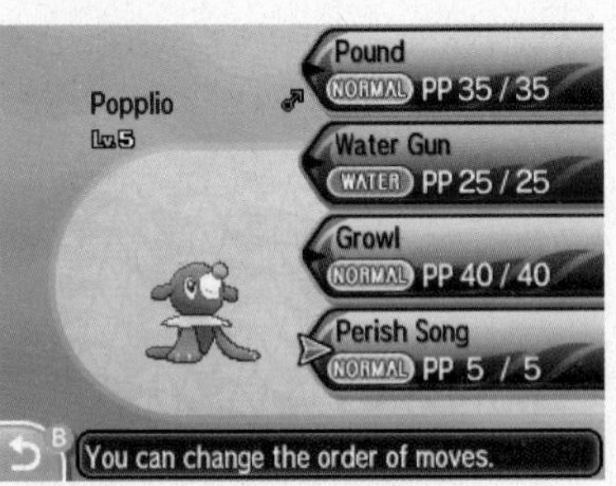

Egg Moves

When Pokémon are hatched from Eggs, they may learn unique moves that their species would normally never learn by leveling up, evolving, or from a TM. These moves are called Egg Moves, and they can be passed down if you're a Pokémon Egg expert. Learn more about that on page 289, and remember that Madam Memorial (p. 210) can also help a Pokémon remember its Egg Moves if it ever forgets them!

Example: Popplio
Perish Song

Popplio can know the Egg Move Perish Song if it's passed down from one of a pair of Pokémon left at the Pokémon Nursery (p. 95).

Evolution cancel

You can stop a Pokémon from evolving by pressing Ⓑ when you see Evolution beginning. This is known as Evolution cancel. Some Pokémon learn different moves than their Evolutions do, which may be a reason to keep your Pokémon from evolving until they have learned all the moves you want them to gain. If you hold off on Evolution for a time, don't worry about missing any of the moves that a later Evolution would have learned: Madam Memorial has you covered. She can teach your fully evolved Pokémon any moves it missed once it finally evolves.

Example: Charjabug
Iron Defense

You can evolve Charjabug into Vikavolt as soon as you want, but Charjabug is the only Pokémon in its Evolution line that can learn Iron Defense. If it evolves into Vikavolt, the chance to learn Iron Defense will be lost forever. Even Madam Memorial can't bring back moves from previous Evolutions!

Know How to Use Your Moves

Moves can do more than just attack your opponent and dish out damage. Consider all the different ways to use moves when you are choosing the perfect four for each of your Pokémon.

Moves can inflict status conditions

Some moves inflict status conditions 100% of the time, letting you put your target in a bind—unless the target is immune to that status condition (p. 235) or happens to be holding the right Berry (p. 348), that is. Other moves deal damage but also have a chance of inflicting a status condition, usually with a lower success rate than non-damaging moves. Check the status condition list on page 49 to review the common status conditions that you can inflict, and decide whether this is the strategy for you.

Move	Type	Effect	Pokémon that can learn this move
Blizzard	Ice	May leave the target Frozen	Glalie, Alolan Sandshrew, Vanilluxe, and others
Poison Powder	Poison	Leaves the target Poisoned	Butterfree, Cottonee, Paras, and others
Sing	Normal	Leaves the target Asleep	Cleffa, Lapras, Popplio, and others
Stun Spore	Grass	Leaves the target with Paralysis	Cutiefly, Exeggcute, Masquerain, and others
Toxic	Poison	Leaves the target Badly Poisoned	Mareanie, Pyukumuku, Trubbish, and others
Will-O-Wisp	Fire	Leaves the target Burned	Froslass, Alolan Marowak, Trevenant, and others

Tip

Protect your Pokémon from status conditions by having them hold Berries that can remove them (p. 348). You can also use Pokémon with types or Abilities that make them immune to status conditions. For example, the Limber Ability helps your Pokémon avoid Paralysis, while the Poison Heal Ability makes your Pokémon regain HP when Poisoned instead of losing it. Komala's Comatose Ability protects it from all status conditions because it will always be Asleep, and a Pokémon cannot be affected by more than one status condition at a time!

Moves can protect your Pokémon from damage

Some moves can protect Pokémon from certain moves or even from all damage altogether. If you need to hold out in battle for a bit longer, these are the moves you'll want your Pokémon to know.

Move	Type	Effect	Pokémon that can learn this move
Detect	Fighting	Protects the user from all attacks that turn	Lucario, Sableye, and others
Protect	Normal	Protects the user from all attacks that turn	Hakamo-o, Shellder, and others
Quick Guard	Fighting	Protects the user and all allies from priority moves	Lucario, Lycanroc (Midday Form), and others
Wide Guard	Rock	Protects the user and allies from multi-target moves (p. 260)	Araquanid, Tirtouga, and others

Moves can help give your Pokémon an advantage

Certain moves can boost your Pokémon's stats, helping them move faster or hit harder during battle. These moves can have a significant impact on a battle's outcome, doubling or even tripling your Pokémon's stats in a flash. You can see how much you or your opponent's stats have been boosted in battle by tapping on a Pokémon's image on the Touch Screen. If a move boosts a stat by 1, then that stat is raised by 50% for the duration of the battle. Boosting a stat by 2 doubles the stat's effect (50% + 50%) unless it is lowered again, and you can just keep on going until your stats are boosted to a maximum of 6 (400% of the original number). With the right moves, your Pokémon can be packing a real wallop in no time!

Move	Type	Effect	Pokémon that can learn this move
Calm Mind	Psychic	Raises the user's Sp. Atk and Sp. Def by 1	Alakazam, Oranguru, and others
Double Team	Normal	Raises the user's evasion by 1	Absol, Mimikyu, and others
Focus Energy	Normal	Raises the user's critical hit rate	Machop, Alolan Raticate, and others
Iron Defense	Steel	Raises the user's Defense by 2	Palossand, Turtonator, and others
Swords Dance	Normal	Raises the user's Attack by 2	Alolan Sandshrew, Scizor, and others
Tailwind	Flying	Doubles the user's Speed (and any ally's Speed) for four turns	Braviary, Pelipper, and others

See Stat Changes

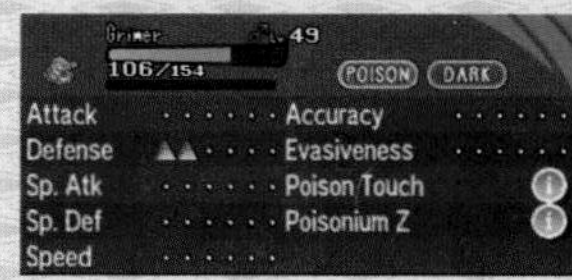

See the changes to your Pokémon's stats in battle by tapping its icon on the lower screen. Here an Alolan Grimer has its Defense raised by 2 (indicated by the two pink arrows) thanks to using Acid Armor.

See any changes affecting your opponent's stats in battle by tapping its icon on the lower screen. Exeggcute has had its Sp. Def lowered by 2 (indicated by the two blue arrows) due to Grimer attacking it with Acid Spray.

Moves can have nasty side effects on your opponents

Just as you can raise your Pokémon's stats with your moves, you can also use moves that lower the stats of opposing Pokémon. Use these moves to strip away the opposing Pokémon's Defense, or lower their Attack so that their moves mean nothing to you. Some moves can make the target flinch, preventing them from using a move that turn. Other moves can confuse the target, which may make them hurt themselves instead of attacking you. What if someone uses a stat-lowering tactic on you? Reset your stats with moves like Haze, or prevent stats from being lowered with moves like Mist. You can also use Pokémon with Abilities like Big Pecks, which prevents Defense from being lowered, or Defiant, which raises the Pokémon's Attack every time one of its other stats is lowered.

Move	Type	Effect	Pokémon that can learn this move
Acid Spray	Poison	Deals damage and lowers the target's Sp. Def by 2	Garbodor, Alolan Muk, Tentacruel, and others
Dynamic Punch	Fighting	Deals damage and confuses the target	Crabominable, Machamp, Poliwrath, and others
Fake Out	Normal	Deals damage and makes the target flinch	Makuhita, Alolan Persian, Sableye, and others
Mud-Slap	Ground	Deals damage and lowers the target's accuracy by 1	Flygon, Grubbin, Mudbray, Trapinch, and others
Parting Shot	Dark	Lowers the target's Attack and Sp. Atk by 1, and then the user switches out for an ally	Pangoro, Silvally, and others
Sky Drop	Flying	Takes the target into the air for one turn, preventing them from taking any action that turn	Braviary, Lunala, and others

Moves can help you control which Pokémon can battle

With the right moves, you can not only get your Pokémon out of battle when the moment is right, you can also mess with your opponent's strategies by either forcing their Pokémon out of battle, or preventing them from switching Pokémon when they might want to.

Move	Type	Effect	Pokémon that can learn this move
Baton Pass	Normal	Switch with an ally, passing along any stat changes	Drifblim, Oricorio, and others
Block	Normal	Prevents the target from leaving battle	Snorlax, Sudowoodo, and others
Circle Throw	Fighting	Forces the target out of the battle	Pangoro, Poliwrath, and others
Dragon Tail	Dragon	Forces the target out of the battle	Flygon, Kommo-o, and others
Mean Look	Normal	Prevents the opponent from leaving battle	Tapu Fini, Umbreon, and others
Roar	Normal	Forces the target out of the battle	Incineroar, Lycanroc, and others
Spider Web	Bug	Prevents the opponent from leaving battle	Araquanid, Ariados, and others
U-turn	Bug	The user attacks, then switches out for an ally	Archeops, Decidueye, and others
Volt Switch	Electric	The user attacks, then switches out for an ally	Emolga, Tapu Koko, and others
Whirlwind	Normal	Forces the target out of the battle	Braviary, Makuhita, and others

Moves can prevent your opponent from moving freely

Strategic Trainers can use moves to control the moves their opponents can use. The following table lists moves that can restrict the opponent's moves and items.

Move	Type	Effect	Pokémon that can learn this move
Disable	Normal	Prevents the target from using their most recent move for four turns	Alolan Grimer, Golduck, and others
Embargo	Dark	Prevents the target from using any held items, or having its Trainer use an item on it, for five turns	Mandibuzz, Weavile, and others
Encore	Normal	Forces the target to use only the last move it used for three more turns	Emolga, Primarina, and others
Heal Block	Psychic	Prevents the target from recovering any HP for five turns	Klefki, Silvally, and others
Taunt	Dark	Forces the target to only use attack moves for three turns	Bastiodon, Oranguru, and others
Torment	Dark	Prevents the target from using the same move in a row	Klefki, Krookodile, and others

Moves can help you get the drop on an opponent

The Speed stat of each Pokémon normally decides which one gets to act first each turn, but some moves don't obey this basic rule of Pokémon battles. These are called priority moves, because they'll strike first even if your Pokémon's Speed stat is lower than your opponent's. If you're close to a knockout, consider these quick hitters to end the battle before your opponent can strike back.

Move	Type	Effect	Pokémon that can learn this move
Aqua Jet	Water	Always strikes first	Carvanha, Golduck, Tirtouga, and others
Bullet Punch	Steel	Always strikes first	Metang, Pangoro, Scizor, and others
Extreme Speed	Normal	Always strikes first	Arcanine, Lucario, and others
Fake Out	Normal	Strikes first and makes target flinch on first turn	Makuhita, Alolan Persian, Sableye, and others
Ice Shard	Ice	Always strikes first	Glaceon, Snorunt, Alolan Vulpix, and others
Mach Punch	Fighting	Always strikes first	Ledian, Ledyba, and others
Shadow Sneak	Ghost	Always strikes first	Ariados, Mimikyu, Sableye, and others
Sucker Punch	Dark	Always strikes first	Gengar, Alolan Raticate, Spinda, and others

Tip

What happens when two opposing Pokémon both use moves of the same priority? Well, then you're back to the Speed stat. Whichever Pokémon has the higher Speed stat gets to use its priority move first.

Moves can help you wait until the opportune time

On the other side of the spectrum, there are also low priority moves, which wait until the end of the turn to be used. This may seem like an odd strategy, but some of these moves often dish out more damage if the user has already taken some damage that turn. If you have a Pokémon with great Defense or Sp. Def, this is one way to hammer opponents when they think they've got you in a corner!

Move	Type	Effect	Pokémon that can learn this move
Avalanche	Ice	Deals double damage if the user was hurt in the same turn	Vanillite, Crabominable, and others
Circle Throw	Fighting	Deals damage and throws the target out of the battle	Pangoro, Poliwrath, and others
Counter	Fighting	Deals back double the physical damage taken that turn	Mudsdale, Pyukumuku, and others
Dragon Tail	Dragon	Deals damage and throws the target out of the battle	Flygon, Kommo-o, and others
Revenge	Fighting	Deals double damage if the user was hurt in the same turn	Machamp, Pinsir, and others

Moves can make sure you hit an evasive opponent

Sometimes it can be hard to hit an opponent that has boosted its evasiveness, or one that has lowered your Pokémon's accuracy with a move like Sand Attack. In these cases, consider moves that are guaranteed to hit. They'll make sure you can deal the damage you need to.

Move	Type	Effect	Pokémon that can learn this move
Aerial Ace	Flying	Never misses	Braviary, Spearow, and others
Aura Sphere	Fighting	Never misses	Lucario, Magearna, and others
Magical Leaf	Grass	Never misses	Comfey, Leafeon, and others
Magnet Bomb	Steel	Never misses	Magnezone, Probopass, and others
Shadow Punch	Ghost	Never misses	Haunter, Gengar, and others
Shock Wave	Electric	Never misses	Electivire, Tapu Koko, and others
Swift	Normal	Never misses	Staryu, Skarmory, and others
Trump Card	Normal	Never misses and power increases as PP decreases	Magearna, Slowking, and others

Tip

If your opponent has used Minimize to raise its evasiveness, try any of these moves: Body Slam, Dragon Rush, Flying Press, Phantom Force, Steamroller, or Stomp. Against any opponent that has used Minimize, these moves never miss and their power is doubled!

Moves can land direct hits or allow you to keep your distance

Check the move tables that begin on page 318, and you'll see that some moves make direct contact with the target, while others don't. If you're wondering why this matters, know that some Pokémon's Abilities—such as Rough Skin—can hurt any Pokémon that makes direct contact with it. There are also Abilities like Static, which may cause opponents that make direct contact with the Pokémon to be affected by Paralysis. You can also have your Pokémon hold an item like a Rocky Helmet, which will cause damage to any opponent that hits it with a direct-contact move.

Moves can take your opponent's size into account

Do you favor adorable little Pokémon? Or maybe hulking beasts are more your style? The effectiveness of certain moves varies depending on the size of your Pokémon, so you should be aware of them. They might be used to target your Pokémon, or they might be a way for your tiny team to pack a big punch. Check out these moves if your team tends toward the extremes.

Move	Type	Effect	Pokémon that can learn this move
Autotomize	Steel	Reduces the Pokémon's weight	Kommo-o, Minior, and others
Grass Knot	Grass	Power increases the heavier the target is	Comfey, Dhelmise, and others
Heavy Slam	Steel	Power increases the heavier the user is compared to the target	Dhelmise, Mudsdale, and others
Low Kick	Fighting	Power increases the heavier the target is	Electivire, Primeape, and others

Tip

These moves can be affected by certain held items, like the Float Stone—which halves a Pokémon's weight while held.

Moves can affect different genders in different ways

Pokémon can be male, female, or have no gender. If they have a gender, then a few tricky moves can be used to play on gender differences. Many Trainers that you meet around Alola tend to use Pokémon of the same gender as themselves, so consider what gender of Pokémon you're likely to encounter while traveling, and plan accordingly. Mind you, this may not work in battles against other Trainers in real life, as they could use Pokémon of any gender at all!

Move	Type	Effect	Pokémon that can learn this move
Attract	Normal	Infatuates targets of the opposite gender, making them less likely to attack	Finneon, Lumineon, and others
Captivate	Normal	Lowers the Sp. Atk of targets of the opposite gender by 2	Froslass, Miltank, and others

Tip

Two Abilities also bring gender into play. Cute Charm can cause infatuation in other Pokémon if they make direct contact with a Pokémon that has this Ability, while Rivalry increases the damage that a Pokémon does to other Pokémon of the same gender.

Moves can interact with held items

Held items can be the key to success for many expert Trainers—so throw them off their game by using a move that takes or knocks away their held item! Some cunning Trainers also have their Pokémon hold a negative-effect item (p. 252), like an Iron Ball, which lowers Speed, with the goal of swapping it with their opponent's held item using one of these surprising moves!

Move	Type	Effect	Pokémon that can learn this move
Acrobatics	Flying	Does double damage if the user is not holding an item	Archeops, Vikavolt, and others
Bug Bite	Bug	Eats the target's Berry, triggering its effects to benefit the user of the move	Dewpider, Golisopod, and others
Covet	Normal	Steals the target's held item if the user has none	Eevee, Mankey, and others
Embargo	Dark	Prevents the target from using any held items, or having its Trainer use an item on it, for five turns	Krookodile, Weavile, and others
Fling	Dark	Flings the user's held item at the target	Alolan Grimer, Alolan Marowak, and others
Incinerate	Fire	Burns up a target's Berry if holding one	Turtonator and others
Knock Off	Dark	Keeps the target from using its held item for the rest of the battle (with some exceptions)	Makuhita, Sableye, and others
Pluck	Flying	Eats the target's Berry, triggering its effects to benefit the user of the move	Archen, Toucannon, and others
Recycle	Normal	Allows the user to reuse an item that had been consumed	Garbodor, Porygon2, and others
Switcheroo	Dark	Swaps the user's held item for the target's held item	Hypno, Alolan Persian, and others
Thief	Dark	Steals the target's held item if the user has none	Crabominable, Honchkrow, and others
Trick	Psychic	Swaps the user's held item for the target's held item	Alakazam, Kadabra, and others

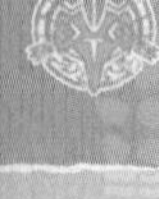

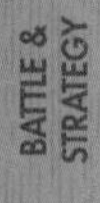

Moves can do a guaranteed amount of damage

If you're up against an opponent with strong defenses, consider using moves that always do a set amount of damage. Though they're not the most powerful, these moves ensure that you can keep chipping away at your opponent.

Move	Type	Effect	Pokémon that can learn this move
Dragon Rage	Dragon	Always does 40 damage	Drampa, Salazzle, and others
Night Shade	Ghost	Always does damage equal to user's level	Ariados, Sableye, and others
Seismic Toss	Fighting	Always does damage equal to user's level	Makuhita, Mankey, and others
Sonic Boom	Normal	Always does 20 damage	Flygon, Magnemite, and others

Moves can guarantee a knockout or do huge damage

Some moves can promise you a knockout against your opponent, although most of these come with relatively low accuracy. They're generally more likely to hit, though, the lower the level of your target is compared to your Pokémon. These moves are therefore ideal for quickly ending battles against low-level wild Pokémon. Other moves will guarantee that your Pokémon faint—but in return, they may be able to either heal their allies or deal some serious damage.

Move	Type	Effect	Pokémon that can learn this move
Explosion	Normal	User deals great damage, then faints	Gigalith, Minior, and others
Final Gambit	Fighting	User inflicts damage equal to its remaining HP, then faints	Mankey, Riolu, and others
Fissure	Ground	If it hits, the target will faint immediately	Alolan Dugtrio, Trapinch, and others
Guillotine	Normal	If it hits, the target will faint immediately	Pinsir, Vikavolt, and others
Healing Wish	Psychic	User faints but heals status conditions and restores HP to the next ally to switch in	Alomomola, Clefairy, and others
Horn Drill	Normal	If it hits, the target will faint immediately	Goldeen, Seaking
Memento	Dark	User faints, sharply lowering the opponent's Attack and Sp. Atk	Alolan Muk, Pyukumuku, and others
Self-Destruct	Normal	User deals great damage, then faints	Alolan Golem, Minior, and others
Sheer Cold	Ice	If it hits, the target will faint immediately	Glalie, Lapras, and others

Moves can help your Pokémon get out of a tight spot

Not all moves do damage to an opponent. There are also moves that can restore HP to your Pokémon, cure status conditions, or reset lowered stats. If your Pokémon's HP hits zero, it'll be out of the battle unless you can revive it with an item, so consider keeping it in fighting form with these moves.

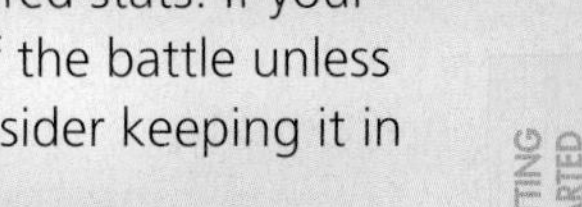

Move	Type	Effect	Pokémon that can learn this move
Aqua Ring	Water	Restores HP gradually every turn	Alomomola, Tapu Fini, and others
Aromatherapy	Grass	Heals status conditions of your entire party	Comfey, Ribombee, and others
Dream Eater	Psychic	Damages a sleeping opponent and restores HP to the user	Lunala, Shiinotic, and others
Floral Healing	Fairy	Restores the target's HP by up to half of its max HP	Comfey
Giga Drain	Grass	Restores HP equal to half the damage dealt to the target	Dhelmise, Shiinotic, and others
Heal Bell	Normal	Heals status conditions of your entire party	Miltank
Healing Wish	Psychic	User faints but heals status conditions and restores HP to the next ally to switch in	Alomomola, Blissey, and others
Leech Seed	Grass	Drains HP from the target to restore the user's HP each turn	Tapu Bulu, Trevenant, and others
Moonlight	Fairy	Restores HP (dependent on weather condition)	Lunala, Umbreon, and others
Morning Sun	Normal	Restores HP (dependent on weather condition)	Espeon, Solgaleo, and others
Pollen Puff	Bug	Restores some HP if the target is an ally; inflicts damage if the target is an opponent	Ribombee
Recover	Normal	Restores half of the user's max HP	Alakazam, Mareanie, and others
Refresh	Normal	Heals the Poisoned, Burned, or Paralysis condition	Blissey, Tapu Fini, and others
Rest	Psychic	Fully restores the user's HP but makes the user fall Asleep for two turns	Probopass, Snorlax, and others
Roost	Flying	Restores half of the user's max HP but takes away its Flying type for that turn	Fearow, Toucannon, and others
Shore Up	Ground	Restores half of the user's max HP	Palossand and Sandygast
Slack Off	Normal	Restores half of the user's max HP	Slowbro and Slowpoke
Strength Sap	Grass	Restores the user's HP equal to the opponent's Attack stat	Morelull and Shiinotic
Synthesis	Grass	Restores HP (dependent on weather condition)	Decidueye, Leafeon, and others
Wish	Normal	Recovers half of the user's max HP at the end of the next turn, or restores the HP of the next ally that switches in	Alomomola

Moves can change Pokémon's Abilities

Pokémon all have Abilities which grant them various benefits, either in battle or out. In most conditions, a Pokémon's Ability does not change, but there are a few special moves that can affect Abilities. They'll throw your opponent for a loop if their strategy depends on their Ability!

Move	Type	Effect	Pokémon that can learn this move
Entrainment	Normal	Makes the target's Ability the same as the user's Ability	Araquanid, Pangoro, and others
Gastro Acid	Poison	Negates the target's Ability	Pyukumuku and others
Gravity	Psychic	Negates the Levitate Ability and removes the immunity of Flying types to Ground-type moves for five turns	Clefairy, Probopass, and others
Role Play	Psychic	Copies the target's Ability	Kadabra and others
Skill Swap	Psychic	Swaps the user's Ability with the target's Ability	Sylveon, Tapu Lele, and others
Worry Seed	Grass	Changes the target's Ability to Insomnia	Exeggcute and others

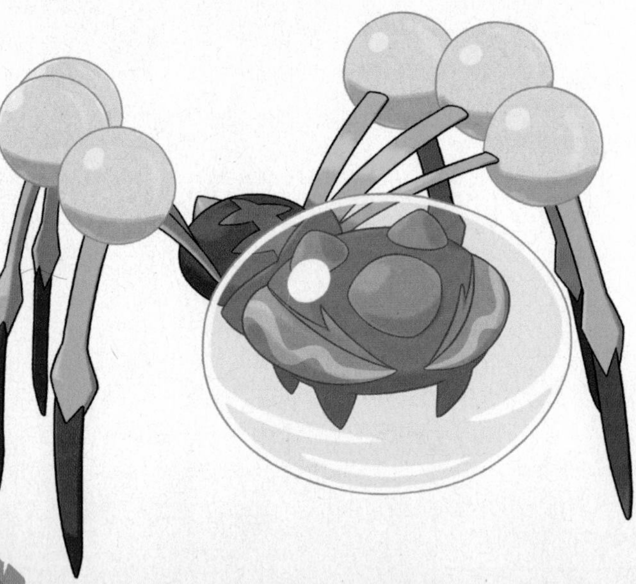

Moves interact with the field

Moves can change the weather conditions in a battle, granting benefits to certain types of Pokémon and negatively affecting others. Turn to page 146 to review how different weather conditions can affect battle, and the moves you can use to trigger them. Some moves can also have their effects altered by the current weather condition—examples of these are listed in the following table. Other moves can affect the terrain in battle, affecting different Pokémon types similar to weather conditions, and potentially causing additional effects as well. Use these moves to turn the field to your team's advantage!

Move	Type	Effect	Pokémon that can learn this move
Blizzard	Ice	This move has 100% accuracy when it's hailing	Froslass, Glalie, and others
Electric Terrain	Electric	Powers up Electric-type moves and prevents Pokémon on the ground from falling Asleep for five turns	Magneton, Togedemaru, and others
Grassy Terrain	Grass	Powers up Grass-type moves and restores a little HP to Pokémon on the ground each turn for five turns	Comfey, Tapu Bulu, and others
Growth	Normal	This move raises the user's Attack and Sp. Atk by 2 instead of the usual 1 in harsh or extremely harsh sunlight	Lurantis, Trevenant, and others
Misty Terrain	Fairy	Halves the damage from Dragon-type moves and protects Pokémon on the ground from status effects for five turns	Primarina, Sylveon, and others
Psychic Terrain	Psychic	Powers up Psychic-type moves and protects Pokémon on the ground from priority moves for five turns	Tapu Lele
Solar Beam	Grass	In harsh sunlight, this move only requires one turn to use instead of the usual two	Fomantis, Solgaleo, and others
Solar Blade	Grass	In harsh sunlight, this move only requires one turn to use instead of the usual two	Lurantis
Thunder	Electric	This move has 100% accuracy when it's raining	Jolteon, Pikachu, and others

Tip

Don't forget that certain moves can target more than one Pokémon at a time! Turn to page 260 for lists of multi-target moves, or check out the range information in the move tables beginning on page 318.

Z-Moves and Their Effects

In addition to knowing about regular moves, having mastery of Z-Moves is a vital step in becoming an expert battler. You learned the basics of using Z-Crystals to unlock the power of your Pokémon's Z-Moves on page 72, but did you know Z-Moves can do more than just pack a punch? It's true! Z-Moves can also have special additional effects that you'll want to consider. In the move tables that begin on page 318, you can see the Z-Move effects of every move than can be learned in the Alola region. But you should start by learning that the Z-Move effects vary depending on the type of Z-Move you trigger.

Two types of Z-Moves

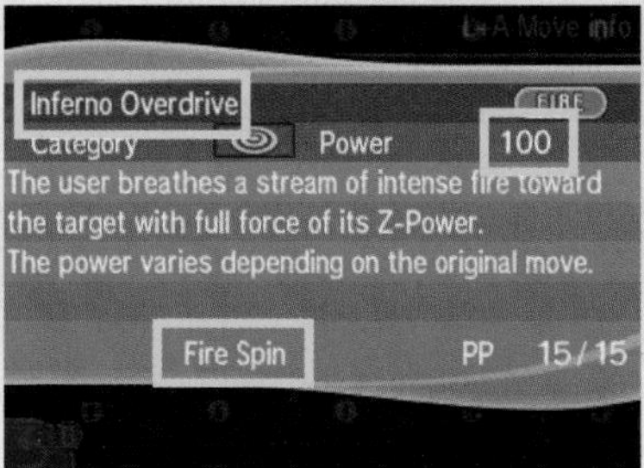

Having a Pokémon hold a Z-Crystal can trigger two different kinds of Z-Moves, depending on the kind of moves the Pokémon knows. When a Pokémon knows a damage-dealing move of the same type as the Z-Crystal, that move will be transformed into the type-specific move for that Z-Crystal. For example, a Pokémon like Arcanine holding Firium Z will have its Fire-type moves, such as Fire Fang, transformed into Inferno Overdrive if it chooses to use its Z-Power. Inferno Overdrive is the Fire-type Z-Move.

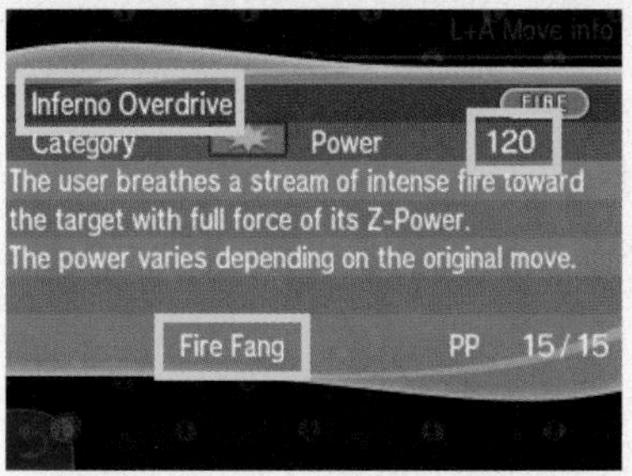

The power of a type-specific Z-Move like Inferno Overdrive can vary depending on the move it's based on. For example, if Arcanine knows Fire Spin with a power of 35 and Fire Fang with a power of 65, both are damage-dealing Fire-type moves that would be transformed into Inferno Overdrive through Z-Power. But you'd want to use the Inferno Overdrive that's based on its Fire Fang move, because it will do more damage based on Fire Fang's greater power. In addition, every type-specific Z-Move has the added Z-Move effect of boosted power. So Inferno Overdrive will always be far more powerful than the move it was based on, whether it was Fire Fang or Fire Spin. But why not go for the maximum power possible?

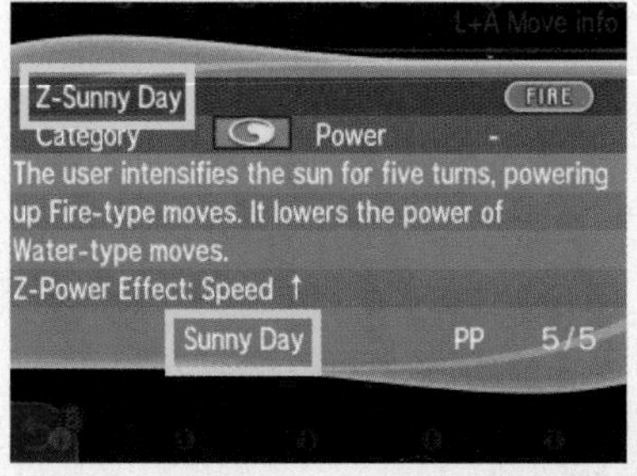

Now say that same Arcanine also knows some non-damaging moves, like Sunny Day. Sunny Day is also a Fire-type move, but it doesn't directly damage an opponent, so it won't transform into Inferno Overdrive. Instead, it turns into Z-Sunny Day when it is powered up by Z-Power. All non-damage-dealing moves get this Z- prefix, and they can have different Z-Move effects on the move's user or on the team, not just boosted power like damage-dealing moves do. In this case, Z-Sunny Day will boost the user's Speed on top of its original effect of turning the weather condition to harsh sunlight (p. 146). The effects will last until the user is switched out of battle or faints.

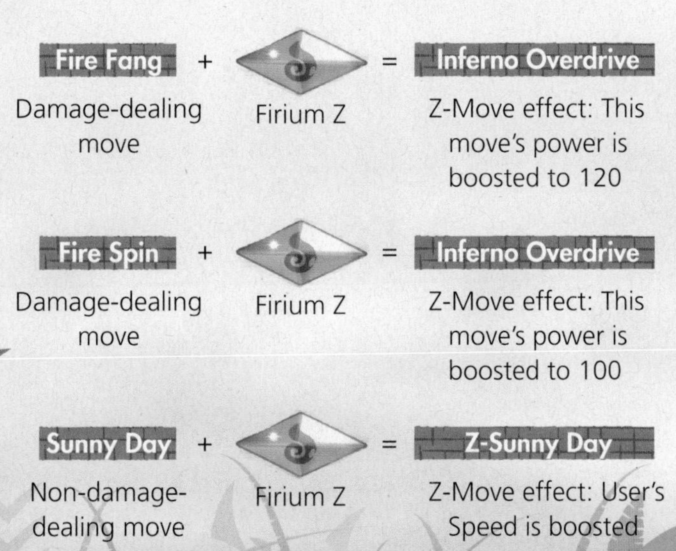

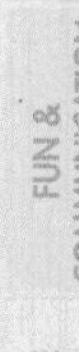
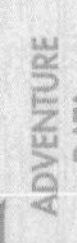

Special Z-Move effects

Arcanine boosted its Speed using its Z-Power!

Non-damaging moves can have a variety of special Z-Move effects, on top of their original effects. The following list reveals all of the various Z-Move effects you may encounter, along with examples of the moves that can trigger them. Use this list, and the full lists on pages 318–333, to plan your best Z-powered strategy!

Attack boosted by 1: Tail Whip, Odor Sleuth, Will-O-Wisp, Hone Claws, etc.

Attack boosted by 2: Mirror Move

Attack boosted by 3: Splash

Defense boosted by 1: Roar, Spikes, Aqua Ring, Mat Block, Strength Sap, etc.

Sp. Atk boosted by 1: Gear Up, Psychic Terrain, Telekinesis, Embargo, etc.

Sp. Atk boosted by 2: Psycho Shift, Heal Block

Sp. Def boosted by 1: Stun Spore, Flatter, Charge, Crafty Shield, Confide, etc.

Sp. Def boosted by 2: Magic Coat, Imprison, Captivate, Aromatic Mist, Powder

Speed boosted by 1: Supersonic, String Shot, Sandstorm, Rain Dance, Electric Terrain, etc.

Speed boosted by 2: Trick, Recycle, Snatch, Me First, Switcheroo, Ally Switch, Bestow

Accuracy boosted by 1: Mimic, Defense Curl, Focus Energy, Sweet Scent, Copycat, Defog, Trick Room

Evasion boosted by 1: Sand Attack, Kinesis, Camouflage, Lucky Chant, etc.

All stats boosted: Purify, Geomancy, Forest's Curse, Trick-or-Treat, Conversion, etc.

Critical Hit Boost: Foresight, Sleep Talk, Acupressure, Heart Swap, Tailwind

Restores HP to the next ally to switch in: Memento, Parting Shot

Restores user's HP: Mist, Teleport, Spite, Stockpile, etc.

Resets all lowered stats: Shore Up, Dragon Dance, Moonlight, Recover, Leech Seed, etc.

Makes all moves target the user: Destiny Bond, Grudge

Z-Crystals and how to obtain them

Many Z-Crystals are obtained as you complete your island challenge, but there are also a few that only diligent adventurers will spot on their own. Every Z-Crystal has been marked throughout the walkthrough, but here's a handy list in case you missed any along the way.

Z-Crystal	Type-Specific Move	How to Obtain
Normalium Z	Breakneck Blitz	Clear one trial (p. 71)
Fightinium Z	All-Out Pummeling	Clear Melemele Island's grand trial (p. 77)
Waterium Z	Hydro Vortex	Clear two trials (p. 103)
Firium Z	Inferno Overdrive	Clear three trials (p. 115)
Grassium Z	Bloom Doom	Clear four trials (p. 123)
Pikanium Z	Catastropika	Receive from a woman in Konikoni City (p. 130)
Rockium Z	Continental Crush	Clear Akala Island's grand trial (p. 133)
Electrium Z	Gigavolt Havoc	Clear five trials (p. 155)
Steelium Z	Corkscrew Crash	Clear five trials (p. 155)
Decidium Z	Sinister Arrow Raid	Receive it from the professor in Malie Garden (p. 156) if you chose Rowlet, or receive it from Hau after becoming Champion
Incinium Z	Malicious Moonsault	Receive it from the professor in Malie Garden (p. 156) if you chose Litten, or receive it from Hau after becoming Champion
Primarium Z	Oceanic Operetta	Receive it from the professor in Malie Garden (p. 156) if you chose Popplio, or receive it from Hau after becoming Champion

Z-Crystal	Type-Specific Move	How to Obtain
Ghostium Z	Never-Ending Nightmare	Clear six trials (p. 165)
Buginium Z	Savage Spin-Out	Pick it up after battling Guzma in the Shady House (p. 174)
Darkinium Z	Black Hole Eclipse	Clear Ula'ula Island's grand trial (p. 176)
Psychium Z	Shattered Psyche	Find it in the Haina Desert (p. 179)
Aloraichium Z	Stoked Sparksurfer	Receive it from a woman in Seafolk Village (p. 191)
Flyinium Z	Supersonic Skystrike	Find it in Ten Carat Hill (p. 85)
Poisonium Z	Acid Downpour	Receive it after battling Plumeria on Poni Island (p. 197)
Groundium Z	Tectonic Rage	Clear Poni Island's grand trial (p. 200)
Fairium Z	Twinkle Tackle	Receive from Mina on Poni Island (p. 201)
Dragonium Z	Devastating Drake	Clear the abandoned trial on Poni Island (p. 203)
Icium Z	Subzero Slammer	Find it on Mount Lanakila (p. 208)
Tapunium Z	Guardian of Alola	Pick it up after becoming Champion and battling Tapu Koko on Melemele Island (p. 216)
Eevium Z	Extreme Evoboost	Complete the "Eevee Trainers" sub-event (p. 217) after becoming Champion

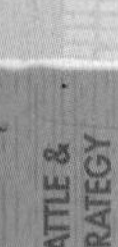

Tip

There may be other Z-Crystals out there that have yet to be discovered. Stay tuned to www.pokemon.com to learn about upcoming distributions and special events that may allow you to learn new Z-Moves!

Use Abilities to Their Fullest

Unlike moves, you don't have as many options when it comes to your Pokémon's Abilities, but that doesn't make them any less important for strategy. Abilities can have huge effects on battles, from powering up your Pokémon's moves to inflicting status conditions on opponents, or even helping your Pokémon heal themselves. Let's check out some of the major categories of Abilities.

Tip

Most Pokémon can have one of two possible Abilities. When you face an opponent in battle, you may not know for sure what Ability it has until it triggers. But you can use this uncertainty against opponents as well!

Abilities that affect attacks

Pangoro's
Mold Breaker
Pangoro breaks the mold!

Abilities can affect moves in a number of ways, from increasing their power to boosting their accuracy. Factor in Ability effects, as they might make up for using moves with lower accuracy or power.

Ability	Effect	Pokémon that can have this Ability
Compound Eyes	Raises accuracy by 30%	Butterfree
Dazzling	Keeps priority attack moves of the opposing Pokémon from working	Bruxish
Guts	Boosts Attack by 50% when the Pokémon has a status condition	Hariyama, Machamp
Infiltrator	Ignores barriers like Reflect and Light Screen	Crobat, Whimsicott
Iron Fist	Increases the power of punching moves	Crabominable, Pangoro
Mold Breaker	User's attacks are not affected by the target's Ability	Pangoro, Rampardos
No Guard	Makes all moves used by and against the user hit their target	Machamp
Prankster	Increases the priority of all non-damaging moves used by the Pokémon	Cottonee, Klefki
Queenly Majesty	Keeps priority attack moves of the opposing Pokémon from working	Tsareena
Rock Head	Protects the Pokémon from recoil damage from moves like Take Down	Bagon, Cubone
Serene Grace	Doubles moves' chances of inflicting their additional effects	Blissey, Chansey
Sheer Force	Raises the power of moves with additional effects by stripping away those effects	Braviary, Rufflet
Skill Link	Moves that have variable hit counts will always hit the max number of times	Cloyster, Toucannon
Super Luck	Boosts the Pokémon's critical-hit ratio	Absol, Honchkrow
Technician	Moves with a power of 60 or less have their power increased by 50%	Alolan Persian, Smeargle

Abilities that affect types and type matchups

Arcanine's
Flash Fire
The power of Arcanine's Fire-type moves rose!

Abilities can even affect type matchups, or help boost moves of a certain type. Look to use these Abilities to your advantage whenever possible.

Ability	Effect	Pokémon that can have this Ability
Adaptability	The power of a move is boosted when used by a Pokémon of the same type	Eevee, Porygon-Z
Blaze	Raises the power of Fire-type moves by 50% when the user's HP drops below 1/3	Incineroar, Litten, Torracat
Corrosion	Allows Steel- and Poison-type opponents to be afflicted with the Poisoned condition	Salandit, Salazzle
Flash Fire	Powers up the Pokémon's Fire-type moves if hit by a Fire-type move	Arcanine, Flareon
Levitate	The Pokémon is immune to Ground-type attacks and moves like Spikes	Mismagius, Vikavolt
Overgrow	Raises the power of Grass-type moves by 50% when the user's HP drops below 1/3	Dartrix, Decidueye, Rowlet
Scrappy	Allows Ghost-type Pokémon to be hit with Normal- and Fighting-type moves	Kangaskhan, Miltank
Steelworker	Boosts the power of Steel-type moves by 50%	Dhelmise
Swarm	Raises the power of Bug-type moves by 50% when the user's HP drops below 1/3	Ariados, Scizor
Torrent	Raises the power of Water-type moves by 50% when the user's HP drops below 1/3	Brionne, Popplio, Primarina

Abilities that help your Pokémon take hits

Geodude's
Sturdy
Geodude endured the hit!

Certain Abilities can help raise your Pokémon defenses, protect them from damage, or even let them absorb attacks of certain types. Some Abilities can even affect healing or restore HP. Sometimes a good defense is the best offense!

Ability	Effect	Pokémon that can have this Ability
Disguise	Protects the Pokémon from all damage one time	Mimikyu
Dry Skin	The Pokémon recovers HP when it is raining or when hit by a Water-type move	Paras, Parasect
Fluffy	Halves the damage from direct-contact attacks (but increases damage from Fire-type moves)	Bewear, Stufful
Ice Body	The Pokémon recovers HP when it's hailing	Glalie, Vanilluxe
Lightning Rod	User draws all Electric-type moves to itself and absorbs them to raise its Sp. Atk	Alolan Marowak, Togedemaru
Shell Armor	Protects the Pokémon from critical hits	Cloyster, Turtonator
Sturdy	Allows the Pokémon to survive a move that would normally knock it out with 1 HP	Alolan Golem, Magnezone
Triage	Gives healing moves higher priority	Comfey
Volt Absorb	Restores HP when hit by an Electric-type move	Jolteon, Lanturn
Water Absorb	Restores HP when hit by a Water-type move	Poliwrath, Vaporeon

Abilities related to negative conditions

Some Abilities can inflict status conditions or other negative conditions, such as confusion or infatuation. Other Abilities can help protect your Pokémon from such conditions, or allow them to recover from them more quickly than usual. Check out these Abilities if you're up against an opponent that you know is likely to inflict status conditions.

Abilities that help inflict negative conditions

Ability	Effect	Pokémon that can have this Ability
Corrosion	Allows Steel- and Poison-type opponents to be Poisoned	Salandit, Salazzle
Effect Spore	Contact with this Pokémon can cause opponents to become Poisoned, fall Asleep, or be affected by Paralysis	Parasect, Shiinotic
Flame Body	Contact with this Pokémon can cause opponents to be Burned	Magmortar, Talonflame
Static	Contact with this Pokémon can cause opponents to be afflicted with Paralysis	Emolga, Pichu
Synchronize	Status conditions inflicted by an opponent will be shared with that opponent	Alakazam, Umbreon

Abilities that help avoid or cure negative conditions

Ability	Effect	Pokémon that can have this Ability
Comatose	Prevents all status conditions due to being permanently Asleep	Komala
Early Bird	Allows the Pokémon to wake from being Asleep quicker	Kangaskhan, Ledian
Hydration	Allows the Pokémon to recover from status conditions when it's raining	Goodra, Wingull
Immunity	Prevents the Pokémon from being Poisoned	Snorlax
Inner Focus	Prevents the Pokémon from flinching	Dragonite, Lucario
Insomnia	Prevents the Pokémon from falling Asleep	Hypno, Spinarak
Leaf Guard	Protects the Pokémon from status conditions during harsh sunlight	Leafeon, Tsareena
Limber	Prevents the Pokémon from being affected by Paralysis	Ditto, Toxapex
Magic Guard	Prevents the Pokémon from taking damage from status conditions	Clefable, Clefairy
Natural Cure	Removes all status conditions if the Pokémon switches out of battle	Staryu, Trevenant
Oblivious	Prevents the Pokémon from becoming infatuated	Slowpoke, Wailord
Own Tempo	Prevents the Pokémon from becoming confused	Mudsdale, Slowpoke
Shed Skin	The Pokémon may spontaneously recover from status conditions	Dragonair, Metapod
Water Veil	Prevents the Pokémon from being Burned	Seaking, Wailord
Vital Spirit	Prevents the Pokémon from falling Asleep	Primeape, Rockruff

Abilities that affect stats

Remember how much of an impact stat changes can have on your Pokémon's performance, easily increasing your Pokémon's stats by 50%, 100% or more (p. 239). Some Abilities can provide these same stat increases, and a few others can help protect certain Pokémon from having their stats affected. Check out the following table and consider how these Abilities might power up your Pokémon team.

Abilities that cause stat increases or decreases

Ability	Effect	Pokémon that can have this Ability
Anger Point	Maxes Attack if hit with a critical hit	Primeape, Tauros
Chlorophyll	Doubles the Pokémon's Speed in harsh sunlight	Exeggcute, Lilligant
Download	Raises either Attack or Sp. Atk when switching into battle	Porygon2, Porygon-Z
Guts	Raises Attack when inflicted with a status condition	Machamp, Makuhita
Hustle	Raises Attack but lowers accuracy of physical moves	Delibird, Alolan Raticate
Intimidate	Lowers the Attack of all opponents when the Pokémon switches in	Arcanine, Salamence
Motor Drive	Raises the Pokémon's Speed if hit by an Electric-type move	Electivire
Moxie	Raises the Pokémon's Attack each time an opponent faints	Krokorok, Krookodile
Sand Rush	Doubles the Pokémon's Speed during a sandstorm	Lycanroc (Midday Form), Stoutland
Sap Sipper	Raises the Pokémon's Attack if hit by a Grass-type move	Drampa, Goodra
Snow Cloak	Raises evasion when it's hailing	Froslass, Alolan Sandslash
Stamina	Raises the Pokémon's Defense by 1 when the Pokémon takes damage	Mudbray, Mudsdale
Steadfast	Raises the Pokémon's Speed each time it flinches	Lucario, Riolu
Swift Swim	Doubles the Pokémon's Speed when it's raining	Magikarp, Relicanth
Tangling Hair	Lowers the Speed stat for any Pokémon that makes direct contact with the Pokémon	Alolan Dugtrio
Unburden	Raises the Pokémon's Speed if they use or lose their held item	Drifblim, Drifloon
Water Compaction	Raises the Pokémon's Defense by 2 when hit by Water-type moves	Palossand, Sandygast
Weak Armor	Decreases Defense but increases Speed by 2 when hit by a physical move	Boldore, Garbodor

Abilities that help avoid or prevent stat decreases

Ability	Effect	Pokémon that can have this Ability
Big Pecks	Protects the Pokémon from having its Defense lowered	Fletchling, Mandibuzz
Clear Body	Protects the Pokémon from having any stats lowered	Metagross, Tentacruel
Hyper Cutter	Protects the Pokémon from having its Attack lowered	Crabominable, Pinsir
Unaware	Stat changes have no effect on the Pokémon	Cosmog

Abilities that activate when Pokémon move in and out of battles

Pyukumuku's
Innards Out
The wild Gumshoos is hurt!

Whether a Pokémon is withdrawn from battle, or forced out by a move such as Roar, certain Abilities trigger only upon exiting battle. Other Abilities affect Pokémon that switch into battle, including the first Pokémon that is sent out at the battle's onset.

Ability	Effect	Pokémon that can have this Ability
Aftermath	Deals damage equal to 1/4 of the Pokémon's max HP if it is knocked out	Drifblim, Drifloon
Forewarn	Reveals one move that the opponent has	Drowzee, Hypno
Electric Surge	Causes Electric Terrain when the Pokémon enters battle	Tapu Koko
Frisk	Reveals what held item an opponent has	Alolan Exeggutor, Trevenant
Grassy Surge	Causes Grassy Terrain when the Pokémon enters battle	Tapu Bulu
Innards Out	Deals equal damage back to an opponent who knocks it out	Pyukumuku
Intimidate	Lowers the Attack of all opponents when the Pokémon switches in	Arcanine, Salamence
Misty Surge	Causes Misty Terrain when the Pokémon enters battle	Tapu Fini
Psychic Surge	Causes Psychic Terrain when the Pokémon enters battle	Tapu Lele
Receiver	The Pokémon copies the Ability of a fainted ally	Passimian
Stakeout	Does double damage to a Pokémon that switches in the same turn	Gumshoos, Yungoos

Abilities that take effect when your Pokémon is hit

Pichu's
Static

No one likes to see their Pokémon take hits, but it's very likely to happen in battle. Some Abilities activate when your Pokémon is hit, however, especially when hit by direct-contact moves. These Abilities can help your Pokémon dish a little damage back to their attackers, making them quite useful.

Ability	Effect	Pokémon that can have this Ability
Cursed Body	May disable a move that is used against the Pokémon	Alolan Marowak
Cute Charm	May infatuate Pokémon of the opposite gender when hit	Sylveon, Wigglytuff
Effect Spore	Contact with this Pokémon can cause opponents to become Poisoned, be affected by Paralysis, or fall Asleep	Parasect, Shiinotic
Flame Body	Contact with this Pokémon can cause opponents to be Burned	Magmortar, Talonflame
Iron Barbs	Contact with this Pokémon damages the attacker	Togedemaru
Pressure	Forces opponents to use more PP to attack this Pokémon	Absol, Weavile
Rough Skin	Contact with this Pokémon damages the attacker	Carvanha, Sharpedo
Static	Contact with this Pokémon can cause opponents to be afflicted with Paralysis	Emolga, Pichu
Weak Armor	Decreases Defense but increases Speed when hit by a physical move	Boldore, Garbodor

Abilities related to the weather and the terrain

Psyduck's
Cloud Nine
The effects of the weather disappeared.

In addition to changing the weather with moves (p. 146), you can also change the weather with certain Abilities. Some Abilities can have special effects when weather conditions are favorable, and a few unique Abilities can create the same special terrains as can be brought about by the moves on page 244.

Ability	Effect	Pokémon that can have this Ability
Chlorophyll	Doubles the Pokémon's Speed in harsh sunlight	Exeggcute, Lilligant
Cloud Nine	Negates all effects of the weather	Golduck, Psyduck
Drizzle	Makes it start to rain when the Pokémon enters battle	Pelipper
Drought	Causes harsh sunlight when the Pokémon enters battle	Torkoal
Electric Surge	Causes Electric Terrain when the Pokémon enters battle	Tapu Koko
Grassy Surge	Causes Grassy Terrain when the Pokémon enters battle	Tapu Bulu
Hydration	Allows the Pokémon to recover from status conditions when it is raining	Goodra, Wingull
Ice Body	The Pokémon recovers HP when it is hailing	Glalie, Vanilluxe
Leaf Guard	Protects the Pokémon from status conditions during harsh sunlight	Leafeon, Tsareena
Misty Surge	Causes Misty Terrain when the Pokémon enters battle	Tapu Fini
Overcoat	Protects the Pokémon from damage taken from hail or a sandstorm	Mandibuzz, Vullaby
Psychic Surge	Causes Psychic Terrain when the Pokémon enters battle	Tapu Lele
Sand Rush	Doubles the Pokémon's Speed during a sandstorm	Lycanroc (Midday Form), Stoutland
Sand Stream	Causes a sandstorm when the Pokémon enters battle	Gigalith
Snow Cloak	Raises evasion when it is hailing	Froslass, Alolan Sandslash
Snow Warning	Makes it start to hail when the Pokémon enters battle	Vanilluxe
Swift Swim	Doubles the Pokémon's Speed when it is raining	Magikarp, Relicanth

Hidden Abilities

Araquanid's
Water Absorb
It doesn't affect Araquanid...

Each Pokémon species can have one or two Abilities. When you catch a Pokémon in the wild, it normally has one of its species' common Abilities—but in special conditions, you may catch a Pokémon with a Hidden Ability! Hidden Abilities are very rare Abilities that wild Pokémon don't normally possess. Trigger enough SOS battles (p. 265), however, and you may find yourself encountering rare Pokémon that have one of these fantastic Abilities! Each individual Pokémon can only have one Ability, so if it has a Hidden Ability, it won't have one of its species' common Abilities.

Use Items Wisely

Don't forget your Bag when you're preparing for battle! Items kept in your Bag are an important part of any robust battle strategy, whether they're items that you plan to use on your Pokémon during battle, or held items that you give your Pokémon to hold in advance so they can use them on their own. You can use as many items from your Bag as you want during battle, but each item you use takes up a turn, preventing your Pokémon from using moves. The advantage to held items is that they're used automatically when their conditions are met, meaning you don't have to sacrifice a turn to reap their benefits.

Tip

Remember that each Pokémon can be given one held item to hold. Turn back to page 47 for a refresher on how to give held items to your Pokémon.

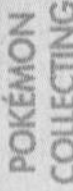

Single-use held items

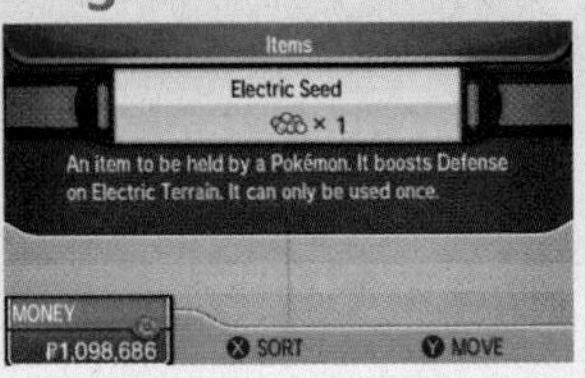

Like Berries, some held items in *Pokémon Sun* and *Pokémon Moon* work only once in battle, and then they're consumed. Be careful about using up these items in random battles against wild Pokémon and regular field Trainers around the Alola region. Try to save them for battles against tough opponents, like those mighty island kahunas!

Item	Effect
Absorb Bulb	Raises the holder's Sp. Atk if hit with a Water-type move
Cell Battery	Raises the holder's Attack if hit with an Electric-type move
Eject Button	Switches the holder out of battle for an ally if hit with an attack
Electric Seed	Raises the holder's Defense in Electric Terrain
Focus Sash	When the holder has full HP, it'll endure a potential KO attack with 1 HP
Grassy Seed	Raises the holder's Defense in Grassy Terrain
Luminous Moss	Raises the holder's Sp. Def if hit with a Water-type move
Misty Seed	Raises the holder's Sp. Def in Misty Terrain
Power Herb	Allows the holder to immediately use a move that normally takes two turns to power up and perform, such as Solar Beam, Sky Attack, or Shadow Force
Psychic Seed	Raises the holder's Sp. Def in Psychic Terrain
Red Card	Forces the opponent to switch out of battle if it hits the holder with an attack
Snowball	Raises the holder's Attack if hit with an Ice-type move
Weakness Policy	Raises the holder's Attack and Sp. Atk sharply if hit with a supereffective move
White Herb	Restores a stat that has been lowered

Tip

Single-use held items won't be consumed when you battle other players via Link Battles (p. 305) or Battle Spot (p. 305), or when you battle in the Battle Tree (p. 224).

Offensive held items

In addition to the type-boosting held items listed on page 235, there are a few more held items that you should remember if you'd like to increase the damage done by your Pokémon's attacks.

Item	Effect
Big Root	Boosts the effects of HP-draining moves like Giga Drain or Horn Leech
Binding Band	Raises the damage done every turn by moves like Bind or Wrap
Expert Belt	Boosts the power of supereffective moves by 20%
King's Rock	Has a 10% chance of making a target flinch when using a simple attack
Life Orb	Boosts the power of moves but takes away some of the holder's HP after each attack
Metronome	Raises the power of a move used in consecutive turns
Muscle Band	Raises the power of physical moves
Razor Fang	Has a 10% chance of making a target flinch when using a simple attack
Wise Glasses	Raises the power of special moves

Defensive held items

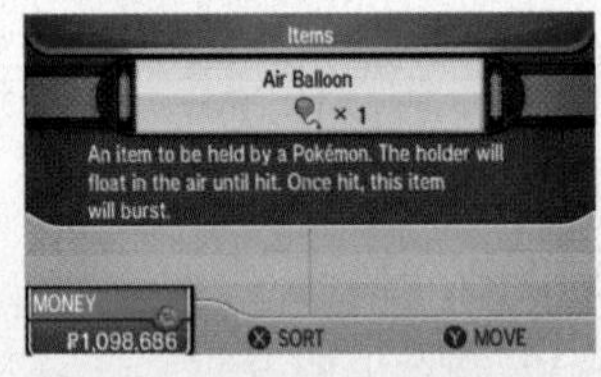

The following held items can give your Pokémon a defensive boost, or help them return a little bit of the damage they receive back on their attackers.

Item	Effect
Air Balloon	Gives the holder immunity to Ground-type moves until damaged by an attack
Focus Band	Has a slight chance of preventing fainting
Focus Sash	When the holder has full HP, it'll endure a potential KO attack with 1 HP
Rocky Helmet	Making contact with the holder will damage an attacker
Protective Pads	Prevents the holder from taking any contact-based side effects from its attacks
Safety Goggles	Makes the holder immune to weather-related damage and powder and spore moves

Time-related held items

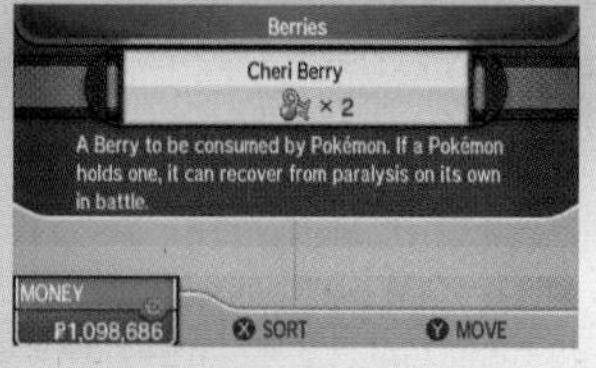

Some held items can help you control the flow of time on the battlefield, giving your Pokémon a chance to move faster or slower, or extending the effects of various moves or conditions.

Item	Effect
Damp Rock	Extends the duration of rain summoned by the holder
Full Incense	Lowers the holder's priority in battle
Grip Claw	Extends the effects of Bind, Clamp, Fire Spin, Infestation, Magma Storm, Sand Tomb, Whirlpool, or Wrap if the holder uses them
Heat Rock	Extends the duration of harsh sunlight summoned by the holder
Icy Rock	Extends the duration of hail summoned by the holder
Lagging Tail	Makes the holder move last in battle
Light Clay	Extends the effects of Light Screen and Reflect if the holder uses either move
Quick Claw	May let the holder move first in battle
Smooth Rock	Extends the duration of a sandstorm summoned by the holder
Terrain Extender	Extends the duration of a terrain change caused by a move or Ability

Stat-boosting held items

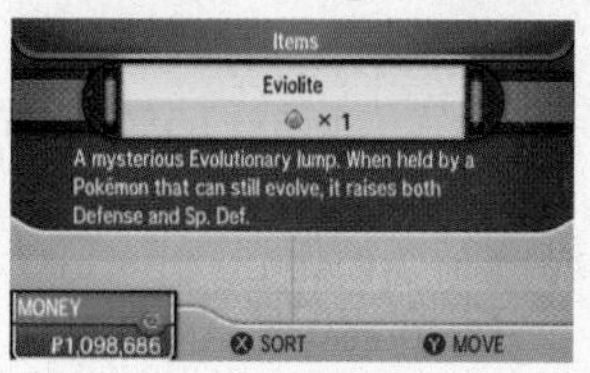

Some held items can help give your Pokémon's stats a little boost, although some of these items also come with drawbacks. Weigh your options carefully, and consider whether or not using moves or Abilities that can also boost stats might be more worthwhile.

Item	Effect
Adrenaline Orb	Raises the holder's Speed if intimidated
Assault Vest	Raises the holder's Sp. Def by 50% but prevents the use of status moves
Bright Powder	Raises the holder's evasion by 10%
Choice Band	Raises the holder's Attack by 50% but only allows the use of the first move selected
Choice Scarf	Raises the holder's Speed by 50% but only allows the use of the first move selected
Choice Specs	Raises the holder's Sp. Atk by 50% but only allows the use of the first move selected
Eviolite	Raises the holder's Defense and Sp. Def if it's still able to evolve
Lax Incense	Raises holder's evasion by 10%
Razor Claw	Raises the critical-hit ratio of the holder's attacks
Scope Lens	Raises the critical-hit ratio of the holder's attacks
Wide Lens	Raises the accuracy of the holder's moves by 10%
Zoom Lens	Raises the accuracy of the holder's moves by 20% if it moves after the target

Berries

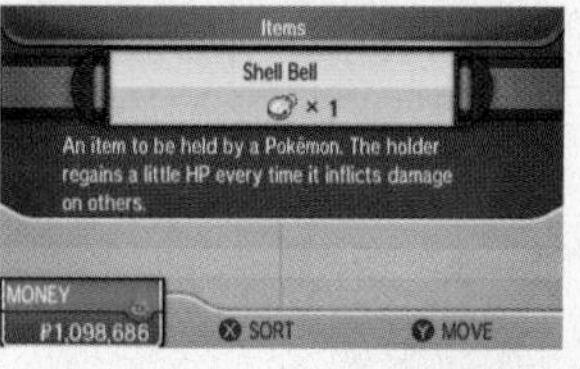

The complete list of Berries can be found on pages 348–349, but here's a breakdown of the types of effects that Berries can have in battle. Just remember that Berries are consumed once eaten by a Pokémon in a normal battle, so try to keep one of each in your Bag so you can use them to grow more Berries in Poké Pelago (p. 309).

Effect	Berries
Allow Pokémon to heal negative conditions in battle	Cheri Berry, Chesto Berry, Pecha Berry, Rawst Berry, Aspear Berry, Persim Berry, Lum Berry
Allow Pokémon to recover HP or PP in battle	Leppa Berry, Oran Berry, Sitrus Berry
Allow Pokémon to escape supereffective damage once	Chilan Berry, Occa Berry, Passho Berry, Rindo Berry, Wacan Berry, Yache Berry, Chople Berry, Kebia Berry, Shuca Berry, Coba Berry, Payapa Berry, Tanga Berry, Charti Berry, Kasib Berry, Haban Berry, Colbur Berry, Babiri Berry, Roseli Berry
Restores HP but may cause confusion	Iapapa Berry, Wiki Berry, Figy Berry, Aguav Berry, Mago Berry
Boosts a stat under certain conditions	Liechi Berry, Ganlon Berry, Petaya Berry, Apicot Berry, Salac Berry, Starf Berry, Kee Berry, Maranga Berry

Healing held items

In addition to Potions and other medicines you can use on your Pokémon during battle, you can also give them a few held items to help them recover some of their HP on their own.

Example Item	Effect
Black Sludge	Restores a small amount of HP each turn to a Poison-type Pokémon that holds it
Leftovers	Restores a small amount of HP each turn to the holder
Shell Bell	Restores a fraction of HP each time that the holder deals damage to another Pokémon

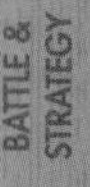
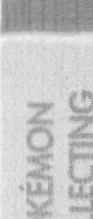

Ending battle on your own terms

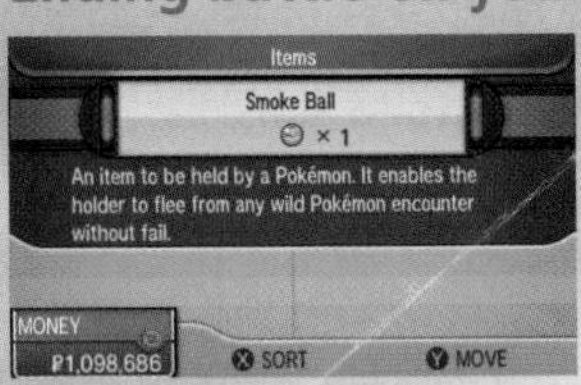

The following unusual items can help you reap greater rewards after battle, or escape from battles that you don't want to fight. Note that items that boost prize money after battle only take effect if the Pokémon that holds them enters the battle, so be sure to switch them in!

Item	Effect
Amulet Coin	Doubles prize money received from battles when held
Lucky Egg	Increases the Exp. Points gained by the holder by 50%
Lucky Incense	Doubles prize money received from battles when held
Shed Shell	Allows the holder to switch out even when a move or Ability would normally prevent it
Smoke Ball	Guaranteed escape from a wild Pokémon encounter when held

Tip

If you don't want to keep buying Repels, give your lead Pokémon some Pure Incense to hold. It will lower the rate at which you encounter wild Pokémon while exploring.

Negative-effect items

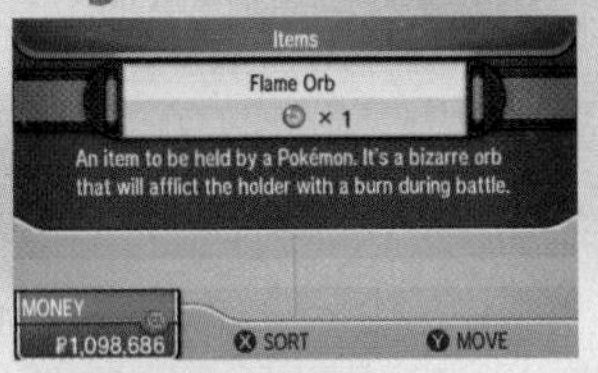

These unusual items actually have negative effects on the holder. You may wonder why such items exist, but remember that page 242 introduced moves that could swap opposing Pokémon's held items. Combine these two into a wicked strategy that can leave your opponent holding onto a whole lot of trouble. Turn to page 254 to discover more ways to combine moves or Abilities and items for unexpected results like this.

Item	Effect
Black Sludge	Damages any non-Poison-type Pokémon that holds it
Flame Orb	Inflicts the holder with a Burn after one turn
Iron Ball	Halves the holder's Speed, and negates the Levitate Ability and Flying-type Pokémon's immunity to Ground-type moves
Ring Target	Negates type immunities for the holder
Sticky Barb	Damages the holder every turn, and sticks to any Pokémon that makes direct contact with the holder and has no held item of its own
Toxic Orb	Inflicts the holder with the Badly Poisoned condition after one turn

Pokémon-specific held items

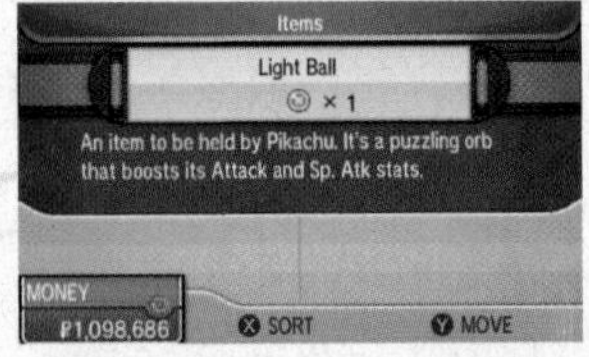

These last few unusual items are intended for particular Pokémon. If these Pokémon are some of your favorites, give them a try!

Item	Effect
Light Ball	Doubles Pikachu's Attack and Sp. Atk when held
Lucky Punch	Boosts Chansey's critical-hit ratio by 2 when held
Metal Powder	Boosts Ditto's Defense when held and when Ditto is in its own form
Quick Powder	Doubles Ditto's Speed when held and when Ditto is in its own form
Stick	Boosts Farfetch'd's critical-hit ratio by 2 when held
Thick Club	Doubles Cubone or Alolan Marowak's Attack when held

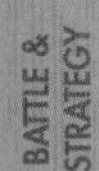

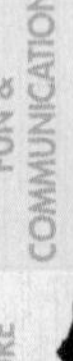

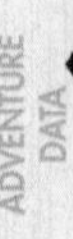

How to Get More Battle Practice

Now that you've learned how to become an expert Pokémon battler, the next step is to put these tips to the test! Fortunately, there's no shortage of ways to practice battling in *Pokémon Sun* and *Pokémon Moon*. You can battle against players beside you or around the world, test your strategies against opponents in the game, or even replay old battles you've enjoyed with Battle Videos.

Battle Buffet

The Battle Buffet in the Hau'oli City Shopping Mall (p. 83) is a great way to challenge your team and see how quickly they can take out other opponents. Your goal is to beat as many opponents in a row as you can within a fixed number of turns, so this is where you can test out those one-hit knockout strategies that you think you've devised.

Available Battle Formats: Single Battle

Battle Tree

Once you've taken on Alola's newly founded Pokémon League and become Champion, you'll be able to take on fearsome Trainers at the Battle Tree (p. 224) in a variety of battle formats to see how many battles you can win in a row. Each victory earns you Battle Points (BP) that can be exchanged for rare goods.

Available Battle Formats: Single Battle, Double Battle, Multi Battle

Link Battles

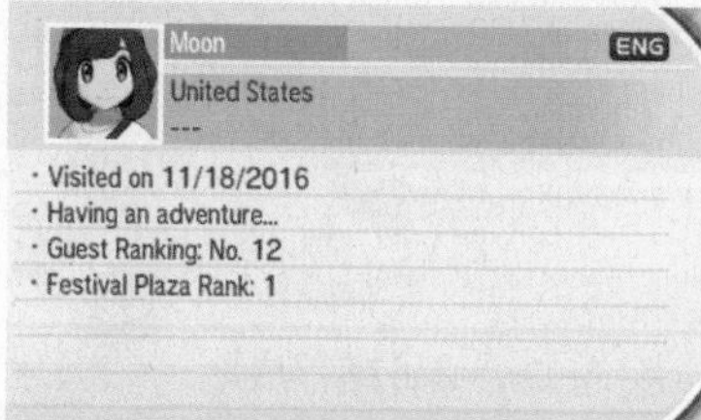

From Festival Plaza (p. 299), select "Battle" on the Touch Screen, and then choose "Link Battle." You'll then be able to select from any of the four available Battle Formats. You can battle with any current visitors to your Festival Plaza or with your VIPs (p. 300). You can also use Quick Link (p. 43) to have Link Battles with nearby friends.

Available Battle Formats: Single Battle, Double Battle, Multi Battle, Battle Royal

Battle Spot

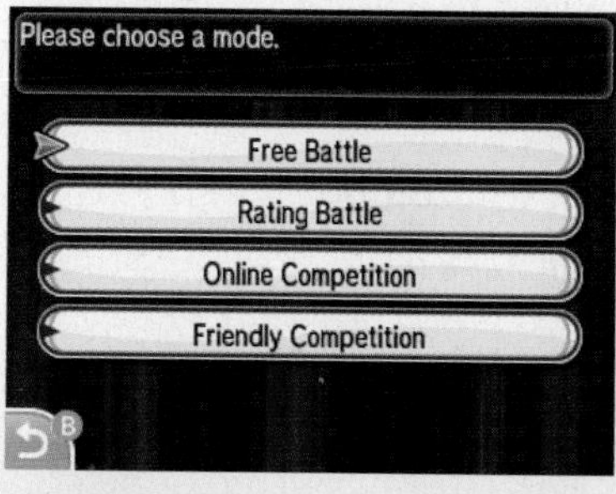

From Festival Plaza (p. 299), select "Battle" on the Touch Screen, and then choose "Visit the Battle Spot." Then choose from the four options for online battles. Free Battles are casual battles that do not affect rating (p. 305). Rating Battles affect your rating on the PGL. Online Competitions are official competitions often featuring prizes, and Friendly Competitions are player-hosted competitions (p. 306).

Available Battle Formats: Single Battle, Double Battle, Battle Royal

Vs. Recorder

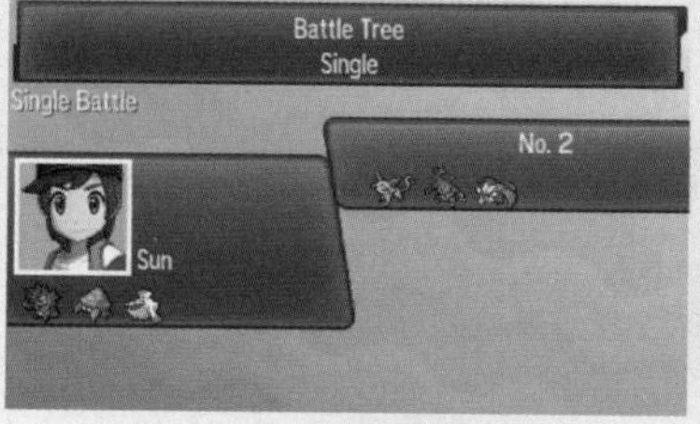

With the Vs. Recorder, you can replay past battles and try out different tactics. Battles can be recorded at the Battle Tree (p. 224), the Battle Royal Dome (p. 108), and at Festival Plaza (p. 299). Access your Battle Videos from the X menu anytime, or download your friends' Battle Videos from the PC in your castle at Festival Plaza (p. 300).

Available Battle Formats: Single Battle, Double Battle, Multi Battle, Battle Royal

Pokémon League

You can also defend your title as Alola's Champion by returning to the Pokémon League (p. 219) and taking on the Elite Four, along with any new challengers. You'll see some familiar faces, as folks from all over Alola show up to try to snatch the new Champion seat away from you.

Available Battle Formats: Single Battle

Master the Art of the Combo

Take what you know about moves, Abilities, and items, and put it all together in a winning strategy

A combo is a combination of Pokémon moves, Abilities, or held items. When you use them together in just the right way, it makes a big difference in battle. Note that some of the combos on the following pages include Pokémon that are not obtainable in the Alola region alone. But your opponents may bring them to *Pokémon Sun* or *Pokémon Moon* using *Pokémon Bank* (p. 316)—just as you can do as well. Be prepared to face these combos, or try to obtain some of these Pokémon from other regions via trades (p. 306) or *Pokémon Bank* to try them out for yourself!

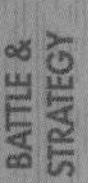

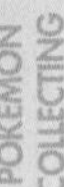

Combo 1 Combine different elements to create clever combos

By combining many different elements, such as moves and Abilities, you can create powerful combos that are far more effective than normal moves. There are so many possible combos that surely some of them are still unknown. Try creating combos by putting together moves, Abilities, and items that seem like they might work. Then, give them a try in battle.

The elements of combos

Move  **Move Combo**

One move can make another move more powerful, or compensate for another move's weakness.

Litten's Fire-type moves can counter Ice-type Pokémon sent out against Rowlet.

Rowlet's Grass-type moves can counter Water-, Ground-, or Rock-type Pokémon sent out against Litten.

Ability  **Move Combo**

An Ability can increase the power of a move or compensate for the weakness of a move.

Pangoro can have the Iron Fist Ability, which increases the power of certain moves it can learn.

Butterfree can have the Compound Eyes Ability, which increases its accuracy and helps it hit with moves like Sleep Powder.

Move  **Item Combo**

Giving the Pokémon an item to hold makes moves powerful or compensates for the weakness of those moves.

Machop dishes out damage with strong physical moves.

Muscle Band increases the power of physical moves, making Machop more effective.

Type  **Move Combo**

When a Pokémon's move will hit its ally, pair it up with a Pokémon of a type that won't take damage from that move.

Porygon can use Discharge to damage all other Pokémon, including its ally.

Mudsdale is a Ground-type Pokémon, so it's immune to Electric-type moves like Discharge.

Main advantages of combos

1. Pull off bigger effects by combining different elements such as moves, Abilities, and items.
2. Sometimes Pokémon can avoid damage from attacks that should have hit them.
3. Sometimes the negative effects of moves, Abilities, or items can be neutralized.

Combo 2

Basic combos for one Pokémon

Here are some very useful old-school combos that can be used by a single Pokémon.

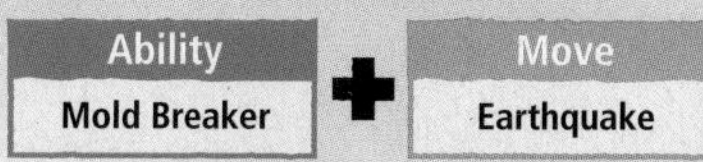

Pinsir
BUG
Ability
Mold Breaker

With the Mold Breaker Ability, a Pokémon can hit a target that is normally protected by its Ability. So Earthquake, a Ground-type move, would hit Pokémon with the Levitate Ability. Use this combo to shake up any Trainers who thought their Pokémon were safe. Get momentum and win!

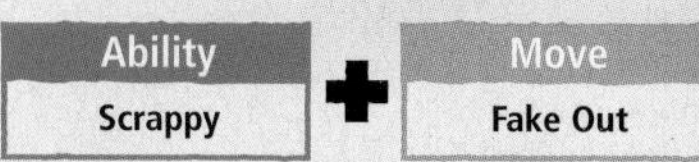

Kangaskhan
NORMAL
Ability
Scrappy

Fake Out shuts down the target when it's used on the same turn its user is sent out. It's very useful until you face a Ghost-type Pokémon—then it becomes completely useless, for Ghost-type Pokémon are immune to Normal-type moves. That is, unless your Pokémon has the Scrappy Ability, which allows Ghost-type Pokémon to be hit with Normal- and Fighting-type moves!

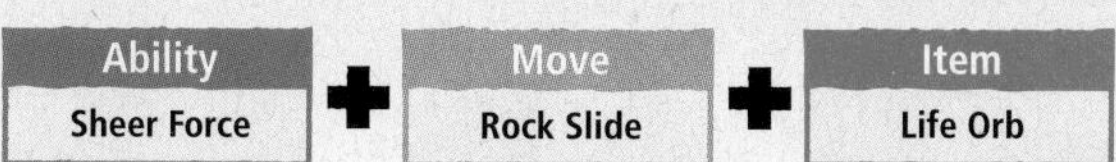

Hariyama
FIGHTING
Hidden Ability
Sheer Force

The move Rock Slide has an additional effect of causing the target to flinch. If a Pokémon with the Sheer Force Ability uses the move, the additional effect doesn't happen, but the move's power increases by 30%. In the case of Hariyama, losing the additional effect of making the target flinch is hardly an issue, because Hariyama is a very slow Pokémon and will likely move last each turn. Give Hariyama a Life Orb to hold, and you'll increase its damage even further. This usually comes with the negative effect of losing a bit of HP every time the holder attacks, but Sheer Force ignores that effect as well when it ignores the additional effect of Rock Slide! That's right: Hariyama won't lose HP at all!

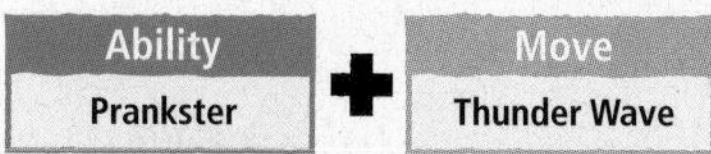

Klefki
STEEL FAIRY
Ability
Prankster

Thunder Wave deals no damage, but it's very useful for slowing the opponent by inflicting them with Paralysis. Pokémon with Paralysis may also fail to attack, so it's best if you can use Thunder Wave before the opponent attacks. That's where Prankster comes in: it increases the priority of all non-damaging moves, making Thunder Wave a priority move and giving you a good chance of using it before the opponent can attack.

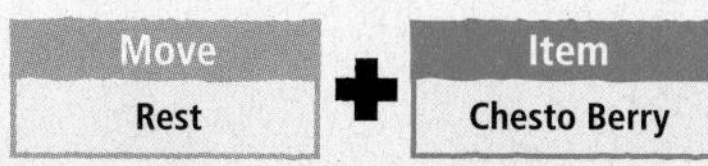

Gigalith
ROCK
Move
Rest

Rest completely restores HP, making it very useful for tough Pokémon with lots of HP. However, Rest also makes the user fall Asleep, making it vulnerable. Give your Pokémon a Chesto Berry to hold, and it will eat it after you use Rest and wake up right away! Since the Pokémon wakes up immediately, it can move during the next turn.

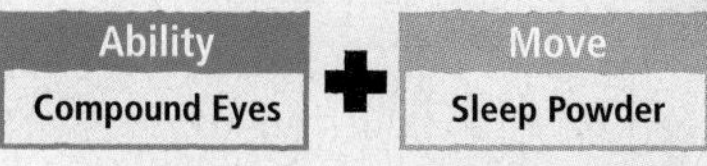

Butterfree
BUG FLYING
Ability
Compound Eyes

Sleep Powder can make the target fall Asleep, but it also has a low accuracy, which can cause it to miss. The Compound Eyes Ability boosts the Pokémon's accuracy by 30%, increasing the odds that Sleep Powder will work.

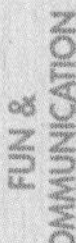

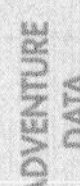

Combo 3 Basic combos for two Pokémon

Here are some very effective combos for Double Battles, where you control more than one Pokémon.

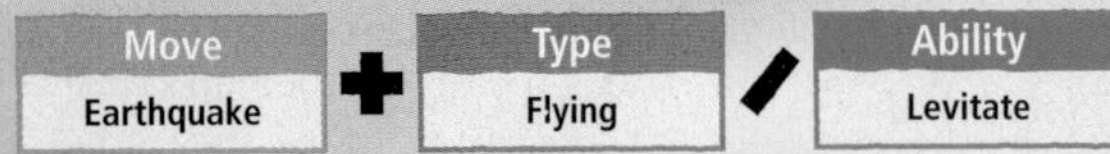

Some moves, like Earthquake, damage all Pokémon except the user, including all enemies and your ally. This makes Earthquake very useful for attacking all enemies at once, but also places the Pokémon on your team at risk. However, with the right Pokémon types or Abilities, you can prevent this unwanted damage to your team. Flying-type Pokémon or Pokémon with the Levitate Ability can't be hit by Ground-type moves, so you can use Earthquake without worrying about damaging your ally! (You can also achieve a similar effect by having your ally use a move like Wide Guard, which protects a Pokémon from any move that targets multiple Pokémon!)

Whiscash
WATER GROUND
Move
Earthquake

Vikavolt
BUG ELECTRIC
Ability
Levitate

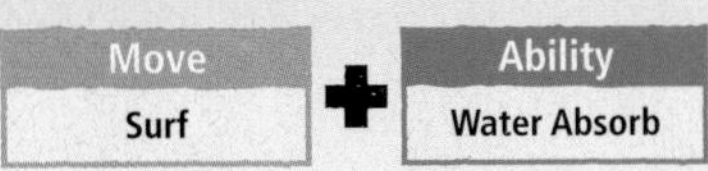

Why not attack and recover HP every turn with this combo? Araquanid and Vaporeon can use Surf, a strong Water-type move that damages all enemies and allies similar to Earthquake. However, if Araquanid and Vaporeon have the Water Absorb Ability, they'll recover HP from Surf instead of being harmed!

Araquanid
WATER BUG
Hidden Ability
Water Absorb

Vaporeon
WATER
Ability
Water Absorb

Combo 4 New combos for one Pokémon in Alola

The Alola region comes with new moves, Abilities, and Pokémon. Let's combine these new elements with some good old standbys to create exciting new strategies!

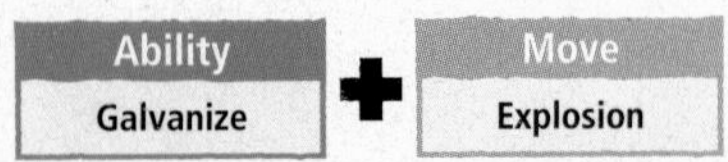

Ever dreamed of defeating Ghost-type Pokémon with the Normal-type move, Explosion? The Galvanize Ability can make this dream a reality! It changes Normal-type moves into Electric-type moves, which Ghost-type Pokémon are not immune to. And in Double Battles if your Pokémon's ally is immune to Electric-type moves (say, a Ground-type Pokémon), this becomes an even more useful combo!

Alolan Golem
ROCK ELECTRIC
Hidden Ability
Galvanize

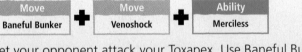

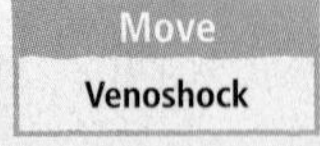

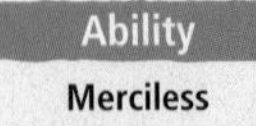

Let your opponent attack your Toxapex. Use Baneful Bunker to protect Toxapex, and the attacker will become Poisoned if it makes direct contact during its attack. Follow up with Venoshock afterward, and it'll be twice as powerful against your Poisoned foe! On top of that, Toxapex's Merciless Ability makes any move score a critical hit if the target is Poisoned. You can also simply use Baneful Bunker every other turn to protect Toxapex and let the opponent suffer from being Poisoned. This is so mean!

Toxapex
POISON WATER
Ability
Merciless

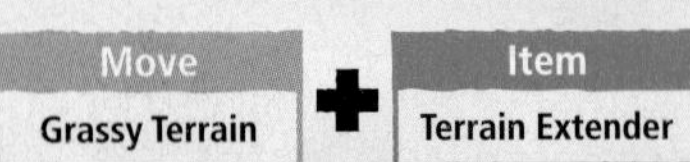

Normally, the effects of terrain moves, such as Grassy Terrain, only last for five turns. You can extend their duration by giving the user a Terrain Extender to hold.

Comfey
FAIRY
Move
Grassy Terrain

Item
Terrain Extender

Ability: Electric Surge + Item: Electric Seed + Move: Thief

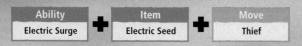

Tapu Koko's Electric Surge Ability creates the Electric Terrain battle condition as it enters battle. Give Tapu Koko an Electric Seed to hold, and it will automatically gain a Defense boost while Electric Terrain is active. Unlike many held items, Electric Seed is consumed when used. Now that Tapu Koko isn't holding anything, why not use Thief to steal an item from the opponent?

Tapu Koko
ELECTRIC FAIRY
Ability
Electric Surge

Item
Electric Seed

New combos for two Pokémon in Alola

The following combos apply Alola's new moves, Abilities, and Pokémon to battles in which you control more than one Pokémon at a time.

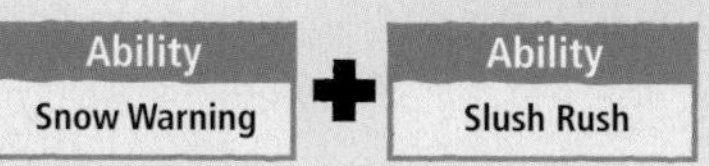

Alolan Sandslash will be faster than usual thanks to its Slush Rush Ability and Alolan Ninetales's Snow Warning Ability!

Alolan Ninetales
ICE FAIRY
Hidden Ability
Snow Warning

Alolan Sandslash
ICE STEEL
Hidden Ability
Slush Rush

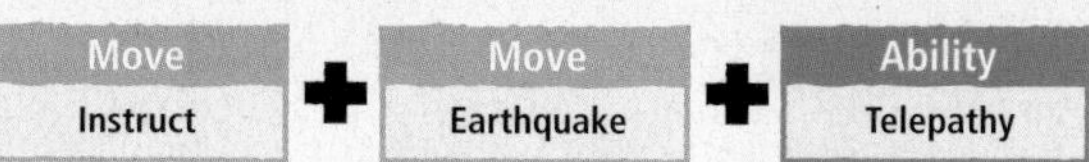

This combo can work with any Pokémon that teams up with Oranguru. Instruct can make your ally (or an opponent) use the same move it just used. Oranguru can avoid the attacks of its allies thanks to its Telepathy Ability, so if Oranguru's ally knows a good supereffective move that damages all opponents, like Surf or Earthquake, have Oranguru use Instruct to make its ally attack twice in a row!

Oranguru
NORMAL PSYCHIC
Ability
Telepathy

Alolan Dugtrio
GROUND STEEL
Move
Earthquake

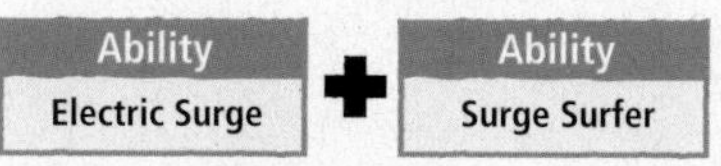

Tapu Koko's and Alolan Raichu's Ability names match perfectly, and they also combine for a nice combo! Alolan Raichu's Surge Surfer Ability doubles its Speed stat on Electric Terrain, a battlefield condition that Tapu Koko creates as it enters battle thanks to its Electric Surge Ability.

Tapu Koko
ELECTRIC FAIRY
Ability
Electric Surge

Alolan Raichu
ELECTRIC PSYCHIC
Ability
Surge Surfer

Pollen Puff can be learned by Ribombee, and it's both an offensive and defensive move at the same time. If used on an opponent, it'll deal damage—but it'll heal the target if it's used on an ally. Oricorio can learn Helping Hand, which boosts the power of an ally's move by 50%. Use Helping Hand on Ribombee to make Pollen Puff deal greater damage or heal for more HP!

Ribombee
BUG FAIRY
Move
Pollen Puff

Oricorio (Pom-Pom Style)
ELECTRIC FLYING
Move
Helping Hand

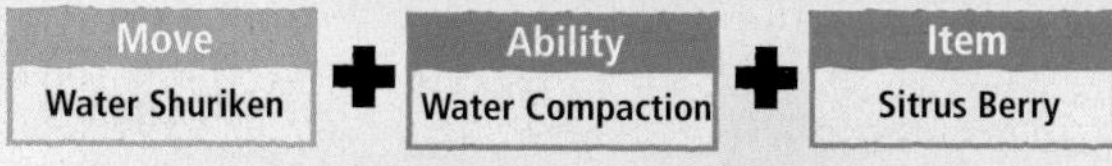

Give your Palossand a Sitrus Berry to hold, then have your Greninja hit Palossand with Water Shuriken. This Water-type move can hit two to five times, and every hit will boost Palossand's Defense sharply thanks to its Water Compaction Ability. If hit enough times, Palossand will eat its Sitrus Berry and recover some HP, all during the same turn!

Greninja
WATER DARK
Move
Water Shuriken

Palossand
GHOST GROUND
Ability
Water Compaction

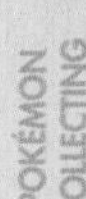

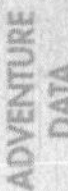

Battle Formats

Five main battle formats are featured in *Pokémon Sun* and *Pokémon Moon*. Each is described below, and more detailed breakdowns and strategies for each format are provided on the following pages.

Single Battles

Single Battles are the most common formats that most Trainers encounter. In this format, two Trainers take each other on by sending out one single Pokémon at a time. Each turn, you and your opponent can each take one action: directing your Pokémon to use a move, using an item on one of your Pokémon, or switching your current Pokémon out for another on your team. In general, the Pokémon with the higher Speed stat gets to use its move first, though some moves are considered "priority moves" and are almost guaranteed to go first (p. 241).

Experience these battles in: wild Pokémon encounters, Trainer battles, Battle Buffet (p. 83), Battle Tree (p. 224), Link Battles (p. 305), Battle Spot (p. 305)

Double Battles

In a Double Battle between two Trainers, each Trainer sends out two Pokémon at a time. You may also encounter Double Battles in which you send out two of your Pokémon to do battle against two other Trainers at the same time, both of whom send out one Pokémon. On each turn, you and your opponent(s) pick two actions. You can direct either or both of your Pokémon to use a move, use items, or switch out one or both of your current Pokémon for another on your team. In Double Battles, the range of your Pokémon's moves becomes much more important, as does the right combination of Abilities, moves, and held items (p. 254).

Experience these battles in: Trainer battles, Battle Tree (p. 224), Link Battles (p. 305), Battle Spot (p. 305)

Multi Battles

One particular subset of the Double Battle is a Multi Battle. In this battle format, two sets of Trainers take each other on by sending out a single Pokémon each. You battle alongside a partner, but you can't control the Pokémon or moves your partner uses. Each turn, all participating Trainers each take one action: directing their Pokémon to use a move, using an item on one of their Pokémon, or switching out their current Pokémon for another on their team.

Experience these battles in: Trainer battles, Battle Tree (p. 224), Link Battles (p. 305)

Battle Royals

New to *Pokémon Sun* and *Pokémon Moon*, the Battle Royal format is a free-for-all affair in which four Trainers each send out one Pokémon. Each Trainer is free to target any of their three opponents, and battle ends as soon as one Trainer runs out of Pokémon. Each turn, each of the four Trainers chooses an action: directing their Pokémon to use a move or switching out their current Pokémon for another on their team. The strategies for this battle format are trickier, since merely keeping your Pokémon from fainting will not be enough to guarantee you a victory.

Experience these battles in: Battle Royal Dome (p. 108), Link Battles (p. 305), Battle Spot (p. 305)

SOS Battles

In a wild Pokémon encounter, a wild Pokémon may call for an ally when it feels threatened. This is known as an SOS battle (p. 63). If an ally appears, the normal Single Battle is suddenly transformed into a two-against-one affair, turning the tables on your Pokémon. To make matters worse, each SOS ally that appears increases the likelihood that additional allies will be called for if one of the wild Pokémon is left on its own again. Unless your Pokémon are vastly more powerful than their opponents, you'll need some strategy to make it through these challenging battles.

Experience these battles in: wild Pokémon encounters

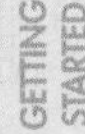

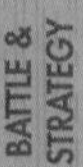

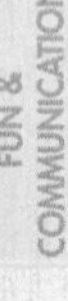

Single Battles

Now that we've introduced the five main battle formats, let's delve a little deeper into format-specific strategies. First up on the list: Single Battles!

When using attack moves

Each turn, the move you choose is used on the opposing Pokémon, your own Pokémon, or the field. If the opposing Pokémon is switched out for a different Pokémon after you select your move, the attack will target the new Pokémon that switches in. A Pokémon switch always occurs first during a turn—before any moves are used (including priority moves). The only exception to this rule is the move Pursuit, which will hit the target Pokémon before it manages to switch out.

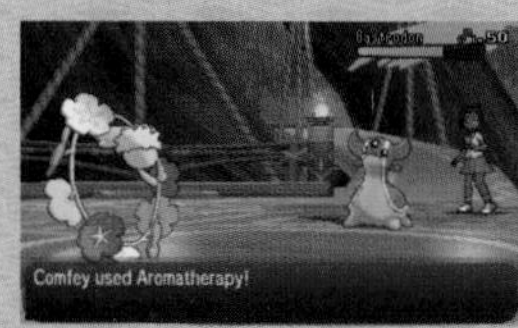

When using status moves

In Single Battles, status moves that your Pokémon uses on itself will only affect itself. Most status moves that can affect your whole team will only affect the user in Single Battles, because the user won't have any other allies in the field. Moves that only target allies (like Aromatic Mist) will fail in Single Battles.

When using Z-Power and Z-Moves

Z-Power can only be used once by each Trainer per battle (p. 72), no matter how many times you switch Pokémon in or out of the battle, so decide carefully when to use Z-Power. Remember that some Z-Moves can have special effects that will continue to affect your Pokémon after they've used the Z-Move. Consider these special effects as well when choosing a Z-Move to use. Check the tables that begin on page 318 to see the special Z-Move effects of each move.

When you affect the field

Some moves and Abilities can affect the entire battlefield. For example, Electric Terrain electrifies the field and protects Pokémon from falling Asleep. If your Pokémon has an Ability or uses a move that affects the entire field, then both your Pokémon and the opposing Pokémon will be affected by its effects.

When you switch out a Pokémon

If you choose to switch out a Pokémon, remember that the switch will occur first during that turn. This means the Pokémon you switch in will be an easy target for any incoming attacks. You can send out a Pokémon that will be super effective against the opposing Pokémon and hope it will be able to withstand this first attack, or you can consider sending out a Pokémon that might be able to resist the incoming attack, even if its moves won't be super effective.

Use combos in Single Battles!

Combos occur whenever you use a clever combination of items, Abilities, or moves to deal a lot of damage. For example, the Sturdy Ability will prevent a full-HP Pokémon from fainting when it's hit with a move that should have knocked it out, leaving it with just one HP instead. You could combine this with a move like Flail, which does more damage the less HP your Pokémon has. Or give a Pokémon that knows the move Trick an Iron Ball to hold. When it uses Trick, it will swap its item with the opponent's item, leaving the opposing Pokémon with an Iron Ball that will drag down its Speed! Always try to think of good ways to combine items, Abilities, and moves, even when you only have one Pokémon in play. Learn more about combos on page 254.

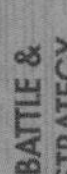

Double Battles

Most of the Single Battle format's general rules apply to Double Battles, but the effects of moves that can hit multiple targets or that affect the whole field come into play even more. You can also set up more involved combos by having your two Pokémon work together—as can your opponent!

When using attack moves

In Double Battles, if you command one of your Pokémon to use an attack that can only target a single Pokémon, then you'll have to choose which Pokémon to hit. If you've fought the opposing Pokémon before, you'll be able to see at a glance whether the attack is effective, super effective, not very effective, or completely ineffective on each of the two opposing Pokémon. You'll also see which of the Pokémon in the field will be hit by your move, should you choose to use it.

Offensive moves that affect multiple targets are listed in the following tables. Some of these moves may not have the greatest power, but they can have worthwhile additional effects, such as lowering your opponents' Speed so that you can keep hitting them first each turn. They may also have Z-Move effects: special effects that are triggered only when you use Z-Power (p. 245). Remember that a move's power is decreased when it hits multiple targets, though. The full list of Pokémon moves starts on page 318.

Damaging Moves That Hit Multiple Opponents					
Move Name	Type	Power	Accuracy	Additional Effects	Z-Move Effects
Acid	Poison	40	100	Has a slight chance of lowering opponents' Sp. Def	This move's power is boosted
Air Cutter	Flying	60	95	More likely to land a critical hit	This move's power is boosted
Blizzard	Ice	110	70	Has a slight chance of leaving opponents Frozen	This move's power is boosted
Bubble	Water	40	100	Has a slight chance of lowering opponents' Speed	This move's power is boosted
Clanging Scales	Dragon	110	100	Lowers the user's Defense	This move's power is boosted
Core Enforcer	Dragon	100	100	Negates the Abilities of any opponents that have used moves that turn and this effect will disappear if the affected Pokémon is switched out of battle	This move's power is boosted
Dazzling Gleam	Fairy	80	100	None	This move's power is boosted
Diamond Storm	Rock	100	95	May raise the user's Defense by 2 for each opponent hit by this move	This move's power is boosted
Disarming Voice	Fairy	40	—	Never misses	This move's power is boosted
Electroweb	Electric	55	95	Lowers opponents' Speed	This move's power is boosted
Eruption	Fire	150	100	The less HP the user has left, the less powerful this move becomes; removes the Frozen status condition from any Pokémon hit by this move	This move's power is boosted
Glaciate	Ice	65	95	Lowers opponents' Speed	This move's power is boosted
Heat Wave	Fire	95	90	Has a slight chance of leaving opponents Burned, and removes the Frozen status condition from any Pokémon hit by this move	This move's power is boosted
Hyper Voice	Normal	90	100	None	This move's power is boosted
Icy Wind	Ice	55	95	Lowers opponents' Speed	This move's power is boosted
Incinerate	Fire	60	100	Burns any Berries that the opponents are holding, making them unusable, and removes the Frozen status condition from any Pokémon hit by this move	This move's power is boosted
Land's Wrath	Ground	90	100	None	This move's power is boosted
Muddy Water	Water	90	85	May lower opponents' accuracy	This move's power is boosted
Origin Pulse	Water	110	85	None	This move's power is boosted
Powder Snow	Ice	40	100	Has a slight chance of leaving opponents Frozen	This move's power is boosted
Precipice Blades	Ground	120	85	None	This move's power is boosted
Razor Leaf	Grass	55	95	More likely to land a critical hit	This move's power is boosted
Razor Wind	Normal	80	100	The user stores power on the first turn, then unleashes this move on the second turn and more likely to land a critical hit	This move's power is boosted
Relic Song	Normal	75	100	Has a slight chance of making opponents fall Asleep	This move's power is boosted
Rock Slide	Rock	75	90	May make opponents flinch	This move's power is boosted
Shell Trap	Fire	150	100	Triggers an explosion if the user is hit with a physical move after setting its Shell Trap, but fails if the user is not hit with any physical moves	This move's power is boosted
Snarl	Dark	55	95	Lowers opponents' Sp. Atk	This move's power is boosted
Struggle Bug	Bug	50	100	Lowers opponents' Sp. Atk	This move's power is boosted
Swift	Normal	60	—	Never misses	This move's power is boosted
Thousand Arrows	Ground	90	100	Hits even Flying types or Pokémon with the Levitate Ability	This move's power is boosted
Thousand Waves	Ground	90	100	Makes opponents unable to flee or switch out of battle	This move's power is boosted
Twister	Dragon	40	100	Has a chance of making opponents flinch	This move's power is boosted
Water Spout	Water	150	100	The less HP the user has left, the less powerful this move becomes	This move's power is boosted

The following table lists moves that will hit multiple opponents—but which also hit your allies. Make sure that your team can take the hit before choosing to use these moves.

Damaging Moves That Hit Multiple Opponents and Your Ally					
Move Name	Type	Power	Accuracy	Additional Effects	Z-Move Effects
Boomburst	Normal	140	100	None	This move's power is boosted
Brutal Swing	Dark	60	100	None	This move's power is boosted
Bulldoze	Ground	60	100	Lowers targets' Speed	This move's power is boosted
Discharge	Electric	80	100	May leave targets with Paralysis	This move's power is boosted
Earthquake	Ground	100	100	None	This move's power is boosted
Explosion	Normal	250	100	The user faints after using this move	This move's power is boosted
Lava Plume	Fire	80	100	May leave targets Burned and heals the Frozen status condition for anyone it hits	This move's power is boosted
Magnitude	Ground	—	100	Power varies between 10 and 150	This move's power is boosted
Parabolic Charge	Electric	65	100	Restores an amount of HP to the user (this amount is equal to half the damage dealt to targets)	This move's power is boosted
Petal Blizzard	Grass	90	100	None	This move's power is boosted
Searing Shot	Fire	100	100	May leave targets Burned, and heals the Frozen status condition for any Pokémon it hits	This move's power is boosted
Self-Destruct	Normal	200	100	The user faints after using this move	This move's power is boosted
Sludge Wave	Poison	95	100	Has a slight chance of leaving targets Poisoned	This move's power is boosted
Sparkling Aria	Water	90	100	Removes the Burned status condition for all Pokémon hit with this move	This move's power is boosted
Surf	Water	90	100	None	This move's power is boosted
Synchronoise	Psychic	120	100	Deals damage to all Pokémon of the same type as the user	This move's power is boosted

Having a greater effect on the field

Not all moves that affect more than one Pokémon are attacks. In Double Battles, you may also want to use status moves that will affect both of your opponents or even everyone on the field. The following tables list the status moves that you can use to affect many Pokémon at once. Consider strategies like changing the weather (p. 146) or the terrain (p. 244) to something that will benefit your team.

Status Moves That Affect Multiple Opponents			
Move Name	Type	Additional Effects	Z-Move Effects
Captivate	Normal	Greatly lowers the opponents' Sp. Atk as long as they are of the opposite gender	The user's Sp. Def is greatly boosted
Cotton Spore	Grass	Greatly lowers the opponents' Speed, but has no effect on Grass-type Pokémon	Any lowered stats will return to normal
Dark Void	Dark	Leaves opponents Asleep	Any lowered stats will return to normal
Growl	Normal	Lowers opponents' Attack	The user's Defense is boosted
Heal Block	Psychic	Prevents opponents from recovering HP through the use of moves, Abilities, or Berries for five turns	The user's Sp. Atk is greatly boosted
Leer	Normal	Lowers opponents' Defense	The user's Attack is boosted
Poison Gas	Poison	Leaves opponents Poisoned	The user's Defense is boosted
Spikes	Ground	Deals damage to any Pokémon that switch into battle after using this move and the damage increases based on the number of times this move is used, until it maxes out after three uses	The user's Defense is boosted
Stealth Rock	Rock	Deals damage to any Pokémon that switch into battle after using this move and damage is affected by type matchup	The user's Defense is boosted
Sticky Web	Bug	Lowers the Speed of any Pokémon that switch into battle after this move was used	The user's Speed is boosted
String Shot	Bug	Greatly lowers opponents' Speed	The user's Speed is boosted
Sweet Scent	Normal	Greatly lowers opponents' evasion	The user's Accuracy is boosted
Tail Whip	Normal	Lowers opponents' Defense	The user's Attack is boosted
Toxic Spikes	Poison	Poisons any Pokémon that switch into battle after using this move and leaves them Badly Poisoned if this move was used twice, but does not work on Poison-type Pokémon	The user's Defense is boosted
Venom Drench	Poison	Lowers the Attack, Sp. Atk, and Speed of any opponents that have been already Poisoned	The user's Defense is boosted

Status Moves That Affect Both Sides of the Battle			
Move Name	Type	Additional Effects	Z-Move Effects
Electric Terrain	Electric	Turns the field for five turns into Electric Terrain (p. 244), which protects all Pokémon on the ground from falling Asleep	The user's Speed is boosted
Fairy Lock	Fairy	Pokémon will not be able to flee or swap out on the next turn	The user's Defense is boosted
Flower Shield	Fairy	Raises the Defense of any Grass types in the field	The user's Defense is boosted
Grassy Terrain	Grass	Turns the field into Grassy Terrain (p. 244) for five turns	The user's Defense is boosted
Gravity	Psychic	Raises the accuracy for all Pokémon in the field for five turns, and brings all Flying-type Pokémon and Pokémon with the Levitate Ability to the ground	The user's Sp. Atk is boosted
Hail	Ice	Changes the weather to hail (p. 146) for five turns	The user's Speed is boosted
Haze	Ice	Removes all stat changes from all Pokémon in the field	Restores the user's HP
Ion Deluge	Electric	Any Normal-type moves used in the same turn will become Electric-type moves	The user's Sp. Atk is boosted
Magic Room	Psychic	This move goes last and for the next five turns, the items of all the Pokémon in the field will have no effect	The user's Sp. Def is boosted
Misty Terrain	Fairy	Turns the field into Misty Terrain (p. 244) for five turns	The user's Sp. Def is boosted
Mud Sport	Ground	Greatly reduces the power of Electric-type moves for five turns	The user's Sp. Def is boosted
Perish Song	Normal	All Pokémon on the field at the time this move is used will faint after three turns	Any lowered stats will return to normal
Psychic Terrain	Psychic	Turns the field into Psychic Terrain (p. 244) for five turns	The user's Sp. Atk is boosted
Rain Dance	Water	Changes the weather to rain (p. 146) for five turns	The user's Speed is boosted
Rototiller	Ground	Raises the Attack and Sp. Atk of any Grass types in the field	The user's Attack is boosted
Sandstorm	Rock	Changes the weather to sandstorm (p. 146) for five turns	The user's Speed is boosted
Sunny Day	Fire	Changes the weather to harsh sunlight (p. 146) for five turns	The user's Speed is boosted
Teeter Dance	Normal	Leaves the targets confused	The user's Sp. Atk is boosted
Trick Room	Psychic	This move goes last and for the next five turns, Pokémon with lower Speed will get to move faster than those with higher Speed; does not prevent priority moves	The user's accuracy is boosted
Water Sport	Water	Greatly reduces the power of Fire-type moves for five turns	The user's Sp. Def is boosted
Wonder Room	Psychic	This move goes last and for the next five turns, all Pokémon's Defense and Sp. Def stats will be swapped	The user's Sp. Def is boosted

When using Z-Moves

Even though you have two Pokémon out in a Double Battle, you can still only use Z-Power once per battle, so decide which Pokémon you want to use your Z-Power on. Remember to consider the special effects that Z-Moves can impart, too (p. 245). You may find some of them beneficial for Double Battles, like Memento and Parting Shot, which will restore HP to whichever Pokémon switches into the battle next for your side.

Combos get creative in Double Battles!

With two Pokémon, two Abilities, and two possible held items at your disposal, you can come up with some interesting combos to dish out during Double Battles. For example, you could have one Pokémon use Sunny Day to make the weather turn to harsh sunlight, and the other use Solar Beam immediately, without having to wait a turn to charge it up like normal. Or send out a pair of Pokémon that work well together, like Gyarados and Salamence: both can learn the move Earthquake from a TM, and neither will take any damage from the move, even though it usually affects everyone on the field. Two Earthquakes in a row will really knock your foes off their feet!

Multi Battles

Multi Battles are a bit different from traditional Double Battles. A Multi Battle is still a 2-on-2 Pokémon battle, but you only control one of the Pokémon on your side of the field—the other is controlled by another Trainer. This makes it harder to set up complicated combos in advance, since you can't be sure what your partner is going to do. Each Trainer is able to use their Z-Power, however, allowing each team to unleash two Z-Moves during the battle. Other than that, the Double Battle strategies we've just covered also apply to Multi Battles.

Battle Royals

Battle Royals are similar to Multi Battles in that you and three other Trainers each send out one Pokémon to use. There are no teams in Battle Royals, though—it's every Trainer for themselves! Your goal is to defeat as many of the other Trainers' Pokémon as possible, while also keeping your Pokémon from fainting. If your team is full of slow but tough Pokémon with good HP, Defense, and Sp. Def stats, other Trainers may think twice before attacking you. However, your Pokémon may be too slow to knock out the other Trainers' Pokémon, which is just as important in this format. It's therefore important to find a good balance among your team.

When using attack moves

In Battle Royals, most move ranges are the same as those of Double Battles. The main difference is that moves with the "Many Others" range will hit all three opposing Pokémon, unlike in Double Battles where they'd only hit the two opposing Pokémon. The power of moves that can hit multiple targets is also halved, making them significantly less effective. Check the move ranges listed in the move tables to see what moves will hit "Many Others" and "Adjacent" (p. 318).

Having a greater effect on the field and "allies"

When a move affects the field in Battle Royals, all other Pokémon are considered to be in the opposing field. If a move's range is "Other Side," it will affect all three opposing Pokémon. If a move's range is "Your Side," it will only affect your Pokémon. Also, any of the other Pokémon can be your "ally" when it comes to using moves such as Helping Hand. In short, all the other Pokémon can be "allies" of yours, but they're also on the other side. A bit tricky, isn't it?

When using Z-Moves

Moves such as Protect and Detect are great defensive moves in Double Battles, so many Trainers will seek to use them in Battle Royals as well. Consider using signature Z-Moves to break through these defensive moves for a knockout. Signature Z-Moves are Z-Moves that are only available to specific species of Pokémon, such as Sinister Arrow Raid for Decidueye.

Building a Balanced Team

Imagine the first Pokémon you send out faints after getting hit by a supereffective move. Would you send out a Pokémon of the same type as the first one, knowing that it'll be vulnerable to the same move? Of course not! Ideally, the second Pokémon should be strong against it. That's how you build a balanced team. Basically, your team should form a Rock-Paper-Scissors kind of relationship, with each Pokémon compensating for its allies' weaknesses.

Pokémon Type Relationships

You learned about type matchups back on page 232. Here we detail some examples of effective type relationships. The first diagram shows that Grass type is strong against Water type, which is strong against Fire type, which is strong against Grass type. Each of these diagrams illustrates a similar relationship.

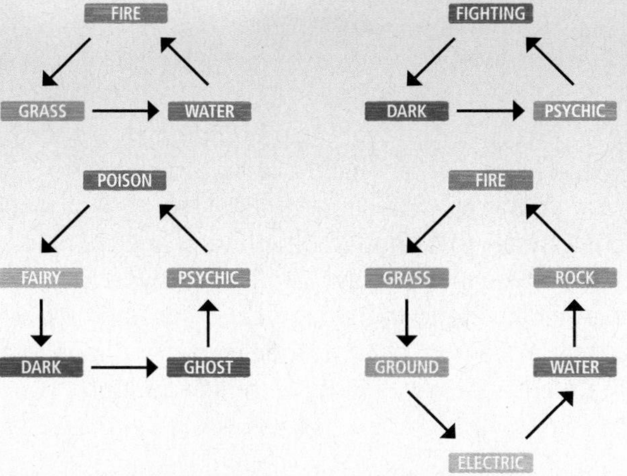

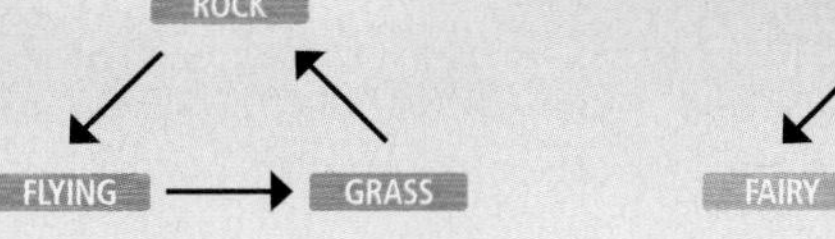

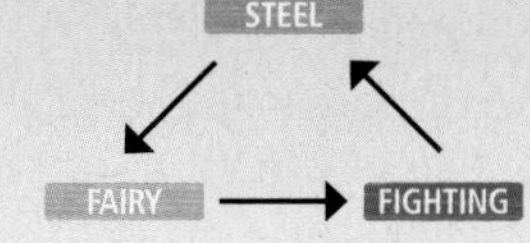

Take a look at the last example on the left here, and imagine this scenario: you have a Ground-type Pokémon, a Water-type Pokémon, and a Fire-type Pokémon. Your opponent has an Electric-type Pokémon, a Rock-type Pokémon, and a Grass-type Pokémon.

GROUND ⟶ ELECTRIC

You send out your Ground-type Pokémon, and your opponent sends out his or her Electric-type Pokémon. Now what happens? Your Ground-type Pokémon has the upper hand, so it will likely either defeat the Electric-type Pokémon, or your opponent chooses to switch it out. Assuming the latter occurs, guess which Pokémon comes next?

GRASS ⟶ GROUND

Your opponent will likely switch in their Grass-type Pokémon. You may not want to continue battling with your Ground-type Pokémon, which is weak against Grass-type moves. Which of its allies do you send out: your Water-type Pokémon, or your Fire-type Pokémon?

FIRE ⟶ GRASS

You should send out your Fire-type Pokémon, of course! It will be strong against the opposing Grass-type Pokémon!

Alolan Pokémon Type Relationships

Here is an example with Alolan Pokémon. As a Flying-type Pokémon, Oricorio is weak against Rock-type moves. That's why you want Makuhita to add its Fighting-type moves to the team—they're especially good against Rock-type Pokémon, which may be sent in by your opponent to counter Oricorio. Makuhita is weak against Psychic-type moves, so you also want to include a Cutiefly—its Bug-type moves will help you deal with any Psychic-type Pokémon that are switched in to counter Makuhita. Cutiefly is weak against Flying-type moves, but for those Flying-type Pokémon that might get sent in to counter it, you have Oricorio, which in its Pom-Pom Style form happens to be an Electric type as well as a Flying type! That Flying-type opponent won't last long against Oricorio's Electric-type moves.

Tip

Give Oricorio different kinds of nectars to change its form and type combinations, then try out different kinds of Rock-Paper-Scissors matchups! It's a very versatile Pokémon.

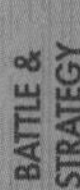

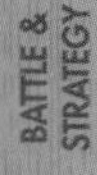

The Importance of Move Variety

If you make a team of Pokémon whose moves are all of the same type or even just a few types, what will you do if you face a Pokémon that's resistant to those types of moves? Ideally, if one of your Pokémon's moves isn't very effective against a particular type of Pokémon, another of its moves should be super effective against that type. Similarly, your team should be able to use both physical moves and special moves. A few status moves never hurt, either! Strive for variety in the types of moves that your team uses, and you'll be able to adapt to any situation.

Forming a Balanced Team

Unlike other regions where you need Pokémon that know HM moves to explore freely, you can use Ride Pokémon to go anywhere in Alola, letting you dedicate your entire team to battling. This gives you a lot of flexibility when it comes to choosing Pokémon for your team! Still, it's wise to travel with three or more Pokémon that can deal with most tough situations. Here's an example of a balanced team whose diversity in Pokémon types and move types gives it a chance to beat almost any rival.

Combine an Alolan Raichu that knows both physical and special Electric- and Psychic-type moves with an Alolan Dugtrio that knows physical Ground- and Steel-type moves, then add a Cloyster that knows both physical and special Water- and Ice-type moves. This team prepares you to do supereffective damage to thirteen different Pokémon types with just three Pokémon, plus you'll be ready for opponents with high Defense as well as those with high Sp. Def!

Organizing Your Teams

Are your PC Boxes full of Pokémon? Do you remember which of them work especially well with each other? How do you keep your combo teams neatly organized? Do you put a team in one Box, separate from the rest? What if a Pokémon from that team works well with other Pokémon as well? That's when you need the Battle Team system! Accessible from any PC, this system lets you create and store up to six unique Battle Teams. The same Pokémon can join multiple Battle Teams, and six teams should be enough for all your battling needs. For example, you could create a Battle Team for each of the following:

- Single Battle Team
- Double Battle Team
- Battle Royal Battle Team
- Online Competition Battle Team
- Live Competition Battle Team
- A team under development

Access your PC Boxes and press ⓧ twice. You'll notice that the "Team 1" Battle Team now appears on the right. Simply choose a Pokémon from your PC Box to place it on Team 1! If you want to change the name of the team, simply tap "Team 1" and change its name to "Single Battle," or anything else you'd like to name it. For further details, just tap the information icon in the bottom-right corner.

Tip

You could say that your party (the Pokémon you explore Alola with) is also a Battle Team, but they can't be used for certain battles that Battle Teams can participate in. There are also Battle Teams called QR Battle Teams, which are teams you can lend out to other players using Battle Team QR Code patterns (p. 268).

Where Your Battle Teams Can Have Fun

Where to Battle	Battle Team	Your Party	QR Battle Team
Alola region adventure	NO	YES	NO
Festival Plaza and Quick Link	YES	YES	YES
Link Battle with distributed regulations data	YES	YES	YES*
Battle Tree	YES	YES	YES
Battle Royal Dome	YES	YES	YES
Battle Spot: Free Battle	YES	YES	YES
Battle Spot: Rating Battle	YES	YES	YES*
Battle Spot: Special Battle	YES	YES	YES*
Battle Spot: Championships Battle	YES	YES	YES*
Battle Spot: Online Competition	YES	NO	NO
Battle Spot: Friendly Competition	YES	NO	NO
Live Competition	YES	NO	NO
Battle Video mock battle	YES	YES	YES

*Case by case. The availability depends on the actual regulations.

Catching the Right Pokémon

Every Pokémon is unique. Even two Pokémon of the same species (two Pikachu, for example) will differ from one another in their stats and Nature. Scour Alola to find the Pokémon that best fit with your strategies!

Using Abilities to Catch Ideal Pokémon

Some Abilities can help you find the Pokémon you want. For example, putting a Pokémon with the Synchronize Ability at the head of your party will let you find more Pokémon with the same Nature as the Pokémon with Synchronize. If you haven't yet learned about Natures and Characteristics and how they may affect the Pokémon you choose for your team, turn to page 269.

Several other Abilities can help you find the Pokémon you want if your lead Pokémon has them. Hustle, Pressure, and Vital Spirit make it easier for you to encounter high-level wild Pokémon. Keen Eye and Intimidate reduce your chances of encountering low-level wild Pokémon. Cute Charm gives you a better chance to find Pokémon of the opposite gender to the Pokémon with Cute Charm. Arena Trap and Illuminate greatly increase your rate of encountering wild Pokémon. Try to find the Ability that best suits the kind of Pokémon you want to catch, and set the Pokémon with that Ability at the head of your party.

Let's say you want to encounter a Pichu, which evolves into Pikachu and then into Alolan Raichu. You might want the lead Pokémon in your party to be a Kadabra with the Synchronize Ability and Modest Nature. Synchronize will increase your chances of finding a Pichu with the same Modest Nature as the Kadabra. Alolan Raichu has slightly stronger base stats in Sp. Atk than Attack, so you might choose to focus on raising a Raichu with high Sp. Atk, even at the cost of its Attack. Modest Nature would give your Pichu high growth in Sp. Atk and decreased growth in Attack, but you won't need a great Attack stat with powerful special attacks like Psychic and Thunderbolt.

Finding Rare Pokémon in SOS Battles

SOS battles are a great way to find Pokémon with high potential. By lowering an opposing Pokémon's HP, you can make it feel nervous and call for help, potentially introducing another wild Pokémon into the battle for a two-on-one affair. The more times a Pokémon calls for help in a battle, the higher the likelihood that its ally Pokémon will have high individual strengths (p. 272), Hidden Abilities (p. 249), or be a differently colored and extremely rare Pokémon of the species known as a Shiny Pokémon. Your chance to encounter these special Pokémon eventually peaks after lots of SOS allies have been called into the battle, and continues at that rate from there on.

To trigger an SOS Battle, enter a wild Pokémon encounter and get the opposing Pokémon's HP into the red. The opposing Pokémon may get scared and call for help. Some Pokémon species are more prone to call for help than others, while others may never call for help. An earlier Evolution of a Pokémon—like Pichu, for example—is pretty likely to call for help.

In addition, the item Adrenaline Orb, which can be bought at Poké Marts all around Alola after completing three trials, makes wild Pokémon more uneasy and thus more likely to call for help. The Pressure, Intimidate, and Unnerve Abilities also increase the chances of a Pokémon calling for help. Other factors that increase the chances of a Pokémon calling for help include:

- Whether the Pokémon called for help last turn and is calling for help this turn
- Whether the ally Pokémon that was called was hit with a supereffective attack on the first turn it appeared
- Whether the Pokémon called for help, but none appeared, the previous turn

Tip

Wild Pokémon that are suffering under status conditions, like Burned or Poisoned, won't call for help.

Building and maintaining an SOS battle chain

Basically, you want to rattle the wild Pokémon to such an extent that it gets scared and calls for help. But if you simply want to build up your chain as quickly as possible in the SOS battle, you may want your lead Pokémon to be something like an Absol with the Pressure Ability and the moves False Swipe and Leer. Pressure will increase the chances that the wild Pokémon will call for help, while False Swipe will ensure that its HP drops into the red without it fainting. Leer is a move that doesn't do damage, which is important on the turns when the wild Pokémon doesn't call for help, and you need to stall until it does. Once you find a wild Pokémon and the battle starts, you can use an Adrenaline Orb to make it jumpy, and then try to knock out each ally Pokémon it calls with supereffective moves, so that the wild Pokémon is more likely to call for help.

Just be careful, because Pressure increases the amount of PP that the opposing Pokémon uses. If it runs out of PP, it will use Struggle and knock itself out, breaking your hard-earned chain! The way around this is to start an SOS battle chain, and after the original wild Pokémon has called a fair number of SOS allies, have your Absol use False Swipe on the current SOS ally and then knock out the original wild Pokémon the following turn. This continues the chain of one low-health Pokémon calling for help. This might result in a turn in which an ally is called and doesn't appear or isn't called for at all, but don't worry: you're only concerned with the number of times a helper has been called, not with whether or not a helper has been called every turn.

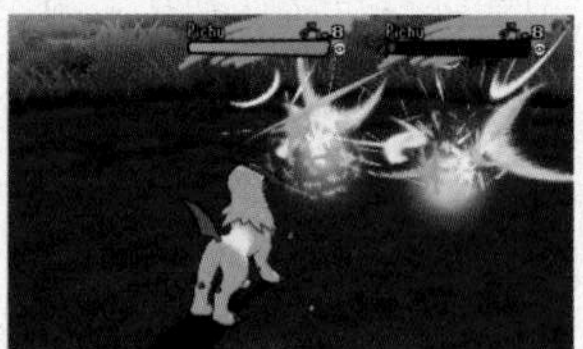

Other things you have to be careful of are moves that hit multiple opponents, like Razor Wind, in the case of Absol. You don't want to accidentally knock out both Pokémon when you are trying to carefully continue your SOS chain!

Tip

Stock up on PP-replenishing items, like Ethers and Elixirs, if you plan on being in an SOS battle for a particularly long time, such as when you're trying to catch a Shiny Pokémon.

Unexpected SOS allies

While a wild Pokémon usually calls one of its own species to help, sometimes a higher Evolution appears. In the case of your Pichu, you may find that it occasionally calls a Pikachu. Knock out Pikachu if you don't want to catch it, and the Pichu will likely call for another Pichu quite soon. Wild Pokémon may also call a different species of Pokémon entirely! For example, Pichu may sometimes call Happiny. However, if you're looking for one specific Pokémon, don't worry: most wild Pokémon will typically call their own species in SOS battles.

Catching your best SOS battle Pokémon

Once lots of SOS allies have been called for, it's time to catch the last one! This one should have several maxed individual strengths, serving as a great starting point for your ideal Alolan Raichu. Or, if you're really patient, you could keep the battle going indefinitely, chaining together the SOS calls until you encounter a Shiny Pokémon. It's up to you! Just be careful that you don't accidentally catch the original wild Pokémon that you encountered. You're looking to catch one of its SOS allies, which is far more likely to have high potential.

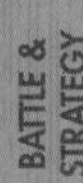

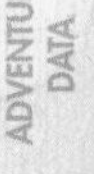

Trading

Trading Pokémon can be a key way to get the Pokémon you want for your team, as well as a great way to fill out your Pokédex and obtain rare Pokémon. In fact, trading is vital if you wish to complete your Pokédex, because some Pokémon only evolve when traded! If you can only obtain a Pokémon in the Alola Pokédex by trading and evolving it, you'll find that information in the Pokémon List on pages 280 to 287.

Tip

Pokémon you receive by trading will gain experience faster than Pokémon you catch in the wild. However, traded Pokémon will have their friendship reduced, and the nicknames of traded Pokémon can't be changed. Also, depending on their level, certain traded Pokémon may not obey you unless you've completed the necessary trials in your island challenge. See the Trainer Passport section (p. 230–231) for details.

Methods of Trading

There are many different ways to trade Pokémon with other players, be they close by or far across the world.

Method 1: Quick Link

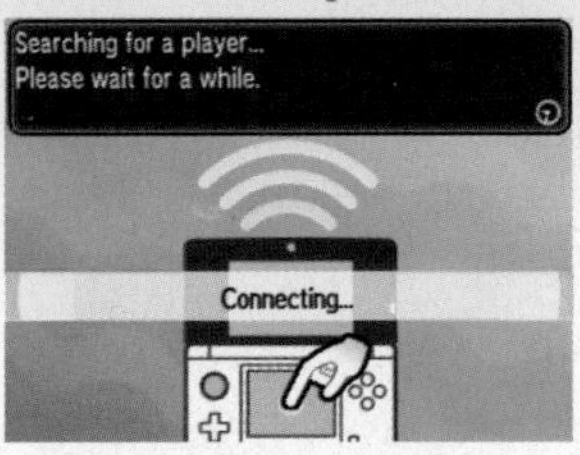

If one of your friends is playing nearby, you can both open your X menus and choose Quick Link on your respective systems to connect and trade. Touch and hold your finger or stylus to your respective Touch Screens, and in a few seconds, your systems should recognize each other, letting you trade.

Method 2: Link Trade

To trade with other players nearby or around the world, go to Festival Plaza (p. 299) and select "Trade" from the Touch Screen, then choose Link Trade. From there, select a player from the Guest list or VIP list, then select your Pokémon and choose to trade.

Method 3: GTS Trade

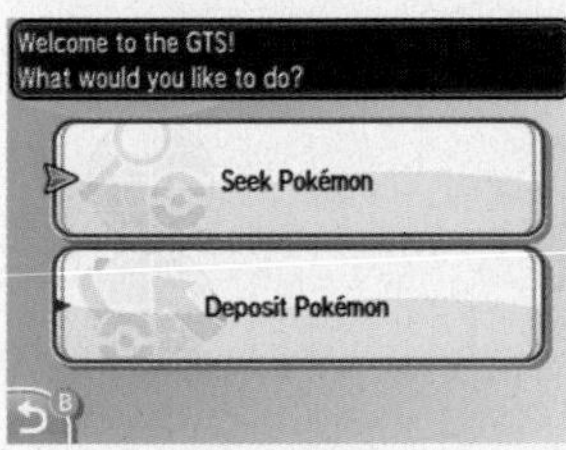

You can also go to Festival Plaza, select "Trade" from the Touch Screen, and then choose GTS (Global Trading System). You'll then have a few options:

Seek Pokémon: Select this option to browse for Pokémon based on a variety of criteria that you choose, such as its name, gender, or level.

Deposit Pokémon: Use this option to drop off a Pokémon, leaving it for others to view. If someone's interested in it, your Pokémon might be traded with a Pokémon that fulfills your search criteria!

Method 4: Wonder Trade

Lastly, you can go to Festival Plaza, select "Trade" from the Touch Screen, and then choose "Wonder Trade." Pick a Pokémon to trade away, then hold your breath as you wait to find out which Pokémon you receive in exchange! You never know which Pokémon you'll get when you use Wonder Trade, making it an exciting and unpredictable way of trading.

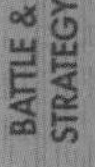

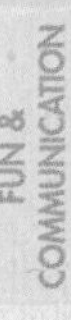

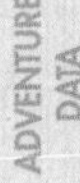

Island Scan

Want to battle and catch some rare Pokémon that aren't typically found in Alola? Island Scan has you covered! This neat feature scans the entire island that you're currently exploring, seeking out exotic Pokémon that aren't registered in the island Pokédex. That's right: Island Scan lets you find rare Pokémon that you can't usually locate in Alola!

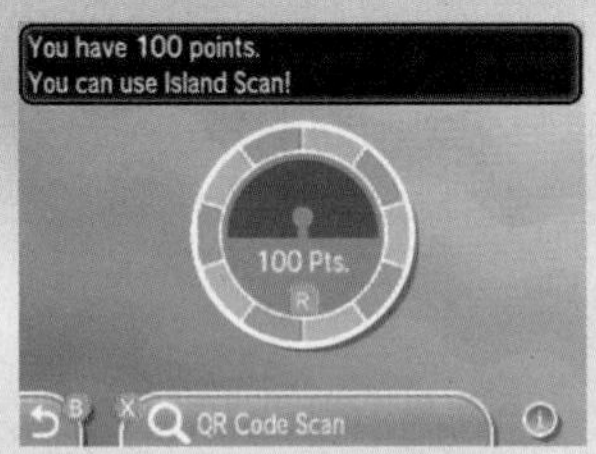

Before you can use Island Scan, you must amass 100 points by scanning QR Code patterns using the QR Scanner (p. 43).

Types of QR Code patterns

Alola Pokédex QR Code: These QR Code patterns are displayed in your Pokédex when you catch a Pokémon. They contain the information of the Pokémon you caught. By scanning an Alola Pokédex QR Code of a Pokémon you haven't seen or caught, you can register that Pokémon in your own Pokédex. You earn 10 points for each scan.

Wonder QR Code: These QR Code patterns can be found all over in the real world (p. 44). You earn 10 points for each scan.

Special QR Code: These QR Code patterns are specially prepared for the QR Scanner. Each QR Code contains the information of a particular Pokémon. You can collect 20 points for each scan.

Using Island Scan

Once you accumulate 100 points, select "Island Scan" or tap Ⓧ on the QR Scanner screen to activate Island Scan, keep pressing Ⓡ or Ⓐ, and before long the Island Scan will detect a trace of a rare Pokémon!

Hurry and search for the silhouetted Pokémon in the location where you picked up its trace. The Pokémon won't linger in that location for long, so get out there and catch it while you can! When time runs out, the trace of the Pokémon will fade, and the Island Scan will end. Island Scans also end if you catch the Pokémon or make it faint.

Pokémon Found with Island Scan

The Pokémon that you trace by Island Scan vary, depending on the island you're currently exploring and the current day of the week.

Melemele Island			Akala Island			Ula'ula Island			Poni Island		
Day	Pokémon	Location	Day	Pokémon	Location	Day	Pokémon	Location	Day	Pokémon	Location
Monday	Totodile	Seaward Cave	Monday	Spheal	Route 7	Monday	Swinub	Tapu Village	Monday	Conkeldurr	Poni Plains
Tuesday	Deino	Ten Carat Hill	Tuesday	Luxio	Route 8	Tuesday	Duosion	Route 16	Tuesday	Togekiss	Poni Gauntlet
Wednesday	Horsea	Kala'e Bay	Wednesday	Honedge	Akala Outskirts	Wednesday	Roselia	Ula'ula Meadow	Wednesday	Leavanny	Poni Meadow
Thursday	Klink	Hau'oli City	Thursday	Venipede	Route 4	Thursday	Staravia	Route 10	Thursday	Serperior	Exeggutor Island
Friday	Chikorita	Route 2	Friday	Bellsprout	Route 5	Friday	Vigoroth	Route 11	Friday	Samurott	Poni Wilds
Saturday	Litwick	Hau'oli Cemetery	Saturday	Marill	Brooklet Hill	Saturday	Axew	Mount Hokulani	Saturday	Emboar	Ancient Poni Path
Sunday	Cyndaquil	Route 3	Sunday	Gothita	Route 6	Sunday	Rhyhorn	Blush Mountain	Sunday	Eelektross	Poni Grove

Other QR Code Patterns

Lastly, there are a few other QR Code patterns that you should know about.

Battle Team QR Code

Link your game with the PGL (p. 315) and you can create a QR Code for one of your Battle Teams and make it public on the PGL website. You can also "rent" other people's QR Battle Teams: just scan their Battle Team QR Code on the PGL when choosing a Battle Team to use in your game. Note that certain battles don't allow for QR Battle Teams (p. 264).

Friendly Competition QR Code

Friendly Competition lets you host original competitions where you set the regulations. Set one up on the PGL (p. 315) and the regulations will be saved in a Friendly Competition QR Code for each player. By scanning in that QR Code, participants will be able to battle according to the competition's regulations.

Live Competition QR Code

Live Competitions are special competitions where you gather together with other players in the same place and have battles. In addition to officially held Live Competitions, now you can host a Live Competition as a Friendly Competition. Set one up from the PGL (p. 315) with special regulations, and have players join by selecting "Live Competition" from the title menu and scanning in the Live Competition QR Code you generate.

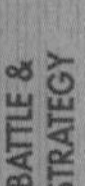

Training the Most Powerful Pokémon

You probably know the basics of training your Pokémon by now. You know that Pokémon level up by earning Exp. Points from battles, and that their stats increase as they level up. You know that there are stats like Attack and Sp. Atk that affect how hard your moves hit, and stats like Defense and Sp. Def which affect how much damage your Pokémon take from hits (p. 7). You probably even know that you can use items in battle, like X Attacks, to give your stats a temporary boost. But do you know all of the factors that will have a permanent effect on your Pokémon's stats?

Factors that affect Pokémon stats

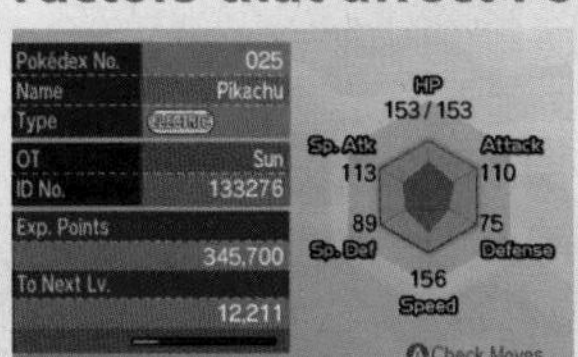

Four factors determine how powerful your particular Pokémon's stats will become: its species strengths, Nature, individual strengths, and base stats. When you catch a Pokémon, you can't change the first two of these factors—but with effort, you can affect a Pokémon's individual strengths and base stats. And if you're an expert Pokémon Egg finder, you can even affect Nature as well by finding a Pokémon Egg that will hatch into a Pokémon with the exact Nature you want. More on that can be found on page 289.

Checking a Pokémon's stat growth

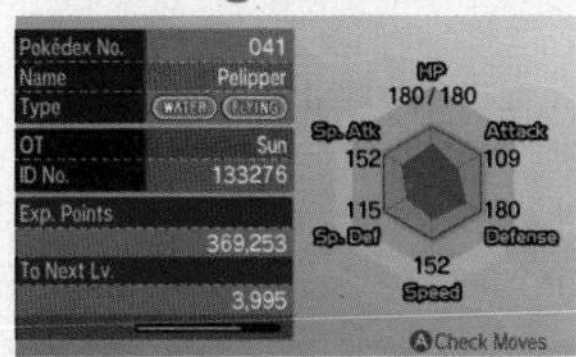

Overall stat growth

Some of these factors can be viewed at your Pokémon's Summary page. Select a Pokémon and look at the top screen. A blue graph is shown by default. This graph shows how your Pokémon's stats are growing. If a particular stat is maxed as high as it can be, the blue area will reach all the way to the graph's outer edge.

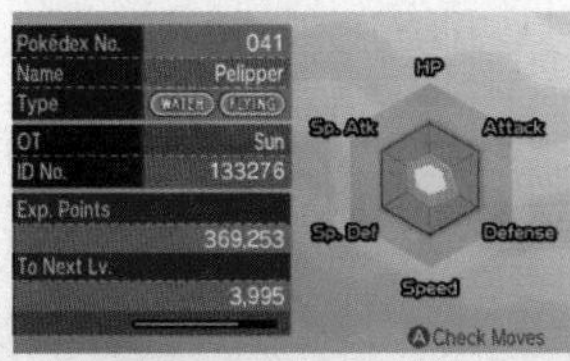

Species strengths (yellow) and base stat growth (orange)

Press ⓨ, and the graph will change. This orange and yellow graph shows two things: the yellow section shows your Pokémon's species strengths, and the orange section shows how your Pokémon's base stats have been growing.

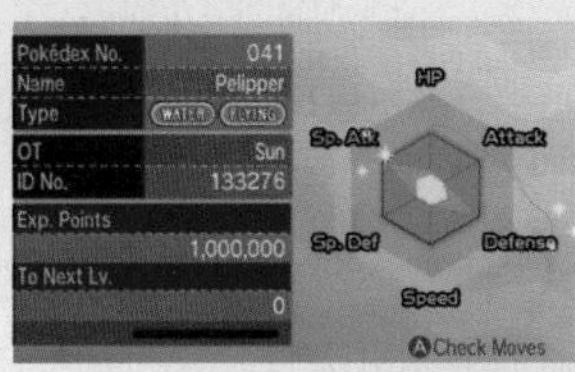

Species strengths (yellow) and maxed out base stat growth (blue)

When a particular base stat has been maxed out, you'll see sparkles appearing near the name of that stat. When your Pokémon has run out of base points and cannot increase any base stats further, this part of the graph will turn blue. See page 272 for more on base points.

Why worry about this stuff?

Is trying to raise the absolute best Pokémon really worth it? Well, that depends on what you want to do with your team. It's not necessary if you simply wish to complete the main story of *Pokémon Sun* and *Pokémon Moon*, though it will make your adventure easier. But if you want to take on difficult challenges like the Battle Buffet (p. 83), the Battle Tree (p. 224), Online Competitions (p. 306), or competitive play, then you'll definitely want to read on!

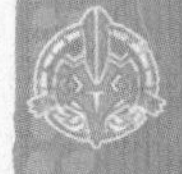

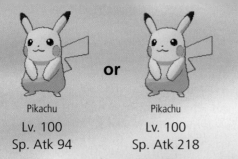

Pikachu
Lv. 100
Sp. Atk 94

or

Pikachu
Lv. 100
Sp. Atk 218

Take two Pikachu, both raised up to Lv. 100 from hours of play. A Pikachu with an ill-suited Nature, poor individual strengths, and no base stat training for Sp. Atk might end up with a Sp. Atk stat of 94. A Pikachu with the right Nature, the best individual strengths, and max base stats might have a Sp. Atk stat of 218. Which one do you think stands a better chance of winning a battle?

Species Strengths

A Pokémon's species affects how quickly its stats will grow as it levels up. The strengths of each species are illustrated in an official Pokédex by the number of colored boxes or dots that appear next to each stat. The greater the species strength for the stat, the more that stat will grow each time the Pokémon levels up. Species strengths can't be changed, so if you want to take the fullest advantage of them, you have to choose the right species of Pokémon for the role you want it to play on your team. Should it be a quick hitter, sacrificing defense to deal serious damage? Or a hardy ally that can absorb a lot of damage while still unleashing powerful attacks? Take a look at these examples:

SPECIES STRENGTHS

HP
Attack
Defense
Sp. Atk
Sp. Def
Speed

Absol

SPECIES STRENGTHS

HP
Attack
Defense
Sp. Atk
Sp. Def
Speed

Bewear

Tip

Absol and Bewear are both great attackers, but the way you use them in battle and the types of moves you teach them will likely differ. Perhaps you'd teach Absol high-priority moves, like Sucker Punch, so that it can quickly land some hits before it takes too much damage. But with Bewear's great HP and an Ability like Fluffy, you could consider powerful moves like Payback—which deals more damage after taking a hit from an opponent—or Double Edge, which damages the user as well as the target.

Absol may have the highest species strength for the Attack stat, but its HP is quite slow to grow, and its Defense and Sp. Def stats aren't particularly impressive. It has a decent Sp. Atk though, allowing it to use both physical and special attacks effectively (p. 7). Absol may hit hard, but can it take a hit?

Then there's Bewear. Its Attack stat will grow nearly as quick as Absol's, but it also has fantastic species strength for HP. If you want a Pokémon that can dish out and take attacks, it might be the wiser choice here for a physical attacker. Just don't expect Bewear to impress as much with special attacks thanks to that lower Sp. Atk growth rate.

Alolan Pokémon with great species strengths

Pokémon whose HP grows quickly	Pokémon whose Attack grows quickly	Pokémon whose Defense grows quickly
Blissey NORMAL	Rampardos ROCK	Cloyster WATER ICE
Wailord WATER	Archeops ROCK FLYING	Bastiodon ROCK STEEL
Alomomola WATER	Wishiwashi (School Form) WATER	Toxapex POISON WATER

Pokémon whose Sp. Atk grows quickly	Pokémon whose Sp. Def grows quickly	Pokémon whose Speed grows quickly
Vikavolt BUG ELECTRIC	Goodra DRAGON	Crobat POISON FLYING
Wishiwashi (School Form) WATER	Probopass ROCK STEEL	Aerodactyl ROCK FLYING
Drampa NORMAL DRAGON	Carbink ROCK FAIRY	Talonflame FIRE FLYING

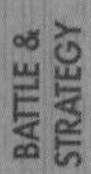

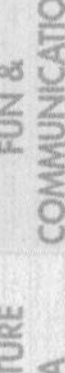

Eevee's Evolutionary Advantages

Eevee's Evolutions often have great species strengths, making them popular choices for any team. You can hatch an Eevee from the Egg you are given at the Pokémon Nursery (p. 288), or catch one in the tall grass in Route 6 if you're lucky.

Below is a guide to Eevee's Evolution's best stats. The stats listed below each particular Evolution indicate that its species strength for that stat is among the top percentile of all Pokémon found in the Alola region.

Vaporeon: HP / Sp. Atk

Jolteon: Speed / Sp. Atk

Flareon: Attack / Sp. Def

Espeon: Sp. Atk / Speed

Umbreon: Sp. Def / Defense

Leafeon: Defense / Attack

Glaceon: Sp. Atk / Defense

Sylveon: Sp. Def / Sp. Atk

Nature

Each Pokémon has an innate Nature, which also affects how its stats grow. Natures can't be changed once you've caught a Pokémon, and they typically make one stat grow more quickly than average, while another stat grows more slowly than it normally would. Check a Pokémon's Summary page to see which stats are affected by its Nature.

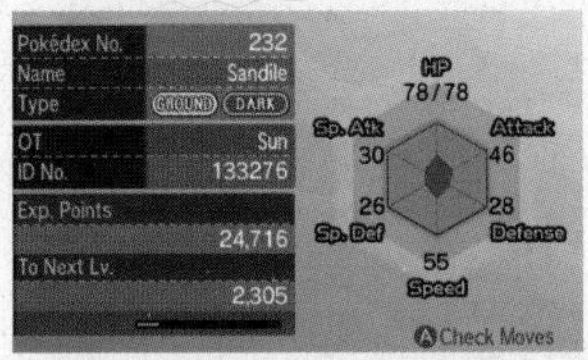

Any pink stat will increase more quickly than average upon leveling up, while any blue stat will increase more slowly than average. Make sure the stat you want to focus on is pink—and also that no stat that your Pokémon really needs is blue. The full table of Natures is on page 340 but here are some of the most coveted Natures:

Nature	Effect	Notes
Adamant	Attack grow faster, Sp. Atk grows slower	Good for physical-move-only users
Jolly	Speed grows faster, Sp. Atk grows slower	Good for physical move users that need to be fast
Modest	Sp. Atk grows faster, Attack grows slower	Good for special-move-only users
Timid	Speed grows faster, Attack grows slower	Good for special move users that need to be fast

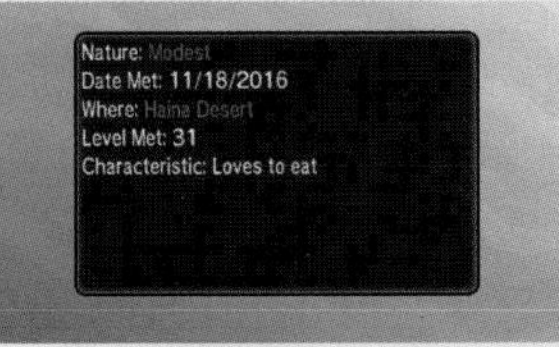

You can pass Natures on to Pokémon that hatch from Eggs, as is described on page 289. Otherwise, you'll just have to try to catch a Pokémon with the Nature you want. There's no item or method that can change the Nature that a Pokémon has after it has been caught or hatched from a Pokémon Egg.

Tip

The Synchronize Ability can help you catch Pokémon with the Nature you want. Put a Pokémon with this Ability at the head of your team, and you'll have a 50/50 chance of encountering wild Pokémon with the same Nature as your team's lead Pokémon. Search Hau'oli City's tall grass for an Abra with the Synchronize Ability and the Nature you want, then put it at the head of your party. You'll then start catching Pokémon with Abra's same Nature in no time.

Individual Strengths

Two Pokémon of the same species and with the same Nature can still differ in how quickly their stats will grow. This difference is partly due to the individual strengths possessed by each Pokémon. Individual Pokémon, even those of the same species, are just naturally a bit better in one area than another. If you think your Pokémon's individual strengths leave something to be desired, then perhaps they could use some Hyper Training! Turn to page 275 to discover how Hyper Training can increase your Pokémon's individual strengths.

After you clear your game and reach the Battle Tree, you can meet a mysterious man. He'll upgrade your PC Boxes to add the Judge function, which lets you check the individual strengths of any Pokémon in your Boxes, if you've kept yourself busy hatching Pokémon Eggs. If your Pokémon's stats are described as having "Outstanding potential!" on the upper screen, then you can rest assured that some of its stats have the highest individual strengths possible.

Tip

If you had to pick one stat to improve your Pokémon's individual strengths for, most Trainers would probably choose Speed. A few points difference in Attack may not make or break a battle, but having a Speed stat even a single point greater than its opponent will mean that your Pokémon gets to dish out its move first in battle!

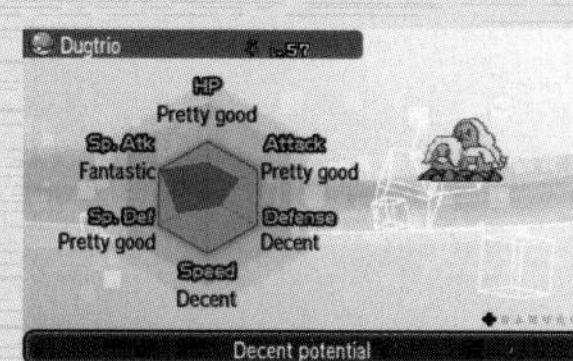

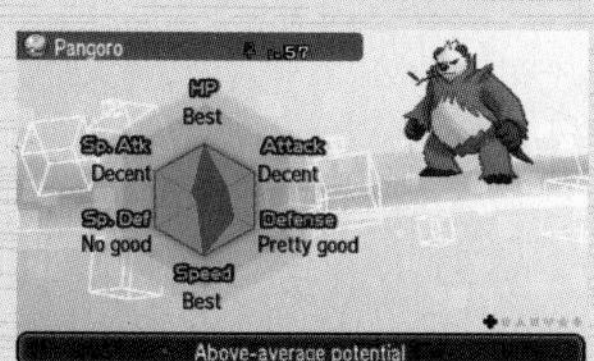

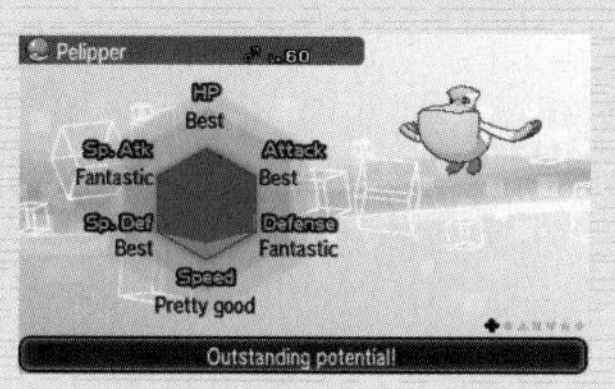

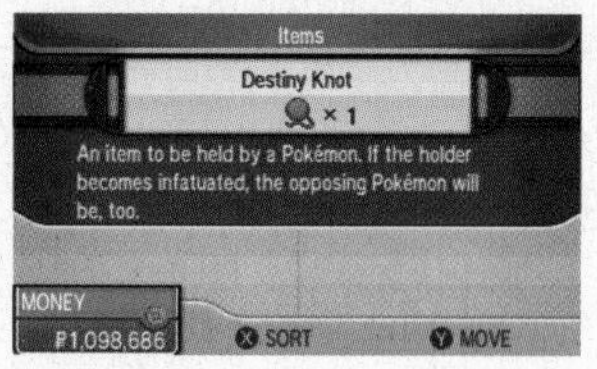

Hyper Training is the only way to change individual strengths for a Pokémon that you've already caught. However, you can also pass individual strengths on to Pokémon that you hatch from Pokémon Eggs by giving the Pokémon that you leave at the Pokémon Nursery special items to hold, like a Power Anklet or a Destiny Knot. (This does not pass on the gains that your Pokémon may have received from Hyper Training, but only the individual strengths they were born with.) See page 288 to learn more about how to pass traits on to Pokémon that hatch from Eggs.

Base Stats

Base stats are stats that can be actively affected each time you win a battle. Each opposing Pokémon that you battle against can affect a different base stat, awarding some base points to your Pokémon's base HP, base Attack, base Defense, base Sp. Atk, base Sp. Def, or base Speed if you defeat it. You accumulate points until your Pokémon has reached the maximum number of base points that any one Pokémon can earn (510 points, to be precise). The number of base points your Pokémon has accumulated for each base stat are then used to calculate its final HP, Attack, Defense, Sp. Atk, Sp. Def, and Speed stats. So increasing base stats will increase your Pokémon's final stats and once you have distributed all 510 base points to your base stats, your Pokémon's base stats will not change unless you purposefully lower them.

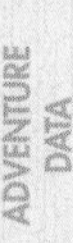

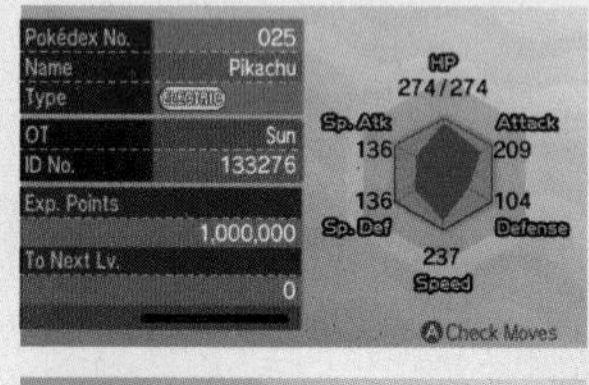

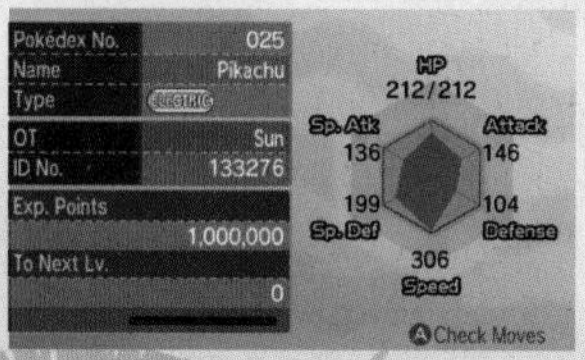

This is just one example of how two seemingly-identical Pikachu could end up with different stats thanks to how their base stats were distributed.

Why would anyone want to lower their Pokémon's base stats? Each base stat can only be raised by a certain number of points (252, to be exact). With a limited amount of points available to you, you can only max out two possible base stats. If your Pokémon has accumulated several points on each of its six base stats through battle, you'll no longer be able to max out two of its base stats—and your Pokémon may end up at a disadvantage to another Pokémon that has successfully maxed out two base stats. This is why you may want to lower the base points that were already added to one of your Pokémon's base stats, as described on page 274. Before we move onto ways to lower base stats, though, let's look at all the ways you can raise them.

Battle to increase base stats

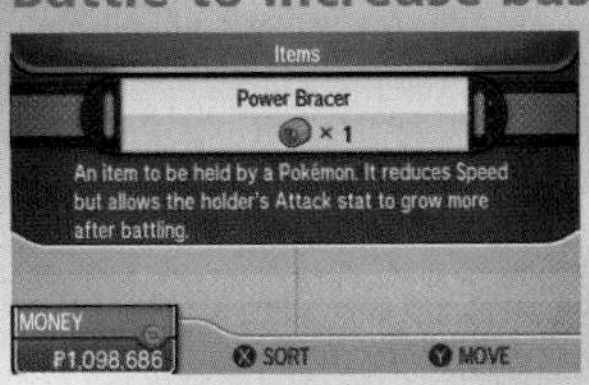

If you choose to raise your Pokémon's base stats through battle, know that a few items can help certain base stats grow faster than normal. The same items that help you pass on individual strengths to Pokémon Eggs will also help your Pokémon's base stats grow if they're held during battles. These items will temporarily reduce your Pokémon's Speed, but they also save you from having to seek out particular Pokémon to battle in the wild. (But you may then have to use Berries or other means to reduce other base stat gains you do not want to keep.)

- **Power Weight**: Increases base HP every time you defeat a Pokémon, but reduces Speed while held
- **Power Bracer**: Increases base Attack stat every time you defeat a Pokémon, but reduces Speed while held
- **Power Belt**: Increases base Defense stat every time you defeat a Pokémon, but reduces Speed while held
- **Power Lens**: Increases base Sp. Atk stat every time you defeat a Pokémon, but reduces Speed while held
- **Power Band**: Increases base Sp. Def stat every time you defeat a Pokémon, but reduces Speed while held
- **Power Anklet**: Increases base Speed stat every time you defeat a Pokémon, but reduces Speed while held
- **Macho Brace**: Doubles all base stat gains earned from battles when held, but reduces Speed while held

Use Festival Plaza to increase base stats

At Festival Plaza, your Pokémon can raise their base stats by playing at the bouncy houses (p. 301). Fill your Festival Plaza with different types of bouncy houses to improve the stats that you want, then select an appropriate course. In just moments, your Pokémon's base stats will improve! You'll need Festival Coins (FC) for each session, though.

Use Poké Pelago to increase base stats

You can also help raise the base stats of whole groups of Pokémon at once using Poké Pelago's Isle Evelup (p. 312). This is the most efficient method, because you can raise the base stats of several Pokémon simultaneously, and it doesn't cost you a thing—except for the Poké Beans you may have used to develop the isle. Select an appropriate drink, and all Pokémon in the group will see their corresponding base stats grow with a bit of time.

Use items to increase base stats

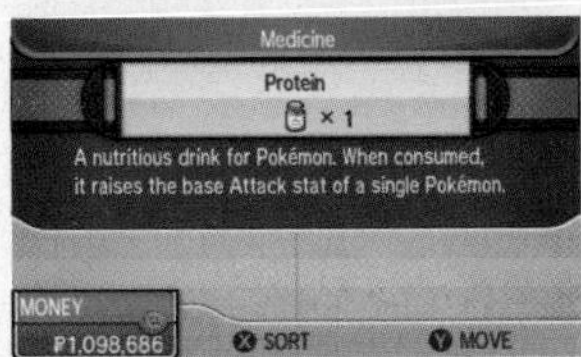

Certain items can also help you increase base stats. The first set of these are all nutritious drinks, which can be purchased at the Pokémon Center on Mount Hokulani (p. 151), or at Festival Plaza in exchange for FC (p. 299) if you're really enjoying communication features.

- **HP Up**: Raises the base HP of a single Pokémon when consumed
- **Protein**: Raises the base Attack stat of a single Pokémon when consumed
- **Iron**: Raises the base Defense stat of a single Pokémon when consumed
- **Calcium**: Raises the base Sp. Atk stat of a single Pokémon when consumed
- **Zinc**: Raises the base Sp. Def stat of a single Pokémon when consumed
- **Carbos**: Raises the base Speed stat of a single Pokémon when consumed

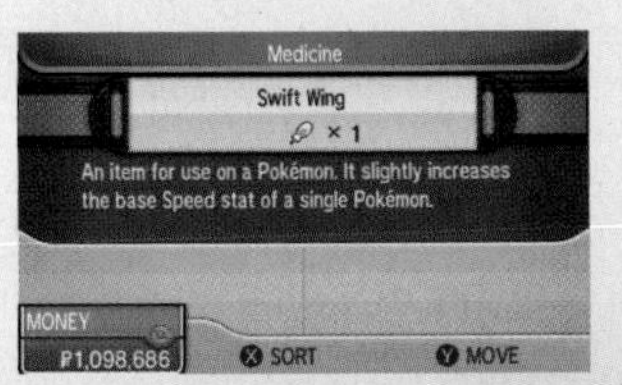

Wing items (namely the Health Wing, Muscle Wing, Resist Wing, Genius Wing, Clever Wing, and Swift Wing) can also raise base stats, but by a lesser degree. These items are also much harder to come by. They sometimes drop after you're ambushed by a bird Pokémon swooping down on you from above, like the ones that dive off the shaking trees on Route 10. But with no way to guarantee which item you'll get, and with each item having such a relatively small effect, it'll be much faster and more efficient to rely on one of the previously detailed methods. Still, if you happen to have any of these Wings in your Bag, feel free to use them!

Keys to maxing out your Pokémon's base stats

As you've learned, you can distribute 510 points to all of a Pokémon's base stats, but each base stat can only be raised by a maximum of 252 points. You could choose to max out two base stats at 252 points each (and have 6 points left over), or you could spread those 510 points among three or more base stats, giving each stat a smaller boost. If your Pokémon has already gained points in various stats through battling, then you may not be able to max out two of its stats. In this case, you'll first need to lower some or all of its base stats to free up some points, then use one of the previously described methods to max only the stats you desire.

Lowering a Pokémon's base stats

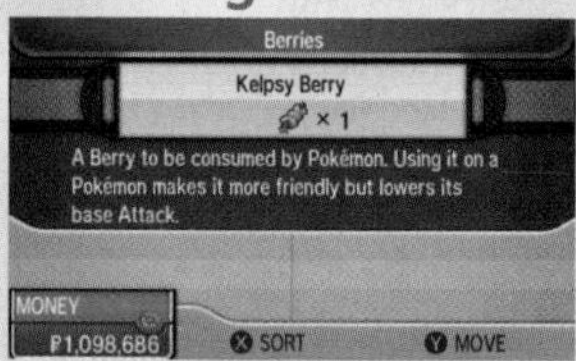

If you want to lower a Pokémon's base stats so that you can start fresh with it, consider using some specific Berries. The following Berries can be found beneath Berry trees in the Alola region, and they lower a Pokémon's base stats when consumed. Once you discover one of these useful Berries, plant it on Poké Pelago's Isle Aplenny (p. 311) to grow more. See page 349 for the full list of Berry trees found around Alola.

- **Pomeg Berry:** Lowers a Pokémon's base HP
- **Kelpsy Berry**: Lowers a Pokémon's base Attack stat
- **Qualot Berry**: Lowers a Pokémon's base Defense stat
- **Hondew Berry**: Lowers a Pokémon's base Sp. Atk stat
- **Grepa Berry**: Lowers a Pokémon's base Sp. Def stat
- **Tamato Berry**: Lowers a Pokémon's base Speed stat

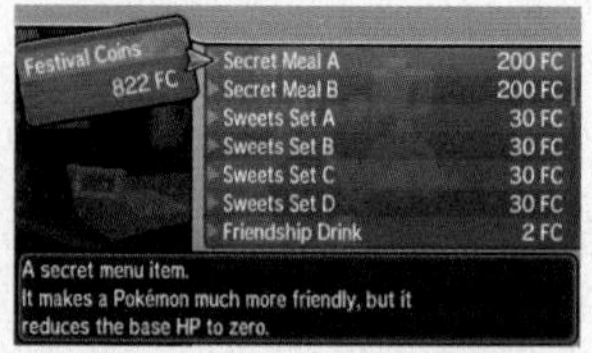

If you've been working on developing your Festival Plaza, then you can also lower your Pokémon's base stats with some special foods bought at the food stalls there (p. 302). You'll need some FC to spend and these meals are only available to real Champions, but it's another great option!

Tip

Pokémon hatched from Pokémon Eggs have no points in their base stats, letting you start fresh with a clean slate. Ah, youth!

What about Characteristics?

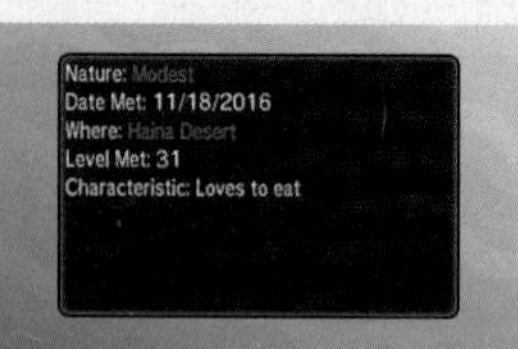

A Characteristic is another bit of information that appears on your Pokémon's Summary page. Wondering what it means? Characteristics don't actually affect how your Pokémon's stats grow. They just give you a clue about where your Pokémon's individual strengths might lie. The full table of Characteristics, and the stats each one matches up with, can be found on page 340.

Hyper Training

Yes
No
What do you say? Want to try some of my Hyper Training to boost your Pokémon's stats?

A fine fellow by the name of Mr. Hyper can be found near the Move Tutors in the Hau'oli City Shopping Mall (p. 81) after you become Champion. Speak with him to put your Pokémon through a performance-enhancing program known as Hyper Training! Hyper Training lets you boost a Pokémon's individual strength for each stat to the max, but only Pokémon that have reached Lv. 100 can undergo Hyper Training. You'll also need to hand Mr. Hyper a Bottle Cap or Gold Bottle Cap in order to put your Pokémon through his program.

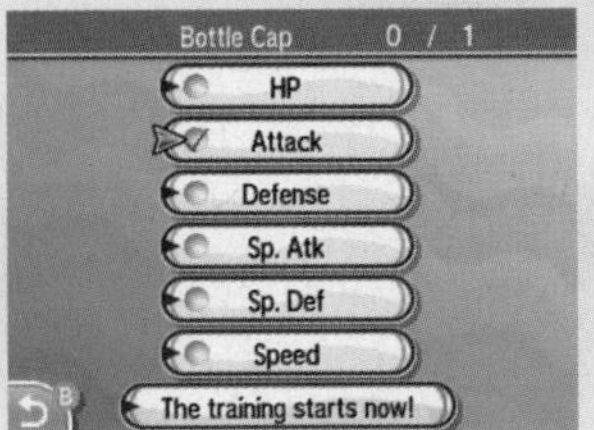
Bottle Cap 0 / 1
HP
Attack
Defense
Sp. Atk
Sp. Def
Speed
The training starts now!

Hyper Training can boost a Pokémon's six stats: HP, Attack, Defense, Sp. Atk, Sp. Def, and Speed. Gold Bottle Caps let you to boost all of these stats, while regular Bottle Caps let you boost just one of them. Once a stat has been boosted through Hyper Training, it reaches its max level and can't be boosted any further through Hyper Training. In addition, you can't use Hyper Training to boost a stat that your Pokémon already had the best possible individual strength for.

Tip

Any individual strengths passed on to Pokémon Eggs found at the Pokémon Nursery will be those from before the Pokémon underwent Hyper Training. The gains a Pokémon gets from Hyper Training cannot be inherited.

Obtaining Bottle Caps

There are several ways to get Bottle Caps and Gold Bottle Caps:

In Festival Plaza (p. 299), you can win Bottle Caps and Gold Bottle Caps as prizes at lottery shops.

In Festival Plaza, your Pokémon may find Bottle Caps in haunted houses.

Yes
No
Maybe...perhaps...by any chance, are you interested in Bottle Caps?

Once you've entered the Hall of Fame, an old man appears in the castle in Festival Piaza. He'll trade you Bottle Caps in exchange for colored shards, which can be found on Isle Aphun (p. 311).

You can score one Bottle Cap each day by winning 30 consecutive battles at the Battle Tree (p. 224). Return to the Battle Tree on the next day to claim your prize.

You can get Bottle Caps by fishing on Poni Island.

Paths to Explore
Path for Rare-Treasure Hunting!
Your Pokémon will explore deep into the underground. They may find rare treasures.
Confirm

Your Pokémon also have a slight chance to find Gold Bottle Caps when they go exploring certain paths on Isle Aphun (p. 311).

Tip

Bottle Caps take some work to find, so if you're looking to put together a competitive team, you may not want to use them on a Pokémon with the wrong Nature. Flip back to page 269 for a refresher on how to maximize your Pokémon's stats.

You can get a Bottle Cap from Captain Mina by beating her at the Poni Gauntlet (p. 223).

Benefits of Affection in Battle

A Pokémon's affection for its Trainer can be a truly advantageous bond. Through the use of Pokémon Refresh, you can increase your Pokémon's level of affection toward you, gaining a number of special benefits that manifest in battle. Note however that these benefits will not occur in Link Battles or in battles waged at battle facilities, such as the Battle Tree and Battle Royal Dome. The table below summarizes some of the main effects of Affection in battle.

Affection Level	♡×2	♡×3	♡×4	♡×5
Effects	Enters battle with a special motion	All the previous effects, plus...	All the previous effects, plus...	All the previous effects, plus...
	Earns a bit more Exp. Points from battle	May occasionally survive what would normally be a one-hit knockout	May spontaneously recover from status conditions	May dodge an opponent's attack
	May see special messages in battle	May see more unique messages in battle	May see more unique messages in battle	More likely to land critical hits

Pokémon Refresh

Everyone needs a little TLC, and Pokémon are no exception. Use Pokémon Refresh to make your Pokémon more affectionate toward you by feeding them yummy Poké Beans and caring for them in a variety of ways.

Opening Pokémon Refresh

Once you have access to Pokémon Refresh, you can use it anytime from the X menu. You can also open Pokémon Refresh by tapping the "Care" button that pops up on the Touch Screen after certain battles, such as when your Pokémon are affected by moves that cause status conditions, or when they use or are hit by moves that can muss up their fur, or make them dirty, sandy, or wet.

The way in which you open Pokémon Refresh matters, because you can only use the special grooming tools after pressing the Care button. So, if you really want to comb, brush, towel off, or blow dry your Pokémon, you'll want it to use or get hit by moves such as Dig, which always makes the Pokémon using it or hit by it dirty—provided the Pokémon is capable of becoming dirty. (Grimer, for example, does not get "dirty.")

Care Button Benefits

There are two benefits to pushing the Care button after a battle. First, if your Pokémon is affected by a status condition, you can cure it without having to use an item—a great way to save your hard-earned money. Second, caring for your Pokémon raises its affection toward you.

Tap and drag the appropriate tool down to the afflicted area on your Pokémon, then rub around until the symptom is relieved and disappears. Don't worry if you pick the wrong tool, you can just choose another until you find the right one. Keep going until hearts appear over your Pokémon's head. That's when you know all its symptoms have been relieved! You'll then be able to pet it, feed it Poké Beans, or switch to a different Pokémon by tapping the Poké Ball button in the Touch Screen's lower right corner.

Petting Your Pokémon

Once you've opened Pokémon Refresh, you can touch your Pokémon with your finger or a stylus, rubbing it and petting it to increase its affection toward you. Most Pokémon have "sweet spots" where they like to be touched, as well as areas of their body that rub them the wrong way (such as Popplio's collar). A Pokémon may react grumpily or sadly if you poke at it or rub its sensitive spots, although neither of these actions will lower its affection toward you.

Tip

Some Pokémon may give you a little shock or singe your hand if you touch them in the right spot. (The hand icon, that is—not your actual hand!) Try it out by petting Pichu's cheeks!

Feeding Your Pokémon

Filling your Pokémon's tummy with tasty Poké Beans is another way to raise its affection toward you. Just tap the Poké Bean icon in the top-left corner to open your supply of Poké Beans, then tap, hold, and drag a Poké Bean to your Pokémon's mouth. Hold it there, and the Pokémon will quickly scarf it down if it's hungry. Just don't let go, or the Poké Bean may fall to the ground—and there's no "five second rule" for Poké Beans!

Tip

A Poké Bean's pattern determines its impact on your Pokémon's affection. You can feed them Plain, Patterned, or Rainbow Beans, which increase its affection either a little, a fair amount, or a lot, respectively. Get more Poké Beans at Pokémon Center cafés or at Poké Pelago (p. 309) once you have access to it!

Checking and Switching Pokémon

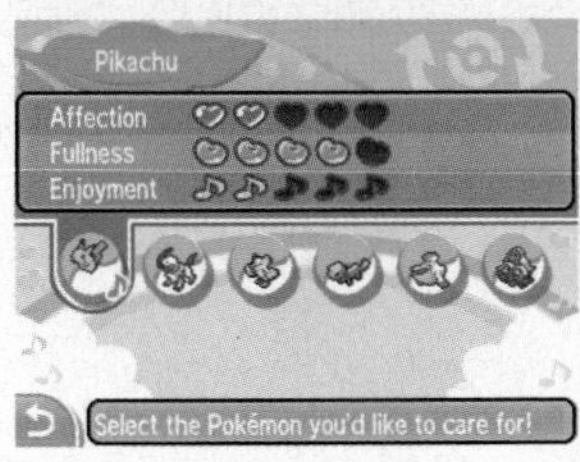

To check your Pokémon's levels or switch in another Pokémon, tap the little Poké Ball button in the Touch Screen's lower right corner. You'll then see the level of affection, fullness, and enjoyment of your Pokémon.

Affection, or how your Pokémon feels about you, is covered in detail on page 276. Raise it by petting your Pokémon or feeding them Poké Beans or malasadas (p. 57).

Fullness indicates how hungry the Pokémon is. It fills when you feed your Pokémon Poké Beans or malasadas, and goes down when you battle or walk around the field.

Enjoyment indicates how satisfied your Pokémon is. It fills when you pet your Pokémon. Once maxed, enjoyment won't go any higher until it goes down again by battling or walking around.

Completing Your Pokédexes

Hundreds of unique Pokémon can be found in the Alola region. Catching one of each species is ideal, but simply battling against a Pokémon is enough to register its basic data in your Pokédex.

Checking Your Progress

25%
Even Pokémon love the big city life sometimezzz...
Kick around in Hau'oli City's grass patches to find 'em!

Rotom happily evaluates your Pokédex for you any time you ask. Tap the dark spot between Rotom's eyes on the Touch Screen to quickly call up the Pokédex (or open your Pokédex from the X menu), then tap "Pokédex Evaluation" at the bottom of the Touch Screen. Listen carefully to Rotom's advice and encouragement, then get out there and find those Pokémon!

Rewards for Completing Island Pokédexes

Completing your Pokédex isn't just fun and informative, it also has several special benefits.

After registering 10 Pokémon, speak to the researcher in Hau'oli City's tourist bureau to receive 10 Ultra Balls!

Get a stamp (p. 230) from the game director at GAME FREAK's office in Heahea City each time you complete an Island Pokédex!

Get a Lucky Egg from Professor Kukui once you've become a Champion and registered at least 50 Pokémon in your Pokédexes.

Tips for Completing Your Pokédex

Technique 1: Catch Wild Pokémon

Many Pokémon can be encountered simply by running through Alola's tall grass, deserts, and caves. You'll also obtain a Fishing Rod during the adventure that lets you fish for certain Pokémon at fishing spots. Once you have a Fishing Rod, use it to catch wild Pokémon in ponds, brooklets, and even the sea!

Technique 2: Evolve Pokémon

Caterpie is evolving!

Many Pokémon can be registered in the Alola Pokédex just by being evolved. There are many different ways to evolve Pokémon, though leveling up is the most common condition. If a certain Pokémon can only be obtained through Evolution, you can be sure to find that information in the Pokémon list beginning on page 280. Check out the entries there to learn some of the surprising ways Pokémon can evolve.

Technique 3: Link Trade Pokémon

Doing a Link Trade with other players is the only way to evolve certain Pokémon, such as Alakazam. Some Pokémon must also be holding a specific item to evolve when traded, such as Slowpoke, which must be holding a King's Rock when traded to evolve into Slowking. Trading is also the only way to find Pokémon that are only available in one version of the game. For more on how to set up a Link Trade, see page 306.

Technique 4: SOS Battles

Chansey appeared!

Some Pokémon in Alola only appear in SOS battles, such as Chansey. Some appear in SOS battles only during particular weather conditions, such as Goomy and Sliggoo, which only appear in SOS Battles when it's raining. SOS battle helpers are more likely to appear under certain conditions. See page 63 for details on SOS battles, and page 121 for a list of the Pokémon allies that may appear in certain weather conditions.

Technique 5: Hatch Pokémon Eggs

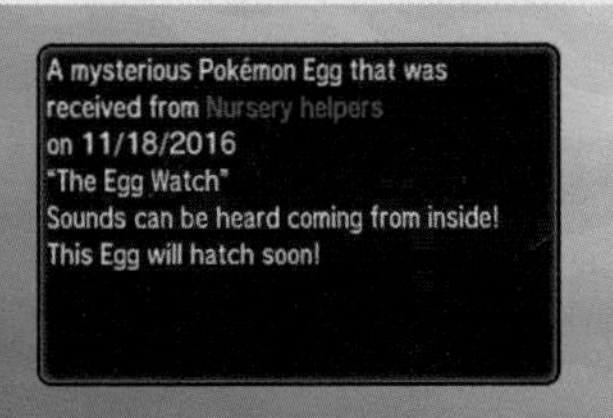

A mysterious Pokémon Egg that was
received from Nursery helpers
on 11/18/2016
"The Egg Watch"
Sounds can be heard coming from inside!
This Egg will hatch soon!

Some Pokémon can't be caught in the wild in Alola, but they can be obtained by finding a Pokémon Egg and hatching it. Gible and Snubbull are both Pokémon that can only be obtained in this way. If you want one for your Pokédex, turn to the section on Pokémon Eggs, beginning on page 288.

Technique 6: Scan QR Code Patterns

Have a friend open their Pokédex and show you a QR Code of a Pokémon you haven't seen or caught yet but they have, then scan its QR Code to register that Pokémon as "Seen" in your Pokédex!

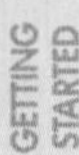

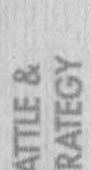

Technique 7: Trade Pokémon with People in Towns

Some people you meet during your adventures around Alola are looking to trade Pokémon. Be sure to make these trades if you have the right Pokémon to offer in return!

Pokémon You Receive	Pokémon You Must Offer	Trader's Location
Machop	Spearow	Pokémon Center on Route 2
Bounsweet	Lillipup	Pokémon Center on Route 5
Poliwhirl	Zubat	Pokémon Center in Konikoni City
Happiny	Pancham	Sushi High Roller in Malie City
Alolan Graveler*	Haunter	Pokémon Center in Tapu Village
Steenee	Granbull	Seafolk Village
Talonflame	Bewear	Poni Gauntlet

*Your new Graveler will immediately evolve into a Golem, as it can only do so via trade!

Technique 8: Isle Abeens in Poké Pelago

Wild Pokémon sometimes show up on Isle Abeens. Tap a Pokémon with "?" on its head to see how it's doing, and it might join your team! Learn more about how to attract more wild Pokémon to Isle Abeens and anything else you want to know about Poké Pelago by turning to page 309.

Technique 9: Restore Fossils

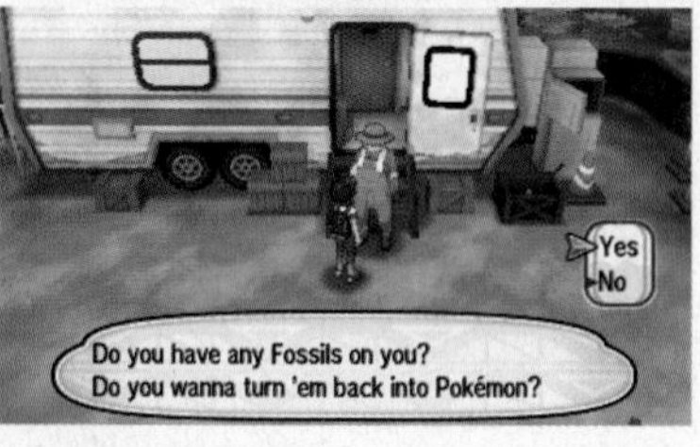

Yes
No
Do you have any Fossils on you?
Do you wanna turn 'em back into Pokémon?

Fossils, such as the Cover Fossil / Armor Fossil that you can buy at Olivia's shop in Konikoni City, can be restored into a Pokémon. Just take them to the Fossil Restoration Center in Dream Park on Route 8 (p. 118).

Island Pokédex Pokémon List

The following pages cover the Pokémon needed to complete your four Island Pokédexes. To complete the Alola Pokédex, you will also need Alola's Legendary Pokémon and to complete Looker's missions after becoming a Champion (p. 221).

Rowlet #001
GRASS FLYING
Receive from Kahuna Hala or receive in a trade from another player
Ability: Overgrow

Dartrix #002
GRASS FLYING
Level up Rowlet to Lv. 17
Ability: Overgrow

Decidueye #003
GRASS GHOST
Level up Dartrix to Lv. 34
Ability: Overgrow

Litten #004
FIRE
Receive from Kahuna Hala or receive in a trade from another player
Ability: Blaze

Torracat #005
FIRE
Level up Litten to Lv. 17
Ability: Blaze

Incineroar #006
FIRE DARK
Level up Torracat to Lv. 34
Ability: Blaze

Popplio #007
WATER
Receive from Kahuna Hala or receive in a trade from another player
Ability: Torrent

Brionne #008
WATER
Level up Popplio to Lv. 17
Ability: Torrent

Primarina #009
WATER FAIRY
Level up Brionne to Lv. 34
Ability: Torrent

Pikipek #010
NORMAL FLYING
Catch in the tall grass on Route 1
Ability: Keen Eye
Skill Link

Trumbeak #011
NORMAL FLYING
Catch in the tall grass on Route 8
Ability: Keen Eye
Skill Link

Toucannon #012
NORMAL FLYING
Level up Trumbeak to Lv. 28
Ability: Keen Eye
Skill Link

Yungoos #013

NORMAL
Catch in the tall grass on Route 1 ☀
Ability: Stakeout
Strong Jaw

Gumshoos #014

NORMAL
Catch in the tall grass in Akala Outskirts ☀
Ability: Stakeout
Strong Jaw

Alolan Rattata #015

DARK NORMAL
Catch in the tall grass on Route 1 ☽
Ability: Gluttony
Hustle

Alolan Raticate #016

DARK NORMAL
Catch in the tall grass in Akala Outskirts ☽
Ability: Gluttony
Hustle

Caterpie #017
BUG
Catch in the tall grass on Route 1 (east)
Ability: Shield Dust

Metapod #018

BUG
Level up Caterpie to Lv. 7
Ability: Shed Skin

Butterfree #019
BUG FLYING
Level up Metapod to Lv. 10
Ability: Compound Eyes

Ledyba #020

BUG FLYING
Catch in the tall grass on Route 1 (east or near Iki Town) ☀
Ability: Swarm
Early Bird

Ledian #021
BUG FLYING
Catch in the tall grass on Route 10 ☀
Ability: Swarm
Early Bird

Spinarak #022
BUG POISON
Catch in the tall grass on Route 1 (east or near Iki Town) ☽
Ability: Swarm
Insomnia

Ariados #023
BUG POISON
Catch in the tall grass on Route 10 ☽
Ability: Swarm
Insomnia

Pichu #024
ELECTRIC
Catch in the tall grass on Route 1 near Iki Town
Ability: Static

Pikachu #025
ELECTRIC
Level up Pichu with high friendship
Ability: Static

Alolan Raichu #026
ELECTRIC PSYCHIC
Use a Thunder Stone on Pikachu
Ability: Surge Surfer

Grubbin #027

BUG
Catch in the tall grass on Route 1 near Iki Town
Ability: Swarm

Charjabug #028

BUG ELECTRIC
Catch in the tall grass on Blush Mountain
Ability: Battery

Vikavolt #029
BUG ELECTRIC
Level up Charjabug in Vast Poni Canyon
Ability: Levitate

Bonsly #030

ROCK
Catch in the tall grass on Route 1 (west)
Ability: Sturdy
Rock Head

Sudowoodo #031

ROCK
Level up Bonsly and have it learn Mimic, or teach it Mimic first and then level it up
Ability: Sturdy
Rock Head

Happiny #032

NORMAL
Receive in exchange for Pancham at Sushi High Roller in Malie City
Ability: Natural Cure
Serene Grace

Chansey #033
NORMAL
Catch in the tall grass in SOS battles on Route 12
Ability: Natural Cure
Serene Grace

Blissey #034
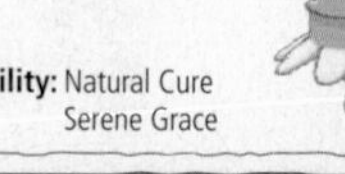
NORMAL
Level up Chansey with high friendship
Ability: Natural Cure
Serene Grace

Munchlax #035

NORMAL
Catch in the tall grass on Route 1 (west)
Ability: Pickup
Thick Fat

Snorlax #036

NORMAL
Level up Munchlax with high friendship
Ability: Immunity
Thick Fat

Slowpoke #037
WATER PSYCHIC
Catch in the tall grass in Hau'oli Outskirts
Ability: Oblivious
Own Tempo

Slowbro #038

WATER PSYCHIC
Catch in the tall grass in SOS battles by Kala'e Bay
Ability: Oblivious
Own Tempo

Slowking #039

WATER PSYCHIC
Receive a Slowpoke with a King's Rock by Link Trade
Ability: Oblivious
Own Tempo

Wingull #040
WATER FLYING
Catch in the tall grass in Hau'oli Outskirts
Ability: Keen Eye
Hydration

Pelipper #041
WATER FLYING
Catch in the tall grass on Route 15
Ability: Keen Eye
Drizzle

Abra #042
PSYCHIC
Catch in the tall grass on Route 2 (south)
Ability: Synchronize
Inner Focus

Kadabra #043
PSYCHIC
Level up Abra to Lv. 16
Ability: Synchronize
Inner Focus

Alakazam #044
PSYCHIC
Link Trade Kadabra
Ability: Synchronize
Inner Focus

Alolan Meowth #045

DARK
Catch in the tall grass on Route 2
Ability: Pickup
Technician

Alolan Persian #046

DARK
Level up Alolan Meowth with high friendship
Ability: Fur Coat
Technician

Magnemite #047
ELECTRIC STEEL
Catch in the tall grass in the Trainers' School
Ability: Magnet Pull
Sturdy

Magneton #048
ELECTRIC STEEL
Level up Magnemite to Lv. 30
Ability: Magnet Pull
Sturdy

Magnezone #049

ELECTRIC STEEL
Level up Magneton in Vast Poni Canyon
Ability: Magnet Pull
Sturdy

Alolan Grimer #050

POISON DARK
Catch in the tall grass in the Trainers' School
Ability: Poison Touch
Gluttony

Alolan Muk #051
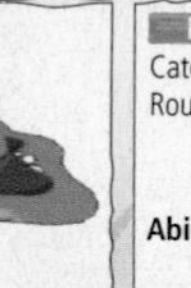
POISON DARK
Level up Alolan Grimer to Lv. 38
Ability: Poison Touch
Gluttony

Growlithe #052
FIRE
Catch in the tall grass on Route 2 (north)
Ability: Intimidate
Flash Fire

Arcanine #053
FIRE
Use a Fire Stone on Growlithe
Ability: Intimidate
Flash Fire

Drowzee #054
PSYCHIC
Catch in the tall grass on Route 2 (south)
Ability: Insomnia
Forewarn

Hypno #055
PSYCHIC
Level up Drowzee to Lv. 26
Ability: Insomnia
Forewarn

Makuhita #056
FIGHTING
Catch on Route 2 (rustling grass)
Ability: Thick Fat
Guts

Hariyama #057
FIGHTING
Level up Makuhita to Lv. 24
Ability: Thick Fat
Guts

Smeargle #058
NORMAL
Catch in the tall grass on Route 2
Ability: Own Tempo
Technician

Crabrawler #059
FIGHTING
Catch in the pile of Berries on Route 10
Ability: Hyper Cutter
Iron Fist

Crabominable #060
FIGHTING ICE
Level up Crabrawler on Mount Lanakila
Ability: Hyper Cutter
Iron Fist

Gastly #061
GHOST POISON
Catch in the tall grass in Hau'oli Cemetery
Ability: Levitate

Haunter #062
GHOST POISON
Catch in the abandoned Thrifty Megamart
Ability: Levitate

Gengar #063
GHOST POISON
Link Trade Haunter
Ability: Cursed Body

Drifloon #064
GHOST FLYING
Catch in the tall grass in Hau'oli Cemetery ☼
Ability: Aftermath
Unburden

Drifblim #065
GHOST FLYING
Level up Drifloon to Lv. 28
Ability: Aftermath
Unburden

Misdreavus #066
GHOST
Catch in the tall grass in Hau'oli Cemetery ☽
Ability: Levitate

Mismagius #067
GHOST
Use a Dusk Stone on Misdreavus
Ability: Levitate

Zubat #068
POISON FLYING
Catch in Verdant Cavern
Ability: Inner Focus

Golbat #069
POISON FLYING
Catch in the abandoned Thrifty Megamart
Ability: Inner Focus

Crobat #070
POISON FLYING
Level up Golbat with high friendship
Ability: Inner Focus

Alolan Diglett #071
GROUND STEEL
Catch on Route 5 (dust clouds)
Ability: Sand Veil
Tangling Hair

Alolan Dugtrio #072
GROUND STEEL
Catch in Vast Poni Canyon (dust clouds)
Ability: Sand Veil
Tangling Hair

Spearow #073
NORMAL FLYING
Catch in the tall grass on Route 2 (north)
Ability: Keen Eye

Fearow #074
NORMAL FLYING
Catch on Route 10 (shaking trees)
Ability: Keen Eye

Rufflet #075
NORMAL FLYING
Catch on Route 3 (Pokémon shadows) ☼ / Obtain it in a Link Trade ☽
Ability: Keen Eye
Sheer Force

Braviary #076
NORMAL FLYING
Level up Rufflet to Lv. 54
Ability: Keen Eye
Sheer Force

Vullaby #077
DARK FLYING
Obtain it in a Link Trade ☼ / Catch on Route 3 (Pokémon shadows) ☽
Ability: Big Pecks
Overcoat

Mandibuzz #078
DARK FLYING
Level up Vullaby to Lv. 54
Ability: Big Pecks
Overcoat

Mankey #079
FIGHTING
Catch in the tall grass on Route 3
Ability: Vital Spirit
Anger Point

Primeape #080
FIGHTING
Level up Mankey to Lv. 28
Ability: Vital Spirit
Anger Point

Delibird #081
ICE FLYING
Catch in the tall grass on Route 3 (north)
Ability: Vital Spirit
Hustle

Oricorio (Pom-Pom Style) #082
ELECTRIC FLYING
Catch in Melemele Meadow (Oricorio's other forms can be registered by using Red, Pink, and Purple Nectar on it)
Ability: Dancer

Cutiefly #083
BUG FAIRY
Catch in the tall grass on Route 3 (north)
Ability: Honey Gather
Shield Dust

Ribombee #084
BUG FAIRY
Catch in the tall grass or flowers in Ula'ula Meadow
Ability: Honey Gather
Shield Dust

Petilil #085
GRASS
Catch in Melemele Meadow ☽ / Obtain it in a Link Trade ☼
Ability: Chlorophyll
Own Tempo

Lilligant #086
GRASS
Use a Sun Stone on Petilil
Ability: Chlorophyll
Own Tempo

Cottonee #087
GRASS FAIRY
Catch in Melemele Meadow ☼ / Obtain it in a Link Trade ☽
Ability: Prankster
Infiltrator

Whimsicott #088
GRASS FAIRY
Use a Sun Stone on Cottonee
Ability: Prankster
Infiltrator

Psyduck #089
WATER
Catch on the water surface on Ten Carat Hill
Ability: Damp
Cloud Nine

Golduck #090
WATER
Catch in the tall grass in Poni Gauntlet
Ability: Damp
Cloud Nine

Magikarp #091
WATER
Catch in the fishing spots in Melemele Sea
Ability: Swift Swim

Gyarados #092
WATER FLYING
Catch in the fishing spots in SOS battles in Melemele Sea
Ability: Intimidate

Barboach #093
WATER GROUND

Catch in the fishing spot in Seaward Cave

Ability: Oblivious
Anticipation

Whiscash #094
WATER GROUND

Catch in the fishing spot in SOS battles in Seaward Cave

Ability: Oblivious
Anticipation

Machop #095
FIGHTING

Receive in exchange for Spearow in the Pokémon Center on Route 2

Ability: Guts
No Guard

Machoke #096
FIGHTING

Catch in Vast Poni Canyon

Ability: Guts
No Guard

Machamp #097
FIGHTING

Link Trade Machoke

Ability: Guts
No Guard

Roggenrola #098
ROCK

Catch in the tall grass or the cave on Ten Carat Hill

Ability: Sturdy
Weak Armor

Boldore #099
ROCK

Catch in the caves in Vast Poni Canyon

Ability: Sturdy
Weak Armor

Gigalith #100
ROCK

Link Trade Boldore

Ability: Sturdy
Sand Stream

Carbink #101
ROCK FAIRY

Catch in the tall grass or the cave on Ten Carat Hill

Ability: Clear Body

Sableye #102
DARK GHOST

Catch in the cave in SOS battles on Ten Carat Hill

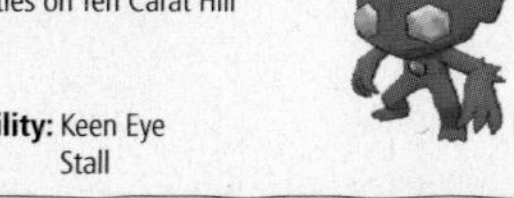

Ability: Keen Eye
Stall

Rockruff #103
ROCK

Catch in the tall grass on Ten Carat Hill

Ability: Keen Eye
Vital Spirit

Lycanroc (Midday Form) #104
ROCK

Catch Midday Form Lycanroc ☀ or Midnight Form Lycanroc ☽ in the tall grass in Vast Poni Canyon

Ability: Keen Eye
Sand Rush

Spinda #105
NORMAL

Catch in the tall grass on Ten Carat Hill

Ability: Own Tempo
Tangled Feet

Tentacool #106
WATER POISON

Catch on the water surface on Route 1

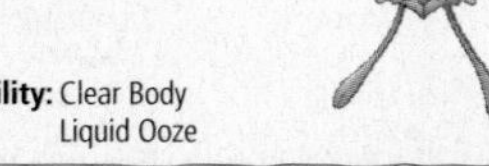

Ability: Clear Body
Liquid Ooze

Tentacruel #107
WATER POISON

Catch on the water surface in Poni Wilds

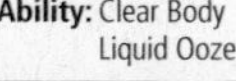

Ability: Clear Body
Liquid Ooze

Finneon #108
WATER

Catch on the water surface on Route 1

Ability: Swift Swim
Storm Drain

Lumineon #109
WATER

Catch on the water surface in Poni Wilds

Ability: Swift Swim
Storm Drain

Wishiwashi #110
WATER

Catch in the fishing spots in Melemele Sea

Ability: Schooling

Luvdisc #111
WATER

Catch in the rare fishing spots in Melemele Sea

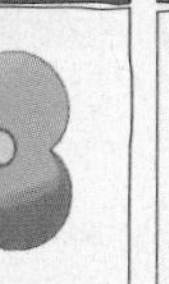

Ability: Swift Swim

Corsola #112
WATER ROCK

Catch in the rare fishing spots in Melemele Sea

Ability: Hustle
Natural Cure

Mareanie #113
POISON WATER

Catch in the fishing spots in SOS battles in Melemele Sea

Ability: Merciless
Limber

Toxapex #114
POISON WATER

Level up Mareanie to Lv. 38

Ability: Merciless
Limber

Shellder #115
WATER

Catch in the fishing spots in Kala'e Bay

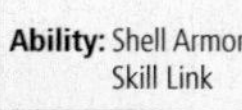

Ability: Shell Armor
Skill Link

Cloyster #116
WATER ICE

Use a Water Stone on Shellder

Ability: Shell Armor
Skill Link

Bagon #117
DRAGON

Catch in the tall grass on Route 3

Ability: Rock Head

Shelgon #118
DRAGON

Catch in the tall grass in SOS battles by Kala'e Bay

Ability: Rock Head

Salamence #119
DRAGON FLYING

Catch in the tall grass in SOS battles on Route 3

Ability: Intimidate

Lillipup #120
NORMAL

Catch in the tall grass in Paniola Ranch

Ability: Vital Spirit
Pickup

Herdier #121
NORMAL

Level up Lillipup to Lv. 16

Ability: Intimidate
Sand Rush

Stoutland #122
NORMAL

Level up Herdier to Lv. 32

Ability: Intimidate
Sand Rush

Eevee #123
NORMAL

Catch in the tall grass on Route 4

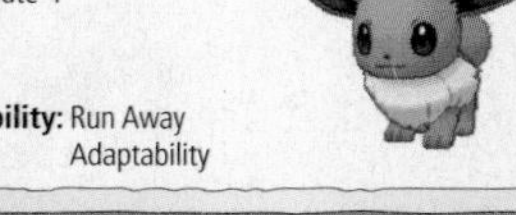

Ability: Run Away
Adaptability

Vaporeon #124
WATER

Use a Water Stone on Eevee

Ability: Water Absorb

Jolteon #125
ELECTRIC

Use a Thunder Stone on Eevee

Ability: Volt Absorb

Flareon #126
FIRE

Use a Fire Stone on Eevee

Ability: Flash Fire

Espeon #127
PSYCHIC

Catch in the tall grass in SOS battles on Route 4 ☀

Ability: Synchronize

Umbreon #128
DARK

Catch in the tall grass in SOS battles on Route 4 ☽

Ability: Synchronize

Leafeon #129
GRASS

Level up Eevee near the moss-covered rock in Lush Jungle

Ability: Leaf Guard

Glaceon #130
ICE

Level up Eevee near the ice-covered rock in a cave on Mount Lanakila

Ability: Snow Cloak

Sylveon #131
FAIRY

Level up an Eevee that is affectionate, and have it learn a Fairy-type move before or after leveling up

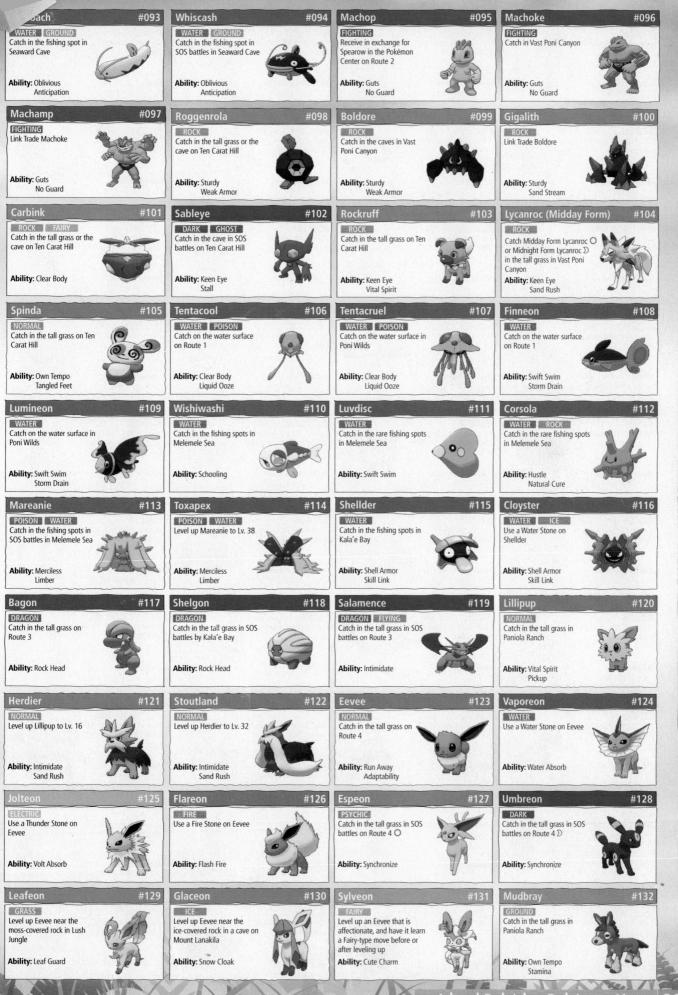

Ability: Cute Charm

Mudbray #132
GROUND

Catch in the tall grass in Paniola Ranch

Ability: Own Tempo
Stamina

Mudsdale #133
GROUND
Level up Mudbray to Lv. 30
Ability: Own Tempo, Stamina

Igglybuff #134
NORMAL FAIRY
Catch in the tall grass on Route 4 ○
Ability: Cute Charm, Competitive

Jigglypuff #135
NORMAL FAIRY
Catch in the tall grass in SOS battles on Route 4 ○
Ability: Cute Charm, Competitive

Wigglytuff #136
NORMAL FAIRY
Use a Moon Stone on Jigglypuff
Ability: Cute Charm, Competitive

Tauros #137
NORMAL
Catch in the tall grass in Poni Plains
Ability: Intimidate, Anger Point

Miltank #138
NORMAL
Catch in the tall grass in Poni Plains
Ability: Thick Fat, Scrappy

Surskit #139
BUG WATER
Catch on the water surface on Brooklet Hill ☽
Ability: Swift Swim

Masquerain #140
BUG FLYING
Catch in the tall grass in Malie Garden ☽
Ability: Intimidate

Dewpider #141
WATER BUG
Catch on the water surface on Brooklet Hill ○
Ability: Water Bubble

Araquanid #142
WATER BUG
Catch in the tall grass in Malie Garden ○
Ability: Water Bubble

Fomantis #143
GRASS
Catch in Lush Jungle (shaking trees)
Ability: Leaf Guard

Lurantis #144
GRASS
Level up Fomantis to Lv. 34 when it is daytime in your game
Ability: Leaf Guard

Morelull #145
GRASS FAIRY
Catch in the tall grass on Brooklet Hill ☽
Ability: Illuminate, Effect Spore

Shiinotic #146
GRASS FAIRY
Level up Morelull to Lv. 24
Ability: Illuminate, Effect Spore

Paras #147
BUG GRASS
Catch in the tall grass in Lush Jungle ○
Ability: Effect Spore, Dry Skin

Parasect #148
BUG GRASS
Level up Paras to Lv. 24
Ability: Effect Spore, Dry Skin

Poliwag #149
WATER
Catch on the water surface on Brooklet Hill
Ability: Water Absorb, Damp

Poliwhirl #150
WATER
Receive in exchange for Zubat in the Pokémon Center in Konikoni City
Ability: Water Absorb, Damp

Poliwrath #151
WATER FIGHTING
Catch in the tall grass in SOS battles in rain in Malie Garden ○
Ability: Water Absorb, Damp

Politoed #152
WATER
Catch in the tall grass in SOS battles in rain in Malie Garden ☽
Ability: Water Absorb, Damp

Goldeen #153
WATER
Catch in the fishing spots in Malie Garden
Ability: Swift Swim, Water Veil

Seaking #154
WATER
Catch in the fishing spots in SOS battles in Malie Garden
Ability: Swift Swim, Water Veil

Feebas #155
WATER
Catch in the fishing spots on Brooklet Hill
Ability: Swift Swim, Oblivious

Milotic #156
WATER
Receive Feebas with a Prism Scale by Link Trade
Ability: Marvel Scale, Competitive

Alomomola #157
WATER
Catch in the rare fishing spots on Brooklet Hill
Ability: Healer, Hydration

Fletchling #158
NORMAL FLYING
Catch in the tall grass in Wela Volcano Park
Ability: Big Pecks

Fletchinder #159
FIRE FLYING
Catch in the tall grass on Route 8
Ability: Flame Body

Talonflame #160
FIRE FLYING
Level up Fletchinder to Lv. 35
Ability: Flame Body

Salandit #161
POISON FIRE
Catch in the tall grass in Wela Volcano Park
Ability: Corrosion

Salazzle #162
POISON FIRE
Level up a female Salandit to Lv. 33
Ability: Corrosion

Cubone #163
GROUND
Catch in the tall grass in Wela Volcano Park
Ability: Rock Head, Lightning Rod

Alolan Marowak #164
FIRE GHOST
Level up Cubone to Lv. 28 when it is nighttime in your game
Ability: Cursed Body, Lightning Rod

Kangaskhan #165
NORMAL
Catch in the tall grass in Wela Volcano Park
Ability: Early Bird, Scrappy

Magby #166
FIRE
Catch in the tall grass in Wela Volcano Park
Ability: Flame Body

Magmar #167
FIRE
Catch in the tall grass in SOS battles in Wela Volcano Park
Ability: Flame Body

Magmortar #168
FIRE
Receive Magmar with a Magmarizer by Link Trade
Ability: Flame Body

Stufful #169
NORMAL FIGHTING
Catch in the tall grass in Akala Outskirts
Ability: Fluffy, Klutz

Bewear #170
NORMAL FIGHTING
Level up Stufful to Lv. 27
Ability: Fluffy, Klutz

Bounsweet #171
GRASS
Catch in the tall grass in Lush Jungle
Ability: Leaf Guard, Oblivious

Steenee #172
GRASS
Receive in exchange for Granbull in Seafolk Village
Ability: Leaf Guard, Oblivious

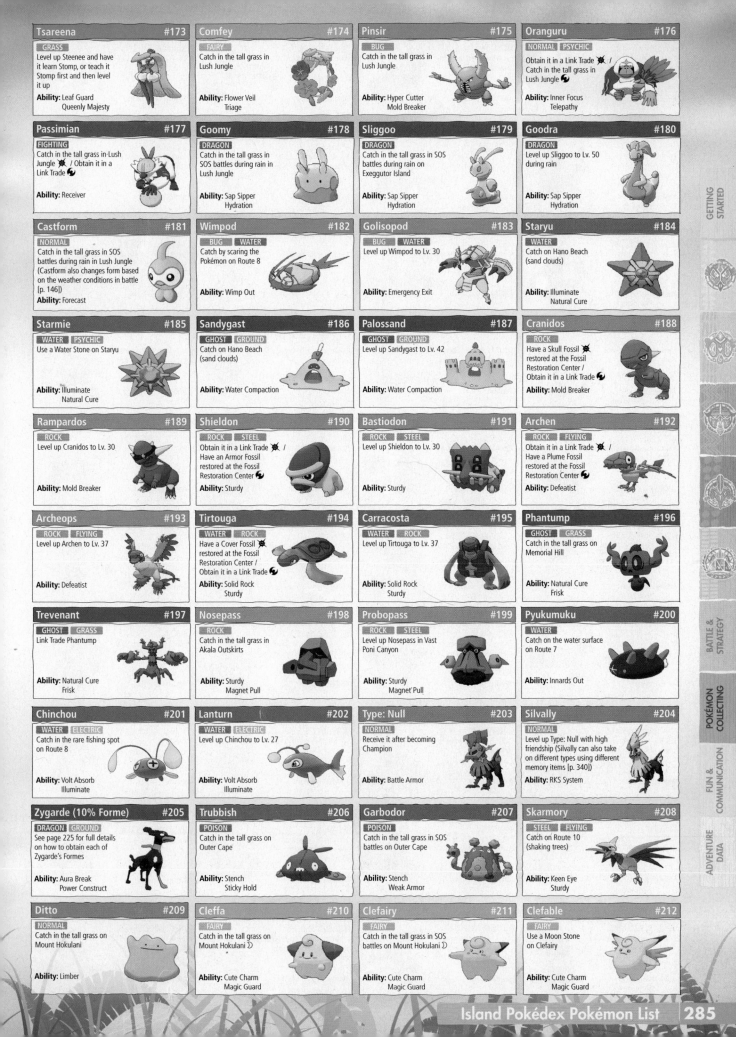

Tsareena #173
GRASS

Level up Steenee and have it learn Stomp, or teach it Stomp first and then level it up

Ability: Leaf Guard
Queenly Majesty

Comfey #174
FAIRY

Catch in the tall grass in Lush Jungle

Ability: Flower Veil
Triage

Pinsir #175
BUG

Catch in the tall grass in Lush Jungle

Ability: Hyper Cutter
Mold Breaker

Oranguru #176
NORMAL PSYCHIC

Obtain it in a Link Trade / Catch in the tall grass in Lush Jungle

Ability: Inner Focus
Telepathy

Passimian #177
FIGHTING

Catch in the tall grass in Lush Jungle / Obtain it in a Link Trade

Ability: Receiver

Goomy #178
DRAGON

Catch in the tall grass in SOS battles during rain in Lush Jungle

Ability: Sap Sipper
Hydration

Sliggoo #179
DRAGON

Catch in the tall grass in SOS battles during rain on Exeggutor Island

Ability: Sap Sipper
Hydration

Goodra #180
DRAGON

Level up Sliggoo to Lv. 50 during rain

Ability: Sap Sipper
Hydration

Castform #181
NORMAL

Catch in the tall grass in SOS battles during rain in Lush Jungle (Castform also changes form based on the weather conditions in battle [p. 146])

Ability: Forecast

Wimpod #182
BUG WATER

Catch by scaring the Pokémon on Route 8

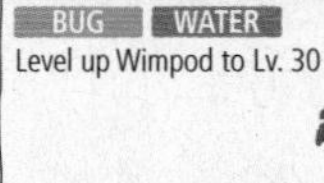

Ability: Wimp Out

Golisopod #183
BUG WATER

Level up Wimpod to Lv. 30

Ability: Emergency Exit

Staryu #184
WATER

Catch on Hano Beach (sand clouds)

Ability: Illuminate
Natural Cure

Starmie #185
WATER PSYCHIC

Use a Water Stone on Staryu

Ability: Illuminate
Natural Cure

Sandygast #186
GHOST GROUND

Catch on Hano Beach (sand clouds)

Ability: Water Compaction

Palossand #187
GHOST GROUND

Level up Sandygast to Lv. 42

Ability: Water Compaction

Cranidos #188
ROCK

Have a Skull Fossil restored at the Fossil Restoration Center / Obtain it in a Link Trade

Ability: Mold Breaker

Rampardos #189
ROCK

Level up Cranidos to Lv. 30

Ability: Mold Breaker

Shieldon #190
ROCK STEEL

Obtain it in a Link Trade / Have an Armor Fossil restored at the Fossil Restoration Center

Ability: Sturdy

Bastiodon #191
ROCK STEEL

Level up Shieldon to Lv. 30

Ability: Sturdy

Archen #192
ROCK FLYING

Obtain it in a Link Trade / Have a Plume Fossil restored at the Fossil Restoration Center

Ability: Defeatist

Archeops #193
ROCK FLYING

Level up Archen to Lv. 37

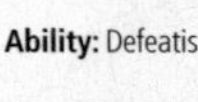

Ability: Defeatist

Tirtouga #194
WATER ROCK

Have a Cover Fossil restored at the Fossil Restoration Center / Obtain it in a Link Trade

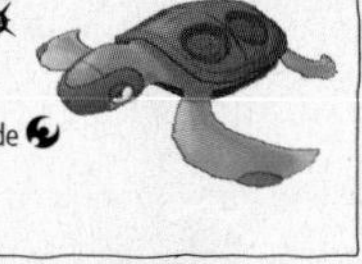

Ability: Solid Rock
Sturdy

Carracosta #195
WATER ROCK

Level up Tirtouga to Lv. 37

Ability: Solid Rock
Sturdy

Phantump #196
GHOST GRASS

Catch in the tall grass on Memorial Hill

Ability: Natural Cure
Frisk

Trevenant #197
GHOST GRASS

Link Trade Phantump

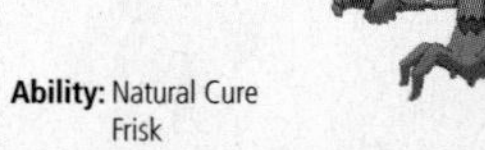

Ability: Natural Cure
Frisk

Nosepass #198
ROCK

Catch in the tall grass in Akala Outskirts

Ability: Sturdy
Magnet Pull

Probopass #199
ROCK STEEL

Level up Nosepass in Vast Poni Canyon

Ability: Sturdy
Magnet Pull

Pyukumuku #200
WATER

Catch on the water surface on Route 7

Ability: Innards Out

Chinchou #201
WATER ELECTRIC

Catch in the rare fishing spot on Route 8

Ability: Volt Absorb
Illuminate

Lanturn #202
WATER ELECTRIC

Level up Chinchou to Lv. 27

Ability: Volt Absorb
Illuminate

Type: Null #203
NORMAL

Receive it after becoming Champion

Ability: Battle Armor

Silvally #204
NORMAL

Level up Type: Null with high friendship (Silvally can also take on different types using different memory items [p. 340])

Ability: RKS System

Zygarde (10% Forme) #205
DRAGON GROUND

See page 225 for full details on how to obtain each of Zygarde's Formes

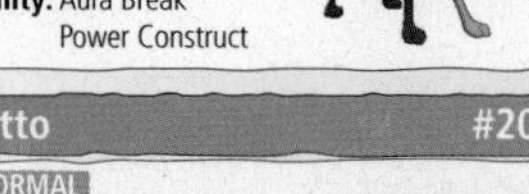

Ability: Aura Break
Power Construct

Trubbish #206
POISON

Catch in the tall grass on Outer Cape

Ability: Stench
Sticky Hold

Garbodor #207
POISON

Catch in the tall grass in SOS battles on Outer Cape

Ability: Stench
Weak Armor

Skarmory #208
STEEL FLYING

Catch on Route 10 (shaking trees)

Ability: Keen Eye
Sturdy

Ditto #209
NORMAL

Catch in the tall grass on Mount Hokulani

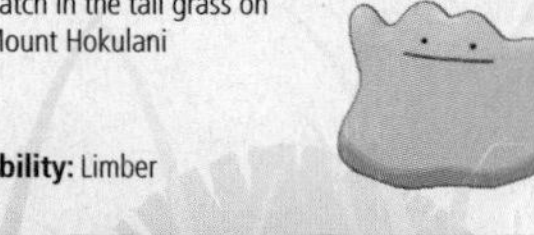

Ability: Limber

Cleffa #210
FAIRY

Catch in the tall grass on Mount Hokulani ☽

Ability: Cute Charm
Magic Guard

Clefairy #211
FAIRY

Catch in the tall grass in SOS battles on Mount Hokulani ☽

Ability: Cute Charm
Magic Guard

Clefable #212
FAIRY

Use a Moon Stone on Clefairy

Ability: Cute Charm
Magic Guard

GETTING STARTED
BATTLE & STRATEGY
POKÉMON COLLECTING
FUN & COMMUNICATION
ADVENTURE DATA

Minior (Meteor Form) #213
ROCK FLYING
Catch in the tall grass on Mount Hokulani (Minior can have one of seven differently colored cores)
Ability: Shields Down

Beldum #214
STEEL PSYCHIC
Catch in the tall grass on Mount Hokulani
Ability: Clear Body

Metang #215
STEEL PSYCHIC
Level up Beldum to Lv. 20
Ability: Clear Body

Metagross #216
STEEL PSYCHIC
Level up Metang to Lv. 45
Ability: Clear Body

Porygon #217
NORMAL
Receive it from an Aether Employee in the Aether House (p. 162)
Ability: Trace
Download

Porygon2 #218
NORMAL
Receive Porygon with an Up-Grade by Link Trade
Ability: Trace
Download

Porygon-Z #219
NORMAL
Receive Porygon2 with a Dubious Disc by Link Trade
Ability: Adaptability
Download

Pancham #220
FIGHTING
Catch in the tall grass on Route 11
Ability: Iron Fist
Mold Breaker

Pangoro #221
FIGHTING DARK
Catch in the tall grass in SOS battles on Route 11
Ability: Iron Fist
Mold Breaker

Komala #222
NORMAL
Catch in the tall grass on Route 11
Ability: Comatose

Torkoal #223
FIRE
Catch in the tall grass on Route 12
Ability: White Smoke
Drought

Turtonator #224
FIRE DRAGON
Catch in the tall grass on Blush Mountain ☀ / Obtain it in a Link Trade ☾
Ability: Shell Armor

Togedemaru #225
ELECTRIC STEEL
Catch in the tall grass on Blush Mountain
Ability: Iron Barbs
Lightning Rod

Elekid #226
ELECTRIC
Catch in the tall grass on Route 12
Ability: Static

Electabuzz #227
ELECTRIC
Catch in the tall grass in SOS battles on Route 12
Ability: Static

Electivire #228
ELECTRIC
Receive Electabuzz with an Electirizer by Link Trade
Ability: Motor Drive

Alolan Geodude #229
ROCK ELECTRIC
Catch in the tall grass on Route 12
Ability: Magnet Pull
Sturdy

Alolan Graveler #230
ROCK ELECTRIC
Catch in the brown tall grass on Route 17
Ability: Magnet Pull
Sturdy

Alolan Golem #231
ROCK ELECTRIC
Link Trade Alolan Graveler
Ability: Magnet Pull
Sturdy

Sandile #232
GROUND DARK
Catch in Haina Desert
Ability: Intimidate
Moxie

Krokorok #233
GROUND DARK
Level up Sandile to Lv. 29
Ability: Intimidate
Moxie

Krookodile #234
GROUND DARK
Level up Krokorok to Lv. 40
Ability: Intimidate
Moxie

Trapinch #235
GROUND
Catch in Haina Desert (sand clouds)
Ability: Hyper Cutter
Arena Trap

Vibrava #236
GROUND DRAGON
Level up Trapinch to Lv. 35
Ability: Levitate

Flygon #237
GROUND DRAGON
Level up Vibrava to Lv. 45
Ability: Levitate

Gible #238
DRAGON GROUND
Leave Gabite or Garchomp at the Pokémon Nursery, and then hatch the Egg that is found (p. 288)
Ability: Sand Veil

Gabite #239
DRAGON GROUND
Catch in SOS battles during a sandstorm in Haina Desert
Ability: Sand Veil

Garchomp #240
DRAGON GROUND
Level up Gabite to Lv. 48
Ability: Sand Veil

Klefki #241
STEEL FAIRY
Catch in the abandoned Thrifty Megamart
Ability: Prankster

Mimikyu #242
GHOST FAIRY
Catch in the abandoned Thrifty Megamart
Ability: Disguise

Bruxish #243
WATER PSYCHIC
Catch in the rare fishing spot on Secluded Shore
Ability: Dazzling
Strong Jaw

Drampa #244
NORMAL DRAGON
Obtain it in a Link Trade ☀ / Catch in the cave on Mount Lanakila ☾
Ability: Berserk
Sap Sipper

Absol #245
DARK
Catch in the tall grass or cave on Mount Lanakila
Ability: Pressure
Super Luck

Snorunt #246
ICE
Catch in the tall grass or cave on Mount Lanakila
Ability: Inner Focus
Ice Body

Glalie #247
ICE
Catch in the tall grass or cave in SOS battles on Mount Lanakila
Ability: Inner Focus
Ice Body

Froslass #248
ICE GHOST
Use a Dawn Stone on Snorunt
Ability: Snow Cloak

Sneasel #249
DARK ICE
Catch in the tall grass or cave on Mount Lanakila
Ability: Inner Focus
Keen Eye

Weavile #250
DARK ICE
Level up Sneasel while holding it is holding a Razor Claw when it is nighttime in your game
Ability: Pressure

Alolan Sandshrew #251
ICE STEEL
Obtain it in a Link Trade ☀ / Catch in the tall grass on Mount Lanakila ☾
Ability: Snow Cloak

Alolan Sandslash #252
ICE STEEL
Use an Ice Stone on Alolan Sandshrew
Ability: Snow Cloak

GETTING STARTED
BATTLE & STRATEGY
POKÉMON COLLECTING
FUN & COMMUNICATION
ADVENTURE DATA

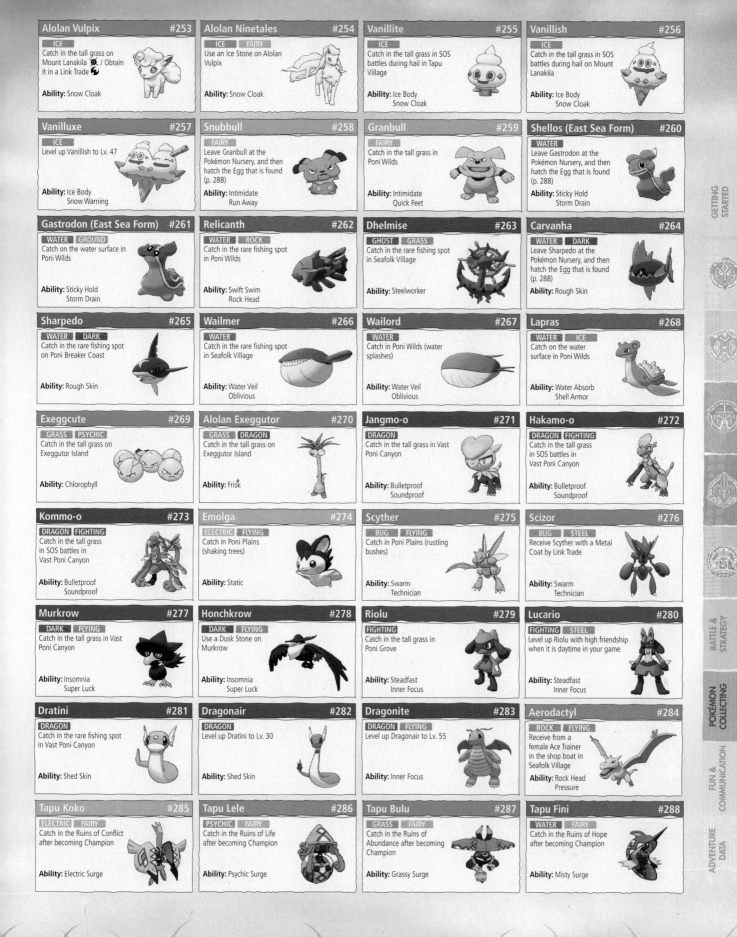

Alolan Vulpix #253
ICE
Catch in the tall grass on Mount Lanakila / Obtain it in a Link Trade

Ability: Snow Cloak

Alolan Ninetales #254
ICE FAIRY
Use an Ice Stone on Alolan Vulpix

Ability: Snow Cloak

Vanillite #255
ICE
Catch in the tall grass in SOS battles during hail in Tapu Village
Ability: Ice Body
Snow Cloak

Vanillish #256
ICE
Catch in the tall grass in SOS battles during hail on Mount Lanakila
Ability: Ice Body
Snow Cloak

Vanilluxe #257
ICE
Level up Vanillish to Lv. 47

Ability: Ice Body
Snow Warning

Snubbull #258
FAIRY
Leave Granbull at the Pokémon Nursery, and then hatch the Egg that is found (p. 288)

Ability: Intimidate
Run Away

Granbull #259
FAIRY
Catch in the tall grass in Poni Wilds

Ability: Intimidate
Quick Feet

Shellos (East Sea Form) #260
WATER
Leave Gastrodon at the Pokémon Nursery, and then hatch the Egg that is found (p. 288)

Ability: Sticky Hold
Storm Drain

Gastrodon (East Sea Form) #261
WATER GROUND
Catch on the water surface in Poni Wilds

Ability: Sticky Hold
Storm Drain

Relicanth #262
WATER ROCK
Catch in the rare fishing spot in Poni Wilds

Ability: Swift Swim
Rock Head

Dhelmise #263
GHOST GRASS
Catch in the rare fishing spot in Seafolk Village

Ability: Steelworker

Carvanha #264
WATER DARK
Leave Sharpedo at the Pokémon Nursery, and then hatch the Egg that is found (p. 288)

Ability: Rough Skin

Sharpedo #265
WATER DARK
Catch in the rare fishing spot on Poni Breaker Coast
Ability: Rough Skin

Wailmer #266
WATER
Catch in the rare fishing spot in Seafolk Village
Ability: Water Veil
Oblivious

Wailord #267
WATER
Catch in Poni Wilds (water splashes)
Ability: Water Veil
Oblivious

Lapras #268
WATER ICE
Catch on the water surface in Poni Wilds

Ability: Water Absorb
Shell Armor

Exeggcute #269
GRASS PSYCHIC
Catch in the tall grass on Exeggutor Island
Ability: Chlorophyll

Alolan Exeggutor #270
GRASS DRAGON
Catch in the tall grass on Exeggutor Island

Ability: Frisk

Jangmo-o #271
DRAGON
Catch in the tall grass in Vast Poni Canyon

Ability: Bulletproof
Soundproof

Hakamo-o #272
DRAGON FIGHTING
Catch in the tall grass in SOS battles in Vast Poni Canyon

Ability: Bulletproof
Soundproof

Kommo-o #273
DRAGON FIGHTING
Catch in the tall grass in SOS battles in Vast Poni Canyon

Ability: Bulletproof
Soundproof

Emolga #274
ELECTRIC FLYING
Catch in Poni Plains (shaking trees)

Ability: Static

Scyther #275
BUG FLYING
Catch in Poni Plains (rustling bushes)
Ability: Swarm
Technician

Scizor #276
BUG STEEL
Receive Scyther with a Metal Coat by Link Trade
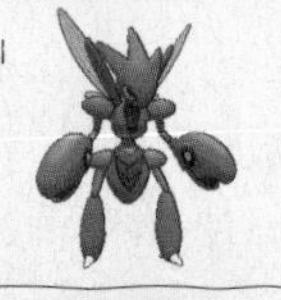
Ability: Swarm
Technician

Murkrow #277
DARK FLYING
Catch in the tall grass in Vast Poni Canyon
Ability: Insomnia
Super Luck

Honchkrow #278
DARK FLYING
Use a Dusk Stone on Murkrow
Ability: Insomnia
Super Luck

Riolu #279
FIGHTING
Catch in the tall grass in Poni Grove

Ability: Steadfast
Inner Focus

Lucario #280
FIGHTING STEEL
Level up Riolu with high friendship when it is daytime in your game

Ability: Steadfast
Inner Focus

Dratini #281
DRAGON
Catch in the rare fishing spot in Vast Poni Canyon

Ability: Shed Skin

Dragonair #282
DRAGON
Level up Dratini to Lv. 30

Ability: Shed Skin

Dragonite #283
DRAGON FLYING
Level up Dragonair to Lv. 55

Ability: Inner Focus

Aerodactyl #284
ROCK FLYING
Receive from a female Ace Trainer in the shop boat in Seafolk Village

Ability: Rock Head
Pressure

Tapu Koko #285
ELECTRIC FAIRY
Catch in the Ruins of Conflict after becoming Champion

Ability: Electric Surge

Tapu Lele #286
PSYCHIC FAIRY
Catch in the Ruins of Life after becoming Champion

Ability: Psychic Surge

Tapu Bulu #287
GRASS FAIRY
Catch in the Ruins of Abundance after becoming Champion

Ability: Grassy Surge

Tapu Fini #288
WATER FAIRY
Catch in the Ruins of Hope after becoming Champion

Ability: Misty Surge

The Pokémon Nursery and Pokémon Eggs

Finding Pokémon Eggs at the Pokémon Nursery in Paniola Ranch can do many things for a Trainer. It can help you obtain more than one of a rare Pokémon, such as the Pokémon you first started your journey with. It can also help you obtain earlier Evolutions of Pokémon that can't always be found in the wild, which is essential if you hope to complete your Alola Pokédex! Pokémon Eggs can also help you obtain Pokémon with great Abilities or moves they'd never have in the wild, giving you a huge advantage in competitive battles against other players.

How to Find Pokémon Eggs

1 Leave a male and female Pokémon together at the Pokémon Nursery or nearly any Pokémon with a Ditto.

Most Pokémon have genders. The Pokémon Egg Group tables shown on the following pages reveal whether a Pokémon only has male or female gender, or if it can appear as either. Some Pokémon are also recorded as "gender unknown," meaning scientists have been unable to determine any gender for them. To find Pokémon Eggs for a gender unknown Pokémon, you must leave it at the Pokémon Nursery with a Ditto: a special Pokémon that lets you find Pokémon Eggs for any Pokémon for which Eggs can be found, including gender unknown ones.

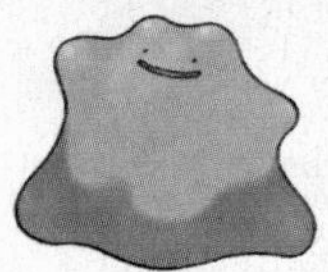
Ditto

2 If the two Pokémon you leave at the Pokémon Nursery are of different species, they must share one Egg Group, unless one of them is a Ditto.

Like types, each Pokémon has at least one Egg Group. Egg Groups have no effect in the game except for when it comes to finding Pokémon Eggs. The two Pokémon you leave at the Pokémon Nursery must share a common Egg Group if you hope to find a Pokémon Egg. The exception is Ditto again, which is the sole member of the "Ditto Group." The Ditto Group is compatible with any other Egg Group. Note that some special Pokémon are listed in the "No Pokémon Eggs Discovered Group." No records have ever been found of these Pokémon discovering Pokémon Eggs, so don't bother leaving them at the Pokémon Nursery in the hope of finding a Pokémon Egg from them.

3 How well your Pokémon get along determines your success at finding a Pokémon Egg

You're more likely to find a Pokémon Egg quickly if the two Pokémon you leave at the Pokémon Nursery like each other. If they don't like each other much, you may find a Pokémon Egg, but it may take a long time. If they don't like playing together at all, you'll never find a Pokémon Egg from them. Talk to the Pokémon Breeder in front of the Pokémon Nursery to find out how your duo are getting along.

Messages from the Breeder	
"They really seem to like hanging out!"	Pokémon Eggs are likely to be found
"They seem to get along all right."	Pokémon Eggs may be found
"They don't seem to like each other very much, though."	Pokémon Eggs are harder to find
"They don't seem to like playing together, though."	Pokémon Eggs will not be found

Tip

The Oval Charm makes it more likely to find Pokémon Eggs. After you've entered the Hall of Fame, you can get the Oval Charm by defeating Morimoto at GAME FREAK's office in Heahea City.

What Will Hatch from Your Pokémon Egg?

Pokémon Eggs hatch into Lv. 1 Pokémon and they inherit many traits from the Pokémon that were left at the Pokémon Nursery when the Pokémon Egg was found. The rules of inheritance are explained over the following page, so read on to learn how to pass on things like Abilities, moves, and individual strengths.

Pokémon Eggs inherit their species from the female Pokémon

Pokémon Eggs you find at the Pokémon Nursery always hatch into Pokémon of the same species as the female Pokémon you leave at the Pokémon Nursery, or an earlier Evolution of that species (if there is one). But if you leave a Ditto at the Pokémon Nursery with another Pokémon, the Pokémon Egg will always be the same species of the non-Ditto Pokémon, even if it was a male Pokémon.

Alolan Dugtrio ♀ FIELD GROUP **Ability:** Tangling Hair

Herdier ♂ FIELD GROUP **Ability:** Intimidate

Pokémon Egg that hatches into Alolan Diglett **Ability:** Tangling Hair or Sand Veil

Pokémon Eggs inherit their Ability from the female Pokémon

Pokémon Eggs also inherit their Ability from the species of the female Pokémon you leave at the Pokémon Nursery. A Pokémon Egg is most likely to have the same Ability as the female Pokémon, but it could also inherit one of the other regular Abilities that its species can have. A Pokémon Egg can only inherit a Hidden Ability if the female left at the Pokémon Nursery has it, though. If you leave a male or gender unknown Pokémon at the Pokémon Nursery with a Ditto, the Pokémon Egg that hatches will inherit its Ability from the other Pokémon.

Tip

An item called an Ability Capsule lets you switch between the two Abilities that a Pokémon species can normally have. Pick up an Ability Capsule in exchange for BP at the Battle Royal Dome, then use it to swap a Pokémon's Ability to one you'd like it to have or to pass down to a Pokémon Egg. Note that an Ability Capsule won't let you switch from a regular Ability to a Hidden Ability (p. 249).

Pokémon Eggs can inherit moves from either Pokémon

Pokémon that hatch from Pokémon Eggs automatically know the basic moves that their species possess at Lv. 1, but they may also know special moves inherited from the Pokémon you leave at the Pokémon Nursery. A Pokémon Egg can inherit a move it'd normally learn at a later level, or a special Egg Move. Egg Moves are moves that a Pokémon would normally never be able to learn by leveling up or from a TM. The moves that Pokémon can learn as Egg Moves can be found in an official Pokédex published by The Pokémon Company International.

Alolan Meowth ♀ FIELD GROUP

Pancham ♂ FIELD GROUP HUMAN-LIKE GROUP knows Parting Shot

Pokémon Egg that hatches into Alolan Meowth knows Parting Shot

Slowpoke ♀ MONSTER GROUP WATER GROUP 1 **Nature:** Adamant

Alolan Marowak ♂ MONSTER GROUP **Nature:** Quiet holding an Everstone

Pokémon Egg that hatches into Slowpoke MONSTER GROUP WATER GROUP 1 **Nature:** Quiet

Pokémon Eggs can inherit their Nature from a Pokémon

Pokémon that hatch from Pokémon Eggs may inherit the Nature of the Pokémon left at the Pokémon Nursery, or it may have any of the other 24 Natures at random. If you want to guarantee that a Pokémon Egg inherits a particular Nature from one of the Pokémon you leave at the Pokémon Nursery, give that Pokémon an Everstone to hold before dropping it off. This guarantees that the Pokémon Egg will hatch into a Pokémon with the same Nature.

Pokémon Eggs can inherit individual strengths with the help of items

With the help of certain held items, individual strengths (p. 272) can be passed down by the Pokémon left at the Pokémon Nursery. All of these items can be obtained in exchange for BP at the Battle Royal Dome (p. 108). If several of your Pokémon have great individual strengths, leave them at the Pokémon Nursery together for a chance to find Pokémon Eggs that are bursting with potential!

Item Name	Individual Strength Inherited
Power Weight	HP of the holder
Power Bracer	Attack of the holder
Power Belt	Defense of the holder
Power Lens	Sp. Atk of the holder
Power Band	Sp. Def of the holder
Power Anklet	Speed of the holder
Destiny Knot	Five of the six battle stats (chosen at random from both Pokémon left at the Pokémon Nursery)

Summary of inheritance rules when not using Ditto

What Pokémon Eggs inherit from female Pokémon	What Pokémon Eggs can inherit from either Pokémon
Species	Moves
Ability (either the same one or another Ability inherent to its species)	Individual strengths
	Nature (with Everstone)

Summary of inheritance rules when using Ditto

What Pokémon Eggs can inherit from the other Pokémon	What Pokémon Eggs can inherit from either Pokémon
Species	Moves
Ability	Individual strengths
	Nature (with Everstone)

Using Pokémon Eggs to Specialize Pokémon

By carefully passing down traits to the Pokémon hatched from Pokémon Eggs, you can end up with a Pokémon that would be impossible to find in the wild. Here's one example of how these traits can be passed down through several generations of Pokémon and Pokémon Eggs to result in a Froslass that's primed for battle!

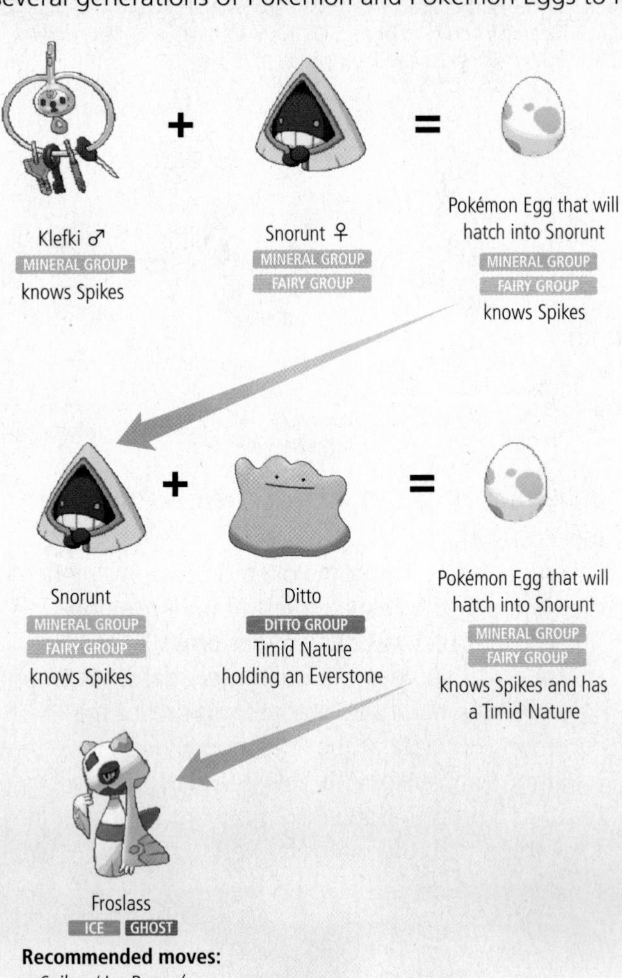

A Timid Nature (p. 271) is good for a Pokémon like Froslass that knows moves like Spikes because this Nature will help its Speed stat grow more quickly so that it can lay down its trap before any other Pokémon moves. Give Froslass a Focus Sash to hold to prevent it from being knocked out by a single hit when it's at full HP. Max out Froslass's base stats for Sp. Atk and Speed using Poké Pelago (p. 309), as well as its individual strengths with Hyper Training (p. 275), and it will become a very fast and very dangerous Pokémon that's great to send out at the start of battle. Use Spikes first so that any Pokémon your opponent sends into battle thereafter will take damage right off the bat. With powerful Ghost-type move Shadow Ball and Ice-type moves like Ice Beam and Blizzard, Froslass will get the same-type attack bonus as well (p. 236). This Froslass also wouldn't be a terrible Pokémon for a Battle Royal, since its Spikes will damage all of the many Pokémon that enter the field, and its Blizzard will hit multiple targets at once!

Tip

If you can obtain a Froslass with the Hidden Ability Cursed Body to pass on, then this Pokémon will be even more dangerous! Cursed Body can disable an opponent's moves if they damage Froslass. Learn more about Hidden Abilities on page 249. You won't be able to find such a Froslass in the wild in Alola, so it's time to hit the GTS (p. 307) if you want to try out this strategy!

Helping Your Pokémon Eggs Hatch

Once you've found a Pokémon Egg, the next step is to help it hatch. Pokémon Eggs naturally hatch over time as you carry them around in your team, but they'll hatch even faster if you place Pokémon with the right Abilities next to them in your party. As explained on page 97, the Abilities Flame Body and Magma Armor will help Pokémon Eggs hatch faster in your party. Magma Armor isn't found in any of the Pokémon native to the Alola region, but Flame Body is!

Alola region Pokémon with the Flame Body Ability: Fletchinder, Talonflame, Magby, Magmar, Magmortar

Tip

You can also leave Pokémon in the hot springs on Poké Pelago's Isle Avue to keep them toasty and help them hatch! Learn how to develop Isle Avue and more on page 309.

A Mythical Pokémon that can find Pokémon Eggs?!

Only one Mythical Pokémon has ever been known to find Pokémon Eggs at a Pokémon Nursery or Day Care. The Mythical Pokémon Manaphy, when left with a Ditto, can find a Pokémon Egg that hatches into a mysterious Pokémon called Phione. While Phione has never been found to evolve into Manaphy, it has also never been found in the wild.

Regional Variants and Pokémon Eggs

Pokémon Eggs you hatch in the Alola region will hatch into their Alolan regional variant if they have one, even if the Pokémon you left at the Pokémon Nursery were not native to Alola. However, if you have a Pokémon that is not an Alolan regional variant hold an Everstone when you drop it off at the Pokémon Nursery, then the Pokémon Eggs you find will hatch into its same form.

Tip

What about Pokémon that can have multiple forms, like Oricorio? A Pokémon Egg will take on the same form as the female Pokémon left at the Pokémon Nursery—or the form of the non-Ditto Pokémon if you leave a Pokémon of any gender with Ditto.

Egg Group Tables

The following pages feature the complete Egg Group tables for all Pokémon discovered to date. The first column shows their number in the Alola Pokédex, which you can use with the preceding Pokémon List (p. 280) to determine the best way to obtain these Pokémon. If there's no number, then the Pokémon can't normally be caught in the Alola region, and you'll probably have to obtain it by bringing it in from another game via *Pokémon Bank* (p. 316) or by receiving it in a trade (p. 306).

Tip

Many Pokémon belong to two Egg Groups, which is the key to passing along surprising features to the Pokémon Eggs that they discover. If a Pokémon belongs to more than one Egg Group, it will appear in the tables in each Egg Group's section.

Key to these tables

Pokémon's name → Accelgor

Alola Pokédex number → 23

If there is no number, then the Pokémon cannot be obtained normally in Alola and will probably have to be found by trading on the GTS (p. 307) or retrieved from *Pokémon Bank* (p. 316).

Genders this Pokémon can have → ♂/♀

Bug Group		
Bug Group Only		
	Accelgor	♂/♀
23	Ariados	♂/♀
	Beautifly	♂/♀
	Beedrill	♂/♀
	Burmy	♂/♀
19	Butterfree	♂/♀

Amorphous Group

Amorphous Group Only

No.	Pokémon	Gender
	Banette	♂/♀
	Chandelure	♂/♀
	Chimecho	♂/♀
65	Drifblim	♂/♀
64	Drifloon	♂/♀
	Duosion	♂/♀
	Dusclops	♂/♀
	Dusknoir	♂/♀
	Duskull	♂/♀
	Eelektrik	♂/♀
	Eelektross	♂/♀
	Frillish	♂/♀
	Gallade	♂
	Gardevoir	♂/♀
61	Gastly	♂/♀
63	Gengar	♂/♀
	Gourgeist	♂/♀
50	Grimer	♂/♀
	Gulpin	♂/♀
62	Haunter	♂/♀
	Jellicent	♂/♀
	Kirlia	♂/♀
	Koffing	♂/♀
	Lampent	♂/♀
	Litwick	♂/♀
	Magcargo	♂/♀
242	Mimikyu	♂/♀
66	Misdreavus	♂/♀
67	Mismagius	♂/♀
51	Muk	♂/♀
187	Palossand	♂/♀
	Pumpkaboo	♂/♀
	Ralts	♂/♀
	Reuniclus	♂/♀
	Rotom	Unknown
186	Sandygast	♂/♀
	Shuppet	♂/♀
	Slugma	♂/♀
	Solosis	♂/♀
	Spiritomb	♂/♀
	Swalot	♂/♀
	Tynamo	♂/♀
	Weezing	♂/♀
	Wobbuffet	♂/♀

Amorphous Group and Fairy Group

No.	Pokémon	Gender
181	Castform	♂/♀

Amorphous Group and Grass Group

No.	Pokémon	Gender
196	Phantump	♂/♀
197	Trevenant	♂/♀

Amorphous Group and Mineral Group

No.	Pokémon	Gender
	Cofagrigus	♂/♀
	Yamask	♂/♀

Amorphous Group and Water Group 1

No.	Pokémon	Gender
261	Gastrodon	♂/♀
260	Shellos	♂/♀
	Stunfisk	♂/♀

Bug Group

Bug Group Only

No.	Pokémon	Gender
	Accelgor	♂/♀
23	Ariados	♂/♀
	Beautifly	♂/♀
	Beedrill	♂/♀
	Burmy	♂/♀
19	Butterfree	♂/♀
	Cascoon	♂/♀
17	Caterpie	♂/♀
28	Charjabug	♂/♀
	Combee	♂/♀
	Durant	♂/♀
	Dustox	♂/♀
	Escavalier	♂/♀
237	Flygon	♂/♀
	Forretress	♂/♀
	Galvantula	♂/♀
	Gligar	♂/♀
	Gliscor	♂/♀
27	Grubbin	♂/♀
	Heracross	♂/♀
	Joltik	♂/♀
	Kakuna	♂/♀
	Karrablast	♂/♀
	Kricketot	♂/♀
	Kricketune	♂/♀
	Larvesta	♂/♀
	Leavanny	♂/♀
21	Ledian	♂/♀
20	Ledyba	♂/♀
18	Metapod	♂/♀
	Mothim	♂
	Nincada	♂/♀
	Ninjask	♂/♀
	Pineco	♂/♀
175	Pinsir	♂/♀
	Scatterbug	♂/♀
276	Scizor	♂/♀
	Scolipede	♂/♀
275	Scyther	♂/♀
	Sewaddle	♂/♀
	Shelmet	♂/♀
	Shuckle	♂/♀
	Silcoon	♂/♀
	Spewpa	♂/♀
22	Spinarak	♂/♀
	Swadloon	♂/♀
235	Trapinch	♂/♀
	Venipede	♂/♀
	Venomoth	♂/♀
	Venonat	♂/♀
	Vespiquen	♀
236	Vibrava	♂/♀
29	Vikavolt	♂/♀
	Vivillon	♂/♀
	Volcarona	♂/♀
	Weedle	♂/♀
	Whirlipede	♂/♀
	Wormadam	♀
	Wurmple	♂/♀
	Yanma	♂/♀
	Yanmega	♂/♀

Bug Group and Fairy Group

No.	Pokémon	Gender
83	Cutiefly	♂/♀
84	Ribombee	♂/♀

Bug Group and Grass Group

No.	Pokémon	Gender
147	Paras	♂/♀
148	Parasect	♂/♀

Bug Group and Human-Like Group

No.	Pokémon	Gender
	Illumise	♀
	Volbeat	♂

Bug Group

Bug Group and Mineral Group

No.	Pokémon	Gender
	Crustle	♂/♀
	Dwebble	♂/♀

Bug Group and Water Group 1

No.	Pokémon	Gender
142	Araquanid	♂/♀
141	Dewpider	♂/♀
140	Masquerain	♂/♀
139	Surskit	♂/♀

Bug Group and Water Group 3

No.	Pokémon	Gender
	Drapion	♂/♀
183	Golisopod	♂/♀
	Skorupi	♂/♀
182	Wimpod	♂/♀

Ditto Group

No.	Pokémon	Gender
209	Ditto	Unknown

Dragon Group

Dragon Group Only

No.	Pokémon	Gender
117	Bagon	♂/♀
	Deino	♂/♀
180	Goodra	♂/♀
178	Goomy	♂/♀
272	Hakamo-o	♂/♀
	Hydreigon	♂/♀
271	Jangmo-o	♂/♀
273	Kommo-o	♂/♀
119	Salamence	♂/♀
118	Shelgon	♂/♀
179	Sliggoo	♂/♀
	Zweilous	♂/♀

Dragon Group and Field Group

No.	Pokémon	Gender
	Arbok	♂/♀
	Ekans	♂/♀
	Scrafty	♂/♀
	Scraggy	♂/♀
	Seviper	♂/♀

Dragon Group and Flying Group

No.	Pokémon	Gender
	Swablu	♂/♀
	Altaria	♂/♀

Dragon Group and Monster Group

No.	Pokémon	Gender
	Axew	♂/♀
	Charizard	♂/♀
	Charmander	♂/♀
	Charmeleon	♂/♀
244	Drampa	♂/♀
	Druddigon	♂/♀
	Fraxure	♂/♀
239	Gabite	♂/♀
240	Garchomp	♂/♀
238	Gible	♂/♀
	Grovyle	♂/♀
	Haxorus	♂/♀
	Heliolisk	♂/♀
	Helioptile	♂/♀
161	Salandit	♂/♀
162	Salazzle	♀
	Sceptile	♂/♀
	Treecko	♂/♀
224	Turtonator	♂/♀
	Tyrantrum	♂/♀
	Tyrunt	♂/♀

Dragon Group

Dragon Group and Water Group 1

No.	Pokémon	Gender
	Horsea	♂/♀
	Seadra	♂/♀
	Kingdra	♂/♀
155	Feebas	♂/♀
156	Milotic	♂/♀
	Skrelp	♂/♀
	Dragalge	♂/♀
281	Dratini	♂/♀
282	Dragonair	♂/♀
283	Dragonite	♂/♀

Dragon Group and Water Group 2

No.	Pokémon	Gender
91	Magikarp	♂/♀
92	Gyarados	♂/♀

Fairy Group

Fairy Group Only

No.	Pokémon	Gender
	Aromatisse	♂/♀
	Audino	♂/♀
34	Blissey	♀
33	Chansey	♀
212	Clefable	♂/♀
211	Clefairy	♂/♀
	Flabébé	♀
	Floette	♀
	Florges	♀
135	Jigglypuff	♂/♀
	Minun	♂/♀
	Plusle	♂/♀
	Slurpuff	♂/♀
	Spritzee	♂/♀
	Swirlix	♂/♀
136	Wigglytuff	♂/♀

Fairy Group and Amorphous Group

No.	Pokémon	Gender
181	Castform	♂/♀

Fairy Group and Bug Group

No.	Pokémon	Gender
83	Cutiefly	♂/♀
84	Ribombee	♂/♀

Fairy Group and Field Group

No.	Pokémon	Gender
	Dedenne	♂/♀
	Delcatty	♂/♀
259	Granbull	♂/♀
	Mawile	♂/♀
	Pachirisu	♂/♀
25	Pikachu	♂/♀
26	Raichu	♂/♀
	Skitty	♂/♀
258	Snubbull	♂/♀
225	Togedemaru	♂/♀

Fairy Group and Flying Group

No.	Pokémon	Gender
	Togetic	♂/♀
	Togekiss	♂/♀

Fairy Group and Grass Group

No.	Pokémon	Gender
	Breloom	♂/♀
	Cherrim	♂/♀
	Cherubi	♂/♀
87	Cottonee	♂/♀
	Hoppip	♂/♀
	Jumpluff	♂/♀
	Roselia	♂/♀
	Roserade	♂/♀
	Shroomish	♂/♀
	Skiploom	♂/♀
88	Whimsicott	♂/♀

Fairy Group

Fairy Group and Mineral Group

No.	Pokémon	Gender
101	Carbink	Unknown
248	Froslass	♀
247	Glalie	♂/♀
246	Snorunt	♂/♀

Fairy Group and Water Group 1

No.	Pokémon	Gender
	Azumarill	♂/♀
	Manaphy	Unknown
	Marill	♂/♀
	Phione	Unknown

Field Group

Field Group Only

No.	Pokémon	Gender
245	Absol	♂/♀
	Aipom	♂/♀
	Ambipom	♂/♀
53	Arcanine	♂/♀
	Beartic	♂/♀
170	Bewear	♂/♀
	Blaziken	♂/♀
	Blitzle	♂/♀
	Bouffalant	♂/♀
	Braixen	♂/♀
	Bunnelby	♂/♀
	Camerupt	♂/♀
	Chesnaught	♂/♀
	Chespin	♂/♀
	Cinccino	♂/♀
	Combusken	♂/♀
	Cubchoo	♂/♀
	Cyndaquil	♂/♀
	Darmanitan	♂/♀
	Darumaka	♂/♀
	Deerling	♂/♀
	Delphox	♂/♀
	Dewott	♂/♀
	Diggersby	♂/♀
71	Diglett	♂/♀
	Donphan	♂/♀
	Drilbur	♂/♀
72	Dugtrio	♂/♀
	Dunsparce	♂/♀
123	Eevee	♂/♀
	Electrike	♂/♀
	Emboar	♂/♀
274	Emolga	♂/♀
127	Espeon	♂/♀
	Espurr	♂/♀
	Excadrill	♂/♀
	Fennekin	♂/♀
126	Flareon	♂/♀
	Furfrou	♂/♀
	Furret	♂/♀
	Girafarig	♂/♀
130	Glaceon	♂/♀
	Glameow	♂/♀
	Gogoat	♂/♀
52	Growlithe	♂/♀
	Grumpig	♂/♀
14	Gumshoos	♂/♀
	Heatmor	♂/♀
121	Herdier	♂/♀
	Hippopotas	♂/♀
	Hippowdon	♂/♀
	Houndoom	♂/♀
	Houndour	♂/♀
6	Incineroar	♂/♀
125	Jolteon	♂/♀
	Kecleon	♂/♀
222	Komala	♂/♀
233	Krokorok	♂/♀

Field Group

No.	Pokémon	Gender
234	Krookodile	♂/♀
129	Leafeon	♂/♀
	Liepard	♂/♀
120	Lillipup	♂/♀
	Linoone	♂/♀
	Litleo	♂/♀
4	Litten	♂/♀
	Luxio	♂/♀
	Luxray	♂/♀
104	Lycanroc	♂/♀
	Mamoswine	♂/♀
	Manectric	♂/♀
79	Mankey	♂/♀
	Meowstic	♂/♀
45	Meowth	♂/♀
	Mightyena	♂/♀
138	Miltank	♀
	Minccino	♂/♀
132	Mudbray	♂/♀
133	Mudsdale	♂/♀
	Munna	♂/♀
	Musharna	♂/♀
254	Ninetales	♂/♀
	Numel	♂/♀
176	Oranguru	♂/♀
	Oshawott	♂/♀
	Panpour	♂/♀
	Pansage	♂/♀
	Pansear	♂/♀
177	Passimian	♂/♀
	Patrat	♂/♀
46	Persian	♂/♀
	Phanpy	♂/♀
	Pignite	♂/♀
	Piloswine	♂/♀
	Ponyta	♂/♀
	Poochyena	♂/♀
80	Primeape	♂/♀
	Purrloin	♂/♀
	Purugly	♂/♀
	Pyroar	♂/♀
	Quilava	♂/♀
	Quilladin	♂/♀
	Rapidash	♂/♀
16	Raticate	♂/♀
15	Rattata	♂/♀
103	Rockruff	♂/♀
	Samurott	♂/♀
232	Sandile	♂/♀
251	Sandshrew	♂/♀
252	Sandslash	♂/♀
	Sawsbuck	♂/♀
	Sentret	♂/♀
	Shinx	♂/♀
	Simipour	♂/♀
	Simisage	♂/♀
	Simisear	♂/♀
	Skiddo	♂/♀
	Skuntank	♂/♀
	Slaking	♂/♀
	Slakoth	♂/♀
58	Smeargle	♂/♀
249	Sneasel	♂/♀
	Spoink	♂/♀
	Stantler	♂/♀
122	Stoutland	♂/♀
169	Stufful	♂/♀
	Stunky	♂/♀
	Swinub	♂/♀
131	Sylveon	♂/♀
137	Tauros	♂
	Teddiursa	♂/♀
	Tepig	♂/♀
	Torchic	♂/♀

Field Group

#	Pokémon	Gender
223	Torkoal	♂/♀
5	Torracat	♂/♀
	Typhlosion	♂/♀
128	Umbreon	♂/♀
	Ursaring	♂/♀
124	Vaporeon	♂/♀
	Vigoroth	♂/♀
253	Vulpix	♂/♀
	Watchog	♂/♀
250	Weavile	♂/♀
13	Yungoos	♂/♀
	Zangoose	♂/♀
	Zebstrika	♂/♀
	Zigzagoon	♂/♀
	Zoroark	♂/♀
	Zorua	♂/♀

Field Group and Dragon Group

#	Pokémon	Gender
	Arbok	♂/♀
	Ekans	♂/♀
	Scrafty	♂/♀
	Scraggy	♂/♀
	Seviper	♂/♀

Field Group and Fairy Group

#	Pokémon	Gender
	Dedenne	♂/♀
	Delcatty	♂/♀
259	Granbull	♂/♀
	Mawile	♂/♀
	Pachirisu	♂/♀
25	Pikachu	♂/♀
26	Raichu	♂/♀
	Skitty	♂/♀
258	Snubbull	♂/♀
225	Togedemaru	♂/♀

Field Group and Flying Group

#	Pokémon	Gender
	Farfetch'd	♂/♀
	Swoobat	♂/♀
	Woobat	♂/♀

Field Group and Grass Group

#	Pokémon	Gender
	Nuzleaf	♂/♀
	Seedot	♂/♀
	Serperior	♂/♀
	Servine	♂/♀
	Shiftry	♂/♀
	Snivy	♂/♀

Field Group and Human-Like Group

#	Pokémon	Gender
	Buneary	♂/♀
	Chimchar	♂/♀
	Infernape	♂/♀
	Lopunny	♂/♀
280	Lucario	♂/♀
	Mienfoo	♂/♀
	Mienshao	♂/♀
	Monferno	♂/♀
220	Pancham	♂/♀
221	Pangoro	♂/♀
105	Spinda	♂/♀

Field Group and Monster Group

#	Pokémon	Gender
	Ampharos	♂/♀
	Exploud	♂/♀
	Flaaffy	♂/♀
	Loudred	♂/♀
	Mareep	♂/♀
	Nidoking	♂
	Nidoran♀	♀
	Nidoran♂	♂
	Nidorino	♂
	Rhydon	♂/♀
	Rhyhorn	♂/♀
	Rhyperior	♂/♀
	Whismur	♂/♀

Field Group

Field Group and Water Group 1

#	Pokémon	Gender
	Bibarel	♂/♀
	Bidoof	♂/♀
8	Brionne	♂/♀
	Buizel	♂/♀
81	Delibird	♂/♀
	Dewgong	♂/♀
	Empoleon	♂/♀
	Floatzel	♂/♀
90	Golduck	♂/♀
	Piplup	♂/♀
7	Popplio	♂/♀
9	Primarina	♂/♀
	Prinplup	♂/♀
89	Psyduck	♂/♀
	Quagsire	♂/♀
	Sealeo	♂/♀
	Seel	♂/♀
	Spheal	♂/♀
	Walrein	♂/♀
	Wooper	♂/♀

Field Group and Water Group 2

#	Pokémon	Gender
266	Wailmer	♂/♀
267	Wailord	♂/♀

Flying Group

Flying Group Only

#	Pokémon	Gender
284	Aerodactyl	♂/♀
76	Braviary	♂
	Chatot	♂/♀
70	Crobat	♂/♀
2	Dartrix	♂/♀
3	Decidueye	♂/♀
	Dodrio	♂/♀
	Doduo	♂/♀
74	Fearow	♂/♀
159	Fletchinder	♂/♀
158	Fletchling	♂/♀
69	Golbat	♂/♀
278	Honchkrow	♂/♀
	Hoothoot	♂/♀
78	Mandibuzz	♀
277	Murkrow	♂/♀
	Natu	♂/♀
	Noctowl	♂/♀
	Noibat	♂/♀
	Noivern	♂/♀
82	Oricorio	♂/♀
	Pidgeot	♂/♀
	Pidgeotto	♂/♀
	Pidgey	♂/♀
	Pidove	♂/♀
10	Pikipek	♂/♀
1	Rowlet	♂/♀
75	Rufflet	♂
	Sigilyph	♂/♀
208	Skarmory	♂/♀
73	Spearow	♂/♀
	Staraptor	♂/♀
	Staravia	♂/♀
	Starly	♂/♀
	Swellow	♂/♀
	Taillow	♂/♀
160	Talonflame	♂/♀
12	Toucannon	♂/♀
	Tranquill	♂/♀
11	Trumbeak	♂/♀
	Unfezant	♂/♀
77	Vullaby	♀
	Xatu	♂/♀
68	Zubat	♂/♀

Flying Group

Flying Group and Dragon Group

#	Pokémon	Gender
	Altaria	♂/♀
	Swablu	♂/♀

Flying Group and Fairy Group

#	Pokémon	Gender
	Togetic	♂/♀
	Togekiss	♂/♀

Flying Group and Field Group

#	Pokémon	Gender
	Farfetch'd	♂/♀
	Swoobat	♂/♀
	Woobat	♂/♀

Flying Group and Water Group 1

#	Pokémon	Gender
	Ducklett	♂/♀
41	Pelipper	♂/♀
	Swanna	♂/♀
40	Wingull	♂/♀

Flying Group and Water Group 3

#	Pokémon	Gender
192	Archen	♂/♀
193	Archeops	♂/♀

Grass Group

Grass Group Only

#	Pokémon	Gender
	Amoonguss	♂/♀
	Bellossom	♂/♀
	Bellsprout	♂/♀
171	Bounsweet	♀
	Carnivine	♂/♀
174	Comfey	♂/♀
269	Exeggcute	♂/♀
270	Exeggutor	♂/♀
143	Fomantis	♂/♀
	Foongus	♂/♀
	Gloom	♂/♀
86	Lilligant	♀
144	Lurantis	♂/♀
	Maractus	♂/♀
145	Morelull	♂/♀
	Oddish	♂/♀
85	Petilil	♀
146	Shiinotic	♂/♀
172	Steenee	♀
	Sunflora	♂/♀
	Sunkern	♂/♀
	Tangela	♂/♀
	Tangrowth	♂/♀
173	Tsareena	♀
	Victreebel	♂/♀
	Vileplume	♂/♀
	Weepinbell	♂/♀

Grass Group and Amorphous Group

#	Pokémon	Gender
196	Phantump	♂/♀
197	Trevenant	♂/♀

Grass Group and Bug Group

#	Pokémon	Gender
147	Paras	♂/♀
148	Parasect	♂/♀

Grass Group and Fairy Group

#	Pokémon	Gender
	Breloom	♂/♀
	Cherrim	♂/♀
	Cherubi	♂/♀
87	Cottonee	♂/♀
	Hoppip	♂/♀
	Jumpluff	♂/♀
	Roselia	♂/♀
	Roserade	♂/♀
	Shroomish	♂/♀
	Skiploom	♂/♀
88	Whimsicott	♂/♀

Grass Group

Grass Group and Field Group

#	Pokémon	Gender
	Nuzleaf	♂/♀
	Seedot	♂/♀
	Serperior	♂/♀
	Servine	♂/♀
	Shiftry	♂/♀
	Snivy	♂/♀

Grass Group and Human-Like Group

#	Pokémon	Gender
	Cacnea	♂/♀
	Cacturne	♂/♀

Grass Group and Mineral Group

#	Pokémon	Gender
	Ferroseed	♂/♀
	Ferrothorn	♂/♀

Grass Group and Monster Group

#	Pokémon	Gender
	Abomasnow	♂/♀
	Bayleef	♂/♀
	Bulbasaur	♂/♀
	Chikorita	♂/♀
	Grotle	♂/♀
	Ivysaur	♂/♀
	Meganium	♂/♀
	Snover	♂/♀
	Torterra	♂/♀
	Tropius	♂/♀
	Turtwig	♂/♀
	Venusaur	♂/♀

Grass Group and Water Group 1

#	Pokémon	Gender
	Lombre	♂/♀
	Lotad	♂/♀
	Ludicolo	♂/♀

Human-Like Group

Human-Like Group Only

#	Pokémon	Gender
42	Abra	♂/♀
44	Alakazam	♂/♀
	Beheeyem	♂/♀
	Bisharp	♂/♀
	Conkeldurr	♂/♀
	Croagunk	♂/♀
54	Drowzee	♂/♀
227	Electabuzz	♂/♀
228	Electivire	♂/♀
	Elgyem	♂/♀
	Gothita	♂/♀
	Gothitelle	♂/♀
	Gothorita	♂/♀
	Gurdurr	♂/♀
57	Hariyama	♂/♀
	Hawlucha	♂/♀
	Hitmonchan	♂
	Hitmonlee	♂
	Hitmontop	♂
55	Hypno	♂/♀
	Jynx	♀
43	Kadabra	♂/♀
97	Machamp	♂/♀
96	Machoke	♂/♀
95	Machop	♂/♀
167	Magmar	♂/♀
168	Magmortar	♂/♀
56	Makuhita	♂/♀
	Medicham	♂/♀
	Meditite	♂/♀
	Mr. Mime	♂/♀
	Pawniard	♂/♀
102	Sableye	♂/♀
	Sawk	♂
	Throh	♂
	Timburr	♂/♀
	Toxicroak	♂/♀

Human-Like Group

Human-Like Group and Bug Group

#	Pokémon	Gender
	Volbeat	♂
	Illumise	♀

Human-Like Group and Field Group

#	Pokémon	Gender
105	Spinda	♂/♀
	Chimchar	♂/♀
	Monferno	♂/♀
	Infernape	♂/♀
	Buneary	♂/♀
	Lopunny	♂/♀
	Mienfoo	♂/♀
	Mienshao	♂/♀
220	Pancham	♂/♀
221	Pangoro	♂/♀
280	Lucario	♂/♀

Human-Like Group and Grass Group

#	Pokémon	Gender
	Cacnea	♂/♀
	Cacturne	♂/♀

Mineral Group

Mineral Group Only

#	Pokémon	Gender
	Aegislash	♂/♀
	Baltoy	Unknown
214	Beldum	Unknown
99	Boldore	♂/♀
	Bronzong	Unknown
	Bronzor	Unknown
	Claydol	Unknown
	Cryogonal	Unknown
263	Dhelmise	Unknown
	Doublade	♂/♀
	Electrode	Unknown
207	Garbodor	♂/♀
229	Geodude	♂/♀
100	Gigalith	♂/♀
231	Golem	♂/♀
	Golett	Unknown
	Golurk	Unknown
230	Graveler	♂/♀
	Honedge	♂/♀
	Klang	Unknown
241	Klefki	♂/♀
	Klink	Unknown
	Klinklang	Unknown
	Lunatone	Unknown
47	Magnemite	Unknown
48	Magneton	Unknown
49	Magnezone	Unknown
216	Metagross	Unknown
215	Metang	Unknown
213	Minior	Unknown
198	Nosepass	♂/♀
	Onix	♂/♀
217	Porygon	Unknown
218	Porygon2	Unknown
219	Porygon-Z	Unknown
199	Probopass	♂/♀
98	Roggenrola	♂/♀
	Shedinja	Unknown
	Solrock	Unknown
	Steelix	♂/♀
31	Sudowoodo	♂/♀
206	Trubbish	♂/♀
256	Vanillish	♂/♀
255	Vanillite	♂/♀
257	Vanilluxe	♂/♀
	Voltorb	Unknown

Mineral Group and Amorphous Group

#	Pokémon	Gender
	Cofagrigus	♂/♀
	Yamask	♂/♀

Mineral Group

Mineral Group and Bug Group

#	Pokémon	Gender
	Crustle	♂/♀
	Dwebble	♂/♀

Mineral Group and Fairy Group

#	Pokémon	Gender
101	Carbink	Unknown
248	Froslass	♀
247	Glalie	♂/♀
246	Snorunt	♂/♀

Mineral Group and Grass Group

#	Pokémon	Gender
	Ferroseed	♂/♀
	Ferrothorn	♂/♀

Monster Group

Monster Group Only

#	Pokémon	Gender
	Aggron	♂/♀
	Amaura	♂/♀
	Aron	♂/♀
	Aurorus	♂/♀
	Avalugg	♂/♀
191	Bastiodon	♂/♀
	Bergmite	♂/♀
188	Cranidos	♂/♀
163	Cubone	♂/♀
165	Kangaskhan	♀
	Lairon	♂/♀
	Larvitar	♂/♀
	Lickilicky	♂/♀
	Lickitung	♂/♀
164	Marowak	♂/♀
	Pupitar	♂/♀
189	Rampardos	♂/♀
190	Shieldon	♂/♀
36	Snorlax	♂/♀
	Tyranitar	♂/♀

Monster Group and Dragon Group

#	Pokémon	Gender
	Axew	♂/♀
	Charizard	♂/♀
	Charmander	♂/♀
	Charmeleon	♂/♀
244	Drampa	♂/♀
	Druddigon	♂/♀
	Fraxure	♂/♀
239	Gabite	♂/♀
240	Garchomp	♂/♀
238	Gible	♂/♀
	Grovyle	♂/♀
	Haxorus	♂/♀
	Heliolisk	♂/♀
	Helioptile	♂/♀
161	Salandit	♂/♀
162	Salazzle	♀
	Sceptile	♂/♀
	Treecko	♂/♀
224	Turtonator	♂/♀
	Tyrantrum	♂/♀
	Tyrunt	♂/♀

Monster Group and Field Group

#	Pokémon	Gender
	Ampharos	♂/♀
	Exploud	♂/♀
	Flaaffy	♂/♀
	Loudred	♂/♀
	Mareep	♂/♀
	Nidoking	♂
	Nidoran♀	♀
	Nidoran♂	♂
	Nidorino	♂
	Rhydon	♂/♀
	Rhyhorn	♂/♀
	Rhyperior	♂/♀
	Whismur	♂/♀

Monster Group and Grass Group

No.	Pokémon	Gender
	Abomasnow	♂/♀
	Bayleef	♂/♀
	Bulbasaur	♂/♀
	Chikorita	♂/♀
	Grotle	♂/♀
	Ivysaur	♂/♀
	Meganium	♂/♀
	Snover	♂/♀
	Torterra	♂/♀
	Tropius	♂/♀
	Turtwig	♂/♀
	Venusaur	♂/♀

Monster Group and Water Group 1

No.	Pokémon	Gender
	Blastoise	♂/♀
	Croconaw	♂/♀
	Feraligatr	♂/♀
268	Lapras	♂/♀
	Marshtomp	♂/♀
	Mudkip	♂/♀
38	Slowbro	♂/♀
39	Slowking	♂/♀
37	Slowpoke	♂/♀
	Squirtle	♂/♀
	Swampert	♂/♀
	Totodile	♂/♀
	Wartortle	♂/♀

Tip

Despite their similar names, Water Group 1, Water Group 2, and Water Group 3 are in fact separate Egg Groups. Don't assume that leaving a Pokémon from Water Group 1 and Water Group 3, for example, will make you able to find a Pokémon Egg. The Pokémon still need to share a common group between them!

Water Group 1

Water Group 1 Only

No.	Pokémon	Gender
	Clamperl	♂/♀
	Froakie	♂/♀
	Frogadier	♂/♀
	Gorebyss	♂/♀
	Greninja	♂/♀
	Huntail	♂/♀
	Mantine	♂/♀
113	Mareanie	♂/♀
	Palpitoad	♂/♀
152	Politoed	♂/♀
149	Poliwag	♂/♀
150	Poliwhirl	♂/♀
151	Poliwrath	♂/♀
200	Pyukumuku	♂/♀
	Seismitoad	♂/♀
114	Toxapex	♂/♀
	Tympole	♂/♀

Water Group 1 and Amorphous Group

No.	Pokémon	Gender
261	Gastrodon	♂/♀
260	Shellos	♂/♀
	Stunfisk	♂/♀

Water Group 1 and Bug Group

No.	Pokémon	Gender
142	Araquanid	♂/♀
141	Dewpider	♂/♀
140	Masquerain	♂/♀
139	Surskit	♂/♀

Water Group 1 and Dragon Group

No.	Pokémon	Gender
	Dragalge	♂/♀
282	Dragonair	♂/♀
283	Dragonite	♂/♀
281	Dratini	♂/♀
155	Feebas	♂/♀
	Horsea	♂/♀
	Kingdra	♂/♀
156	Milotic	♂/♀
	Seadra	♂/♀
	Skrelp	♂/♀

Water Group 1 and Fairy Group

No.	Pokémon	Gender
	Azumarill	♂/♀
	Manaphy	Unknown
	Marill	♂/♀
	Phione	Unknown

Water Group 1 and Field Group

No.	Pokémon	Gender
	Bibarel	♂/♀
	Bidoof	♂/♀
8	Brionne	♂/♀
	Buizel	♂/♀

Water Group 1

No.	Pokémon	Gender
81	Delibird	♂/♀
	Dewgong	♂/♀
	Empoleon	♂/♀
	Floatzel	♂/♀
90	Golduck	♂/♀
	Piplup	♂/♀
7	Popplio	♂/♀
9	Primarina	♂/♀
	Prinplup	♂/♀
89	Psyduck	♂/♀
	Quagsire	♂/♀
	Sealeo	♂/♀
	Seel	♂/♀
	Spheal	♂/♀
	Walrein	♂/♀
	Wooper	♂/♀

Water Group 1 and Flying Group

No.	Pokémon	Gender
	Ducklett	♂/♀
41	Pelipper	♂/♀
	Swanna	♂/♀
40	Wingull	♂/♀

Water Group 1 and Grass Group

No.	Pokémon	Gender
	Lombre	♂/♀
	Lotad	♂/♀
	Ludicolo	♂/♀

Water Group 1 and Monster Group

No.	Pokémon	Gender
	Blastoise	♂/♀
	Croconaw	♂/♀
	Feraligatr	♂/♀
268	Lapras	♂/♀
	Marshtomp	♂/♀
	Mudkip	♂/♀
38	Slowbro	♂/♀
39	Slowking	♂/♀
37	Slowpoke	♂/♀
	Squirtle	♂/♀
	Swampert	♂/♀
	Totodile	♂/♀
	Wartortle	♂/♀

Water Group 1 and Water Group 2

No.	Pokémon	Gender
157	Alomomola	♂/♀
	Inkay	♂/♀
	Malamar	♂/♀
	Octillery	♂/♀
262	Relicanth	♂/♀
	Remoraid	♂/♀

Water Group 1 and Water Group 3

No.	Pokémon	Gender
195	Carracosta	♂/♀
	Clauncher	♂/♀
	Clawitzer	♂/♀

Water Group 1

No.	Pokémon	Gender
	Corphish	♂/♀
112	Corsola	♂/♀
	Crawdaunt	♂/♀
	Kabuto	♂/♀
	Kabutops	♂/♀
	Omanyte	♂/♀
	Omastar	♂/♀
194	Tirtouga	♂/♀

Water Group 2

Water Group 2 Only

No.	Pokémon	Gender
93	Barboach	♂/♀
	Basculin	♂/♀
243	Bruxish	♂/♀
264	Carvanha	♂/♀
201	Chinchou	♂/♀
108	Finneon	♂/♀
153	Goldeen	♂/♀
202	Lanturn	♂/♀
109	Lumineon	♂/♀
111	Luvdisc	♂/♀
	Qwilfish	♂/♀
154	Seaking	♂/♀
265	Sharpedo	♂/♀
94	Whiscash	♂/♀
110	Wishiwashi	♂/♀

Water Group 2 and Dragon Group

No.	Pokémon	Gender
92	Gyarados	♂/♀
91	Magikarp	♂/♀

Water Group 2 and Field Group

No.	Pokémon	Gender
266	Wailmer	♂/♀
267	Wailord	♂/♀

Water Group 2 and Water Group 1

No.	Pokémon	Gender
157	Alomomola	♂/♀
	Inkay	♂/♀
	Malamar	♂/♀
	Octillery	♂/♀
262	Relicanth	♂/♀
	Remoraid	♂/♀

Water Group 3

Water Group 3 Only

No.	Pokémon	Gender
	Anorith	♂/♀
	Armaldo	♂/♀
	Barbaracle	♂/♀
	Binacle	♂/♀
116	Cloyster	♂/♀
60	Crabominable	♂/♀
59	Crabrawler	♂/♀
	Cradily	♂/♀

Water Group 3

No.	Pokémon	Gender
	Kingler	♂/♀
	Krabby	♂/♀
	Lileep	♂/♀
115	Shellder	♂/♀
185	Starmie	Unknown
184	Staryu	Unknown
106	Tentacool	♂/♀
107	Tentacruel	♂/♀

Water Group 3 and Bug Group

No.	Pokémon	Gender
	Drapion	♂/♀
183	Golisopod	♂/♀
	Skorupi	♂/♀
182	Wimpod	♂/♀

Water Group 3 and Flying Group

No.	Pokémon	Gender
192	Archen	♂/♀
193	Archeops	♂/♀

Water Group 3 and Water Group 1

No.	Pokémon	Gender
195	Carracosta	♂/♀
	Clauncher	♂/♀
	Clawitzer	♂/♀
	Corphish	♂/♀
112	Corsola	♂/♀
	Crawdaunt	♂/♀
	Kabuto	♂/♀
	Kabutops	♂/♀
	Omanyte	♂/♀
	Omastar	♂/♀
194	Tirtouga	♂/♀

No Eggs Discovered

No.	Pokémon	Gender
	Arceus	Unknown
	Articuno	Unknown
	Ash-Greninja	♂
	Azelf	Unknown
	Azurill	♂/♀
30	Bonsly	♂/♀
	Budew	♂/♀
	Celebi	Unknown
	Chingling	♂/♀
210	Cleffa	♂/♀
	Cobalion	Unknown
	Cresselia	♀
	Darkrai	Unknown
	Deoxys	Unknown
	Dialga	Unknown
	Diancie	Unknown
226	Elekid	♂/♀
	Entei	Unknown
	Genesect	Unknown
	Giratina	Unknown
	Groudon	Unknown
32	Happiny	♀
	Heatran	♂/♀
	Ho-Oh	Unknown

No Eggs Discovered

No.	Pokémon	Gender
	Hoopa	Unknown
134	Igglybuff	♂/♀
	Jirachi	Unknown
	Keldeo	Unknown
	Kyogre	Unknown
	Kyurem	Unknown
	Landorus	♂
	Latias	♀
	Latios	♂
	Lugia	Unknown
292	Lunala	Unknown
166	Magby	♂/♀
	Mantyke	♂/♀
	Meloetta	Unknown
	Mesprit	Unknown
	Mew	Unknown
	Mewtwo	Unknown
	Mime Jr.	♂/♀
	Moltres	Unknown
35	Munchlax	♂/♀
	Nidoqueen	♀
	Nidorina	♀
	Palkia	Unknown
24	Pichu	♂/♀
	Raikou	Unknown
	Rayquaza	Unknown
	Regice	Unknown
	Regigigas	Unknown
	Regirock	Unknown
	Registeel	Unknown
	Reshiram	Unknown
279	Riolu	♂/♀
	Shaymin	Unknown
204	Silvally	Unknown
	Smoochum	♀
291	Solgaleo	Unknown
	Suicune	Unknown
287	Tapu Bulu	Unknown
288	Tapu Fini	Unknown
285	Tapu Koko	Unknown
286	Tapu Lele	Unknown
	Terrakion	Unknown
	Thundurus	♂
	Togepi	♂/♀
	Tornadus	♂
203	Type: Null	Unknown
	Tyrogue	♂
	Unown	Unknown
	Uxie	Unknown
	Victini	Unknown
	Virizion	Unknown
	Volcanion	Unknown
	Wynaut	♂/♀
	Xerneas	Unknown
	Yveltal	Unknown
	Zapdos	Unknown
	Zekrom	Unknown
205	Zygarde	Unknown

Fun & Communication

Catching, training, and battling with Pokémon sure is fun, but Alola has a lot more to offer than these all-important activities. Here you'll learn about the many other fun and unique activities you can enjoy around Alola when you're looking to take a break from the norm.

Customizing Your Character

When you first began your adventure, you made several choices that determined your character's appearance. The name, gender, and skin tone you selected at your adventure's outset can't be changed, but almost everything else about your character's appearance can be customized in a variety of ways. On page 55, you learned about the many different hair color and style options available to you at salons. You also learned how to change the color of your character's eyes with contact lenses. Now all you need is the perfect outfit to complete your look! The apparel shops around Alola are ready to help you out, and the following pages catalog every item you can obtain in the Alola region.

Color Options

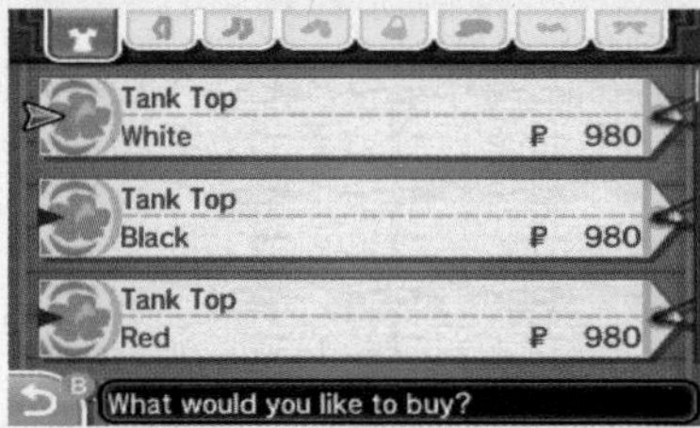

Most clothes are available in a variety of colors, but you'll also find that some colors are only available in *Pokémon Sun* or *Pokémon Moon*. If you're yearning for a certain color but only have one version of the game, don't worry! There are two ways to get items in colors that you can't find off the rack.

Dye houses (p. 302)

In Festival Plaza, you can set up special dye houses that let you color white items in a huge array of shades. You'll learn more about dye houses in the Festival Plaza section (p. 299), but know that they'll allow you to dye your clothes in a variety of hues that you won't find in stores. In the tables on the following pages, you can easily see which items can be dyed because they are identified with a icon.

Special orders

While visiting Festival Plaza, you might meet a visitor who's wearing something special—something that really catches your eye. Once you've reached Rank 10 (p. 299), your guests can help you buy the same items that they're wearing in exchange for Festival Coins (FC)!

Tip

Your personalized character will appear in other people's Festival Plazas, as well as during other communication features, such as Link Battles. Create the perfect look and show the world your savvy sense of style!

Fashion Item Tables

The following pages cover the complete lineup of the apparel shops and other stores you find around Alola. Items or colors marked with are only available at shops in *Pokémon Sun*, and those marked with can only be bought at shops in *Pokémon Moon*.

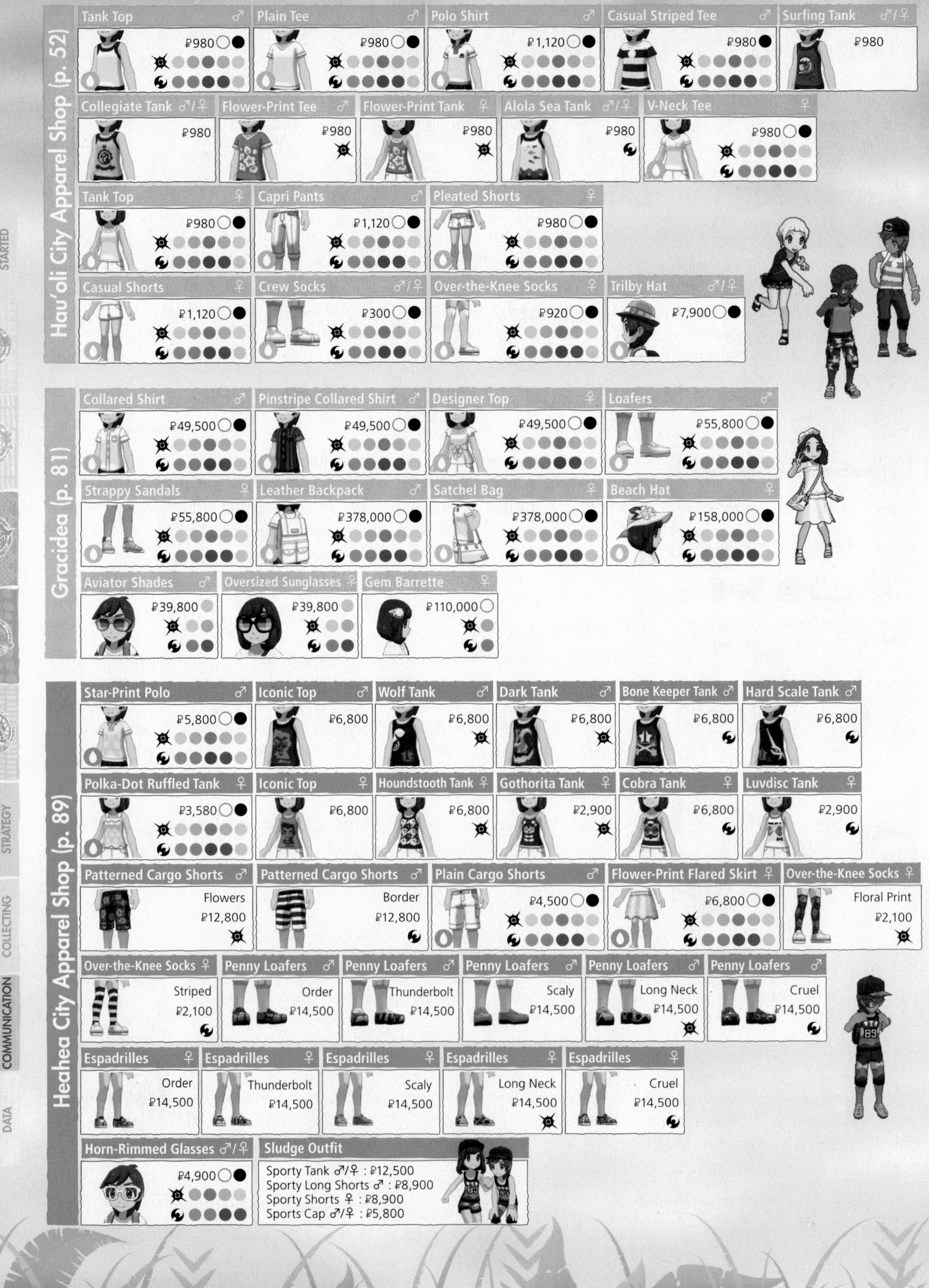

Hau'oli City Apparel Shop (p. 52)

- Tank Top ♂ — ₽980
- Plain Tee ♂ — ₽980
- Polo Shirt ♂ — ₽1,120
- Casual Striped Tee ♂ — ₽980
- Surfing Tank ♂/♀ — ₽980
- Collegiate Tank ♂/♀ — ₽980
- Flower-Print Tee ♂ — ₽980
- Flower-Print Tank ♀ — ₽980
- Alola Sea Tank ♂/♀ — ₽980
- V-Neck Tee ♀ — ₽980
- Tank Top ♀ — ₽980
- Capri Pants ♂ — ₽1,120
- Pleated Shorts ♀ — ₽980
- Casual Shorts ♀ — ₽1,120
- Crew Socks ♂/♀ — ₽300
- Over-the-Knee Socks ♀ — ₽920
- Trilby Hat ♂/♀ — ₽7,900

Gracidea (p. 81)

- Collared Shirt ♂ — ₽49,500
- Pinstripe Collared Shirt ♂ — ₽49,500
- Designer Top ♀ — ₽49,500
- Loafers ♂ — ₽55,800
- Strappy Sandals ♀ — ₽55,800
- Leather Backpack ♂ — ₽378,000
- Satchel Bag ♀ — ₽378,000
- Beach Hat ♀ — ₽158,000
- Aviator Shades ♂ — ₽39,800
- Oversized Sunglasses ♀ — ₽39,800
- Gem Barrette ♀ — ₽110,000

Heahea City Apparel Shop (p. 89)

- Star-Print Polo ♂ — ₽5,800
- Iconic Top ♂ — ₽6,800
- Wolf Tank ♂ — ₽6,800
- Dark Tank ♂ — ₽6,800
- Bone Keeper Tank ♂ — ₽6,800
- Hard Scale Tank ♂ — ₽6,800
- Polka-Dot Ruffled Tank ♀ — ₽3,580
- Iconic Top ♀ — ₽6,800
- Houndstooth Tank ♀ — ₽6,800
- Gothorita Tank ♀ — ₽2,900
- Cobra Tank ♀ — ₽6,800
- Luvdisc Tank ♀ — ₽2,900
- Patterned Cargo Shorts ♂ — Flowers — ₽12,800
- Patterned Cargo Shorts ♂ — Border — ₽12,800
- Plain Cargo Shorts ♂ — ₽4,500
- Flower-Print Flared Skirt ♀ — ₽6,800
- Over-the-Knee Socks ♀ — Floral Print — ₽2,100
- Over-the-Knee Socks ♀ — Striped — ₽2,100
- Penny Loafers ♂ — Order — ₽14,500
- Penny Loafers ♂ — Thunderbolt — ₽14,500
- Penny Loafers ♂ — Scaly — ₽14,500
- Penny Loafers ♂ — Long Neck — ₽14,500
- Penny Loafers ♂ — Cruel — ₽14,500
- Espadrilles ♀ — Order — ₽14,500
- Espadrilles ♀ — Thunderbolt — ₽14,500
- Espadrilles ♀ — Scaly — ₽14,500
- Espadrilles ♀ — Long Neck — ₽14,500
- Espadrilles ♀ — Cruel — ₽14,500
- Horn-Rimmed Glasses ♂/♀ — ₽4,900

Sludge Outfit

Sporty Tank ♂/♀ : ₽12,500
Sporty Long Shorts ♂ : ₽8,900
Sporty Shorts ♀ : ₽8,900
Sports Cap ♂/♀ : ₽5,800

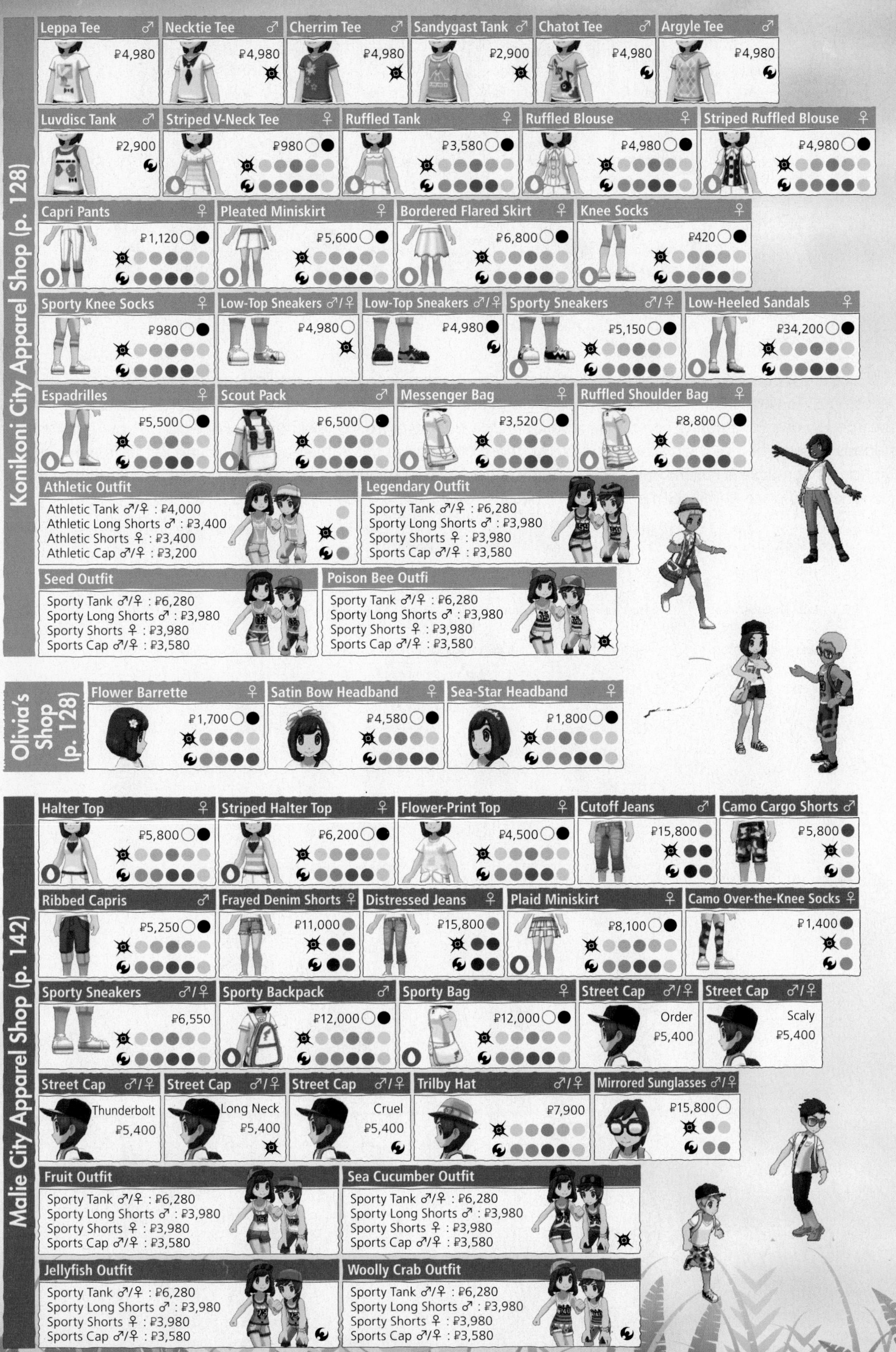

Konikoni City Apparel Shop (p. 128)

Leppa Tee	♂	₽4,980
Necktie Tee	♂	₽4,980
Cherrim Tee	♂	₽4,980
Sandygast Tank	♂	₽2,900
Chatot Tee	♂	₽4,980
Argyle Tee	♂	₽4,980
Luvdisc Tank	♂	₽2,900
Striped V-Neck Tee	♀	₽980
Ruffled Tank	♀	₽3,580
Ruffled Blouse	♀	₽4,980
Striped Ruffled Blouse	♀	₽4,980
Capri Pants	♀	₽1,120
Pleated Miniskirt	♀	₽5,600
Bordered Flared Skirt	♀	₽6,800
Knee Socks	♀	₽420
Sporty Knee Socks	♀	₽980
Low-Top Sneakers	♂/♀	₽4,980
Low-Top Sneakers	♂/♀	₽4,980
Sporty Sneakers	♂/♀	₽5,150
Low-Heeled Sandals	♀	₽34,200
Espadrilles	♀	₽5,500
Scout Pack	♂	₽6,500
Messenger Bag	♀	₽3,520
Ruffled Shoulder Bag	♀	₽8,800

Athletic Outfit
Athletic Tank ♂/♀ : ₽4,000
Athletic Long Shorts ♂ : ₽3,400
Athletic Shorts ♀ : ₽3,400
Athletic Cap ♂/♀ : ₽3,200

Legendary Outfit
Sporty Tank ♂/♀ : ₽6,280
Sporty Long Shorts ♂ : ₽3,980
Sporty Shorts ♀ : ₽3,980
Sports Cap ♂/♀ : ₽3,580

Seed Outfit
Sporty Tank ♂/♀ : ₽6,280
Sporty Long Shorts ♂ : ₽3,980
Sporty Shorts ♀ : ₽3,980
Sports Cap ♂/♀ : ₽3,580

Poison Bee Outfi
Sporty Tank ♂/♀ : ₽6,280
Sporty Long Shorts ♂ : ₽3,980
Sporty Shorts ♀ : ₽3,980
Sports Cap ♂/♀ : ₽3,580

Olivia's Shop (p. 128)

Flower Barrette	♀	₽1,700
Satin Bow Headband	♀	₽4,580
Sea-Star Headband	♀	₽1,800

Malie City Apparel Shop (p. 142)

Halter Top	♀	₽5,800
Striped Halter Top	♀	₽6,200
Flower-Print Top	♀	₽4,500
Cutoff Jeans	♂	₽15,800
Camo Cargo Shorts	♂	₽5,800
Ribbed Capris	♂	₽5,250
Frayed Denim Shorts	♀	₽11,000
Distressed Jeans	♀	₽15,800
Plaid Miniskirt	♀	₽8,100
Camo Over-the-Knee Socks	♀	₽1,400
Sporty Sneakers	♂/♀	₽6,550
Sporty Backpack	♂	₽12,000
Sporty Bag	♀	₽12,000
Street Cap (Order)	♂/♀	₽5,400
Street Cap (Scaly)	♂/♀	₽5,400
Street Cap (Thunderbolt)	♂/♀	₽5,400
Street Cap (Long Neck)	♂/♀	₽5,400
Street Cap (Cruel)	♂/♀	₽5,400
Trilby Hat	♂/♀	₽7,900
Mirrored Sunglasses	♂/♀	₽15,800

Fruit Outfit
Sporty Tank ♂/♀ : ₽6,280
Sporty Long Shorts ♂ : ₽3,980
Sporty Shorts ♀ : ₽3,980
Sports Cap ♂/♀ : ₽3,580

Sea Cucumber Outfit
Sporty Tank ♂/♀ : ₽6,280
Sporty Long Shorts ♂ : ₽3,980
Sporty Shorts ♀ : ₽3,980
Sports Cap ♂/♀ : ₽3,580

Jellyfish Outfit
Sporty Tank ♂/♀ : ₽6,280
Sporty Long Shorts ♂ : ₽3,980
Sporty Shorts ♀ : ₽3,980
Sports Cap ♂/♀ : ₽3,580

Woolly Crab Outfit
Sporty Tank ♂/♀ : ₽6,280
Sporty Long Shorts ♂ : ₽3,980
Sporty Shorts ♀ : ₽3,980
Sports Cap ♂/♀ : ₽3,580

Flea Market (p. 142)
Penny Loafers ♂ Rare Order ₽50,000
Penny Loafers ♂ Rare Thunderbolt ₽50,000
Penny Loafers ♂ Rare Scaly ₽50,000
Penny Loafers ♂ Rare Long Neck ₽50,000
Penny Loafers ♂ Rare Cruel ₽50,000
Espadrilles ♀ Rare Order ₽50,000
Espadrilles ♀ Rare Thunderbolt ₽50,000
Espadrilles ♀ Rare Scaly ₽50,000
Espadrilles ♀ Rare Long Neck ₽50,000
Espadrilles ♀ Rare Cruel ₽50,000
Street Cap ♂/♀ Rare Order ₽25,000
Street Cap ♂/♀ Rare Thunderbolt ₽25,000
Street Cap ♂/♀ Rare Scaly ₽25,000
Street Cap ♂/♀ Rare Long Neck ₽25,000
Street Cap ♂/♀ Rare Cruel ₽25,000

Skull Tank ♂/♀
₽10,000
After clearing the main story (p. 217)

Ribbons

Ribbons are special awards that your Pokémon receive when you accomplish special feats or reach special milestones. To view a Pokémon's ribbons, simply bring up its Summary page and then press ✚. Ribbons may be awarded to one Pokémon or several, depending on the circumstance. For example, all Pokémon in your party earn ribbons through battle-based achievements, like those obtained at the Battle Royal Dome and Battle Tree. However, Ribbons that require a Pokémon to meet certain criteria, such as the Best Friends Ribbon, are only awarded to the Pokémon you place at the head of your party, because only that Pokémon is evaluated.

Ribbon	Name	Recipient	How to Obtain
	Alola Champion Ribbon	All party Pokémon	Enter the Hall of Fame
	Battle Royal Master Ribbon	All Battle Team Pokémon	Become No. 1 in a Master Rank Battle Royal match
	Battle Tree Great Ribbon	All Battle Team Pokémon	Win against a Battle Legend in a Single/Double/Multi Battle in the Battle Tree.
	Battle Tree Master Ribbon	All Battle Team Pokémon	Win against a Battle Legend in a Super Single/Double/Multi Battle in the Battle Tree.
	Best Friends Ribbon	Lead party Pokémon	Place a Pokémon with a max affection level as your lead Pokémon, and speak to a girl in Malie Community Center.
	Effort Ribbon	Lead party Pokémon	Place a Pokémon with max base stats as your lead Pokémon, and speak to a woman in the Battle Royal Dome.
	Footprint Ribbon	Lead party Pokémon	Show a Pokémon that has leveled up by 30 levels or more since you met the Pokémon to the Pokémon Breeder in Hano Grand Resort.

Festival Plaza

Run by Captain Sophocles, Festival Plaza is a wondrous place where you can take a break from your daily routine and connect with other *Pokémon Sun* and *Pokémon Moon* players nearby or around the world through the magic of communication features. Festival Plaza certainly is festive, but Sophocles needs your help to liven up the place and make it even more spectacular!

To visit Festival Plaza, simply press ⓧ to open the X menu, then choose "Festival Plaza" once it is available to you. You'll then be whisked away to this magical place, where you'll find two ways of communicating with other players: local wireless communication and via the Internet. You're connected to local wireless communication by default, but you can switch between these two modes anytime you like by tapping the blue icon at the lower right corner on the lower screen.

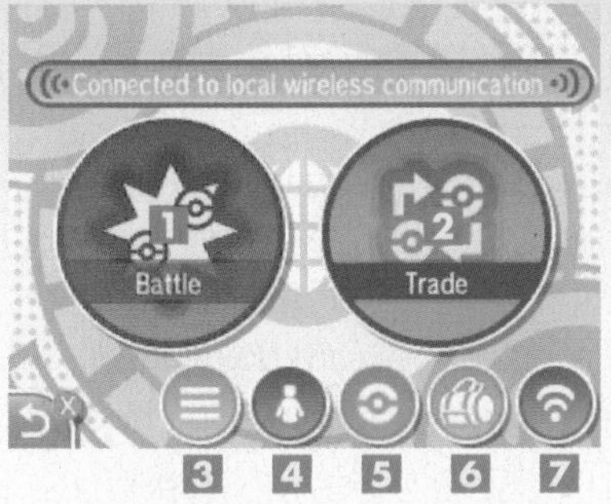

1. **Battle**: Have a battle against nearby players or players from around the world.
2. **Trade**: Trade Pokémon with nearby players or players from around the world.
3. **Player Lists**: View your guest list, VIP list, and block list.
4. **Profile**: Check the status of your Festival Plaza and adjust your character's catchphrases.
5. **Pokémon**: View your current party Pokémon.
6. **Bag**: View the items currently stored in your Bag.
7. **Connection**: Switch between local wireless communication and Internet communication methods.

Festival Plaza Rank

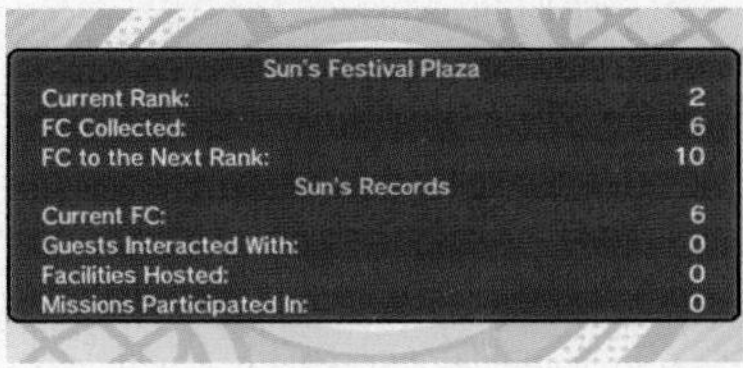

Your Festival Plaza Rank is a measurement of how much you've accomplished at Festival Plaza. Your Festival Plaza Rank increases by earning Festival Coins (FC), and you earn FC by chatting with visitors and responding to their requests. You can also use FC for products and services in various facilities around Festival Plaza. Tap the purple icon on the Touch Screen to check your Profile and see your current rank, along with the number of FC you've collected so far.

Rank	Coins you need for the next Rank	Rank	Coins you need for the next Rank
1	6	11–20	100
2	10	21–30	120
3	15	31–40	150
4	30	41–50	180
5	40	51–60	210
6	50	61–70	240
7	60	71–80	270
8	70	81–90	270
9	80	91–100	270
10	90	101–	300

Rank Rewards

Sophocles gives you special rewards each time your Festival Plaza Rank goes up. Talk to everyone who visits your Festival Plaza to earn lots of FC and score these sweet prizes from Sophocles!

Rank	Sophocles's present
Rank 4	Makes it possible to play missions
Rank 8	Makes it possible for your visitors to introduce their favorite facilities to you
Rank 10	Makes it possible to order outfits your visitors wear
Rank 20	Makes it possible to change the name of your Festival Plaza
Rank 30 (After clearing the game)	Adds premium services
Rank 40 (After clearing the game)	Makes it possible to change songs
Rank 50	Makes it possible to change the design of your castle
Rank 60	Adds a theme to redecorate your castle's exterior
Rank 70	Adds a theme to redecorate your castle's exterior
Rank 100	Makes the message "I reached Festival Plaza Rank 100!" available
All others	Introduces a new facility to you

Your Home Is Your Castle

Festival Plaza's central castle is your headquarters in Festival Plaza. Visit it to participate in global missions (p. 304), check out Battle Videos (p. 308), or use Game Sync (p. 315). You can also talk to the staff inside to move your facilities around, alter the design of your castle (after reaching Rank 50), or change the song played in Festival Plaza (after Rank 40). You can also page someone from your guest list or VIP list to make them appear in your Festival Plaza, or receive FC from people you've traded or battled with!

Theme: Basic

Theme: Glitz

Theme: A Fairy Tale

Theme: Subdued Tone

Communicating with Visitors

Talking to visitors is a simple and fun way of interacting in Festival Plaza. If a visitor's speech bubble is blue, speaking to them will help you learn more about them. Ask them, "How have you been lately?" and your visitor will tell you how he or she has been doing lately. Saying "Let me see how you are doing" will give you the chance to view their records from the game. You can also choose to register visitors as VIPs, which lets you easily find them in the future even if they get bumped from your guest list.

When you reach Rank 8, you will be able to ask visitors if they know any good facilities. If a visitor recommends a facility to you, you can host it in your Festival Plaza, using FC to replace one of your existing facilities with the new one. Just choose carefully—once you replace one of your old facilities, you won't be able to host it again until you find another guest who will recommend it to you or Sophocles introduces it to you as a Rank reward!

After Rank 10, you can also compliment a visitor's outfit. If your visitor is the same gender as you, they can recommend their favorite fashion item, allowing you to order it for yourself using FC.

If a visitor's speech bubble is red, talking to them will earn you FC. Listen to their stories, answer their questions, or take them to facilities they're interested in, then rake in the FC!

Player Lists

Tap the yellow icon with the three white lines on the Touch Screen to view the three player lists:

Guest List: View the list of players who have recently visited your Festival Plaza. Up to 50 players will be listed, and players with the oldest update times will be deleted from the list as new players appear in your Festival Plaza.

VIP List: Add guests who've come to Festival Plaza to your VIP list if you'd like that person to continue to hang out in your Festival Plaza. Speak to a player and select "I'll register you as my VIP!" to add them to your VIP List.

Block List: If you don't want to communicate with certain people, you can add them to your block list when they ask you for a battle or to trade. Players added to your block list won't appear in your Festival Plaza anymore.

Using Facilities

Festival Plaza is filled with all sorts of nifty facilities. You can host different facilities as a reward from Sophocles or after a recommendation from a visitor, as previously mentioned. Facilities also have ranks, from one star to five stars. The higher your Festival Plaza Rank is, the higher the rank of the facilities you can host. Higher-ranked facilities provide more products and services, and your chances of winning a great item in a lottery shop increase as its rank goes up. It pays to host great facilities!

Lottery Shops

Visit a lottery shop to draw a lottery ticket once a day. If you're lucky, you may be able to draw one more time!

Prize	Big Dreams	Gold Rush	Treasure Hunt
1st	Master Ball	Big Nugget	Gold Bottle Cap
2nd	Rare Candy	Nugget	Bottle Cap
3rd	PP Max	PP Max	PP Max
4th	PP Up	PP Up	PP Up
5th	Max Revive	Max Revive	Max Revive
6th	Max Elixir	Max Elixir	Max Elixir
7th	Max Ether	Max Ether	Max Ether
8th	Ultra Ball	Ultra Ball	Ultra Ball
9th	Full Heal	Full Heal	Full Heal
10th	Berry Juice	Berry Juice	Berry Juice

Haunted Houses

Let your Pokémon play in a haunted house, and it'll come out with an item. If you're lucky, your Pokémon will come out with several items! Using a haunted house costs 10 FC.

Ghosts' Den	Trick Room	Confuse Ray	
Sacred Ash	Sacred Ash	Sacred Ash	Hard to pick up
Bottle Cap	Bottle Cap	Bottle Cap	↑
PP Up	Max Revive	Max Elixir	
Heart Scale	Heart Scale	Heart Scale	
Patterned Bean	Patterned Bean	Patterned Bean	
Festival Ticket	Festival Ticket	Festival Ticket	
HP Up	Iron	Calcium	
Protein	Carbos	Zinc	
Full Heal	Hyper Potion	Ultra Ball	↓
Hard Stone	Hard Stone	Hard Stone	Easy to pick up

Bouncy Houses

Bring your Pokémon to a bouncy house to let it train while it plays! The more stars a course has, the more your Pokémon's base stats (p. 272) will grow by playing there.

Course	Effect
Course A	Raises the Pokémon's base HP
Course B	Raises the Pokémon's base Attack stat
Course C	Raises the Pokémon's base Defense stat
Course D	Raises the Pokémon's base Sp. Atk stat
Course E	Raises the Pokémon's base Sp. Def stat
Course F	Raises the Pokémon's base Speed stat

Course Rank	Price
1★	5 FC
2★	10 FC
3★	15 FC
4★	30 FC
5★	50 FC
6★	100 FC
7★	200 FC

Note: 6★ and 7★ stages are only available to Champions!

Facility Name	Available Courses
Thump-Bump Park ★	Course B (1★/6★), Course D (1★/6★)
Thump-Bump Park ★★	Course B (1★/2★/6★), Course D (1★/2★/6★)
Thump-Bump Park ★★★	Course B (1★/2★/3★/6★), Course D (1★/2★/3★/6★)
Thump-Bump Park ★★★★	Course B (1★/2★/3★/4★/6★), Course D (1★/2★/3★/4★/6★)
Thump-Bump Park ★★★★★	Course B (1★/2★/3★/4★/5★/6★/7★), Course D (1★/2★/3★/4★/5★/6★/7★)
Clink-Clunk Land ★	Course C (1★/6★), Course E (1★/6★)
Clink-Clunk Land ★★	Course C (1★/2★/6★), Course E (1★/2★/6★)
Clink-Clunk Land ★★★	Course C (1★/2★/3★/6★), Course E (1★/2★/3★/6★)
Clink-Clunk Land ★★★★	Course C (1★/2★/3★/4★/6★), Course E (1★/2★/3★/4★/6★)
Clink-Clunk Land ★★★★★	Course C (1★/2★/3★/4★/5★/6★/7★), Course E (1★/2★/3★/4★/5★/6★/7★)
Stomp-Stomp House ★	Course A (1★/6★), Course F (1★/6★)
Stomp-Stomp House ★★	Course A (1★/2★/6★), Course F (1★/2★/6★)
Stomp-Stomp House ★★★	Course A (1★/2★/3★/6★), Course F (1★/2★/3★/6★)
Stomp-Stomp House ★★★★	Course A (1★/2★/3★/4★/6★), Course F (1★/2★/3★/4★/6★)
Stomp-Stomp House ★★★★★	Course A (1★/2★/3★/4★/5★/6★/7★), Course F (1★/2★/3★/4★/5★/6★/7★)

Food Stalls

Treat your Pokémon to meals at food stalls for a variety of special benefits. The FC cost and benefit to your Pokémon vary depending on the menu item you select—from boosting and lowering your Pokémon's base stats (p. 272) to making them more friendly (p. 130) and even raising their level. There are a set number of dishes available at a time, and once they've run out for the day, you may be out of luck! Come back again the next day to treat your Pokémon again. Also notice that some food stalls aren't available in both versions of the game. The one-star varieties are all available in both versions, though, so you can at least get a taste for their offerings!

Item Name	Rare Breakfast	Rare Lunch	Rare Brunch	Rare Desert	Rare Appetizer	Rare Dinner*
Effect	Raises Lv. by 1 (up to Lv. 30)	Raises Lv. by 1 (up to Lv. 40)	Raises Lv. by 1 (up to Lv. 50)	Raises Lv. by 1 (up to Lv. 60)	Raises Lv. by 1 (up to Lv. 70)	Raises Lv. by 7 (up to Lv. 80)
Cost	4 FC	10 FC	20 FC	30 FC	40 FC	100 FC
Availability	Rare Kitchen ★ and up	Rare Kitchen ★★ and up	Rare Kitchen ★★★ and up	Rare Kitchen ★★★★ and up	Rare Kitchen ★★★★★ ☀	Rare Kitchen ★ and up
Item Name	**Rare Buffet***	**HP Lunch**	**Attack Lunch**	**Defense Lunch**	**Sp. Atk Lunch**	**Sp. Def Lunch**
Effect	Raises Lv. by 9 (up to Lv. 90)	Raises base HP	Raises base Atk	Raises base Def	Raises base Sp. Atk	Raises base Sp. Def
Cost	300 FC	20 FC	20 FC	20 FC	20 FC	20 FC
Availability	Rare Kitchen ★★★★★ ☀	Battle Table ★ and up	Battle Table ★ and up	Battle Table ★ and up	Battle Table ★ and up	Battle Table ★ and up
Item Name	**Speed Lunch**	**Level-Up Lunch 3***	**Level-Up Lunch 5***	**Friendship Drink**	**Friendship Lunch**	**Friendship Combo**
Effect	Raises base Speed	Raises Lv. by 3 (up to Lv. 70)	Raises Lv. by 5 (up to Lv. 80)	Small friendship boost	Medium friendship boost	Big friendship boost
Cost	20 FC	100 FC	200 FC	2 FC	10 FC	20 FC
Availability	Battle Table ★ and up	Battle Table ★ and up	Battle Table ★★★★★ ☀	Friendship Parlor ★ and up, Friendship Café ★ and up	Friendship Parlor ★ and up, Friendship Café ★ and up	Friendship Parlor ★ and up, Friendship Café ★ and up
Item Name	**Sweets Set A**	**Sweets Set B**	**Sweets Set C**	**Sweets Set D**	**Sweets Set E**	**Sweets Set F**
Effect	Raises friendship / Lowers base HP	Raises friendship / Lowers base Atk	Raises friendship / Lowers base Def	Raises friendship / Lowers base Sp. Atk	Raises friendship / Lowers base Sp. Def	Raises friendship / Lowers base Speed
Cost	30 FC	30 FC	30 FC	30 FC	30 FC	30 FC
Availability	Friendship Parlor ★ and up, Friendship Café ★★★ and up ☾	Friendship Parlor ★★ and up ☀, Friendship Café ★★★★ and up ☾	Friendship Parlor ★★ and up ☀, Friendship Café ★★★★★ ☾	Friendship Parlor ★★★ and up ☀, Friendship Café ★ and up	Friendship Parlor ★★★★ and up ☀, Friendship Café ★★ and up ☾	Friendship Parlor ★★★★★ ☀, Friendship Café ★★ and up ☾
Item Name	**Secret Meal A***	**Secret Meal B***	**Secret Meal C***	**Secret Meal D***	**Secret Meal E***	**Secret Meal F***
Effect	Raises friendship / Resets base HP	Raises friendship / Resets base Atk	Raises friendship / Resets base Def	Raises friendship / Resets base Sp. Atk	Raises friendship / Resets base Sp. Def	Raises friendship / Resets base Speed
Cost	200 FC	200 FC	200 FC	200 FC	200 FC	200 FC
Availability	Friendship Parlor ★ and up	Friendship Parlor ★★★ and up ☀	Friendship Parlor ★★★★★ ☀	Friendship Café ★ and up	Friendship Café ★★★ and up ☾	Friendship Café ★★★★★ ☾

Note: Meals marked with an asterisk are only available after entering the Hall of Fame.

Dye Houses

Visit a dye house to have your white clothing and fashion items dyed into different colors. It costs 100 FC to dye a white item, but only 10 FC to remove the dye and make the item white again. Alternatively, you can choose to dye an item using Berries. By using Berries, you can have fashion items dyed in colors that your particular dye house doesn't usually carry. You'll need lots of Berries, though, so get growing in Poké Pelago (p. 309)! Refer to the table on the right to see what Berries you need to dye various colors, and remember to check out the tables on pages 348 and 349 if you need tips on where to find Berries around Alola.

Color	Berry	Qty.	Berry	Qty.	Berry	Qty.
Pastel Red	Pomeg Berry	15	Tamato Berry	15	Cheri Berry	15
Dark Red	Occa Berry	30	Figy Berry	30	Liechi Berry	30
Pastel Yellow	Sitrus Berry	15	Qualot Berry	15	Grepa Berry	15
Dark Yellow	Aspear Berry	30	Iapapa Berry	30	Wacan Berry	30
Pastel Green	Hondew Berry	15	Rawst Berry	15	Lum Berry	15
Dark Green	Aguav Berry	30	Salac Berry	30	Rindo Berry	30
Pastel Blue	Kelpsy Berry	15	Oran Berry	15	Maranga Berry	15
Dark Blue	Passho Berry	30	Yache Berry	30	Coba Berry	30
Pastel Orange	Leppa Berry	15	Kee Berry	15	Sitrus Berry	15
Dark Orange	Chople Berry	30	Charti Berry	30	Shuca Berry	30
Pastel Navy	Apicot Berry	15	Kelpsy Berry	15	Chesto Berry	15
Dark Navy Blue	Passho Berry	30	Coba Berry	30	Payapa Berry	30
Pastel Purple	Chesto Berry	15	Wiki Berry	15	Ganlon Berry	15
Dark Purple	Kasib Berry	30	Colbur Berry	30	Payapa Berry	30
Pastel Pink	Pecha Berry	15	Persim Berry	15	Mago Berry	15
Dark Pink	Mago Berry	30	Petaya Berry	30	Roseli Berry	30

Dye houses with one star can dye items only to pastel colors; dye houses with three stars can dye items only to dark colors; and dye houses with five stars can do both with Berries. When you dye an item by paying FC, one-star shops can only dye pastel colors, while three-star shops can dye both pastel and dark colors. And five-star dye houses can additionally dye special bright colors in exchange for a nice chunk of FC!

The dye houses available to you will also vary based on the version of the game you are playing. Team Red, Team Green, Team Orange, and Team Purple shops can be constructed at your Festival Plaza if you are playing *Pokémon Sun*, while Team Yellow, Team Blue, Team Navy Blue, and Team Pink will be available in *Pokémon Moon*.

Goody Shop

Pop by a goody shop to buy rare items in exchange for FC. As your Festival Plaza Rank goes up, goody shops carry more items.

Product Name	Price	Content	Shops
Ball Set A	12 FC	12 Poké Balls	Ball Shop ★ and up, General Store ★ and ★★
Ball Set B	24 FC	12 Great Balls	Ball Shop ★★ and up ☾, General Store ★★★ and up
Ball Set C	48 FC	12 Ultra Balls	Ball Shop ★★★, General Store ★★★★★ ☾
Ball Set D*	24 FC	12 Dive Balls	Ball Shop ★ and up
Ball Set E*	24 FC	12 Nest Balls	Ball Shop ★ and up
Ball Set F*	24 FC	12 Repeat Balls	Ball Shop ★★ and up ☾
Ball Set G*	24 FC	12 Timer Balls	Ball Shop ★★ and up ☾
Ball Set H*	24 FC	12 Dusk Balls	Ball Shop ★★★ ☾
Ball Set I*	24 FC	12 Heal Balls	Ball Shop ★★★ ☾
Ball Set J*	24 FC	12 Quick Balls	Ball Shop ★★★ ☾
Ball Set K*	24 FC	12 Premier Balls	Ball Shop ★★★ ☾
Value Product*	10 FC	1 Big Pearl	General Store ★ and up
Lemonade Set	24 FC	12 Lemonades	General Store ★ ★★★★ ☾, Soft Drink Parlor ★ and up
Honey Set	10 FC	4 Honeys	General Store ★ and up, Battle Store ★ and up
Toy Set	10 FC	4 Poké Toys	Battle Store ★ and up
Water Set	12 FC	12 Fresh Waters	General Store ★ and ★★, Soft Drink Parlor ★ and up
Milk Set	30 FC	12 Moomoo Milks	Soft Drink Parlor ★ and up
Sinnoh Set	10 FC	4 Old Gateaux	General Store ★★★ and up
Johto Set	10 FC	4 Rage Candy Bars	General Store ★ and up
Hoenn Set	10 FC	4 Lava Cookies	General Store ★★ and up
Unova Set	10 FC	4 Casteliacones	General Store ★★★★ and up
Kalos Set	10 FC	4 Shalour Sables	General Store ★★★★★ ☾
Unusual Product	200 FC	1 PP Up	General Store ★★★★★ ☾
Soda Set	18 FC	12 Soda Pops	General Store ★★★ and ★★★★, Soft Drink Parlor ★ and up
Repel Set	24 FC	12 Max Repels	Battle Store ★ and up
Battle Set A	10 FC	4 Guard Spec.	Battle Store ★★★ ☾
Battle Set B	10 FC	4 Dire Hits	Battle Store ★★★ ☾
Battle Set C	10 FC	4 X Accuracies	Battle Store ★★★ ☾
Battle Set D	10 FC	4 X Attacks	Battle Store ★ and up
Battle Set E	10 FC	4 X Defenses	Battle Store ★ and up
Battle Set F	10 FC	4 X Sp. Atks	Battle Store ★★ and up ☾
Battle Set G	10 FC	4 X Sp. Defs	Battle Store ★★ and up ☾
Battle Set H	10 FC	4 X Speeds	Battle Store ★ and up
HP Set	60 FC	4 HP Ups	Pharmacy ★★★ ☼
Attack Set	60 FC	4 Proteins	Pharmacy ★★★ ☼
Defense Set	60 FC	4 Irons	Pharmacy ★★★ ☼
Speed Set	60 FC	4 Carbos	Pharmacy ★★★ ☼
Sp. Atk Set	60 FC	4 Calciums	Pharmacy ★★★ ☼
Sp. Def Set	60 FC	4 Zincs	Pharmacy ★★★ ☼
Medicine Set	16 FC	4 Hyper Potions	Pharmacy ★ and up
Full Heal Set	16 FC	4 Full Heals	Pharmacy ★ and up
Revive Set	25 FC	4 Revives	Pharmacy ★★★ ☼
Unusual Med A*	100 FC	1 Max Revive	Pharmacy ★★★ ☼
Unusual Med B*	50 FC	1 Ether	Pharmacy ★ and up

Fortune-Teller Tents

Fortune tellers recommend activities for you to try in Festival Plaza. Try these activities to find that you have better luck than usual. For example, you may get more items, more FC, and so on. Fortune tellers also make it possible for you to use a certain phrase in Festival Plaza. Fortune tellers charge 10 FC for their services.

Missions

Missions are special games that you can enjoy with other people who are playing in Festival Plaza. During a mission, all participants share a common goal and compete for their best score, with each player earning FC based on their score. You can either host a mission or participate in a mission hosted by another person.

Hosting and Participating in a Mission

Once you reach Rank 4, talk to the receptionist in front of the castle (not the one inside) to take part in missions. She'll give you three Festival Tickets per day. Facilities sometimes give out tickets, too. You can host a mission by using a Festival Ticket or you can participate in missions hosted by others without using any Festival Tickets. Tap the blue arrows on the bottom screen when viewing missions to see any missions currently hosted by other players.

Mission List

Mission	Tips	Conditions for unlocking
Japanese lesson!	Find people who say "Konnichiwa!" "Arigatō!" or "Sayōnara!"	None
English lesson!	Find people who say "Hello!" "Thank you!" or "Bye!"	None
French lesson!	Find people who say "Bonjour !" "Merci !" or "Au revoir !"	None
Italian lesson!	Find people who say "Buongiorno!" "Grazie!" or "Ciao!"	None
German lesson!	Find people who say "Guten Tag!" "Danke!" or "Tschüss!"	None
Spanish lesson!	Find people who say "¡Hola!" "¡Gracias!" or "¡Adiós!"	None
Korean lesson!	Find people who say "Annyeonghaseyo!" "Gomawo!" or "Annyeonghi gaseyo!"	None
Traditional and simplified Chinese lesson!	Find people who say "Nǐhǎo!" "Xièxie!" or "Zàijiàn!"	None
Type matchup tests!	Select a type that's super effective against the Pokémon people mention!	None
Find [*varies*]-type enthusiasts! Part 1	They will talk about Pokémon commonly seen in Alola.	None
Find fans!	Find people dressed like you.	Do 10 missions
Big costume contest!	Find the people who don't fit in.	Do 10 missions
Send people to [*varies*]!	Satisfy your visitors to succeed!	Do 10 missions
Cross-cultural communications!	Find people who greet you in other languages.	Do 10 missions
See through people's disguise!	Find people trying to hide behind glasses and hats.	Do 10 missions
True selves are the best!	Find people not hiding behind glasses or hats.	Do 10 missions
Greet experienced Trainers!	Find people who say, "I'm an experienced Trainer."	Do 20 missions
Give a message to beginners!	Find people who say, "I'm a beginner Trainer."	Do 20 missions
Find people in love!	Find people who say, "I have someone I love!"	Do 20 missions
Find lonely people!	Find people who say, "I don't have anyone I love."	Do 20 missions
Survey about male friends!	Find people who say, "I have a lot of male friends."	Do 20 missions
Survey about female friends!	Find people who say, "I have a lot of female friends."	Do 20 missions
Find big brothers and sisters!	Find people who say, "I'm the oldest among my siblings."	Do 20 missions
Find middle children!	Find people who say, "I'm in the middle among my siblings."	Do 20 missions
Find youngest children!	Find people who say, "I'm the youngest among my siblings."	Do 20 missions
Find only children!	Find people who say, "I'm the only child."	Do 20 missions
Personality matters most!	Find people who say, "Personality matters."	Do 20 missions
Looks matter most!	Find people who say, "Looks matter."	Do 20 missions
Secrets are something to keep!	Find people who say, "I will keep secrets at all costs."	Do 20 missions
Secrets are something to leak!	Find people who say, "I will tell secrets to people."	Do 20 missions
Chill out in your free time?	Find people who say, "I like to stay at home when I'm free."	Do 20 missions
Active in my free time!	Find people who say, "I like to go out when I'm free."	Do 20 missions
Research red!	Find people dressed all in red.	Do 20 missions
Research yellow!	Find people dressed all in yellow.	Do 20 missions
Research green!	Find people dressed all in green.	Do 20 missions
Research blue!	Find people dressed all in blue.	Do 20 missions
Research orange!	Find people dressed all in orange.	Do 20 missions
Research navy blue!	Find people dressed all in navy blue.	Do 20 missions
Research purple!	Find people dressed all in purple.	Do 20 missions
Research pink!	Find people dressed all in pink.	Do 20 missions
Show off muscles!	Find people pleased to see you.	Become Champion
Break boulders quickly!	Break as many boulders as you can.	Become Champion
Inverse type matchup tests!	Pick the type that's usually weak against the Pokémon people mentioned!	Become Champion
Find [*varies*]-type enthusiasts! Part 2	People will talk about Pokémon not found in Alola!	Become Champion

Global Missions

Sun,
welcome to global missions!

A global mission is a large-scale mission hosted via the Internet that all *Pokémon Sun* and *Pokémon Moon* players can participate in. In these missions, your score will be based on activities you complete during your normal adventure, such as how many Pokémon you've caught in Alola. If you are connected to the Internet, speak with the global mission receptionist in the castle to take part. You can check how you're doing by talking with her and when the mission is over, Festival Coins will be distributed to all participants equally if the mission was a success!

Battle

While visiting Festival Plaza, tap the "Battle" button on the Touch Screen to access a variety of ways to battle with players near and far.

Link Battle

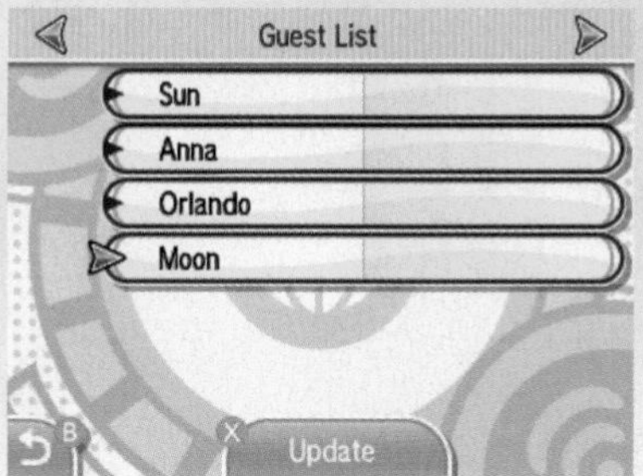

Tap "Battle" on the Touch Screen in Festival Plaza, then select "Link Battle" to battle with players on your guest list or VIP list. You can choose from four different battle formats (p. 258): Single Battles, Double Battles, Multi Battles, and Battle Royal. You can also select from three different battle rules, as explained below.

Battle Rules:

Normal Rules: All Pokémon will be set to Lv. 50, whether their level is higher or lower.

Flat Rules: Any Pokémon above Lv. 50 will be set to Lv. 50.

No Restrictions: There are no restrictions and Pokémon's levels will not be changed.

Battle Spot

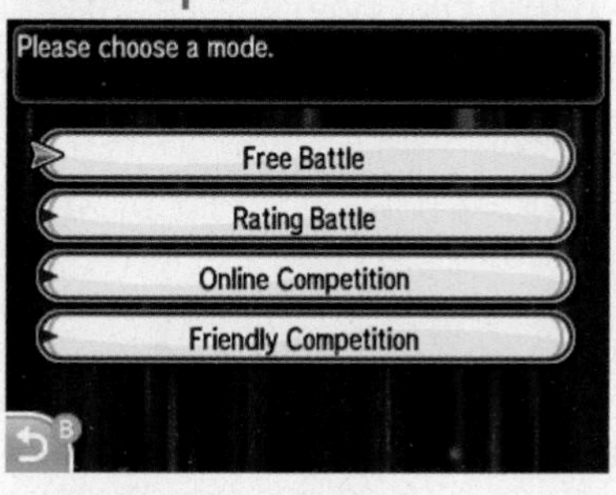

Battle Spot uses your Internet connection to match you instantly with another player in the world who's also looking for a battle at the same time as you. Even if you can't find a Link Battle partner, you can still find a player to battle with via Battle Spot. There are four modes of battles you can enjoy: Free Battle, Rating Battle, Online Competition, and Friendly Competition.

Free Battle

You can freely participate in a Free Battle without registering at the Pokémon Global Link (PGL) (p. 315). You also don't have to worry about your results too much, because the results won't be saved. You'll battle with a player who chose the same battle format and battle rules. Here, too, you can choose among Single Battles, Double Battles, and Battle Royal. You can also choose whether or not to allow "special Pokémon" (see below).

Rating Battle

Rating Battles are serious business. In a Rating Battle, your rating on the PGL (p. 315) will go up or down depending on your battle results, and your rating will be shown on the PGL website for the world to see! You'll need to register at the PGL before you can participate in Rating Battles, and your Nintendo 3DS system will be registered on the server. If you change your system, your results will be reset. Choose between Single Battles, Double Battles, Special Battles, and Championships Battles.

Tip

Special Battles have different regulations each season. Please visit the PGL (Pokemon.com/PGL) for details. Championships Battles use the same regulations as the Pokémon World Championships for the year. It's perfect for advanced players who want to compete in the Pokémon World Championships.

Tip

The following special Pokémon cannot participate in Rating Battles: Ho-Oh, Celebi, Kyogre, Groudon, Rayquaza, Jirachi, Deoxys, Dialga, Palkia, Giratina, Phione, Manaphy, Darkrai, Shaymin, Arceus, Victini, Reshiram, Zekrom, Kyurem, Keldeo, Meloetta, Genesect, Xerneas, Yveltal, Zygarde, Diancie, Hoopa, Volcanion, Cosmog, Cosmoem, Solgaleo, Lunala, and other Legendary and Mythical Pokémon.

Online Competition

Online Competitions are special events held over the Internet. To participate, you'll need to register and enter a competition at the PGL website (p. 315) during the entry period. After completing your entry, you can download your Digital Player ID. Once the competition starts, you'll register your Battle Team and start battling. Battles will be held over a short period of time, such as three or four days, and then rankings will be determined.

Tip

You can't change your Battle Team until the competition ends. Choose your Pokémon wisely!

In Online Competitions, there's a limit to the number of battles a player can have each day. Once you've reached the day's limit, you'll need to wait until the next day to continue your progress. If you don't reach the battle limit, then your remaining battles can be carried over to a later day.

Tip

Online Competitions can be divided by age group into two separate competitions, and competitions for younger players may have special restrictions on when participants can battle in a day. Please check the PGL website for the competition info and regulations.

GETTING STARTED

Friendly Competition

A Friendly Competition is a battle competition that a player can host. You can host either an Online Competition or a Live Competition.

Create a Competition

You can create your own competition at the PGL website, and you can set your competition name, regulations, and make the competition public or private.

Participate in a Competition

In order to participate in an Online Competition, you need to enter the competition at the PGL. If the competition is public or you're specified as a participant of a private competition, you can enter the competition. A Digital Player ID for each player will be displayed on the PGL, and by scanning in that QR Code, participants will be able to battle according to the competition's regulations. For Live Competitions, you don't have to meet any conditions or register at the PGL. Go to the title menu, select "Live Competition," and obtain the Digital Player ID to participate in the competition. There is only one Digital Player ID for a Live Competition. You can share and distribute it as an image data.

Trade

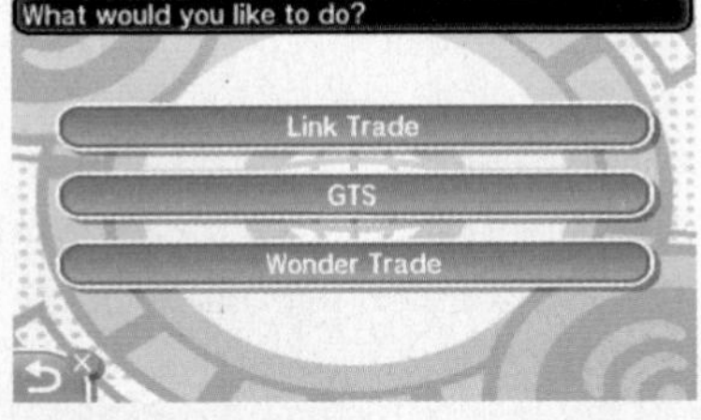

While visiting Festival Plaza, tap the "Trade" button on the Touch Screen to access a variety of ways to trade with players near and far.

Link Trade

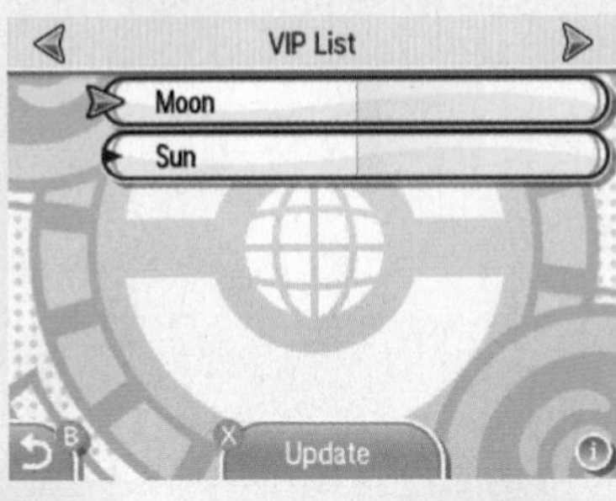

Tap "Trade" on the lower screen in Festival Plaza, and select "Link Trade" to trade with a player on your guest list or VIP list. You'll trade a Pokémon in your party or box. You can keep trading until one of you decides to quit.

Tip

You can trade Pokémon with an item, but Z-Crystals will be removed from Pokémon.

BATTLE & STRATEGY
POKÉMON COLLECTING
FUN & COMMUNICATION
ADVENTURE DATA

GTS (Global Trade Station)

With the GTS, you can trade Pokémon with people all over the world via the Internet. You can search for the exact Pokémon you want from all the many Pokémon other players have offered. If you have the Pokémon another player wants and you're willing to trade it, go ahead and make the trade! You can also simply deposit a Pokémon for trading and input certain conditions for the Pokémon you would like to receive in return.

To use the GTS, simply tap "Trade" on the lower screen in Festival Plaza, and select "GTS." You'll then have two ways to trade: Seek Pokémon or Deposit Pokémon.

Seek Pokémon

1. Choose a Pokémon you want

This function lets you search for desired Pokémon by name. Choose the first letter of a Pokémon from the menu, then pick the Pokémon from the list that appears. For Pokémon that you haven't seen yet, choose "What Pokémon?" and then type its name. You can usually also specify the desired Pokémon's gender and level. Once you're done specifying the conditions, tap "Search with these conditions!"

2. Choose a trading partner

Players who've offered Pokémon that match the conditions you've specified will be displayed. Browse through your options and pick a player you want to trade with. You can filter the players by the following conditions:

- Players who are seeking Pokémon that you have
- Players who are in the same region as you
- Players who are in a different region

3. Trade!

Choose a Pokémon that the trading partner wants, and select "Yes." The Pokémon will then be traded. Enjoy your new Pokémon!

Deposit a Pokémon

1. Choose a Pokémon to deposit

This function lets you deposit Pokémon for other players to browse over the GTS. Choose a Pokémon you want to deposit from your party or PC Boxes, then select "Deposit."

2. Specify conditions

Search for a Pokémon that you want by its name. Choose the first letter of a Pokémon from the menu, then pick the Pokémon from the list that appears. For Pokémon that you haven't seen yet, choose "What Pokémon?" and then type its name. You can also specify its gender and level, and select a message to display to would-be traders.

3. Deposit your Pokémon and wait for a trade

Tap "Deposit Pokémon," and your Pokémon will be deposited. Now just sit back and wait! Check the GTS after a while to see if the trade is complete. If it is, you'll receive the Pokémon that you wanted.

> **Tip**
>
> If you want to take back a Pokémon that you've deposited to the GTS, tap "See Summary of [Pokémon species name]," and then tap "Take back."

> **Tip**
>
> You cannot deposit a Pokémon Egg for trading over the GTS.

Wonder Trade

With Wonder Trade, you never know what kind of Pokémon you'll get. Select a Pokémon of your own to offer for trade, and you'll receive a Pokémon chosen at random from among all the Pokémon that players around the world have offered. It's a very exciting way to trade Pokémon!

> **Tip**
>
> You can't trade the following Pokémon with the GTS or Wonder Trade:
>
> 1. Mythical Pokémon brought from past games using *Poké Transporter*: Mew, Celebi, Jirachi, Deoxys, Phione, Manaphy, Darkrai, Shaymin, Arceus, Victini, Keldeo, Meloetta, and Genesect.
> 2. Pokémon that were obtained in *Pokémon X*, *Pokémon Y*, *Pokémon Omega Ruby*, *Pokémon Alpha Sapphire*, *Pokémon Sun*, or *Pokémon Moon* that have a special ribbon.

Battle Video

A Battle Video is a video of a battle that's been saved via a Vs. Recorder. Battle Videos can be viewed later, made public, or used for "mock battles" in which you can recreate the battle from the Vs. Recorder data. To view Battle Videos, boot up the PC in the castle in Festival Plaza, and select "View Battle Video."

Search for a Battle Video

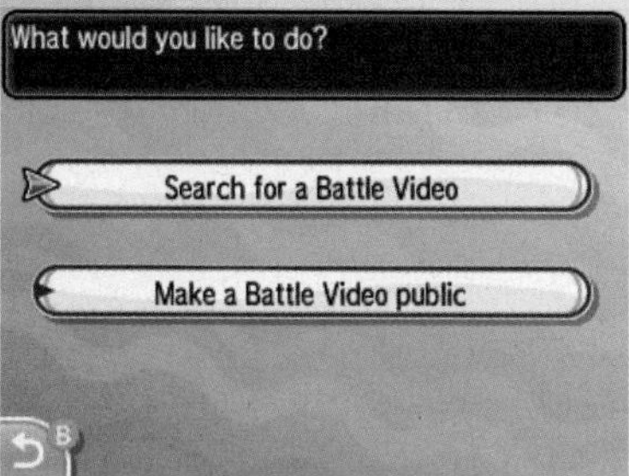

A Battle Video that has been made public has a Battle Video code. Enter a Battle Video code, and you can view the Battle Video. You can ask other players to share their Battle Video Codes or find them on the PGL website.

Make a Battle Video Public

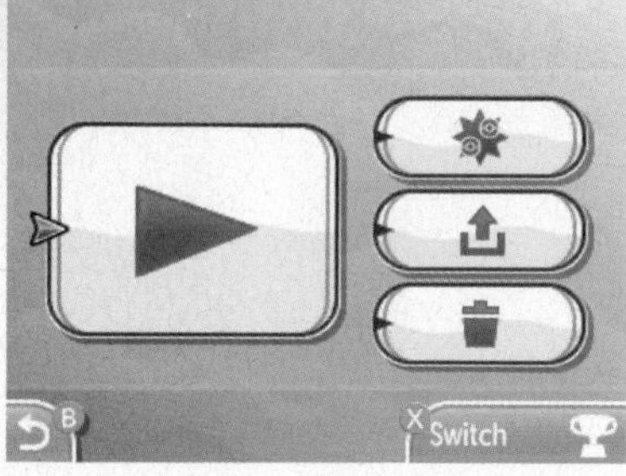

The PC in Festival Plaza's castle can also be used to make your Battle Videos public by pressing the upper right button. But remember that once you make it public, you won't be able to withdraw it until the next day. Select a Battle Video you've saved to your SD Card and press Ⓐ. You can also simply play the Battle Video from here, use it for a mock battle, or delete it to make room for more.

Tip

You can play your Battle Videos, use them as mock battles, or delete them from the X menu, too. Simply open the X menu and then select "Battle Video."

Mock Battles

If you record a battle that you've had with another player, such as a Link Battle in Festival Plaza, you can attempt it over and over again with mock battles! Select an eligible Battle Video from your Vs. Recorder (accessible from the X Menu) and then select the battle icon. You will be asked to choose which battle you want to use for the recreated battle. Your opponent's team will stay the same, but you can choose from your in-game party, one of your Battle Teams, or a QR Battle Team (p. 268) you are borrowing from someone else. Try different set-ups to see how the battle might have unfolded under another set of circumstances!

Game Sync

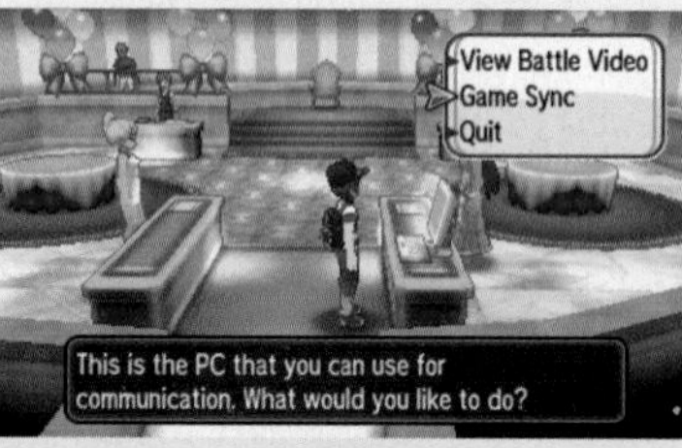

Game Sync is a service that connects your game with the PGL (p. 315). You can use Game Sync to send your saved data to the PGL. Boot up the PC in the castle in Festival Plaza, and select "Game Sync" to get started.

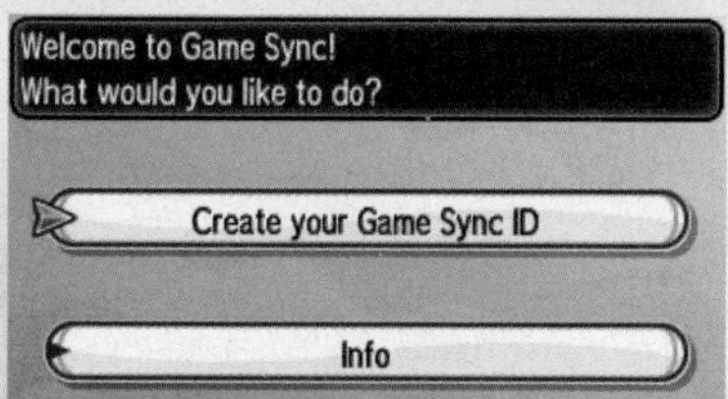

When you use Game Sync for the first time, a Game Sync ID will be issued. Register your Game Sync ID at the PGL, and your game will be linked with the PGL. Please see page 315 for details.

Tip

Once you've registered your Game Sync ID at the PGL, Game Sync will occur automatically when you connect to the Internet in Festival Plaza. If you ever need to check your Game Sync ID, simply log on to the PC inside the castle and select "Check Game Sync ID."

Poké Pelago

Poké Pelago is a special group of islands that exist solely for the delight of the Pokémon you've deposited in your PC Boxes. It's overseen by Mohn, a friendly caretaker who lives in a Raft Hut and helps keep Poké Pelago running. At first, Poké Pelago features just one island, Isle Abeens. But with a bit of effort, you can develop up to five different islands, each with their own unique benefits. All it takes is a little help from the Pokémon in your PC Boxes—and a healthy supply of Poké Beans!

> **Tip**
>
> You can't explore Poké Pelago if you don't have any Pokémon in your PC Boxes. Visit Poké Pelago after placing some Pokémon in your PC Boxes.

Poké Beans

Plain Bean

Patterned Bean

Rainbow Bean

Poké Beans are delicious treats enjoyed by Pokémon, and they have a variety of uses. You can use Poké Beans to develop Poké Pelago islands, or you can place them in a developed island's crate to enjoy that island's special Poké Bean effects (more on those in a bit). Poké Beans come in three types: Plain Beans, Patterned Beans, and Rainbow Beans. For variety, Plain Beans and Patterned Beans also come in seven different colors.

> **Tip**
>
> Poké Beans can also be fed to hungry Pokémon in Pokémon Refresh, increasing their affection for you (p. 276).

Each Poké Pelago island features a Poké Bean crate. Just tap an island's crate to place some Poké Beans in it. The more Poké Beans you place in a crate, the longer the Poké Beans' effects last! Poké Bean effects vary from island to island, as noted in the following sections.

Raft Hut

The Raft Hut has been Mohn's private abode ever since he decided to turn Alola's uninhabited islands into peaceful resorts for Pokémon. It may not look like much, but Mohn built the Raft Hut all by himself! Tap the little raft icon  in the Touch Screen's lower-right corner to visit the Raft Hut anytime you need Mohn's assistance. He'll help you develop isles, exchange Poké Beans, or send out Bean Bottles in the hopes that they'll reach other players.

Developing Isles

Develop Isles
You need
15
15
Isle Aplenny Development Phase 1
Develop this isle to create a space where Pokémon can enjoy growing Berries.
Up to six Berries can be grown on this isle.

By developing isles, you can create all-new Poké Pelago islands, or develop your existing isles even further. Developing isles requires you to have a certain number of Pokémon in your PC Boxes. You'll also need lots of Plain Beans to develop isles.

> **Tip**
>
> The number of Poké Beans you can place in an island's crate increases as you develop the island. You can place 20 Poké Beans in a crate for Phase 1 islands, 30 for Phase 2 islands, and 50 for Phase 3 islands.

Development	Poké Beans Needed	Pokémon Needed
Isle Abeens Development Phase 1	Available from start	
Isle Abeens Development Phase 2	30	15
Isle Abeens Development Phase 3	90	30
Isle Aplenny Development Phase 1	15	15
Isle Aplenny Development Phase 2	60	30
Isle Aplenny Development Phase 3	135	45
Isle Aphun Development Phase 1	30	30

Development	Poké Beans Needed	Pokémon Needed
Isle Aphun Development Phase 2	90	45
Isle Aphun Development Phase 3	180	60
Isle Evelup Development Phase 1	45	45
Isle Evelup Development Phase 2	120	60
Isle Evelup Development Phase 3	225	75
Isle Avue Development Phase 1	60	60
Isle Avue Development Phase 2	150	75
Isle Avue Development Phase 3	270	90

Exchanging Poké Beans

Plain Beans are needed to develop Poké Pelago isles. If you have rare Patterned or Rainbow Beans, Mohn will happily exchange them for Plain Beans. He'll give you three Plain Beans for each Patterned Bean, and seven Plain Beans for each Rainbow Bean. What a guy!

Sending Bean Bottles

A Bean Bottle is just what it sounds like: a bottle filled with Poké Beans! Talk to Mohn if you'd like to send out a Bean Bottle in the hopes that another player will receive it. Place seven Poké Beans in a Bean Bottle, then send it out with Mohn's help. After a while, you'll find a Bean Bottle sent out by another player somewhere in Poké Pelago. Tap the sparkling bottle to get Poké Beans!

Isle Abeens

Poké Bean Effect: Increases the chance of wild Pokémon coming to the island

Isle Abeens is the only isle that's developed at first, and it's your main source of Poké Beans. Tap the tall beanstalk in the middle of the isle to shake it, then watch as those Poké Beans come tumbling down! Poké Beans grow very quickly, so if no new Poké Beans shake loose, just wait a while and then try tapping the beanstalk again.

Tip

The more Pokémon you have in your PC Boxes, the faster Isle Abeens's beanstalk will produce Poké Beans. Perhaps your Pokémon are encouraging them to flourish?

Wild Pokémon sometimes wander over to play on Isle Abeens. You can easily spot a wild Pokémon by the "?" that appears above it. Tap the wild Pokémon for a closer look, and it may decide to stick around the island and join your team the next day!

Tip

Wild Pokémon that visit Isle Abeens are so eager to join your team that you won't need to throw any Poké Balls to catch them.

Pokémon	When Poké Pelago is unlocked	After reaching Ula'ula Island	After reaching Poni Island	After entering the Hall of Fame
Pikipek	○	○	○	○
Wingull	○	○	○	○
Kadabra	△	△	△	△
Magnemite	◎	○	○	○
Gastly	◎	○	○	○
Drifblim	△	△	△	△
Mismagius	—	—	—	△
Zubat	○	○	○	○
Spearow	○	○	○	○
Rufflet ☀	△	△	△	△
Vullaby ☾	△	△	△	△
Carbink	◎	○	○	○
Shellder	○	○	○	○

Pokémon	When Poké Pelago is unlocked	After reaching Ula'ula Island	After reaching Poni Island	After entering the Hall of Fame
Poliwag	—	◎	○	○
Fletchling	—	◎	○	○
Pinsir	—	◎	○	○
Staryu	—	◎	○	○
Trevenant	—	△	△	△
Pyukumuku	—	◎	○	○
Skarmory	—	—	◎	○
Metang	—	—	△	△
Klefki	—	—	◎	○
Lapras	—	—	—	◎
Emolga	—	—	—	◎
Scyther	—	—	—	◎
Murkrow	△	△	△	△

◎ frequent ○ average △ rare — never

Isle Aplenny

Poké Bean Effect: Makes Berry plants grow faster

Isle Aplenny's rich soil makes it a perfect place for growing Berries. After developing Isle Aplenny, simply tap the isle's sign and let Mohn know which Berries you'd like to plant. You can plant up to six Berries in one field, and you'll be able to harvest your Berries after a while. After you've fully developed the isle, you'll have three fields at your disposal, letting you plant up to 18 Berries at a time. You will also be able to harvest more Berries from each Berry tree as you develop Isle Aplenny further.

Tip

You'll need to find Berries before you can plant them. Look for Berries beneath Berry trees around Alola, such as the one near Route 2's Pokémon Center. See page 348 for a complete list of Berries and their effects, as well as information about how long each takes to grow and how many Berries you can expect to harvest.

Isle Aphun

Poké Bean Effect: Shortens the time for Pokémon to come back from exploration

Isle Aphun features a dark, mysterious cave that your Pokémon can explore for fun and profit. After developing Isle Aphun, tap its sign to send your Pokémon on an exploration adventure! More paths will become available as you continue to develop the isle, and your Pokémon may discover items as they explore. The items they find will vary depending on the exploration path and the isle's current development phase. Tap the isle's treasure box to obtain any items that your Pokémon have found.

Path	Items Found	Rarity
Path for Odd-Shard Hunting! (Phase 1)	Red Shard / Blue Shard / Yellow Shard / Green Shard	◎
	Hard Stone / Revive / Star Piece	○
Path for Brilliant-Stone Hunting! (Phase 2)	Hard Stone / Everstone / Float Stone	◎
	Fire Stone / Thunder Stone / Water Stone / Leaf Stone / Ice Stone / Sun Stone / Moon Stone / Oval Stone	○
	Shiny Stone / Dusk Stone / Dawn Stone / Light Clay	△
Path for Interesting-Item Hunting! (Phase 2)	Red Shard / Blue Shard / Yellow Shard / Green Shard / Hard Stone / Everstone / Float Stone	◎
	Revive / Star Piece / Fire Stone / Thunder Stone / Water Stone / Leaf Stone / Ice Stone / Sun Stone / Moon Stone / Oval Stone	○
	Shiny Stone / Dusk Stone / Dawn Stone / Light Clay	△
Path for Rare-Treasure Hunting (Phase 3)	Hard Stone / Pearl	◎
	Big Pearl / Nugget / Rare Bone / Pearl String	○
	Big Nugget / Comet Shard	△
	Gold Bottle Cap	▲
Path for Interesting-Item Hunting! (Phase 3)	Red Shard / Blue Shard / Yellow Shard / Green Shard / Hard Stone / Everstone / Float Stone / Pearl	◎
	Revive / Star Piece / Fire Stone / Thunder Stone / Water Stone / Leaf Stone / Ice Stone / Sun Stone / Moon Stone / Oval Stone / Big Pearl / Nugget / Rare Bone / Pearl String	○
	Shiny Stone / Dusk Stone / Dawn Stone / Light Clay / Big Nugget / Comet Shard	△
	Gold Bottle Cap	▲

◎ frequent ○ average △ rare ▲ almost never

Isle Evelup

Poké Bean Effect: Reduces the time required to complete each session

Isle Evelup is a simple place where your Pokémon can play, exercise, and grow. After developing Isle Evelup, tap the isle's sign to invite a group of up to six Pokémon to play on the play gym. Fully developing the isle lets you invite up to three groups (18 Pokémon) to play at the same time.

After picking your Pokémon, choose a drink for them to enjoy while they play. The drink you choose determines the manner in which your Pokémon will grow while playing. Drinks can increase their Exp. Points to help them level up or boost their base stats (p. 272) while they frolic on the play gym.

After you've selected a drink, choose how many play sessions you'd like your Pokémon to enjoy. Each play session lasts for 30 minutes, and the benefits of the drink you selected are bestowed to the Pokémon after each session is complete.

Tip

If you want to make your Pokémon quit in the middle of their play, tap the sign. The results for the number of sessions your Pokémon have already finished will be reflected on each Pokémon.

Isle Avue

Poké Bean Effect: Makes Pokémon become friendly toward you faster

Isle Avue is a sublime place where your Pokémon can enjoy a soothing soak in steamy, natural hot springs. After developing Isle Avue, tap the isle's sign to invite up to six Pokémon to soak in the spring, making them more friendly (p. 130) toward you. Fully developing the isle adds two more hot springs, letting up to 18 Pokémon bask in the relaxing experience. You can also soak Pokémon Eggs found at the Pokémon Nursery (p. 97) in Isle Avue's hot springs, helping them hatch faster than normal.

Don't leave your Pokémon for 24 hours or more in the hot springs, or they'll start feeling dizzy and become less friendly toward you!

Poké Finder

Shortly after you're given the Rotom Dex, you're granted access to the Poké Finder. This special camera lets you snap photos of Pokémon you spot in the wild around Alola. Share your photos with people living in the Pokémon world, and they'll give you a "thumbs-up" if they like your pics. Get lots of thumbs-ups, and your Poké Finder will be upgraded, letting you take even better shots!

Version	Thumbs-Up Needed	New Functionality
Ver. 1 (Default)	—	—
Ver. 2	1,500	Zoom function added
Ver. 3	10,000	Zoom function improved
Ver. 4	100,000	Zoom function maxed
Ver. 5	1,500,000	Calling Pokémon function added

Taking Great Photos

Looking for lots of thumbs-ups? Here are some tips that will make people in Alola rate your photos highly.

Catching the Pokémon head-on

Capturing a Pokémon face on will get you better results than catching it from the side. Photographing the back of a Pokémon will not be likely to get you a thumbs-up from most people.

Getting in close to the Pokémon

People want to see every detail of the wonderful Pokémon that can be found in Alola. The closer you get to the Pokémon, the more thumbs-ups you'll probably receive. But be warned: if you get too close and cut off some of the Pokémon, you may find people start complaining. The more that you cut off, the fewer thumbs-ups you'll get.

Catching a rare scene

Pokémon can perform a number of different actions, and some are rarer than others. Getting a snapshot of a Pokémon while it is performing one of these rarer moves will definitely get people excited!

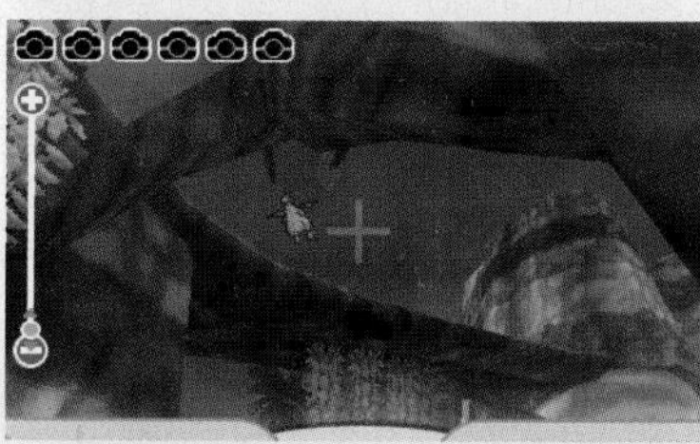

Finding a rare Pokémon

There are also a number of different Pokémon that tend to appear in the environs of each photo spot. Some appear commonly, but some are quite rare. If you manage to come across one of these rare Pokémon, take the best shots of it you can and be ready for the thumbs-ups to start pouring in!

Tip

Wondering if you got a great shot? Turn up the volume! The chime that plays when you snap a picture will change depending on how well it fits the criteria above. Rotom's comments may also help give you a little hint.

Tip

You can save your favorite photos to the SD Card in your Nintendo 3DS system and from there you can share them with friends if you want. See who gets the coolest shots!

Photo Spots

Poké Finder photo spots are marked on the maps throughout this guide, but here's the complete list in case you're having trouble finding any.

Melemele Island Photo Spots

Location	Name	Pokémon That Appear (those in **bold** are rare)
	Hau'oli City (p. 52) (Shopping District)	Growlithe, Alolan Meowth ☽, Pikachu, Rockruff ○
	Hau'oli City (p. 52) (Beachfront)	**Drifloon** ○, Pelipper, Wingull
	Hau'oli Cemetery (p. 60)	Gastly ☽, Pikipek ○, Zubat ☽
	Melemele Meadow (p. 74)	Cutiefly, Oricorio (Pom-Pom Style)
	Kala'e Bay (p. 87) (need Lapras Paddle or Sharpedo Jet)	Corsola, Alolan Dugtrio, Slowpoke

Akala Island Photo Spots

Location	Name	Pokémon That Appear (those in **bold** are rare)
	Paniola Ranch (p. 95)	Eevee, Espeon ○, Lillipup, Umbreon ☽
	Royal Avenue (p. 108)	Butterfree ○, Oricorio (Pa'u Style) ☽
	Brooklet Hill (p. 100)	Dewpider ○, Poliwag, Politoed, Surskit ☽
	Wela Volcano Park (p. 113)	Cubone, Fletchling, Salandit, **Talonflame** ○
	Route 8 (p. 118)	Crabrawler, Alolan Rattata ☽ , Yungoos ○
	Lush Jungle (p. 120) (West side)	Bounsweet ○, Comfey, Fomantis ☽, **Goodra**, Morelull ☽, Paras ○

Ula'ula Island Photo Spots

Location	Name	Pokémon That Appear (those in **bold** are rare)
	Mount Hokulani (p. 151)	Beldum, Clefable ☽, Clefairy ☽, **Magnezone** ☽, Metang
	Blush Mountain (p. 159)	Elekid, Magneton, **Porygon-Z**, Togedemaru
	Route 13 (p. 160)	**Flygon**, Gible, Sandile
	Thrifty Megamart (p. 163) (Abandoned Site)	Gastly, Gengar, Haunter, Mimikyu
	Ula'ula Meadow (p. 169)	Ariados ☽, Ledian ○, Oricorio (Baile Style)
	Mount Lanakila (p. 208) (Peak)	Absol ○, **Froslass** ☽, Sneasel ☽, Vanillish, Vanillite

Poni Island Photo Spots

Location	Name	Pokémon That Appear (those in **bold** are rare)
	Vast Poni Canyon (p. 198) (Exterior)	Gigalith, Hakamo-o, Jangmo-o, **Lucario**
	Poni Coast (p. 222)	Bewear, Fearow
	Poni Meadow (p. 223)	**Dragonite**, Oricorio (Sensu Style) ☽, Ribombee

The Pokémon Global Link

The Pokémon Global Link, abbreviated as PGL, is a website that can be linked to your *Pokémon Sun* or *Pokémon Moon* game. Join the community of Pokémon Trainers and see how other people are playing and competing in Pokémon. You need to register at the PGL to take part in Rating Battles, Online Competitions, and Friendly Competitions. You can also rent another player's Battle Team by scanning a Battle Team QR Code generated on the PGL. For details, please see page 268 or visit the PGL website (Pokemon.com/PGL).

How to sign up

Screenshot image subject to change

Signing up for the PGL is absolutely no charge, but you do need to purchase *Pokémon Sun* or *Pokémon Moon* to use some of the features. To sign up, create a Pokémon Trainer Club account. Go to Pokemon.com/PGL on your computer or mobile device. You may have to select your region the first time. Select "Sign Up!" under the log-in area on the left-hand side of the page. Enter your birth date and country. Be truthful, because if you are ever found to be using false information during a competition, you could be disqualified!

Next, choose a username and password, and enter an email address you'd like to associate with your account. You can opt in or out for receiving marketing emails from The Pokémon Company International. Then verify your email and accept the terms of use for the PGL website, and you're done!

Game Sync

Game Sync is a service that can connect your game with the PGL website. You can use Game Sync to send your saved data to the PGL. By linking your game with the PGL, you can participate in Rating Battles and competitions, and rent Battle Teams.

Linking your game to the PGL is easy and can be completed in three short steps.

1. Start by generating a Game Sync ID in your game

Press ⓧ to open the X menu, and then select "Festival Plaza." Enter the castle and boot up the PC and select "Game Sync." You'll be asked if you want to connect to the Internet and then to save your game. If you're not currently in an environment where you can connect to the Internet, you won't be able to connect to Game Sync.

2. Choose "Create your Game Sync ID" from the menu that appears, and then select "Yes"

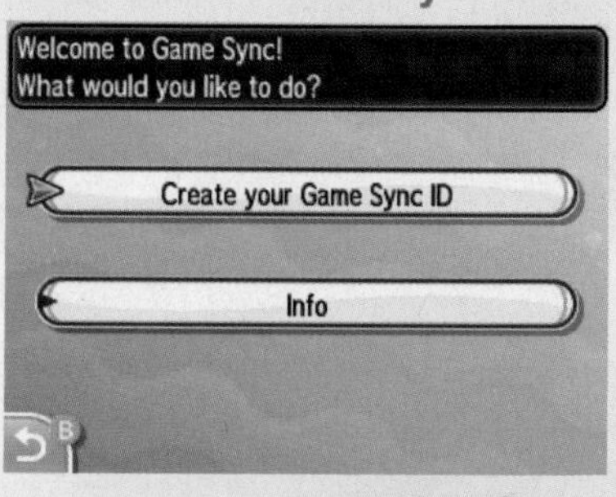

Your game will be authenticated online and you will be issued a Game Sync ID. Your Game Sync ID will be a 16-digit series of letters and numbers, which you'll need to enter at the PGL website to connect your game.

3. With your Game Sync ID handy, visit the PGL at Pokemon.com/PGL and log in

If you don't already have a PGL account, choose to sign up and follow the instructions (or have a parent help out) to activate your PGL account and enter your Game Sync ID when done!

Miiverse

Miiverse is a game-based online social hub run by Nintendo where you can share your experiences, ask questions, and even post artwork to share with other players. If your Nintendo 3DS system is up to date, you should see the Miiverse icon in the upper-right corner of the HOME Menu. Your HOME Menu is the first screen you see when you turn on your Nintendo 3DS system. If you're already playing your game, press the HOME button to reach the HOME Menu. You won't have to close your game to access the Miiverse, so feel free to pop in and out of it anytime. You will need to have a Nintendo Network ID to use Miiverse, so please visit Nintendo's official website for instructions if you aren't sure how to set one up.

Tip

You can also view the Miiverse from your computer or mobile device by visiting https://miiverse.nintendo.net/.

Miiverse Features

Here are some of the neat things you can do on Miiverse:

Post hand-written notes and drawings: Share your creative side with all the Trainers in Alola! Other Miiverse visitors may like your drawing and give it a "Yeah!" The most popular drawings can be seen on the front page of the Miiverse community for the game you're playing.

Create a Play Journal: Keep track of what you've done in your adventures as you complete your island challenge. Capture exciting moments, write down reminders of things you want to go back and try later, or journal your personal experience of *Pokémon Sun* and *Pokémon Moon* however you'd like!

Discussions: Chat with other players on a variety of topics. You can share hints with other players, ask questions when you're stuck, look for other players to battle or trade with, or just enjoy being part of the community.

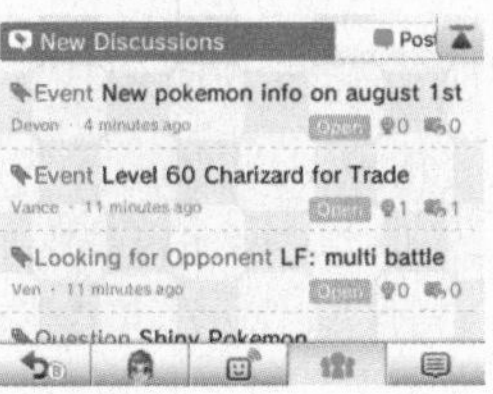

Tip

You can hide spoilers when posting on Miiverse. Be considerate of other players and don't spoil the secrets of the Alola region for them!

 and 

Pokémon Bank is an application and service that lets you deposit, store, and manage your Pokémon in private Boxes on the Internet. *Pokémon Bank* is a paid service, with an annual charge for usage. In addition to allowing you to store a greater number of Pokémon than any single game can contain, it will also allow you to bring Pokémon from your previous games to *Pokémon Sun* and *Pokémon Moon* beginning in early 2017! You will be able to transfer Pokémon directly from *Pokémon X*, *Pokémon Y*, *Pokémon Omega Ruby*, and *Pokémon Alpha Sapphire* using *Pokémon Bank*, as well as from the virtual console versions of *Pokémon Red*, *Pokémon Blue*, and *Pokémon Yellow: Special Pikachu Edition*.

You can even transfer Pokémon from older games using the linked application *Poké Transporter*, which is available to *Pokémon Bank* subscribers free of charge. Visit the *Pokémon Bank* official website for more instructions on how to bring your old pals to the latest Pokémon games!

Tip

You may find yourself unable to use *Pokémon Bank* or *Poké Transporter* to deposit any Pokémon created by software unauthorized by The Pokémon Company and Nintendo, and their affiliates, into your online Boxes, or to move these Pokémon between online Boxes. Also note that your Pokémon cannot be returned to older games once they have been transferred to *Pokémon Sun* or *Pokémon Moon*.

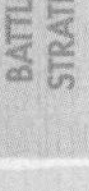

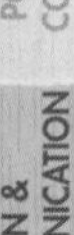

Adventure Data

Moves

Move	Type	Kind	Pow.	Acc.	PP	Range	DA	Z-Move Pow./ Effects	Battle Effects
Absorb	Grass	Special	20	100	25	Normal	—	100	Restores HP by up to half of the damage dealt to the target.
Accelerock	Rock	Physical	40	100	20	Normal	◯	100	Always strikes first. The user with the higher Speed goes first if similar moves are used.
Acid	Poison	Special	40	100	30	Many Others	—	100	A 10% chance of lowering the targets' Sp. Def by 1. Its power is reduced by 25% when it hits multiple Pokémon in a Double Battle. Its power is reduced by 50% when it hits multiple Pokémon in a Battle Royal.
Acid Armor	Poison	Status	—	—	20	Self	—	Resets negative stat changes.	Raises the user's Defense by 2.
Acid Spray	Poison	Special	40	100	20	Normal	—	100	Lowers the target's Sp. Def by 2.
Acrobatics	Flying	Physical	55	100	15	Normal	◯	100	This move's power is doubled if the user isn't holding an item.
Acupressure	Normal	Status	—	—	30	Self / Ally	—	Critical hits land more easily.	Raises a random stat by 2.
Aerial Ace	Flying	Physical	60	—	20	Normal	◯	120	A sure hit.
Aeroblast	Flying	Special	100	95	5	Normal	—	180	Critical hits land more easily.
After You	Normal	Status	—	—	15	Normal	—	Raises the user's Speed.	The user helps the target and makes it use its move right after the user, regardless of its Speed. It fails if the target was going to use its move right after anyway, or if the target has already used its move this turn.
Agility	Psychic	Status	—	—	30	Self	—	Resets negative stat changes.	Raises the user's Speed by 2.
Air Cutter	Flying	Special	60	95	25	Many Others	—	120	Critical hits land more easily. Its power is reduced by 25% when it hits multiple Pokémon in a Double Battle. Its power is reduced by 50% when it hits multiple Pokémon in a Battle Royal.
Air Slash	Flying	Special	75	95	15	Normal	—	140	A 30% chance of making the target flinch (unable to use moves on that turn).
Ally Switch	Psychic	Status	—	—	15	Self	—	Raises the user's Speed by 2.	This move goes first. The user switches places with an ally.
Amnesia	Psychic	Status	—	—	20	Self	—	Resets negative stat changes.	Raises the user's Sp. Def by 2.
Anchor Shot	Steel	Physical	80	100	20	Normal	◯	160	The target cannot escape. If used during a Trainer battle, the opposing Trainer cannot switch Pokémon. When used on a Ghost type, no additional effect takes place.
Ancient Power	Rock	Special	60	100	5	Normal	—	120	A 10% chance of raising the user's Attack, Defense, Speed, Sp. Atk, and Sp. Def stats by 1.
Aqua Jet	Water	Physical	40	100	20	Normal	◯	100	Always strikes first. The user with the higher Speed goes first if similar moves are used.
Aqua Ring	Water	Status	—	—	20	Self	—	Raises the user's Defense.	Restores 1/16 of max HP every turn.
Aqua Tail	Water	Physical	90	90	10	Normal	◯	175	A regular attack.
Arm Thrust	Fighting	Physical	15	100	20	Normal	◯	100	Attacks 2–5 times in a row in a single turn.
Aromatherapy	Grass	Status	—	—	5	Your Party	—	Restores the user's HP.	Heals status conditions of all your Pokémon, including those in your party.
Aromatic Mist	Fairy	Status	—	—	20	1 Ally	—	Raises the user's Sp. Def by 2.	Raises one ally's Sp. Def by 1.
Assist	Normal	Status	—	—	20	Self	—	None	Uses a random move from one of the Pokémon in your party that is not in battle.
Assurance	Dark	Physical	60	100	10	Normal	◯	120	Move's power is doubled if the target has already taken some damage in the same turn.
Astonish	Ghost	Physical	30	100	15	Normal	◯	100	A 30% chance of making the target flinch (unable to use moves on that turn).
Attack Order	Bug	Physical	90	100	15	Normal	—	175	Critical hits land more easily.
Attract	Normal	Status	—	100	15	Normal	—	Resets negative stat changes.	Leaves the target unable to attack 50% of the time. Only works if the user and the target are of different genders.
Aura Sphere	Fighting	Special	80	—	20	Normal	—	160	A sure hit.
Aurora Beam	Ice	Special	65	100	20	Normal	—	120	A 10% chance of lowering the target's Attack by 1.
Aurora Veil	Ice	Status	—	—	20	Your Side	—	Raises the user's Speed.	Damage from opponents' physical and special attacks is halved for 5 turns. This move can only be used when the weather condition is hail. Effect lasts 5 turns even if the user is switched out. Effect is weaker in Double Battles and Battle Royal.
Autotomize	Steel	Status	—	—	15	Self	—	Resets negative stat changes.	Raises the user's Speed by 2 and lowers its weight by 220 lbs.
Avalanche	Ice	Physical	60	100	10	Normal	◯	120	Always strikes last. This move's power is doubled if the user has taken damage from the target that turn.
Baby-Doll Eyes	Fairy	Status	—	100	30	Normal	—	Raises the user's Defense.	Always strikes first. Lowers the target's Attack by 1.
Baneful Bunker	Poison	Status	—	—	10	Self	—	Raises the user's Defense.	The user takes no damage in the same turn this move is used. If an opposing Pokémon uses a move that makes direct contact, the attacker will be inflicted with the Poison status condition. Fails more easily when used repeatedly.
Barrage	Normal	Physical	15	85	20	Normal	—	100	Attacks 2–5 times in a row in a single turn.
Barrier	Psychic	Status	—	—	20	Self	—	Resets negative stat changes.	Raises the user's Defense by 2.
Baton Pass	Normal	Status	—	—	40	Self	—	Resets negative stat changes.	User swaps out with an ally Pokémon and passes along any stat changes.
Beak Blast	Flying	Physical	100	100	15	Normal	—	180	Charges up and attacks on the same turn. If an opposing Pokémon uses a move that makes direct contact while the user is charging up, this move inflicts the Burned status condition on the attacker.
Beat Up	Dark	Physical	—	100	10	Normal	—	100	Attacks once for each Pokémon in your party, including the user. Does not count Pokémon that have fainted or have status conditions.

Move	Type	Kind	Pow.	Acc.	PP	Range	DA	Z-Move Pow./ Effects	Battle Effects
Belch	Poison	Special	120	90	10	Normal	—	190	Cannot be used without first eating a Berry.
Belly Drum	Normal	Status	—	—	10	Self	—	Restores the user's HP.	The user loses half of its maximum HP but raises its Attack to the maximum.
Bestow	Normal	Status	—	—	15	Normal	—	Raises the user's Speed by 2.	If the target is not holding an item and the user is, the user can give that item to the target. Fails if the user is not holding an item or the target is holding an item.
Bide	Normal	Physical	—	—	10	Self	○	100	Inflicts twice the damage received during the next 2 turns. Cannot choose moves during those 2 turns.
Bind	Normal	Physical	15	85	20	Normal	○	100	Inflicts damage equal to 1/8 the target's max HP for 4–5 turns. The target cannot flee during that time.
Bite	Dark	Physical	60	100	25	Normal	○	120	A 30% chance of making the target flinch (unable to use moves on that turn).
Blast Burn	Fire	Special	150	90	5	Normal	—	200	The user can't move during the next turn. If the target is Frozen, it will be thawed.
Blaze Kick	Fire	Physical	85	90	10	Normal	○	160	A 10% chance of inflicting the Burned status condition on the target. Critical hits land more easily. If the target is Frozen, it will be thawed.
Blizzard	Ice	Special	110	70	5	Many Others	—	185	A 10% chance of inflicting the Frozen status condition on the targets. Is 100% accurate in the hail weather condition. Its power is reduced by 25% when it hits multiple Pokémon in a Double Battle. Its power is reduced by 50% when it hits multiple Pokémon in a Battle Royal.
Block	Normal	Status	—	—	5	Normal	—	Raises the user's Defense.	The target cannot escape. If used during a Trainer battle, the opposing Trainer cannot switch Pokémon. Has no effect on Ghost-type Pokémon.
Blue Flare	Fire	Special	130	85	5	Normal	—	195	A 20% chance of inflicting the Burned status condition on the target. If the target is Frozen, it will be thawed.
Body Slam	Normal	Physical	85	100	15	Normal	○	160	A 30% chance of inflicting the Paralysis status condition on the target. If the target has used Minimize, this move will be a sure hit and its power will be doubled.
Bolt Strike	Electric	Physical	130	85	5	Normal	○	195	A 20% chance of inflicting the Paralysis status condition on the targets.
Bone Club	Ground	Physical	65	85	20	Normal	—	120	A 10% chance of making the target flinch (unable to use moves on that turn).
Bone Rush	Ground	Physical	25	90	10	Normal	—	140	Attacks 2–5 times in a row in a single turn.
Bonemerang	Ground	Physical	50	90	10	Normal	—	100	Attacks twice in a row in a single turn.
Boomburst	Normal	Special	140	100	10	Adjacent	—	200	Its power is reduced by 25% when it hits multiple Pokémon in a Double Battle. Its power is reduced by 50% when it hits multiple Pokémon in a Battle Royal. Strikes the target even if it is using Substitute.
Bounce	Flying	Physical	85	85	5	Normal	○	160	The user flies into the air on the first turn and attacks on the second. A 30% chance of inflicting the Paralysis status condition on the target.
Brave Bird	Flying	Physical	120	100	15	Normal	○	190	The user takes 1/3 of the damage inflicted.
Brick Break	Fighting	Physical	75	100	15	Normal	○	140	This move is not affected by Aurora Veil or Reflect. It removes the effect of Aurora Veil, Light Screen, and Reflect.
Brine	Water	Special	65	100	10	Normal	—	120	This move's power is doubled if the target's HP is at half or below.
Brutal Swing	Dark	Physical	60	100	20	Adjacent	○	120	A regular attack. Its power is reduced by 25% when it hits multiple Pokémon in a Double Battle. Its power is reduced by 50% when it hits multiple Pokémon in a Battle Royal.
Bubble	Water	Special	40	100	30	Many Others	—	100	A 10% chance of lowering the targets' Speed by 1. Its power is reduced by 25% when it hits multiple Pokémon in a Double Battle. Its power is reduced by 50% when it hits multiple Pokémon in a Battle Royal.
Bubble Beam	Water	Special	65	100	20	Normal	—	120	A 10% chance of lowering the target's Speed by 1.
Bug Bite	Bug	Physical	60	100	20	Normal	○	120	If the target is holding a Berry, the user eats that Berry and uses its battle effect if it has one.
Bug Buzz	Bug	Special	90	100	10	Normal	—	175	A 10% chance of lowering the target's Sp. Def by 1. Strikes the target even if it is using Substitute.
Bulk Up	Fighting	Status	—	—	20	Self	—	Raises the user's Attack.	Raises the user's Attack and Defense by 1.
Bulldoze	Ground	Physical	60	100	20	Adjacent	—	120	Lowers the target's Speed by 1. Its power is reduced by 25% when it hits multiple Pokémon in a Double Battle. Its power is reduced by 50% when it hits multiple Pokémon in a Battle Royal.
Bullet Punch	Steel	Physical	40	100	30	Normal	○	100	Always strikes first. The user with the higher Speed goes first if similar moves are used.
Bullet Seed	Grass	Physical	25	100	30	Normal	—	140	Attacks 2–5 times in a row in a single turn.
Burn Up	Fire	Special	130	100	5	Normal	—	195	After attacking, the user is no longer Fire type.
Calm Mind	Psychic	Status	—	—	20	Self	—	Resets negative stat changes.	Raises the user's Sp. Atk and Sp. Def by 1.
Camouflage	Normal	Status	—	—	20	Self	—	Raises the user's evasion.	Changes the user's type to match the environment: Cave: Rock type. Dirt / Sand: Ground type. Electric Terrain: Electric type. Grass / Grassy Terrain: Grass type. Indoors / Link Battle: Normal type. Misty Terrain: Fairy type. Psychic Terrain / Ultra Space: Psychic type. Snow/Ice: Ice type. Volcano: Fire type. Water Surface / Puddle / Shoal: Water type.
Captivate	Normal	Status	—	100	20	Many Others	—	Raises the user's Sp. Def by 2.	Lowers the targets' Sp. Atk by 2. Only works if the user and the targets are of different genders.
Celebrate	Normal	Status	—	—	40	Self	—	Raises all of the user's stats.	No effect.
Charge	Electric	Status	—	—	20	Self	—	Raises the user's Sp. Def.	Doubles the attack power of an Electric-type move used the next turn. Raises the user's Sp. Def by 1.
Charge Beam	Electric	Special	50	90	10	Normal	—	100	A 70% chance of raising the user's Sp. Atk by 1.
Charm	Fairy	Status	—	100	20	Normal	—	Raises the user's Defense.	Lowers the target's Attack by 2.
Chatter	Flying	Special	65	100	20	Normal	—	120	When the user is Chatot, this move also makes the target confused. Strikes the target even if it is using Substitute.
Chip Away	Normal	Physical	70	100	20	Normal	○	140	Damage dealt is not affected by the opposing Pokémon's stat changes.
Circle Throw	Fighting	Physical	60	90	10	Normal	○	120	Always strikes last. Ends wild Pokémon battles after attacking. When battling multiple wild Pokémon or if the wild Pokémon's level is higher than the user's, no additional effect takes place. In a battle with a Trainer, this move forces another Pokémon to switch in. If there is no Pokémon to switch in, no additional effect takes place.
Clamp	Water	Physical	35	85	15	Normal	○	100	Inflicts damage equal to 1/8 the target's max HP for 4–5 turns. The target cannot flee during that time.

Move	Type	Kind	Pow.	Acc.	PP	Range	DA	Z-Move Pow./ Effects	Battle Effects
Clanging Scales	Dragon	Special	110	100	5	Many Others	—	185	As an additional effect, lowers the user's Defense by 1. Its power is reduced by 25% when it hits multiple Pokémon in a Double Battle. Its power is reduced by 50% when it hits multiple Pokémon in a Battle Royal.
Clear Smog	Poison	Special	50	—	15	Normal	—	100	Eliminates every stat change of the target.
Close Combat	Fighting	Physical	120	100	5	Normal	◯	190	Lowers the user's Defense and Sp. Def by 1.
Coil	Poison	Status	—	—	20	Self	—	Resets negative stat changes.	Raises the user's Attack, Defense, and accuracy by 1.
Comet Punch	Normal	Physical	18	85	15	Normal	◯	100	Attacks 2–5 times in a row in a single turn.
Confide	Normal	Status	—	—	20	Normal	—	Raises the user's Sp. Def.	A sure hit. Lowers the target's Sp. Atk by 1. Strikes the target even if it is using Baneful Bunker, Detect, King's Shield, Mat Block, Protect, Spiky Shield, or Substitute.
Confuse Ray	Ghost	Status	—	100	10	Normal	—	Raises the user's Sp. Atk.	Makes the target confused.
Confusion	Psychic	Special	50	100	25	Normal	—	100	A 10% chance of making the target confused.
Constrict	Normal	Physical	10	100	35	Normal	◯	100	A 10% chance of lowering the target's Speed by 1.
Conversion	Normal	Status	—	—	30	Self	—	Raises all of the user's stats.	Changes the user's type to that of one of its moves.
Conversion 2	Normal	Status	—	—	30	Normal	—	Restores the user's HP.	Changes the user's type to one that is strong against the last move the target used.
Copycat	Normal	Status	—	—	20	Self	—	Increases the user's accuracy.	Uses the last move used.
Core Enforcer	Dragon	Special	100	100	10	Many Others	—	140	Nullifies Abilities of targets that used a move on the same turn. Fails with certain Abilities, however.
Cosmic Power	Psychic	Status	—	—	20	Self	—	Raises the user's Sp. Def.	Raises the user's Defense and Sp. Def by 1.
Cotton Guard	Grass	Status	—	—	10	Self	—	Resets negative stat changes.	Raises the user's Defense by 3.
Cotton Spore	Grass	Status	—	100	40	Many Others	—	Resets negative stat changes.	Lowers the targets' Speed by 2. Has no effect on Grass-type Pokémon.
Counter	Fighting	Physical	—	100	20	Varies	◯	100	If the user is attacked physically, this move inflicts twice the damage done to the user. Always strikes last.
Covet	Normal	Physical	60	100	25	Normal	◯	120	When the target is holding an item and the user is not, the user can steal that item. A regular attack if the target is not holding an item.
Crabhammer	Water	Physical	100	90	10	Normal	◯	180	Critical hits land more easily.
Crafty Shield	Fairy	Status	—	—	10	Your Side	—	Raises the user's Sp. Def.	Protects the user and allies from status moves used in the same turn. Does not protect against damage-dealing moves.
Cross Chop	Fighting	Physical	100	80	5	Normal	◯	180	Critical hits land more easily.
Cross Poison	Poison	Physical	70	100	20	Normal	◯	140	Critical hits land more easily. A 10% chance of inflicting the Poison status condition on the target.
Crunch	Dark	Physical	80	100	15	Normal	◯	160	A 20% chance of lowering the target's Defense by 1.
Crush Claw	Normal	Physical	75	95	10	Normal	◯	140	A 50% chance of lowering the target's Defense by 1.
Crush Grip	Normal	Physical	—	100	5	Normal	◯	190	The more HP the target has left, the greater the move's power becomes (max 120).
Curse	Ghost	Status	—	—	10	Varies	—	Ghost type: restores all of the user's HP. Other types: Raises the user's Attack.	Lowers the user's Speed by 1 and raises its Attack and Defense by 1. If used by a Ghost-type Pokémon, the user loses half of its maximum HP, but the move lowers the target's HP by 1/4 of its maximum every turn.
Cut	Normal	Physical	50	95	30	Normal	◯	100	A regular attack.
Dark Pulse	Dark	Special	80	100	15	Normal	—	160	Has a 20% chance of making the target flinch (unable to use moves on that turn).
Dark Void	Dark	Status	—	50	10	Many Others	—	Resets negative stat changes.	Inflicts the Asleep status condition on the targets.
Darkest Lariat	Dark	Physical	85	100	10	Normal	◯	160	Damage dealt is not affected by the opposing Pokémon's stat changes.
Dazzling Gleam	Fairy	Special	80	100	10	Many Others	—	160	Its power is reduced by 25% when it hits multiple Pokémon in a Double Battle. Its power is reduced by 50% when it hits multiple Pokémon in a Battle Royal.
Defend Order	Bug	Status	—	—	10	Self	—	Raises the user's Defense.	Raises the user's Defense and Sp. Def by 1.
Defense Curl	Normal	Status	—	—	40	Self	—	Increases the user's accuracy.	Raises the user's Defense by 1.
Defog	Flying	Status	—	—	15	Normal	—	Increases the user's accuracy.	Lowers the target's evasion by 1. Nullifies the effects of Aurora Veil, Light Screen, Reflect, Safeguard, Mist, Spikes, Toxic Spikes, and Stealth Rock on the target's side.
Destiny Bond	Ghost	Status	—	—	5	Self	—	Follow Me	If the user faints due to damage from a Pokémon, that Pokémon faints as well. Fails when used in succession.
Detect	Fighting	Status	—	—	5	Self	—	Raises the user's evasion.	The user evades all moves that turn. If used in succession, its chance of failing rises.
Diamond Storm	Rock	Physical	100	95	5	Many Others	—	180	A 50% chance of raising the user's Defense by 2. Its power is reduced by 25% when it hits multiple Pokémon in a Double Battle. Its power is reduced by 50% when it hits multiple Pokémon in a Battle Royal.
Dig	Ground	Physical	80	100	10	Normal	◯	160	The user burrows underground on the first turn and attacks on the second.
Disable	Normal	Status	—	100	20	Normal	—	Resets negative stat changes.	The target can't use the move it just used for 4 turns.
Disarming Voice	Fairy	Special	40	—	15	Many Others	—	100	A sure hit. Strikes the targets even if they are using Substitute. Its power is reduced by 25% when it hits multiple Pokémon in a Double Battle. Its power is reduced by 50% when it hits multiple Pokémon in a Battle Royal.
Discharge	Electric	Special	80	100	15	Adjacent	—	160	A 30% chance of inflicting the Paralysis status condition on the target. Its power is reduced by 25% when it hits multiple Pokémon in a Double Battle. Its power is reduced by 50% when it hits multiple Pokémon in a Battle Royal.
Dive	Water	Physical	80	100	10	Normal	◯	160	The user dives deep on the first turn and attacks on the second.
Dizzy Punch	Normal	Physical	70	100	10	Normal	◯	140	A 20% chance of making the target confused.
Doom Desire	Steel	Special	140	100	5	Normal	—	200	Attacks the target after 2 turns. This move is affected by the target's type.

Move	Type	Kind	Pow.	Acc.	PP	Range	DA	Z-Move Pow./ Effects	Battle Effects
Double Hit	Normal	Physical	35	90	10	Normal	○	140	Attacks twice in a row in a single turn.
Double Kick	Fighting	Physical	30	100	30	Normal	○	100	Attacks twice in a row in a single turn.
Double Slap	Normal	Physical	15	85	10	Normal	○	100	Attacks 2–5 times in a row in a single turn.
Double Team	Normal	Status	—	—	15	Self	—	Resets negative stat changes.	Raises the user's evasion by 1.
Double-Edge	Normal	Physical	120	100	15	Normal	○	190	The user takes 1/3 of the damage inflicted.
Draco Meteor	Dragon	Special	130	90	5	Normal	—	195	Lowers the user's Sp. Atk by 2.
Dragon Ascent	Flying	Physical	120	100	5	Normal	○	190	Lowers the user's Defense and Sp. Def by 1.
Dragon Breath	Dragon	Special	60	100	20	Normal	—	120	A 30% chance of inflicting the Paralysis status condition on the target.
Dragon Claw	Dragon	Physical	80	100	15	Normal	○	160	A regular attack.
Dragon Dance	Dragon	Status	—	—	20	Self	—	Resets negative stat changes.	Raises the user's Attack and Speed by 1.
Dragon Hammer	Dragon	Physical	90	100	15	Normal	○	175	A regular attack.
Dragon Pulse	Dragon	Special	85	100	10	Normal	—	160	A regular attack.
Dragon Rage	Dragon	Special	—	100	10	Normal	—	100	Deals a fixed 40 points of damage.
Dragon Rush	Dragon	Physical	100	75	10	Normal	○	180	A 20% chance of making the target flinch (unable to use moves on that turn). If the target has used Minimize, this move will be a sure hit and its power will be doubled.
Dragon Tail	Dragon	Physical	60	90	10	Normal	○	120	Attacks last. Ends wild Pokémon battles after attacking. When battling multiple wild Pokémon or if the wild Pokémon's level is higher than the user's, no additional effect takes place. In a battle with a Trainer, this move forces another Pokémon to switch in. If there is no Pokémon to switch in, no additional effect takes place.
Drain Punch	Fighting	Physical	75	100	10	Normal	○	140	Restores HP by up to half of the damage dealt to the target.
Draining Kiss	Fairy	Special	50	100	10	Normal	○	100	Restores HP by up to 3/4 of the damage dealt to the target.
Dream Eater	Psychic	Special	100	100	15	Normal	—	180	Only works when the target is Asleep. Restores HP by up to half of the damage dealt to the target.
Drill Peck	Flying	Physical	80	100	20	Normal	○	160	A regular attack.
Drill Run	Ground	Physical	80	95	10	Normal	○	160	Critical hits land more easily.
Dual Chop	Dragon	Physical	40	90	15	Normal	○	100	Attacks twice in a row in a single turn.
Dynamic Punch	Fighting	Physical	100	50	5	Normal	○	180	Makes the target confused.
Earth Power	Ground	Special	90	100	10	Normal	—	175	A 10% chance of lowering the target's Sp. Def by 1.
Earthquake	Ground	Physical	100	100	10	Adjacent	—	180	Does twice the damage if targets are underground due to using Dig. Its power is reduced by 25% when it hits multiple Pokémon in a Double Battle. Its power is reduced by 50% when it hits multiple Pokémon in a Battle Royal.
Echoed Voice	Normal	Special	40	100	15	Normal	—	100	If this move is used every turn, no matter which Pokémon uses it, its power increases (max 200). If no Pokémon uses it in a turn, the power returns to normal. Strikes the target even if it is using Substitute.
Eerie Impulse	Electric	Status	—	100	15	Normal	—	Raises the user's Sp. Def.	Lowers the target's Sp. Atk by 2.
Egg Bomb	Normal	Physical	100	75	10	Normal	—	180	A regular attack.
Electric Terrain	Electric	Status	—	—	10	Both Sides	—	Raises the user's Speed.	Electrifies the field for 5 turns. During that time, Pokémon on the ground will be able to do 50% more damage with Electric-type moves and cannot fall Asleep.
Electrify	Electric	Status	—	—	20	Normal	—	Raises the user's Sp. Atk.	Changes any attack used by the target in the same turn into an Electric-type move.
Electro Ball	Electric	Special	—	100	10	Normal	—	160	The faster the user is than the target, the greater the move's power (max 150).
Electroweb	Electric	Special	55	95	15	Many Others	—	100	Lowers the targets' Speed by 1. Its power is reduced by 25% when it hits multiple Pokémon in a Double Battle. Its power is reduced by 50% when it hits multiple Pokémon in a Battle Royal.
Embargo	Dark	Status	—	100	15	Normal	—	Raises the user's Sp. Atk.	The target can't use items for 5 turns. The Trainer also can't use items on that Pokémon.
Ember	Fire	Special	40	100	25	Normal	—	100	A 10% chance of inflicting the Burned status condition on the target. If the target is Frozen, it will be thawed.
Encore	Normal	Status	—	100	5	Normal	—	Raises the user's Speed.	The target is forced to keep using the last move it used. This effect lasts 3 turns.
Endeavor	Normal	Physical	—	100	5	Normal	○	160	Inflicts damage equal to the target's HP minus the user's HP.
Endure	Normal	Status	—	—	10	Self	—	Resets negative stat changes.	Leaves the user with 1 HP when hit by a move that would KO it. If used in succession, its chance of failing rises.
Energy Ball	Grass	Special	90	100	10	Normal	—	175	A 10% chance of lowering the target's Sp. Def by 1.
Entrainment	Normal	Status	—	100	15	Normal	—	Raises the user's Sp. Def.	Makes the target's Ability the same as the user's. Fails with certain Abilities, however.
Eruption	Fire	Special	150	100	5	Many Others	—	200	If the user's HP is low, this move has lower power. If the targets are Frozen, they will be thawed. Its power is reduced by 25% when it hits multiple Pokémon in a Double Battle. Its power is reduced by 50% when it hits multiple Pokémon in a Battle Royal.
Explosion	Normal	Physical	250	100	5	Adjacent	—	200	The user faints after using it. Its power is reduced by 25% when it hits multiple Pokémon in a Double Battle. Its power is reduced by 50% when it hits multiple Pokémon in a Battle Royal.
Extrasensory	Psychic	Special	80	100	20	Normal	—	160	A 10% chance of making the target flinch (unable to use moves on that turn).
Extreme Speed	Normal	Physical	80	100	5	Normal	○	160	Always strikes first. Faster than other moves that strike first, except Fake Out. If two Pokémon use this move, or if the other Pokémon uses the move Feint or First Impression, the one with the higher Speed goes first.
Facade	Normal	Physical	70	100	20	Normal	○	140	This move's power is doubled if the user has a Paralysis, Poison, or Burned status condition.
Fairy Lock	Fairy	Status	—	—	10	Both Sides	—	Raises the user's Defense.	The target cannot escape during the next turn. If used during a Trainer battle, the opposing Trainer cannot switch Pokémon. Has no effect on Ghost-type Pokémon.
Fairy Wind	Fairy	Special	40	100	30	Normal	—	100	A regular attack.
Fake Out	Normal	Physical	40	100	10	Normal	○	100	Always strikes first and makes the target flinch (unable to use moves on that turn). Only works on the first turn after the user is sent out. Faster than other moves that strike first.

Move	Type	Kind	Pow.	Acc.	PP	Range	DA	Z-Move Pow./ Effects	Battle Effects
Fake Tears	Dark	Status	—	100	20	Normal	—	Raises the user's Sp. Atk.	Lowers the target's Sp. Def by 2.
False Swipe	Normal	Physical	40	100	40	Normal	○	100	Always leaves 1 HP, even if the damage would have made the target faint.
Feather Dance	Flying	Status	—	100	15	Normal	—	Raises the user's Defense.	Lowers the target's Attack by 2.
Feint	Normal	Physical	30	100	10	Normal	—	100	Always strikes first. Faster than other moves that strike first, except Fake Out. If two Pokémon use this move, or if the other Pokémon uses the move Extreme Speed or First Impression, the one with the higher Speed goes first. Strikes the target even if it is using Baneful Bunker, Detect, King's Shield, Mat Block, Protect, Quick Guard, Spiky Shield, or Wide Guard, and eliminates the effects of those moves.
Feint Attack	Dark	Physical	60	—	20	Normal	○	120	A sure hit.
Fell Stinger	Bug	Physical	50	100	25	Normal	○	100	When the Pokémon knocks out an opponent with this move, its Attack goes up 3.
Fiery Dance	Fire	Special	80	100	10	Normal	—	160	A 50% chance of raising the user's Sp. Atk by 1. If the target is Frozen, it will be thawed.
Final Gambit	Fighting	Special	—	100	5	Normal	—	180	Does damage to the target equal to the user's remaining HP. If the move lands, the user faints. If the move does not land, the user will not faint.
Fire Blast	Fire	Special	110	85	5	Normal	—	185	A 10% chance of inflicting the Burned status condition on the target. If the target is Frozen, it will be thawed.
Fire Fang	Fire	Physical	65	95	15	Normal	○	120	A 10% chance of inflicting the Burned status condition or making the target flinch (unable to use moves on that turn). If the target is Frozen, it will be thawed.
Fire Lash	Fire	Physical	80	100	15	Normal	○	160	Lowers the target's Defense by 1.
Fire Pledge	Fire	Special	80	100	10	Normal	—	160	When combined with Water Pledge or Grass Pledge, the power and effect change. If combined with Water Pledge, the power is 150 and it becomes a Water-type move. This makes it more likely that your team's moves will have additional effects for 4 turns. If combined with Grass Pledge, the power is 150 and it remains a Fire-type move. This damages opposing Pokémon, except Fire types, for 4 turns. If the target is Frozen, it will be thawed.
Fire Punch	Fire	Physical	75	100	15	Normal	○	140	A 10% chance of inflicting the Burned status condition on the target. If the target is Frozen, it will be thawed.
Fire Spin	Fire	Special	35	85	15	Normal	—	100	Inflicts damage equal to 1/8 the target's max HP for 4–5 turns. The target cannot flee during that time. If the target is Frozen, it will be thawed.
First Impression	Bug	Physical	90	100	10	Normal	○	175	Always strikes first. Only works on the first turn after the user is sent out. Faster than other moves that strike first, except Fake Out. If two Pokémon use this move, or if the other Pokémon uses the move Extreme Speed or Feint, the one with the higher Speed goes first.
Fissure	Ground	Physical	—	30	5	Normal	—	180	The target faints with one hit if the user's level is equal to or greater than the target's level. The higher the user's level is compared to the target's, the more accurate the move is.
Flail	Normal	Physical	—	100	15	Normal	○	160	The lower the user's HP is, the greater the move's power becomes (max 200).
Flame Burst	Fire	Special	70	100	15	Normal	—	140	It deals damage equal to 1/16 of the max HP of opposing Pokémon next to the target during Double Battles or Battle Royals. If the target is Frozen, it will be thawed.
Flame Charge	Fire	Physical	50	100	20	Normal	○	100	Raises the user's Speed by 1. If the target is Frozen, it will be thawed.
Flame Wheel	Fire	Physical	60	100	25	Normal	○	120	A 10% chance of inflicting the Burned status condition on the target. If the target is Frozen, it will be thawed. This move can be used even if the user is Frozen. If the user is Frozen, this also thaws the user.
Flamethrower	Fire	Special	90	100	15	Normal	—	175	A 10% chance of inflicting the Burned status condition on the target. If the target is Frozen, it will be thawed.
Flare Blitz	Fire	Physical	120	100	15	Normal	○	190	User takes 1/3 of the damage done to the target. A 10% chance of inflicting the Burned status condition on the target. If the target is Frozen, it will be thawed. This move can be used even if the user is Frozen. If the user is Frozen, this also thaws the user.
Flash	Normal	Status	—	100	20	Normal	—	Raises the user's evasion.	Lowers the target's accuracy by 1.
Flash Cannon	Steel	Special	80	100	10	Normal	—	160	A 10% chance of lowering the target's Sp. Def by 1.
Flatter	Dark	Status	—	100	15	Normal	—	Raises the user's Sp. Def.	Makes the target confused, but also raises its Sp. Atk by 1.
Fleur Cannon	Fairy	Special	130	90	5	Normal	—	195	Lowers the user's Sp. Atk by 2.
Fling	Dark	Physical	—	100	10	Normal	—	100	The user attacks by throwing its held item at the target. Power and effect vary depending on the item.
Floral Healing	Fairy	Status	—	—	10	Normal	—	Resets negative stat changes.	Restores a target other than the user's HP by up to half of its maximum HP. If Grassy Terrain is in effect, it recovers 2/3 of the target's maximum HP.
Flower Shield	Fairy	Status	—	—	10	Varies	—	Raises the user's Defense.	Raises the Defense of any Grass-type Pokémon by 1.
Fly	Flying	Physical	90	95	15	Normal	○	175	The user flies into the air on the first turn and attacks on the second.
Flying Press	Fighting	Physical	100	95	10	Normal	○	170	This move is both Fighting type and Flying type. If the target has used Minimize, it will be a sure hit and its power will be doubled.
Focus Blast	Fighting	Special	120	70	5	Normal	—	190	A 10% chance of lowering the target's Sp. Def by 1.
Focus Energy	Normal	Status	—	—	30	Self	—	Increases the user's accuracy.	Heightens the critical-hit ratio of the user's subsequent moves.
Focus Punch	Fighting	Physical	150	100	20	Normal	○	200	Always strikes last. The move misses if the user is hit before this move lands.
Follow Me	Normal	Status	—	—	20	Self	—	Resets negative stat changes.	This move goes first. Opposing Pokémon aim only at the user.
Force Palm	Fighting	Physical	60	100	10	Normal	○	120	A 30% chance of inflicting the Paralysis status condition on the target.
Foresight	Normal	Status	—	—	40	Normal	—	Critical hits land more easily.	Attacks land easily regardless of the target's evasion. Makes Ghost-type Pokémon vulnerable to Normal- and Fighting-type moves.
Forest's Curse	Grass	Status	—	100	20	Normal	—	Raises all of the user's stats.	Gives the target the Grass type.
Foul Play	Dark	Physical	95	100	15	Normal	○	175	The user turns the target's power against it. Damage varies depending on the target's Attack and Defense.
Freeze Shock	Ice	Physical	140	90	5	Normal	—	200	Builds power on the first turn and attacks on the second. A 30% chance of inflicting the Paralysis status condition on the target.

Move	Type	Kind	Pow.	Acc.	PP	Range	DA	Z-Move Pow./ Effects	Battle Effects
Freeze-Dry	Ice	Special	70	100	20	Normal	—	140	Super effective even against Water-type Pokémon. A 10% chance of inflicting the Frozen status condition.
Frenzy Plant	Grass	Special	150	90	5	Normal	—	200	The user can't move during the next turn.
Frost Breath	Ice	Special	60	90	10	Normal	—	120	Always delivers a critical hit.
Frustration	Normal	Physical	—	100	20	Normal	○	160	The lower the user's friendship, the greater this move's power (max 102).
Fury Attack	Normal	Physical	15	85	20	Normal	○	100	Attacks 2–5 times in a row in a single turn.
Fury Cutter	Bug	Physical	40	95	20	Normal	○	100	This move doubles in power with every successful hit (max 160). Power returns to normal once it misses.
Fury Swipes	Normal	Physical	18	80	15	Normal	○	100	Attacks 2–5 times in a row in a single turn.
Fusion Bolt	Electric	Physical	100	100	5	Normal	—	180	Attack's power is doubled if used immediately after Fusion Flare.
Fusion Flare	Fire	Special	100	100	5	Normal	—	180	Attack's power is doubled if used immediately after Fusion Bolt. If the target is Frozen, it will be thawed. This move can be used even if the user is Frozen. If the user is Frozen, this also thaws the user.
Future Sight	Psychic	Special	120	100	10	Normal	—	190	Attacks the target after 2 turns. This move is affected by the target's type.
Gastro Acid	Poison	Status	—	100	10	Normal	—	Raises the user's Speed.	Disables the target's Ability. Fails with certain Abilities, however.
Gear Grind	Steel	Physical	50	85	15	Normal	○	180	Attacks twice in a row in a single turn.
Gear Up	Steel	Status	—	—	20	Your Party	—	Raises the user's Sp. Atk.	Raises the Attack and Sp. Atk of allies with either the Plus or Minus Abilities.
Geomancy	Fairy	Status	—	—	10	Self	—	Raises all of the user's stats.	Builds power on the first turn and increases the user's Sp. Atk, Sp. Def, and Speed by 2 on the second.
Giga Drain	Grass	Special	75	100	10	Normal	—	140	Restores HP by up to half of the damage dealt to the target.
Giga Impact	Normal	Physical	150	90	5	Normal	○	200	The user can't move during the next turn.
Glaciate	Ice	Special	65	95	10	Many Others	—	120	Lowers the targets' Speed by 1. Its power is reduced by 25% when it hits multiple Pokémon in a Double Battle. Its power is reduced by 50% when it hits multiple Pokémon in a Battle Royal.
Glare	Normal	Status	—	100	30	Normal	—	Raises the user's Sp. Def.	Inflicts the Paralysis status condition on the target.
Grass Knot	Grass	Special	—	100	20	Normal	○	160	The heavier the target is compared to the user, the greater the move's power becomes (max 120).
Grass Pledge	Grass	Special	80	100	10	Normal	—	160	When combined with Water Pledge or Fire Pledge, the power and effect change. If combined with Water Pledge, the power is 150 and it remains a Grass-type move. This lowers the Speed of opposing Pokémon for 4 turns. If combined with Fire Pledge, the power is 150 and it becomes a Fire-type move. This damages all non-Fire types for 4 turns. If the target is Frozen, it will be thawed.
Grass Whistle	Grass	Status	—	55	15	Normal	—	Raises the user's Speed.	Inflicts the Asleep status condition on the target. Strikes the target even if it is using Substitute.
Grassy Terrain	Grass	Status	—	—	10	Both Sides	—	Raises the user's Defense.	Covers the field with grass for 5 turns. During that time, Pokémon on the ground will be able to do 50% more damage with Grass-type moves and will recover 1/16 of the Pokémon's maximum HP each turn. Damage done to Pokémon on the ground by Earthquake, Bulldoze, or Magnitude is halved.
Gravity	Psychic	Status	—	—	5	Both Sides	—	Raises the user's Sp. Atk.	Raises the accuracy of all Pokémon in battle for 5 turns. Ground-type moves will now hit a Pokémon with the Levitate Ability or a Flying-type Pokémon. Prevents the use of Bounce, Fly, High Jump Kick, Jump Kick, Magnet Rise, Sky Drop, Splash, and Telekinesis. Pulls any airborne Pokémon to the ground.
Growl	Normal	Status	—	100	40	Many Others	—	Raises the user's Defense.	Lowers the targets' Attack by 1. Strikes the targets even if they are using Substitute.
Growth	Normal	Status	—	—	20	Self	—	Raises the user's Sp. Atk.	Raises the user's Attack and Sp. Atk by 1. Raises them by 2 when the weather condition is sunny or extremely harsh sunlight.
Grudge	Ghost	Status	—	—	5	Self	—	Follow Me	Any move that causes the user to faint will have its PP dropped to 0.
Guard Split	Psychic	Status	—	—	10	Normal	—	Raises the user's Speed.	The user and the target's Defense and Sp. Def are added, then divided equally between them.
Guard Swap	Psychic	Status	—	—	10	Normal	—	Raises the user's Speed.	Swaps Defense and Sp. Def changes between the user and the target.
Guillotine	Normal	Physical	—	30	5	Normal	○	180	The target faints with one hit if the user's level is equal to or greater than the target's level. The higher the user's level is compared to the target's, the more accurate the move is.
Gunk Shot	Poison	Physical	120	80	5	Normal	—	190	A 30% chance of inflicting the Poisoned status condition on the target.
Gust	Flying	Special	40	100	35	Normal	—	100	It even hits Pokémon that are in the sky due to using moves such as Fly and Bounce, dealing them twice the usual damage.
Gyro Ball	Steel	Physical	—	100	5	Normal	○	160	The slower the user is than the target, the greater the move's power becomes (max 150).
Hail	Ice	Status	—	—	10	Both Sides	—	Raises the user's Speed.	Changes the weather condition to hail for 5 turns, dealing damage every turn equal to 1/16 of its max HP to each Pokémon in the field that is not an Ice type.
Hammer Arm	Fighting	Physical	100	90	10	Normal	○	180	Lowers the user's Speed by 1.
Happy Hour	Normal	Status	—	—	30	Your Side	—	Raises all of the user's stats.	Doubles the amount of prize money received after battle.
Harden	Normal	Status	—	—	30	Self	—	Raises the user's Defense.	Raises the user's Defense by 1.
Haze	Ice	Status	—	—	30	Both Sides	—	Restores the user's HP.	Eliminates every stat change of the targets.
Head Charge	Normal	Physical	120	100	15	Normal	○	190	The user takes 1/4 of the damage inflicted.
Head Smash	Rock	Physical	150	80	5	Normal	○	200	The user takes 1/2 of the damage inflicted.
Headbutt	Normal	Physical	70	100	15	Normal	○	140	A 30% chance of making the target flinch (unable to use moves on that turn).
Heal Bell	Normal	Status	—	—	5	Your Party	—	Restores the user's HP.	Heals status conditions of all your Pokémon, including those in your party. Affects the target even if it is using Substitute.
Heal Block	Psychic	Status	—	100	15	Many Others	—	Raises the user's Sp. Atk by 2.	Targets cannot have HP restored by moves, Abilities, or held items for 5 turns.

Move	Type	Kind	Pow.	Acc.	PP	Range	DA	Z-Move Pow./ Effects	Battle Effects
Heal Order	Bug	Status	—	—	10	Self	—	Resets negative stat changes.	Restores HP by up to half of the user's maximum HP.
Heal Pulse	Psychic	Status	—	—	10	Normal	—	Resets negative stat changes.	Restores the target's HP by up to half of its maximum HP.
Healing Wish	Psychic	Status	—	—	10	Self	—	None	The user faints, but fully heals the next Pokémon's HP and status conditions.
Heart Stamp	Psychic	Physical	60	100	25	Normal	○	120	A 30% chance of making the target flinch (unable to use moves on that turn).
Heart Swap	Psychic	Status	—	—	10	Normal	—	Critical hits land more easily.	Swaps all stat changes between the user and the target.
Heat Crash	Fire	Physical	—	100	10	Normal	○	160	The heavier the user is compared to the target, the greater the move's power becomes (max 120). If the target is Frozen, it will be thawed. If the target has used Minimize, this move will be a sure hit and its power will be doubled.
Heat Wave	Fire	Special	95	90	10	Many Others	—	175	A 10% chance of inflicting the Burned status condition on the targets. If the targets are Frozen, they will be thawed. Its power is reduced by 25% when it hits multiple Pokémon in a Double Battle. Its power is reduced by 50% when it hits multiple Pokémon in a Battle Royal.
Heavy Slam	Steel	Physical	—	100	10	Normal	○	160	The heavier the user is compared to the target, the greater the move's power becomes (max 120).
Helping Hand	Normal	Status	—	—	20	1 Ally	—	Resets negative stat changes.	Always strikes first. Strengthens the attack power of one ally's moves by 50%.
Hex	Ghost	Special	65	100	10	Normal	—	160	Deals twice the usual damage to a target affected by status conditions.
Hidden Power	Normal	Special	60	100	15	Normal	—	120	Type changes depending on the user.
High Horsepower	Ground	Physical	95	95	10	Normal	○	175	A regular attack.
High Jump Kick	Fighting	Physical	130	90	10	Normal	○	195	If this move misses, the user loses half of its maximum HP.
Hold Back	Normal	Physical	40	100	40	Normal	○	100	Always leaves 1 HP, even if the damage would have made the target faint.
Hold Hands	Normal	Status	—	—	40	1 Ally	—	Raises all of the user's stats.	No effect.
Hone Claws	Dark	Status	—	—	15	Self	—	Raises the user's Attack.	Raises Attack and accuracy by 1.
Horn Attack	Normal	Physical	65	100	25	Normal	○	120	A regular attack.
Horn Drill	Normal	Physical	—	30	5	Normal	○	180	The target faints with one hit if the user's level is equal to or greater than the target's level. The higher the user's level is compared to the target's, the more accurate the move is.
Horn Leech	Grass	Physical	75	100	10	Normal	○	140	Restores HP by up to half of the damage dealt to the target.
Howl	Normal	Status	—	—	40	Self	—	Raises the user's Attack.	Raises the user's Attack by 1.
Hurricane	Flying	Special	110	70	10	Normal	—	185	A 30% chance of making the target confused. Is 100% accurate in the rain / heavy rain weather conditions and 50% accurate in the sunny / extremely harsh sunlight weather conditions. It can hit Pokémon that are in the sky due to using moves such as Fly and Bounce.
Hydro Cannon	Water	Special	150	90	5	Normal	—	200	The user can't move during the next turn.
Hydro Pump	Water	Special	110	80	5	Normal	—	185	A regular attack.
Hyper Beam	Normal	Special	150	90	5	Normal	—	200	The user can't move during the next turn.
Hyper Fang	Normal	Physical	80	90	15	Normal	○	160	A 10% chance of making the target flinch (unable to use moves on that turn).
Hyper Voice	Normal	Special	90	100	10	Many Others	—	175	Strikes the targets even if they are using Substitute. Its power is reduced by 25% when it hits multiple Pokémon in a Double Battle. Its power is reduced by 50% when it hits multiple Pokémon in a Battle Royal.
Hyperspace Fury	Dark	Physical	100	—	5	Normal	—	180	A sure hit. Strikes the target even if it is using Baneful Bunker, Detect, King's Shield, Mat Block, Protect, or Spiky Shield. Fails when used by Hoopa Confined. Can only be used by Hoopa Unbound.
Hyperspace Hole	Psychic	Special	80	—	5	Normal	—	160	A sure hit. Strikes the target even if it is using Baneful Bunker, Detect, King's Shield, Mat Block, Protect, or Spiky Shield.
Hypnosis	Psychic	Status	—	60	20	Normal	—	Raises the user's Speed.	Inflicts the Asleep status condition on the target.
Ice Ball	Ice	Physical	30	90	20	Normal	○	100	Attacks consecutively over 5 turns or until it misses. Cannot choose other moves during this time. Damage dealt doubles with each successful hit (max 480). Its power is doubled if used after Defense Curl.
Ice Beam	Ice	Special	90	100	10	Normal	—	175	A 10% chance of inflicting the Frozen status condition on the target.
Ice Burn	Ice	Special	140	90	5	Normal	—	200	Builds power on the first turn and attacks on the second. A 30% chance of inflicting the Burned status condition on the targets.
Ice Fang	Ice	Physical	65	95	15	Normal	○	120	A 10% chance of inflicting the Frozen status condition or making the target flinch (unable to use moves on that turn).
Ice Hammer	Ice	Physical	100	90	10	Normal	○	180	Lowers the user's Speed by 1.
Ice Punch	Ice	Physical	75	100	15	Normal	○	140	A 10% chance of inflicting the Frozen status condition on the target.
Ice Shard	Ice	Physical	40	100	30	Normal	—	100	Always strikes first. The user with the higher Speed goes first if similar moves are used.
Icicle Crash	Ice	Physical	85	90	10	Normal	—	160	A 30% chance of making the target flinch (unable to use moves on that turn).
Icicle Spear	Ice	Physical	25	100	30	Normal	—	140	Attacks 2–5 times in a row in a single turn.
Icy Wind	Ice	Special	55	95	15	Many Others	—	100	Lowers the targets' Speed by 1. Its power is reduced by 25% when it hits multiple Pokémon in a Double Battle. Its power is reduced by 50% when it hits multiple Pokémon in a Battle Royal.
Imprison	Psychic	Status	—	—	10	Self	—	Raises the user's Sp. Def by 2.	Opposing Pokémon cannot use a move if the user knows that move as well.
Incinerate	Fire	Special	60	100	15	Many Others	—	120	Burns up the Berry or Gem being held by the targets, which makes them unusable. If the targets are Frozen, they will be thawed. Its power is reduced by 25% when it hits multiple Pokémon in a Double Battle. Its power is reduced by 50% when it hits multiple Pokémon in a Battle Royal.
Inferno	Fire	Special	100	50	5	Normal	—	180	Inflicts the Burned status condition on the target. If the target is Frozen, it will be thawed.

Move	Type	Kind	Pow.	Acc.	PP	Range	DA	Z-Move Pow./ Effects	Battle Effects
Infestation	Bug	Special	20	100	20	Normal	◯	100	Inflicts damage equal to 1/8 the target's max HP for 4–5 turns. The target cannot flee during that time.
Ingrain	Grass	Status	—	—	20	Self	—	Raises the user's Sp. Def.	Restores 1/16 of max HP every turn. The user cannot be switched out after using this move. Ground-type moves will now hit the user even if it is a Flying-type Pokémon or has the Levitate Ability.
Instruct	Psychic	Status	—	—	15	Normal	—	Raises the user's Sp. Atk.	The target is forced to use the same move it just used.
Ion Deluge	Electric	Status	—	—	25	Both Sides	—	Raises the user's Sp. Atk.	Attacks first. Changes any Normal-type moves used in the same turn into Electric-type moves.
Iron Defense	Steel	Status	—	—	15	Self	—	Resets negative stat changes.	Raises the user's Defense by 2.
Iron Head	Steel	Physical	80	100	15	Normal	◯	160	A 30% chance of making the target flinch (unable to use moves on that turn).
Iron Tail	Steel	Physical	100	75	15	Normal	◯	180	A 30% chance of lowering the target's Defense by 1.
Judgment	Normal	Special	100	100	10	Normal	—	180	A regular attack. This move's type changes according to the plate that Arceus is holding.
Jump Kick	Fighting	Physical	100	95	10	Normal	◯	180	If this move misses, the user loses half of its maximum HP.
Karate Chop	Fighting	Physical	50	100	25	Normal	◯	100	Critical hits land more easily.
Kinesis	Psychic	Status	—	80	15	Normal	—	Raises the user's evasion.	Lowers the target's accuracy by 1.
King's Shield	Steel	Status	—	—	10	Self	—	Resets negative stat changes.	The user evades all attacks that turn. If an opposing Pokémon uses a move that makes direct contact, its Attack will be lowered by 2. Fails more easily when used repeatedly.
Knock Off	Dark	Physical	65	100	20	Normal	◯	120	The target drops its held item. It gets the item back after the battle. This move does 50% more damage to opponents holding items.
Land's Wrath	Ground	Physical	90	100	10	Many Others	—	185	Its power is reduced by 25% when it hits multiple Pokémon in a Double Battle. Its power is reduced by 50% when it hits multiple Pokémon in a Battle Royal.
Laser Focus	Normal	Status	—	—	30	Self	—	Raises the user's Attack.	The user's next move will always be a critical hit.
Last Resort	Normal	Physical	140	100	5	Normal	◯	200	Fails unless the user has used each of its other moves at least once.
Lava Plume	Fire	Special	80	100	15	Adjacent	—	160	A 30% chance of inflicting the Burned status condition on the target. If the targets are Frozen, they will be thawed. Its power is reduced by 25% when it hits multiple Pokémon in a Double Battle. Its power is reduced by 50% when it hits multiple Pokémon in a Battle Royal.
Leaf Blade	Grass	Physical	90	100	15	Normal	◯	175	Critical hits land more easily.
Leaf Storm	Grass	Special	130	90	5	Normal	—	195	Lowers the user's Sp. Atk by 2.
Leaf Tornado	Grass	Special	65	90	10	Normal	—	120	A 50% chance of lowering the target's accuracy by 1.
Leafage	Grass	Physical	40	100	40	Normal	—	100	A regular attack.
Leech Life	Bug	Physical	80	100	10	Normal	◯	160	Restores HP by up to half of the damage dealt to the target.
Leech Seed	Grass	Status	—	90	10	Normal	—	Resets negative stat changes.	Steals 1/8 of the target's max HP every turn and absorbs it to restore the user. Keeps working even after the user switches out. Does not work on Grass types.
Leer	Normal	Status	—	100	30	Many Others	—	Raises the user's Attack.	Lowers the targets' Defense by 1.
Lick	Ghost	Physical	30	100	30	Normal	◯	100	A 30% chance of inflicting the Paralysis status condition on the target.
Light Screen	Psychic	Status	—	—	30	Your Side	—	Raises the user's Sp. Def.	Halves the damage to the Pokémon on your side from special moves. Effect lasts 5 turns even if the user is switched out. Effect is weaker in Double Battles and Battle Royal.
Liquidation	Water	Physical	85	100	10	Normal	◯	160	A 20% chance of lowering the target's Defense by 1.
Lock-On	Normal	Status	—	—	5	Normal	—	Raises the user's Speed.	The user's next move will be a sure hit.
Lovely Kiss	Normal	Status	—	75	10	Normal	—	Raises the user's Speed.	Inflicts the Asleep status condition on the target.
Low Kick	Fighting	Physical	—	100	20	Normal	◯	160	The heavier the target is compared to the user, the greater the move's power becomes (max 120).
Low Sweep	Fighting	Physical	65	100	20	Normal	◯	120	Lowers the target's Speed by 1.
Lucky Chant	Normal	Status	—	—	30	Your Side	—	Raises the user's evasion.	The Pokémon on your side take no critical hits for 5 turns.
Lunar Dance	Psychic	Status	—	—	10	Self	—	None	The user faints, but fully heals the next Pokémon's HP, PP, and status conditions.
Lunge	Bug	Physical	80	100	15	Normal	◯	160	A 100% chance of lowering the target's Attack by 1.
Luster Purge	Psychic	Special	70	100	5	Normal	—	140	Has a 50% chance of lowering the target's Sp. Def by 1.
Mach Punch	Fighting	Physical	40	100	30	Normal	◯	100	Always strikes first. The user with the higher Speed goes first if similar moves are used.
Magic Coat	Psychic	Status	—	—	15	Self	—	Raises the user's Sp. Def by 2.	Always strikes first. Reflects moves with effects like Leech Seed or those that inflict status conditions such as Asleep, Poisoned, Paralysis, or Confused.
Magic Room	Psychic	Status	—	—	10	Both Sides	—	Raises the user's Sp. Def.	Always strikes last. No held items will have any effect for 5 turns. Fling cannot be used to throw items while Magic Room is in effect. The effect ends if the move is used again.
Magical Leaf	Grass	Special	60	—	20	Normal	—	120	A sure hit.
Magma Storm	Fire	Special	100	75	5	Normal	—	180	Inflicts damage over 4–5 turns. The target cannot flee during that time. If the targets are Frozen, they will be thawed.
Magnet Bomb	Steel	Physical	60	—	20	Normal	—	120	A sure hit.
Magnet Rise	Electric	Status	—	—	10	Self	—	Raises the user's evasion.	Nullifies Ground-type moves for 5 turns.
Magnetic Flux	Electric	Status	—	—	20	Your Party	—	Raises the user's Sp. Def.	Raises the Defense and Sp. Def of allies with either the Plus or Minus Abilities.
Magnitude	Ground	Physical	—	100	30	Adjacent	—	140	This move's power varies among 10, 30, 50, 70, 90, 110, and 150. Does twice the damage if targets are underground due to using Dig. Its power is reduced by 25% when it hits multiple Pokémon in a Double Battle. Its power is reduced by 50% when it hits multiple Pokémon in a Battle Royal.

Move	Type	Kind	Pow.	Acc.	PP	Range	DA	Z-Move Pow./ Effects	Battle Effects
Mat Block	Fighting	Status	—	—	10	Your Side	—	Raises the user's Defense.	Protects the user and allies from damage-dealing moves used in the same turn. Only works on the first turn after the user is sent out. Does not protect against status moves.
Me First	Normal	Status	—	—	20	Varies	—	Raises the user's Speed by 2.	Copies the target's chosen move and uses it with 50% greater power. Fails if it does not strike first.
Mean Look	Normal	Status	—	—	5	Normal	—	Raises the user's Sp. Def.	The target cannot escape. If used during a Trainer battle, the opposing Trainer cannot switch Pokémon. Has no effect on Ghost-type Pokémon.
Meditate	Psychic	Status	—	—	40	Self	—	Raises the user's Attack.	Raises the user's Attack by 1.
Mega Drain	Grass	Special	40	100	15	Normal	—	120	Restores HP by up to half of the damage dealt to the target.
Mega Kick	Normal	Physical	120	75	5	Normal	○	190	A regular attack.
Mega Punch	Normal	Physical	80	85	20	Normal	○	160	A regular attack.
Megahorn	Bug	Physical	120	85	10	Normal	○	190	A regular attack.
Memento	Dark	Status	—	100	10	Normal	—	Restores the HP of the next ally that enters the field.	The user faints, but the target's Attack and Sp. Atk are lowered by 2.
Metal Burst	Steel	Physical	—	100	10	Varies	—	100	Targets the Pokémon that most recently damaged the user with a move. Inflicts 1.5 times the damage taken.
Metal Claw	Steel	Physical	50	95	35	Normal	○	100	A 10% chance of raising the user's Attack by 1.
Metal Sound	Steel	Status	—	85	40	Normal	—	Raises the user's Sp. Atk.	Lowers the target's Sp. Def by 2. Strikes the target even if it is using Substitute.
Meteor Mash	Steel	Physical	90	90	10	Normal	○	175	Has a 20% chance of raising the user's Attack by 1.
Metronome	Normal	Status	—	—	10	Self	—	None	Uses one move randomly chosen from all possible moves.
Milk Drink	Normal	Status	—	—	10	Self	—	Resets negative stat changes.	Restores HP by up to half of the user's maximum HP.
Mimic	Normal	Status	—	—	10	Normal	—	Increases the user's accuracy.	Copies the target's last-used move (copied move has a PP of 5). Fails if used before the opposing Pokémon uses a move.
Mind Reader	Normal	Status	—	—	5	Normal	—	Raises the user's Sp. Atk.	The user's next move will be a sure hit.
Minimize	Normal	Status	—	—	10	Self	—	Resets negative stat changes.	Raises the user's evasion by 2.
Miracle Eye	Psychic	Status	—	—	40	Normal	—	Raises the user's Sp. Atk.	Attacks land easily regardless of the target's evasion. Makes Dark-type Pokémon vulnerable to Psychic-type moves.
Mirror Coat	Psychic	Special	—	100	20	Varies	—	100	If the user is attacked with a special move, this move inflicts twice the damage done to the user. Always strikes last.
Mirror Move	Flying	Status	—	—	20	Normal	—	Raises the user's Attack by 2.	Uses the last move that the target used.
Mirror Shot	Steel	Special	65	85	10	Normal	—	120	A 30% chance of lowering the target's accuracy by 1.
Mist	Ice	Status	—	—	30	Your Side	—	Restores the user's HP.	Protects against stat-lowering moves and additional effects for 5 turns.
Mist Ball	Psychic	Special	70	100	5	Normal	—	140	Has a 50% chance of reducing the target's Sp. Atk by 1.
Misty Terrain	Fairy	Status	—	—	10	Both Sides	—	Raises the user's Sp. Def.	Covers the field with mist for 5 turns. During that time, Pokémon on the ground take half damage from Dragon-type moves and cannot be afflicted with new status conditions or confusion.
Moonblast	Fairy	Special	95	100	15	Normal	—	175	A 30% chance of lowering the target's Sp. Atk by 1.
Moongeist Beam	Ghost	Special	100	100	5	Normal	—	180	Ignores the effects of the target's Ability.
Moonlight	Fairy	Status	—	—	5	Self	—	Resets negative stat changes.	Recovers 1/2 of the user's maximum HP in normal weather conditions. Recovers 2/3 of the user's maximum HP in sunny or extremely harsh sunlight weather conditions. Recovers 1/4 of the user's maximum HP in rain/heavy rain/sandstorm/hail weather conditions.
Morning Sun	Normal	Status	—	—	5	Self	—	Resets negative stat changes.	Recovers 1/2 of the user's maximum HP in normal weather conditions. Recovers 2/3 of the user's maximum HP in sunny or extremely harsh sunlight weather conditions. Recovers 1/4 of the user's maximum HP in rain/heavy rain/sandstorm/hail weather conditions.
Mud Bomb	Ground	Special	65	85	10	Normal	—	120	A 30% chance of lowering the target's accuracy by 1.
Mud Shot	Ground	Special	55	95	15	Normal	—	100	Lowers the target's Speed by 1.
Mud Sport	Ground	Status	—	—	15	Both Sides	—	Raises the user's Sp. Def.	Lowers the power of Electric-type moves to 1/3 of normal for 5 turns.
Mud-Slap	Ground	Special	20	100	10	Normal	—	100	Lowers the target's accuracy by 1.
Muddy Water	Water	Special	90	85	10	Many Others	—	175	A 30% chance of lowering the targets' accuracy by 1. Its power is reduced by 25% when it hits multiple Pokémon in a Double Battle. Its power is reduced by 50% when it hits multiple Pokémon in a Battle Royal.
Multi-Attack	Normal	Physical	90	100	10	Normal	○	185	A regular attack. This move's type changes according to the memory disc that Silvally is holding.
Mystical Fire	Fire	Special	75	100	10	Normal	—	140	Lowers the target's Sp. Atk by 1.
Nasty Plot	Dark	Status	—	—	20	Self	—	Resets negative stat changes.	Raises the user's Sp. Atk by 2.
Natural Gift	Normal	Physical	—	100	15	Normal	—	160	This move's type and power change according to the Berry held by the user. The Berry is consumed when this move is used. This move fails if the user is not holding a Berry.
Nature Power	Normal	Status	—	—	20	Normal	—		This move varies depending on the environment: Cave: Power Gem. Dirt/Sand: Earth Power. Grass / Grassy Terrain: Energy Ball. Electric Terrain: Thunderbolt. Ice: Ice Beam. Indoors / Link Battle: Tri Attack. Misty Terrain: Moonblast. Psychic Terrain / Ultra Space: Psychic. Snow: Frost Breath. Volcano: Lava Plume. Water Surface / Puddles / Shoals: Hydro Pump.
Nature's Madness	Fairy	Special	—	90	10	Normal	—	100	Halves the target's HP.
Needle Arm	Grass	Physical	60	100	15	Normal	○	120	A 30% chance of making the target flinch (unable to use moves on that turn).
Night Daze	Dark	Special	85	95	10	Normal	—	160	A 40% chance of lowering the target's accuracy by 1.

Move	Type	Kind	Pow.	Acc.	PP	Range	DA	Z-Move Pow./ Effects	Battle Effects
Night Shade	Ghost	Special	—	100	15	Normal	—	100	Deals a fixed amount of damage equal to the user's level.
Night Slash	Dark	Physical	70	100	15	Normal	○	140	Critical hits land more easily.
Nightmare	Ghost	Status	—	100	15	Normal	—	Raises the user's Sp. Atk.	Lowers the target's HP by 1/4 of maximum after each turn. Fails if the target is not Asleep.
Noble Roar	Normal	Status	—	100	30	Normal	—	Raises the user's Defense.	Lowers the target's Attack and Sp. Atk by 1. Strikes the target even if it is using Substitute.
Nuzzle	Electric	Physical	20	100	20	Normal	○	100	Inflicts the Paralysis status condition on the target.
Oblivion Wing	Flying	Special	80	100	10	Normal	—	160	Restores HP by up to 3/4 of the damage dealt to the target.
Octazooka	Water	Special	65	85	10	Normal	—	120	A 50% chance of lowering the target's accuracy by 1.
Odor Sleuth	Normal	Status	—	—	40	Normal	—	Raises the user's Attack.	Attacks land easily regardless of the target's evasion. Makes Ghost-type Pokémon vulnerable to Normal- and Fighting-type moves.
Ominous Wind	Ghost	Special	60	100	5	Normal	—	120	A 10% chance of raising the user's Attack, Defense, Speed, Sp. Atk, and Sp. Def stats by 1.
Origin Pulse	Water	Special	110	85	10	Many Others	—	185	Its power is reduced by 25% when it hits multiple Pokémon in a Double Battle. Its power is reduced by 50% when it hits multiple Pokémon in a Battle Royal.
Outrage	Dragon	Physical	120	100	10	1 Random	○	190	Attacks consecutively over 2–3 turns. Cannot choose other moves during this time. The user becomes Confused after using this move.
Overheat	Fire	Special	130	90	5	Normal	—	195	Lowers the user's Sp. Atk by 2. If the target is Frozen, it will be thawed.
Pain Split	Normal	Status	—	—	20	Normal	—	Raises the user's Defense.	The user and target's HP are added, then divided equally between them.
Parabolic Charge	Electric	Special	65	100	20	Adjacent	—	120	Restores HP by up to half of the damage dealt to the target. Its power is reduced by 25% when it hits multiple Pokémon in a Double Battle. Its power is reduced by 50% when it hits multiple Pokémon in a Battle Royal.
Parting Shot	Dark	Status	—	100	20	Normal	—	Restores the HP of the next ally that enters the field.	Lowers the target's Attack and Sp. Atk. After attacking, user switches out with another Pokémon in the party. Strikes the target even if it is using Substitute.
Pay Day	Normal	Physical	40	100	20	Normal	—	100	Increases the amount of prize money received after battle (the user's level, multiplied by the number of attacks, multiplied by 5).
Payback	Dark	Physical	50	100	10	Normal	○	100	This move's power is doubled if the user strikes after the target.
Peck	Flying	Physical	35	100	35	Normal	○	100	A regular attack.
Perish Song	Normal	Status	—	—	5	Adjacent	—	Resets negative stat changes.	All adjacent Pokémon in battle will faint after 3 turns, unless switched out. Strikes the target even if it is using Substitute.
Petal Blizzard	Grass	Physical	90	100	15	Adjacent	—	175	Its power is reduced by 25% when it hits multiple Pokémon in a Double Battle. Its power is reduced by 50% when it hits multiple Pokémon in a Battle Royal.
Petal Dance	Grass	Special	120	100	10	1 Random	○	190	Attacks consecutively over 2–3 turns. Cannot choose other moves during this time. The user becomes Confused after using this move.
Phantom Force	Ghost	Physical	90	100	10	Normal	○	175	User disappears on the first turn and attacks on the second. Strikes the target even if it is using Baneful Bunker, Detect, King's Shield, Mat Block, Protect, Spiky Shield, or Substitute. If the target has used Minimize, it will be a sure hit and its power will be doubled.
Pin Missile	Bug	Physical	25	95	20	Normal	—	140	Attacks 2–5 times in a row in a single turn.
Play Nice	Normal	Status	—	—	20	Normal	—	Raises the user's Defense.	A sure hit. Lowers the target's Attack by 1. Strikes the target even if it is using Baneful Bunker, Detect, King's Shield, Mat Block, Protect, Spiky Shield, or Substitute.
Play Rough	Fairy	Physical	90	90	10	Normal	○	175	A 10% chance of lowering the target's Attack by 1.
Pluck	Flying	Physical	60	100	20	Normal	○	120	If the target is holding a Berry, the user eats that Berry and uses its battle effect if it has one.
Poison Fang	Poison	Physical	50	100	15	Normal	○	100	A 50% chance of inflicting the Badly Poisoned status condition on the target. Damage from being Badly Poisoned increases with every turn.
Poison Gas	Poison	Status	—	90	40	Many Others	—	Raises the user's Defense.	Inflicts the Poisoned status condition on the targets.
Poison Jab	Poison	Physical	80	100	20	Normal	○	160	A 30% chance of inflicting the Poisoned status condition on the target.
Poison Powder	Poison	Status	—	75	35	Normal	—	Raises the user's Defense.	Inflicts the Poisoned status condition on the targets. Has no effect on Grass-type Pokémon.
Poison Sting	Poison	Physical	15	100	35	Normal	—	100	A 30% chance of inflicting the Poisoned status condition on the target.
Poison Tail	Poison	Physical	50	100	25	Normal	○	100	A 10% chance of inflicting the Poisoned status condition on the target. Critical hits land more easily.
Pollen Puff	Bug	Special	90	100	15	Normal	—	175	When targeting an ally, it restores HP by up to half of the target's maximum HP.
Pound	Normal	Physical	40	100	35	Normal	○	100	A regular attack.
Powder	Bug	Status	—	100	20	Normal	—	Raises the user's Sp. Def by 2.	Always attacks first. Has no effect on Grass-type Pokémon. Deals damage equal to 1/4 of max HP if the target uses a Fire-type move in the same turn.
Powder Snow	Ice	Special	40	100	25	Many Others	—	100	A 10% chance of inflicting the Frozen status condition on the targets. Its power is reduced by 25% when it hits multiple Pokémon in a Double Battle. Its power is reduced by 50% when it hits multiple Pokémon in a Battle Royal.
Power Gem	Rock	Special	80	100	20	Normal	—	160	A regular attack.
Power Split	Psychic	Status	—	—	10	Normal	—	Raises the user's Speed.	The user and the target's Attack and Sp. Atk are added, then divided equally between them.
Power Swap	Psychic	Status	—	—	10	Normal	—	Raises the user's Speed.	Swaps Attack and Sp. Atk changes between the user and the target.
Power Trick	Psychic	Status	—	—	10	Self	—	Raises the user's Attack.	Swaps original Attack and Defense stats (does not swap stat changes).
Power Trip	Dark	Physical	20	100	10	Normal	○	160	With each level that the user's stats increase, the move's power increases by 20 (max 860).
Power Whip	Grass	Physical	120	85	10	Normal	○	190	A regular attack.
Power-Up Punch	Fighting	Physical	40	100	20	Normal	○	100	Raises the user's Attack by 1.
Precipice Blades	Ground	Physical	120	85	10	Many Others	—	190	Its power is reduced by 25% when it hits multiple Pokémon in a Double Battle. Its power is reduced by 50% when it hits multiple Pokémon in a Battle Royal.

Move	Type	Kind	Pow.	Acc.	PP	Range	DA	Z-Move Pow./ Effects	Battle Effects
Present	Normal	Physical	—	90	15	Normal	—	100	This move's power varies among 40 (40% chance), 80 (30% chance), and 120 (10% chance). It also has a 20% chance of healing the target by 1/4 of its maximum HP.
Prismatic Laser	Psychic	Special	160	100	10	Normal	—	200	The user can't move during the next turn.
Protect	Normal	Status	—	—	10	Self	—	Resets negative stat changes.	The user evades all moves that turn. If used in succession, its chance of failing rises.
Psybeam	Psychic	Special	65	100	20	Normal	—	120	A 10% chance of making the target confused.
Psych Up	Normal	Status	—	—	10	Normal	—	Restores the user's HP.	Copies the target's stat changes to the user.
Psychic	Psychic	Special	90	100	10	Normal	—	175	A 10% chance of lowering the target's Sp. Def by 1.
Psychic Fangs	Psychic	Physical	85	100	10	Normal	○	160	This move is not affected by Aurora Veil or Reflect. It removes the effect of Aurora Veil, Light Screen, and Reflect.
Psychic Terrain	Psychic	Status	—	—	10	Both Sides	—	Raises the user's Sp. Atk.	Covers the field with psychic energy for 5 turns. During that time, Pokémon on the ground will be able to do 50% more damage with Psychic-type moves and will evade first-strike moves.
Psycho Boost	Psychic	Special	140	90	5	Normal	—	200	Lowers the user's Sp. Atk by 2.
Psycho Cut	Psychic	Physical	70	100	20	Normal	—	140	Critical hits land more easily.
Psycho Shift	Psychic	Status	—	100	10	Normal	—	Raises the user's Sp. Atk by 2.	Shifts the user's Paralysis, Poisoned, Badly Poisoned, Burned, or Asleep status conditions to the target and heals the user.
Psyshock	Psychic	Special	80	100	10	Normal	—	160	Damage depends on the user's Sp. Atk and the target's Defense.
Psystrike	Psychic	Special	100	100	10	Normal	—	180	Damage depends on the user's Sp. Atk and the target's Defense.
Psywave	Psychic	Special	—	100	15	Normal	—	100	Inflicts damage equal to the user's level multiplied by a random value between 0.5 and 1.5.
Punishment	Dark	Physical	—	100	5	Normal	○	160	With each level that the target's stats increase, the move's power becomes greater (max 200).
Purify	Poison	Status	—	—	20	Normal	—	Raises all of the user's stats.	Heals the target's status conditions. After healing the target's status conditions, it restores the user's HP by up to half of the user's maximum HP.
Pursuit	Dark	Physical	40	100	20	Normal	○	100	Does twice the usual damage if the target is switching out.
Quash	Dark	Status	—	100	15	Normal	—	Raises the user's Speed.	The user suppresses the target and makes it move last that turn. Fails if the target has already used its move that turn.
Quick Attack	Normal	Physical	40	100	30	Normal	○	100	Always strikes first. The user with the higher Speed goes first if similar moves are used.
Quick Guard	Fighting	Status	—	—	15	Your Side	—	Raises the user's Defense.	Protects the user and its allies from first-strike moves.
Quiver Dance	Bug	Status	—	—	20	Self	—	Resets negative stat changes.	Raises the user's Sp. Atk, Sp. Def, and Speed by 1.
Rage	Normal	Physical	20	100	20	Normal	○	100	Attack rises by 1 with each hit the user takes.
Rage Powder	Bug	Status	—	—	20	Self	—	Resets negative stat changes.	This move goes first. Opposing Pokémon aim only at the user. Has no effect on Grass-type Pokémon.
Rain Dance	Water	Status	—	—	5	Both Sides	—	Raises the user's Speed.	Changes the weather condition to rain for 5 turns, strengthening Water-type moves by 50% and reducing the power of Fire-type moves by 50%.
Rapid Spin	Normal	Physical	20	100	40	Normal	○	100	Releases the user from moves such as Bind, Leech Seed, Spikes, and Wrap.
Razor Leaf	Grass	Physical	55	95	25	Many Others	—	100	Critical hits land more easily. Its power is reduced by 25% when it hits multiple Pokémon in a Double Battle. Its power is reduced by 50% when it hits multiple Pokémon in a Battle Royal.
Razor Shell	Water	Physical	75	95	10	Normal	○	140	A 50% chance of lowering the target's Defense by 1.
Razor Wind	Normal	Special	80	100	10	Many Others	—	160	The user stores power on the first turn and attacks on the second. Critical hits land more easily. Its power is reduced by 25% when it hits multiple Pokémon in a Double Battle. Its power is reduced by 50% when it hits multiple Pokémon in a Battle Royal.
Recover	Normal	Status	—	—	10	Self	—	Resets negative stat changes.	Restores HP by up to half of the user's maximum HP.
Recycle	Normal	Status	—	—	10	Self	—	Raises the user's Speed by 2.	A held item that has been used can be used again.
Reflect	Psychic	Status	—	—	20	Your Side	—	Raises the user's Defense.	Halves the damage to the Pokémon on your side from physical moves. Effect lasts 5 turns even if the user is switched out. Effect is weaker in Double Battles and Battle Royal.
Reflect Type	Normal	Status	—	—	15	Normal	—	Raises the user's Sp. Atk.	The user becomes the same type as the target.
Refresh	Normal	Status	—	—	20	Self	—	Restores the user's HP.	Heals Poisoned, Badly Poisoned, Paralysis, and Burned conditions.
Relic Song	Normal	Special	75	100	10	Many Others	—	140	10% chance of inflicting the Asleep status condition on the targets. Its power is reduced by 25% when it hits multiple Pokémon in a Double Battle. Its power is reduced by 50% when it hits multiple Pokémon in a Battle Royal. After using the move, Meloetta undergoes a Forme Change. Strikes the targets even if they are using Substitute.
Rest	Psychic	Status	—	—	10	Self	—	Resets negative stat changes.	Fully restores HP, but makes the user Asleep for 2 turns.
Retaliate	Normal	Physical	70	100	5	Normal	○	140	This move's power is doubled if an ally fainted in the previous turn.
Return	Normal	Physical	—	100	20	Normal	○	160	This move's power is affected by friendship. The higher the user's friendship, the greater the move's power (max 102).
Revelation Dance	Normal	Special	90	100	15	Normal	—	175	This move's type becomes the same as the user's first type.
Revenge	Fighting	Physical	60	100	10	Normal	○	120	Attacks last. This move's power is doubled if the user has taken damage from the target that turn.
Reversal	Fighting	Physical	—	100	15	Normal	○	160	The lower the user's HP is, the greater the move's power becomes (max 200).
Roar	Normal	Status	—	—	20	Normal	—	Raises the user's Defense.	Ends wild Pokémon battles. In a battle with a Trainer, this move forces the opposing Trainer to switch Pokémon. When there are no Pokémon to switch in, this move fails. Attacks last. If the opposing Pokémon's level is higher than the user's, this move fails. In a battle with more than one wild Pokémon, this move fails. Strikes the target even if it is using Substitute. Strikes the target even if it is using Baneful Bunker, Detect, King's Shield, Mat Block, Protect, Spiky Shield, or Substitute.
Roar of Time	Dragon	Special	150	90	5	Normal	—	200	The user can't move during the next turn.

Move	Type	Kind	Pow.	Acc.	PP	Range	DA	Z-Move Pow./ Effects	Battle Effects
Rock Blast	Rock	Physical	25	90	10	Normal	—	140	Attacks 2–5 times in a row in a single turn.
Rock Climb	Normal	Physical	90	85	20	Normal	○	175	A 20% chance of making the target confused.
Rock Polish	Rock	Status	—	—	20	Self	—	Resets negative stat changes.	Raises the user's Speed by 2.
Rock Slide	Rock	Physical	75	90	10	Many Others	—	140	A 30% chance of making the targets flinch (unable to use moves on that turn). Its power is reduced by 25% when it hits multiple Pokémon in a Double Battle. Its power is reduced by 50% when it hits multiple Pokémon in a Battle Royal.
Rock Smash	Fighting	Physical	40	100	15	Normal	○	100	A 50% chance of lowering the target's Defense by 1.
Rock Throw	Rock	Physical	50	90	15	Normal	—	100	A regular attack.
Rock Tomb	Rock	Physical	60	95	15	Normal	—	120	Lowers the target's Speed by 1.
Rock Wrecker	Rock	Physical	150	90	5	Normal	—	200	The user can't move during the next turn.
Role Play	Psychic	Status	—	—	10	Normal	—	Raises the user's Speed.	Copies the target's Ability. Fails with certain Abilities, however.
Rolling Kick	Fighting	Physical	60	85	15	Normal	○	120	A 30% chance of making the target flinch (unable to use moves on that turn).
Rollout	Rock	Physical	30	90	20	Normal	○	100	Attacks consecutively over 5 turns or until it misses. Cannot choose other moves during this time. Damage dealt doubles with every successful hit (max 480). Does twice the damage if used after Defense Curl.
Roost	Flying	Status	—	—	10	Self	—	Resets negative stat changes.	Restores HP by up to half of the user's maximum HP, but takes away the Flying type from the user for that turn.
Rototiller	Ground	Status	—	—	10	Adjacent	—	Raises the user's Attack.	Raises the Attack and Sp. Atk of Grass-type Pokémon by 1.
Round	Normal	Special	60	100	15	Normal	—	120	When multiple Pokémon use this move in a turn, the first one to use it is followed immediately by the others. Attack's power is doubled when following another Pokémon using the same move. Strikes the target even if it is using Substitute.
Sacred Fire	Fire	Physical	100	95	5	Normal	—	180	A 50% chance of inflicting the Burned status condition on the target. If the target is Frozen, it will be thawed. This move can be used even if the user is Frozen. If the user is Frozen, this also thaws the user.
Sacred Sword	Fighting	Physical	90	100	15	Normal	○	175	Ignores the stat changes of the opposing Pokémon, except for Speed.
Safeguard	Normal	Status	—	—	25	Your Side	—	Raises the user's Speed.	Protects the Pokémon on your side from status conditions and confusion for 5 turns. Effects last even if the user switches out.
Sand Attack	Ground	Status	—	100	15	Normal	—	Raises the user's evasion.	Lowers the target's accuracy by 1.
Sand Tomb	Ground	Physical	35	85	15	Normal	—	100	Inflicts damage equal to 1/8 the target's max HP for 4–5 turns. The target cannot flee during that time.
Sandstorm	Rock	Status	—	—	10	Both Sides	—	Raises the user's Speed.	Changes the weather condition to sandstorm for 5 turns. Raises the Sp. Def of Rock-type Pokémon by 50% for the length of the sandstorm. All Pokémon other than Rock, Steel, and Ground types take damage each turn equal to 1/16 of their max HP.
Scald	Water	Special	80	100	15	Normal	—	160	A 30% chance of inflicting the Burned status condition on the target. This move can be used even when the user is Frozen. Using this move will thaw the user, relieving the Frozen status condition.
Scary Face	Normal	Status	—	100	10	Normal	—	Raises the user's Speed.	Lowers the targets' Speed by 2.
Scratch	Normal	Physical	40	100	35	Normal	○	100	A regular attack.
Screech	Normal	Status	—	85	40	Normal	—	Raises the user's Attack.	Lowers the target's Defense by 2. Strikes the target even if it is using Substitute.
Searing Shot	Fire	Special	100	100	5	Adjacent	—	180	A 30% chance of inflicting the Burned status condition on the targets. If the targets are Frozen, they will be thawed. Its power is reduced by 25% when it hits multiple Pokémon in a Double Battle. Its power is reduced by 50% when it hits multiple Pokémon in a Battle Royal.
Secret Power	Normal	Physical	70	100	20	Normal	—	140	A 30% chance of one of the following additional effects, depending on the environment: Cave: Target flinches. Dirt/Sand: Lowers accuracy by 1. Grass / Grassy Terrain: Asleep status condition. Indoors / Electric Terrain / Link Battle: Inflicts Paralysis status condition. Misty Terrain: Lowers Sp. Atk by 1. Psychic Terrain / Ultra Space: Lowers Defense by 1. Snow/Ice: Inflicts Frozen status condition. Swamp: Lowers Speed by 1. Volcano: Burned status condition. Water Surface / Puddles / Shoals: Lowers Attack by 1.
Secret Sword	Fighting	Special	85	100	10	Normal	—	160	Damage depends on the user's Sp. Atk and the target's Defense.
Seed Bomb	Grass	Physical	80	100	15	Normal	—	160	A regular attack.
Seed Flare	Grass	Special	120	85	5	Normal	—	190	A 40% chance of lowering the target's Sp. Def by 2.
Seismic Toss	Fighting	Physical	—	100	20	Normal	○	100	Deals a fixed amount of damage equal to the user's level.
Self-Destruct	Normal	Physical	200	100	5	Adjacent	—	200	The user faints after using it. Its power is reduced by 25% when it hits multiple Pokémon in a Double Battle. Its power is reduced by 50% when it hits multiple Pokémon in a Battle Royal.
Shadow Ball	Ghost	Special	80	100	15	Normal	—	160	A 20% chance of lowering the target's Sp. Def by 1.
Shadow Bone	Ghost	Physical	85	100	10	Normal	—	160	A 20% chance of lowering the target's Defense by 1.
Shadow Claw	Ghost	Physical	70	100	15	Normal	○	140	Critical hits land more easily.
Shadow Force	Ghost	Physical	120	100	5	Normal	○	190	Makes the user invisible on the first turn and attacks on the second. Strikes the target even if it is using Baneful Bunker, Detect, King's Shield, Mat Block, Protect, Spiky Shield, or Substitute. If the target has used Minimize, this move will be a sure hit and its power will be doubled.
Shadow Punch	Ghost	Physical	60	—	20	Normal	○	120	A sure hit.
Shadow Sneak	Ghost	Physical	40	100	30	Normal	○	100	Always strikes first. The user with the higher Speed goes first if similar moves are used.
Sharpen	Normal	Status	—	—	30	Self	—	Raises the user's Attack.	Raises the user's Attack by 1.
Sheer Cold	Ice	Special	—	30	5	Normal	—	180	The target faints with one hit if the user's level is equal to or greater than the target's level. The higher the user's level is compared to the target's, the more accurate the move is. Accuracy is lowered when a Pokémon that is not an Ice type uses it. Does not hit Ice-type Pokémon.
Shell Smash	Normal	Status	—	—	15	Self	—	Resets negative stat changes.	Lowers the user's Defense and Sp. Def by 1 and raises the user's Attack, Sp. Atk, and Speed by 2.

Move	Type	Kind	Pow.	Acc.	PP	Range	DA	Z-Move Pow./ Effects	Battle Effects
Shell Trap	Fire	Special	150	100	5	Many Others	—	200	Sets a trap at the start of the turn. When the user is hit by a physical attack during that turn, the trap explodes and deals damage.
Shift Gear	Steel	Status	—	—	10	Self	—	Resets negative stat changes.	Raises the user's Speed by 2 and Attack by 1.
Shock Wave	Electric	Special	60	—	20	Normal	—	120	A sure hit.
Shore Up	Ground	Status	—	—	10	Self	—	Resets negative stat changes.	Restores HP by up to half of the user's maximum HP. Recovers 2/3 of the user's maximum HP in the sandstorm weather condition.
Signal Beam	Bug	Special	75	100	15	Normal	—	140	A 10% chance of making the target confused.
Silver Wind	Bug	Special	60	100	5	Normal	—	120	A 10% chance of raising the user's Attack, Defense, Speed, Sp. Atk, and Sp. Def stats by 1.
Simple Beam	Normal	Status	—	100	15	Normal	—	Raises the user's Sp. Atk.	Changes the target's Ability to Simple. Fails with certain Abilities, however.
Sing	Normal	Status	—	55	15	Normal	—	Raises the user's Speed.	Inflicts the Asleep status condition on the target. Strikes the target even if it is using Substitute.
Sketch	Normal	Status	—	—	1	Normal	—	Raises all of the user's stats.	Copies the last move used by the target. The user then forgets Sketch and learns the new move.
Skill Swap	Psychic	Status	—	—	10	Normal	—	Raises the user's Speed.	Swaps Abilities between the user and target. Fails with certain Abilities, however.
Skull Bash	Normal	Physical	130	100	10	Normal	○	195	Builds power on the first turn and attacks on the second. It raises the user's Defense stat by 1 on the first turn.
Sky Attack	Flying	Physical	140	90	5	Normal	—	200	Builds power on the first turn and attacks on the second. Critical hits land more easily. A 30% chance of making the target flinch (unable to use moves on that turn).
Sky Drop	Flying	Physical	60	100	10	Normal	○	120	The user takes the target into the sky, and then damages it by dropping it during the next turn. Does not damage Flying-type Pokémon. Pokémon weighing over 440.9 lbs. cannot be lifted.
Sky Uppercut	Fighting	Physical	85	90	15	Normal	○	160	It even hits Pokémon that are in the sky due to having used moves such as Fly and Bounce.
Slack Off	Normal	Status	—	—	10	Self	—	Resets negative stat changes.	Restores HP by up to half of the user's maximum HP.
Slam	Normal	Physical	80	75	20	Normal	○	160	A regular attack.
Slash	Normal	Physical	70	100	20	Normal	○	140	Critical hits land more easily.
Sleep Powder	Grass	Status	—	75	15	Normal	—	Raises the user's Speed.	Inflicts the Asleep status condition on the target. Has no effect on Grass-type Pokémon.
Sleep Talk	Normal	Status	—	—	10	Self	—	Critical hits land more easily.	Only works when the user is Asleep. Randomly uses one of the user's moves.
Sludge	Poison	Special	65	100	20	Normal	—	120	A 30% chance of inflicting the Poisoned status condition on the target.
Sludge Bomb	Poison	Special	90	100	10	Normal	—	175	A 30% chance of inflicting the Poisoned status condition on the target.
Sludge Wave	Poison	Special	95	100	10	Adjacent	—	175	A 10% chance of inflicting the Poisoned status condition on the target. Its power is reduced by 25% when it hits multiple Pokémon in a Double Battle. Its power is reduced by 50% when it hits multiple Pokémon in a Battle Royal.
Smack Down	Rock	Physical	50	100	15	Normal	—	100	Ground-type moves will now hit a Pokémon with the Levitate Ability or a Flying-type Pokémon. They will also hit a Pokémon that is in the sky due to using a move such as Fly or Bounce.
Smart Strike	Steel	Physical	70	—	10	Normal	○	140	A sure hit.
Smelling Salts	Normal	Physical	70	100	10	Normal	○	140	Deals twice the usual damage to targets with Paralysis, but heals that status condition.
Smog	Poison	Special	30	70	20	Normal	—	100	A 40% chance of inflicting the Poisoned status condition on the target.
Smokescreen	Normal	Status	—	100	20	Normal	—	Raises the user's evasion.	Lowers the target's accuracy by 1.
Snarl	Dark	Special	55	95	15	Many Others	—	100	Lowers the targets' Sp. Atk by 1. Its power is reduced by 25% when it hits multiple Pokémon in a Double Battle. Its power is reduced by 50% when it hits multiple Pokémon in a Battle Royal. Strikes the targets even if they are using Substitute.
Snatch	Dark	Status	—	—	10	Self	—	Raises the user's Speed by 2.	Steals the effects of recovery or stat-changing moves used by the target on that turn and applies them to the user.
Snore	Normal	Special	50	100	15	Normal	—	100	Only works when the user is Asleep. A 30% chance of making the target flinch (unable to use moves on that turn). Strikes the target even if it is using Substitute.
Soak	Water	Status	—	100	20	Normal	—	Raises the user's Sp. Atk.	Changes the target's type to Water.
Soft-Boiled	Normal	Status	—	—	10	Self	—	Resets negative stat changes.	Restores HP by up to half of the user's maximum HP.
Solar Beam	Grass	Special	120	100	10	Normal	—	190	Builds power on the first turn and attacks on the second. In sunny or extremely harsh sunlight weather conditions, attacks on the first turn. In rain/heavy rain/sandstorm/ hail weather conditions, the power is halved.
Solar Blade	Grass	Physical	125	100	10	Normal	○	190	Builds power on the first turn and attacks on the second. In sunny or extremely harsh sunlight weather conditions, attacks on the first turn. In rain / heavy rain / sandstorm / hail weather conditions, the power is halved.
Sonic Boom	Normal	Special	—	90	20	Normal	—	100	Deals a fixed 20 points of damage.
Spacial Rend	Dragon	Special	100	95	5	Normal	—	180	Critical hits land more easily.
Spark	Electric	Physical	65	100	20	Normal	○	120	A 30% chance of inflicting the Paralysis status condition on the target.
Sparkling Aria	Water	Special	90	100	10	Adjacent	—	175	Heals the Burned status condition from its targets. Its power is reduced by 25% when it hits multiple Pokémon in a Double Battle. Its power is reduced by 50% when it hits multiple Pokémon in a Battle Royal.
Speed Swap	Psychic	Status	—	—	10	Normal	—	Raises the user's Speed.	Switches the user's Speed with the target's Speed.
Spider Web	Bug	Status	—	—	10	Normal	—	Raises the user's Defense.	The target cannot escape. If used during a Trainer battle, the opposing Trainer cannot switch Pokémon. Has no effect on Ghost-type Pokémon.
Spike Cannon	Normal	Physical	20	100	15	Normal	—	100	Attacks 2–5 times in a row in a single turn.
Spikes	Ground	Status	—	—	20	Other Side	—	Raises the user's Defense.	Damages Pokémon as they are sent out to the opposing side. Power rises with each use, up to 3 times (1st time: 1/8 of maximum HP, 2nd time: 1/6 of maximum HP, and 3rd time: 1/4 of maximum HP). Ineffective against Flying-type Pokémon and Pokémon with the Levitate Ability.

Move	Type	Kind	Pow.	Acc.	PP	Range	DA	Z-Move Pow./ Effects	Battle Effects
Spiky Shield	Grass	Status	—	—	10	Self	—	Raises the user's Defense.	The user takes no damage in the same turn this move is used. If an opposing Pokémon uses a move that makes direct contact, the attacker will be damaged for 1/8 of its maximum HP. Fails more easily when used repeatedly.
Spirit Shackle	Ghost	Physical	80	100	10	Normal	—	160	The target cannot escape. If used during a Trainer battle, the opposing Trainer cannot switch Pokémon. When used on a Ghost type, no additional effect takes place.
Spit Up	Normal	Special	—	100	10	Normal	—	100	The more times the user has used Stockpile, the greater the move's power becomes (max 300). Fails if the user has not used Stockpile first. Nullifies Defense and Sp. Def stat increases caused by Stockpile.
Spite	Ghost	Status	—	100	10	Normal	—	Restores the user's HP.	Takes 4 points from the PP of the target's last used move.
Splash	Normal	Status	—	—	40	Self	—	Raises the user's Attack by 3.	No effect.
Spore	Grass	Status	—	100	15	Normal	—	Resets negative stat changes.	Inflicts the Asleep status condition on the target. Has no effect on Grass-type Pokémon.
Spotlight	Normal	Status	—	—	15	Normal	—	Raises the user's Sp. Def.	Designates which Pokémon will be attacked.
Stealth Rock	Rock	Status	—	—	20	Other Side	—	Raises the user's Defense.	Damages Pokémon as they are sent out to the opposing side. Damage is subject to type matchups.
Steam Eruption	Water	Special	110	95	5	Normal	—	185	A 10% chance of inflicting the Burned status condition on the target. If the target is Frozen, it will be thawed.
Steamroller	Bug	Physical	65	100	20	Normal	○	120	A 30% chance of making the targets flinch (unable to use moves on that turn). If the target has used Minimize, this move will be a sure hit and its power will be doubled.
Steel Wing	Steel	Physical	70	90	25	Normal	○	140	A 10% chance of raising the user's Defense by 1.
Sticky Web	Bug	Status	—	—	20	Other Side	—	Raises the user's Speed.	Lowers the Speed of any Pokémon sent out to the opposing side by 1.
Stockpile	Normal	Status	—	—	20	Self	—	Restores the user's HP.	Raises the user's Defense and Sp. Def by 1. Can be used up to 3 times.
Stomp	Normal	Physical	65	100	20	Normal	○	120	A 30% chance of making the targets flinch (unable to use moves on that turn). If the target has used Minimize, this move will be a sure hit and its power will be doubled.
Stomping Tantrum	Ground	Physical	75	100	10	Normal	○	140	If the user's attack missed during the previous turn, this move's power is doubled.
Stone Edge	Rock	Physical	100	80	5	Normal	—	180	Critical hits land more easily.
Stored Power	Psychic	Special	20	100	10	Normal	—	160	With each level that the user's stats increase, the move's power increases by 20 (max 860).
Storm Throw	Fighting	Physical	60	100	10	Normal	○	120	Always delivers a critical hit.
Strength	Normal	Physical	80	100	15	Normal	○	160	A regular attack.
Strength Sap	Grass	Status	—	100	10	Normal	—	Raises the user's Defense.	Lowers the target's Attack by 1. Restores the user's HP by an amount equal to the target's Attack.
String Shot	Bug	Status	—	95	40	Many Others	—	Raises the user's Speed.	Lowers the targets' Speed by 2.
Struggle	Normal	Physical	50	—	1	Normal	○	-	This move becomes available when all other moves are out of PP. The user takes damage equal to 1/4 of its maximum HP. Inflicts damage regardless of type matchup.
Struggle Bug	Bug	Special	50	100	20	Many Others	—	100	Lowers the targets' Sp. Atk by 1. Its power is reduced by 25% when it hits multiple Pokémon in a Double Battle. Its power is reduced by 50% when it hits multiple Pokémon in a Battle Royal.
Stun Spore	Grass	Status	—	75	30	Normal	—	Raises the user's Sp. Def.	Inflicts the Paralysis status condition on the target. Has no effect on Grass-type Pokémon.
Submission	Fighting	Physical	80	80	20	Normal	○	160	The user takes 1/4 of the damage inflicted.
Substitute	Normal	Status	—	—	10	Self	—	Resets negative stat changes.	Uses 1/4 of maximum HP to create a copy of the user.
Sucker Punch	Dark	Physical	70	100	5	Normal	○	140	This move attacks first and deals damage only if the target's chosen move is an attack move.
Sunny Day	Fire	Status	—	—	5	Both Sides	—	Raises the user's Speed.	Changes the weather condition to sunny for 5 turns, strengthening Fire-type moves by 50% and reducing the power of Water-type moves by 50%.
Sunsteel Strike	Steel	Physical	100	100	5	Normal	○	180	Ignores the effects of the target's Ability.
Super Fang	Normal	Physical	—	90	10	Normal	○	100	Halves the target's HP.
Superpower	Fighting	Physical	120	100	5	Normal	○	190	Lowers the user's Attack and Defense by 1.
Supersonic	Normal	Status	—	55	20	Normal	—	Raises the user's Speed.	Makes the target confused. Strikes the target even if it is using Substitute.
Surf	Water	Special	90	100	15	Adjacent	—	175	Does twice the damage if the target is using Dive when attacked. Its power is reduced by 25% when it hits multiple Pokémon in a Double Battle. Its power is reduced by 50% when it hits multiple Pokémon in a Battle Royal.
Swagger	Normal	Status	—	85	15	Normal	—	Resets negative stat changes.	Makes the target confused, but also raises its Attack by 2.
Swallow	Normal	Status	—	—	10	Self	—	Resets negative stat changes.	Restores HP, the amount of which is determined by how many times the user has used Stockpile. Fails if the user has not used Stockpile first. Nullifies Defense and Sp. Def stat increases caused by Stockpile.
Sweet Kiss	Fairy	Status	—	75	10	Normal	—	Raises the user's Sp. Atk.	Makes the target confused
Sweet Scent	Normal	Status	—	100	20	Many Others	—	Increases the user's accuracy.	Lowers the targets' evasion by 2.
Swift	Normal	Special	60	—	20	Many Others	—	120	A sure hit. Its power is reduced by 25% when it hits multiple Pokémon in a Double Battle. Its power is reduced by 50% when it hits multiple Pokémon in a Battle Royal.
Switcheroo	Dark	Status	—	100	10	Normal	—	Raises the user's Speed by 2.	Swaps items between the user and the target.
Swords Dance	Normal	Status	—	—	20	Self	—	Resets negative stat changes.	Raises the user's Attack by 2.

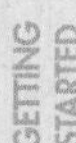

Move	Type	Kind	Pow.	Acc.	PP	Range	DA	Z-Move Pow./ Effects	Battle Effects
Synchronoise	Psychic	Special	120	100	10	Adjacent	—	190	Inflicts damage on any Pokémon of the same type as the user. Its power is reduced by 25% when it hits multiple Pokémon in a Double Battle. Its power is reduced by 50% when it hits multiple Pokémon in a Battle Royal.
Synthesis	Grass	Status	—	—	5	Self	—	Resets negative stat changes.	Recovers 1/2 of the user's maximum HP in normal weather conditions. Recovers 2/3 of the user's maximum HP in sunny or extremely harsh sunlight weather conditions. Recovers 1/4 of the user's maximum HP in rain/heavy rain/sandstorm/hail weather conditions.
Tackle	Normal	Physical	40	100	35	Normal	◯	100	A regular attack.
Tail Glow	Bug	Status	—	—	20	Self	—	Resets negative stat changes.	Raises the user's Sp. Atk by 3.
Tail Slap	Normal	Physical	25	85	10	Normal	◯	140	Attacks 2–5 times in a row in a single turn.
Tail Whip	Normal	Status	—	100	30	Many Others	—	Raises the user's Attack.	Lowers the targets' Defense by 1.
Tailwind	Flying	Status	—	—	15	Your Side	—	Critical hits land more easily.	Doubles the Speed of the Pokémon on your side for 4 turns.
Take Down	Normal	Physical	90	85	20	Normal	◯	175	The user takes 1/4 of the damage inflicted.
Taunt	Dark	Status	—	100	20	Normal	—	Raises the user's Attack.	Prevents the target from using anything other than attack moves for 3 turns.
Tearful Look	Normal	Status	—	—	20	Normal	—	Raises the user's Defense.	Lowers the target's Attack and Sp. Atk. Strikes the target even if it is using Baneful Bunker, Detect, King's Shield, Mat Block, Protect, or Spiky Shield.
Techno Blast	Normal	Special	120	100	5	Normal	—	190	A regular attack. This move's type changes according to the drive that Genesect is holding.
Teeter Dance	Normal	Status	—	100	20	Adjacent	—	Raises the user's Sp. Atk.	Makes the target confused.
Telekinesis	Psychic	Status	—	—	15	Normal	—	Raises the user's Sp. Atk.	Makes the target float for 3 turns. All moves land regardless of their accuracy except for Ground-type moves and one-hit KO moves such as Fissure, Guillotine, Horn Drill, and Sheer Cold.
Teleport	Psychic	Status	—	—	20	Self	—	Restores the user's HP.	Ends wild Pokémon battles.
Thief	Dark	Physical	60	100	25	Normal	◯	120	When the target is holding an item and the user is not, the user can steal that item. When the target is not holding an item, this move will function as a normal attack.
Thousand Arrows	Ground	Physical	90	100	10	Many Others	—	180	Will also hit Pokémon with the Levitate Ability or Flying-type Pokémon. Ground-type moves will now hit Pokémon with the Levitate Ability or Flying-type Pokémon. Its power is reduced by 25% when it hits multiple Pokémon in a Double Battle. Its power is reduced by 50% when it hits multiple Pokémon in a Battle Royal.
Thousand Waves	Ground	Physical	90	100	10	Many Others	—	175	The targets cannot escape. If used during a Trainer battle, the opposing Trainer cannot switch Pokémon. Its power is reduced by 25% when it hits multiple Pokémon in a Double Battle. Its power is reduced by 50% when it hits multiple Pokémon in a Battle Royal.
Thrash	Normal	Physical	120	100	10	1 Random	◯	190	Attacks consecutively over 2–3 turns. Cannot choose other moves during this time. The user becomes Confused after using this move.
Throat Chop	Dark	Physical	80	100	15	Normal	◯	160	The target will not be able to use sound moves for 2 turns.
Thunder	Electric	Special	110	70	10	Normal	—	185	A 30% chance of inflicting the Paralysis status condition on the target. Is 100% accurate in the rain or heavy rain weather condition and 50% accurate in the sunny or extremely harsh sunlight weather condition. It hits even Pokémon that are in the sky due to using moves such as Fly and Bounce.
Thunder Fang	Electric	Physical	65	95	15	Normal	◯	120	A 10% chance of inflicting the Paralysis status condition or making the target flinch (unable to use moves on that turn).
Thunder Punch	Electric	Physical	75	100	15	Normal	◯	140	A 10% chance of inflicting the Paralysis status condition on the target.
Thunder Shock	Electric	Special	40	100	30	Normal	—	100	A 10% chance of inflicting the Paralysis status condition on the target.
Thunder Wave	Electric	Status	—	90	20	Normal	—	Raises the user's Sp. Def.	Inflicts the Paralysis status condition on the target. Does not work on Ground types.
Thunderbolt	Electric	Special	90	100	15	Normal	—	175	A 10% chance of inflicting the Paralysis status condition on the target.
Tickle	Normal	Status	—	100	20	Normal	—	Raises the user's Defense.	Lowers the target's Attack and Defense by 1.
Topsy-Turvy	Dark	Status	—	—	20	Normal	—	Raises the user's Attack.	Reverses the effects of any stat changes affecting the target.
Torment	Dark	Status	—	100	15	Normal	—	Raises the user's Defense.	Makes the target unable to use the same move twice in a row.
Toxic	Poison	Status	—	90	10	Normal	—	Raises the user's Defense.	Inflicts the Badly Poisoned status condition on the target. Damage from being Badly Poisoned increases with every turn. It never misses if used by a Poison-type Pokémon.
Toxic Spikes	Poison	Status	—	—	20	Other Side	—	Raises the user's Defense.	Lays a trap of poison spikes on the opposing side that inflict the Poisoned status condition on Pokémon that switch into battle. Using Toxic Spikes twice inflicts the Badly Poisoned condition. The damage from the Badly Poisoned condition increases every turn. Toxic Spikes' effects end when a Poison-type Pokémon switches into battle. Ineffective against Flying-type Pokémon and Pokémon with the Levitate Ability.
Toxic Thread	Poison	Status	—	100	20	Normal	—	Raises the user's Speed.	Inflicts the Poisoned status condition on the target and lowers its Speed by 1.
Transform	Normal	Status	—	—	10	Normal	—	Restores the user's HP.	The user transforms into the target. The user has the same moves and Ability as the target (all moves have 5 PP).
Tri Attack	Normal	Special	80	100	10	Normal	—	160	A 20% chance of inflicting the Paralysis, Burned, or Frozen status condition on the target.
Trick	Psychic	Status	—	100	10	Normal	—	Raises the user's Speed by 2.	Swaps items between the user and the target.
Trick Room	Psychic	Status	—	—	5	Both Sides	—	Increases the user's accuracy.	Always strikes last. For 5 turns, Pokémon with lower Speed go first. First-strike moves still go first. Self-canceling if used again while Trick Room is still in effect.
Trick-or-Treat	Ghost	Status	—	100	20	Normal	—	Raises all of the user's stats.	Gives the target the Ghost type in addition to its original type(s).
Triple Kick	Fighting	Physical	10	90	10	Normal	◯	120	Attacks 3 times in a row in a single turn. Power raises from 10 to 20 to 30 as long as it continues to hit.
Trop Kick	Grass	Physical	70	100	15	Normal	◯	140	A 100% chance of lowering the target's Attack by 1.

Move	Type	Kind	Pow.	Acc.	PP	Range	DA	Z-Move Pow./ Effects	Battle Effects
Trump Card	Normal	Special	—	—	5	Normal	○	160	A sure hit. The lower the user's PP is, the greater the move's power becomes (max 200).
Twineedle	Bug	Physical	25	100	20	Normal	—	100	Attacks twice in a row in a single turn. A 20% chance of inflicting the Poison status condition on the target.
Twister	Dragon	Special	40	100	20	Many Others	—	100	A 20% chance of making the targets flinch (unable to use moves on that turn). It even hits Pokémon that are in the sky due to using moves such as Fly and Bounce, dealing them twice the usual damage. Its power is reduced by 25% when it hits multiple Pokémon in a Double Battle. Its power is reduced by 50% when it hits multiple Pokémon in a Battle Royal.
U-turn	Bug	Physical	70	100	20	Normal	○	140	After attacking, the user switches out with another Pokémon in the party.
Uproar	Normal	Special	90	100	10	1 Random	—	175	The user makes an uproar for 3 turns. During that time, no Pokémon can fall Asleep. Strikes the target even if it is using Substitute.
V-create	Fire	Physical	180	95	5	Normal	○	220	Lowers the user's Defense, Sp. Def, and Speed by 1. If the target is Frozen, it will be thawed.
Vacuum Wave	Fighting	Special	40	100	30	Normal	—	100	Always strikes first. The user with the higher Speed goes first if similar moves are used.
Venom Drench	Poison	Status	—	100	20	Many Others	—	Raises the user's Defense.	Lowers the Attack, Sp. Atk, and Speed of opposing Pokémon afflicted with Poison or Badly Poisoned status conditions by 1.
Venoshock	Poison	Special	65	100	10	Normal	—	120	Does twice the damage to a target that has the Poison or Badly Poisoned status condition.
Vice Grip	Normal	Physical	55	100	30	Normal	○	100	A regular attack.
Vine Whip	Grass	Physical	45	100	25	Normal	○	100	A regular attack.
Vital Throw	Fighting	Physical	70	—	10	Normal	○	140	Always strikes later than normal, but has perfect accuracy.
Volt Switch	Electric	Special	70	100	20	Normal	—	140	After attacking, the user switches out with another Pokémon in the party.
Volt Tackle	Electric	Physical	120	100	15	Normal	○	190	The user takes 1/3 of the damage inflicted. A 10% chance of inflicting the Paralysis status condition on the target.
Wake-Up Slap	Fighting	Physical	70	100	10	Normal	○	140	Does twice the usual damage to a target that is Asleep, but heals that status condition.
Water Gun	Water	Special	40	100	25	Normal	—	100	A regular attack.
Water Pledge	Water	Special	80	100	10	Normal	—	160	When combined with Fire Pledge or Grass Pledge, the power and effect change. If combined with Fire Pledge, the power is 150 and it remains a Water-type move. This makes it more likely that your team's moves will have additional effects for 4 turns. If combined with Grass Pledge, the power is 150 and it becomes a Grass-type move. This lowers the Speed of opposing Pokémon for 4 turns.
Water Pulse	Water	Special	60	100	20	Normal	—	120	A 20% chance of making the target confused.
Water Shuriken	Water	Special	15	100	20	Normal	—	100	Always strikes first. The user with the higher Speed goes first if similar moves are used. Attacks 2–5 times in a row in a single turn. When used by Ash-Greninja that has undergone a form change due to its Battle Bond, the move's power is raised to 20 and it attacks 3 times in a row in a single turn.
Water Sport	Water	Status	—	—	15	Both Sides	—	Raises the user's Sp. Def.	Lowers the power of Fire-type moves to 1/3 of normal for 5 turns.
Water Spout	Water	Special	150	100	5	Many Others	—	200	If the user's HP is low, this move has lower power. Its power is reduced by 25% when it hits multiple Pokémon in a Double Battle. Its power is reduced by 50% when it hits multiple Pokémon in a Battle Royal.
Waterfall	Water	Physical	80	100	15	Normal	○	160	A 20% chance of making the target flinch (unable to use moves on that turn).
Weather Ball	Normal	Special	50	100	10	Normal	—	160	In special weather conditions, this move's type changes and its attack power doubles. Sunny / extremely harsh sunlight weather condition: Fire type. Rain / heavy rain weather condition: Water type. Hail weather condition: Ice type. Sandstorm weather condition: Rock type.
Whirlpool	Water	Special	35	85	15	Normal	—	100	Inflicts damage equal to 1/8 the target's max HP for 4–5 turns. The target cannot flee during that time. Does twice the damage if the target is using Dive when attacked.
Whirlwind	Normal	Status	—	—	20	Normal	—	Raises the user's Sp. Def.	Ends wild Pokémon battles. In a battle with a Trainer, this move forces the opposing Trainer to switch Pokémon. When there are no Pokémon to switch in, this move fails. Attacks last. If the opposing Pokémon's level is higher than the user's, this move fails. In a battle with more than one wild Pokémon, this move fails. Strikes the target even if it is using Baneful Bunker, Detect, King's Shield, Mat Block, Protect, Spiky Shield, or Substitute.
Wide Guard	Rock	Status	—	—	10	Your Side	—	Raises the user's Defense.	Protects your side from the effects of any moves used that turn that target multiple Pokémon.
Wild Charge	Electric	Physical	90	100	15	Normal	○	175	The user takes 1/4 of the damage inflicted.
Will-O-Wisp	Fire	Status	—	85	15	Normal	—	Raises the user's Attack.	Inflicts the Burned status condition on the target.
Wing Attack	Flying	Physical	60	100	35	Normal	○	120	A regular attack.
Wish	Normal	Status	—	—	10	Self	—	Raises the user's Sp. Def.	Restores 1/2 of maximum HP at the end of the next turn. Works even if the user has switched out.
Withdraw	Water	Status	—	—	40	Self	—	Raises the user's Defense.	Raises the user's Defense by 1.
Wonder Room	Psychic	Status	—	—	10	Both Sides	—	Raises the user's Sp. Def.	Always strikes last. Each Pokémon's Defense and Sp. Def stats are swapped for 5 turns. The effect ends if the move is used again.
Wood Hammer	Grass	Physical	120	100	15	Normal	○	190	The user takes 1/3 of the damage inflicted.
Work Up	Normal	Status	—	—	30	Self	—	Raises the user's Attack.	Raises the user's Attack and Sp. Atk by 1.
Worry Seed	Grass	Status	—	100	10	Normal	—	Raises the user's Speed.	Changes the target's Ability to Insomnia. Fails with certain Abilities, however.
Wrap	Normal	Physical	15	90	20	Normal	○	100	Inflicts damage equal to 1/8 the target's max HP for 4–5 turns. The target cannot flee during that time.
Wring Out	Normal	Special	—	100	5	Normal	○	190	The more HP the target has left, the greater the move's power becomes (max 120).
X-Scissor	Bug	Physical	80	100	15	Normal	○	160	A regular attack.
Yawn	Normal	Status	—	—	10	Normal	—	Raises the user's Speed.	Inflicts the Asleep status condition on the target at the end of the next turn unless the target switches out.
Zap Cannon	Electric	Special	120	50	5	Normal	—	190	Inflicts the Paralysis status condition on the target.
Zen Headbutt	Psychic	Physical	80	90	15	Normal	○	160	A 20% chance of making the target flinch (unable to use moves on that turn).
Zing Zap	Electric	Physical	80	100	10	Normal	○	160	A 30% chance of making the target flinch (unable to use moves on that turn).

How to Obtain TMs

No.	Move	Type	How to Obtain	Price
TM01	Work Up	Normal	Get from a Rising Star in the Trainers' School	—
TM02	Dragon Claw	Dragon	Find at the trial site in the Vast Poni Canyon	—
TM03	Psyshock	Psychic	Lake of the Moone ☀ / Find at Lake of the Sunne ☾	—
TM04	Calm Mind	Psychic	Buy at the Seafolk Village Poké Mart	₽10,000
TM05	Roar	Normal	Find in Kala'e Bay	—
TM06	Toxic	Poison	Find at the dock in Aether Paradise	—
TM07	Hail	Ice	Buy at the Royal Avenue Poké Mart	₽50,000
TM08	Bulk Up	Fighting	Buy at the TM shop in Konikoni City	₽10,000
TM09	Venoshock	Poison	Buy at the TM shop in Konikoni City	₽10,000
TM10	Hidden Power	Normal	Get from a Pokémon Breeder at the Pokémon Nursery	—
TM11	Sunny Day	Fire	Buy at the Royal Avenue Poké Mart	₽50,000
TM12	Taunt	Dark	Get from a man in a trailer on Route 13	—
TM13	Ice Beam	Ice	Find on Mount Lanakila	—
TM14	Blizzard	Ice	Buy at the Seafolk Village Poké Mart	₽30,000
TM15	Hyper Beam	Normal	Buy at the Seafolk Village Poké Mart	₽50,000
TM16	Light Screen	Psychic	Buy at the Heahea City Poké Mart	₽10,000
TM17	Protect	Normal	Buy at the Heahea City Poké Mart	₽10,000
TM18	Rain Dance	Water	Buy at the Royal Avenue Poké Mart	₽50,000
TM19	Roost	Flying	Buy at the Malie City Poké Mart	₽10,000
TM20	Safeguard	Normal	Buy at the Heahea City Poké Mart	₽10,000
TM21	Frustration	Normal	Get from an Oranguru in the malasada shop in Malie City ☽	—
TM22	Solar Beam	Grass	Buy at the Seafolk Village Poké Mart	₽10,000
TM23	Smack Down	Rock	Buy at the Malie City Poké Mart	₽10,000
TM24	Thunderbolt	Electric	Find in Poni Plains*	—
TM25	Thunder	Electric	Buy at the Seafolk Village Poké Mart	₽30,000
TM26	Earthquake	Ground	Find at Resolution Cave entrance*	—
TM27	Return	Normal	Get from a Police Officer in the malasada shop in Malie City ☽	—
TM28	Leech Life	Bug	Find in Akala Outskirts	—
TM29	Psychic	Psychic	Get from Wicke in Aether Paradise	—
TM30	Shadow Ball	Ghost	Find on Route 14	—
TM31	Brick Break	Fighting	Find in Verdant Cavern	—
TM32	Double Team	Normal	Buy at the TM shop in Konikoni City	₽10,000
TM33	Reflect	Psychic	Buy at the Heahea City Poké Mart	₽10,000
TM34	Sludge Wave	Poison	Buy at the Seafolk Village Poké Mart	₽10,000
TM35	Flamethrower	Fire	Find in the third cave in the Vast Poni Canyon	—
TM36	Sludge Bomb	Poison	Find in the Shady House	—
TM37	Sandstorm	Rock	Buy at the Royal Avenue Poké Mart	₽50,000
TM38	Fire Blast	Fire	Buy at the Seafolk Village Poké Mart	₽30,000
TM39	Rock Tomb	Rock	Find in Wela Volcano Park	—
TM40	Aerial Ace	Flying	Buy at the Malie City Poké Mart	₽10,000
TM41	Torment	Dark	Find on Route 5 (south)	—
TM42	Facade	Normal	Buy at the Malie City Poké Mart	₽10,000
TM43	Flame Charge	Fire	Get from Colress on Route 8	—
TM44	Rest	Psychic	Get from Hypno in Thrifty Megamart	—
TM45	Attract	Normal	Get from Machamp caddy in Hano Grand Hotel	—
TM46	Thief	Dark	Find in Verdant Cavern	—
TM47	Low Sweep	Fighting	Buy at the TM shop in Konikoni City	₽10,000
TM48	Round	Normal	Get from a Janitor as a reward for cleaning the mall at the shopping mall ☽	—
TM49	Echoed Voice	Normal	Find in Hau'oli City Shopping District	—
TM50	Overheat	Fire	Find in Poni Meadow*	—
TM51	Steel Wing	Steel	Buy at the Malie City Poké Mart	₽10,000
TM52	Focus Blast	Fighting	Buy at the Seafolk Village Poké Mart	₽30,000
TM53	Energy Ball	Grass	Find on Route 8	—
TM54	False Swipe	Normal	Get from Kukui after Hala's grand trial	—
TM55	Scald	Water	Find in Brooklet Hill	—
TM56	Fling	Dark	Get from a mourning woman at the Hau'oli Cemetery ☽	—
TM57	Charge Beam	Electric	Find on Route 5 (south)	—
TM58	Sky Drop	Flying	Get from an Ace Trainer after defeating all Trainers on Route 8	—
TM59	Brutal Swing	Dark	Find on Route 5 (north)	—
TM60	Quash	Dark	Get from an Ace Trainer after defeating all Trainers around Poni Plains*	—
TM61	Will-O-Wisp	Fire	Find in Konikoni City	—
TM62	Acrobatics	Flying	Find in the Farthest Hollow in Ten Carat Hill	—
TM63	Embargo	Dark	Get from a Scientist in the Geothermal Power Plant ○	—
TM64	Explosion	Normal	Find in Ten Carat Hill	—
TM65	Shadow Claw	Ghost	Buy at the TM shop in Konikoni City	₽10,000
TM66	Payback	Dark	Buy at the Malie City Poké Mart	₽10,000
TM67	Smart Strike	Steel	Get from Kukui after Mallow's trial	—
TM68	Giga Impact	Normal	Buy at the Seafolk Village Poké Mart	₽50,000
TM69	Rock Polish	Rock	Buy at the Malie City Poké Mart	₽10,000
TM70	Aurora Veil	Ice	Buy at the Heahea City Poké Mart	₽30,000
TM71	Stone Edge	Rock	Buy at the Seafolk Village Poké Mart	₽30,000
TM72	Volt Switch	Electric	Find on Mount Hokulani	—
TM73	Thunder Wave	Electric	Find on Route 7	—
TM74	Gyro Ball	Steel	Find on Route 11	—
TM75	Swords Dance	Normal	Buy at the Malie City Poké Mart	₽10,000
TM76	Fly	Flying	Get from a woman in Malie Library	—
TM77	Psych Up	Normal	Get from a Collector after defeating all Trainers on Route 12	—
TM78	Bulldoze	Ground	Buy at the Malie City Poké Mart	₽10,000
TM79	Frost Breath	Ice	Find on the Ancient Poni Path	—
TM80	Rock Slide	Rock	Find in Melemele Sea	—
TM81	X-Scissor	Bug	Find on Route 16	—
TM82	Dragon Tail	Dragon	Buy at the TM shop in Konikoni City	₽10,000
TM83	Infestation	Bug	Find on Route 3	—
TM84	Poison Jab	Poison	Find on Route 17	—
TM85	Dream Eater	Psychic	Find in Haina Desert (Area 4)	—
TM86	Grass Knot	Grass	Find in Lush Jungle	—
TM87	Swagger	Normal	Get from Guzma's mom in his house on Route 2	—
TM88	Sleep Talk	Normal	Find in Paniola Town	—
TM89	U-turn	Bug	Buy at the Malie City Poké Mart	₽10,000
TM90	Substitute	Normal	Get from Professor Kukui in the Pokémon Research Lab*	—
TM91	Flash Cannon	Steel	Find in Seafolk Village	—
TM92	Trick Room	Psychic	Get from Kahili at Hano Grand Resort*	—
TM93	Wild Charge	Electric	Find on Route 15	—
TM94	Surf	Water	Get from Swimmer Girls on Poni Breaker Coast*	—
TM95	Snarl	Dark	Get from a Veteran after defeating all Trainers on Mount Hokulani	—
TM96	Nature Power	Normal	Get from a Trial Guide after defeating all Trainers on Route 5	—
TM97	Dark Pulse	Dark	Find on Poni Coast*	—
TM98	Waterfall	Water	Get from Swimmer Girls on Poni Breaker Coast*	—
TM99	Dazzling Gleam	Fairy	Find in the Vast Poni Canyon	—
TM100	Confide	Normal	Find in the Hau'oli Cemetery	—

Note: TMs marked with an asterisk can only be obtained after entering the Hall of Fame.

Abilities

Ability	Effect in Battle	Effect when the Pokémon is the lead in your party
Adaptability	The power boost received by using a move of the same type as the Pokémon will be 100% instead of 50%.	—
Aerilate	Changes Normal-type moves to Flying type and increases their power by 20%.	—
Aftermath	Knocks off 1/4 of the attacking Pokémon's maximum HP when a direct attack causes the Pokémon to faint.	—
Air Lock	Eliminates effects of weather on Pokémon.	—
Analytic	The power of its move is increased by 30% when the Pokémon moves last.	—
Anger Point	Raises the Pokémon's Attack to the maximum when hit by a critical hit.	—
Anticipation	Warns if your opponent's Pokémon has supereffective moves or one-hit KO moves when the Pokémon enters battle.	—
Arena Trap	Prevents the opponent's Pokémon from fleeing or switching out. Ineffective against Flying- or Ghost-type Pokémon and Pokémon with the Levitate Ability.	Makes it easier to encounter wild Pokémon.
Aroma Veil	Protects the team from Attract, Disable, Encore, Heal Block, Taunt, and Torment.	—
Aura Break	Reverses the effects of the Fairy Aura Ability and lowers the power of Fairy-type moves by 25%. Reverses the Dark Aura Ability and lowers the power of Dark-type moves by 25%.	—
Bad Dreams	Lowers the HP of any opposing Pokémon that are Asleep by 1/8 of their maximum HP every turn.	—
Battery	Raises the power of an ally's special moves by 30%.	—
Battle Armor	Opposing Pokémon's moves will not hit critically.	—
Battle Bond	The Pokémon changes form when it defeats a Pokémon.	—
Beast Boost	When the Pokémon knocks out another Pokémon with a move, its most prominent stat goes up 1.	—
Berserk	Raises Sp. Atk by 1 when the Pokémon takes a hit that causes its HP to become 1/2 or less.	—
Big Pecks	Prevents Defense from being lowered.	—
Blaze	Raises the power of Fire-type moves by 50% when the Pokémon's HP drops to 1/3 or less.	—
Bulletproof	Protects against Acid Spray, Aura Sphere, Barrage, Bullet Seed, Egg Bomb, Electro Ball, Energy Ball, Focus Blast, Gyro Ball, Ice Ball, Magnet Bomb, Mist Ball, Mud Bomb, Octazooka, Rock Wrecker, Searing Shot, Seed Bomb, Shadow Ball, Sludge Bomb, Weather Ball, and Zap Cannon.	—
Cheek Pouch	Eating a Berry not only grants its usual benefits, but also restores 1/3 of the Pokémon's maximum HP.	—
Chlorophyll	Doubles Speed in the sunny or extremely harsh sunlight weather conditions.	—
Clear Body	Protects against stat-lowering moves and Abilities.	—
Cloud Nine	Eliminates effects of weather on Pokémon.	—
Color Change	Changes the Pokémon's type into the type of the move that just hit it.	—
Comatose	The Pokémon is permanently affected by the Asleep status condition. It can use moves while Asleep.	—
Competitive	When an opponent's move or Ability lowers the Pokémon's stats, the Pokémon's Sp. Atk rises by 2.	—
Compound Eyes	Raises accuracy by 30%.	Raises encounter rate with wild Pokémon holding items.
Contrary	Makes stat changes have an opposite effect (increase instead of decrease and vice versa).	—
Corrosion	Makes the Pokémon able to inflict the Poisoned status condition on Steel types and Poison types.	—
Cursed Body	Provides a 30% chance of inflicting Disable on the move the opponent used to hit the Pokémon. (Cannot use that move for three turns.)	—
Cute Charm	Provides a 30% chance of causing infatuation when hit with a direct attack.	Raises encounter rate of wild Pokémon of the opposite gender.
Damp	Prevents Pokémon on either side from using Explosion or Self-Destruct. Nullifies the Aftermath Ability.	—
Dancer	The Pokémon immediately follows and uses the same move when another Pokémon in battle uses a dance move.	—
Dark Aura	Raises the power of Dark-type moves by 1/3. Affects all Pokémon in the field.	—
Dazzling	Prevents the opposing Pokémon from using priority attacking moves.	—
Defeatist	The Pokémon's Attack and Sp. Atk gets halved when HP becomes half or less.	—
Defiant	When an opponent's move or Ability lowers the Pokémon's stats, the Pokémon's Attack rises by 2.	—
Delta Stream	Makes the weather strong winds when the Pokémon enters battle. This weather makes Flying-type Pokémon receive half the damage from supereffective moves against them.	—
Desolate Land	Makes the weather extremely harsh sunlight when the Pokémon enters battle. This weather raises the power of Fire-type moves by 50%, reduces that of Water-type moves to zero, and prevents the Frozen status condition.	—
Disguise	Once per battle, this Ability prevents damage when hit by a move. Then the Pokémon's form changes.	—
Download	When the Pokémon enters battle, this Ability raises its Attack by 1 if the opposing Pokémon's Defense is lower than its Sp. Def, and raises its Sp. Atk by 1 if the opposing Pokémon's Sp. Def is lower than its Defense. If the opponent's Defense and Sp. Def are the same, this Ability raises its Sp. Atk by 1.	—
Drizzle	Makes the weather rain for five turns when the Pokémon enters battle. Does nothing when the weather is extremely harsh sunlight, heavy rain, or strong winds.	—
Drought	Makes the weather sunny for five turns when the Pokémon enters battle. Does nothing when the weather is extremely harsh sunlight, heavy rain, or strong winds.	—
Dry Skin	Restores HP by 1/4 of the Pokémon's maximum HP when the Pokémon is hit by a Water-type move. Restores HP by 1/8 of its maximum HP at the end of every turn in the rain or heavy rain weather condition. However, the damage the Pokémon receives from Fire-type moves increases by 25%. Takes damage of 1/8 of its maximum HP at the end of every turn in the sunny or extremely harsh sunlight weather condition.	—

Ability	Effect in Battle	Effect when the Pokémon is the lead in your party
Early Bird	Causes the Pokémon to wake quickly from the Asleep status condition.	—
Effect Spore	Provides a 30% chance of inflicting the Poisoned, Paralysis, or Asleep status conditions when hit with a direct attack. Grass-type Pokémon are immune to this effect.	—
Electric Surge	Turns the field into Electric Terrain for five turns when the Pokémon enters battle.	—
Emergency Exit	The Pokémon switches places with a party Pokémon automatically when its HP drops to 1/2 or less.	—
Fairy Aura	Raises the power of Fairy-type moves by 1/3. Affects all Pokémon in the field.	—
Filter	Decreases the damage received from supereffective moves by 25%.	—
Flame Body	Provides a 30% chance of inflicting the Burned status condition when hit with a direct attack.	Facilitates hatching Pokémon Eggs in your party.
Flare Boost	Increases the power of special moves by 50% when Burned.	—
Flash Fire	When the Pokémon is hit by a Fire-type move, rather than taking damage, its Fire-type moves increase power by 50%.	—
Flower Gift	Raises Attack and Sp. Def of the Pokémon and its allies by 50% in the sunny or extremely harsh sunlight weather condition.	—
Flower Veil	Grass-type allies cannot have their stats lowered, and they are protected from being inflicted with status conditions.	—
Fluffy	Halves the damage taken from moves that make direct contact. Doubles the damage taken from Fire-type moves.	—
Forecast	Changes Castform's form and type. Sunny or extremely harsh sunlight weather conditions: changes to Fire type. Rain or heavy rain weather conditions: changes to Water type. Hail weather condition: changes to Ice type.	—
Forewarn	Reveals a move an opponent knows when the Pokémon enters battle. Damaging moves with high power are prioritized.	—
Friend Guard	Reduces damage done to allies by 25%.	—
Frisk	Checks an opponent's held item when the Pokémon enters battle.	—
Full Metal Body	Protects against stat-lowering moves and Abilities.	—
Fur Coat	Halves the damage taken from physical moves.	—
Gale Wings	Gives priority to Flying-type moves when HP is full.	—
Galvanize	Changes Normal-type moves to Electric type and increases their power by 20%.	—
Gluttony	Allows the Pokémon to use its held Berry sooner when it has low HP.	—
Gooey	Lowers by 1 the Speed of an attacker who makes direct contact.	—
Grass Pelt	Raises Defense by 50% when the field is affected by Grassy Terrain.	—
Grassy Surge	Turns the field into Grassy Terrain for five turns when the Pokémon enters battle.	—
Guts	Attack stat rises by 50% when the Pokémon is affected by a status condition.	—
Harvest	Provides at every turn end a 50% chance of restoring the Berry the Pokémon used, and a 100% chance when the weather condition is sunny or extremely harsh sunlight.	—
Healer	At the end of every turn, it provides a 33% chance that an ally Pokémon's status condition will be healed.	—
Heatproof	Halves damage from Fire-type moves and from the Burned status condition.	—
Heavy Metal	Doubles the Pokémon's weight.	—
Honey Gather	If the Pokémon isn't holding an item, it will sometimes be left holding Honey after a battle (even if it didn't participate). Its chance of finding Honey increases with its level.	—
Huge Power	Doubles Attack.	—
Hustle	Raises Attack by 50%, but lowers the accuracy of the Pokémon's physical moves by 20%.	Makes it easier to encounter high-level wild Pokémon.
Hydration	Cures status conditions at the end of each turn during the rain or heavy rain weather conditions.	—
Hyper Cutter	Prevents Attack from being lowered.	—
Ice Body	Restores HP by 1/16 of the Pokémon's maximum HP at the end of every turn in the hail weather condition rather than taking damage.	—
Illuminate	No effect.	Makes it easier to encounter wild Pokémon.
Illusion	Appears in battle disguised as the last Pokémon in the party.	—
Immunity	Protects against the Poisoned status condition.	—
Imposter	Transforms itself into the Pokémon it is facing as it enters battle.	—
Infiltrator	Moves can hit ignoring the effects of Aurora Veil, Light Screen, Mist, Reflect, Safeguard, or Substitute.	—
Innards Out	Upon fainting, the Pokémon does damage to the attacker equal to its last remaining HP.	—
Inner Focus	The Pokémon doesn't flinch as an additional effect of a move.	—
Insomnia	Protects against the Asleep status condition.	—
Intimidate	When this Pokémon enters battle, it lowers the opposing Pokémon's Attack by 1.	Lowers encounter rate with low-level wild Pokémon.
Iron Barbs	Reduces the HP of an opponent that hits the Pokémon with a direct attack by 1/8 of its maximum HP.	—
Iron Fist	Increases the power of Bullet Punch, Comet Punch, Dizzy Punch, Drain Punch, Dynamic Punch, Fire Punch, Focus Punch, Hammer Arm, Ice Punch, Mach Punch, Mega Punch, Meteor Mash, Power-Up Punch, Shadow Punch, Sky Uppercut, and Thunder Punch by 20%.	—
Justified	When the Pokémon is hit by a Dark-type move, Attack goes up by 1.	—
Keen Eye	Prevents accuracy from being lowered. Ignores evasiveness-raising moves.	Lowers encounter rate with low-level wild Pokémon.
Klutz	The Pokémon can't use held items.	—
Leaf Guard	Protects the Pokémon from status conditions when in the sunny or extremely harsh sunlight weather conditions.	—

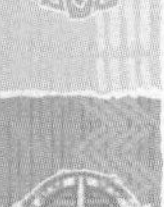

Ability	Effect in Battle	Effect when the Pokémon is the lead in your party
Levitate	Gives full immunity from all Ground-type moves.	—
Light Metal	Halves the Pokémon's weight.	—
Lightning Rod	Draws all Electric-type moves to the Pokémon. When the Pokémon is hit by an Electric-type move, rather than taking damage, its Sp. Atk goes up by 1.	—
Limber	Protects against the Paralysis status condition.	—
Liquid Ooze	When an opposing Pokémon uses an HP-draining move, it damages the user instead.	—
Magic Bounce	Reflects status moves that lower stats or inflict status conditions.	—
Magic Guard	The Pokémon will not take damage from anything other than direct damage. Nullifies the Aftermath, Bad Dreams, Innards Out, Iron Barbs, Liquid Ooze, and Rough Skin Abilities, the hail and sandstorm weather conditions, and the Burned, Poisoned, and Badly Poisoned status conditions. The effects of Bind, Clamp, Curse, Fire Pledge, Fire Spin, Flame Burst, Infestation, Leech Seed, Magma Storm, Nightmare, Sand Tomb, Spikes, Stealth Rock, Whirlpool, and Wrap are negated, as are the item effects from Black Sludge, Life Orb, Rocky Helmet, and Sticky Barb. The Pokémon also receives no recoil or move-failure damage from attacks. Receives no damage from attacking a Pokémon that has used the Spiky Shield move or damage from using a Fire-type move after the Powder move has been used.	—
Magician	The Pokémon seizes the item of an opponent it hits with a move. Fails if the Pokémon is already holding an item.	—
Magma Armor	Prevents the Frozen status condition.	Facilitates hatching Pokémon Eggs in your party.
Magnet Pull	Prevents Steel-type opponents from fleeing or switching out.	Raises encounter rate with wild Steel-type Pokémon.
Marvel Scale	Defense stat increases by 50% when the Pokémon is affected by a status condition.	—
Mega Launcher	Raises the power of Aura Sphere, Dark Pulse, Dragon Pulse, Origin Pulse, and Water Pulse by 50%. Heal Pulse will restore 75% of the target's maximum HP.	—
Merciless	The Pokémon delivers critical hits as long as the target has the Poisoned status condition.	—
Minus	Raises Sp. Atk by 50% when another ally has the Ability Plus or Minus.	—
Misty Surge	Turns the field into Misty Terrain for five turns when the Pokémon enters battle.	—
Mold Breaker	Allows the Pokémon to use moves on targets regardless of their Abilities. Does not nullify Abilities that have effects after an attack. For example, the Pokémon can score a critical hit against a target with Battle Armor, but it will still take damage from Rough Skin.	—
Moody	Raises one stat by 2 and lowers another by 1 at the end of every turn.	—
Motor Drive	When the Pokémon is hit by an Electric-type move, its Speed goes up by 1 and damage and effects of the move are nullified.	—
Moxie	When the Pokémon knocks out another Pokémon with a move, its Attack goes up 1.	—
Multiscale	Halves damage when HP is full.	—
Multitype	Type changes according to the plate or Z-Crystal Arceus is holding.	—
Mummy	Changes the Ability of the opponent that hits the Pokémon with a direct attack to Mummy.	—
Natural Cure	Cures the Pokémon's status conditions when it switches out.	—
No Guard	Moves used by or against the Pokémon always strike their targets.	Makes it easier to encounter wild Pokémon.
Normalize	Changes all of the Pokémon's moves to Normal type and increases their power by 20%.	—
Oblivious	Protects against infatuation. Immune to Captivate and Taunt.	—
Overcoat	Protects the Pokémon from weather damage, such as hail and sandstorm. Protects it from Cotton Spore, Poison Powder, Powder, Rage Powder, Sleep Powder, Spore, and Stun Spore. Immune to the Effect Spore Ability.	—
Overgrow	Raises the power of Grass-type moves by 50% when the Pokémon's HP drops to 1/3 or less.	—
Own Tempo	Protects against confusion.	—
Parental Bond	Causes attacks to strike twice, with the second hit dealing only one fourth the normal damage. Does not affect moves that naturally strike multiple times or moves that strike multiple targets.	—
Pickpocket	Steals an item when hit with a direct attack. It fails if the Pokémon is already holding an item.	—
Pickup	At the end of every turn, the Pokémon picks up the item that the opposing Pokémon used that turn. Fails if the Pokémon is already holding an item.	If the Pokémon has no held item, it sometimes picks one up after battle (even if it didn't participate). It picks up different items depending on its level.
Pixilate	Changes Normal-type moves to Fairy type and increases their power by 20%.	—
Plus	Raises Sp. Atk by 50% when another ally has the Ability Plus or Minus.	—
Poison Heal	Restores 1/8 of the Pokémon's maximum HP at the end of every turn if the Pokémon has the Poisoned or Badly Poisoned status condition rather than taking damage.	—
Poison Point	Provides a 30% chance of inflicting the Poisoned status condition when the Pokémon is hit by a direct attack.	—
Poison Touch	Provides a 30% chance of inflicting the Poisoned status condition when the Pokémon uses a direct attack.	—
Power Construct	The Pokémon changes its form to Complete Form when the Pokémon's HP drops to 1/2 or less.	—
Power of Alchemy	Copies the Ability of a defeated ally.	—
Prankster	Gives priority to status moves. Fails if the target is a Dark type.	—
Pressure	When the Pokémon is hit by an opponent's move, it depletes 1 additional PP from that move.	Makes it easier to encounter high-level wild Pokémon.
Primordial Sea	Makes the weather heavy rain when the Pokémon enters battle. This weather raises the power of Water-type moves by 50% and reduces that of Fire-type moves to zero.	—
Prism Armor	Decreases the damage received from supereffective moves by 25%.	—
Protean	Changes the Pokémon's type to the same type as the move it is about to use.	—

Ability	Effect in Battle	Effect when the Pokémon is the lead in your party
Psychic Surge	Turns the field into Psychic Terrain for five turns when the Pokémon enters battle.	—
Pure Power	Doubles its Attack stat.	—
Queenly Majesty	Prevents the opposing Pokémon from using priority attacking moves.	—
Quick Feet	Increases Speed by 50% when the Pokémon is affected by status conditions.	Lowers wild Pokémon encounter rate.
Rain Dish	Restores HP by 1/16 of the Pokémon's maximum HP at the end of every turn in the rain or heavy rain weather conditions.	—
Rattled	When the Pokémon is hit by a Ghost-, Dark-, or Bug-type move, Speed goes up by 1.	—
Receiver	Copies the Ability of a defeated ally.	—
Reckless	Raises the power of moves by 20% with recoil damage.	—
Refrigerate	Changes Normal-type moves to Ice type and increases their power by 20%.	—
Regenerator	Restores 1/3 its maximum HP when withdrawn from battle.	—
Rivalry	If the target is the same gender, the Pokémon's Attack goes up by 25%. If the target is of the opposite gender, its Attack goes down by 25%. No effect when the gender is unknown.	—
RKS System	Type changes according to the memory disc the Pokémon is holding.	—
Rock Head	No recoil damage from moves like Take Down and Double-Edge.	—
Rough Skin	Knocks off 1/8 of the attacking Pokémon's maximum HP when the Pokémon makes a direct attack.	—
Run Away	Allows the Pokémon to always escape from a battle with a wild Pokémon.	—
Sand Force	Raises the power of Ground-, Rock-, and Steel-type moves by 30% in the sandstorm weather condition. Sandstorm does not damage the Pokémon.	—
Sand Rush	Doubles Speed in the sandstorm weather condition. Sandstorm does not damage the Pokémon.	—
Sand Stream	Makes the weather sandstorm for five turns when the Pokémon enters battle. Rock-type Pokémon's Sp. Def increases by 50% and Pokémon other than Rock, Steel, and Ground types take damage of 1/16 of the Pokémon's maximum HP during the weather sandstorm. Does nothing when the weather is extremely harsh sunlight, heavy rain, or strong winds.	—
Sand Veil	The accuracy of the opposing Pokémon's move decreases by 20% in the sandstorm weather condition. Sandstorm does not damage the Pokémon with this Ability.	Lowers encounter rate with wild Pokémon in the sandstorm weather condition.
Sap Sipper	When the Pokémon is hit by a Grass-type move, rather than taking damage, its Attack goes up by 1.	—
Schooling	If the Pokémon's level is 20 or above, it takes another form. It changes back to its previous form when its HP drops to 1/4 or less.	—
Scrappy	Allows the Pokémon to hit Ghost-type Pokémon with Normal- and Fighting-type moves. (The type matchup changes from "It doesn't affect..." to normal.)	—
Serene Grace	Doubles chances of moves inflicting additional effects.	—
Shadow Shield	Halves damage when HP is full.	—
Shadow Tag	Prevents the opposing Pokémon from fleeing or switching out. If both your and the opposing Pokémon have this Ability, the effect is canceled. Does not affect Ghost types.	—
Shed Skin	At the end of every turn, provides a 33% chance of curing the Pokémon's status conditions.	—
Sheer Force	When moves with an additional effect are used, power increases by 30%, but the additional effect is lost.	—
Shell Armor	Opposing Pokémon's moves will not hit critically.	—
Shield Dust	Protects the Pokémon from additional effects of moves.	—
Shields Down	The Pokémon changes its form from a defensive one to an offensive one when its HP drops to half or less.	—
Simple	Doubles the effects of stat changes.	—
Skill Link	Moves that strike successively strike the maximum number of times (2-5 times means it always strikes 5 times).	—
Slow Start	Halves Attack and Speed for 5 turns after the Pokémon enters battle.	—
Slush Rush	Doubles Speed in the hail weather condition. Hail does not damage the Pokémon.	—
Sniper	Moves that deliver a critical hit deal 125% more damage.	—
Snow Cloak	The accuracy of the opposing Pokémon's move decreases by 20% in the hail weather condition. Hail does not damage Pokémon with this Ability.	Lowers encounter rate with wild Pokémon in the hail weather condition.
Snow Warning	Makes the weather hail for five turns when the Pokémon enters battle. Pokémon other than Ice types take damage of 1/16 of the Pokémon's maximum HP during the weather hail. Does nothing when the weather is extremely harsh sunlight, heavy rain, or strong winds.	—
Solar Power	Raises Sp. Atk by 50%, but takes damage of 1/8 of the Pokémon's maximum HP at the end of every turn in the sunny or extremely harsh sunlight weather conditions.	—
Solid Rock	Decreases the damage received from supereffective moves by 25%.	—
Soul-Heart	Raises Sp. Atk by 1 every time another Pokémon faints.	—
Soundproof	Protects the Pokémon from sound-based moves: Boomburst, Bug Buzz, Chatter, Clanging Scales, Confide, Disarming Voice, Echoed Voice, Grass Whistle, Growl, Heal Bell, Hyper Voice, Metal Sound, Noble Roar, Parting Shot, Perish Song, Roar, Round, Screech, Sing, Snarl, Snore, Sparkling Aria, Supersonic, and Uproar.	—
Speed Boost	Raises Speed by 1 at the end of every turn.	—
Stakeout	The Pokémon deals double the damage to the new target if the original target is replaced by another of its party.	—
Stall	The Pokémon's moves are used last in the turn.	—
Stamina	Raises Defense by 1 every time the Pokémon takes move damage.	—
Stance Change	Changes from Shield Forme to Blade Forme when an attack move is used. Changes from Blade Forme to Shield Forme when King's Shield is used.	—
Static	A 30% chance of inflicting the Paralysis status condition when hit with a direct attack.	Raises encounter rate with wild Electric-type Pokémon.
Steadfast	Raises Speed by 1 every time the Pokémon flinches.	—

Ability	Effect in Battle	Effect when the Pokémon is the lead in your party
Steelworker	Increases the power of Steel-type moves by 50%.	—
Stench	Has a 10% chance of making the target flinch when the Pokémon uses a move to deal damage.	Lowers wild Pokémon encounter rate.
Sticky Hold	Prevents the Pokémon's held item from being stolen.	Makes Pokémon bite more often when fishing.
Storm Drain	Draws all Water-type moves to the Pokémon. When the Pokémon is hit by a Water-type move, rather than taking damage, Sp. Atk goes up by 1.	—
Strong Jaw	Raises the power of Bite, Crunch, Fire Fang, Hyper Fang, Ice Fang, Poison Fang, and Thunder Fang by 50%.	—
Sturdy	Protects the Pokémon against one-hit KO moves like Horn Drill and Sheer Cold. Leaves the Pokémon with 1 HP if hit by a move that would knock it out when its HP is full.	—
Suction Cups	Nullifies moves like Dragon Tail, Roar, and Whirlwind, and items like a Red Card, which would force Pokémon to switch out.	Makes Pokémon bite more often when fishing.
Super Luck	Heightens the critical-hit ratio of the Pokémon's moves.	—
Surge Surfer	Doubles Speed when the field is affected by Electric Terrain.	—
Swarm	Raises the power of Bug-type moves by 50% when the Pokémon's HP drops to 1/3 or less.	—
Sweet Veil	Protects the team against the Asleep status condition.	—
Swift Swim	Doubles Speed in the rain or heavy rain weather conditions.	—
Symbiosis	When an ally uses its item, the Pokémon gives its own item to that ally.	—
Synchronize	When the Pokémon receives the Poisoned, Paralysis, or Burned status condition, this inflicts the same condition.	Raises encounter rate with wild Pokémon with the same Nature.
Tangled Feet	Raises evasion when the Pokémon is confused.	—
Tangling Hair	Lowers by 1 the Speed of an attacker that makes direct contact.	—
Technician	If the move's power is 60 or less, its power will increase by 50%. Also takes effect if a move's power is altered by itself or by another move.	—
Telepathy	Prevents damage from allies.	—
Teravolt	Use moves on targets regardless of their Abilities. Does not nullify Abilities that have effects after an attack. For example, the Pokémon can score a critical hit against the target with Battle Armor, but it will still take damage from Rough Skin.	—
Thick Fat	Halves damage from Fire- and Ice-type moves.	—
Tinted Lens	Nullifies the type disadvantage of the Pokémon's not-very-effective moves: 1/2 damage turns into regular damage, 1/4 damage turns into 1/2 damage.	—
Torrent	Raises the power of Water-type moves by 50% when the Pokémon's HP drops to 1/3 or less.	—
Tough Claws	Raises the power of direct attacks by 30%.	—
Toxic Boost	Increases the power of physical moves by 50% when it has the Poisoned or Badly Poisoned status condition.	—
Trace	Makes the Pokémon's Ability the same as the opponent's, except for certain Abilities like Trace.	—
Triage	Gives priority to healing moves.	—
Truant	Allows the Pokémon to use a move only once every other turn.	—
Turboblaze	Use moves on targets regardless of their Abilities. Does not nullify Abilities that have effects after an attack. For example, the Pokémon can score a critical hit against the target with Battle Armor, but it will still take damage from Rough Skin.	—
Unaware	Ignores the stat changes of the opposing Pokémon, except Speed.	—
Unburden	Doubles Speed if the Pokémon loses or consumes a held item. Its Speed returns to normal if the Pokémon holds another item. No effect if the Pokémon starts out with no held item.	—
Unnerve	Prevent the opposing Pokémon from eating Berries.	—
Victory Star	The accuracy of the Pokémon and its allies is 10% higher.	—
Vital Spirit	Protects against the Asleep status condition.	Makes it easier to encounter high-level wild Pokémon.
Volt Absorb	When the Pokémon is hit by an Electric-type move, HP is restored by 25% of its maximum HP rather than taking damage.	—
Water Absorb	When the Pokémon is hit by a Water-type move, HP is restored by 25% of its maximum HP rather than taking damage.	—
Water Bubble	Halves damage from Fire-type moves. Prevents the Burned status condition.	—
Water Compaction	Raises Defense by 2 every time the Pokémon is hit by a Water-type move.	—
Water Veil	Prevents the Burned status condition.	—
Weak Armor	When the Pokémon is hit by a physical attack, Defense goes down by 1, but Speed goes up by 1.	—
White Smoke	Protects against stat-lowering moves and Abilities.	Lowers wild Pokémon encounter rate.
Wimp Out	The Pokémon switches places with a party Pokémon automatically when its HP drops to half or less during a Trainer battle. If a wild Pokémon has this Ability, it will flee battle when its HP drops to half or less.	—
Wonder Guard	Protects the Pokémon against all moves except supereffective ones.	—
Wonder Skin	Makes status moves more likely to miss.	—
Zen Mode	When over half its HP is lost, the Pokémon changes form.	—

Pokémon Natures

Each individual Pokémon has a Nature, which affects how its stats grow when it levels up. Most Natures will cause one stat to increase more quickly and one stat to increase more slowly than others. A few Natures, however, provide no benefit and no liability. Your Pokémon's Nature will also affect which flavors it likes and dislikes when it comes to malasadas and certain Berries.

Nature	Increased stat	Decreased stat	Favorite flavor	Disliked flavor
Adamant	ATK	SP. ATK	Spicy	Dry
Bashful	—	—	—	—
Bold	DEF	ATK	Sour	Spicy
Brave	ATK	SPD	Spicy	Sweet
Calm	SP. DEF	ATK	Bitter	Spicy
Careful	SP. DEF	SP. ATK	Bitter	Dry
Docile	—	—	—	—
Gentle	SP. DEF	DEF	Bitter	Sour
Hardy	—	—	—	—
Hasty	SPD	DEF	Sweet	Sour
Impish	DEF	SP. ATK	Sour	Dry
Jolly	SPD	SP. ATK	Sweet	Dry
Lax	DEF	SP. DEF	Sour	Bitter
Lonely	ATK	DEF	Spicy	Sour
Mild	SP. ATK	DEF	Dry	Sour
Modest	SP. ATK	ATK	Dry	Spicy
Naive	SPD	SP. DEF	Sweet	Bitter
Naughty	ATK	SP. DEF	Spicy	Bitter
Quiet	SP. ATK	SPD	Dry	Sweet
Quirky	—	—	—	—
Rash	SP. ATK	SP. DEF	Dry	Bitter
Relaxed	DEF	SPD	Sour	Sweet
Sassy	SP. DEF	SPD	Bitter	Sweet
Serious	—	—	—	—
Timid	SPD	ATK	Sweet	Spicy

Pokémon Characteristics

On top of having a Nature, each individual Pokémon has a Characteristic. This also affects how the Pokémon's stats grow when it levels up. Characteristics give a hint of which of the Pokémon's stats likely has the highest individual strength.

Stat that grows easily	Characteristic
HP	Loves to eat
	Takes plenty of siestas
	Nods off a lot
	Scatters things often
	Likes to relax
ATTACK	Proud of its power
	Likes to thrash about
	A little quick tempered
	Likes to fight
	Quick tempered
DEFENSE	Sturdy body
	Capable of taking hits
	Highly persistent
	Good endurance
	Good perseverance
SP. ATK	Highly curious
	Mischievous
	Thoroughly cunning
	Often lost in thought
	Very finicky
SP. DEF	Strong willed
	Somewhat vain
	Strongly defiant
	Hates to lose
	Somewhat stubborn
SPEED	Likes to run
	Alert to sounds
	Impetuous and silly
	Somewhat of a clown
	Quick to flee

Items

Item	Description	Main way to obtain	Price
Ability Capsule	Allows a Pokémon with two Abilities (excluding Hidden Abilities) to switch between these Abilities.	Win 50 straight battles at the Battle Tree	—
Absolite	When held, it allows Absol to Mega Evolve into Mega Absol during battle.	Get for 64 BP at the Battle Tree	64 BP
Absorb Bulb	Raises the holder's Sp. Atk by 1 when it is hit by a Water-type move. It goes away after use.	Sometimes held by wild Petilil or Cottonee	—
Adamant Orb	When held by Dialga, it boosts the power of Dragon-and Steel-type moves by 20%.	Buy at Antiquities of the Ages in Hau'oli shopping mall	₽10,000
Adrenaline Orb	Using it makes wild Pokémon more likely to call for help. If held by a Pokémon, it boosts Speed when intimidated. It can only be used once.	Route 4 / Ula'ula Meadow / Ancient Poni Path	₽300
Aerodactylite	When held, it allows Aerodactyl to Mega Evolve into Mega Aerodactyl during battle.	Get for 64 BP at the Battle Tree	64 BP
Air Balloon	The holder floats and Ground-type moves will no longer hit the holder. The balloon pops when the holder is hit by an attack.	Receive from a girl in Malie Garden during the day (after completing the Ula'ula Grand Trial)	—
Alakazite	When held, it allows Alakazam to Mega Evolve into Mega Alakazam during battle.	Get for 64 BP at the Battle Tree	64 BP
Amulet Coin	Doubles the prize money from a battle if the Pokémon holding it joins in.	Paniola Ranch	—
Antidote	Cures the Poisoned status condition.	Buy at any Poké Mart (from the start)	₽200
Armor Fossil	A Pokémon Fossil. When restored, it becomes Shieldon.	Buy at Olivia's shop in Konikoni City	₽7,000
Assault Vest	Raises Sp. Def when held by 50%, but prevents the use of status moves.	Get for 48 BP at the Battle Tree	48 BP

Item	Description	Main way to obtain	Price
Awakening	Cures the Asleep status condition.	Buy at any Poké Mart (from the start)	₽100
Balm Mushroom	A fragrant mushroom. It can be sold at shops for a high price.	Sometimes picked up by a Pokémon with the Pickup Ability	—
Berry Juice	Restores the HP of one Pokémon by 20 points.	Receive at a lottery shop as a prize in Festival Plaza	—
Big Malasada	The Alola region's local specialty—fried bread. It can be used once to heal all the status conditions and confusion of a Pokémon.	Buy at Malasada Shops around Alola	₽350
Big Mushroom	A big mushroom. It can be sold at shops for a high price.	Hau'oli Cemetery / Berry Fields / Heahea City / Malie Garden	—
Big Nugget	A big nugget of pure gold. It can be sold at shops for a high price.	Defeat five Trainers at a bridge in Malie Garden (after defeating Team Skull Boss)	—
Big Pearl	A big pearl. It can be sold at shops for a high price.	Route 8 / Poni Gauntlet / Fishing spots (except Poni Island)	—
Big Root	When the holder uses an HP-draining move, it increases the amount of HP recovered by 30%.	Lush Jungle	—
Binding Band	When held, the damage done to a target by moves like Bind or Wrap will be 1/6 of the target's maximum HP every turn.	Get for 48 BP at the Battle Royal Dome	48 BP
Black Belt	When held by a Pokémon, it boosts the power of Fighting-type moves by 20%.	Sometimes held by wild Makuhita	—
Black Glasses	When held by a Pokémon, it boosts the power of Dark-type moves by 20%.	Hano Beach / Often held by wild Krookodile	—
Black Sludge	If the holder is a Poison-type Pokémon, it restores 1/16 of its maximum HP every turn. If the holder is any other type, it loses 1/8 of its maximum HP every turn.	Sometimes held by wild Grimer or Garbodor	—
Blastoisinite	When held, it allows Blastoise to Mega Evolve into Mega Blastoise during battle.	Defeat Red at the Battle Tree	—
Blue Orb	A shiny blue orb that is said to have a legend tied to it. It's known to have a deep connection with the Hoenn region.	Buy at Antiquities of the Ages in Hau'oli shopping mall	₽10,000
Blue Shard	Can be exchanged for Bottle Caps in Festival Plaza.	Sometimes found by your Pokémon on Isle Aphun in Poké Pelago	—
Bottle Cap	A beautiful bottle cap that gives off a silver gleam. Some people are happy to receive one.	Fishing spots on Poni Island	—
Bright Powder	Lowers the opponent's accuracy.	Get for 48 BP at the Battle Royal Dome	48 BP
Bug Memory	When held by Silvally, its type changes to Bug type.	Receive from Gladion (after becoming Champion)	—
Burn Drive	When held by Genesect, it changes Genesect's Techno Blast move so it becomes Fire type.	Receive from Colress on Route 8 (after becoming Champion)	—
Burn Heal	Cures the Burned status condition.	Buy at any Poké Mart (from the start)	₽300
Calcium	Raises the base Sp. Atk stat of a Pokémon.	Buy at the Poké Mart on Mount Hokulani	₽10,000
Carbos	Raises the base Speed stat of a Pokémon.	Poni Plains / Buy at the Poké Mart on Mount Hokulani	₽10,000
Casteliacone	Heals all the status problems and confusion of a single Pokémon.	Buy a drink at the Pokémon Center café on a Wednesday	—
Cell Battery	Increases Attack by 1 when the holder is hit with Electric-type moves. It goes away after use.	Sometimes held by wild Charjabug	—
Charcoal	When held by a Pokémon, it boosts the power of Fire-type moves by 20%.	Wela Volcano Park	—
Charizardite X	When held, it allows Charizard to Mega Evolve into Mega Charizard X during battle.	Defeat Red at the Battle Tree	—
Charizardite Y	When held, it allows Charizard to Mega Evolve into Mega Charizard Y during battle.	Defeat Red at the Battle Tree	—
Chill Drive	When held by Genesect, it changes Genesect's Techno Blast move so it becomes Ice type.	Receive from Colress on Route 8 (after becoming Champion)	—
Choice Band	The holder can use only one of its moves, but the power of physical moves increases by 50%.	Get for 48 BP at the Battle Tree	48 BP
Choice Scarf	The holder can use only one of its moves, but Speed increases by 50%.	Get for 48 BP at the Battle Tree	48 BP
Choice Specs	The holder can use only one of its moves, but the power of special moves increases by 50%.	Get for 48 BP at the Battle Tree	48 BP
Cleanse Tag	Helps keep wild Pokémon away if the holder is the first one in the party.	Memorial Hill	—
Clever Wing	Slightly increases the base Sp. Def stat of a single Pokémon. It can be used until the max of base stats.	Sometimes dropped on Ula'ula Island by Skarmory	—
Comet Shard	A shard that fell to the ground when a comet approached. It can be sold at shops for a high price.	Poni Coast / Haina Desert	—
Cover Fossil	A Pokémon Fossil. When restored, it becomes Tirtouga.	Buy at Olivia's shop in Konikoni City ☀	₽7,000
Damp Rock	Extends the duration of the rainy weather by three turns when held.	Receive from a woman after taking a quiz at the community center in Malie City	—
Dark Memory	When held by Silvally, its type changes to Dark type.	Receive from Gladion (after becoming Champion)	—
Dawn Stone	It can evolve male Kirlia and female Snorunt.	Sometimes found by your Pokémon on Isle Aphun in Poké Pelago	—
Deep Sea Scale	When held by Clamperl, it doubles Sp. Def. Link Trade Clamperl while it holds the Deep Sea Scale to evolve it into Gorebyss.	Sometimes held by wild Chinchou or Relicanth	—
Deep Sea Tooth	When held by Clamperl, it doubles Sp. Atk. Link Trade Clamperl while it holds the Deep Sea Tooth to evolve it into Huntail.	Sometimes held by wild Carvanha or Sharpedo	—
Destiny Knot	When a Pokémon holding it is inflicted with Infatuation, the Pokémon shares the condition with its attacker.	Get for 48 BP at the Battle Royal Dome	48 BP
Dire Hit	Significantly raises the critical-hit ratio of the Pokémon on which it is used. It can be used only once and wears off if the Pokémon is withdrawn.	Buy at the Poké Mart in Hau'oli City	₽1,000
DNA Splicers	A pair of splicers that fuse Kyurem and Zekrom or Reshiram.	Receive from an Ether Employee in Aether Paradise (after becoming Champion)	—
Douse Drive	When held by Genesect, it changes Genesect's Techno Blast move so it becomes Water type.	Receive from Colress on Route 8 (after becoming Champion)	—

Item	Description	Main way to obtain	Price
Draco Plate	When held by a Pokémon, it boosts the power of Dragon-type moves by 20%. (When held by Arceus, it shifts Arceus's type to Dragon type.)	Hau'oli City Shopping District	—
Dragon Fang	When held by a Pokémon, it boosts the power of Dragon-type moves by 20%.	Sometimes held by Bagon, Shelgon, or Salamence	—
Dragon Memory	When held by Silvally, its type changes to Dragon type.	Receive from Gladion (after becoming Champion)	—
Dragon Scale	Link Trade Seadra while it holds the Dragon Scale to evolve it into Kingdra.	Sometimes held by wild Dratini, Dragonair, or Dragonite	—
Dread Plate	When held by a Pokémon, it boosts the power of Dark-type moves by 20%. (When held by Arceus, it shifts Arceus's type to Dark type.)	Buy at Antiquities of the Ages in Hau'oli shopping mall	₽10,000
Dubious Disc	Link Trade Porygon2 while it holds the Dubious Disc to evolve it into Porygon-Z.	Receive from Faba after defeating him at Aether Paradise (after becoming Champion)	—
Dusk Stone	It can evolve Doublade, Lampent, Misdreavus, and Murkrow.	Poni Wilds	—
Earth Plate	When held by a Pokémon, it boosts the power of Ground-type moves by 20%. (When held by Arceus, it shifts Arceus's type to Ground type.)	Hau'oli Outskirts	—
Eject Button	If the holder is hit by an attack, it switches places with a party Pokémon. It goes away after use.	Get for 32 BP at the Battle Tree	32 BP
Electirizer	Link Trade Electabuzz while it holds the Electirizer to evolve it into Electivire.	Receive from the guy in the southwest houseboat in Seafolk Village	—
Electric Memory	When held by Silvally, its type changes to Electric type.	Receive from Gladion (after becoming Champion)	—
Electric Seed	It boosts Defense of a Pokémon on Electric Terrain by 1 during battle. It can only be used once.	Sometimes held by wild Togedemaru	—
Elixir	Restores the PP of all of a Pokémon's moves by 10 points.	Route 12 / Vast Poni Canyon / Resolution Cave	—
Energy Powder	Restores the HP of one Pokémon by 60 points. Very bitter (lowers a Pokémon's friendship).	Buy at the herb vendor in Konikoni City	₽500
Energy Root	Restores the HP of one Pokémon by 120 points. Very bitter (lowers a Pokémon's friendship).	Buy at the herb vendor in Konikoni City	₽1,200
Escape Rope	Use it to escape instantly from a cave or a dungeon.	Buy at any Poké Mart (from the start)	₽1,000
Ether	Restores the PP of a Pokémon's move by 10 points.	Hau'oli City Shopping District / Route 5 / Paniola Ranch	—
Everstone	Prevents the Pokémon that holds it from evolving.	Visit Ilima's house and defeat him (after completing the Melemele grand trial)	—
Eviolite	Raises Defense and Sp. Def by 50% when held by a Pokémon that can still evolve.	Konikoni City	—
Expert Belt	Raises the power of supereffective moves by 20%.	Seaward Cave	—
Fairy Memory	When held by Silvally, its type changes to Fairy type.	Receive from Gladion (after becoming Champion)	—
Festival Ticket	A ticket that allows you to host a mission in Festival Plaza.	Receive daily from the woman in Festival Plaza (after reaching Rank 4)	—
Fighting Memory	When held by Silvally, its type changes to Fighting type.	Receive from Gladion (after becoming Champion)	—
Fire Memory	When held by Silvally, its type changes to Fire type.	Receive from Gladion (after becoming Champion)	—
Fire Stone	It can evolve Eevee, Growlithe, Pansear, and Vulpix.	Buy at Olivia's jewelry shop in Konikoni City	₽3,000
Fist Plate	When held by a Pokémon, it boosts the power of Fighting-type moves by 20%. (When held by Arceus, it shifts Arceus's type to Fighting type.)	Buy at Antiquities of the Ages in Hau'oli shopping mall	₽10,000
Flame Orb	Inflicts the Burned status condition on the holder during battle.	Defeat all the Trainers in Ula'ula Meadow	—
Flame Plate	When held by a Pokémon, it boosts the power of Fire-type moves by 20%. (When held by Arceus, it shifts Arceus's type to Fire type.)	Trainers' School	—
Float Stone	Halves the holder's weight.	Get for 48 BP at the Battle Royal Dome	48 BP
Flying Memory	When held by Silvally, its type changes to Flying type.	Receive from Gladion (after becoming Champion)	—
Focus Band	Has a 10% chance of leaving the holder with 1 HP when it receives damage that would cause it to faint.	Receive from a Police Officer in Route 9 Police Station (after completing the Akala grand trial)	—
Focus Sash	A holder with full HP is left with 1 HP when it is hit by a move that would cause it to faint. Then the item disappears.	Defeat all the Trainers in the Poni Wilds	—
Fresh Water	Restores the HP of one Pokémon by 30 points.	Buy at a vending machine	Varies
Full Heal	Cures all status conditions and confusion.	Buy at any Poké Mart (after completing 5 trials)	₽400
Full Incense	When held by a Pokémon, it makes the holder move later.	Buy at the incense vendor in Konikoni City	₽5,000
Full Restore	Restore the HP of a Pokémon and cures status conditions and confusion.	Buy at any Poké Mart (after completing 7 trials)	₽3,000
Garchompite	When held, it allows Garchomp to Mega Evolve into Mega Garchomp during battle.	Get for 64 BP at the Battle Tree	64 BP
Gengarite	When held, it allows Gengar to Mega Evolve into Mega Gengar during battle.	Get for 64 BP at the Battle Tree	64 BP
Genius Wing	Slightly increases the base Sp. Atk stat of a single Pokémon. It can be used until the base stat reaches its maximum value.	Sometimes dropped on Poni Island by Braviary and Mandibuzz	—
Ghost Memory	When held by Silvally, its type changes to Ghost type.	Receive from Gladion (after becoming Champion)	—
Glalitite	When held, it allows Glalie to Mega Evolve into Mega Glalie during battle.	Get for 64 BP at the Battle Tree	64 BP
Gold Bottle Cap	A beautiful bottle cap that gives off a golden gleam. Some people are happy to receive one.	Sometimes found by your Pokémon on Isle Aphun in Poké Pelago	—
Gracidea	A flower to convey gratitude. Shaymin will change its Forme if Gracidea is used on it (except at night).	Receive from a clerk in the Gracidea apparel shop in Hau'oli shopping mall	—
Grass Memory	When held by Silvally, its type changes to Grass type.	Receive from Gladion (after becoming Champion)	—
Grassy Seed	It boosts Defense of a Pokémon on Grassy Terrain by 1 during battle. It can only be used once.	Malie Garden / Sometimes held by wild Bounsweet	—
Green Shard	Can be exchanged for Bottle Caps in Festival Plaza.	Sometimes found by your Pokémon on Isle Aphun in Poké Pelago	—

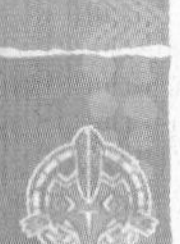

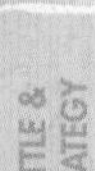

Item	Description	Main way to obtain	Price
Grip Claw	Extends the duration of moves like Bind and Wrap to seven turns.	Sometimes held by wild Sandshrew	—
Griseous Orb	When held by Giratina, it changes it into its Origin Forme, and boosts the power of Dragon- and Ghost-type moves by 20%.	Buy at Antiquities of the Ages in Hau'oli shopping mall	₽10,000
Ground Memory	When held by Silvally, its type changes to Ground type.	Receive from Gladion (after becoming Champion)	—
Guard Spec.	Prevents stat reduction among the Trainer's party Pokémon for five turns. It can be used only once.	Buy at the Poké Mart in Hau'oli City	₽1,500
Gyaradosite	When held, it allows Gyarados to Mega Evolve into Mega Gyarados during battle.	Get for 64 BP at the Battle Tree	64 BP
Hard Stone	When held by a Pokémon, it boosts the power of Rock-type moves by 20%.	Ten Carat Hill / Sometimes held by wild Roggenrola or Boldore	—
Heal Powder	Cures all status conditions and confusion. Very bitter (lowers a Pokémon's friendship).	Buy at the herb vendor in Konikoni City	₽300
Health Wing	Slightly increases the base HP of a single Pokémon. It can be used until the max of base stats.	Sometimes dropped on Ula'ula and Poni Islands by Fearow	—
Heart Scale	A pretty, heart-shaped scale that is extremely rare. Highly sought-after by certain people.	Seafolk Village's floating restaurant / Fishing spots on Akala Island / Often held by wild Luvdisc	—
Heat Rock	When held by a Pokémon, it extends the duration of the sunny weather by three turns.	Receive from a woman after taking a quiz at the community center in Malie City	—
Honey	Attracts wild Pokémon where wild Pokémon can appear.	Buy at any Poké Mart (after completing 2 trials)	₽300
HP Up	Raises the base HP of a Pokémon.	Royal Avenue / Buy at the Poké Mart on Mount Hokulani	₽10,000
Hyper Potion	Restores the HP of one Pokémon by 120 points.	Buy at any Poké Mart (after completing 4 trials)	₽1,500
Ice Heal	Cures the Frozen status condition.	Buy at any Poké Mart (from the start)	₽100
Ice Memory	When held by Silvally, its type changes to Ice type.	Receive from Gladion (after becoming Champion)	—
Ice Stone	It can evolve Alolan Vulpix and Alolan Sandshrew.	Po Town	—
Icicle Plate	When held by a Pokémon, it boosts the power of Ice-type moves by 20%. (When held by Arceus, it shifts Arceus's type to Ice type.)	Hau'oli City Beachfront	—
Icy Rock	Extends the duration of the hail by three turns when held.	Receive from a woman after taking a quiz at the community center in Malie City	—
Insect Plate	When held by a Pokémon, it boosts the power of Bug-type moves by 20%. (When held by Arceus, it shifts Arceus's type to Bug type.)	Hau'oli City Shopping District	—
Iron	Raises the base Defense stat of a Pokémon.	Shady House / Buy at the Poké Mart on Mount Hokulani	₽10,000
Iron Ball	Halves the holder's Speed. If the holder has the Levitate Ability or is a Flying-type Pokémon, Ground-type moves can hit it.	Get for 16 BP at the Battle Tree	16 BP
Iron Plate	When held by a Pokémon, it boosts the power of Steel-type moves by 20%. (When held by Arceus, it shifts Arceus's type to Steel type.)	Buy at Antiquities of the Ages in Hau'oli shopping mall	₽10,000
Kangaskhanite	When held, it allows Kangaskhan to Mega Evolve into Mega Kangaskhan during battle.	Get for 64 BP at the Battle Tree	64 BP
Key Stone	A stone filled with an unexplained power. It makes Pokémon that battle with a Mega Stone Mega Evolve.	Receive from Dexio (after becoming Champion)	—
King's Rock	When the holder successfully inflicts damage, the target may also flinch. Link Trade Poliwhirl or Slowpoke while they hold a King's Rock to evolve them.	Sometimes held by wild Slowbro, Hariyama, Poliwhirl, or Politoed	—
Lagging Tail	When held by a Pokémon, it makes it move later.	Sometimes held by wild Slowpoke	—
Lava Cookie	Lavaridge Town's famous specialty. Cures all status conditions and confusion.	Buy a drink at the Pokémon Center café on a Saturday	—
Lax Incense	Boosts the holder's evasion.	Buy at the incense vendor in Konikoni City	₽5,000
Leaf Stone	It can evolve Exeggcute, Gloom, Nuzleaf, Pansage, and Weepinbell.	Buy at Olivia's jewelry shop in Konikoni City	₽3,000
Leftovers	It restores 1/16 of the holder's maximum HP every turn.	Often held by wild Munchlax or Snorlax	—
Lemonade	Restores the HP of one Pokémon by 70 points.	Buy at a vending machine	Varies
Life Orb	Lowers the holder's HP each time it attacks, but raises the power of moves by 30%.	Resolution Cave	—
Light Ball	Doubles the power of both physical and special moves when held by Pikachu.	Resolution Cave / Sometimes held by wild Pikachu	—
Light Clay	Extends the duration of moves like Reflect, Light Screen, and Aurora Veil by three turns.	Sometimes held by wild Mudbray or Mudsdale	—
Lucarionite	When held, it allows Lucario to Mega Evolve into Mega Lucario during battle.	Get for 64 BP at the Battle Tree	64 BP
Luck Incense	Doubles prize money from a battle if the holding Pokémon joins in.	Buy at the incense vendor in Konikoni City	₽11,000
Lucky Egg	Increases the number of Experience Points received from battle by 50%.	Receive from Professor Kukui when your Pokédex is filled by a few dozen Pokémon (after becoming Champion)	—
Lucky Punch	It is a pair of gloves that boosts Chansey's critical-hit ratio.	Receive from a Rising Star in the northeast houseboat in Seafolk Village	—
Luminous Moss	Increases Sp. Def by 1 when the holder is hit with Water-type moves. It goes away after use.	Sometimes held by wild Corsola	—
Lumiose Galette	A popular pastry sold in Lumiose City. Cures all status conditions and confusion for one Pokémon.	Buy a drink at the Pokémon Center café on a Monday	—
Lustrous Orb	When held by Palkia, it boosts the power of Dragon- and Water-type moves by 20%.	Buy at Antiquities of the Ages in Hau'oli shopping mall	₽10,000
Magmarizer	Link Trade Magmar while it holds the Magmarizer to evolve it into Magmortar.	Receive from the guy in the southwest houseboat in Seafolk Village	—
Magnet	When held by a Pokémon, it boosts the power of Electric-type moves by 20%.	Sometimes held by wild Nosepass	—
Max Elixir	Completely restores the PP of all of a Pokémon's moves.	Sometimes picked up by a Pokémon with the Pickup Ability	—

Item	Description	Main way to obtain	Price
Max Ether	Completely restores the PP of a Pokémon's move.	Receive from Hau in Diglett's Tunnel	—
Max Potion	Completely restores the HP of a single Pokémon.	Buy at any Poké Mart (after completing 6 trials)	₽2,500
Max Repel	Prevents weak wild Pokémon from appearing for a long while after its use.	Buy at any Poké Mart (after completing 5 trials)	₽900
Max Revive	Revives a fainted Pokémon and fully restores its HP.	Seaward Cave / Lush Jungle / Shady House	—
Meadow Plate	When held by a Pokémon, it boosts the power of Grass-type moves by 20%. (When held by Arceus, it shifts Arceus's type to Grass type.)	Hau'oli City Shopping District	—
Mental Herb	The holder shakes off the effects of Attract, Disable, Encore, Heal Block, Taunt, and Torment. It goes away after use.	Sometimes held by wild Pancham	—
Metagrossite	When held, it allows Metagross to Mega Evolve into Mega Metagross during battle.	Get for 64 BP at the Battle Tree	64 BP
Metal Coat	When held by a Pokémon, it boosts the power of Steel-type moves by 20%. Link Trade Onix or Scyther while they hold a Metal Coat to evolve them.	Sometimes held by wild Magnemite, Skarmory, or Beldum	—
Metal Powder	When held by Ditto, Defense doubles.	Sometimes held by wild Ditto	—
Metronome	When held, it raises the power of a move used consecutively by that Pokémon (up to a maximum increase of 100%)	Receive from the Veteran in Grand Hano Resort	—
Mind Plate	When held by a Pokémon, it boosts the power of Psychic-type moves by 20%. (When held by Arceus, it shifts Arceus's type to Psychic type.)	Hau'oli Outskirts	—
Miracle Seed	When held by a Pokémon, it boosts the power of Grass-type moves by 20%.	Route 8 / Sometimes held by wild Fomantis	—
Misty Seed	It boosts Sp. Def of a Pokémon on Misty Terrain by 1 during battle. It can only be used once.	Poni Gauntlet / Sometimes held by wild Comfey	—
Moomoo Milk	Restores the HP of one Pokémon by 100 points.	Often held by wild Miltank	—
Moon Stone	It can evolve Clefairy, Jigglypuff, Munna, Nidorina, Nidorino, and Skitty.	Route 13	—
Muscle Band	When held by a Pokémon, it boosts the power of physical moves by 10%.	Visit Lana's house in Konikoni City and defeat Lana and her little sisters (after completing the Akala grand trial)	—
Muscle Wing	Slightly increases the base Attack stat of a single Pokémon. It can be used until the max of base stats.	Sometimes dropped on Poni Island by Braviary and Mandibuzz	—
Mystic Water	When held by a Pokémon, it boosts the power of Water-type moves by 20%.	Sometimes held by wild Dewpider, Araquanid, or Goldeen	—
Never-Melt Ice	When held by a Pokémon, it boosts the power of Ice-type moves by 20%.	Seaward Cave	—
Normal Gem	It boosts the power of a Normal-type move by 30% one time. It goes away after use.	Route 15	—
Nugget	A nugget of pure gold. It can be sold at shops for a high price.	Route 1 / Ten Carat Hill / Malie City Outer Cape	—
Odd Incense	When held by a Pokémon, it boosts the power of Psychic-type moves by 20%.	Buy at the incense vendor in Konikoni City	₽2,000
Old Gateau	The Old Chateau's hidden specialty. It can heal all the status conditions and confusion.	Buy a drink at the Pokémon Center café on a Thursday	—
Oval Charm	An oval charm said to increase the chance of Pokémon Eggs being found at the Nursery.	Receive from Morimoto at GAME FREAK's office in Heahea City after defeating him (after becoming Champion)	—
Oval Stone	Level up Happiny between 4 a.m. and 7:59 p.m. while it holds the Oval Stone to evolve it into Chansey.	Often held by wild Happiny	—
Paralyze Heal	Cures the Paralysis status condition.	Buy at any Poké Mart (from the start)	₽300
Pearl	A pretty pearl. It can be sold at shops for a low price.	Fishing spots / often held by wild Shellder	—
Pearl String	Very large pearls that sparkle in a pretty silver collar. It can be sold at shops for a high price.	Hano Beach / Poni Wilds / Fishing spots on Melemele Island	—
Pink Nectar	It changes the form of Oricorio.	Sparkling spots near the flowering shrubs in the middle of Royal Avenue	—
Pinsirite	When held, it allows Pinsir to Mega Evolve into Mega Pinsir during battle.	Get for 64 BP at the Battle Tree	64 BP
Pixie Plate	When held by a Pokémon, it boosts the power of Fairy-type moves by 20%. (When held by Arceus, it shifts Arceus's type to Fairy type.)	Buy at Antiquities of the Ages in Hau'oli shopping mall	₽10,000
Plume Fossil	A Pokémon Fossil. When restored, it becomes Archen.	Buy at Olivia's shop in Konikoni City	₽7,000
Poison Barb	When held by a Pokémon, it boosts the power of Poison-type moves by 20%.	Melemele Meadow	—
Poison Memory	When held by Silvally, its type changes to Poison type.	Receive from Gladion (after becoming Champion)	—
Poké Doll	Ensures that the holder can successfully run from a wild Pokémon encounter.	Receive from Lillie in Hau'oli City's Marina (after becoming Champion)	—
Poké Toy	Ensures that the holder can successfully run from a wild Pokémon encounter.	Buy a Toy Set at a goody shop in Festival Plaza	—
Potion	Restores the HP of one Pokémon by 20 points.	Buy at any Poké Mart (from the start)	₽200
Power Anklet	Halves the holder's Speed, but makes the Speed base stat easier to raise.	Get for 16 BP at the Battle Royal Dome	16 BP
Power Band	Halves the holder's Speed, but makes the Sp. Def base stat easier to raise.	Get for 16 BP at the Battle Royal Dome	16 BP
Power Belt	Halves the holder's Speed, but makes the Defense base stat easier to raise.	Get for 16 BP at the Battle Royal Dome	16 BP
Power Bracer	Halves the holder's Speed, but makes the Attack base stat easier to raise.	Get for 16 BP at the Battle Royal Dome	16 BP
Power Herb	The holder can immediately use a move that requires a one-turn charge. It goes away after use.	Poni Meadow	—
Power Lens	Halves the holder's Speed, but makes the Sp. Atk base stat easier to raise.	Get for 16 BP at the Battle Royal Dome	16 BP
Power Weight	Halves the holder's Speed, but makes the HP base stat easier to raise.	Get for 16 BP at the Battle Royal Dome	16 BP
PP Max	Increases the max number of PP as high as it will go.	Defeat all the Trainers on Route 15	—
PP Up	Increases the max number of PP by one level.	Route 16	—
Pretty Wing	A beautiful feather. It can be sold at shops for a low price.	Sometimes dropped by Pokémon flying overhead on Route 3	—
Prism Scale	Link Trade Feebas while it holds the Prism Scale to evolve it into Milotic.	Exeggutor Island / Fishing spots on Ula'ula Island	—

Item	Description	Main way to obtain	Price
Prison Bottle	A bottle believed to have been used to seal away the power of a certain Pokémon long, long ago.	Receive from an Ether Employee in Aether Paradise (after becoming Champion)	—
Protective Pads	These pads protect the holder from effects caused by making direct contact with the target.	Get for 48 BP at the Battle Tree	48 BP
Protector	Link Trade Rhydon while it holds the Protector to evolve it into Rhyperior.	Receive from Kiawe's father in his house in Paniola Town (after becoming Champion)	—
Protein	Raises the base Attack stat of a Pokémon.	Buy at the Poké Mart on Mount Hokulani	₽10,000
Psychic Memory	When held by Silvally, its type changes to Psychic type.	Receive from Gladion (after becoming Champion)	—
Psychic Seed	It boosts Sp. Def of a Pokémon on Psychic Terrain by 1 during battle. It can only be used once.	Sometimes held by wild Exeggcute	—
Pure Incense	Helps keep wild Pokémon away if the holder is the first one in the party.	Buy at the incense vendor in Konikoni City	₽6,000
Purple Nectar	It changes the form of Oricorio.	Sparkling spots in Poni Meadow	—
Quick Claw	Allows the holder to strike first sometimes.	Receive from a woman in Trainers' School	—
Quick Powder	When held by Ditto, Speed doubles.	Often held by wild Ditto	—
Rage Candy Bar	Mahogany Town's famous snack. Heals all the status conditions and confusion of a Pokémon.	Buy a drink at the Pokémon Center café on a Tuesday	—
Rare Bone	A rare bone. It can be sold at shops for a high price.	Sometimes found by your Pokémon on Isle Aphun in Poké Pelago	—
Rare Candy	Raises a Pokémon's level by 1.	Brooklet Hill / Route 6 / Aether Paradise / Po Town	—
Razor Claw	Boosts the holder's critical-hit ratio.	Often held by wild Kommo-o	—
Razor Fang	When the holder hits a target with an attack, there is a 10% chance the target will flinch.	Sometimes held by wild Bruxish	—
Reaper Cloth	Link Trade Dusclops while it holds the Reaper Cloth to evolve it into Dusknoir.	Receive from the little girl in the Malie City Pokémon Center (after completing the Ula'ula grand trial)	—
Red Card	If the holder is hit by an attack that makes direct contact, the opposing Trainer is forced to switch out the attacking Pokémon. It goes away after use.	Defeat all the Trainers on Route 3	—
Red Nectar	It changes the form of Oricorio.	Sparkling spots in Ula'ula Meadow	—
Red Orb	A shiny red orb that is said to have a legend tied to it. It's known to have a deep connection with the Hoenn region.	Buy at Antiquities of the Ages in Hau'oli shopping mall	₽10,000
Red Shard	Can be exchanged for Bottle Caps in Festival Plaza.	Sometimes found by your Pokémon on Isle Aphun in Poké Pelago	—
Repel	Prevents weak wild Pokémon from appearing for a while after its use.	Buy at any Poké Mart (from the start)	₽400
Resist Wing	Slightly increases the base Defense stat of a single Pokémon. It can be used until the max of base stats.	Sometimes dropped on Ula'ula Island by Skarmory	—
Reveal Glass	A looking glass necessary to change Tornadus, Thundurus, and Landorus from Incarnate Forme into Therian Forme.	Receive from Professor Burnet at the Dimensional Research Lab (after completing the Akala grand trial)	—
Revival Herb	Revives a fainted Pokémon. Very bitter (lowers a Pokémon's friendship).	Buy at the herb vendor in Konikoni City	₽2,800
Revive	Revives a fainted Pokémon and restores half of its HP.	Buy at any Poké Mart (after completing 2 trials)	₽2,000
Ring Target	Moves that would otherwise have no effect will hit the holder.	Get for 16 BP at the Battle Tree	16 BP
Rock Incense	When held by a Pokémon, it boosts the power of Rock-type moves by 20%.	Buy at the incense vendor in Konikoni City	₽2,000
Rock Memory	When held by Silvally, its type changes to Rock type.	Receive from Gladion (after becoming Champion)	—
Rocky Helmet	When the bearer is hit with an attack that makes direct contact, it damages the attacker for 1/6 of its maximum HP.	Get for 48 BP at the Battle Tree	48 BP
Rose Incense	When held by a Pokémon, it boosts the power of Grass-type moves by 20%.	Buy at the incense vendor in Konikoni City	₽2,000
Sablenite	When held, it allows Sableye to Mega Evolve into Mega Sableye during battle.	Get for 64 BP at the Battle Tree	64 BP
Sachet	Link Trade Spritzee while it holds the Sachet to evolve it into Aromatisse.	Receive from the Punk Girl at Mallow's restaurant in Konikoni City (after becoming Champion)	—
Sacred Ash	Revives fainted Pokémon in a party and fully restores their HP.	Sometimes picked up by your Pokémon at a haunted house in Festival Plaza	—
Safety Goggles	Protect the holder from weather-related damage, from certain moves (Cotton Spore, Poison Powder, Powder, Rage Powder, Sleep Powder, Spore, and Stun Spore), and from the Effect Spore Ability.	Receive from the Hiker in Haina Desert at night (after completing the Ula'ula grand trial)	—
Salamencite	When held, it allows Salamence to Mega Evolve into Mega Salamence during battle.	Get for 64 BP at the Battle Tree	64 BP
Scizorite	When held, it allows Scizor to Mega Evolve into Mega Scizor during battle.	Get for 64 BP at the Battle Tree	64 BP
Scope Lens	Boosts the holder's critical-hit ratio.	Receive from a man after defeating his Tauros in Paniola Ranch	—
Sea Incense	When held by a Pokémon, it boosts the power of Water-type moves by 20%.	Buy at the incense vendor in Konikoni City	₽2,000
Shalour Sable	Shalour City's famous shortbread. It can be used once to heal all the status conditions and confusion of a Pokémon.	Buy a drink at the Pokémon Center café on a Friday	—
Sharp Beak	When held by a Pokémon, it boosts the power of Flying-type moves by 20%.	Route 3 / Sometimes held by wild Spearow or Fearow	—
Sharpedonite	When held, it allows Sharpedo to Mega Evolve into Mega Sharpedo during battle.	Get for 64 BP at the Battle Tree	64 BP
Shed Shell	Always allows the holder to be switched out.	Sometimes held by wild Goomy or Sliggoo	—
Shell Bell	Restores the holder's HP by up to 1/8th of the damage dealt to the target.	Receive from Delibird in the city hall in Hau'oli City (after completing the Melemele Grand Trial)	—
Shiny Charm	A shiny charm said to increase the change of finding a Shiny Pokémon in the wild.	Receive from the game director after completing the Alola Pokédex and showing it to him at GAME FREAK's office in Heahea City	—

Item	Description	Main way to obtain	Price
Shiny Stone	It can evolve Floette, Minccino, Togetic, and Roselia.	Ancient Poni Path	—
Shock Drive	When held by Genesect, it changes Genesect's Techno Blast move so it becomes Electric type.	Receive from Colress on Route 8 (after becoming Champion)	—
Silk Scarf	When held by a Pokémon, it boosts the power of Normal-type moves by 20%.	Receive from the woman outside the apparel shop in Hau'oli City	—
Silver Powder	When held by a Pokémon, it boosts the power of Bug-type moves by 20%.	Berry Fields	—
Skull Fossil	A Pokémon Fossil. When restored, it becomes Cranidos.	Buy at Olivia's shop in Konikoni City	₽7,000
Sky Plate	When held by a Pokémon, it boosts the power of Flying-type moves by 20%. (When held by Arceus, it shifts Arceus's type to Flying type.)	Buy at Antiquities of the Ages in Hau'oli shopping mall	₽10,000
Slowbronite	When held, it allows Slowbro to Mega Evolve into Mega Slowbro during battle.	Get for 64 BP at the Battle Tree	64 BP
Smoke Ball	Allows the holder to successfully run away from wild Pokémon.	Po Town / Sometimes held by wild Salandit	—
Smooth Rock	Extends the duration of the sandstorm weather by three turns when held.	Receive from a woman after taking a quiz at the community center in Malie City	—
Snowball	Increases Attack by 1 when the holder is hit with Ice-type moves. It goes away after use.	Sometimes held by wild Snorunt or Vulpix	—
Soda Pop	Restores the HP of one Pokémon by 50 points.	Buy at a vending machine	Varies
Soft Sand	When held by a Pokémon, it boosts the power of Ground-type moves by 20%.	Melemele Sea / Sometimes held by wild Diglett or Dugtrio	—
Soothe Bell	The holder's friendship improves more quickly.	Receive from the Pokémon Breeder on Route 3	—
Soul Dew	When held by Latios or Latias, it boosts the power of Dragon- and Psychic-type moves by 20%.	Receive from an Ether Employee in Aether Paradise (after becoming Champion)	—
Spell Tag	When held by a Pokémon, it boosts the power of Ghost-type moves by 20%.	Memorial Hill / Sometimes held by wild Sandygast or Palossand	—
Splash Plate	When held by a Pokémon, it boosts the power of Water-type moves by 20%. (When held by Arceus, it shifts Arceus's type to Water type.)	Buy at Antiquities of the Ages in Hau'oli shopping mall	₽10,000
Spooky Plate	When held by a Pokémon, it boosts the power of Ghost-type moves by 20%. (When held by Arceus, it shifts Arceus's type to Ghost type.)	Hau'oli Cemetery	—
Star Piece	A red gem. It can be sold at shops for a high price.	Route 2 / Poni Plains	—
Stardust	Lovely, red-colored sand. It can be sold at shops for a low price.	Often held by wild Staryu or Starmie	—
Steel Memory	When held by Silvally, its type changes to Steel type.	Receive from Gladion (after becoming Champion)	—
Stick	When held by Farfetch'd, it raises the critical-hit ratio of its moves.	Receive from an Aether Employee in Aether Paradise	—
Sticky Barb	Damages the holder by 1/8 of its maximum HP every turn. It latches on to the attacker that touches the holder if the attacker doesn't have an item.	Fishing spots on Poni Island	—
Stone Plate	When held by a Pokémon, it boosts the power of Rock-type moves by 20%. (When held by Arceus, it shifts Arceus's type to Rock type.)	Buy at Antiquities of the Ages in Hau'oli shopping mall	₽10,000
Strange Souvenir	An ornament depicting a mysterious Pokémon that has been venerated as a guardian deity for an extremely long time in the Alola region.	Receive from the Gentleman in the community center in Malie City	—
Sun Stone	It can evolve Cottonee, Gloom, Helioptile, Petilil, and Sunkern.	Blush Mountain	—
Super Potion	Restores the HP of one Pokémon by 60 points.	Buy at any Poké Mart (after completing 1 trial)	₽700
Super Repel	Prevents weak wild Pokémon from appearing for a long while after its use.	Buy at any Poké Mart (after completing 3 trials)	₽700
Sweet Heart	Restores the HP of one Pokémon by 20 points.	Buy a drink at the Pokémon Center café on a Sunday	—
Swift Wing	Slightly increases the base Speed stat of a single Pokémon. It can be used until the max of base stats.	Sometimes dropped on Ula'ula and Poni Islands by Fearow	—
Terrain Extender	An item to be held by a Pokémon. It extends the effects of terrain by three turns.	Resolution Cave	—
Thick Club	When held by Cubone or Marowak, the power of Physical Moves is doubled.	Sometimes held by wild Cubone	—
Thunder Stone	It can evolve Eelektrik, Eevee, and Pikachu.	Buy at Olivia's jewelry shop in Konikoni City	₽3,000
Tiny Mushroom	A tiny mushroom. It can be sold at shops for a low price.	Route 11 / Hau'oli City Shopping District	—
Toxic Orb	Inflicts the Badly Poisoned status condition on the holder during battle.	Get for 16 BP at the Battle Tree	16 BP
Toxic Plate	When held by a Pokémon, it boosts the power of Poison-type moves by 20%. (When held by Arceus, it shifts Arceus's type to Poison type.)	Hau'oli City Shopping District	—
Twisted Spoon	When held by a Pokémon, it boosts the power of Psychic-type moves by 20%.	Receive from the Janitor after defeating him and his son in Malie City Outer Cape	—
Up-Grade	Link Trade Porygon while it holds the Up-Grade to evolve it into Porygon2.	Receive from an Aether Employee in Aether House (after completing the Ula'ula Grand Trial)	—
Venusaurite	When held, it allows Venusaur to Mega Evolve into Mega Venusaur during battle.	Defeat Red at the Battle Tree	—
Water Memory	When held by Silvally, its type changes to Water type.	Receive from Gladion (after becoming Champion)	—
Water Stone	It can evolve Eevee, Lombre, Panpour, Poliwhirl, Shellder, and Staryu.	Buy at Olivia's jewelry shop in Konikoni City	₽3,000
Wave Incense	When held by a Pokémon, it boosts the power of Water-type moves by 20%.	Buy at the incense vendor in Konikoni City	₽2,000
Weakness Policy	Increases Attack and Sp. Atk by 2 if the holder is hit with a move that it's weak to.	Get for 32 BP at the Battle Tree	32 BP
Whipped Dream	Link Trade Swirlix while it holds a Whipped Dream to evolve it into Slurpuff.	Receive from the Punk Girl at Mallow's restaurant in Konikoni City (after becoming Champion)	—
White Herb	Restores lowered stats. It goes away after use.	Get for 24 BP at the Battle Tree	24 BP
Wide Lens	Raises the holder's accuracy by 10%.	Talk to a Corsola in front of the Pokémon Research Lab (after obtaining a Fishing Rod)	—
Wise Glasses	When held by a Pokémon, it boosts the power of special moves by 10%.	Get for 48 BP at the Battle Royal Dome	48 BP

Item	Description	Main way to obtain	Price
X Accuracy	Raises the accuracy of a Pokémon by 2 during battle.	Buy at the Poké Mart in Hau'oli City	₽1,000
X Attack	Raises the Attack stat of a Pokémon by 2 during battle.	Buy at the Poké Mart in Hau'oli City	₽1,000
X Defense	Raises the Defense stat of a Pokémon by 2 during battle.	Buy at the Poké Mart in Hau'oli City	₽2,000
X Sp. Atk	Raises the Sp. Atk stat of a Pokémon by 2 during battle.	Buy at the Poké Mart in Hau'oli City	₽1,000
X Sp. Def	Raises the Sp. Def stat of a Pokémon by 2 during battle.	Buy at the Poké Mart in Hau'oli City	₽2,000
X Speed	Raises the Speed of a Pokémon by 2 during battle.	Buy at the Poké Mart in Hau'oli City	₽1,000
Yellow Nectar	It changes the form of Oricorio.	Sparkling spots in Melemele Meadow	—
Yellow Shard	Can be exchanged for Bottle Caps in Festival Plaza.	Sometimes found by your Pokémon on Isle Aphun in Poké Pelago	—
Zap Plate	When held by a Pokémon, it boosts the power of Electric-type moves by 20%. (When held by Arceus, it shifts Arceus's type to Electric type.)	Buy at Antiquities of the Ages in Hau'oli shopping mall	₽10,000
Zinc	Raises the base Sp. Def stat of a Pokémon.	Buy at the Poké Mart on Mount Hokulani	₽10,000
Zoom Lens	Raises the holder's accuracy by 20% when it moves after the opposing Pokémon.	Get for 48 BP at the Battle Royal Dome	48 BP

Note: For a list of Z-Crystals and where to find them, turn to page 246. For a list of TMs and how to obtain them, turn to page 334.

Poké Balls Available in Alola

	Name	Description	Main Way to Obtain in Alola	Effect in Battle	Price
	Poké Ball	Standard Poké Ball with a decent success rate	Buy it at the Thrifty Megamart on Royal Avenue or at any Poké Mart		₽100/200
	Great Ball	High-performance Poké Ball with a high success rate	Buy it at the Thrifty Megamart on Royal Avenue or at any Poké Mart (after completing one trial)		₽300/600
	Ultra Ball	Ultra high-performance Poké Ball with a very high success rate	Buy it at any Poké Mart (after completing four trials)		₽800
	Master Ball	Guaranteed to catch any Pokémon	Receive one from Gladion		
	Luxury Ball	Quickly makes the caught Pokémon feel friendly toward you	Buy it at the Route 2 Poké Mart		₽1,000
	Heal Ball	Restores HP and removes status conditions for the caught Pokémon	Buy it at the Thrifty Megamart on Royal Avenue or at the Route 2 Poké Mart		₽150/300
	Nest Ball	Best for catching low-level Pokémon	Buy it at the Thrifty Megamart on Royal Avenue or at the Route 2 Poké Mart		₽500/ 1,000
	Repeat Ball	Best for catching a Pokémon species you've caught before	Buy it at the Paniola Town Poké Mart		₽1,000
	Net Ball	Best for catching Water- or Bug-type Pokémon	Buy it at the Paniola Town Poké Mart		₽1,000
	Dive Ball	Best for catching Pokémon that live underwater	Buy it at the Route 8 Poké Mart		₽1,000
	Dusk Ball	Best for catching Pokémon at night or in dark places like caves	Buy it at the Route 8 Poké Mart		₽1,000
	Quick Ball	Best for using at the very outset of a battle	Buy it at the Route 8 Poké Mart		₽1,000
	Timer Ball	Best for using when a battle has lasted many turns	Buy it at the Thrifty Megamart on Royal Avenue or at the Paniola Town Poké Mart		₽500/ 1,000
	Premier Ball	Rare Poké Ball made to celebrate an event of some sort	Buy 10 or more Poké Balls at a time		
	Fast Ball	Best for catching Pokémon that normally run away	Find one on Mount Hokulani		
	Level Ball	Best for catching Pokémon with a lower level than your Pokémon	Find one on Mount Hokulani		
	Lure Ball	Best for catching Pokémon found through fishing	Receive one from Samson Oak (p. 159)		
	Heavy Ball	Best for catching Pokémon that weigh a lot	Find one on Mount Hokulani		
	Love Ball	Best for catching Pokémon of the opposite gender to your Pokémon	Receive one from Samson Oak (p. 145)		
	Friend Ball	Immediately makes the caught Pokémon feel friendly toward you	Receive one from Samson Oak (p. 148)		
	Moon Ball	Best for catching Pokémon that evolve with a Moon Stone	Receive one from Samson Oak (p. 152)		
	Beast Ball	Best for catching Ultra Beasts	Receive from Wicke when assisting Looker after becoming Champion		

Note: There are other Poké Balls that cannot be obtained in *Pokémon Sun* or *Pokémon Moon*. But if you obtain a Pokémon via a trade, special event, or other means, check out the special effects of other unique balls like Cherish Balls or Sport Balls when your Pokémon pop into battle!

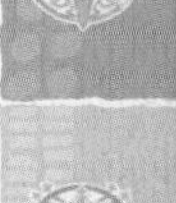

Berries

	Name	Pokémon Effects	Dye Color	Avg. Hours to Grow	Typical Harvest	Main Way to Obtain in Alola
	Aguav Berry	Restores some HP when in a pinch, but confuses Pokémon that don't like bitter flavors	Dark Green	24	3-9	Berry tree on Route 4 (p. 92)
	Apicot Berry	Raises the holder's Sp. Def when in a pinch	Pastel Navy Blue	72	2-8	Berry tree on Secluded Shore (p. 157)
	Aspear Berry	Allows a Pokémon to recover from being Frozen during battle	Dark Yellow	24	4-12	Berry tree on Secluded Shore (p. 157)
	Babiri Berry	Lessens the damage from one supereffective Steel-type attack when held	—	48	2-6	Central Berry tree in Poni Wilds (p. 192)
	Bluk Berry	An unusual Berry not normally found in the Alola region	—	24	4-12	Thrifty Megamart (p. 109)
	Charti Berry	Lessens the damage from one supereffective Rock-type attack when held	Dark Orange	48	2-6	Northwest Berry tree in Poni Wilds (p. 192)
	Cheri Berry	Allows a Pokémon to cure its own Paralysis during battle	Pastel Red	24	4-12	Berry tree on Route 3 (p. 73)
	Chesto Berry	Allows a Pokémon to wake itself from being Asleep during battle	Pastel Navy Blue / Pastel Purple	24	4-12	Berry tree on Route 2 (p. 60)
	Chilan Berry	Lessens the damage from one supereffective Normal-type attack when held	—	48	2-6	Northwest Berry tree in Poni Wilds (p. 192)
	Chople Berry	Lessens the damage from one supereffective Fighting-type attack when held	Dark Orange	48	2-6	Northwest Berry tree in Poni Wilds (p. 192)
	Coba Berry	Lessens the damage from one supereffective Flying-type attack when held	Dark Blue / Dark Navy Blue	48	2-6	Northeast Berry tree in Poni Wilds (p. 192)
	Colbur Berry	Lessens the damage from one supereffective Dark-type attack when held	Dark Purple	48	2-6	Northwest Berry tree in Poni Wilds (p. 192)
	Figy Berry	Restores some HP when in a pinch, but confuses Pokémon that don't like spicy flavors	Dark Red	24	3-9	Berry tree on Route 4 (p. 92)
	Ganlon Berry	Raises the holder's Defense when in a pinch	Pastel Purple	72	2-8	Berry tree on Route 17 (p. 170)
	Grepa Berry	Increases a Pokémon's friendship (p. 130) and lowers its base Sp. Def (p. 272)	Pastel Yellow	48	5-14	Berry tree on Route 10 (p. 149)
	Haban Berry	Lessens the damage from one supereffective Dragon-type attack when held	—	48	2-6	Northeast Berry tree in Poni Wilds (p. 192)
	Hondew Berry	Increases a Pokémon's friendship (p. 130) and lowers its base Sp. Atk (p. 272)	Pastel Green	48	5-14	Berry tree on Route 10 (p. 149)
	Iapapa Berry	Restores some HP when in a pinch, but confuses Pokémon that don't like sour flavors	Dark Yellow	24	3-9	Berry tree on Route 4 (p. 92)
	Kasib Berry	Lessens the damage from one supereffective Ghost-type attack when held	Dark Purple	48	2-6	Northeast Berry tree in Poni Wilds (p. 192)
	Kebia Berry	Lessens the damage from one supereffective Poison-type attack when held	—	48	2-6	Northeast Berry tree in Poni Wilds (p. 192)
	Kee Berry	Increases the holder's Defense if hit with a physical move	Pastel Orange	72	2-8	Berry tree on Route 10 (p. 149)
	Kelpsy Berry	Increases a Pokémon's friendship (p. 130) and lowers its base Attack (p. 272)	Pastel Blue / Pastel Navy Blue	48	5-14	Berry tree on Route 10 (p. 149)
	Lansat Berry	Raises the holder's critical-hit ratio when in a pinch	—	72	2-4	Win 100 times in a row at the Battle Tree
	Leppa Berry	Allows a Pokémon to restore 10 PP to a move during battle	Pastel Orange	24	4-12	Berry tree on Route 2 (p. 60)
	Liechi Berry	Raises the holder's Attack when in a pinch	Dark Red	72	2-8	Northeast Berry tree in Poni Wilds (p. 192)
	Lum Berry	Allows a Pokémon to recover from any status condition or confusion during battle	Pastel Green	48	4-10	Berry tree on Route 4 (p. 92)
	Mago Berry	Restores some HP when in a pinch but confuses Pokémon that don't like sweet flavors	Pastel Pink / Dark Pink	24	3-9	Berry tree on Route 4 (p. 92) / Thrifty Megamart (p. 109)
	Maranga Berry	Increases the holder's Sp. Def if hit with a special move	Pastel Blue	72	2-8	Berry tree in Poni Plains (p. 222)
	Occa Berry	Lessens the damage from one supereffective Fire-type attack when held	Dark Red	48	2-6	Northwest Berry tree in Poni Wilds (p. 192)
	Oran Berry	Allows a Pokémon to recover 10 HP during battle	Pastel Blue	24	4-12	Berry tree in the Berry Fields (p. 60) / Thrifty Megamart (p. 109)
	Passho Berry	Lessens the damage from one supereffective Water-type attack when held	Dark Blue / Dark Navy Blue	48	2-6	Central Berry tree in Poni Wilds (p. 192)
	Payapa Berry	Lessens the damage from one supereffective Psychic-type attack when held	Dark Navy Blue / Dark Purple	48	2-6	Central Berry tree in Poni Wilds (p. 192)
	Pecha Berry	Allows a Pokémon to cure its own Poisoned condition during battle	Pastel Pink	24	4-12	Berry tree on Route 3 (p. 73)
	Persim Berry	Allows a Pokémon to cure its own confusion during battle	Pastel Pink	24	4-12	Berry tree in the Berry Fields (p. 60)
	Petaya Berry	Raises the holder's Sp. Atk when in a pinch	Dark Pink	72	2-8	Central Berry tree in Poni Wilds (p. 192)
	Pinap Berry	An unusual Berry not normally found in the Alola region	—	24	4-12	Thrifty Megamart (p. 109)
	Pomeg Berry	Increases a Pokémon's friendship (p. 130) and lowers its base HP (p. 272)	Pastel Red	48	5-14	Berry tree on Route 10 (p. 149)
	Qualot Berry	Increases a Pokémon's friendship (p. 130) and lowers its base Defense (p. 272)	Pastel Yellow	48	5-14	Berry tree on Route 10 (p. 149)

	Name	Pokémon Effects	Dye Color	Avg. Hours to Grow	Typical Harvest	Main Way to Obtain in Alola
	Rawst Berry	Allows a Pokémon to cure its own Burned condition during battle	Pastel Green	24	4-12	Berry tree on Route 5 (p. 98) / Thrifty Megamart (p. 109)
	Rindo Berry	Lessens the damage from one supereffective Grass-type attack when held	Dark Green	48	2-6	Northeast Berry tree in Poni Wilds (p. 192)
	Roseli Berry	Lessens the damage from one supereffective Fairy-type attack when held	Dark Pink	48	2-6	Central Berry tree in Poni Wilds (p. 192)
	Salac Berry	Raises the holder's Speed when in a pinch	Dark Green	72	2-8	Northwest Berry tree in Poni Wilds (p. 192)
	Shuca Berry	Lessens the damage from one supereffective Ground-type attack when held	Dark Orange	48	2-6	Northwest Berry tree in Poni Wilds (p. 192)
	Sitrus Berry	Allows a Pokémon to recover a percentage of its max HP during battle	Pastel Yellow / Pastel Orange	48	5-15	Berry tree on Route 16 (p. 167) / Thrifty Megamart (p. 109)
	Starf Berry	Raises one of the holder's stats when in a pinch	—	72	2-4	Win 200 times in a row at the Battle Tree
	Tamato Berry	Increases a Pokémon's friendship (p. 130) and lowers its base Speed (p. 272)	Pastel Red	48	5-14	Thrifty Megamart (p. 109)
	Tanga Berry	Lessens the damage from one supereffective Bug-type attack when held	—	48	2-6	Northeast Berry tree in Poni Wilds (p. 192)
	Wacan Berry	Lessens the damage from one supereffective Electric-type attack when held	Dark Yellow	48	2-6	Central Berry tree in Poni Wilds (p. 192)
	Wiki Berry	Restores some HP when in a pinch, but confuses Pokémon that don't like dry flavors	Pastel Purple	24	3-9	Berry tree on Route 4 (p. 92)
	Yache Berry	Lessens the damage from one supereffective Ice-type attack when held	Dark Blue	48	2-6	Central Berry tree in Poni Wilds (p. 192)

Berry Tree Locations

Island	Berries you can find there	Location		Crabrawler Encounters
Melemele	Oran, Persim	Berry Fields off of Route 2		—
Melemele	Oran, Chesto, Leppa, Persim, Sitrus	North of Pokémon Center on Route 2		△
Melemele	Chesto, Pecha, Cheri, Leppa, Sitrus	East end of Route 3		△
Akala	Pecha, Lum, Mago, Figy, Wiki, Aguav, Iapapa	North end of Route 4		△
Akala	Pecha, Cheri, Rawst, Persim, Lum	West side of Route 5		△
Akala	Oran, Chesto, Cheri, Pecha, Lum, Persim, Sitrus	Middle of Route 8		△
Ula'ula	Pomeg, Kelpsy, Qualot, Hondew, Grepa, Tamato, Kee	Middle of Route 10		◎

Island	Berries you can find there	Location		Crabrawler Encounters
Ula'ula	Aspear, Cheri, Chesto, Leppa, Apicot	off of Route 12		△
Ula'ula	Oran, Sitrus, Aspear, Pecha, Persim, Lum	West side of Route 16		△
Ula'ula	Sitrus, Leppa, Pecha, Rawst, Lum, Ganlon	North end of Route 17		△
Poni	Salac, Shuca, Chilan, Chople, Colbur, Charti, Occa	Northwest corner of Poni Wilds		△
Poni	Passho, Roseli, Yache, Wacan, Payapa, Babiri, Petaya	Center of Poni Wilds		△
Poni	Rindo, Kasib, Coba, Kebia, Tanga, Haban, Liechi	Northeast corner of Poni Wilds		△
Poni	Occa, Passho, Rindo, Wacan, Shuca, Yache, Maranga	Northwest corner of Poni Plains		◎

◎ frequent △ rare — never

Shops

Poké Mart (Normal Wares)

Items available from the start	
Antidote	₽200
Awakening	₽100
Burn Heal	₽300
Escape Rope	₽1,000
Ice Heal	₽100
Paralyze Heal	₽300
Poké Ball	₽200
Potion	₽200
Repel	₽400
Items added after completing one trial	
Great Ball	₽600
Super Potion	₽700
Items added after completing two trials	
Honey	₽300
Revive	₽2,000
Items added after completing three trials	
Adrenaline Orb	₽300
Super Repel	₽700

Items added after completing four trials	
Hyper Potion	₽1,500
Ultra Ball	₽800
Items added after completing five trials	
Full Heal	₽400
Max Repel	₽900
Items added after completing six trials	
Max Potion	₽2,500
Items added after completing seven trials	
Full Restore	₽3,000

Other Shops

Royal Avenue

Thrifty Megamart—Clerk A	
Great Ball	₽300
Heal Ball	₽150
Nest Ball	₽500
Poké Ball	₽100
Timer Ball	₽500
Thrifty Megamart—Clerk B	
Antidote	₽100
Awakening	₽50
Burn Heal	₽150
Ice Heal	₽50
Paralyze Heal	₽150
Potion	₽100
Repel	₽200
Thrifty Megamart—Clerk C	
Strange Souvenir	₽1,500

Konikoni City

Olivia's Jewelry Shop	
Fire Stone	₽3,000
Leaf Stone	₽3,000
Thunder Stone	₽3,000
Water Stone	₽3,000
TM Shop	
TM08 Bulk Up	₽10,000
TM09 Venoshock	₽10,000
TM32 Double Team	₽10,000
TM47 Low Sweep	₽10,000
TM65 Shadow Claw	₽10,000
TM82 Dragon Tail	₽10,000
Incense Shop	
Full Incense	₽5,000
Lax Incense	₽5,000
Luck Incense	₽11,000
Odd Incense	₽2,000
Pure Incense	₽6,000
Rock Incense	₽2,000
Rose Incense	₽2,000
Sea Incense	₽2,000
Wave Incense	₽2,000
Herb Seller	
Energy Powder	₽500
Energy Root	₽1,200
Heal Powder	₽300
Revival Herb	₽2,800

Poké Mart (Special Wares)

Hau'oli City	
Dire Hit	₽1,000
Guard Spec.	₽1,500
X Accuracy	₽1,000
X Attack	₽1,000
X Defense	₽2,000
X Sp. Atk	₽1,000
X Sp. Def	₽2,000
X Speed	₽1,000
Route 2	
Dire Hit	₽1,000
Guard Spec.	₽1,500
Heal Ball	₽300
Luxury Ball	₽1,000
Nest Ball	₽1,000
Super Potion	₽700
X Accuracy	₽1,000
X Attack	₽1,000
X Defense	₽2,000
X Sp. Atk	₽1,000
X Sp. Def	₽2,000
X Speed	₽1,000

Heahea City	
TM16 Light Screen	₽10,000
TM17 Protect	₽10,000
TM20 Safeguard	₽10,000
TM33 Reflect	₽10,000
TM70 Aurora Veil	₽30,000
Paniola Town	
Net Ball	₽1,000
Repeat Ball	₽1,000
Timer Ball	₽1,000
Royal Avenue	
TM07 Hail	₽50,000
TM11 Sunny Day	₽50,000
TM18 Rain Dance	₽50,000
TM37 Sandstorm	₽50,000

Route 8	
Dire Hit	₽1,000
Dive Ball	₽1,000
Dusk Ball	₽1,000
Guard Spec.	₽1,500
Quick Ball	₽1,000
X Accuracy	₽1,000
X Attack	₽1,000
X Defense	₽2,000
X Sp. Atk	₽1,000
X Sp. Def	₽2,000
X Speed	₽1,000
Malie City	
TM19 Roost	₽10,000
TM23 Smack Down	₽10,000
TM40 Aerial Ace	₽10,000
TM42 Facade	₽10,000
TM51 Steel Wing	₽10,000
TM66 Payback	₽10,000
TM69 Rock Polish	₽10,000
TM75 Swords Dance	₽10,000
TM78 Bulldoze	₽10,000
TM89 U-turn	₽10,000

Mount Hokulani	
Calcium	₽10,000
Carbos	₽10,000
HP Up	₽10,000
Iron	₽10,000
Protein	₽10,000
Zinc	₽10,000
Seafolk Village	
TM04 Calm Mind	₽10,000
TM14 Blizzard	₽30,000
TM15 Hyper Beam	₽50,000
TM22 Solar Beam	₽10,000
TM25 Thunder	₽30,000
TM34 Sludge Wave	₽10,000
TM38 Fire Blast	₽30,000
TM52 Focus Blast	₽30,000
TM68 Giga Impact	₽50,000
TM71 Stone Edge	₽30,000

Type Matchup Chart

Types are assigned both to moves and to the Pokémon themselves. These types can greatly affect the amount of damage dealt or received in battle, so if you learn how they line up against one another, you'll give yourself an edge in battle.

If your Pokémon has two types, the strengths and weaknesses of both types will be used to calculate that Pokémon's weaknesses and strengths. If both types share the same weakness, the Pokémon will take four times the damage. (For example, Grass types and Ice types are both weak to Fire, and each will take 2× damage from a Fire-type move. A Grass- and Ice-type Pokémon will be twice as weak, and take 4× the damage from a Fire-type move.) However, two resistances can combine in the same way. (Fire types and Water types are both resistant to Fire-type attacks, taking only 1/2 the usual damage. A Fire- and Water-type Pokémon would be twice as resistant, and only take 1/4 the usual damage from a Fire-type move.) Finally, a strength and weakness will cancel each other out. (Grass types take 2× damage from Fire-type attacks, and Water types take 1/2 damage from Fire-type attacks. A Grass- and Water-type Pokémon will simply take normal damage from a Fire-type attack, not more or less.)

Defending Pokémon's Type (columns) / **Attacking Pokémon's Move Type** (rows)

	Normal	Fire	Water	Grass	Electric	Ice	Fighting	Poison	Ground	Flying	Psychic	Bug	Rock	Ghost	Dragon	Dark	Steel	Fairy
Normal													▲	×			▲	
Fire		▲	▲	◉		◉						◉	▲		▲		◉	
Water		◉	▲	▲					◉				◉		▲			
Grass		▲	◉	▲				▲	◉	▲		▲	◉		▲		▲	
Electric			◉	▲	▲				×	◉					▲			
Ice		▲	▲	◉		▲			◉	◉					◉		▲	
Fighting	◉					◉		▲		▲	▲	▲	◉	×		◉	◉	▲
Poison				◉				▲	▲				▲	▲			×	◉
Ground		◉		▲	◉			◉		×		▲	◉				◉	
Flying				◉	▲		◉					◉	▲				▲	
Psychic							◉	◉			▲					×	▲	
Bug		▲		◉			▲	▲		▲	◉			▲		◉	▲	▲
Rock		◉				◉	▲		▲	◉		◉					▲	
Ghost	×										◉			◉		▲		
Dragon															◉		▲	×
Dark							▲				◉			◉		▲		▲
Steel		▲	▲		▲	◉							◉				▲	◉
Fairy		▲					◉	▲							◉	◉	▲	

Key

◉	Very effective "It's super effective!"	× 2
No icon	Normal damage	× 1
▲	Not too effective "It's not very effective..."	× 1/2
×	No effect "It doesn't affect..."	× 0

Ineffective status conditions and moves depending on type

Type	Effect
Fire	• Immune to the Burned condition
Grass	• Immune to Leech Seed • Immune to powder and spore moves
Electric	• Immune to the Paralysis condition
Ice	• Immune to the Frozen condition • Take no damage from hail • Immune to Sheer Cold
Poison	• Immune to the Poisoned and Badly Poisoned conditions, even when switched in with Toxic Spikes in play • Nullify Toxic Spikes so no other Pokémon will be Poisoned when switching in. (Note: if the Poison-type Pokémon is also a Flying type, has the Levitate Ability, or holds an Air Balloon, this nullifying effect will not occur.)
Ground	• Immune to Thunder Wave* • Take no damage from sandstorms
Flying	• Cannot be damaged by Spikes when switching in • Immune to the Poisoned and Badly Poisoned conditions, when switching in with Toxic Spikes in play
Rock	• Take no damage from sandstorms • Sp. Def goes up in a sandstorm
Ghost	• Cannot be affected by moves and Abilities that prevent Pokémon from fleeing from battle
Dark	• Immune to the effect of status moves used by Pokémon with the Prankster Ability
Steel	• Take no damage from sandstorms • Immune to the Poisoned and Badly Poisoned conditions, even when switched in with Toxic Spikes in play

*Types usually don't have effects on status moves, but Thunder Wave won't work against Ground-type Pokémon.

Credits

Writer
Steve Stratton (Prima Games)

Editors
Kellyn Ballard
Rachel Payne
Blaise Selby

Technical Advisor
Jillian Nonaka

Researchers
Hisato Yamamori
Sayuri Munday
Ben Regal
Bryson Clark

Fact-Check
Mayu Todo
Bryan Olsson
Guillaume Didier
Clémence Amoric
Lylia Khrissate
Alice Troiani
Kathleen Kalms
Ireneusz Radko
Christopher Derbort
Eva Rodriguez Grana
Diego Luque de la Campa (JAC Recruitment)

Screenshots
Jeff Hines
Robert Colling

Design
Chris Franc
Kevin Lalli
Justin Gonyea
Hiromi Kimura

Project Managers
Yoshi Uemura
Mikiko Ryu

Production
Prima Games
Jamie Knight Bryson
Elise Winter
Vanessa Perez
Mark Hughes

Acknowledgements
Heather Dalgleish
Yutaka Kamai
Phaedra Long
Steven Thomason
Yasuhiro Usui
Anja Weinbach

The Pokémon Company
INTERNATIONAL

THE OFFICIAL ALOLA REGION STRATEGY GUIDE

ISBN: 978-0744017-47-2 [standard edition]
ISBN: 978-0744017-48-9 [collector's edition]
ISBN: 978-0744017-86-1 [vault edition]

Published in the United States by
The Pokémon Company International
601 108th Ave NE Suite 1600
Bellevue, WA 98004 USA

1st Floor Building, 4 Chiswick Park
566 Chiswick High Road
London, W4 5YE United Kingdom

Printed in the United States of America.

Australian warranty statement:

This product comes with guarantees that cannot be excluded under the Australian Consumer Law. You are entitled to a replacement or refund for a major failure and for compensation for any other reasonably foreseeable loss or damage. You are also entitled to have the goods repaired or replaced if the goods fail to be of acceptable quality and the failure does not amount to a major failure.

This product comes with a one-year warranty from date of purchase. Defects in the product must have appeared within one year from date of purchase in order to claim the warranty. All warranty claims must be facilitated back through the retailer of purchase, in accordance with the retailer's returns policies and procedures. Any cost incurred as a result of returning the product to the retailer of purchase are the full responsibility of the consumer.

AU wholesale distributor:
Bluemouth Interactive Pty Ltd,
Suite 1502, 9 Yarra Street, South Yarra
Victoria, 3141 Australia
+613 9646 4011

Email: support@bluemouth.com.au